Information Technology Law in Australia

Information Technology Law in Australia

George Cho

This book was originally published as a monograph in the International Encyclopaedia of Laws/Privacy and Technology Law.

Founding Editor: Roger Blanpain
General Editor: Frank Hendrickx
Volume Editors: Jos Dumortier, Pieter Gryffroy, Ruben Roex & Yung Shin Van Der Sype

Wolters Kluwer

Published by:
Kluwer Law International B.V.
PO Box 316
2400 AH Alphen aan den Rijn
The Netherlands
E-mail: lrs-sales@wolterskluwer.com
Website: www.wolterskluwer.com/en/solutions/kluwerlawinternational

Sold and distributed by:
Wolters Kluwer Legal & Regulatory U.S.
920 Links Avenue
Landisville, PA 17538
United States of America
E-mail: customer.service@wolterskluwer.com

ISBN 978-94-035-2296-8

e-Book: ISBN 978-94-035-2536-5
web-PDF: ISBN 978-94-035-2546-4

The Author

George Cho, PhD, is an Emeritus Professor of GeoInformatics and Law at the University of Canberra, Australia. George was the Chair of Academic Board (2008-2013) the peak academic body on quality and standards and in 2018 he was Deputy Vice-Chancellor Research and Innovation at the University of Canberra and from 2019 Executive Dean of the Faculty of Science and Technology until his retirement in 2022. He obtained an Honours degree in Arts from the University of Malaya, Master of Arts from the University of British Columbia and a PhD from the Australian National University. He also gained a Graduate Certificate in Higher Education from the University of Canberra and a Graduate LLB degree from the Australian National University. He was admitted as a barrister and solicitor of the Supreme Court of the Australian Capital Territory and the High Court of Australia and is a barrister-at-law in the Supreme Court of New South Wales. He practises law *pro bono* for the Welfare Rights and Legal Centre Night Time Legal Advice Service in Canberra. George was made a member of the Order of Australia in 2005 for his services to higher education and for his contributions to the study of geographic information systems and the law.

George has published numerous books and journal articles on law and geography including *Geographic Information Science: Mastering the Legal Issues* (John Wiley 2005); *Marketers and the Law* (LBC Sydney, 2000, with Clark and Hoyle); *E-business: Law and Management for the 21st Century* (Info-Sys International Publications, Canberra 2000, with Clark and Hoyle); *Y2K: Avoiding the Legal Byte* (Prospect Publications, 1999, with Clark and Hoyle); *Geographic Information Systems and the Law* (John Wiley, 1998), *Cyber Law in Australia* (Wolters Kluwer, 2020) and twenty other prior book publications. George has also written book chapters in various texts including *Commercial and Economic Law in Australia* (Griggs *et al.* Kluwer Law Intl. Alphen aan den Rijn, 2018); 'E-commerce law' in *The International Encyclopaedia of Laws*; and 'E-commerce: Legal and Policy Framework' in *Managers and the Law: A Guide for Business Decision Makers*, edited by Griggs, Clark and Iredale (Sydney: Lawbook Co, 2009); and *Australian Commercial and Economic Law* (The Hague, Kluwer Law International, 1999). He is an international member of the editorial boards of the *Journal of Law and Information Science, GIS Law, International Journal of Geoinformatics,* and *Coordinates*. He has delivered papers to international and national conferences on topics related to information systems, intellectual property and e-commerce.

George has written this monograph following the format and structure of the Wolters Kluwer series in the International Encyclopaedia of Laws. While this volume has used material from his previous book *Cyber Law in Australia* (2020) (2nd ed.) in the Wolters Kluwer series he is grateful to the contributors of the previous work *Cyber Law Suppl. 50* (2015) by Clark, Cho, Hoyle and McLaren for their work. Further, the present work has benefitted from material published E.E. Clark (2003) 'Managing the Transformation to e-Government: An Australian Perspective', *Thunderbird International Business Review*, Vol. 45(4), July-August, pp. 377-397, John Wiley & Sons; and, E. Clark & R. Prentice (2000) 'Circuit Layouts' in Butterworths, *Halsbury's Laws of Australia*, vol. 15, Intellectual Property.

This monograph is dedicated in loving memory and tribute to his mother Theresa Ho who passed away in 2021 aged 100.

Table of Contents

List of Abbreviations

2-D	Two-Dimensional
2LD	Second Level Domain Names
3-D	Three-Dimensional
5G	Fifth Generation Cellular Standard
A$DC	A dollar Digital Coin
ABA	Australian Broadcasting Authority
ABACUS	Australian Business Assessment of Computer User Security
ABC	Australian Broadcasting Corporation
ABN	Australian Business Number
ABS	Australian Bureau of Statistics
ACA	Australian Communications Authority
ACCC	Australian Competition and Consumer Commission
ACIC	Australian Criminal Intelligence Commission
ACIP	Advisory Council on Intellectual Property
ACL	Australian Consumer Law
ACLC	Annual Carrier Licence Charge
ACMA	Australian Communications and Media Authority
ACORN	Australian Cybercrime Online Reporting Network
ACSC	Australian Cybersecurity Centre
ACT	Australian Capital Territory
ad	Advertising
ADBC	Australian Digital Business Council
ADC	Australian Digital Council
ADF	Australian Defence Force
ADHA	Australian Digital Health Agency
ADI	Authorised Deposit-taking Institutions
ADMA	Australian Direct Marketing Association
AEC	Australian Electoral Commission
AFACT	Australian Federation Against Copyright Theft

List of Abbreviations

AFCA	Australian Financial Complaints Authority
AFP	Australian Federal Police
AFSL	Australian Financial Services Licence
AGD	Attorney General's Department
AGIMO	Australian Government Information Management Office
AHMAC	Australian Health Ministers' Advisory Council
AHMC	Australian Health Ministers' Conference
AHPRA	Australian Health Practitioner Regulation Agency
AHTCC	Australian Hi-Tech Crime Centre
AI	Artificial Intelligence
AIC	Australian Institute of Criminology
AIHW	Australian Institute of Health and Welfare
AML/CTF Act	*Anti-Money Laundering and Counter Terrorism Financing Act* 2006
AML/CTF	Anti-money Laundering and Counter-Terrorism Financing
ANU	Australian National University
ANZ	Australia New Zealand Banking Group Ltd.
AON	Australian Office of Nanotechnology
APAC	Asia Pacific
APCA	Australian Payments Clearing Association
APCERT	Asia Pacific Computer Emergency Response Team
APEC	Asia-Pacific Economic Cooperation
APH	Australian Parliament House
APMA	Australian Pharmaceutical Manufacturers Association
APO	Australian Patents Office
APP	Australian Privacy Principles
APRA	Australian Prudential Regulation Authority
APS	Australian Public Service
AR	Augmented Reality
ARA	Australian Retail Association
ARGMD	Australian Regulatory Guidelines for Medical Devices
ARNECC	Australian Registrars' National E-conveyancing Council
ARTG	Australian Register of Therapeutic Goods
ASCII	American Standard Code for Information Interchange
ASD	Australian Signals Directorate
ASIC	Australian Securities and Investments Commission
ASIO	Australian Security Intelligence Organisation
Assistance & Access Act	*Telecommunications and Other Legislation Amendment (Assistance and Access) Act* 2018

ASPI	Australian Strategic Policy Institute
ASTRA	Australian Subscription Television and Radio Association
ASX	Australian Securities Exchange
ATM	Automated Teller Machines
ATMOSS	Australian Trade Mark Online Search System
ATO	Australian Tax Office
AUD	Australian Dollar
auDA	.au Domain Administration
auDRP	au Dispute Resolution Policy
AUSFTA	Australia-US Free Trade Agreement 2004
AUSTLII	Australian Legal Information Institute
AUSTRAC	Australian Transaction Reports and Analysis Centre
AVMS	*Audiovisual Media Services Directive*
B2B	Business to Business
B2C	Business to Consumer
B2G	Business to Government
BCA	Business Council of Australia
BECS	Bulk Electronic Clearing System
BGP	Border Gateway Protocol
BLV	Blind and Low Vision
BNPL	Buy Now Pay Later
BSA	*Broadcasting Services Act* 1992
BSB	Bank State Branch
BTTPS	Business Transactions Through Payment Systems
Budapest Convention	*Budapest Convention on Cyber-Crime*
C2G	Consumer to Government
CAANZ	Consumer Affairs Australia New Zealand
CAC	Computer Access Crimes
CAD	Computer-Aided Design
CAF	Consumer Affairs Forum
CAOIA	*Copyright Amendment (Online Infringement) Act* 2018
Carly's Law	*Criminal Code Amendment (Protection of Minors Online) Act* 2017
CA	*Copyright Act* 1968
CAs	Certification Authorities
CASSPrs	Crypto Asset Secondary Service Providers
CBDC	Central Bank Digital Currency
CCA	*Competition and Consumer Act* 2010
ccTLD	Country code Top-Level Domain Names

List of Abbreviations

cctv	Closed Circuit Television
CDC	Computer Disruption Crimes
CDR	Consumer Data Right
CDR Rules	*Competition and Consumer (Consumer Data Right) Rules* 2020
CD-ROM	Compact Disk Read-Only-Memory
CEA	*Commonwealth Electoral Act* 1918
CERT	Computer Emergency Response Team
CGDN	Community Geographic Domain Names
CGT	Capital Gains Tax
CISC	Cyber and Infrastructure Security Centre (prev. Critical Infrastructure Centre)
CLA	*Circuit Layouts Act* 1989
CLAA	*Cybercrime Legislation Amendment Act* 2012
CLI	Calling Line Identification
CLOUD Act	Clarifying Lawful Overseas Use of Data Act (US)
CLR	*Commonwealth Law Review*
CND	Calling Number Display
CNNIC	China Internet Network Information Centre
COAG	Council of Australian Governments
COTS	Commercial-Off-the-Shelf
COVID-19	Coronavirus-19
CPI	Consumer Price Index
CRB	Credit Reporting Body
Criminal Code	*Criminal Code Act* 1995
CSG	Customer Service Guarantee
CSIAP	Cybersecurity Strategy Industry Advisory Panel
CSIRO	Commonwealth Scientific and Industrial Research Organisation
CSP	Carriage Service Providers
Cth	Commonwealth
CUECIC	Convention on the Use of Electronic Communications in International Contracts
DAO	Digital Autonomous Organizations
Data Retention Act	*Telecommunications (Interception and Access) Amendment (Data Retention) Act 2015*
DBCDE	Department of Broadband, Communications and the Digital Economy
DC	Digital Certificates
DCE	Digital currency exchanges

DDOS	Distributed denial of service
DDSO	Digital data service obligation
DeFi	Decentralized Finance
DER	Digital Education Revolution
DESE	Department of Education, Skills and Employment
DFAT	Department of Foreign Affairs and Trade
DIGI	Digital Industry Group Inc
DIO	Defence Intelligence Organisation
DLT	Distributed ledger technology
DMCA	*Digital Millennium Copyright Act* (US) 1998
DNS	Domain Name System
DOI	Digital Object Identifier
DP-REG	Digital Platform Regulators Forum
DRE	Direct Recording Electronic
DRM	Digital Rights Management
DRN	Defence Restricted Network
DSGL	Defence and Strategic Goods List
DTA	Digital Transformation Agency
EAR	Export Administration Regulations
EC	European Council/Commission
ECANZ	Electoral Council of Australia and New Zealand
ECEG	Electronic Commerce Expert Group
ECNL	e-Conveyancing National Law
EDI	Electronic Data Interchange
EFT Code	Electronic Funds Transfer Code of Conduct
EFTPOS	Electronic Funds Transfers Point of Sale
EGDI	e-Government Development Index
EHR	Electronic Health Records
EIU	Economist Intelligence Unit
EL	Eligible Layout
ELN	Electronic Lodgement Network
EP	Entrepreneurs' Programme
EPAL	EFTPOS Payments Australia Limited
EPROM	Erasable Programmable Read-Only Memory
eSafety Commissioner	Office of the Children's eSafety Commissioner
ETA	*Electronic Transactions Act* 1999
ETSI	European Telecommunication Standards Institute
EU	European Union

List of Abbreviations

EVACS	Electronic Voting and Counting System
FA Scheme	Foreign Arrangements Scheme
FCA	Federal Court of Australia
FCDO	Foreign, Commonwealth and Development Office, United Kingdom
FDI	Foreign Direct Investment
FIRB	Foreign Investment Review Board
FIU	Financial Intelligence Unit
FMI	Financial Market Infrastructures
FOS	Financial Ombudsman Service
FSAC	Financial Sector Advisory Council
FSR	*Financial Sector Reform Amendments and Transitional Provisions Act* 1998
FTA	Free-to-air
FTR Act	*Financial Transaction Reports Act* 1988
FVEY	Five Eyes alliance
G-20	Group of 20 Developed Countries
G2B	Government to Business
G2G	Government to Government
GAC	Government Advisory Committee
GATT	General Agreement on Tariffs and Trade
GBE	Government Business Enterprise
GDP	Gross Domestic Product
GFIN	Global Financial Innovation Network
GIF	Graphic Interchange Format
GIS	Geographical Information Systems/Science
GNSO	Generic Names Supporting Organization
GnuPG	GNU Privacy Guard
GovDXP	Government Digital Experience Platform
GP	General Practitioners
GPL	GNU General Public Licence
GPS	Global Positioning Systems
GST	Goods and Services Tax
gTLD	Generic Top-Level Domain Names
GUI	Graphical User Interface
GVA	Gross Value Added
Hague System	Hague System for the International Registration of Industrial Designs
HCA	High Court of Australia
HCPIL	Hague Conference on Private International Law

HI	Health Identifier
HI Act	*Healthcare Identifiers Act 2010*
HRC	Human Rights Commission
HTML	Hypertext Markup Language
IaaS	Infrastructure as a Service
IANA	Internet Assigned Numbers Authority
IC	Integrated Circuit
ICANN	Internet Corporation for Assigned Names and Numbers
ICCPR	International Covenant on Civil and Political Rights
ICO	Initial Coin Offerings
ICT	Information Communication Technology
IGAct	*Interactive Gambling Act* 2001
IGA	Intergovernmental Agreement
IGO	Intergovernmental Organizations
iMS	Instant Messaging Services
INN	International Non-proprietary Names
INSLM	Independent National Security Legislation Monitor
International IDEA	International Institute for Democracy and Electoral Assistance
IOT	Internet of Things
IoTAA	Internet of Things Alliance Australia
IOT Code of Practice	*Code of Practice: Securing the Internet of Things for Consumers*
IP	Intellectual Property
IPFS	Interplanetary File System
IPIC Treaty	Treaty on Intellectual Property in Respect of Integrated Circuits
IPO Act	*Telecommunications Legislation Amendment (International Production Orders) Act 2021*
IPR	Intellectual Property Rights
IPU	Inter-Parliamentary Union
ISP	Internet Service Providers
ITU	International Telecommunications Union
JCSCs	Joint Cybersecurity Centres
JPEG	Joint Photographic Experts Group
JSCEM	Joint Standing Committee on Electoral Matters
KYC	Know Your Customer
LIFD	Low Impact Facilities Determination
MACM Act	*Mutual Assistance in Criminal Matters Act* 1987
MCCOC	Model Criminal Code Officers Committee

List of Abbreviations

MDAP	Model Defamation Amendment Provisions 2020
MDP	Model Defamation Provisions
Model Code	National Model Criminal Code
MOR	Model Operating Requirements
MPR	Model Participation Rules
MTAA	Medical Technology Association of Australia
NAA	National Archives of Australia
NBN	National Broadband Network
NCCP	*National Consumer Credit Protection Act* 2009
NDB Scheme	Notifiable Data Breaches Scheme
NDES	*National Digital Economy Strategy*
NDIS	National Disability Insurance Scheme
NECDL	National E-Conveyancing Development Ltd
NECO	National E-Conveyancing Office
NECS	National E-Conveyancing System
NEHTA	National Electronic Health Transition Authority
NFC	Near Field Communication
NFT	Non-fungible Tokens
NI	Norfolk Island
NICTA	National ICT Australia
NISA	National Innovation and Science Agenda
NITV	National Indigenous Television
NOIE	National Office for the Information Economy
NPA	National Partnership Agreement
NPP	New Payments Platform
NSW	New South Wales
NT	Northern Territory
OAIC	Office of the Australian Information Commissioner
OCAC	Office of Communications Access and Cybercrime
ODR	Online Dispute Resolution
OECD	Organisation for Economic Co-operation and Development
OGIT	Office of Government Information Technology
OHCHR	Office of the High Commissioner for Human Rights
ONDC	Office of National Data Commissioner
OSP	Online Service Providers
OSS	Open-Source Software
OT	Operational Technology
OTC	Overseas Telecommunications Commission

P2B	Platform to Business
P2C	Platform to Consumer
PaaS	Platform-as-a-Service
PaCSON	Pacific Cybersecurity Operational Network
Paris Convention	International Convention for the Protection of Industrial Property
PCEHR	Personally Controlled Electronic Health Record
PEPPOL	Pan-European Public Procurement OnLine
PEXA	Property Exchange Australia Ltd
PGD	Pretty Good Democracy
PIN	Personal identification number
PJCIS	Parliamentary Joint Committee on Intelligence and Security
PKAF	Public Key Authentication Framework
PKI	Public Key Infrastructure
PKT	Public Key Technology
PM&C	Prime Minister & Cabinet
PMG	Postmaster General
POC Act	*Proceeds of Crime Act* 2002
POS	Point of Sale
PROM	Programmable Read-Only Memory
PSB	Payments System Board
PSEA	Paid Search Engine Advertising
PSO	Positive Security Obligations
Qld	Queensland
RaaS	Ransomware-as-a-Service
RBA	Reserve Bank of Australia
R&D	Research and Development
Revenge porn law	*Enhancing Online Safety (Non-consensual Sharing of Intimate Images) Act* 2018
RFT	Request for Tender
RITS	Reserve Bank Information and Transfer System
RMG	Resource Management Guides
RMIT	Royal Melbourne Institute of Technology
RSS	Really Simple Syndication
RTGS	Real-Time Gross Settlement
SA	South Australia
SaaS	Software-as-a-Service
SaMD	Software Classified as a Medical Device

List of Abbreviations

SAVM Act	*Criminal Code Amendment (Sharing of Abhorrent Violent Material) Act* 2019
SBS	Special Broadcasting Services
SCADA	Supervisory Control and Data Acquisition
SCAG	Standing Committee of Attorneys-General
SCPA	*Semiconductor Chip Protection Act* 1984 (US)
SEO	Search Engine Optimization
SET	Secure Electronic Transaction
SFA	Standard Form Service Agreement
SME	Small and Medium Enterprises
SMPT	Simple Mail Transport Protocol
SMS	Short Messaging Service
SOAC Act	*Crimes Legislative Amendment (Sex Offences Against Children) Act* 2010
SOCI Act	*Security of Critical Infrastructure Act* 2020
SOE	Statement of Expectations
SSL	Secure Socket Layers
SVC	Stored Value Cards
TAF	Telecommunications Access Forum
TAN	Technical Assistance Notice
TAR	Technical Assistance Request
TCCC	Transnational Crime Coordination Centre
TCN	Technical Capability Notice
TCP Code	Telecommunications Consumer Protections Code
TCP/IP	Transmission Control Protocol Internet Protocol
TCPSS	*Telecommunications (Consumer Protection and Services Standards) Act* 1999
TDIF	Trusted Digital Identity Framework
Telecom	Australian Telecommunications Commission
TG Act	*Therapeutic Goods Act* 1989
TGA	Therapeutic Goods Administration
TIAA	*Telecommunications (Interception and Access) Act* 1979
TIO	Telecommunication Industry Ombudsman
TISN	Trusted Information Sharing Network
TLD	Top Level Domain
TMT	Telecommunications, Media and Technology
TOLA	*Telecommunications and Other Legislation Amendment (Assistance and Access) Act* 2018
TOR	The Onion Router
TPA	*Trade Practices Act* 1974

TPM	Technological Protection Measures
TRIPS	Trade-Related Intellectual Property Rights
TSSR	Telecommunications Sector Security Reforms
UDHR	Universal Declaration of Human Rights
UDR	Unregistered Design Right
UDRP	Uniform Domain Name Dispute Resolution Policy
UFIT	University Foreign Interference Taskforce
UGC	User Generated Content
UI	User Interface
UNCITRAL	UN Commission on International Trade Law
UNESCO	UN Economic, Social and Cultural Organization
UNIDROIT	UN International Institute for the Unification of Private Law
URL	Universal Resource Locator
USDCoin	US Dollar Coin
USO	Universal Service O
USP	Universal Service Provider
UX	User Experience
VEC	Victoria Electoral Commission
VOD	Video on Demand
VPN	Virtual Private Networks
VR	Virtual Reality
VUI	Voice-Controlled User Interface
WA	Western Australia
WCO	World Customs Organization
WCT	WIPO Copyright Treaty
WIPO	World Intellectual Property Organization
WPI	Wage Price Index
WPPT	WIPO Performance and Phonograms Treaty
WTO	World Trade Organization
WWW	World Wide Web
XML	Extensible Mark-Up Language

List of Abbreviations

Preface

This volume on Information Technology Law in Australia is presented in six parts each addressing a specific topic following the Kluwer Information Technology Law series format. In addition to the *Introduction* and *Summary and Conclusions*, the focus here is the way Australian policy and legal frameworks have responded to the pervasive and dynamic developments in the cyber world. The monograph avoids any discussion on the impact of information technology law on privacy and data protection in Australia as there is a separate monograph that comprehensively addresses the topic in the Kluwer Information Technology Law Series *International Encyclopedia of Privacy and Technology Law – Privacy and Data Protection.*

In the *General Introduction*, Chapter 1 gives readers a background to Australia in terms of its geography, cultural composition and political system. This is followed by a brief outline of the population, the economy and social and cultural milieu of Australians. In Chapter 2 the *Australian Telecommunication and Digital Infrastructure* surveys the responses to the difficult challenges presented by the rapidly changing information economy. There are the matters of the 'regalian' functions of a sovereign state in terms of finance, laws and national security that run in parallel to the mundane day-to-day organization and delivery of public services such as health, education, justice and government services. The twinning of law and e-government are described as well as the government's leading role in promoting the digital economy. The proper function of these aspects of the economy are intrinsically bound with rules of law, an economic system and a set of cultural values that underpin all such activity. Public and private endeavours assist in the overall performance of the nation-state competing on an international stage. In Chapter 3 the *Information Technology Market* operating within the national economy is discussed. COVID-19 containment measures have witnessed restricted economic activities leading to a large fall in gross domestic product in 2020. Yet, Australia's use of digital technologies remains unabated given the data on participation rates in the digital economy either in terms of Internet activity or the household use of information technology. Chapter 4 continues the theme of *e-Commerce Activity* and the pandemic's impact on m-commerce and health delivery and the overall contribution of information communication technology to the Australian economy.

Part I Telecommunications, Media and Technology Regulation is the substantive section that lays the foundational theme of the Australian telecommunications, media and technology regulatory environment. Such an environment is presented in eight chapters with Chapter 1 on the legal status of standards and technical specifications and market regulation. Chapter 2 deals with the anti-competition and access regime that are underpinned by the need for consumer protection in the telecommunication sector. This is followed by Chapter 3 on the application of competition law to the telecommunication market and reforms to the competition regime. Chapters 4, 5 and 6 discuss the regulation of the technology market, the regulation of media and broadcasting activity and the regulation of media and online services respectively. These chapters are predicated on the regulation of anti-competitive conduct and consumer protection, from the point of view of media ownership, broadcast rules and online content on digital platforms. The regulation necessarily centres on cyber safety and prevention of harm from cybercriminal activity. Chapter 7 is an evaluation of the conflict of laws as applied to online environments given that jurisdictional issues are a major consideration on the borderless Internet. A corollary to this is the development of uniform rules in terms of the choice of law determinations. Chapter 8 is on the regulation of cryptographic goods and services and a review of dual-use goods. The focus here is on the regulatory framework that better manages national security risks of espionage, sabotage and foreign interference of Australia's telecommunication networks and facilities.

Part II Online Public Services. Chapter 1 outlines the legal and policy framework for e-government in Australia. The theme here is that e-government and governance is a business of the state. Antecedents to e-government policy statements and initiatives and e-readiness measures and performance suggest that the success is due in part to the use of integrated service delivery in social security and health services. The pandemic response underscores the pivotal role that information communication technology plays in the delivery of services. Chapter 2 sketches the legal framework for e-health delivery within the Australian healthcare system. The national e-Health Strategy proposes a staged approach that leverages capacities, variations across the health sector and levels of government. The manner in which the regulatory and legal frameworks are fashioned to support healthcare strategy from identifiers, through to therapeutic goods, liability and litigation as well as emergency measures to counter the COVID-19 pandemic and security obligations touching on critical infrastructures are unpicked and described here. Chapter 3 is about the Australian electoral system and the modalities of electronic voting. Whether any design of electronic online voting can ensure voter secrecy and absolute integrity in vote counting can achieve the same excitement and passion as the traditional face-to-face methods is assessed here. The Australian parliament suggests that electoral system is in no position to introduce any large-scale means of electronic voting at any time soon without catastrophically compromising electoral integrity and other considerations of costs, integrity, voter identity and secrecy. Chapter 4 is on other e-government services foremost being the national e-conveyancing project. The regulatory framework to facilitate implementing e-conveyancing nationally is discussed and its performance reviewed. e-Invoicing is a further governmental transnational initiative that is supported by the necessary legislation and mandates. Business transactions through an electronically based payment and invoicing system to provide a further means of facilitating supplies and payments is also presented. The Trans-Tasman agreement between Australia and New Zealand for e-invoicing is discussed.

Part III Online Transactions. Chapter 1 addresses online transactions from the perspective of e-commerce and the Internet. The legal framework afforded by the

Electronic Transactions Act 1999 permits e-commerce to fit into the same processes as traditional paper-based transactions and gives consumers a choice to use the most efficacious means to transact commerce. In Chapter 2 electronic contracts are addressed to highlight its distinctive aspects unapparent in the conventional form and to restate the principles of contract law for an electronic environment. There is a discussion on consumer protection in the use of self-executing 'smart' contracts and distributed ledger technology 'blockchains' and the emergent issues arising therefrom. This is followed in Chapter 3 of a discussion on digital signatures and the public key infrastructure framework. The issues of integrity, vulnerability, security and authentication are common themes for both e-signatures and the public key infrastructure framework. Model laws on signatures and remote witnessing is also discussed. In Chapter 4 the developments in public key infrastructure processes that introduce digital certificates, the possibilities for e-procurement and e-tendering are discussed given the need for trust mechanisms and security tools for e-commerce transactions. Chapter 5 discusses online financial services and consumer retail payment systems and how consumers, businesses and financial institutions transfer funds to one another to satisfy their respective obligations. The regulatory framework underpinning these relationships are presented to highlight the different and alternative payment instruments. The trends and developments in the enforcement of the regulations and funds transfer codes are discussed within the newly developed national payments platform. In these discussions the underlying concern for consumer protection is foremost given the emergence of neo-banks, digital assets and cryptocurrencies mixing in with traditional payment systems. In Chapter 6 the law of evidence in the digital environment is presented. The framework for the law of evidence is shown to require flexibility with an extension to the norms of evidence given its electronic nature and its intangibility. The admissibility of electronic mail and other media such as text messages and 'screen shots' challenge authenticity thresholds for their admissibility in court. A discussion on electronic archiving of public documents and the regulatory environment is also presented here. Chapter 7 focuses on consumer protection in online sales and service under State and Territory laws with the Commonwealth powers limited to corporations and interstate trade. Australian Consumer Law applying to all Australian businesses who deal with consumers and regulating all manner of business conduct is elaborated. In Chapter 8 online liability addresses the central question of 'who did what wrongful conduct' in cyberspace. The characterization of the role of various participants is as important as the media by which the business is conducted. Common law and statutory liability are discussed generally and then specifically under copyright law, defamation, the Australian consumer law and statutory and intermediary liability. The latter two items are pertinent in addressing vilification and abhorrent violent material posted online.

Part IV Digital Property Rights highlights the parallels with traditional intellectual property rights. Chapter 1 is about patent protection for software under the *Patents Act* 1990. Digital patents cover computer-implemented inventions most typically those that use software to achieve the desired results. The protection is for the design processes that deliver functionality to the inventions. The debate on the patentability of artificial intelligent inventions because of a lack of an 'inventor' is presented here. In Chapter 2 copyright protection for software is presented together with other protection methods such as trademarks, open-source software licences and the exemptions for embedded software in medical devices. Chapter 3 presents trademarks in a digital context. The legal framework that distinguishes between 'use' as in deployment and 'use' as in illustration is explained here as is the unregistered trademark. Aspects of trademark law that are raised by online triggered ads, online trading, online brands, trademark dilution and other trademark infringements are discussed. Australian trends and global impacts of trademarks are also given here. Chapter 4 is about the protection of digital designs. The law governing digital design assets and online services is presented including 3D printing, graphical user interfaces for virtual and non-physical designs and typefaces and fonts. The unregistered design right is presented together with the design-copyright law overlap and prospective reforms that are on the horizon for virtual and non-physical designs such as the use of non-fungible tokens to protect digital assets. In Chapter 5 copyright protection for digital assets is discussed considering online information technology data. Protective methods such as the digital fingerprinting of documents, digital rights management laws, geo-blocking that controls access to digital content from physical locations and safe harbour principles that deal with copyright infringement are discussed at length. Chapter 6 focuses on the legal bases for the protection of electronic databases. Copyright norms prescribed by the *Copyright Act* 1968 applied to electronic data are examined as well as other legal protections under patent, contract, confidential information, passing-off, criminal law and unfair competition. A brief examination of technological protection measures is included here. In Chapter 7 electronic data rights within the consumer data right provisions are discussed. Chapter 8 presents the legal protection of circuit layouts given the importance of integrated circuits in all electronic equipment. The protection given under the *Circuit Layouts Act* 1989 like those in copyright law is discussed in terms of the relationships with other intellectual property rights such as trade secrets, and patent law together with infringements and enforcement remedies. In Chapter 9 the Internet Domain Names system is presented from the viewpoint of its administration, licensing and registration and dispute resolution procedures. Australian and international reforms of the domain names system are also presented.

Part V Cybersecurity Legal Issues is about digital security of a nation's cyberspace and the defence of national digital assets. In Chapter 1 the defence of networks and digital assets from malicious attacks through regulation and national preparedness is presented. Data on cyberattacks and its implications are given here. Chapter 2 presents the national security framework – a set if processes and policies positioned to secure the threat environment. The key roles of entities such as the Department of Home Affairs and the Australian Signals Directorate are highlighted together with the key cybersecurity trends, issues and challenges in the decade of the 2020s. The Cybersecurity Strategy of 2020 is discussed together with the Australian Surveillance Framework that together have brought about regulatory changes impacting on the telecommunication industry. In Chapter 3 the legal frameworks for sector-specific obligations are discussed considering the *Security of Critical Infrastructure Act* 2020. Amendments to this Act in 2021 now cover a greater number of asset classes across eleven sectors together with an economy-wide approach to raise businesses' cybersecurity capabilities and responsibilities. Privacy in terms of notifiable data breaches, data protection and consumer protection have been acknowledged under this security regime. Chapter 4 outlines the respective public and private sector roles under the Act and examines the impact on the various sectors of the economy including the financial, health, communication, utilities and higher education respectively. In Chapter 5 reform of the cybersecurity strategy is analysed by examining proposals for governance standards, minimum standards for personal information, standards for smart devices, disclosure policies, small business 'health checks' and legal remedies for consumers. The key in these proposals is how regulation may be strengthened to better protect the nation from cybersecurity threats and the legal options available for redress. Chapter 6 describes Australian international and global citizenship given that international engagement is important to ensure cyberspace and critical technologies lead to a safe and secure world. Australia's participation in the Paris Call for trust and security in cyberspace underscores the government's commitment to cybersecurity.

Part VI Cybercrime. In Chapter 1 a classification scheme for cybercrime attempts to distinguish between cyber-dependent crimes from cyber-enabled crimes. The nature and extent of cybercrime based on industry and government statistics demonstrates its impact on society and the economy. Chapter 2 lays out Commonwealth cybercrime legislation under uniform Criminal Code provisions applicable to all jurisdictions as well as legislative amendments not only to enable adoption of the Cybercrime Convention but also to regulate mutual assistance to other nations. This chapter also examines telecommunications and cybercrime offences such as unauthorized interception and access, content regulation, online safety, the general prohibition of online abhorrent and violent material, suicide related material, money laundering and the financing of terrorism and anti-discrimination laws. In Chapter 3 State and Territory cybercrime laws are discussed in a highly selective manner, if only to exemplify different approaches to address a similar problem posed by cybercrimes. Chapter 4 examines the topic of the computer and systems as a target of criminal activity. The criminal use of the domain name system is examined first followed by unauthorized access such as hacking and cracking. Next, the legal codes in selected States are discussed separately to show variations on a theme. Then distributed denial of service attacks is presented with a following section on malware infection of information technology systems. Hardware and software tools used to commit cybercrime is discussed next together with a discussion of unsolicited penetration testing of information technology systems and identity theft and fraud. By way of contrast Chapter 5 examines computers and systems as tools and attack vectors. Crimes such as online fraud represented as phishing, electronic theft of data and information, posting of offensive content and revenge porn, sexting, online sabotage and information warfare are given within the cybercrime context and the existing legislation. Chapter 6 is about traditional crimes in a digital context. The discussion begins with offences against the person and personnel that spans offences against decency, hate speech, defamation, cyberbullying and cyberstalking as common law and criminal offences. This is followed by outlining financial criminal offences from online fraud to theft, extortion, money laundering and other financial frauds. In the e-business sector, advertising fraud is discussed as an online crime that affects both consumers and businesses alike. Cybercrime touching on nation-state security posed by a 'parallel' Internet and dark web that is used by criminals is also discussed here. In Chapter 7 cybercrime law enforcement and criminal procedures in Australia are outlined. The respective roles of the Australian Hi-Tech Crime Centre and the Transnational Crime Coordination Centre are described. Data retention, interception of electronic communications, network searches and seizure of data policies are outlined. Court procedures and jurisdictional issues are presented together with defences and mitigating factors in cybercriminal activity. Chapter 8 presents the national cybercrime strategy and prospective legislation in relation to ransomware payments, social media defamation and basic expectations on user safety online. Chapter 9 describes Australian participation in international and regional agreements in terms of the Cybercrime Convention, law enforcement, cooperative agreement with neighbouring countries, US Cloud Agreement on the access to electronic data to counter serious crime, international production orders to access data of communication service providers overseas and the cyber and critical technology partnership with the UK.

Summary and Conclusions is a reflective section on information technology law in Australia and a postscript to this volume. The themes running through this monograph are summarized and prospective legislation and policy developments on the horizon are outlined. As the Web 3.0, metaverse and 5G technology would probably dominate the Internet, these megatrends are discussed together with the legal infrastructure that may be necessary to guide, limit, regulate and encourage the development of technology for the benefit of netizens, the nation-state and the world.

This monograph has been reviewed by the Author and the Australian law current as of November 2022.

General Introduction

1. This General Introduction consists of four chapters. Chapter 1 gives readers a background to Australia in terms of its geography, cultural composition and political system. This is followed by a brief outline of its population, the economy and social and cultural milieu of Australians. Chapter 2 surveys the *Australian Telecommunication and Digital Infrastructure* as the sector responds to the difficult challenges presented by the rapidly changing information economy. The 'regalian' functions of a sovereign state are presented in terms of finance, laws and national security that run in parallel to the mundane day-to-day organization and delivery of public services such as health, education, justice and government services. The twinning of law and e-government are described as is the government's leading role in promoting the digital economy. The proper function of these aspects of the economy are intrinsically bound with rules of law, an economic system and a set of cultural values that underpin all such activity. These endeavours assist in the overall performance of the nation-state competing on an international stage. In Chapter 3 the *Information Technology Market* operating within the national economy is discussed. COVID-19 containment measures have witnessed restricted economic activities leading to a large fall in gross domestic product in 2020. Yet, Australia's use of digital technologies remains unabated given the data on participation rates in the digital economy either in terms of Internet activity or the household use of information technology. Chapter 4 continues the theme of *e-Commerce Activity* and the pandemic's impact on m-commerce and health delivery and the overall contribution of information communication technology to the Australian economy.

Chapter 1. Background to the Country

§1. Geography

2. Australia is the lowest, flattest and, apart from Antarctica, the driest of the continents. Australia comprises a land area of almost 7.7 million sq. kilometres.[1] This land mass makes Australia the sixth largest land area of all countries in the world exceeded only by Brazil, China, the United States of America, Canada and Russia.

3. Australia is an island continent situated in the Southern Hemisphere between the Indian Ocean and the South Pacific. Except for the coastal areas, much of Australia is dry and arid. Australia's nearest neighbours are Papua New Guinea and Indonesia to the north, New Zealand to the southeast and the Melanesian and Polynesian islands to the east.

4. In a jurisdictional and economic sense, Australia extends well beyond the mainland continent and Tasmania, including about 12,000 islands. While most of these islands are small, the 1982 United Nations Convention on the Law of the Sea grants Australian jurisdiction over large tracts of the ocean and seafloor that surround them. Australia also administers a portion of Antarctica, the Australian Antarctic Territory.

§2. Cultural Composition

5. Although recent migrants are more likely to be from Asia, many Australians continue to be of Anglo-Saxon origin, and the dominant culture, language, manners and customs remain like those found in other Anglo-Saxon countries such as England, Canada and the United States. Recent migrants who have acquired permanent Australian resident status were born overseas comprise about 8 per cent of Australia's population aged 15 and over. The United Kingdom (14 per cent) and India (13 per cent) provided the highest number of recent migrants, followed by the People's Republic of China and Taiwan with 10 per cent.[2] Australia in the twenty-first century is a multicultural country that is home to significant numbers of migrants from many other countries, including Italy, Greece and Vietnam.

6. There were estimated to be about 800,000 Aboriginal and Torres Strait Islander people in Australia on 30 June 2019, or 3.3 per cent of the total population.[3] Most of these indigenous Australians live in non-remote areas (79.8 per cent), and

1. Australian Bureau of Statistics (ABS) 2012 1301.0 – *Year Book Australia, 2012. See* GeoScience Australia at https://www.ga.gov.au/scientific-topics/national-location-information/dimensions/australias-size-compared.
2. *Ibid.* ABS 2012 1301.0 – *Year Book Australia*, 2012.
3. *See* Australian Institute of Health and Welfare (2019) *Australia's Welfare in brief'*, Cat. No. AUS227, Canberra: AIHW, pg. 60 at https://www.aihw.gov.au/reports/australias-welfare/australias-welfare-2017-in-brief/contents/indigenous-australians.

the indigenous population is much younger than the non-indigenous population. The median age was 21.8 years for indigenous and 37.6 years for non-indigenous.

7. Indigenous Australians experience widespread socioeconomic disadvantage and health inequality. Factors like discrimination and racism, violence, alcohol and drug use and high psychological distress have a negative impact on their social and emotional well-being. Poor social and emotional well-being, in turn, affect employment, income, living conditions and opportunities. Their struggle for recognition and a rightful share of Australia's considerable wealth continues in the new century.

§3. Political System

I. The Constitution and System of Government

8. Australia has a federal system of government within which there are four divisions: Commonwealth, state, territory and local governments.[4]

9. The formal powers of the Commonwealth Parliament are constitutionally limited to areas of national importance such as trade and commerce, taxation, postal services, foreign relations, defence, immigration, naturalization, quarantine, currency and coinage, weights and measures, copyright, patents and trademarks.[5]

10. However, High Court decisions, Commonwealth-state agreements and use by the Commonwealth of the constitutional power to make grants to the states and territories, have seen the Commonwealth gain influence on other matters including industrial relations, financial regulation, companies and securities, health and welfare and education.

11. All powers not specifically granted by the Constitution to the Commonwealth government are reserved to the states.

12. Where there is an inconsistency between state and commonwealth law, the commonwealth legislation prevails.[6]

13. More than half of Parliament's time is taken up with the consideration of proposed legislation. Between 150 and 250 Bills are passed each year, and most are non-contentious, either being 'good governance' legislation necessary for the orderly processes of government, or Bills that propose alterations to existing legislation. Most of the Bills are government Bills; legislation sponsored by private members is rare.

4. Australian Parliament House, Parliamentary Library 2011, *Parliamentary Handbook of the Commonwealth of Australia* (32nd ed., Canberra).
5. Commonwealth of Australia Constitution Act 1900 (Imp) 63 and 64 Vic, c 12 (Imp).
6. Australian Constitution Act 1900, s. 92.

14. The Australian nation was created by the federation of the six British self-governing colonies of New South Wales (NSW), Tasmania, Queensland, Western Australia (WA), Victoria and South Australia (SA). Under the constitutional arrangements that came into existence in 1901, significant powers were retained by these states. State administrative responsibilities include education, police, public health, public transport, agriculture, roads, community services, corrective services, mineral resources, emergency services, ports and the oversight of local government.

15. The state governments derive their powers from the former British Colonies established by British Act of Parliament. However, today, all Australian states have their own constitutions and complete political independence from Britain. All states, except Queensland, have a bicameral legislature with an upper house serving review functions. Queensland has a unicameral parliament.

16. The Northern Territory (NT) and the Australian Capital Territory (ACT) came under the control of the Commonwealth Government in 1911. The NT (since 1978) and the ACT (since 1989) are self-governing territories with powers almost matching those of the states.

17. The Australian political system is one of democratically elected governments – general elections must be held at least once every three years. The governmental framework in Australia draws on features from both the British parliamentary system and the American checks and balances system. Australia is a constitutional monarchy with allegiance to the Queen who maintains a representative at Commonwealth and state levels. By virtue of the *Australia Act* 1986 (Cth), however, Australia terminated all British control over the former colonies. There is much debate about whether Australia should become a republic and have a president.

18. The government is formed by the majority party in the lower house of Parliament, the leader of which serves as Prime Minister assisted by a cabinet comprised of other members of Parliament drawn from both the House of Representatives (lower house) and Senate (upper house). Membership in the House of Representatives representing geographic regions based upon proportion of population (totalling 151 members) while the Senate is comprised of an equal number of senators (12) from each state and two from each of the territories giving a total of seventy-six senators.

19. Since WWII the balance of political power has shifted markedly in favour of the federal government. This is especially so since 1942, when the Commonwealth government began collecting income tax revenue that was then reapportioned to the states on an agreed formula. The Commonwealth government has used its 'external affairs' powers to commit Australia to various treaty obligations, which have enabled the Commonwealth government in turn to override any inconsistent state laws.[7]

II. Judicial Power

20. The highest court in Australia is the High Court, which consists of seven justices, though it is unusual for the court to sit *en banc*.[8] The High Court hears appeals from the state Supreme Courts and is the final Court of Appeal in the Australian legal system.[9] It also acts as the guardian and interpreter of the Australian Constitution. The High Court has original jurisdiction in matters such as indictable Commonwealth offences.

21. Also, on the federal level is the Family Court of Australia, which governs marriage disputes as prescribed under the *Family Law Act* 1975 (Cth).

22. The Federal Court of Australia was created by the *Federal Court of Australia Act* 1976 (Cth) and began to exercise its jurisdiction on 1 February 1977. The Federal Court of Australia has original jurisdiction in other federal matters, such as industrial law, patents, trademarks, bankruptcy and antitrust. The Federal Court sits in all capital cities as well as other locations from time to time throughout Australia.

23. The Federal Court's original jurisdiction is conferred by over 150 statutes of the Parliament. The Federal Court also has a broad range of appellate jurisdiction.

24. The Federal Court shares first instance jurisdiction with the Supreme Courts of the States and Territories around intellectual property (IP) such as copyright, patents, trademarks, designs and circuit layouts.[10]

25. Appeal from the Federal Court is to the Full Court of the Federal Court and to the High Court. Each of the States and Territories has its own court system that is comprised of various administrative tribunals, inferior courts, a court of general jurisdiction and a Court of Appeal.

---

7. *See* for example *Commonwealth of Australia v. State of Tasmania* (1983) 158 CLR 1, in which the Commonwealth government relied on its obligations pursuant to a world heritage area designation to block the construction of a dam.
8. French for 'on the bench'. The term is used when all judges of a particular court hear a case.
9. Until 1986 it was possible to have an appeal from a state Supreme Court to the Privy Council in England. This avenue of appeal ended with the passage of the *Australia Act* 1986 (Cth).
10. *See* Federal Court jurisdiction at http://www.fedcourt.gov.au/about/jurisdiction.

III. Political Parties

26. Australian parliaments have been dominated by the tightly controlled parties since the early twentieth century. Strong party discipline and party unity has made political attitudes more predictable and tended to narrow the parliamentary debate.

27. Australia today has two major political parties: The Australian Labor Party, which on most matters is further to the political left than the more conservative Liberal-National Party coalition, which ruled Australia from the 1950s through the 1970s, and again during much of the past two decades. During the 1980s, the Australian Labor Party was in the majority, led for most of that time by Bob Hawke and by Paul Keating. From 1996-2007 Australia was led by the Liberal-National party coalition under the leadership of John Howard. Kevin Rudd was elected Prime Minister in 2007 and replaced in June 2010 by Julia Guillard, who became Australia's twenty-seventh Prime Minister and the first woman to win that position. In June 2013, Mr Rudd's party returned him to the leadership, and he once again became Prime Minister. The 2013 election saw the return to government of the Liberal-National Party Coalition and the election of Tony Abbott as Australia's Prime Minister, subsequently deposed by Malcolm Turnbull in 2015 and then replaced by Scott Morrison in 2018.

28. Other political parties attract significant support but in small numbers. The Democratic Party for a time had controlled the balance of power in the Federal Senate by agreeing to cast its votes with either labour or liberal to give them a majority. The National Party represents agricultural interests and usually forms a coalition with the conservative Liberal party. In the 2016 Federal Elections for the Forty-fifth Parliament of Australia the Greens, the Nick Xenophon Team, Katter's Australian Party and independents Wilkie and McGowan won a seat each. For the first time since federation, the post-election opposition won more seats than the post-election government in the two most populous states, NSW, and Victoria.

29. The 2019 Federal Elections for the Forty-sixth Parliament of Australia saw the election of a Coalition with a three-seat majority of seventy-seven seats, with Labor winning sixty-eight whilst the remaining six seats were won by members from the minor parties including, the Australian Greens, Centre Alliance, Katter's Australian Party and three independents.

§4. Population

30. Though occupying a land mass as large as the size of the continental United States, much of Australia is a sparsely populated dry desert. Most of the population of approximately 22.4 million live on the fertile coastal regions of the east and south-west coast, and approximately half of the population resides in the seven capital cities. Of these capital cities, Sydney has approximately 4.6 million people, Melbourne 4.2 million, Brisbane 2.1 million, Perth 1.8 million and Adelaide 1.2 million people with Canberra having 462,000 and Darwin 147,000 people. Ironically, despite its large land mass and small population, Australia has a population density that makes it one of the most urbanized countries in the world. Australia's unemployment rate was 4.5 per cent in August 2021.[11]

31. Australia is one of the most urbanized countries in the world with almost 64 per cent of its population living in its five largest cities, which, along with most of the remaining population, is clustered predominantly along the coastal fringe, primarily in the east and southeast of the country. Half the continent contains 0.3 per cent of the population, and 84 per cent of the population occupies only 1 per cent of the continent.[12]

§5. Economy

32. According to the Heritage Economic Freedom Index, Australia ranks third of all countries behind Hong Kong (first) and Singapore (second). Over the twenty years the Heritage Economic Freedom Index has been in existence, Australia has been among the top ten in terms of overall improvement – a testament to its long-term commitment and achievements in economic reform.[13] The inflation rate has been low (3.5 per cent) and Australia attracts approximately AUD 1 trillion a year in foreign direct investment (FDI).[14]

33. Australia is a developed country and rich in natural resources. Farming and mining continue to be major exports along with a rapidly growing service industry and minor manufacturing. Australia's leading farm products are cattle, wheat and wool, followed by dairy products. Australia's major sources of economic activity include agriculture (including forestry and fishing), mining and quarrying, manufacturing, tourism, and education and financial services (including insurance, real estate and business).[15]

34. Australia is the world's largest exporter of wool and a major exporter of sugar, beef and wheat, rice, eggs, cotton, potatoes and vegetables. Major mining exports are bauxite, industrial diamonds, lead, copper, gold, iron ore, manganese, silver, aluminium, zinc and nickel.

11. Australian Bureau of Statistics (2021) 6202.0 -- *Labour Force Australia* (August 2021) at https://www.abs.gov.au/statistics/labour/employment-and-unemployment/labour-force-australia/latest-release#media-releases.
12. *See ABS Australia* Yearbook 2012 Catalogue 1301.0 at http://www.abs.gov.au/ausstats/abs@.nsf/Lookup/1301.0Main+Features782012.
13. *See* Heritage Economic Freedom Index at http://www.heritage.org/index/.
14. *See* Austrade (2021) https://www.austrade.gov.au/news/economic-analysis/who-invests-in-australia-analysing-2020-s-4-trillion-record-for-foreign-investmenthttp://www.heritage.org/index/country/australia.
15. *See* Reserve Bank of Australia (2022) at https://www.rba.gov.au/snapshots/economy-indicators-snapshot/.

35. Major service industries include financial services, tourism, transport, communication and education.

36. Manufacturing exports include processed foods, clothing, shoes and household appliances.

37. Australia also has a significant fishing industry, exporting lobsters, abalone, oysters, prawns, scallops, salmon and tuna.

38. Australia's major two-way trading partners are China followed by Japan. Approximately 70 per cent of Australia's trade is conducted with Asia-Pacific Economic Cooperation (APEC) nation members.[16]

39. Australia has been an active player in the G-20 summit and internationally through its participation in World Trade Organization (WTO) and other international organizations.[17] In addition it has multiple bilateral and other free trade agreements with other countries beginning 1983 till 2022.[18]

40. As an advanced economy, Australia has also been among the leading countries in its promotion of both e-government and e-commerce. It consequently has introduced and continues to work on providing the necessary legal infrastructure to promote these developments.

§6. Social and Cultural Values

41. Australia has a mixed free enterprise economy, and it has significantly deregulated some industries, such as banking and aviation. Like many Western democracies, Australia has increasingly moved to a view of government as a guide for general policy, as opposed to a primary deliverer of services. This has led to significant outsourcing of traditional government activities to the private sector and to a blurring of public and private sector economic activity.

42. The social and cultural values that shape and form the foundation of Australia's legal system are found in the traditional freedoms of a free enterprise economy. These include private ownership of property and the right to make a profit from it, freedom of contract, commerce and industry to engage in any pursuit one chooses, freedom of association, whereby one is free to join with others in a commercial venture and freedom of labour, whereby one is free to contract to work in any position as mutually agreed between employer and employee.

16. Department of Foreign Affairs and Trade (2010) Composition of Trade Australia at https://www.dfat.gov.au/publications/stats-pubs/cot-cy-2010.pdf.
17. Wiseman, JR (1988) Global Nation: Australia? Australia and the Politics of Globalization (Cambridge University Press 1998).
18. Department of Foreign Affairs and Trade (2022) at https://www.dfat.gov.au/trade/agreements/in-force/free-trade-agreements-in-force.

43. Australia's cultural values are increasingly shaped by a global economy, as trade barriers have come down, and Australian businesses have operated on an international stage. Economic and social values have also been impacted by Australia's rapid uptake of information technology. The growth of e-commerce has further accelerated Australia's global outlook and presents significant challenges to existing commercial laws, which are premised in a world of paper commerce.

Chapter 2. Telecommunications and Digital Infrastructure

§1. Australia's Challenges in the Information Economy

44. Telecommunications infrastructure is understood in general terms to include landline telephone usage, mobile phones, television sets, personal computers, the Internet and other means of communication. A telecommunications infrastructure index may be computed from these elements per 1000 persons in the jurisdiction.

45. An obvious face of digital infrastructure is having a reliable and fit-for-purpose mobile and fixed phone and broadband services. Without this, access to digital services that is used everyday by Australians like banking, healthcare, entertainment and communicating with family, friends and at work would be impossible.

46. Digital infrastructures also include location-based technologies, such as global positioning systems (GPS), that is increasingly driving the development of new products and services around the world. Advances in location-based technology are needed to support emerging applications that require highly precise location information including automated vehicles and drones.

47. In regional areas, improved broadband services and location-based technology supports innovation and the delivery of services to remote areas in the farming, construction and mining industries.

48. Demonstrably the accelerating growth of the Internet of Things (IOT) is evidenced by the increasing number of Australian families investing in technology to enable smart homes where lighting, heating and security systems can all be controlled with mobile applications and devices.[19] The pace at which adoption of such innovation is dependent on continuing private sector and government investment.

49. Any national digital infrastructure also needs to be secure. A key strategy in reducing national security risks in the adopting of new technologies (including infrastructure such as 5G and the IOT) is the promotion of security-by-design where technologies are designed from the ground up to be secure and not as a future consideration.[20]

50. The federal government does not directly subsidize the construction of broadband infrastructure or the use of retail broadband services. However, in 2009, the government set up a state-owned corporation, National Broadband Network (NBN) Co to design, build and operate a wholesale-only next generation network. Currently, NBN relies on government funding, and earns revenue primarily by selling wholesale access to its network to retail telecommunications operators.

---

19. *See* Department of Industry (2018) *Australia's Tech Future* at https://www.industry.gov.au/sites/default/files/2018-12/australias-tech-future.pdf.
20. *Ibid.* Australia's Tech Future.

51. The NBN is being built in partnership with the private sector and represents one of the largest nation-building infrastructure projects in Australian history.[21] The NBN will:

- connect 90 per cent of all Australian homes, schools and workplaces with broadband services with speeds up to 100 megabits per second, 100 times faster than those currently used by many households and businesses;
- connect all other premises in Australia with next generation wireless and satellite technologies that will deliver broadband speeds of 12 megabits per second; and,
- directly support up to 25,000 local jobs every year, on average, over the eight-year life of the project.

52. The rollout of Australia's NBN was seriously over-budget and behind schedule under the Labor Government. Since 2016 the government has taken its time in both reappraising the underlying business model on which the broadband is based with a view to substantially reducing the costs. As well there are serious regulatory, financial and practical problems to be overcome. Most prominent of these is how to find a cost-effective way to reach remote and rural areas.

53. At the end of 2020 the NBN formally announced the completion of the network. At the end of the 2020 financial year, almost 12 million premises were ready to connect and approximately 8.2 million homes and businesses already connected to the NBN.[22]

54. The COVID-19 pandemic affected the telecommunications industry during 2020-2021. During this period residential consumers and small businesses continued to rely on phone and Internet services to work, study from home and stay connected to family and friends at unprecedented levels.

55. As broadband and online applications became essential to support remote working, education, entertainment and social connection, NBN reported 81 per cent higher daytime peaks for downstream traffic than the pre-pandemic baseline.[23]

56. In this globalized world with the challenges of the knowledge and information economy, Australia has several natural advantages and disadvantages. Advantages include a well-educated population with a high take-up rate of new technology, a solid base of scientific, engineering and technical expertise and an improved regulatory framework. Australia is also advantaged because of its multicultural society and depth of cultural awareness. This multicultural talent enables Australia to develop and sustain international and global cross-cultural networks upon which tomorrow's business will be based.

---

21. *See* Department of Communications at https://www.communications.gov.au/what-we-do/internet/national-broadband-network.
22. *See* National Broadband Network (2022) https://www.nbnco.com.au/corporate-information/about-nbn-co/corporate-plan/weekly-progress-report.
23. ACCC Communications Market Report 2019-20 at https://www.accc.gov.au/system/files/20-47RPT_Communications_Market_Report_FA.pdf.

57. The disadvantages include distance from major markets, small and aging population, lack of venture capital, under-funded research and education, small size of Australian firms, existence of few head offices of international companies, over-dependence on mining and agriculture, and threats of a significant brain drain of Australia's best and brightest to Europe, US and elsewhere. These disadvantages have been recognized in the National Strategic Framework for the Information Economy report in December 1998, a picture which is largely unchanged in the 2020s and beyond.[24]

58. While Australia has its competitive advantages, new challenges have emerged. According to the Business Council of Australia (BCA) and others, there is a dire need to respond quickly with several key reforms, including the need, among others to invest in infrastructure; sustain and even grow its population; repair federal finances; engage in regulatory (financial system, taxation and labour) reforms; reduce the amount of regulatory red tape; and pass laws and regulatory systems that better facilitate the growth of startups and sustainable development.[25]

59. A digital transformation of the economy has been touted to overcoming some of the burdens and baggage of the information age. According to Dutta & Lanvin (2020) digital transformation of any nation involves at least four levels of McKinsey's typology.[26] These include:

1. 'the "regalian" functions of a sovereign state (for example, in fiscal matters, laws and regulations, national security);
2. the day-to-day organization and delivery of public services (health, education, justice and most government services);
3. the proper functioning of the economy and society according to some set of accepted rules (typically a constitution), a particular economic system, as well as a set of cultural and confessional values; and,
4. the overall efficiency and performance of the national economy, as it competes on the international scene'.

60. As its first steps in this transformation the adoption of a digital by default for all transactions is a prime necessity. Such a strategy specifies explicit savings targets to drive change and proposes decisive actions to remove legislative barriers to digital transactions.

---

24. *See* NOIE 1988, A Strategic Framework for the Information Economy – Identifying Priorities for Action, National Office for the Information Economy (December 1998), at https://www.noie.gov.au/nationalstrategy/index.html.
25. Business Council of Australia, *Action Plan for Enduring Prosperity* (2013) at http://www.acbc.com.au/.
26. Dutta, S & Lanvin, B (eds.) (2020) *The Network Readiness Index 2020. Accelerating Digital Transformation in a post-COVID Global Economy*, Portulans Institute at: https://networkreadinessindex.org/wp-content/uploads/2020/11/NRI-2020-V828-11-2020.pdf.

§2. Law and e-Government

61. An essential element and tool for achieving an effective Information Economy is a legal infrastructure that provides the guidance and certainty which is required for domestic and foreign businesses to invest in that growth.[27] An Information Economy will not eventuate organically unless there is a legal infrastructure in place to promote and support it. The legal infrastructure required to support this new architecture and government initiatives in e-commerce includes the provision of ICT infrastructure; regulations governing content; domain names; protection of intellectual property rights (IPR); recognition of electronic signatures and public key encryption; electronic procurement; recognizing electronic forms of contract in B2B international trade; consumer protection; responsive criminal and civil law; protection of privacy; online dispute resolution (ODR); and augmenting cybersecurity and curbing cybercrime.

62. For a legal system to be relevant, and to keep up with this new e-government environment, it is also important to see law as part of a wider system with many convergent parts if e-government is to succeed.[28]

63. E-government is to be considered as part of the larger context of the country's innovation system. The infrastructure provided by e-government becomes a major factor in the promotion of innovation.

64. The Australian legal framework should aim to ensure that people's digital data are protected and gives them a *de facto* right to digital government.

65. The country has a central e-government portal that is home to more than 900 Australian government websites. In brief, the portal provides a simple and secure way to access online government services such as employment, the Australian Taxation Office (ATO), Services Australia: Child Support, My Aged Care, My Health Record and the National Disability Insurance Scheme.

§3. Government's Role in Promoting the Digital Economy

66. A 'digital economy' is characterized by the range of economic and social activities that are enabled by information and communications technologies. It includes activities like banking, e-commerce and e-business, and accessing education or entertainment using the Internet and connected devices. The digital economy is an integral part of the economy. Such an economy impacts on all industries and business types and influences the way people interact with each other everyday. It

27. Ramsfield, J (2000) *The Law as Architecture* (West-Thomson); Banathy, B (1996) *Designing Social Systems in a Changing World* (Plenum Press).
28. Bhatnagar, SC (2002) *E-government: From Vision to Implementation: A Practical Guide with Case Studies* (Sage Publications); and Zahir, I & Lov, P (2013) *Evaluating Information Systems* (Routledge).

also recognizes that as sectors become data driven their economic structures change, industry boundaries blur and the basis of competition evolves.

67. The *National Digital Economy Strategy* (NDES) (2011) set out the vision for realizing the benefits of the NBN to position Australia as a leading digital economy by 2020.[29] The Australian Government Information Management Office (AGIMO) was tasked to achieve the stated goal of improved online government service delivery and engagement by 2020 where four out of five Australians will choose to engage with the government through the Internet or other type of online services.

68. *Advancing Australia as a Digital Economy* (2013) updated the 2011 NDES and laid out the next steps towards delivering the vision for 2020 and beyond.[30] The strategic update provided an overview of individual initiatives and outlines new initiatives representing the progress being made by the Australian government to embrace the digital future.[31]

69. In 2017 the Department of Industry, Innovation and Science (2017) paper *The Digital Economy: Opening Up the Conversation* began the dialogue with all Australians where the government sought ideas to help develop the strategy.[32] The responses helped identify the key issues, challenges and opportunities, and the way forward.[33]

70. The *Digital Economy Strategy* 2018 set out how the government, the private sector and community can work together to build competitive strengths and build new ones. The aims were to develop world-leading digital business capability for globally engaged, innovative, high-growth businesses of all sizes. In addition, the strategy would drive a culture and mindset that supports lifelong learning; a global outlook and to help respond positively to change; and address the 'digital divide' in skills and confidence to help all Australians to succeed in a digital economy.[34]

71. In support of its *Digital Economy Strategy* 2018 the government established several agencies responsible for the different elements that make up e-commerce

29. Steward, A (2016) *AGIMO: The Australian Government releases the National Digital Economy Strategy* (2011) at https://www.finance.gov.au/blog/2011/05/31/australian-government-releases-national-digital-economy-strategy/ (last updated 01 Aug. 2016).
30. Australian Government Department of Broadband, Communications and the Digital Economy (DBCDE) 2013 *Advancing Australia as a Digital Economy: An Update to the National Digital Economy Strategy* (see Index of Initiatives in the Executive Summary, p. x) and also *ICT Reports Advancing Australia as a Digital Economy* – DBCDE June 2013 at http://ict-industry-reports.com.au/advancing-australia-as-a-digital-economy/.
31. Prime Minister and Cabinet, Transforming the Commonwealth's Digital Agenda (14 Oct. 2016), at https://ministers.pmc.gov.au/taylor/2016/transforming-commonwealths-digital-agenda.
32. Digital Economy at https://industry.gov.au/innovation/Digital-Economy/Pages/default.aspx.
33. Australian Government Department of Industry, Innovation and Science (2017) *The Digital Economy: Opening Up the Conversation* at https://www.industry.gov.au/innovation/Digital-Economy/Documents/Digital-Economy-Strategy-Consultation-Paper.pdf.
34. *Ibid. The Digital Economy.*

discussed below. In addition, there has been a subtle shift towards the implementation of a 'digital by default' strategy, like the one adopted in the United Kingdom. A manifestation of this is the switch from an 'opt-in' arrangement for myGov to a default 'opt-out' strategy discussed below.

72. The government's digital transformation vision is the modernization of Australian public services by 2025. This includes a strong focus on making public agencies user-centric and widening the accessibility of digital services to ensure their availability for all. To embed the national digital transformation into sub-national and local structures, an Australian Digital Council was formed. Australian investment strategies are focussed on a range of emerging technologies underpinned by the National Innovation and Science Agenda (NISA) and a digital economy strategy set out in Australia's Tech Future.[35]

73. Australia's ongoing commitment to remaining a leader in e-government is also demonstrated in the Australian Department of Finance launch of an interactive system called GovShare for all Australian Public Service (APS) agencies. As of 1 December 2017, GovShare was decommissioned in favour of the Digital Transformation Agency (DTA) assuming responsibilities of the system.[36] The system will enable agencies to share documents, spreadsheets, find contacts and discuss problems through an online forum. Australia is striving for a whole-of-government open-source cloud-based content management system.[37] The DTA plans to implement wide-scale change in digital capability across government departments, benefiting the public and other users of government services. For instance, the *Data Availability and Transparency Act* 2022 (Cth) (DATA Act) establishes a new regulatory framework for the controlled sharing of Commonwealth public sector data.[38]

74. Other instances of the changed approach are the Department of Human Services myGov service. The myGov service permits people to access government services from Medicare, Centrelink, Child Support, the Department of Health, the Department of Veterans' Affairs and the National Disability Insurance Agency using one username and password online and via mobile apps. The Department of Human Services through myGov is a conduit to more than 200 services in over 20 other Commonwealth agencies and departments.[39]

75. One example is the myGov digital mailbox service that provides secure electronic mail delivery channels for official correspondence. This service links with the Australia Post Digital Mailbox facility with the potential to link with commercial providers.

35. *Supra* Dutta, S & Lanvin, B (2020).
36. As announced on the Govshare website at https://www.govshare.gov.au.
37. *See* Digital Transformation Agency at https://dta.gov.au.
38. *See* text of the Act at https://www.legislation.gov.au/Details/C2022A00011.
39. *See* Commission of Audit Report at https://australianpolitics.com/downloads/budgets/2014/14-05-01_commission-of-audit-report1_phase1.pdf pp. 230.

76. Since 2014 the ATO through its new e-tax products and new web and mobile services has used a similar platform to deliver its services. The Australian Taxation Office reports that it is required by legislation to send over 10 million notices of assessment in hard copy. It sends a further 17 million letters each year on activity statement material.[40] With myGov the ATO has offered online tax returns for individuals and introduced Standard Business Reporting, which allows firms to lodge tax returns with government agencies directly from the software they use for financial reporting. The introduction of the SuperTICK service for superannuation funds to check client identity is a further example.[41]

77. Other government services available online include the Department of Immigration and Border Protection and the Australian Customs and Border Protection Service.[42] The Department of Immigration and Border Protection has processed visas electronically since the 1990s through the Electronic Travel Authority, which links into airline booking systems. The Australian Customs and Border Protection Service uses electronic cargo manifests to assess risks associated with imported goods and has been giving eligible travellers the option to self-process through passport control. By using SmartGate, the ePassport and face recognition technology customs and immigration checks usually conducted by an officer is no longer necessary.[43]

78. The myGov portal is a secure way to access government services online with one login and one password.[44] The advent of digital and mobile technology has made many government services, information provision and other linked services available online.

79. The Australian Government National Commission of Audit has recommended that the government adopt a transformative strategy to become digital by default for all transactions. The strategy should specify an explicit savings target to drive change; it should act decisively to remove legislative barriers to digital transactions; and it should set concrete milestones, including switching from an 'opt-in' arrangement for myGov to a default 'opt-out'.[45]

80. Other Commonwealth agencies that facilitate the digital economy and its regulators are mentioned below.

81. Australian Communications and Media Authority (ACMA) responsible for the regulation of broadcasting, radio communications, telecommunications and

---

40. *Ibid.* at p. 238.
41. *See* ATO https://www.ato.gov.au/super/superstream/in-detail/validation-services/supertick-user-guide/.
42. *See* Australian Customs website at https://www.customs.gov.au/.
43. *See* Australian Border Force at https://www.abf.gov.au/entering-and-leaving-australia/smartgates/arrivals.
44. About myGov at https://my.gov.au/mygov/content/html/about.html.
45. National Commission of Audit (2014) at https://australianpolitics.com/downloads/budgets/2014/14-05-01_commission-of-audit-report1_phase1.pdf.

online content. This is in addition to responsibilities on monitoring information on the Internet, radio and TV, phones and licences for consumers and industry.

82. Australian Competition and Consumer Commission (ACCC) provides guidelines for consumers in relation to Internet commerce. The guidelines make clear that competition rules will govern an e-commerce environment, just as it does traditional business contexts.

83. Australian Government Information Management Office (AGIMO) at the Department of Finance works across the whole-of-government to maintain Australia's position as a leader in the productive application of information and communications technologies to government administration, information and services.

84. Consumer Affairs Division of Treasury which has proactively produced a new code described in Building Consumer Sovereignty in E-commerce: A Best Practice Model for Business.

85. Data61 an entity established after funding for the *National ICT Australia Ltd* (NICTA), an ICT Research Centre of Excellence, ceased in 2015. Data61 in conjunction with the *Commonwealth Scientific and Industrial Research Organisation (CSIRO)* is an important part of Australia's innovation system that seeks to generate new opportunities for Australian industry.

86. Department of Communications (previously known as the Department of Broadband, Communications and the Digital Economy (DBCDE)) is the lead Australian government agency working to support all Australians to realize the full potential of the digital economy.

87. IPAustralia administers intellectual property (IP) rights and legislation relating to copyright, patents, trademarks, designs and plant breeder's rights.[46]

88. Office of the Privacy Commissioner has the remit for privacy matters, now integrated into the Office of the Australian Information Commissioner (OAIC).

89. State Governments and Grant Assistance. Each of the State and Territory governments also offer a range of services and provide information to assist both businesses and consumers in relation to e-commerce. For example, the Victorian Government e-Business site,[47] Business Victoria which provides information about how to start a business, building a website, social media, grants, risk management, government tenders.[48]

---

46. *See* IPAustralia at http://www.ipaustralia.gov.au/.
47. *See* Victoria Government at http://www.vic.gov.au/business-industry/business-practice-management/e-business.html.
48. *See* Business Victoria at http://www.business.vic.gov.au/operating-a-business/developing-your-business/online-business-and-technology.

90. The Australian government also offers grant assistance through business grants programmes for investment and innovative projects[49] and from the Australian Business Financing Centre.[50] Australian entrepreneurs have received funding and assistance from various government agencies and funded government programmes.

---

49. *See* Australian Government Grants at https://business.gov.au/.
50. *See* Australian Government Grants at http://www.australiangovernmentgrants.org/articles.php?indlist=online.

Chapter 3. Information Technology Market

§1. National Economy

91. The COVID-19 pandemic has presented the greatest global economic challenge since the Great Depression. The spread of the virus and the restrictions implemented to contain it has led to a slowdown in economic activity and employment over the period 2020-2021. Fortunately, Australia's has experienced some favourable economic and health outcomes compared to most other countries. However, while Australia was one of the few countries that avoided a recession following the global financial crisis between mid-2007 and early 2009, for the first time in over thirty years the Australian economy is under a recession in 2020-2021. Government surpluses have been expended during this period and Australia begins the second decade of the twenty-first century with significant debts.[51]

92. COVID-19 containment measures have restricted economic activities and has led to the largest fall in GDP on record in the June quarter of 2020. The easing of containment measures is expected to drive Australia's recovery with improving business and consumer confidence. Government economic support in spending and investment will assist the recovery.[52]

93. According to the Budget papers for 2020-2021 in 2020, real GDP is expected to fall by 3.75 per cent, before growing by 4.25 per cent in 2021. The Australian economy rose 0.7 per cent in seasonally adjusted measures with the GDP showing a rise of 1.4 per cent in 2020-2021. Seasonally adjusted estimates for August 2021 shows that the unemployment rate decreased to 4.5 per cent; employment to population ratio decreased to 62.2 per cent and underemployment rate increased to 9.3 per cent.

94. In the June quarter 2021 the seasonally adjusted wage price index (WPI) rose 0.4 per cent over the quarter and 1.7 per cent over the year. Also, the WPI rose 0.5 per cent in the private sector and 0.4 per cent in the public sector.

95. The Consumer Price Index (CPI) rose 0.8 per cent the June quarter whereas over the twelve months to the June 2021 quarter, the CPI rose 3.8 per cent.

96. Labour market conditions have also improved, including through a marked reduction in the number of people working zero hours for economic reasons.

97. The government's economic support since the onset of the COVID-19 pandemic, totalling AUD 257 billion, is unprecedented. There remains substantial uncertainty and the extent of long-lasting economic effects arising from the pandemic. This uncertainty stems from further and continuing spread of the virus and

---

51. *Australia Budget Papers 2020-21* at https://archive.budget.gov.au/2020-21/bp1/download/bp1_w.pdf.
52. *Ibid.* Australia Budget Papers 2020-21.

its mutations and the effectiveness of containment measures. Much would depend on the success of health interventions such as the efficacy of vaccines and other medical treatments. Together these would affect overall economic activity in the country (Table 1).

Table 1 Major Economic Parameters:[a] Outcome and Forecasts 2019-2024

	Outcome	*Forecasts*			
	2019-2020	*2020-2021*	*2021-2022*	*2022-2023*	*2023-2024*
Real GDP per cent	-0.2	-1.5	4.75	2.75	3
Employment per cent	-4.3	2.75	1.75	1	1.75
Unemployment rate per cent	7.0	7.25	6.5	6	5.5
Consumer price index (CPI)	-0.3	1.75	1.5	1.75	2
Wage price index (WPI)	1.8	1.25	1.5	2	2.25
Nominal GDP per cent	1.7	-1.75	3.25	4.5	5

Sources: Budget 2020-2021: Budget Strategy and Outlook Budget Paper No. 1, 2020-2021, pp. 1-8, ABS cat. 5206 Australian National Accounts: National Income, Expenditure and Product; ABS cat. 5202 Labour Force, Australia; ABS cat. 6345 Wage Price Index, Australia; ABS cat. 6401 Consumer Price Index, Australia; and Treasury.

[a] Real GDP and nominal GDP are percentage change on preceding year. The consumer price index, employment and the wage price index are through the year growth to the June quarter. The unemployment rate is the rate for the June quarter.

§2. Australia's Use of Digital Technology

98. Key indicators of business use of IT include Internet access; the use of broadband; web presence; social media presence; and Internet commerce (that is, the placing and receiving of orders via the Internet) (*see* Table 2).[53]

99. For the first time, over half of businesses in the retail trade industry (59 per cent) had a web presence, while 56 per cent had a social media presence.

100. More than a third of businesses reported having received orders via the Internet (37 per cent), with income obtained from these orders totalling an estimated

53. ABS 2018 8166.0 – *Summary of IT Use and Innovation in Australian Business, 2016-2017.*

AUD 394 billion in 2016-2017. The scope of Internet income estimates includes both B2B and B2C orders and as such is not adjusted to include only the value-added component of a sale.[54]

Table 2 Australia: Business Use of Information Technology – Selected Indicators[(a)] 2014-2015 to 2016-2017

		2014-2015	*2015-2016*	*2016-2017*
Estimated number of businesses[(b)]	'000	776	799	831
Businesses with[(c)]:				
Internet access	%	94.8	95.3	95.4
web presence	%	48.6	50.1	51.1
social media presence	%	34.0	38.2	40.4
Businesses with Internet access[(c)]:				
broadband as main connection	%	99.2	99.3	99.4
Businesses that:				
placed orders via the Internet	%	55.7	57.0	59.3
received orders via the Internet	%	33.8	36.8	37.1
Internet income[(d)]	AUD billion	285.5	321.4	394.3

Notes:
(a) Proportions are of all businesses in each output category.
(b) Business counts are provided for contextual information only.
(c) As at the end of the reference period, 30 June.
(d) ABS uses the Organization for Economic Co-operation and Development (OECD)[55] narrow definition of e-commerce transactions when collecting data on Internet orders and Internet income. Internet income is defined as income resulting from goods and services ordered over the Internet where the commitment to purchase is via the Internet.

101. While 95.4 per cent of Australian businesses had Internet access about half (51.1 per cent) had an online presence in 2016-2017.

54. Further data relating to the proportion of income from Internet orders received, see ABS 2018, *Selected Characteristics of Australian Business* (cat. no. 8167.0).
55. *See* OECD at http://www.keepeek.com/Digital-Asset-Management/oecd/science-and-technology/oecd-guide-to-measuring-the-information-society-2011_9789264113541-en.

102. In terms of online orders, the proportion of businesses that placed orders online increased from 55.7 per cent in 2014-2015 to 59.3 per cent in 2016-2017. However, there is a noticeable gap between those businesses placing orders online and those accepting orders online. There was very little difference when it came to the latter, with 37.1 per cent in 2016-2017 compared to 33.8 per cent in 2014-2015 of Australian businesses accepting orders online.

103. Despite the stagnation in the share of businesses that accepted orders online, the income earned from online orders has grown significantly. In total, AUD 285.5 billion was earned by Australian businesses through online orders in 2014-2015 which increased to AUD 394.3 billion in 2016-2017, an increase of 38.1 per cent over the period.[56]

104. In terms of telephony usage, the demand for fixed line voice services remained steady at 6.2 million in 2019-2020, but the number of services has fallen by 31 per cent since 2015-2016. The number of mobile phone services declined slightly in 2019-2020 to approximately 28 million. However, this is 11 per cent above 2015-2016 levels.

105. End-users favour mobile phone services over fixed line services for voice calls. Mobile phone voice call minutes increased to 69.9 billion minutes in 2019-2020, an increase of 18 per cent since 2015-2016. However, fixed line voice call minutes fell to 9.6 billion minutes in 2019-2020, a decrease of 50 per cent since 2015-2016.

106. In 2019-2020 fixed line broadband services made up 90 per cent of the total volume of data downloaded with mobile services making up the remaining 10 per cent. This split has been relatively consistent in recent years.[57]

§3. Australian Participation in the Digital Economy

I. Internet Activity

107. Internet subscribers. There were 14.7 million Internet subscribers in Australia at the end of June 2018.[58] This is an increase of 3.6 per cent from the end of December 2017. Fibre connections grew by 69.8 per cent between 2017 and 2018 reaching 3.6 million subscribers.

108. Data downloads. The total volume of data downloaded in the three months ended 30 June 2018 was 3.8 million Terabytes (or 3.8 Exabytes). This is a 7.0 per

56. ABS 2018 8166.0 – *Summary of IT Use and Innovation in Australian Business, 2016-2017.*
57. ACCC *Communications Market Report 2019-20* at https://www.accc.gov.au/system/files/20-47RPT_Communications_Market_Report_FA.pdf.
58. ABS 2018 8153.0 – *Internet Activity, Australia, June 2018.*

cent increase in data downloads when compared with the three months ended on 31 December 2017 and a 28.1 per cent increase compared with the three months ended on June 2017.

109. Data downloaded via fixed line broadband (3.7 million Terabytes) accounted for 96.8 per cent of all Internet downloads in the three months ended 30 June 2018.

110. Mobile handset subscribers. As of 30 June 2018, there were approximately 27.0 million mobile handset subscribers in Australia. This is an increase of 1.1 per cent since December 2017.

111. The volume of data downloaded via mobile handsets for the three months ended on 30 June 2018 was 246,765 Terabytes. This was a 21.5 per cent increase in data downloads via mobile handsets when compared with the three months ended on 30 December 2017 and a 40.9 per cent increase in downloads compared to the three months ended on 30 June 2017.

II. Household Use of Information Technology

112. The proportion of households with access to the Internet at home has been steadily climbing since 2004-2005 but remained constant between 2014-2015 and 2016-2017 at 86 per cent.[59]

113. For households with children aged under 15, 97 per cent had access to the Internet compared with 82 per cent of households without children under 15.

114. Households located in major cities were more likely to have Internet access at home (88 per cent) than those in remote or very remote parts of Australia (77 per cent).

115. Devices to access Internet at home. Desktop or laptop computers are used by 91 per cent of connected households. Similarly, mobile, or smart phones are also used by 91 per cent of connected households.

116. Tablets were the next most popular type of device used by 66 per cent of households to connect to the internet. Internet connected TVs had the largest increase in usage by households, from 27 per cent in 2014-2015 to 42 per cent in 2016-2017. Internet connected music or video player devices showed a drop in usage from 26 per cent in 2014-2015 to 19 per cent in 2016-2017.

59. ABS 2018 8146.0 – *Household Use of Information Technology, Australia, 2016-2017.*

117. Child protection online indicators. In 2016-2017, 14 per cent of connected households with children aged 5-14 stated a child had been exposed to inappropriate material and 5 per cent of these households stated a child aged 5-14 had been subject to cyberbullying.

118. Internet users and cybersecurity indicators. In 2016-2017, 5 per cent of Internet users stated they had experienced abuse of personal information and 9 per cent of Internet users stated they had experienced damage or loss caused by a virus or other computer infection.

119. Internet access by persons. In 2016-2017, 87 per cent of people were Internet users (persons aged 15 and over who accessed the Internet in the last three months). People aged 15 to 17 were the highest proportion of Internet users (98 per cent) compared with the older age group (65 years and over) which had the lowest proportion of Internet users (55 per cent).

120. The three most popular online activities were entertainment, social networking and banking (all 80 per cent). The proportion of Internet users accessing the Internet for health services or health research has increased from 22 per cent of Internet users in 2014-2015 to 46 per cent in 2016-2017.

121. In Australia there are around four times more mobile handset subscribers than fixed Internet subscribers.[60] It is reported that by December 2018 more searches on Google Search were being undertaken on mobile devices than on desktop computers.[61]

122. The 2019 *University of Canberra Digital News Report* found that that 33 per cent of Australian consumers report accessing news through social media, with 25 per cent using search engines to search for news brands and 20 per cent using search engines to search for news stories.[62]

123. However, it appears that there is much to be done in terms of access to technology as well as the necessary levels of digital literacy for all Australians. The *Australian Digital Inclusion Index* – a collaboration between the ARC Centre of Excellence for Automated Decision-Making & Society at Royal Melbourne Institute of Technology (RMIT), the Centre for Social Impact at Swinburne University of Technology and Telstra reported that one in four people in Australia are digitally excluded and one in ten are 'highly excluded'.[63] In measuring the digital divide the index measures access, affordability and digital ability.

---

60. Australian Bureau of Statistics, *Household Use of Information Technology*, 8 Feb. 2010; and 28 Mar. 2018.
61. Australian Communications and Media Authority, *Communications Report 2017-18*, 9 Jan. 2019, p. 8.
62. Fisher, C, Park, S, Lee, JY, Fuller, G & Sang, Y (2019) *Digital News Report: Australia 2019*, News and Media Research Centre, University of Canberra, June 2019, p. 15.
63. *See* Australian Digital Inclusion Index at https://www.digitalinclusionindex.org.au/?utm_source=sendgrid.com&utm_medium=email&utm_campaign=website.

124. The *Annual Report of the Telecommunications Industry Ombudsman for 2020-21* reports that the largest proportion of complaints were about Internet services, a trend observed over the last three years.[64] Internet services complaints accounted for 33.4 per cent in 2020-2021 compared to 33.7 per cent in 2019-2020. However, the overall volume of Internet complaints continued the downwards trend from the previous year and dropped by 7.1 per cent in 2020-2021.

125. In 2020-2021, mobile services continued to be the second most complained about service type with 32.7 per cent of complaints compared to 31.2 per cent in the previous year. Mobile complaints reduced by 1.5 per cent compared to the previous year. Mobile services were the most dominant service type in the second and third quarter as complaints about internet services decreased in these periods.

126. The proportion and volume of complaints relating to landline services has reduced in 2020. The volume dropped by 18.3 per cent and this service type made up 10.9 per cent of all complaints. The proportion of complaints about multiple service types increased from 21.5 per cent to 22.3 per cent, and the volume decreased by 2.4 per cent.

64. Telecommunications Industry Ombudsman *Annual Report 2020-21* at https://www.tio.com.au/sites/default/files/2021-09/TIO_AR_Accessible_LR.pdf.

Chapter 4. e-commerce Activity

127. Australia is a leading country both in e-government and in moving toward an information economy. The government in Australia, like its counterparts in the United States,[65] United Kingdom,[66] Canada[67] and elsewhere, has sought to transform itself into an e-government while at the same time promoting e-business generally.

128. With the world economy recovering from the COVID-19 pandemic crisis and as a direct result of significant investment by the Australian government in digital infrastructure, it is a safe prediction that the Australian information economy will continue to grow in all areas: B2C, B2B and e-government.

129. As demonstrated by Australia's Internet usage statistics quoted above, the size and importance of e-commerce and e-government activity will become increasingly substantial. The efficiencies brought about by e-commerce are expected to produce changed employment patterns. Post-pandemic, some areas will grow; others will contract. Demand is likely to be strongest in the areas related to tourism, education and associated activities. While all States and territories have benefitted from efficiency gains, there will be some major adjustments required for those regions relying on traditional export activities.

130. Looking to the future, Australia's presence in a rapidly growing Asian region looks promising. Julian Linklaters Report predicts the exponential growth in broadband connections in emerging markets to grow from AUD 1.3 to 3.7 billion in five years creating substantial opportunities for Australian telecommunications equipment providers, developers and content providers.[68] For example, the report shows that most opportunities in content and applications will come in the form of mobile financial services, which are expected to grow to 876 million users by 2017 generating a market value of almost AUD 30 billion.

131. Cloud ICT services spent by customers in emerging markets was AUD 2.2 billion in 2012 and is set to grow to AUD 10.4 billion by 2017.[69] Cloud ICT – whether infrastructure-as-a-service (IaaS), software-as-a-service (SaaS) or platform-as-a-service (PaaS) – will open new markets for the Australian ICT industry.

132. Mobile health is set to generate around AUD 8.8 billion of annual revenues for telecommunications, media and technology (TMT) providers in emerging

65. *See* US Census Bureau of the Department of Commerce at https://www.census.gov/retail/mrts/www/data/pdf/ec_current.pdf.
66. *See* UK Office for National Statistics at https://www.ons.gov.uk/businessindustryandtrade/itandinternetindustry/bulletins/ecommerceandictactivity/2019.
67. *See* Government of Canada at https://www.tradecommissioner.gc.ca/guides/e-commerce-electronique.aspx?lang=eng#wb-cont.
68. Linklaters, J (2013) *Generation Next: 5 Pathways to TMT Growth in Emerging Markets* at http://www.tmtgenerationnext.com.
69. *Ibid.*

markets by 2017, as governments use broadband infrastructure to improve health outcomes and maximize healthcare resources. The deployment of mobile health services is becoming a standard component of healthcare delivery.[70]

133. Finally, m-Commerce is predicted a continued growth trajectory. According to Mims, by 2014, smartphone adoption in emerging markets will experience an exponential growth.[71] The total number of mobile subscriptions globally, however, will exceed 7 billion by 2014, according to the International Telecommunications Union (ITU).

134. One estimate of the potential benefits to the Australian economy through digitalization is as much as AUD 315 billion over the next decade, with the potential to create up to a quarter of a million new jobs by 2025.[72]

135. Limited access to physical stores during the pandemic has driven growth in e-commerce throughout 2020. A survey of Australian businesses in August 2020 showed this shift to online activity increased average online revenue between AUD 105,000 and AUD 708,000 for small businesses. This shift to digital purchases is expected to persist, with home deliveries expected to remain 25 per cent higher than before March 2020.[73]

136. In estimating the contribution of ICT to the Australian economy, the accelerated trend towards digital technology contributed to the 6.0 per cent growth of activity in the ICT sector between the 2018-2019 and 2019-2020 financial year. The growth of the sector may be measured by looking at its direct contribution to gross value added (GVA), which measures the total value of the goods and services generated by an industry after accounting for the costs of production. GVA estimates of telecommunications services and computer system design and related services suggest the ICT sector directly contributed AUD 57.4 billion to Australia's economy in the 2019-2020 financial year.[74]

137. The IMD World Digital Competitiveness Ranking, produced by the IMD World Competitiveness Centre, measures the capacity and readiness of sixty-four economies to adopt and explore digital technologies as a key driver for economic

---

70. *See also* Deloitte (2019) *Technology, Media & Telecommunications (TMT) Predictions 2019* at https://www2.deloitte.com/au/en/pages/technology-media-and-telecommunications/articles/tmt-predictions.html.
71. Mims, C (2014) In 2014 the next Billion Will Access the Mobile Internet – at AUD 20 a Handset (6 Jan., at http://qz.com/163621/in-2014-the-next-billion-will-access-the-mobile-internet-at-20-a-handset/.
72. Alphabeta Advisors (2018) *Digital Innovation: Australia's AUD 315b Opportunity*, https://alphabeta.com/wp-content/uploads/2018/09/csiro-data61_digital-innovation-report.pdf.
73. Deloitte Access Economics, (2020) *Australia's eCommerce revolution: how it saved businesses in COVID-19 and future strategies to thrive* (report commissioned by Australia Post, October 2020) <https://auspost.com.au/content/dam/auspost_corp/media/documents/ ecommerce-report-2020.pdf>.
74. Australian Computer Society (2021) *Australia's Digital Pulse Future directions for Australia's Technology workforce 2021* at https://www2.deloitte.com/au/en/pages/economics/articles/australias-digital-pulse.html.

transformation in business, government and wider society.[75] The World Competitiveness Ranking is based on 334 competitiveness criteria.

138. Top-performing economies are characterized by varying degrees of investment in innovation, diversified economic activities and supportive public policy. Strength in these areas prior to the pandemic allowed these economies to address the economic implications of the crisis more effectively.

139. According to the IMD World Competitiveness Centre ranking for 2021, Australia's digital competitiveness ranking was twenty out of sixty-four countries. Australia is ranked sixth within the peer group ranking in the Asia-Pacific region.[76]

140. In the global environment, Australia is a participant in the OECD and international fora dealing with e-commerce issues. Australia has been an active participant in the World Intellectual Property Organization's (WIPO) programme on e-commerce and domain names, including implementation of standards consistent with the WIPO Copyright Treaty (WCT), and the WIPO Performance and Phonograms Treaty (WPPT).

141. Australia is also active with other initiatives including:

- APEC coordination of e-commerce blueprint, Telecommunications working group.
- United Nations Commission on International Trade Law (UNCITRAL) working group on e-commerce.
- OECD.
- World Customs Organizations (WCO).
- Bilateral e-commerce agreements with the United States, Singapore, Hong Kong and Canada.

75. *See* IMD International Institute for Management Development at https://www.imd.org/centers/world-competitiveness-center/.
76. *See* IMD International Institute for Management Development at https://worldcompetitiveness.imd.org/countryprofile/Au/digital.

Part I. Telecommunications, Media and Technology Regulation

Chapter 1. Legal Status of Standards and Technical Specifications

§1. Introduction

142. The regulation of digital markets in Australia has long been underpinned by the regulation of information communications technology (ICT) *per se*. This is a recognition of the effects of communications and technological convergence in the market so that a holistic approach may be necessary to ensure completeness in coverage. Furthermore, with fresh developments in this sphere of activity, there is an increasing regulatory need to bring the telecommunications, media and technology (TMT) including broadcasting industries closer together with their respective regulatory agencies.

143. Telecommunications regulation in Australia has been shaped by the realities of the communications infrastructure, its history and markets, the vast land mass but small and very unevenly distributed population and small market depth.

144. While the vast bulk of the population lives in the cities, the rural constituencies historically have exercised a significant influence on Australia's policies.[77]

145. Since Federation (1901) the Commonwealth government has been responsible for the regulation of telecommunications under the Constitution. The policy imperative is that there be universal and affordable access to the voice network and untimed local calls.[78] Such access has required delivery of services be made within and between Australia's three largest cities, namely Sydney, Melbourne and Brisbane as well as to the sparsely populated regional and remote areas beyond Australia's 'East Coast spine', on relatively comparable terms.

146. The challenge is further accentuated by such features of Australia's topography, severe temperature gradients, flooding, cyclones and other natural and human-induced disasters. For most of the twentieth century, the vehicle chosen to

---

77. *See* Australian Bureau of Statistics *Australia Yearbook 2012* Catalogue 1301.0 at http://www.abs.gov.au/ausstats/abs@.nsf/Lookup/1301.0Main+Features782012.
78. *Post and Telegraph Act* 1901 (Cth).

deliver this universal affordable telecommunication service is the provision of services by government through a statutorily created monopoly carrier whose operations involved the use of cross-subsidies and protection against competition.

§2. Legislation and Market Regulation

147. For the first half of the twentieth century, the Commonwealth Government assumed responsibility for telecommunications.[79] In 1975, domestic telecommunication functions were moved from the Postmaster General's Department (PMG) to the statutory body known as Australian Telecommunications Commission (Telecom). Telecom was given the exclusive right to install, maintain and operate domestic telecommunications infrastructure and attach lines or equipment to the telecommunications system. The Overseas Telecommunications Commission (OTC), established in 1946, retained its functions in relation to overseas telecommunications. In 1985, a national satellite telecommunications system was established, operated by AUSSAT Pty Ltd, a company jointly owned by Telecom and the Commonwealth Government.[80]

148. From 1975 to 1991 administrative and legislative changes occurred in the provision of telecommunications services in Australia and their regulation, and the first steps were taken to move to competition in the provision of telecommunications. This was largely in response to the growth of private networks by commercial organizations, the increase in demand for communications services as the economy became more service-based and a concern that Telecom's regulatory functions represented a conflict of interest inconsistent with the government's position on trade practices reform.[81]

149. In 1989, the Commonwealth established an independent regulator, AUSTEL.[82] Limited competition for commercial operators was permitted in some areas. However, Telecom retained its monopoly over basic telephony to cross subsidize uniform tariff charges and service provision in regional and remote Australia.[83]

150. The *Telecommunications Act* 1991 (Cth) established a regime under which a limited monopoly was granted to two carriers, Telecom[84] and Optus Communications.[85] Additionally, the *Telecommunications Act* 1991 (Cth) influenced changes in the lead-up to the government's declared intention to open telecommunications

79. *Post and Telegraph Act* 1901 (Cth), *Wireless Telegraphy Act* 1905 (Cth) and *Overseas Telecommunications Commission Act* 1946 (Cth).
80. Raiche, H (2004) *The Policy Context, in Australian Telecommunications Regulations* (Grant, A ed., UNSW Press).
81. *Ibid.* at p. 5.
82. *Telecommunications Act* 1989 (Cth).
83. Raiche *supra.*
84. After its merger with OTC (or AOTC as it then was) in 1992 was renamed TELSTRA in 1995.
85. Following a tender process to determine the Australia's 'second carrier', Optus' majority shareholders at the time were: UK Cable and Wireless and US RBOT.

to full competition by 1997. These changes included the broadening of competition to the Public Switched Telephone Network (PSTN) and the broadening of AUSTEL's powers to deal with interconnection between carriers, competition among operators, and consumer protection.[86]

151. The *Telecommunications Act* 1997 (Cth) established the Australian Communication and Media Authority (ACMA) that sought to open the field to full competition with the aim of creating an internationally competitive industry. This included the establishment of an access scheme that aimed to give all Australians equitable access to standard telecommunications services. The *Telecommunications Act* 1997 (Cth) also attempted to promote, wherever possible, self-regulation of the industry. The Act also contained consumer provisions including customer service guarantees (CSG), emergency call services, untimed local calls and confidentiality of information routed through the network.

152. The ACMA is a statutory authority within the Federal Government portfolio of Communications. The ACMA is Australia's regulator for broadcasting; the Internet; radio communications; and telecommunications. In July 2005 the Australian Communications Authority (ACA) was merged with the Australian Broadcasting Authority (ABA) that became a part of ACMA. The ACMA licenses Australia's telecommunications carriers and regulates fixed line and mobile telecommunications.

153. In September 2009, the Minister for Communications, Broadband, and the Digital Economy announced extensive reforms to the legislation regulating telecommunications. The legislative reforms followed extensive public consultation through the publication of the *National Broadband Network: Regulatory Reform for the Twenty-first Century Broadband* discussion paper released in April 2009. The thrust of the reforms focused on the structural separation of Telstra.[87]

154. In terms of consumer protection, the *Telecommunications Act* 1997 (Cth) is supported by telecommunications-specific amendments to the *Competition and Consumer Act* 2010 (Cth) (CCA) and later by the enactment of other telecommunications-specific consumer protection legislation. For example, the *Telecommunications Act* 1997 (Cth) s. 3 when read together with Parts XIB and XIC of the *Competition and Consumer Act* 2010 (Cth); the *Telecommunications (Consumer Protection and Services Standards) Act* 1999 (Cth) (TCPSS); and *Broadcasting Services Act* 1992 (Cth) (Schedules 5 and 7).

---

86. Raiche *supra*.
87. *See* DBCDE at http://ict-industry-reports.com.au/wp-content/uploads/sites/4/2012/08/2009-Digital-Economy-Future-Directions-Snapshot-DBCDE-2009.pdf.

§3. Standards and Technical Specifications

155. ACMA's remit is supported by various legislative instruments that regulate products as well as provide technical standards.[88] Specific sections of the general legislation on equipment rules includes s 376 *Telecommunications Act* 1997 (Cth) (technical standards); s 158 *Radiocommunications Act* 1992 (Cth) (non-standard transmitters); and s 156 *Radiocommunications Act* 1992 (Cth) (equipment rules).

156. In general, technical standards refer to industry standards such as the Australian standards from Standards Australia, international standards from the International Electrotechnical Commission, European Telecommunication Standards Institute, European Committee for Electrotechnical Standardization, Standards from the Communications Alliance and the Australian Radiation Protection and Nuclear Safety Agency.

157. Telecommunications standards for customer equipment and customer cabling refer to Schedule 1 of the Telecommunications (Labelling Notice for Customer Equipment and Customer Cabling) Instrument 2015.

158. Radiocommunications standards for transmitters and receivers are within the *Radiocommunications Act* 1992 (Cth) as amended by the *Radiocommunications Legislation Amendment (Reform and Modernisation) Act* 2020 (Cth). As part of these amendments, provisions relating to standards, labelling notices, permits and permissions were replaced with a broader power for the ACMA to make equipment rules. The Radiocommunications Equipment (General) Rules 2021 give more flexibility and options to regulate equipment and the supply of equipment.

159. Parental lock standards are found in the Broadcasting Services (Parental Lock) Technical Standard 2020. Parental lock is a feature of digital TV receivers. It allows control access to programmes based on their classification (for example, G, PG, M or MA). Parents and guardians use parental lock to protect their children from inappropriate or harmful TV content. Penalties for breaching the Act can reach up to AUD 165,000.

§4. Telecommunication Legislation

160. The *Telecommunications Act* 1997 (Cth) establishes a system for regulating telecommunications in Australia. The main object of this Act, when read together with Parts XIB and XIC of the *CCA*, is to provide a regulatory framework that promotes:

– the long-term interests of end users of carriage services or of services provided by means of carriage services that are reasonably accessible to all on an equitable basis and efficiently and economically as practicable;

88. *See* ACMA at https://www.acma.gov.au/technical-standards.

- the development of the telecommunications industry that is efficient and responsive to the needs and international competitiveness of the Australian telecommunications market and industry; and,
- the availability of accessible and affordable carriage services and responsible practices that enhance the welfare of Australians.

161. A graphical summary of the *Telecommunications Act* 1997 (Cth) is given in Figure 1.

Figure 1 A Graphical Summary of the Telecommunications Act 1997 (Cth)

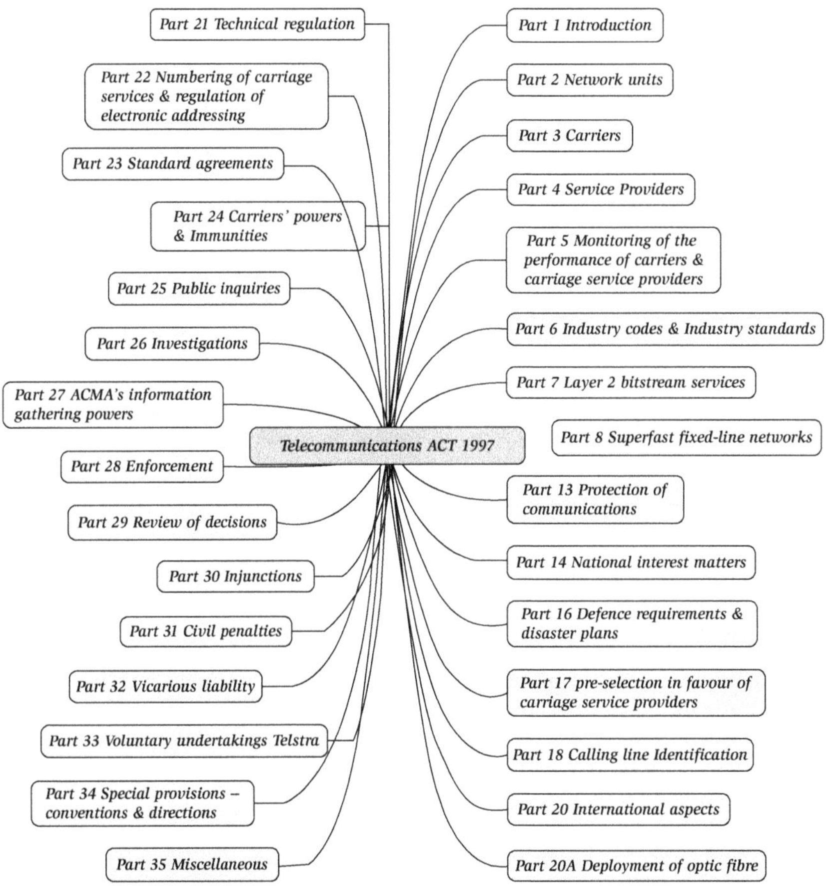

I. The Regulatory Policy Environment

162. The Parliament's goal in regulating the telecommunication industry is one that:

- promotes the greatest practicable use of industry self-regulation; and,
- does not impose undue financial and administrative burdens on participants in the Australian telecommunications industry and maximizes the effectiveness of regulation.

163. The main entities regulated by the *Telecommunications Act* 1997 (Cth) are carriers and service providers.

164. A *carrier* is the holder of a carrier licence granted under the *Telecommunications Act* 1997 (Cth). The owner of a *network unit* that is used to supply carriage services to the public must hold a carrier licence subject to certain exemptions (section 41).

165. Two types of *service providers* are carriage service providers and content service providers.

166. A *carriage* service provider (CSP) supplies certain carriage services. A *content* service provider supplies certain content services. Service providers must comply with service provider rules.

§5. Non-Binding Self-Regulation

167. While ACMA maintains a register of telecommunications industry codes and standards, the telecommunication industry itself provides guidelines and specifications and codes of practice.[89] A distinction is made between standards, guidelines and specifications.

168. *Standards* cover a range of technical topics. Most of these define the technical parameters such as customer equipment, for example, phones, modems and phone exchange equipment.

169. *Guidelines* cover a range of topics including consumer, operational and technical matters. Their compliance is voluntary and indirectly enforceable in a contract or through adoption by a regulator.

170. *Specifications* are voluntary documents that are technical in nature and used to assist in integrating telecommunication networks.

171. The Communications Alliance creates Industry Codes that define good industry practice. In many cases these Codes are enforceable by the Australian government regulators.[90] To date there are twenty-seven different codes that address issues with customers, equipment, network integration, safety, cooperative handling

89. *See* https://www.acma.gov.au/register-telco-industry-codes-and-standards.
90. Communications Alliance Ltd at https://www.commsalliance.com.au/Documents/all/codes.

procedures, broadband services on phone lines, customer rights and provider obligations and others. As there are too many codes to describe individually, a highly selective set of relevant codes are described in brief below.

I. Telecommunications Consumer Protections (TCP) Code

172. The TCP Code is a code of conduct for the Telecommunications Industry in Australia.[91] It provides community safeguards in the areas of sales, service and contracts, billing, credit and debt management and changing suppliers. The TCP Code also sets out a framework of code compliance and monitoring. This Code applies to all CSPs in Australia and is enforceable by the ACMA.

173. The TCP Code has rules for providers as well as protection for customers who use mobile phone, landline and Internet services. Provider rules include communication and dealing with customers, content of advertising and sales information, bills and disputes, customer payment methods, credit assessment of new customers and helping customers switch service providers.

174. Communications Compliance (CommCom) is an independent body responsible for overseeing the conduct of the Code Compliance Framework outlined in Chapter 10 of the TCP Code.[92] CommCom also promotes compliance with the TCP Code through industry guidance and educational initiatives.

175. A Communications Alliance working committee with representatives from industry, consumers, government and regulators revised the TCP Code which was registered by the ACMA on 1 July 2019. The TCP Code commenced on 1 August 2019.

176. CSPs who provide telecommunications services to consumers are required to submit an annual attestation to, and assessment of compliance with the Code by ACMA.

II. iCode

177. The *iCode* is a voluntary Internet Industry Code of Practice for Internet service providers for industry self-regulation in cybersecurity. The first edition was published by the Internet Industry Association as Version 1.0 on 1 June 2010. The *iCode* is designed to:[93]

91. *See* ACMA https://www.acma.gov.au/telecommunications-consumer-protections-code, and https://www.commsalliance.com.au/Documents/all/codes/c628.
92. *See* Communications Compliance Ltd at https://commcom.com.au/.
93. *See* Communications Alliance Ltd at https://www.commsalliance.com.au/Documents/all/codes/icode.

- instil cybersecurity culture within Australian Internet Service Providers (ISP) and their customers;
- provide consistent messaging and plain language information to customers;
- assist those customers who experience repeated compromises to their devices and develop a strategy to minimize the effect of such compromises to other customers on the ISP's network as well as customers on other ISPs' networks;
- encourage ISP to identify compromised devices on their networks;
- encourage ISP to identify, communicate with each other and report any cybersecurity issue that may affect Australia's critical infrastructure, or may have a national security dimensions; and,
- implement these measures in a manner that protects the privacy of customers, consistent with relevant legislative obligations.

III. Internet Gambling Code

178. The Interactive Gambling Code aims to:[94]

- establish confidence in, and encourage the use of, the Internet;
- provide a mechanism for ISP to meet their legal obligations in dealing with designated Internet gambling matters; and,
- promote positive user relations with the Internet industry.

IV. Content Services Code

179. The Content Services Code aims to:[95]

- provide guidelines for Designated Content/Hosting Service Providers, to assist their compliance with legal obligations and to promote the adoption of responsible processes and procedures for dealing with content issues;
- provide a clear, efficient and responsible self-regulatory content assessment regime in regard to the provision by Commercial Content Service Providers of Commercial Content Services;
- promote community confidence in and encouraging availability of appropriate information, educational and entertainment digital content using the Internet, mobile phones and other delivery technologies; and,
- provide a transparent mechanism for complaint handling in relation to content and ensuring that complaints are handled in a fair and efficient manner.

---

94. *See* Communications Alliance Ltd at https://www.commsalliance.com.au/Documents/all/codes/interactive_gambling_code.
95. *See* Communications Alliance Ltd at https://www.commsalliance.com.au/Documents/all/codes/content_services.

V. Internet Industry Codes of Practice

180. The Internet Industry Codes of Practice – Internet and Mobile Content aims to:[96]

- provide guidelines for Content Hosts, ISP and Mobile Carriers to ensure compliance with their legal obligations and promote the adoption of responsible processes and procedures for dealing with content issues;
- provide a clear, efficient and responsible self-regulatory content assessment regime in regard to the provision of mobile content;
- promote end user confidence in, and encouraging the use of, the Internet; and,
- provide a transparent mechanism for complaint handling in relation to content and ensuring that complaints are handled in a fair and efficient manner.

§6. Emerging Issues

181. From time to time the interaction between the legislation, code of practice and policy imperatives suggest the need for consultation and resolution. One issue of note are proposals for amendments to telecommunication carrier powers and immunities.[97] Telecommunication companies have powers to enter land and instal and maintain some types of facilities under immunities from state and territory laws when doing so. These carrier powers and immunities regime are set out under Schedule 3 to the *Telecommunications Act* 1997 and are critical to the efficient construction and maintenance of telecommunications networks.

182. In 2021 the Department of Infrastructure prepared exposure drafts of amendments to the *Telecommunications Code of Practice 2018* (Code of Practice) and *Telecommunications (Low-impact Facilities) Determination 2018* (LIFD) to assist stakeholder understanding of the effects of the proposed changes and sought stakeholder feedback on the proposed changes.[98]

183. The regulatory regime is intended to assist carriers to efficiently construct and maintain telecommunications infrastructure, and to provide Australians with essential communications services. Under the regime carriers may undertake certain construction and related activities on land *without the consent* of the landowner or occupier. Such a regime has excited some debate and controversy including some landowners and occupiers objecting to the exercise of these rights by carriers.

96. *See* Communications Alliance Ltd at https://www.commsalliance.com.au/Documents/all/codes/internet_and_mobile_codes.
97. Flannery, A (2021) 'Recent judicial consideration of the tele-communications carrier powers and immunities regime: Broad interpretation given to "maintenance"' at https://www.holdingredlich.com/recent-judicial-consideration-of-the-tele-communications-carrier-powers-and-immunities-regime-broad-interpretation-given-to-maintenance.
98. *See* Department of Infrastructure (2021) at https://www.infrastructure.gov.au/have-your-say/amendments-telecommunications-carrier-powers-and-immunities-framework-tranche-one (1 Mar).

184. To protect landowners and occupiers, the amendments to the Code of Practice provides that a carrier must consult with an objecting landowner or occupier. Any disputes must be referred to the Telecommunications Industry Ombudsman (TIO).

185. In *Queensland v. Telecommunications Industry Ombudsman* [2021] FCA 522, the state of Queensland took Optus to the Federal Court in relation to two disputes that could not be resolved under the Code of Practice processes. The Federal Court attempted an interpretation of the meaning of 'maintenance' in Schedule 3 of the *Telecommunications Act* 1997. The Court confirmed the TIO's position that the term maintenance should not be given a restricted meaning based on its general meaning but should be given an interpretation consistent with the broad definition in Schedule 3. The State has appealed this decision.

Chapter 2. Legal Status: Standard Terms and Conditions

§1. Introduction

186. Of particular importance under telecommunications access regulations are those that relate to consumer protection, marketplace competition and service standards. The *Competition and Consumer Act* 2010 (Cth) contains two parts specifically relating to the telecommunications market industry (Part XIB) and to telecommunications access regimes (Part XIC). In Part XIB the focus is on anti-competitive conduct and record keeping rules. Within these are 16 Divisions that specify, among others, enforcement and competition rules, and telecommunication charges that consumers pay. Part XIC specifies access obligations, supply of services as well as procedural rules.

§2. Anti-competition Regime: Part XIB CCA

187. Part XIB of the CCA complements the anti-competition provisions contained in Part IV which has a generic application to all businesses including the telecommunications industry.

188. The legislation also makes it clear that the competition notice regime applies to content services – such as subscription television services – delivered by carriers and CSPs.

189. In this monograph a discussion of the regulation of anti-competitive conduct in the telecommunication marketplace is undertaken in Part I. Chapter 4 Regulation of the Telecommunication and Technology Market §1 Regulation of Anti-competitive conduct *infra.*

§3. Access Regulations: Part XIC CCA

190. Part XIC of the CCA sets out the Telecommunications Access Regulations. This part outlines the nature of declared services and the standard access obligations expected from telecommunications providers. In identifying a declared service, the distinction is made between those provided by the NBN and those that are not part of the NBN corporation.

191. A carriage service other than an NBN corporation is a *declared service* where declared by the Competition and Consumer Commission subject to any provisos (section 152AL).

192. All carriers and CSPs who provide declared services are required to comply with *standard access obligations* (category A section 152AR and category B section 152AXB of the CCA) in relation to those services. The *standard access obligations* facilitate the provision of access to declared services by service providers so that service providers can provide carriage services and/or content services. The obligations are subject to mutual agreement between the parties overseen by the Competition and Consumer Commission.

193. A graphical summary of provisions of Parts XIB and XIC of the CCA is given in Figure 2.

Figure 2 A Graphical Summary of the Competition and Consumer Act 2010*: Parts XIB & XIC*

§4. Conditions and Obligations

I. Object of Section 152AB CCA

194. The object of section 152AB in the *Competition and Consumer Act* 2010 (Cth) (CCA) is to promote the *long-term interests of end users* of carriage services. Other objectives include the promotion of competition in markets for listed services; achievement of 'any-to-any' connectivity in relation to carriage services involving end users; and encouraging the economically efficient use and investment in infrastructure where listed services are supplied.

195. Section 152AE of the Act extends to each eligible territory (within the meaning of the *Telecommunications Act* 1997 (Cth)) and applies to external territories.

196. Part XIC of the CCA contains specific provisions relating to the Government-owned company, the NBN, and its role in the ICT industry. An important feature of the telecommunications industry is that competitors must make use of each other's networks. This is because communications services generally require 'any-to-any' connectivity – the capacity of any end user of the service to contact any other end user, regardless of the identity of the suppliers or the network to which they are connected.

197. This regime reflects the policy imperatives of promoting any-to-any connectivity; diversity and competition in the supply of carriage, content and other services; and ensuring access to services on reasonable terms and conditions and other ancillary services such as interconnection, billing, access to customer equipment such as pay TV set-top boxes.

198. Guiding principles of this regime are shaped by incentives to develop industry-based solutions to access issues, reliance on commercial resolution, a pathway to administrative solutions where disputes exist and to provide commercial certainty while minimizing regulatory imposts.

II. Service Declaration Section 152AL CCA

199. A key element of the scheme is the concept of *declared services*. 'Access obligations' only arise following the declaration of a service. Under section 152AL of the *Competition and Consumer Act* 2010 (Cth) a service may be declared by the ACCC in two ways:

1. The Telecommunications Access Forum (TAF) may recommend that the ACCC declare a service.
2. By an ACCC public inquiry. The procedures for public inquiries are detailed in Part 25 of the *Telecommunications Act* 1997 (Cth).

200. The ACCC can designate a body or association to be the TAF (section 152AI). A TAF must have membership open to all carriers and CSPs, be capable of making recommendations regarding the declaration of services, the preparation of draft access codes, and have a written constitution.

§5. Consumer Protection in the Telecommunications Sector

201. The interests of consumers of telecommunications services are protected by legislative provisions, either directly or indirectly. The areas of importance are Universal Service Obligation (USO); Customer Service Guarantee (CSG); confidentiality provisions; Telecommunications Industry Ombudsman; equipment standards; billing; and content regulation.

202. The provisions are found in the *Telecommunications (Consumer Protection and Services Standards) Act* 1999 (TCPSS), as well as in codes and standards made under the *Telecommunications Act* 1997 (Cth). These provisions are discussed in this chapter except billing, equipment and content regulation, which are outside the scope of this section. A graphical summary of the TCPSS is given in Figure 3.

Figure 3 A Graphical Summary of the Telecommunications (Consumer Protection and Services Standards) Act *1999 (TCPSS)*

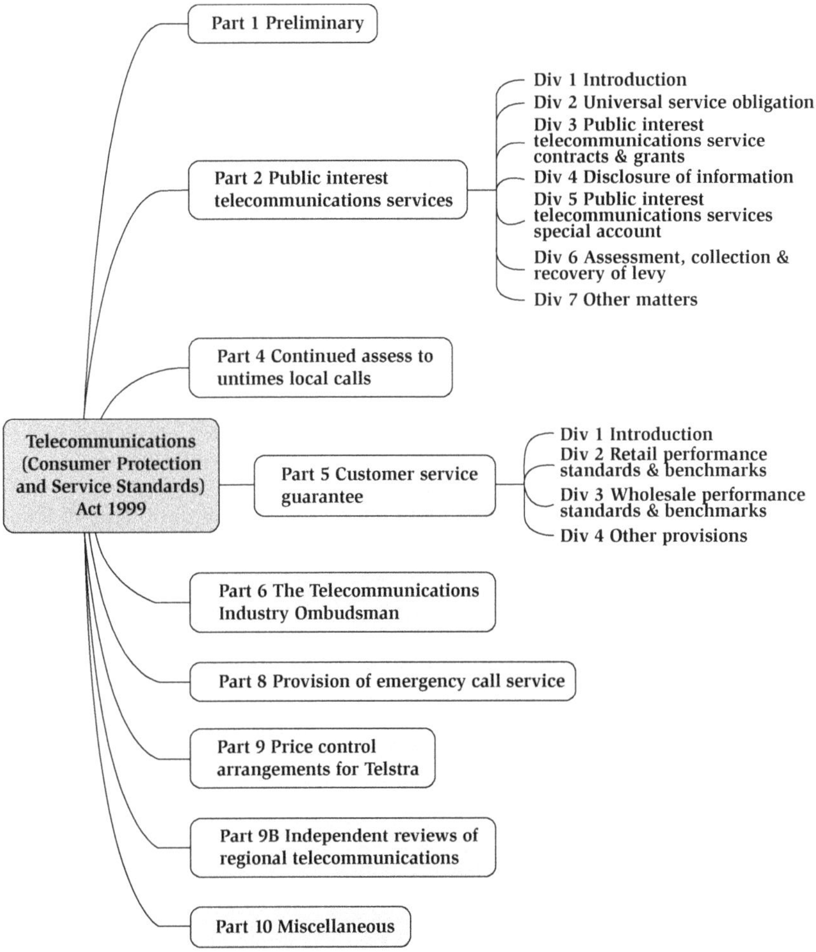

I. Universal Service Obligation (USO)

203. The universal service obligation (USO) is the obligation placed on a universal service provider (USP) to ensure that standard telephone services, pay phones and prescribed carriage services are reasonably accessible to all Australians on an equitable basis, in whatever part of Australia they reside in or in which they carry on business.

204. Telstra is currently the sole USP, but additional USPs may be declared in the future. As the USP, Telstra is obligated to have a policy statement and marketing plan approved by ACMA. The policy statement and marketing plan outlines how Telstra proposes to meet its obligations as USP, including its obligations to those with disabilities, those with special needs and priority customers.

205. A central object of the USO regime is that the losses arising while fulfilling the USO are to be shared among carriers. The minister may expand the funding base to include CSPs but no announcements have been made to date.

206. A separate obligation related to the USO is the digital data service obligation (DDSO). The DDSO is the obligation placed on a digital data service provider to ensure that digital data services are accessible to all people in Australia on an equitable basis, wherever they reside or conduct their business. The DDSO consists of two obligations – the general DDSO for people in general digital data service areas (approximately 96 per cent of the population) and the special DDSO for people in special digital data service areas (approximately 4 per cent of the population, usually living or working at more than 4.5 km from their local telephone exchange). A special and general digital data service provider is obliged to have in place a special and a general digital data service plan that sets out how it will fulfil its obligations as the digital data service provider within each area.

207. Telstra, as the primary USP, must offer service to all customers in the contestable Universal Service Areas, but other carriers may be approved by ACMA as competing USP for those areas.

II. Customer Service Guarantee (CSG)

208. CSG is designed to encourage service improvement and prevent poor service. Telecommunications companies are required to meet minimum performance requirements for specified services and compensate customers when they fail to meet these requirements.

209. The CSG Standard covers the supply of standard telephone services, including voice-grade services used to connect to the Internet or for a facsimile machine. Enhanced call-handling features that require activation by a phone company are also covered, including call waiting, call forwarding, call-barring, caller number ID and calling number display (CND) blocking. These services are commonly referred to as CSG services.

210. Phone companies must meet maximum time frames for the connection of a CSG service; the repair of a fault or service difficulty; and attending to appointments with customers.

211. The CSG only applies where a phone company offers a CSG service at a customer's location. It does not apply to mobile phone services; Internet services; customer equipment, such as the telephone handset; disconnection of services; or preselection (change of phone company or 'churn') delays.

212. The CSG does not apply to customers with more than five phone lines.

III. Telecommunications Industry Ombudsman (TIO)

213. Part 6 of the TCPSS provides that carriers and eligible CSPs must enter the scheme which provides for the Telecommunications Industry Ombudsman (TIO) to investigate, make determinations in relation to and give directions relating to complaints about carriage services by the end users of those services.[99]

214. The TIO is empowered to issue an evidentiary certificate stating that a CSPs has contravened a CSG performance standard and setting out particulars of the contravention; investigate complaints about breaches of performance standards under the CSG; and investigate complaints about the application of Mass Service Disruption Notices under the CSG.

215. The functions of the TIO are given in clause 3 of the constitution of the TIO while clause 4 outlines other powers and responsibilities.[100]

99. Section 128(4), CCA.
100. *See* TIO Constitution at https://www.tio.com.au/sites/default/files/2020-12/CONSTITUTION%20as%20amended%2015%20December%202020.pdf.

Chapter 3. Competition Law Applied to Telecommunications Market

§1. Competition Law and Telecommunications Reforms

216. The Minister for Communications, Broadband and the Digital Economy announced on 15 September 2009 extensive reforms to the legislation regulating the telecommunications. The three principal reforms proposed have now been implemented as discussed in the following sections.[101] The policy reforms were aimed at addressing Telstra's high level of integration to promote greater competition and consumer benefits; streamlining and simplifying the competition regime to provide more certain and quicker outcomes for telecommunications companies; and strengthening consumer safeguards to ensure services standards are maintained at a high level.

I. Structural Separation of Telstra

217. The first element of the reform relates to the structural separation of Telstra. The government's view was that Telstra was one of the most highly integrated telecommunications companies in the world across the fixed line copper, cable and mobile platforms.

218. The NBN established by the Commonwealth government on 7 April 2009 is the first step in the implementation of the structural separation of Telstra. NBN is wholly owned by the Commonwealth of Australia as a Government Business Enterprise (GBE), incorporated under the *Corporations Act* 2001 (Cth) and operates in accordance with the *Public Governance, Performance and Accountability Act* 2013 (Cth).

219. This initiative by the government created a wholesale entity to provide all retail telecommunication companies with access to the network. NBN is to design, build and operate Australia's wholesale broadband access network and underpinned by the goal to connect Australia and bridge the digital divide. This meant that Telstra still had its own copper and fibre network and the NBN was creating its own fibre network. On 23 June 2010, Telstra entered a contract with the government's

101. *See* DBCDE at http://ict-industry-reports.com.au/wp-content/uploads/sites/4/2012/08/2009-Digital-Economy-Future-Directions-Snapshot-DBCDE-2009.pdf. *See also* discussions in Feetham, M & Abbott, C 2009 Australia: The National Broadband Network And Regulatory Reforms at https://www.mondaq.com/australia/telecoms-mobile-cable-communications/84420/the-national-broadband-network-and-regulatory-reforms; Groshinski, K, Webb, K, & McCarthy, J 2009 'Historic reforms to telecommunications regulation' at https://www.claytonutz.com/knowledge/2009/october/historic-reforms-to-telecommunications-regulation; and, National Broadband Network: *Regulatory Reform for 21st Century Broadband. Discussion Paper*, April 2009 at https://www.accc.gov.au/system/files/NBN%20Regulatory%20Reform%20for%20the%2021st%20Century%20Broadband%20-%20low%20res%20web.pdf.

NBN to transfer its existing network for AUD 11 billion. The effect of such a contract is that the vertical separation of Telstra will be completed when the contract has been finalized.

220. Since its establishment, the NBN has been mandated through its Statement of Expectations (SoE) together with relevant policy directives. NBN's current objectives are set out in the 24 August 2016 SoE.[102]

II. Reforms to the Competition Regime

221. The legislation to reform the arrangements in Part XIB have been enacted and now form part of the CCA so that the ACCC can address breaches of competition law and conduct damaging to the market.[103]

222. The legislation also makes it clear that the competition notice regime applies to content services – such as subscription television services – delivered by carriers and CSPs.

223. The reform of the access regime would streamline the arrangements found in the repealed Part XIC of the *Trade Practices Act* 1974 (Cth) (TPA) now replaced by Part XIC of the CCA, discussed above. The new law allows parties to access regulated services with the ACCC to determine the terms and conditions and principles that apply and the binding rules of conduct to address problems with the supply of regulated wholesale services.

III. Universal Service Obligations

224. The third legislative reforms strengthen the USOs by enabling the minister to specify the standards, terms and conditions of services, connection and repair periods and reliability requirements of the standard telephone service. Telstra is required to meet new minimum performance benchmarks. Failure by Telstra to meet the requirements will expose Telstra to a civil penalty of up to AUD 10 million.

225. The legislation also includes more stringent rules on the removal of pay phones and new provisions to allow people concerned about a pay phone removal to apply to the ACMA to direct Telstra not to remove a pay phone.

---

102. *See* NBN Co at https://www.nbnco.com.au/content/dam/nbnco2/2018/documents/Policies/soe-shareholder-minister-letter.pdf.
103. *Telecommunications Legislation Amendment (Competition and Consumer Safeguards) Act* 2010 (Cth).

226. The legislation provides for new minimum performance benchmarks to require telephone companies to meet or exceed the CSG time periods for a certain proportion of cases. Failure to comply will result in civil penalties or on-the-spot fines.

227. The legislation also provides the ACMA with increased powers to issue infringement notices, (on-the-spot) fines instead of commencing procedures in court.

228. The government has announced the exemption of carriers with a revenue less than AUD 25 million per annum from paying an annual carrier licence charge (ACLC) and reporting to the ACMA, as costs of compliance are often considerably higher than their monetary contribution.[104] The purpose of the ACLC is to fund activities of the ACMA, the ACCC and the Department of Communications in regulating telecommunications services provided by licensed carriers to ensure that those who receive the government activities meet the cost of those activities.

104. *See Telecommunications (Carrier Licence Charges) Act* (Cth) 1997 at http://classic.austlii.edu.au/au/legis/cth/consol_act/tlca1997377/. *See also* ACMA at www.acma.gov.au/Industry/Telco/Carriers-and-service-providers/Licence-fees-annual-levies-and-charges/eligible-revenue-portal-current-year.

Chapter 4. Regulation of the Telecommunications and Technology Market

§1. Regulation of Anti-competitive Conduct

229. Part XIB of the *Competition and Consumer Act* 2010 (Cth) sets up the Regulation of Anti-competitive Conduct and Record-keeping Rules.[105] This part sets up a special regime for regulating anti-competitive conduct in the telecommunications industry.

230. The circumstances in which carriers and CSPs are said to *engage in anti-competitive conduct* are stated in section 151AK. In general, a carrier or CSPs must not engage in anti-competitive conduct. This rule is called the *competition rule.*

231. The Commission may issue a notice stating that a specified carrier or CSP has engaged, or is engaging, in anti-competitive conduct. The notice is called a *Part A competition notice*. The enforcement of the competition rule is instituted when a Part A competition notice is in force at the time of the alleged conduct.

232. In Part XIC, the ACCC administers the regulation of anti-competitive conduct in telecommunications markets, and legislation regulating international telecommunications operators[106] engaging in 'unacceptable conduct'. Such conduct includes the use of market power or of any legal rights or legal status in a manner that is, or is likely to be, contrary to Australia's national interest given in Division 3 of Part 20 of the *Telecommunications Act* 1997 (Cth).[107]

§2. The Competition Notice Regime

233. The key themes of the competition notice regime contained in Part XIB are: (1) the competition rule; (2) anti-competitive conduct; (3) competition notices; (4) advisory notices; and (5) exemption orders.

234. *Anti-competitive conduct* is defined under section 151AJ of the CCA. That section sets out the two circumstances under which a carrier or a CSP will engage in anti-competitive conduct for the purposes of Part XIB. Those two circumstances

105. For a comprehensive treatment of the scheme as originally implemented, see Commonwealth of Australia, *Anticompetitive Conduct in Telecommunications Markets: An Information Paper* (August 1999).

106. International telecommunications are operators that provide carriage services from overseas that may originate, terminate, or pass-through Australia, the supply of goods or services for use in connection with the provision of such carriage services, or the installation, maintenance, operation, or provision of access to a telecommunications network or facility where the network or facility is used to provide such a carriage service: s. 367(6) of the *Telecommunications Act* 1997 (Cth).

107. Section 367(1) of the *Telecommunications Act* 1997 (Cth).

include taking advantage of market power by a carrier or CSP with the effect of substantially lessening competition in the telecommunication market or taking advantage of that power and engaging in other conduct that would reduce competition in the telecommunication market

235. *Part A competition notices* allow the ACCC to quickly respond to conduct it considers is in contravention of the competition rule and foreshadow court action against such conduct.

236. *Part B competition notices* enable the ACCC to give particulars of conduct or a defined kind of conduct under a Part A notice, enabling the ACCC to provide the detailed, particularized information required for *prima facie* evidence purposes for use in its own court action or court actions mounted by third parties.

237. The ACCC may vary or revoke an advisory notice.[108] If it does, it must give the carrier or CSP concerned written notice of the variation or revocation. The notice will cease to be in force if the Part A competition notice ceases to be in force.

238. A carrier or CSP proposing to engage in conduct which may breach the competition rule may apply to the ACCC for an exemption order. Subdivision B of Division 3 of Part XIB of the CCA sets out the circumstances under which a carrier or CSP may be granted an *exemption order*. The ACCC may grant an exemption order where it is satisfied that the resultant public benefit outweighs any public detriment of lessened competition; or the conduct will not breach the competition rule.

§3. The e-Communications Market

239. The competition rule applies only to carriers or CSPs.[109] As noted previously, a 'carrier' means a person who holds a carrier licence issued under the *Telecommunications Act* 1997 (Cth), and a CSP is a person who supplies to the public certain communications services (as defined in Part 4 Division 3 of the Act).

240. A *'telecommunications market'* is defined in section 151AF of the CCA to mean a market in which carriage services; goods or services for use in connection with a carriage service; access to facilities; and content services are supplied or acquired carriage service.

241. Under the *Telecommunications Act* 1997 (Cth), '*carriage service*' is defined to mean 'a service for carrying communications by means of guided or unguided electromagnetic energy'.[110]

108. Section 151AQB(5), CCA.
109. Section 151AK, CCA.
110. Section 7, CCA.

242. '*Communication*' is broadly defined in the *Telecommunications Act* 1997 (Cth) to include communications between people and/or things and includes speech, music, data, text, visual images, signals, or any other form or combination of forms.[111] A service is a 'carriage service' therefore where the service consists of 'carrying' communications by means of electromagnetic energy.

243. '*Carrying*' communications (as opposed to initiating or modifying that communication) is defined in the *Telecommunications Act* 1997 (Cth) to include transmission, switching, or receipt of that communication.

244. In the ACCC's view the 'telecommunications market', may include carriage services; value-added services for use in connection with a carriage service such as call manipulation (for example, diversion, call waiting), the use of calling line identification (CLI), or message services (for example, voice mail, paging); the supply of physical components of telecommunications networks used by carriers or CSPs in the provision of carriage services; information and related services used in connection with carriage services (for example, 'help desk' consultancy services, directory assistance services, account management services, or customer billing information); other rights (services) used as inputs for creating, offering, or accessing a carriage service (including rights relating to assets such as spectrum or IPR such as patents); any bundled or tied package where one component of that package is a carriage service, a good or service for use in connection with a carriage service, or access to facilities; or any goods or services whose 'use', have some nexus with an underlying carriage service.

245. *Market definition* is fundamental to the evaluation of any anti-competitive conduct under section 151AJ(2), as with other provisions in Part IV of the CCA.

246. Market definition provides the basis on which to assess the telecommunications market in which a carrier or CSP does or does not have market power; and whether in that market or another market there has been, or will be, a 'substantial lessening of competition'.

247. Part XIB of the CCA aims to facilitate vigorous competition in the telecommunications industry by preventing members of the industry with a substantial degree of power in a telecommunications market from engaging in anti-competitive conduct. Carriers and CSPs with substantial market power should not be able to take advantage of that market power to stifle competition.[112]

248. The CCA makes illegal, agreements, arrangements, or understandings to fix the prices at which goods or services are bought or sold.[113] If two or more carriers or CSPs are observed to vary their prices by the same amount and at the same time,

---

111. *Ibid.*
112. *Trade Practices Amendment (Telecommunications) Bill* 1996, Explanatory Memorandum, 6.
113. Section 45A, CCA.

this may indicate that they are acting in collusion in breach of the CCA. Nevertheless, in a strongly competitive market where the cross-elasticity of demand for the services of each supplier is very high, individual service providers cannot afford to allow their prices to differ significantly from those set by their competitors.

Chapter 5. Regulation of Media and Broadcasting Activities

§1. Broadcasting Services

249. A major pillar of the regulation of the telecommunication, media and technology market is the *Broadcasting Services Act* 1992 (Cth) (BSA).[114] Under section 1 of the Act national broadcasters who operate a transmitter are subject to restrictions regarding the services that may be transmitted in digital mode. Owners and operators of broadcasting transmission towers must give digital broadcasters and data casters access to the towers for the purposes of installing or maintaining digital transmitters.

250. Schedule 5 sets up a system for regulating certain aspects of the Internet industry. One prime example is where the Internet content hosted outside Australia is transmitting prohibited content. The Commissioner may refer the Internet content host to a law enforcement agency and to the relevant ISP to deal with the issue in accordance with specified industry code or standard. Section 8 of the Act defines the Internet Service Provider (ISP) as persons who supply or proposes to supply an Internet carriage service to the public.

251. Part 5 on Industry Codes and Standards provides that bodies and associations that represent ISPs may develop industry codes. Compliance with an industry code is to be on a voluntary basis unless directed by the Commissioner. The Commissioner has a reserve power to make an industry standard if there are no industry codes or if an industry code is deficient. Finally, the Commissioner may make online provider determinations regulating ISP.

252. Part 6 gives online provider rules. Section 85 states that a Federal Court may order a person to cease supplying Internet carriage services.

253. Part 8 refers to protection from civil and criminal proceedings. Section 88 provides for the protection against civil proceedings for ISP.

254. Section 90 in this Schedule applies to State or Territory laws operating concurrently.

255. Schedule 7 on Content Services relates to complaints to the Commissioner about prohibited content or potential prohibited content, in relation to certain services. These actions include takedown notice; service cessation notice; and a link-deletion notice.

256. Schedule 8 Online Content Services empowers ACMA to make online content service provider rules about gambling promotional content provided on an online content service in conjunction with live coverage of a sporting event.

---

114. *See* text of the Act at https://www.legislation.gov.au/Details/C2018C00375.

257. The ACMA may exempt an online content service, or an online content service provider, from the online content service provider rules. In addition, ACMA may give remedial directions to an online content service provider if the provider contravenes the online content service provider rules.

258. Figure 4 is a graphical summary of Schedules 5 & 7 of the *Broadcasting Services Act* 1992 (Cth).

Figure 4 A Graphical Summary of the Broadcasting Services Act *1992 (Cth) Schedules 5 and 7*

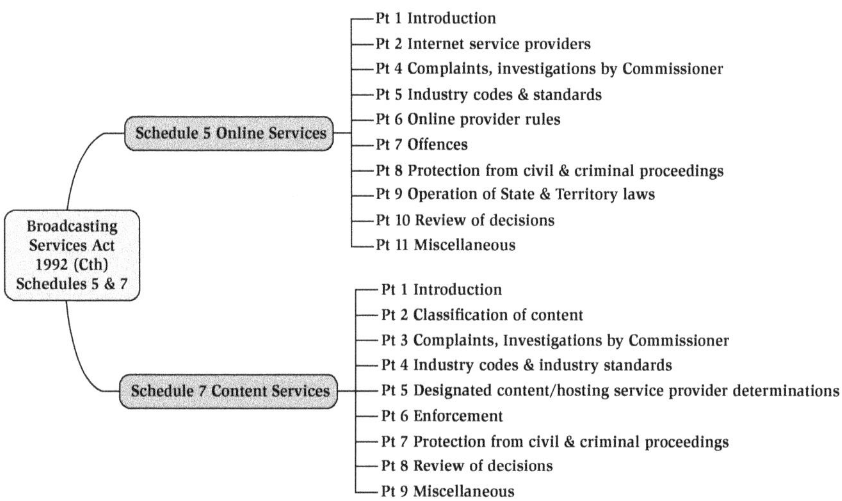

§2. MEDIA REGULATION IN AUSTRALIA: ISSUES AND REFORM

259. A key issue challenging media regulation in Australia is the disruptive nature of digital technologies to traditional business models. Such digital disruption in turn is transforming who produces content, what content is being produced, how it is distributed and how it is consumed.

260. In addition, the effect of globalization has domestic implications. In 2011, for example, the government undertook a Convergence Review which found that there were many elements in the current regulatory regime that were either outdated, unnecessary or ineffective rules besetting the telecommunications environment.[115] The review highlighted several areas of concern including media control rules in terms of ownership, the rise of multinational platform service providers and new forms of media consumption in viewing and reading habits.

115. *See Convergence Review Report* at https://apo.org.au/sites/default/files/resource-files/2012-04/apo-nid29219_5.pdf.

261. As noted previously the BSA sets out most of the regulatory regime for traditional television and radio broadcasting in Australia as well as provisions for regulating parts of the Internet industry. The ACMA is conferred functions and powers to regulate and monitor the broadcasting industry generally. Different types of broadcasting licences as well as co-regulatory codes of practice for commercial and community free-to-air (FTA) radio and television sectors are in place.

262. The ABC and SBS are national broadcasters having their own charters and obligations.

263. Print news media and online activities have self-regulating standards of practice. The Australian Press Council is the responsible body and works in addition to codes of conduct under the auspices of the Independent Media Council.

264. Interestingly, Internet social media platforms such as Facebook and YouTube are not currently under any type of licence and hence are unregulated under the BSA.

I. Inquiries

265. To ensure a strong and robust media industry the government has undertaken several inquiries. Among these include the *Report of the Independent Inquiry into the Media and Media Regulation* (the Finkelstein Inquiry). The Inquiry found that the print newspaper industry was struggling to adjust to the digital environment and in particular the sector's ability to monetize content that could lead to a decline in the quality of journalism.[116]

266. A further inquiry is the Digital Platforms Inquiry by the ACCC in 2017 to consider the impact of platform service providers on competition in the Australian media market as well as 'on the level of choice and quality of news and journalistic content to consumers'.[117] A preliminary report has found that traditional media print and online platforms have faced major financial challenges because of the decline in advertising in its businesses.[118]

267. The ACCC inquiry also discussed the issue of transnational companies such as Google and Facebook playing an increasingly serious role in controlling the exposure and consumption of all kinds of news that do not contribute to the public interest in Australia.

---

116. *See* Finkelstein Inquiry at https://apo.org.au/sites/default/files/resource-files/2012-02/apo-nid28522.pdf.
117. *See* ACCC at https://www.accc.gov.au/focus-areas/inquiries-finalised/digital-platforms-inquiry-0.
118. *See* ACCC at https://www.accc.gov.au/publications/digital-platforms-inquiry-final-report.

II. Recent Media Reform

268. The discussion following focuses on ownership while the next chapter deals with content in social media and the Internet. Social media is conceived here as the communication of content over a range of online experiences. Often most people think of social media networking sites such as Facebook (now Meta) and *MySpace*. However, social media interactions also transcend virtual worlds such as *World of Warcraft*, *Second Life*, blogs, wikis and file sharing sites and software such as *YouTube* and *Flickr*.

269. In 2020-2021 the government put together a broadcast and content reform package aimed at improving the sustainability of Australia's free-to-air (FTA) broadcasting sector, protect children from exposure to gambling advertising and to support the creation of high quality Australian content on screen and in print.[119] Other items on the package include adjustments to the anti-siphoning regime, the abolition of outdated media ownership rules and the provision of funding of under-represented sports on pay TV discussed below.

270. Broadcast Pricing Reforms. Digital online service providers have disrupted traditional business models of Australian broadcasters for audiences and advertising revenue. This has resulted in the fragmentation of audiences and consequent diminution of advertising revenue for commercial broadcasters. To assist broadcasters, compete, under the *Broadcast and Reform Package,* the government has proposed abolishing broadcasting licence fees and introducing a price for the use of broadcast spectrum that better reflects its use as well as recognizing its intrinsic value.

271. Restrictions on gambling advertising. The reform package will restrict gambling advertising and promotions during live sports programmes to reduce the exposure of children to gambling. These steps are implemented via broadcast industry Codes of Practice.

272. Supporting Australian content. A joint review by the Department of Communications and the Arts, ACMA and Screen Australia is inquiring into the support measures needed for producing and delivering Australian and children's screen content in the new multi-platform environment.

273. Amending anti-siphoning scheme. Amendments to the anti-siphoning scheme now means the outdated and redundant provisions have been removed and the anti-siphoning list streamlined. In the digital media era events of national and cultural significance will be available to FTA broadcasters.

274. Funding under-represented sports. The Australian government has provided AUD 30 million to Foxtel from 2017 to 2021 to support television and online

119. Department of Infrastructure, Transport, Regional Development and Communications (2017) (DITRDC) *Broadcast and Content Reform Package* at https://www.infrastructure.gov.au/media-technology-communications/media-laws-regulation/broadcast-content-reform-package (17 Jan).

coverage of sports that receive low or no broadcast exposure to encourage women's sports, niche sports and sports that have high levels of community participation.

III. Ownership Issues

275. The specific controls over media ownership contained in the *Broadcasting Services Act* 1992 (Cth) include television,[120] radio,[121] cross-media control[122], subscription television broadcasting licences[123] and foreign investment controls.

276. In reforming the broadcasting sector, the government in 2017 introduced the *Broadcasting Legislation Amendment (Broadcasting Reform) Act* 2017 (Cth) to amend media regulations.[124] A major effect of the amendment is to encourage a diversity of ownership and to prevent the common ownership of newspapers, television and radio broadcasting licences in a particular licence region.[125]

277. Under the *Broadcasting Reform Act* 2017 the government will repeal two media control and ownership rules in the *Broadcasting Services Act* 1992 (Cth) that currently prevent a person from controlling:

(1) commercial television licences that collectively reach more than 75 per cent of the Australian population (75 per cent reach rule); and,
(2) more than two of the three regulated forms of media – commercial radio, commercial TV and associated newspapers) in the one commercial radio licence area (two out of two rule).

278. The government, however, is maintaining the other diversity rules including the '5/4' rule, the 'one-to-a-market' rule and the 'two-to-a-market' rule. These have the effect of providing a safety net for voice diversity. The '5/4' rule ensures that at least there are five independent media 'voices' in metropolitan commercial radio licence areas in mainland state capital cities and at least four in regional commercial radio licence areas. The market rules specify that no person or company may hold no more than one TV licence or two radio licences in a licence area.[126]

---

120. *Broadcasting Services Act* 1992 (Cth) ss 53, 55,57 & 58.
121. *Broadcasting Services Act* 1992 (Cth) ss 54 & 55.
122. *Broadcasting Services Act* 1992 (Cth) ss 60 & 61.
123. *Broadcasting Services Act* 1992 (Cth) ss 109.
124. *See* Department of Infrastructure at https://www.infrastructure.gov.au/media-technology-communications/media-laws-regulation/broadcast-content-reform-package.
125. *See* detailed discussions on media ownership regulation in Australia in Gardiner-Garden, J & Chowns, J (2006) *Media Ownership Regulation in Australia* at https://www.aph.gov.au/about_parliament/parliamentary_departments/parliamentary_library/publications_archive/archive/mediaregulation.
126. *See* Dwyer, T (2016) 'What changes to Australia's media ownership laws are being proposed' at https://theconversation.com/explainer-what-changes-to-australias-media-ownership-laws-are-being-proposed-55509.

279. There are also foreign ownership restrictions. In the telecommunications sector the Foreign Investment Review Board (FIRB) must be notified if a foreign person(s) acquires a 'substantial interest' in an Australian corporation whose assets exceed AUD 266 million. Substantial interest is deemed to be where a single foreign person holds 20 per cent or more, or several foreign persons hold 40 per cent or more of the issued shares, units or voting power of the target corporation.

280. For investments in the media sector FIRB must be notified if a foreign person seeks to acquire 5 per cent or more of an Australian media business regardless of value. A foreign person is an individual not ordinarily a resident in Australia or a corporation where one or more foreign persons hold a combined total of 20 per cent of more of issues shares, units or voting power.

281. ACMA is to be notified of foreign persons who have 2.5 per cent or more interests in an Australian media company.

282. Merger and acquisitions in the telecommunications and media technology sectors are subject to the general merger control regime overseen by the ACCC.[127]

IV. Spectrum Policy

283. The government is in the process of replacing the current spectrum management system with a simplified single licensing scheme.[128] The Spectrum Pricing Review found that the existing management arrangements were slow, rigid, administratively cumbersome and unnecessarily costly for users. A staged approach to amend the existing *Radiocommunications Act* 1992 (Cth) is underway.[129]

284. On 17 December 2020, the *Radiocommunications Legislation Amendment (Reform and Modernisation) Act* 2020 (Cth) (the Modernisation Act) received Royal Assent, amending the *Radiocommunications Act* 1992 (Cth). The amendments made by the Modernisation Act adds flexibility to the way the spectrum is managed; provides greater clarity to licensees; simplifies and streamlines spectrum management and planning processes; and ensures that spectrum management is fit-for purpose in a challenging, dynamic environment. The provisions of the Modernisation Act come into force on 17 June 2021.

285. ACMA's 2020-2024 five-year spectrum outlook includes mobile broadband spectrum planning projects being undertaken and for implementation.[130]

---

127. *See also* s. 50 of the CCA.
128. Department of Communications and the Arts (2018), *Spectrum Pricing – Review*, (Feb) at https://www.communications.gov.au/what-we-do/spectrum/spectrum-reform.
129. *See* ACMA (2021) Radcomms licensing and allocation reform at https://www.acma.gov.au/radcomms-licensing-and-allocation-reform.
130. ACMA (2020), *Five-Year Spectrum Outlook 2020–2024: The ACMA's spectrum management work programme – consultation draft*, (Apr).

Chapter 6. Regulation of Media and Online Services

§1. Regulation of Broadcast Content

286. Australian broadcast content regulation consists of an interrelated framework comprising both regulatory mechanisms as well as funding to secure domestic content. The Australian government and ACMA are responsible for regulating the screen industry and to provide information for compliance purposes. Screen Australia is the Federal funding agency for screen content.[131] Separately regulated are commercial FTA broadcasters, subscription television broadcasters, national television broadcasters and video-on-demand (VOD) services.

287. Commercial FTA TV Broadcasters. TV broadcasters have a primary responsibility to ensure that the content of broadcast materials reflect community standards as per the Commercial TV Industry Code of Practice. Some aspects of programming for FTA and subscription TV are regulated by ACMA. The regulations cover minimum levels of Australian content, in advertising and the anti-siphoning of sport.

- The *Broadcasting Services Act* 1992 (Cth) requires all commercial FTA licensees to broadcast minimum amounts on primary and non-primary channels between 6 a.m. and midnight.
- From 1 January 2008, as part of the changes introduced by the *Broadcasting Services Amendment (Media Ownership) Act* 2006 (Cth), ACMA has been required to ensure that specified regional commercial television broadcasting licensees in Queensland, New South Wales, Victoria and Tasmania broadcast minimum amounts of material of local significance pursuant to the *Broadcasting Services Local Programming Determination 2018.*[132]
- The *Broadcasting Services (Australian Content in Advertising) Standard 2018* requires a commercial broadcaster to ensure that Australian produced advertisements occupy at least 80 per cent of the total advertising time broadcast per year between 6 a.m. and midnight.[133]
- Current content standards specified in the Broadcasting Services (Australian Content and Children's Television) Standards 2020 commenced on 1 January 2020.
- Captions must be shown on all programmes broadcast between 6 a.m. and midnight.
- The anti-siphoning scheme is aimed at FTA broadcasters a first opportunity to buy TV rights to major events included on the anti-siphoning list.[134]

---

131. *See* Screen Australia (2018) at https://www.screenaustralia.gov.au/fact-finders/television/industry-trends/content-regulation.
132. *See* ACMA at https://www.acma.gov.au/local-tv-content-regional-areas.
133. *See* ACMA at https://www.acma.gov.au/australian-content-tv-ads.
134. *See* Department of Infrastructure at https://www.infrastructure.gov.au/media-centre/publications/anti-siphoning.

288. Subscription TV Broadcasters. Programme broadcasting requirements are governed by a code of practice published on the Australian Subscription Television and Radio Association (ASTRA) website.[135] Other aspects of programming on FTA and subscription TV are regulated by ACMA including new eligible drama expenditure scheme and anti-siphoning scheme.

289. National TV Broadcasters. The nation's publicly funded FTA broadcasters are the ABC, SBS and National Indigenous TV (NITV). Public broadcasters do not have quota requirements and their respective charters set out their respective functions.

- The ABC is precluded from advertising on its broadcasting services while the SBS may do so with certain restrictions.
- ABC and SBS must show captions on all programmes broadcast between 6 a.m. and midnight.
- The anti-siphoning scheme permits FTA TV broadcasters a chance to show major events included on the anti-siphoning list.

290. Video-on-Demand Services. Large video-on-demand (VOD) services have been requested to voluntarily report on their level of investment in Australian content to ACMA from 1 January 2021. Consultations are in process to introduce content investment obligations that reach certain thresholds.[136]

291. The Australian interrelated framework approach differs markedly from the European Union *Audiovisual Media Services Directive* (the *AVMS Directive*) 2007 which adopts a technologically neutral definition of *audiovisual media service* that applies across all audiovisual mass media, including television, the Internet and mobile devices and whether scheduled or on demand.[137]

§2. Regulation of Online Content

292. The regulation of Australian online content is informed by concerns for cyber-safety and harm including cybercrime activity. The Broadcast and Content Reform Package includes legislative measures to restrict online gambling promotion.[138]

---

135. *See* ASTRA at http://www.astra.org.au/
136. *See* Department of Infrastructure at https://www.infrastructure.gov.au/media-technology-communications/television/modernising-australian-screen-content-settings.
137. Directive 2007/65/EC of the European Parliament and of the Council of 11 Dec. 2007 (amending Council Directive 89/552/EEC). Also see: European Commission 'The Television Without Frontiers Directive: Regulatory Framework' available at: http://ec.europa.eu/avpolicy/reg/tvwf/index_en.htm.
138. *See* test of the *Interactive Gambling Act* 2001 (Cth) at http://classic.austlii.edu.au/au/legis/cth/consol_act/iga2001193/ and ACMA at https://www.acma.gov.au/about-interactive-gambling-act.

293. Criminal and civil responses to harmful online content were legislated including penalties for posting, threatening to post, intimate images on the Internet without consent. So also new offences were enacted that criminalize acts done online to prepare or plan to cause harm to, or engage in, sexual activity with a person under the age of 16.[139]

294. In April 2019, the Australian Parliament passed legislation that created new offences that will apply to providers of Internet, hosting or content services who fail to refer to police 'abhorrent violent material that records or streams conduct that occurring' in Australia; and do not 'expeditiously' take down 'abhorrent violent material' capable of being accessed within Australia.[140] This legislation is in response to the live streaming of violent material by the perpetrator of the terrorist incident in Christchurch, New Zealand.[141]

295. Christchurch Call. The Christchurch Call was initiated by the NZ Prime Minister Jacinda Arden and the President of France Emmanuel Macron in the wake of the March 2019 Christchurch terror attacks that was live streamed on social media. The Call is an attempt to bring countries and tech companies to end the use of social media to organize and promote terrorism and violent extremism. Australian has signed the summit pledge.[142]

296. In response to recommendations of the Royal Commission into Institutional Responses to Child Sexual Abuse[143] proposed new offences for the possession or control of 'child abuse material' in the form of data held in a computer or on a data storage device.[144] This Bill seeks to amend the *Crimes Act* 1914 (Cth) to insert community safety as a factor.

297. Cyber-safety. This term describes initiatives and resources to help people manage their online activity. In Australia, offensive online behaviours are punishable by prison sentences. These offences include cyber harassment, cyberstalking and cyberbullying as well as image-based harm. However, the primary focus is on the better management of online risks through an education process.

298. A Draft Online Safety Charter has been developed by the Commonwealth government. This Charter is underpinned by two fundamental principles:

---

139. Penalties are in *Enhancing Online Safety (Non-consensual Sharing of Intimate Images) Act* 2018 (Cth); and criminalization in *Criminal Code Amendment (Protecting Minors Online) Act* 2017 (Cth).
140. *See Criminal Code Amendment (Sharing of Abhorrent Violent Material) Act* 2019 (Cth).
141. *See* Radio NZ at https://embed.radionz.co.nz/news/chch-terror.
142. *See* Minister of Home Affairs at https://minister.homeaffairs.gov.au/KarenAndrews/Pages/christchurch-call-further-bolsters-online-safety.aspx.
143. *See* Child Abuse Royal Commission at https://www.childabuseroyalcommission.gov.au/.
144. *See Crimes Legislation Amendment (Sexual Crimes Against Children and Community Protection Measures) Bill* 2017 (Cth). *See also Criminal Code Amendment (Protection of Minors Online) Act* 2017 (Cth) ('Carly's Law').

1. standards of behaviour online should reflect the standards that apply offline, and,
2. content that is harmful to users, particularly children, should be appropriately restricted.[145]

299. Under the *Enhancing Online Safety Act* 2015 (Cth) the Australian eSafety Commissioner promotes online safety for all Australians.[146] The Online Content Scheme provides a complaints process for prohibited content based on categories in the National Classification Scheme.[147]

300. The *Spam Act* 2003 (Cth) makes it illegal to send commercial electronic messages with an Australian link without the express or inferred consent of the recipient.[148] All manner of electronic messages is included under this legislation. In addition, commercial electronic messages must contain a functional unsubscribe mechanism and accurate information about who authorized the sending of the message. Certain exemptions exist for purely factual messages from government bodies, registered political parties, registered charities and educational institutions.

301. The *Do Not Call Register* is designed to prevent unsolicited telemarketing calls being made to telephone and fax numbers.[149] This free public service permits users to register their telephone or fax number on the Do Not Call Register. Once registered, unsolicited telemarketing calls or marketing faxes are prohibited to be sent to that number. Like spam, some exemptions apply.

302. The *Telecommunications and Other Legislation Amendment Act* 2017 (Cth) (TOLA Act) Schedule 1 Part 1 Main amendments to the *Telecommunications Act* 1997 (Cth) section 5 requires all carriers, CSPs and carriage service intermediaries to protect their telecommunications networks and facilities from unauthorized interference or access to confidential communications. A further requirement of the Act is competent supervision and effective control over the networks and facilities owned or operated by them.

303. The *Telecommunications (Interception and Access) Amendment (Data Retention) Act* 2015 (Cth) mandates that carriers and CSPs are subject to a metadata retention regime.[150] Metadata refers to phone numbers of the parties to a call or message, the time and duration of a call, the email address of sender and recipient and the time the email message was sent. The content of a communication or

145. *See* Department of Infrastructure at https://www.infrastructure.gov.au/have-your-say/online-safety-charter-consultation.
146. *See* text of the Act at https://www.legislation.gov.au/Series/C2015A00024.
147. *See* Department of Infrastructure, Transport, Regional Development and Communications Classification Scheme at http://www.classification.gov.au/About/Pages/National-Classification-Scheme.aspx. *See Broadcasting Services Act* 1992 (Cth) Schedules 5 & 7.
148. *Spam Act* 2003 (Cth), Schedule 1.
149. *Do Not Call Register Act* 2006 (Cth), Schedules 1 and 1A.
150. *Telecommunications (Interception and Access) Amendment (Data Retention) Act* 2015 (Cth).

web-browsing history is not part of the metadata. Metadata relating to communications of their subscribers are required to be retained for two years.

304. The government enacted industry assistance and access laws under the *Telecommunications and Other Legislation Amendment (Assistance and Access) Act* 2018 on 8 December 2018. The legislation requires all domestic and foreign designated communication providers to provide voluntary assistance to law enforcement and security agencies to access certain communications. Issues of appropriate safeguards for protecting the rights of individuals and whether the requirements remain proportionate to the threat to national security is under review by a Parliamentary Committee.[151] A major concern is the preservation and protection of classified and commercial-in-confidence material.

305. Section 313 of the *Telecommunications Act* 1997 (Cth) provides Australian government agencies, including state government agencies, with the ability to obtain assistance from the telecommunications industry when upholding Australian laws.[152]

306. The Australian government has also assisted the Special Rapporteur on Freedom of Opinion and Expression's report to the UN Human Rights Council on online content regulation as part of the multi-year examination of Freedom of Expression and the Private Sector in the Digital Age.[153]

§3. Regulation of Digital Online Platforms

I. Digital Online Platforms

307. Digital online platforms provide consumers with services that have revolutionized the way they communicate with each other, access news and information and interact with business. However, with reference to the role of global digital platforms in the supply of news and journalism in Australia, there remain important questions to be addressed. The main question is the responsibility such platforms hold as gateways to information and business and the extent of their accountability for their influence. These questions arise because of the digital platforms' market power and presence across multiple markets, the impact on the ability of content creators to monetize their content, and the lack of transparency in its operations for advertisers, media businesses and consumers.

---

151. *See* https://www.aph.gov.au/Parliamentary_Business/Committees/Joint/Intelligence_and_Security/AmendmentsTOLAAct2018.
152. *Telecommunications Act* 1997 s313 (Cth) at https://www.comlaw.gov.au/Details/C2012C00584.
153. *See* OHCHR at https://www.ohchr.org/Documents/Issues/Opinion/ContentRegulation/Australia.docx.

308. The ACCC 2017 Digital Platforms Inquiry Terms of Reference identified three categories of digital platforms namely: digital search engines, social media platforms and digital content aggregators.[154]

309. In adopting the recommendations of the Digital Platforms Inquiry final report, the Australian government passed a new law that will require digital platforms like Facebook and Google to pay local media outlets and publishers to link their content in news feeds or search results.

310. On February 25, 2021, the Australian Parliament passed the *Treasury Laws Amendment (News Media and Digital Platforms Mandatory Bargaining Code) Act* 2021 (Cth).[155] The Act establishes a 'mandatory code of conduct that applies to news media businesses and digital platform corporations when bargaining in relation to news content made available by digital platform services'. The mandatory code will also establish appropriate enforcement, penalty and binding dispute resolution mechanisms. The Act 'seeks to address a bargaining power imbalance that exists between digital platforms and Australian news businesses' which was identified in the Final Report of the ACCC's *Digital Platforms Inquiry*.

311. The Act adds a new part IVBA to the *Competition and Consumer Act* 2010 (Cth) to establish the news media and digital platforms mandatory bargaining code.[156]

312. The implementation of the Code essentially means that Australia will become the first country globally where a government-appointed arbitrator can decide on the final price that either platform will have to pay Australian news publishers, provided a commercial deal cannot be reached independently. It will also mean that news media businesses are fairly remunerated for the content they generate and in turn help sustain public interest journalism in Australia.

II. Interactive Gambling

313. The *Interactive Gambling Act* 2001 (Cth) (IGAct) makes it illegal to provide some interactive gambling activities, such as 'online casinos', to anyone in Australia.[157] Any game of chance, including games of mixed chance and skill played over the Internet, is prohibited if it is provided to someone who is physically in Australia.

314. The Act aims to limit the harmful effects of gambling on the Australian community. It targets the providers of interactive gambling.

---

154. *See* ACCC at https://www.accc.gov.au/focus-areas/inquiries-finalised/digital-platforms-inquiry-0.
155. *See* text of the Act at https://www.legislation.gov.au/Details/C2021A00021.
156. *See* text of the Act at https://www.legislation.gov.au/Details/C2021C00055.
157. *See* text of the Act at https://www.legislation.gov.au/Details/C2020C00027.

315. Internet service providers are obliged to adopt the Interactive Gambling Industry Code for online gambling hosted outside Australia[158]. It includes a provision for ISPs to provide one of the approved filters listed in Schedule 1 of the Code.

316. Furthermore, it is illegal to advertise interactive online gambling to an Australian audience. This prohibition is established under Part 7A of the IGAct and applies to all forms of electronic and non-electronic media – the Internet, broadcast services, print media, billboards and hoardings.

317. Internet service providers as intermediaries are generally protected under the *Criminal Code* and common law from liability for third-party content that is innocently transmitted over their networks.[159]

III. Interactive Online Marketplaces

318. Online marketplaces have taken on the business model of using the platform-as-a-service (PaaS) used extensively by platforms such as Amazon, ebay, Uber, Airbnb and Deliveroo. In general consumers can contract with online marketplace providers subject to their respective terms of use and local regulatory requirements governing such transactions. These may be characterized as platform-to-business (P2B), platform-to-consumer (P2C) and business-to-consumer (B2C).

319. Australia does not currently have a single regulatory framework aimed at P2B dealings. Instead, there are a multiplicity of regulatory regimes that impact on how online marketplace providers operate and engage with their business users and individuals. In general, the applicable regimes include:

- the Australian consumer law (ACL) regime governed by the *Competition and Consumer Act* 2010 (Cth) that relevantly fall within the definition of a 'consumer' under the CCA and enforced by the ACCC. The regulations generally apply to statutory guarantees and warranties, unfair contracts regime, misleading or deceptive conduct, and the making of false or misleading representations about goods or services;
- Australian privacy laws under the *Privacy Act* 1988 (Cth); and,
- other industry-specific regulations depending on the type of goods or service and industry-specific regulations.

320. Australia's existing regulations aim to help promote fairness, transparency and disclosure between online marketplaces, the businesses and individuals they engage with.

158. *See* Communications Alliance (2010) at https://www.commsalliance.com.au/__data/assets/pdf_file/0019/44605/gambling_code_nov2010.pdf.
159. *See* the recent High Court decision in *Fairfax Media Publications Pty Ltd & Ors v. Voller* [2021] HCA 27.

Chapter 7. International Private Law Applied to Online Environment

§1. CONFLICT OF LAWS

321. Private international law, often referred to as 'Conflict of Laws', is a body of law which deals with disputes that involve the laws of more than one country because some of their constituent elements relate to more than one jurisdiction. The 'borderless' online environment is one where such conflict of laws may arise.

322. The International Institute for the Unification of Private Law (UNIDROIT) is an independent intergovernmental organization with its seat in Rome set up in 1926. Its purpose is to study needs and methods for modernizing, harmonizing and coordinating private and commercial law as between states and groups of states. Established based on a multilateral agreement, the UNIDROIT Statute, membership is restricted to states acceding to the Statute. UNIDROIT has sixty-three Member States and Australia since 1973.

323. From 2015-2018, several UNIDROIT Member States sent proposals for the development of a model law on several related topics ranging from business informatics to distributed ledger technology (including blockchain) and inheritance of digital assets for inclusion in the 2020-2022 Work Programme.

324. A similar proposal relating to the legal aspects of smart contracts and artificial intelligence was presented to the UN Commission on International Trade Law (UNCITRAL) and UNIDROIT and member states subsequently organized two joint exploratory workshops, in May 2019[160] and March 2020[161], respectively.

325. As this topic of private international law is discussed in various chapters of this monograph relating to online transactions, intellectual property rights, cybersecurity law and cybercrime, the discussion below is necessarily in general terms only. Private international law is a matter of 'jurisdiction' where either the parties are in multiple jurisdictions or where the dispute arises in a foreign jurisdiction but litigated in a home country. The context also arises in foreign ownership of assets and the supply of assets from another jurisdiction.

326. In Australia, investments in the media sector require a notification to the Foreign Investment Review Board (FIRB) if a foreign person seeks to acquire more than 5 per cent of an Australian media business, regardless of value.[162] A *foreign*

---

160. *See* UNIDROIT (2019) at https://www.unidroit.org/english/news/2019/190506-unidroit-uncitral-workshop/conclusions-e.pdf.

161. *See* UNIDROIT (2021) Digital assets and private law at https://www.unidroit.org/work-in-progress/digital-assets-and-private-law/#1456405893720-a55ec26a-b30a.

162. Henderson, A & Halforty, I (2021) The Technology, Media and Telecommunications Review: Australia, at https://thelawreviews.co.uk/title/the-technology-media-and-telecommunications-review/australia.

person is defined as an individual who is not ordinarily a resident in Australia or a corporation where one or more foreign persons hold a combined total of 20 per cent or more of the issued shares, units or voting power.

327. In addition, from September 2018, a foreign person with company interests of more than 2.5 per cent in an Australian media company is required to notify the ACMA of its interests within thirty days.[163]

328. The ACMA maintains a publicly available register of foreign owners of media assets.

329. The foreign investment notification rules for the media and telecommunications sectors apply even to investors from countries that have free trade agreements with Australia, such as Chile, China, Japan, New Zealand, South Korea and the United States.

330. Australia has also flagged national security concerns about the involvement of Chinese companies in the building of 5G networks. For example, on 23 August 2018 the Departments of Home Affairs and Communications and the Arts issued a joint statement that banned Huawei and ZTE from supplying 5G network equipment due to national security concerns. The concern was that the involvement of such vendors who were likely to be subject to extrajudicial directions from a foreign government. Such 'interference' may conflict with Australian law and obligations, for example, unauthorized access or interference as legislated by the *Telecommunications and Other Legislation Amendment Act* 2017 (Cth).[164]

331. The challenge is for the Commonwealth to develop uniform rules with respect to the choice of law determinations. Arguably, the Commonwealth could enact such legislation pursuant to section 51 (XXV) of the Australian Constitution which allows the Commonwealth to make laws with respect to: 'The recognition throughout the Commonwealth of the laws, the public Acts and records, and the judicial proceedings of the State.'

332. An alternative approach would be to have all Australian States and Territories adopt a model code or to have an amendment to the Constitution giving the Commonwealth Government the power to make laws with respect to principles of choice of law and the development of procedural rules, including uniform conflict of laws rules.

---

163. *Broadcasting Legislation Amendment (Foreign Media Ownership, Community Radio and Other Measures) Act* 2018, s. 74F.
164. Hon Mitch Fifield, Minister for Communications and the Arts and the Hon Scott Morrison, Acting Minister for Home Affairs, Government Provides 5G Security Guidance To Australian Carriers, Departments of Home Affairs and Communications and the Arts, 23 Aug. 2018, https://www.minister.communications.gov.au/minister/mitch-fifield/news/government-provides-5g-security-guidance-australian-carriers.

333. Conflicts of law may be brought about by means of an international agreement. For example, the Preliminary Draft Convention on Jurisdiction and Foreign Judgments in Civil and Commercial matters adopted by the Hague Conference on Private International Law (HCPIL) could be more rigorously pursued.[165]

§2. Online Environments

334. Private international law in online environments can be fraught with traps and unintended consequences. Thus far it seems that governments have relied on the self- and private regulation of the Internet and domestic legislation steps in only when private regulation proves unsatisfactory. For lawyers, this means that there is little available in the form of case law or legislation that regulates this space. Instead, lawyers must rely on codes and industry standards.

335. Cross-border issues arise where it is difficult to determine where a content provider is domiciled. Even when a location is determined, the existence of the Internet in cyberspace means that a business can shift locations in a matter of hours. Locating a server is not the same thing as finding the legal identity behind the machine. At the same time, allowing users to sue content providers in the local court of each user means that the content provider can be sued in multiple jurisdictions simultaneously for essentially the same act. Australian law on these issues is unsettled. Australia has looked to the US, where decisions have emanated on the issue of Internet jurisdiction.[166]

336. E-business trading can take place across national borders and may even take place when one party is unaware of the physical location of the other party. This situation contrasts greatly with that of bricks-and-mortar transactions where jurisdiction is determined either by the physical presence of the party or the presence of physical property within that jurisdiction. In the case of e-business, its feature of being able to reach across multiple jurisdictions gives rise to many legal uncertainties about which jurisdiction's laws will apply and under what circumstances. For example, if a consumer in Australia orders a book or tennis racquet from a website in Topeka, Kansas, sent from a warehouse in Chennai, which consumer or liability law applies? This in turn poses a problem for Internet sites because owners of those sites can never be sure when their site might subject them to the laws of any country or state. In fact, a situation may arise that an Internet

---

165. HCPIL at http://www.hcch.net/e/conventions (on 30 Oct. 1999).

166. *See* for example, *Playboy Enterprises Inc. v. Chuckleberry Publishing Inc.* (1999) F. Supp. 1032, where the acceptance of jurisdiction of a US court in relation to a website in Italy was based on the interactive nature of the site; *State of* Minnesota *v. Granite Gate Resources* (1997) No. C6-95-7227, where a company located outside the US used a website to advertise its planned e-gambling site and indicated it would be legally accessible in Minnesota. The Minnesota Court held this to be a breach of the fair-trading laws.

trader may be sued in numerous jurisdictions at the same time for the one act. Alternatively, as in the Yahoo case, the same activity may be found to be legitimate in one jurisdiction, but a criminal offence in another.[167]

I. Jurisdiction: General Principles

337. Jurisdiction refers to the power of any government's laws and court system to bind a party or make a judgment in relation to a party or matter. Jurisdiction may be limited by geography, by the subject matter that the court may deal with, by the type of relief that can be sought, and the point of law or fact to be decided. The limits of a court's jurisdiction are usually defined by statute and the common law.

338. Jurisdictional clauses in many commercial cases apply where the parties themselves through an express stipulation in a contract may provide that any dispute between the parties arising out of the contract must be resolved by a court in a designated jurisdiction. However, if the contract is silent as to jurisdiction or it is not otherwise clearly indicated by the parties, the court will have to apply normal jurisdictional principles with a clear case to be made out that the exercise of jurisdiction is warranted.

II. Territorial Restrictions and Other Jurisdictions

339. There may also be territorial restriction laws. Except for a few cases such as Australian citizens or companies acting abroad, the laws of a State normally do not have application outside of the territorial boundaries of that State. This fact makes litigation on the Internet a very difficult challenge. Internet transactions can cross the borders of numerous countries in an instant. In this sense, it is said that the Internet can potentially be a lawless frontier. At the same time, it is also true that the problem with Internet transactions is that too many laws apply. This is because the transmission of the digital information may be subject to every one of the jurisdictions through which that information may flow through. This territorial nexus is seen in criminal law statutes that typically require there to be a jurisdictional connection. This means that either the defendant must be located there or one of the elements of the offence occurred there. This also means that the same conduct may give rise to different legal consequences in more than one State.

340. Another important, but technical, distinction is based upon personal *in personam* jurisdiction as opposed to jurisdiction over the thing itself, that is, '*in rem*' jurisdiction. It is not possible to bring an action against the person without giving that person notice, that is, personal service of process. However, where the 'thing'

167. *Yahoo Inc. v. La Ligue Contre Le Racisme et L'Antisemitisme* USC Northern District of California, San Jose Division 7 Nov 2001. The issue in the instant case is whether it is consistent with the laws of the US for another nation to regulate speech by a US resident within the US on the basis that such speech can be accessed by Internet users in that nation.

or '*res*' is situated in the jurisdiction, a court may determine and exercise its jurisdiction over the '*res*' even though personal jurisdiction may be absent. An apt example is in real estate transactions, where a court will have no difficulty finding jurisdiction because the thing itself (the '*res*') is physically located there.

341. The question in a technology communications context is whether a court can exercise its '*in rem*' jurisdiction over items that are 'virtually' located in that jurisdiction, for example, a domain name. In other cases, the presence will be partly physical and partly virtual, for example, a web server.

342. In cases where personal jurisdiction is required, a case cannot be heard in a court where process cannot be served on the defendant. Thus, the general rule is that no action can be taken against defendants until they have been served with an originating process. This general rule applies to cases in which the court is said to be exercising its jurisdiction *in personam*. Service of process is seen as necessary to ground the court's jurisdiction. Note that even if the court has jurisdiction, it may decide that the forum is an inappropriate one and that on policy grounds the case should be heard elsewhere.

343. A court may also exercise its powers over the subject matter, hence a subject matter jurisdiction. In some cases, the jurisdiction is limited by the type of case. For example, one could not attempt to get a divorce in a Small Claims Court. In other cases, the factor limiting the court's jurisdiction is the amount in dispute. Again, taking the example of the Small Claims Court, if the jurisdictional limit is disputes involving AUD 5,000 or less, then one could not file a case seeking AUD 10,000 in compensation.

III. Jurisdiction in Online Environments

344. In an Australian context in *Macquarie Bank v. Berg (*(1999) NSW SC 526), Macquarie Bank sought an injunction against Berg, a disgruntled former employee, who established a 'lemon' site through which he made allegedly defamatory statements about his former employer. The Court refused to exercise jurisdiction over Berg in relation to the injunction because it could only be enforceable within the territorial limits of New South Wales (NSW). Pragmatically, there was no way to limit such an order to a particular jurisdiction. To impose the injunction on a website would be in effect to impose NSW law on the rest of the world, something her Honour in her discretion declined to do.

345. In *Gutnick v. Dow Jones Inc.* (2001) VSC 305 (28 August 2001) multiple jurisdictions were involved. In November 2000, Joseph Gutnick, a well-known Melbourne identity, filed defamation action in the Victorian Supreme Court against Dow Jones & Co. a Delaware Corporation located in the US. Dow Jones is the publisher of the print and online editions of *Barrons Magazine*. The defamation related to various statements made about the plaintiff in the 30 October 2000 issue of *Barrons*. In its unsuccessful defence Dow Jones argued that the Victorian court had no jurisdiction; there was improper service of process; and the US and not Victoria was the most convenient and appropriate forum. It was conceded that an article is published when it becomes capable of being comprehended by a reader.

346. The *Gutnik* decision was recently affirmed on appeal to the High Court of Australia (*Dow Jones & Company Inc. v. Gutnick* (2002) H.C.A. 56 (10 December 2002)). In a unanimous decision, all seven High Court justices decided that Gutnick had the right to sue for defamation at his primary residence and the place he was best known. Victoria was considered the place where damage to his reputation occurred. The High Court decided that defamation did not occur at the time of publishing, but only after a third party read the publication and thought less of the individual who was defamed.[168]

347. Jurisdictional issues have also come into play in considering the extraterritorial effects of statutory regimes involving areas such as online securities, financial institutions and other vendors of such instruments that have many opportunities available to them online. However, advertising such products on the Internet may lead to uncertainties, the most obvious of which is whether such an offering complies with the regulations of the various jurisdictions.[169]

348. Information on a website about various financial offerings may indeed be a 'public offer' and subject to the laws of those jurisdictions reached by the website. In Australia, the offer of securities on the Internet and accessible from Australia means that Australian law will apply.[170]

349. A technological solution may provide some hope to the impasse. New technology is being developed which can allow a business to select their customers and jurisdictional reach of their website through geo-blocking, a technology that restricts access to Internet content based upon the user's geographical location. Alternatively, software may allow consumers to designate the countries, laws, or protections desired, and an expert system or artificial intelligence will match those preferences with websites that meet the specified criteria. For B2B commerce, a contract will prove decisive. In other words, the parties will continue to specify in their contractual arrangements what laws are to govern the relationship.

350. Arguably the Internet may indeed be a new and separate legal frontier. A proposal for reform is to assign Internet law disputes to their own territory, that is, to cyberspace. In other words, perhaps the industry should move to a form of self-regulation, using cyber courts and other mechanisms to resolve disputes. Indeed, such a regime could be enforced by key players such as ISP who require agreement to accede to the regime as a condition for use of the Internet. While this approach

---

168. *See* AUSTLII (2002) at http://austlii.law. uts.edu.au/au/cases/cth/high_ct/2002/56.html.
169. *See* Goueff, S (2001) Offering Financial Services on the Web: Experiencing the World Wide (Legal) Web', *World Internet Law Report* 2, no. 2 (February 2001): 26.
170. Australian Securities and Investments Commission (ASIC) Policy Statement No. 141, issued on 2 Mar. 2000.

is appealing in its simplicity, it is difficult to imagine that a traditional court would give up its jurisdictional powers, especially when the welfare of its citizenry is at stake and where such emotive moral issues as gambling and online pornography are involved.

351. Also relevant in such matters is the issue of appropriate venue and choice of laws. Even if a court exercises jurisdiction, it may refuse to do so if it finds that the forum is inconvenient. The issue of a forum raised in Australia in the *Gutnick* case suggests that the existence of a website will be insufficient to support a finding of a proper venue under the Federal statute.

352. Assuming a court has jurisdiction over the parties, the choice of law is the next procedural question to be resolved. Parties to an electronic or other contract can choose the law that will apply to the contract in question. If the contract does not state expressly the law to be applied, then it may be possible to imply what law the parties intended to apply.

353. The general rule of most states is that the courts should honour the parties' choice of law unless it would violate a fundamental policy of the state. An example might be a situation where there is an unequal bargaining position where an NSW Court might insist on applying the NSW *Contracts Review Act* 1980 (NSW).

Chapter 8. Regulation of Cryptography and Dual-use Goods

§1. CRYPTOGRAPHY

354. Cryptography is taken here to mean the use of technology to 'scramble' information into an unreadable form for humans. Computers have revolutionized the way messages are disguised and how access is made impossible without the appropriate keys. These computer ciphers use a method or algorithm and a key to code and decode messages or files. While the algorithm might be public, the key is always kept secret. Thus, anyone who has the key will be able to decrypt the message or file. While there are several types of ciphers the more common are secret key cryptography (also known as symmetrical because the same key is used for encryption and decryption) and public key cryptography (asymmetrical as different keys are used for encryption and decryption).[171]

355. Cryptography is used by governments and businesses to ensure that confidential information may be stored, transmitted and used over public networks in a secure manner. To date there are no direct controls by way of legislation to control the use and import of cryptographic software or hardware to Australia. However, there are restrictions to the export of cryptographic technology discussed below.

356. Some limits were initially placed on the use of cryptographic tools. The *Telecommunications and Other Legislation Amendment (Assistance and Access) Act* 2018 (Cth) (Assistance and Access Act)[172] extends law enforcement assistance obligations under Australia's *Telecommunications Act* 1997 (Cth) and related legislation to a much broader range of suppliers of communications services and equipment, software providers and device manufacturers, both within Australia and overseas. The Act attempts to leverage and mandate the technical assistance of industry to equip law enforcement and intelligence agencies with the means required to investigate serious crime whilst balancing the public interest in maintaining strong encrypted communication systems.

357. While encryption of messages and files may be used freely within Australia, the *Cybercrime Act* 2001 (Cth) provides that law enforcement agencies may compel the disclosure of encryption keys, passwords and other tools to obtain the necessary evidence.

---

171. *See* Electronic Frontiers Australia (2005) at https://www.efa.org.au/Issues/Crypto/cryptfaq.html, (30 Apr).
172. *See* text of the Act at https://www.legislation.gov.au/Details/C2018A00148.

358. An early development of public policy on the domestic use of cryptography in Australia is found in the 1996 Walsh Report. The gist of the report was in favour of free access to cryptography to the public.[173]

359. The provisions of the *Telecommunications and Other Legislation Amendment (Assistance and Access) Act* 2018 *(Cth) (Assistance and Access Act)* is subject to an ongoing review by the Parliamentary Joint Committee on Intelligence and Security (PJCIS) and by the Independent National Security Legislation Monitor (INSLM).[174]

360. Encryption software is readily available from the Internet. Examples include Pretty Good Privacy (PGP)[175] for email encryption and digital signatures and its variant GNU Privacy Guard (GnuPG).[176] Open-source toolkits are also available such as OpenSSL where commercial-grade full-featured tools assist in implementing robust security.[177]

361. Australian export controls on cryptographic tools are regulated under the *Customs (Prohibited Exports Regulations)* - Schedule 13E[178] and the *Customs Act* 1901 section 112 (Prohibited Exports)[179]. The prohibited export items are listed in the Defence and Strategic Goods List of the Australian Controls on the Export of Defence and Dual-Use Goods and crypto software is identified under Part 3.[180]

362. Either a Defence permit or licence listed in the Defence and Strategic Goods List (DSGL) 2019 published under the *Customs Act* 1901 (Cth) para. 112(2A)(aa) by the Minister of Defence is necessary for the export of such goods.[181]

---

173. *See* Walsh Report 1996 at https://www.efa.org.au/Issues/Crypto/Walsh/walsh.htm. The full name of the report is the *Review of policy relating to encryption technologies*, the outcome of a study conducted in 1996 by Gerard Walsh, a former deputy director-general of the Australian Security Intelligence Organisation (ASIO). An unredacted copy is found on the Electronic Frontiers Australia website quoted above.
174. *See* Department of Home Affairs (2019) Lawful access to telecommunications and the Assistance and Access Act 2018 at https://www.homeaffairs.gov.au/about-us/our-portfolios/national-security/lawful-access-telecommunications/data-encryption (9 Sept); Walker-Munro (2020) 'A shot in the dark: Australia's proposed encryption laws and the "disruption calculus"' at https://law.adelaide.edu.au/system/files/media/documents/2020-04/ALR_40%283%29_08_Walker-Munro_Web.pdf; and Hardy, K (2020) 'Australia's encryption laws: practical need or political strategy?' at https://experts.griffith.edu.au/8598-keiran-hardy/publications. *See also* INSLM Report at https://www.inslm.gov.au/sites/default/files/2020-07/INSLM_Review_TOLA_related_matters.pdf.
175. Zimmermann, PR (1999) 'Why I Wrote PGP.' Essays on PGP. Phil Zimmermann & Associates LLC at https://www.philzimmermann.com/EN/essays/WhyIWrotePGP.html.
176. *See* GNU at https://gnupg.org/.
177. *See* Open SSL at http://www.openssl.org.
178. *See* text of the Act at http://www.austlii.edu.au/au/legis/cth/consol_reg/cer439/s13e.html.
179. *See* text of the Act at http://www.austlii.edu.au/au/legis/cth/consol_act/ca1901124/s112.html.
180. *See* Department of Defence at http://www.defence.gov.au/dmo/id/export/Export_Control_Guidelines_03.pdf.
181. *See Defence and Strategic Goods List 2019* at https://www.legislation.gov.au/Details/F2019L00424/Download.

363. Australian controls are based on the international Wassenaar Arrangement.[182] Australia is one of thirty-three participant States of the arrangement.

364. The Wassenaar Arrangement has assumed the status of a treaty with the prohibitions and export controls embedded in relevant legislation. While, the Wassenaar Arrangement sets general parameters for import and export controls, they are not binding and are implemented depending on the circumstances of each member state.

365. The Wassenaar Arrangement on Export Controls for Conventional Arms and Dual-Use Goods and Technologies was established in 1995. Participating States undertake to ensure that exports of these items do not contribute to the development or enhancement of military capabilities which undermine international and regional security and stability. There are two lists, a munitions list; and a dual-use goods and technology list of which the latter list is highly relevant for the present discussion.

366. Limited exemptions to export control are available and the personal use exemption allows encryption software to be taken out of the country under certain defined conditions. Examples include software installed on a notebook computer, devices such as smartcard readers and others used in the banking and finance industry.

I. Cryptographic Software Tools as Goods?

367. Under the *Customs Act* 1901 (Cth) the definition of 'goods' is an inclusive one and where computer software made available for download comes within the ordinary meaning of the term. But in *Vickers v. Young* the presiding Judge characterized property as either movable or immovable under private international law of succession and on this basis found it unlikely that software made available for download would be 'goods' for the purposes of the *Customs Act.*[183]

368. However, two other cases considered whether the licensing of software constitutes a supply of goods for the purposes of the sales of goods legislation. In *Toby Constructions Products Pty Ltd v. Computa Bar (Sales) Pty Ltd*, a computer system comprising hardware and software constituted a sale of goods within the meaning of the relevant legislation while casting doubt as to whether the mere licensing of software constituted a sale of goods.[184] In *St Albans City and District*

---

182. *See* Department of Foreign Affairs and Trade (n.d.) at https://www.dfat.gov.au/international-relations/security/non-proliferation-disarmament-arms-control/export-control-regimes/Pages/wassenaar-arrangement. *See also* Wassenaar Agreement at http://www.wassenaar.org.
183. (1982) 65 FLR 260.
184. [1983] 2 NSWLR 48 at 54.

Council v. International Computers Limited the English Court of Appeal opined that mere licensing of software was not a supply of 'goods' within the relevant statutory definition.[185]

369. In the US, Congress may lack the power to restrict exports of encryption software in some forms under first amendment arguments.[186] In Australia, under the *Customs Act* 1901 (Cth) there is a suggestion that Australian cryptographers may succeed in a test case if they were to argue that computer software containing strong encryption available for download from an Australian server constitutes an exempt export good.[187]

370. The *Defence Trade Controls Act* 2012 (Cth) specifies several circumstances where the supply or publication of DSGL-listed software or technology does not require a permit, for example, verbal discussions and publication of Part 2 DSGL-listed software and technology do not require a permit.[188]

II. Review of Legislation and Amendments

371. A review of the TOLA 2017 led to the *Telecommunications Legislation Amendment (International Production Orders) Act* 2021 (Cth) (IPO Act) which received assent on 23 July 2021.[189] This IPO Act provides a framework for Australian agencies to obtain independently authorized international production orders for interception, stored communications and telecommunications data directly to designated communications providers in foreign countries with which Australia has a designated international agreement.

372. A review of the Telecommunications Sector Security Reforms (TSSR), found within the TOLA 2017, established a regulatory framework to better manage the national security risks of espionage, sabotage and foreign interference to Australia's telecommunications networks and facilities.

373. The TSSR was implemented from 18 September 2018. The reforms contain key elements such as obligations for the protection of networks and facilities from unauthorized access and interference; notification to the government of planned changes to their systems and services that could comprise the security obligation; the exercise of powers, such as an information gathering power of the Secretary of the Department of Home Affairs; and, the directions power permitting the

---

185. [1996] 4 All ER 481.
186. *See* Electronic Frontiers Foundation (2008) at https://www.eff.org/cases/bernstein-v-us-dept-justice?page=1 (21 Apr).
187. *See* Gunning, P (1998) 'Distributing encryption software by the Internet: loopholes in Australian export controls' at http://www2.austlii.edu.au/itlaw/articles/Gunning_Encryption.html.
188. Department of Defence 'Australian Export Controls and ICT' Guide at https://cecs.anu.edu.au/sites/default/files/staff/announcement/australian_export_controls_and_ict.pdf.
189. *See* Australian Parliament at https://www.aph.gov.au/Parliamentary_Business/Bills_LEGislation/Bills_Search_Results/Result?bId=r6511.

Minister of Home Affairs to direct a carrier, CSP or intermediary to do or not do a specified thing to reasonably necessary to protect networks and facilities from national security risks.[190]

374. The *Surveillance Legislation Amendment (Identify and Disrupt) Act* 2021 (Cth) creates a data disruption warrant, a network activity warrant and an account takeover warrant.[191]This Act also amends other legislation including:

- the *Surveillance Devices Act* 2004 (Cth) and *Telecommunications (Interception and Access) Act* 1979 (Cth) to authorize the issue of data disruption warrants to enable the Australian Federal Police (AFP) and the Australian Criminal Intelligence Commission (ACIC) to disrupt data by modifying, adding, copying or deleting data in order to frustrate the commission of serious offences online; and make minor technical corrections;
- the *Surveillance Devices Act* 2004 (Cth) to introduce network activity warrants to enable the AFP and ACIC to collect intelligence on serious criminal activity by permitting access to the devices and networks used to facilitate criminal activity; and,
- the *Crimes Act* 1914 (Cth) to introduce an account takeover warrant to enable the AFP and ACIC to take over a person's online account for the purposes of gathering evidence to further a criminal investigation; and make minor amendments to the controlled operations regime to ensure controlled operations can be conducted effectively in the online environment.

§2. Dual-Use Goods

375. There is a lack of an internationally binding definition of 'dual-use' goods as different instruments in various jurisdictions define the term dissimilarly. While generally linked to military capabilities, nuclear proliferation has been included in the gamut of weapons of mass destruction and other human security approaches.[192] The Minister for Defence's statement emphasizes that the DSG List 2019 is compatible with human rights security in accordance with Part 3 of the *Human Rights (Parliamentary Scrutiny) Act* 2011 (Cth).[193]

376. In the US, the Export Administration Regulations (EAR) define dual-use as '(those items having) civil applications as well as terrorism and military or weapons

---

190. *See* Department of Home Affairs (2022) at https://www.homeaffairs.gov.au/nat-security/Pages/telecommunications-sector-security-reforms.aspx (23 Feb).
191. Royal assent on 3 Sep. 2021 at https://www.aph.gov.au/Parliamentary_Business/Bills_Legislation/Bills_Search_Results/Result?bId=r6623.
192. *See* Vella, V (2017) 'Is there a common understanding of dual-use? The case of cryptography', at https://strategictraderesearch.org/wp-content/uploads/2017/09/Is-there-a-Common-Understanding-of-Dual-use-The-Case-of-Cryptography.pdf.
193. *See* Explanatory Statement issued by the Authority of the Minister for Defence at https://www.legislation.gov.au/Details/F2019L00424/Download.

of mass destruction-related applications'.[194] Encryption software and technology may be marked as being controlled for special reasons including the more general national security and anti-terrorism reasons for control.

377. The European Union (EU) Article II.I of European Council (EC) Regulation 428/2009 defines dual-use as 'items, including software and technology, which can be used for both civil and military purposes' and includes non-explosive uses and assisting in any way in the manufacture of nuclear weapons.[195] Interestingly amendments to the regulation proposes certain cyber surveillance technology be added to the definition as these tools that may be used in the commission of serious violations of human rights or international humanitarian law and may pose serious threats to international and essential security of the EU.[196]

194. US Department of Commerce Bureau of Industry and Security, 'EAR – Part 730,' BIS, January 4, 2017, p. 2 at https://www.bis.doc.gov/index.php/regulations/export-administration-regulations-ear.
195. European Council Regulation (EC) No. 428/2009 of 5 May 2009 Setting up a Community Regime for the Control of Exports, Transfer, Brokering and Transit of Dual-use Items, Official Journal of the European Union (L134/1) of May 29, 2009.
196. European Union Commission, 'Proposal for a Regulation of the European Parliament and of the Council Setting Up a Union Regime for the Control of Exports, Transfer, Brokering, Technical Assistance and Transit of Dual-Use items (recast)', COM (2016) 616 final, Brussels, 2016 at http ://trade.ec.europa.eu/doclib/docs/2016/september/tradoc_154976.pdf.

Part II. Online Public Services

Chapter 1. Legal and Policy Framework for e-Government

§1. Introduction

378. While there is no uniform or generally accepted definition, a consensus is that e-Government may be conceived of as the 'e-business of the state'. The UN Global E-government Readiness Report 2004 defined e-government as 'the use of information communications technology (ICT) and its application by governments for the provision of information and basic public services to people'.[197]

379. E-government in the form of online public services is the application of ICT to transform the efficiency, effectiveness, transparency and accountability of informational and transactional exchanges within government, between governments and government agencies at federal, state, and local levels, citizens and businesses; and to empower citizens through access and use of information and knowledge. Both e-government and e-business use the same infrastructure, hardware and at times also software as e-government.

380. Australia is recognized as one of the leading countries in the rapid move to an Information Economy, and the Australian government has played a pivotal role in this transformation. The commentary below outlines some of the emergent key issues for Australia as it progresses towards its policy goal of achieving e-government.

381. A prerequisite for e-governments is the necessary infrastructure conditions to promote a knowledge or information economy. Whilst, governments can promote e-business, the government itself must be exemplary in its adoption and deployment of new technologies and electronic media as the means to achieve such aims. Undoubtedly, the government is the largest agency in the lives of business and consumers. E-government may be seen as a key factor in increasing the overall competitiveness of the economy.

---

197. United Nations (2004) Global E-government Readiness Report: Towards Access for Opportunity, Geneva: Department of Economic and Social Affairs & Division for Public Administration and Development Management, UN Publication, 1-182 (2004).

382. It is significant to note that the 2014 National Commission of Audit findings is that e-government services are often preferred by citizens, businesses and other government customers because they are more convenient and generally cheaper and more accurate. The audit report recommends that the government accelerate the transition to online service delivery by setting an ambitious digital strategy that makes myGov the default means of engaging with government supported by 'opt-out' provisions; remove legislative barriers; and strengthen the myGov online credential.[198]

383. The evolving technologies, data and analytics and artificial intelligence present significant opportunities to deliver better outcomes for the public and the ability to do so more efficiently and effectively. Digital technologies offer improved citizen and business experience. As evidenced previously millions of Australians have already securely accessed a range of government services online everyday, including the myGov gateway to over 200 government services through 20 government agencies, myTax, and myHealth Record.[199]

§2. Antecedents to e-Government

384. By way of background, an initial policy statement for the promotion of e-commerce was the *Investing for Growth* policy statement on 8 December 1997. This statement outlined the government's intention and the various initiatives to enable Australian business to benefit from the global information age.[200] In pursuit of this policy the Commonwealth established the National Office for the Information Economy (NOIE) in 1997 to develop, coordinate and oversee broad policy relating to establishing the regulatory, legal and physical infrastructure environment for online activities and facilitating e-commerce. NOIE was replaced by the AGIMO on the 8 April 2004.

385. A later e-commerce policy was set out in *A Strategic Framework for the Information Economy – Identifying Priorities for Action* in January 1999.[201] In this framework effective approaches to consumer protection were to be developed. Such protections were designed to ensure B2C e-commerce compatibility with B2B e-commerce and government services online.

---

198. Towards Responsible Government Report of the National Commission of Audit. Phase One. February 2014, pp. lxvii, 236-239 at https://australianpolitics.com/downloads/budgets/2014/14-05-01_commission-of-auditreport1_phase1.pdf.
199. Department of Industry (2018) *Australia's Tech Future* at https://www.industry.gov.au/sites/default/files/2018-12/australias-tech-future.pdf.
200. Australia (1997) *Investing for Growth. The Howard Government's Plan for Australian Industry* at https://www.disr.gov.au/growth/.
201. NOIE (2009) *A Strategic Framework for the Information Economy – Identifying Priorities for Action*, National Office for the Information Economy, December 1998, at https://www.noie.gov.au/nationalstrategy/index.html.

386. The e-commerce policy framework identified ten priorities, including the need to develop a legal and regulatory framework to facilitate e-commerce to encourage more consumers and businesses to conduct more of their business online. The Strategic Framework also recognized the need for Australia to influence the emerging international rules and conventions for e-commerce.

387. Since the Strategic Framework policy there have been significant regulatory reform to introduce more competition and to promote greater consumer protection in the Australian information technology and telecommunication sector. Many of the submissions received in response to the *National Broadband Network: Regulatory Reform for Twenty-First Century Broadband Discussion Paper* released by the government on 7 April 2009 have been supportive of the policy.

388. The Government's *Digital Economy: Future 2009* policy conceives the digital economy as comprising of 'the global network of economic and social activities that are enabled by information and communications technologies, such as the Internet, mobile and sensor networks'.[202]

§3. E-GOVERNMENT POLICY INITIATIVES

389. The Digital Education Revolution (DER) is designed to build digital media literacy among school children. In 2008, the Australian government committed more than AUD 2.1 billion to the DER initiative – an intervention designed to generate an immediate, large-scale boost to enhance the integration of ICT into teaching and learning in Australian schools. The initiative involved investment in computers and software, school-based infrastructure, leadership, professional development and digital resources across all Australian education systems and sectors. The objective of the DER was to create ubiquitous access to the tools necessary for students to take advantage of new technologies.[203]

390. Enterprise Connect was launched on 21 May 2008 to provide advisory services tailored to the needs of Australian small and medium-sized enterprises (SMEs). Matched grants were also provided to assist participants implement the advice received.

391. The closure of Enterprise Connect was announced in May 2014 with most programme activities concluded by December 2014. In its place a new

202. *See* DBCDE (2009) at http://ict-industry-reports.com.au/wp-content/uploads/sites/4/2012/08/2009-Digital-Economy-Future-Directions-Report-DBCDE-2009.pdf.

203. Australian Government (2008) Success through Partnership: Achieving a National Vision for ICT in Schools – Strategic Plan to Guide the Implementation of the Digital Education Revolution Initiative and Related Initiatives. *See* reviews in Australian Government (2011) Digital Education Revolution Evaluation Strategy, April 2011, Department of Education, Employment and Workplace Relations, Canberra; and The Auditor-General (2011) Digital Education Revolution Program – National Secondary Schools Computer Fund, Audit Report No. 30 2010–11 Performance Audit, Australian National Audit Office, Canberra.

Entrepreneurs' Programme (EP) was announced in May 2014. EP drew together some of the key elements of several closing programmes including Enterprise Connect. EP is an important pillar of both the National Industry and Competitiveness Agenda and the National Innovation and Science Agenda (NISA).[204]

392. The government's *Information Policy* by the Office of the Australian Information Commissioner (OAIC) promotes 'open government', the free flow of information and about how government handles and uses public sector information that it holds.[205] The OAIC's *Principles on Open Public Sector Information* is designed to help agencies implement best practice information management. Agencies are encouraged to embed these principles in their internal policies and procedures on information management to help build a culture of proactive information disclosure and community engagement.[206]

§4. E-READINESS

393. Over the last two decades, Australia has been rated among the top countries in e-readiness by the Economist Intelligence Unit (EIU), the business arm of *The Economist* group. In a report for 2002, Australia slipped from second to sixth overall e-readiness. The metric is based upon a composite measure of IT infrastructure, good overall business environment, uptake of the Internet by consumers, a stable economic and political climate, telephone penetration, online security and IP protection.[207]

394. In 2020, a sample of 141 countries were assessed for digital readiness using seven indicators and slightly changed methodology. Australia was assessed as still in the top ten ranked countries in the world. However, this is a 'never-ending journey' and even leading countries face a constant need to develop their digital readiness to remain competitive relative to their peers and keep ahead of technology developments.[208]

395. Using a different set of criteria, the CISCO Australian *Digital Readiness Index 2020* provides both a snapshot of Australia's evolving digital capability and

204. Enterprise Connect (2019) at https://www.industry.gov.au/sites/default/files/2019-06/business-performance-of-enterprise-connect-participants.pdf. For the Entrepreneurs Programme see https://business.gov.au/grants-and-programs/entrepreneurs-programme.
205. *See* OAIC at http://www.oaic.gov.au/information-policy/about-information-policy.
206. *See* OAIC at https://www.oaic.gov.au/information-policy/information-policy-resources/principles-on-open-public-sector-information.
207. AAP (2002) Our E-Readiness Slips: Report, *Canberra Times* 15 (25 Jul. 2002).
208. *See* Prime Minister & Cabinet (2021) at https://digitaleconomy.pmc.gov.au/sites/default/files/2021-07/digital-economy-strategy.pdf.

a guide for government and industry relative to where additional investments are needed to ensure Australia continues to develop as a digitally capable and inclusive society.[209]

396. The resulting indices place countries in the survey into three categories of digital readiness.

1. *Activate*: the lowest stage of digital readiness, indicating the need for interventions that target basic needs as a foundation for building more advanced digital readiness capabilities.
2. *Accelerate*: a moderate stage of digital readiness with ongoing requirements for investment in basic needs but demonstrating potential for benefits through improvements in other areas, such as ease of doing business. The breadth of countries included in the Accelerate group resulting in subsequently splitting it into two further subclasses – Accelerate Low and Accelerate High.
3. *Amplify*: the highest stage of digital readiness, showing significant existing benefits and great potential for further uplift from additional investment in infrastructure and higher-level skills development.

397. In 2017, Australia scored highly across all seven components of digital readiness and ranked in the Amplify group with an overall score of 17.3 out of a possible 25. This placed Australia among global leaders including the US, Singapore and numerous European nations.

398. In 2019, Australia's digital readiness score increased from 17.3 to 17.9 out of a possible 25 points. However, while Australia retained its global Amplify ranking in 2019, its ranking fell two places to twelfth as two other countries improved their rankings.

399. The 2019 global results showed the continued high correlation between digital readiness and per capita gross domestic product (GDP), with high GDP countries such as Singapore, the US and Luxembourg all ranking in the top ten.

400. It is also worth noting that the 2019 results saw Singapore advance to the number one position globally, overtaking the US, which dropped to third position with the inclusion of Luxembourg in second place. This was again despite the US maintaining its score across most components of digital readiness. These results show the highly competitive global environment and the importance of continued investment to retain and develop Australia's overall state of digital readiness.

---

209. *See* CISCO (2020) at https://www.cisco.com/c/dam/m/en_au/digital-readiness/pdfs/cisco-wp-driAustralia2020.pdf. The digital readiness of a country is determined by analysing seven components, standardized and summed to give an overall digital readiness score out of a possible total of twenty points.

§5. Australian e-Government Performance

401. According to a biennial UN e-government survey in 2016 Australia has maintained its place as the second-best country after the UK for e-government.[210]

402. The UN noted a sharp global rise in the number of countries using one stop service platforms. In 2003, only forty-five countries had a one-stop-platform, and only thirty-three countries provided online transactions. According to the 2016 survey, 90 countries now offer one or more single entry portal for public information or online services, and 148 provide at least one form of online transactional services.

403. Australia has risen on e-participation rates from seventh to equal second with Japan in 2016.

404. The *e-participation index* assesses the provision of government information on the Internet, online public consultations and the involvement of citizens in decision processes.

405. The *e-government development index* measures the adequacy of telecommunication infrastructure, the promotion and use of ICT and the availability of online services.

406. The top ten countries in rank order in 2016 according to the e-government development index are: the UK, Australia, South Korea, Singapore, Finland, Sweden, the Netherlands, New Zealand, Denmark and France.

407. The UN e-Government Survey in 2020 shows that most of the world's governments are embracing digital transformation.[211] Australia ranked fifth on the global e-Government Development Index (EGDI), behind Denmark, Finland, Estonia and South Korea.

408. The rankings demonstrate continued leadership and focus on e-government innovation. As well the higher rankings attained by the top fifteen to twenty countries the rankings reflect the relative levels of economic, social and political developments in the countries concerned. More importantly, there appears a high correlation between investments in telecommunications, human capital and the provision of government online services.

---

210. *See* UN (2016) E-participation Rising, but UK Now Beats Australia at e-Government at http://publicadministration.un.org/egovkb/en-us/Resources/E-Government-Survey-in-Media/ID/1866/E-participation-Rising-but-UK-Now-Beats-Australia-at-e-Government posted August 04, 2016. *See also* Donaldson, D (2016) 'e-participation rising, but UK now beats Australia at e-government', at https://www.themandarin.com.au/68452-uk-beating-australia-at-e-government/.

211. *See* UN (2020) at https://www.un.org/development/desa/publications/publication/2020-united-nations-e-government-survey.

409. The rise in rankings is neither surprising nor unexpected as the Australian government has taken comprehensive steps towards digital transformation.[212] In 2016, in pursuit of its digital agenda, a Digital Transformation Agency (DTA) was established to oversee the migration of government services to online platforms like myGov and Australia.gov.au.[213]

410. As noted in the UN report Australia's success in e-government is due in part to the use of joined-up, integrated service delivery in social security and health and other services. Digitally joined-up services allow governments to make some services conditional in return for citizens fulfilling certain obligations. Australia's ambitious plan is to complete digital transformation of government by 2025. This plan is overseen by the DTA and other bodies like the Australian Digital Council (ADC)[214]. The ADC is equivalent to a ministerial council of the Council of Australian Governments (COAG) and performs an intergovernmental coordinating role.[215]

411. In summary, the digital transformation strategy is underpinned by five core initiatives:

1. *A unified digital identity* to obviate the need for separate login accounts and passwords. At present two separate digital identities – myGovID (for government services online) and Australia Post Digital iD (for government and private sector services) are in place. The Trusted Digital Identity Framework (TDIF) provides access to all types of services from tax records to Medicare, drivers licence, bank accounts with a single login system.[216] The myGovID allows access to eighty government services that links data across services such as Medicare, Centrelink and the Australian Tax Office (ATO). The exposure draft to the *Trusted Digital Identity Bill* 2021 (Cth) proposes an expansion of powers to outsource the process of identity verification to approved Australian businesses and that the proposed digital identity system will be entirely voluntary.[217] The Bill is yet to pass parliament and is in the consultation stage at the end of 2021.

---

212. *See* Australian Parliament House (2019) at https://www.aph.gov.au/About_Parliament/Parliamentary_Departments/Parliamentary_Library/pubs/rp/rp1819/Quick_Guides/PSDigitalTransformation (2 Apr).
213. *See* Digital Transformation Agency at https://www.dta.gov.au/digital-government-strategy.
214. *See* PMC at https://www.directory.gov.au/portfolios/prime-minister-and-cabinet/department-prime-minister-and-cabinet/data-and-digital-ministers-meeting.
215. *See* COAG at https://www.coag.gov.au.
216. *See* DTA (2019) at https://www.dta.gov.au/blogs/how-were-developing-policy-behind-digital-identity (1 Feb). *See also* https://www.dta.gov.au/our-projects/digital-identity/trusted-digital-identity-framework.
217. *See* DTA (2021) at https://www.digitalidentity.gov.au/sites/default/files/2021-09/Trusted%20Digital%20Identity%20Bill%202021%20exposure%20draft.docx. *See also* Nabben, K (2021) The government wants to expand the 'digital identity' system that lets Australians access services. There are many potential pitfalls, *The Conversation* 27 Oct 2021 at https://theconversation.com/the-government-wants-to-expand-the-digital-identity-system-that-lets-australians-access-services-there-are-many-potential-pitfalls-170550.

2. *A focus on citizen experience*. The development by Deloitte of a Government Digital Experience Platform (GovDXP) aims to emulate and provide an online experience like on social media platforms.[218]
3. *Personalization and customization for government services*. E-governance platforms that offer personalized services to improve user experience (UX) such as using only available citizen data and removing services that are not applicable based on socioeconomic and demographic data. A pensioner's experience will be different from that of a student.
4. *Data analytic tools bringing benefits beyond enhanced user experience*. At a policy level appropriate changes may be made based on citizen behaviour. Data from user-behaviour may focus on direct feedback from users in an iterative process.
5. *Enhancing privacy and trust*. As government agencies have access to and accumulate sensitive personal data cyber-safety security is imperative. Arguably the success of digital transformation projects in government agencies will require high levels of trust among citizens. This would be in addition to transparency in the process of data sharing and a citizen's access to data and where it is shared as well as permissions to use such information between departments and agencies within government.

412. The *Data Availability and Transparency Act* 2022 and the *Data Availability and Transparency (Consequential Amendments) Act* 2022 passed both Houses of Parliament with bipartisan support on 30 March 2022.[219] First introduced in December 2020, these Acts will significantly change the way that public sector data can be collected, shared and used. The Acts will permit Commonwealth bodies to share public sector data with state and federal governments and public Australian universities. The Act establishes the Office of the National Data Commissioner (ONDC) and the National Data Advisory Council. Consequential amendments have been made to the *Administrative Decisions (Judicial Review) Act* 1977 (Cth), *Australian Security Intelligence Organisation Act* 1979 (Cth), *Freedom of Information Act* 1982 (Cth) and *Privacy Act* 1988 (Cth) in relation to the operation of the data sharing scheme.

413. The COVID-19 pandemic amply demonstrates a crisis that has been dealt with through various forms of e-governance from ICT like the Internet through to smartphone apps to deliver essential services to the population at large under lockdown. The public's experience with e-commerce and other online services in private and public have whetted appetites with higher expectations for on-demand services in virtual settings. Digital transformation in government services and delivery appears to be the next logical step.

218. *See* Deloitte selected as systems integrator for GovDXP platform (2 Mar. 2021) at https://www.consultancy.com.au/news/3057/deloitte-selected-as-systems-integrator-for-govdxp-platform.
219. *See Data Availability and Transparency Act* 2022 (Cth) (DATA Act) text at https://www.legislation.gov.au/Details/C2022A00011; and *Data Availability and Transparency (Consequential Amendments) Act* 2022 text at https://www.legislation.gov.au/Details/C2022A00012.

Chapter 2. Legal Framework for e-Health

§1. Australian HealthCare System

414. Health issues have dominated the global landscape with the COVID-19 pandemic emergency requiring the full attention of many governments and health-care professionals worldwide. The pandemic has required large-scale government interventions at all levels. The health-related incidents of SARS, MERS, H1N1 swine flu, Ebola and myriad other epidemics pale by comparison to the pandemic during the period 2020-2021 and beyond. While the timely and effective delivery of healthcare services to young and old is being tested when epidemics and pandemics occur yet in the twenty-first century it appears that many nations are still reliant on processes and procedures of yesteryears to combat these challenges. Globally many governments are in the process of reforming their healthcare service delivery in using modern technology to assist in the timely and cost-effective use of available resources. Such reforms in the health sector are aimed at providing better health-care and better hospital treatments.[220]

415. The Australian healthcare system is both large and complex. In 2008 the healthcare industry employed over 850,000 people and services a diverse population of over 26 million residents across the vast continent. In 2020 there were more than 586,000 registered health practitioners in Australia including 334,000 nurses and midwives, 133,400 allied health professionals, 98,400 medical practitioners and 20,600 dental practitioners.[221]

416. The services are provided through a complex network of public and private providers working across over 1,000 hospitals and many more additional general practitioners, specialists, community health, allied health and aged care environments.

417. Both public and private hospital sectors provide services for admitted and non-admitted patients. There were 693 public hospitals in Australia in 2017-2018 and 657 private hospitals including day hospital facilities in 2016-2017. In 2017-2018 AUD 74 billion was spent on Australia's public and private hospitals. Spending per person on hospital care increased by an average of 2.1 per cent per year between 2013-2014 and 2017-2018.[222]

418. Most healthcare delivery is via face-to-face sessions, some in remote areas rely on either radio telephone and videoconferencing services such as Skype or sporadic and infrequent flying doctor services.

---

220. *See* the Department of Health (2020) Health Reform Agreement at https://www.health.gov.au/initiatives-and-programs/2020-25-national-health-reform-agreement-nhra (29 May).
221. AIHW (2020) Australia's Health 2020: In Brief at https://www.aihw.gov.au/getmedia/2aa9f51b-dbd6-4d56-8dd4-06a10ba7cae8/aihw-aus-232.pdf.aspx?inline=true.
222. *Ibid*. AIHW (2020) Australia's Health 2020.

419. It is estimated that in the period 2005-2006 Australia spent one in every eleven dollars on health that equated to AUD 87 billion or approximately nine per cent of the GDP.[223]

420. Expenditures on health as a proportion of Australian GDP have more than doubled over the last forty-five years, from 3.8 per cent in 1960-1961 to 9.0 per cent in 2005-2006.[224] The AIHW expects that healthcare spending as a proportion of GDP is expected to continue increasing to an estimated 16-20 per cent of GDP by 2045.[225]

421. Over the past two decades health expenditure in Australia has grown faster than either inflation or population growth. In the twenty-year period to 2017-2018, total health expenditure in Australia increased from AUD 77.5 billion to AUD 185.4 billion in real terms and spending per person increased from AUD 4,189 to AUD 7,485. As a proportion of GDP, health expenditure increased from 7.6 per cent in 1997-1998 to 10 per cent in 2017-2018.[226]

422. In June 2019, 11.2 million Australians (44 per cent of the population) had some form of private patient hospital cover, and 13.6 million (53 per cent) had some form of general treatment cover.[227]

423. Besides expenditure growth there are real challenges in terms of finding enough skilled healthcare workers across the whole sector to satisfy current, let alone future levels of demand. Such trends raise the issue of the sustainability of the Australian healthcare system.

424. The following discussion provides the contextual background to e-health and its scope. Then the policy developments for this sector are reviewed before examining the legislation that regulates this important industry. The final section looks towards the future and likely developments in the regulation of the e-health industry.

I. e-Health: Definition

425. E-Health has been used to describe a form of healthcare practice that is supported by electronic processes and communications. However, the subject matter of

---

223. AIHW (2008) *Australia's Health*, Canberra: AIHW. *See also* Australian Health Ministers' Conference (AHMC) 2008 *National Digital Strategy: Summary*, December at https://www.digitalhealth.gov.au/about-us/national-digital-health-strategy-and-framework-for-action and *supra* AIHW (2020) Australia's Health 2020: In Brief.
224. AIHW (2008) Health Expenditure Data Cubes, September, Canberra: AIHW.
225. AIHW (2008) Long-term Trends in Health Expenditure, September, Canberra: AIHW.
226. AIHW (2020) Australia's Health 2020: Data Insights at https://www.aihw.gov.au/reports-data/australias-health.
227. AIHW (2020) Australia's Health 2020: In Brief *supra*.

e-health reveals that it is extensive and covers both the delivery of health services using technologies as well as the workings of those technologies. There are numerous definitions for e-Health.[228]

426. The World Health Organisation defines e-Health as:

> the cost-effective and secure use of information and communications technologies in support of health and health-related fields, including health-care services, health surveillance, health literature, and health education, knowledge and research.[229]

427. The Council of Australian Governments (COAG) takes e-Health to mean ICT to improve the coordination and integration of healthcare delivery to individuals.[230]

428. Eysenbach's (2001) definition of e-health as a term and concept is more expansive in that:

> *e-health* is an emerging field in the intersection of medical informatics, public health and business referring to health services and information delivered or enhanced through the Internet and related technologies. In a broader sense, the term characterizes not only a technical development, but also a state-of-mind, a way of thinking, an attitude, and a commitment for networked, global thinking, to improve health care locally, regionally, and worldwide by using information and communication technology.[231]

429. Unsurprisingly, the term e-health has been inconsistently used and commonly misunderstood by many. The term has been used interchangeably with health informatics and sometimes taken as a subset of health informatics. A very narrow interpretation is one where healthcare practice is intrinsically linked with the Internet.

430. Health informatics involves the collection, analysis and movement of health information and data. Health informatics has brought about the automation of many labour-intensive health procedures, thereby saving dollars. Health informatics has developed and employed technology to transmit medical information,

228. Oh, H, Rizo, C, Enkin, M & Jadad, A (2005) 'What is eHealth (3): a systematic review of published definitions', *Journal of Medical Internet Research*, vol. 7, no. 1, 2005 at http://www.jmir.org/2005/1/e1/.
229. World Health Organisation (WHO) (2005) *e Health resolution 2005* at http://www.who.int/healthacademy/news/en/.
230. *See* COAG (2009) National Partnership Agreement on e-Health, Intergovernmental Agreement on Federal Financial Relations, Canberra: Australian Parliament House.
231. *See* Eysenbach, G (2001) What is e-health? *J Med Internet Res* 2001; 3(2):e20 at http://www.jmir.org/2001/2/e20.

thereby reducing mistaken interpretations and related adverse patient outcomes. Additionally, health informatics is used to observe disease trends and population health outcomes.[232]

431. The Health Informatics Society of Australia defines health informatics as:

> an evolving scientific discipline that deals with the collection, storage, retrieval, communication and optimal use of health-related data, information and knowledge. The discipline utilizes the methods and technologies of the information sciences for the purposes of problem solving and decision-making thus assuring quality healthcare in all basic and applied areas of biomedical sciences.[233]

432. *Telemedicine* is reliant on health informatics for its delivery. Telemedicine 'systematically applies information technologies to public health practice. Public health informatics employs a wide variety of tools and techniques to reach its goal of preventive health, a practice that telemedicine similarly attains. Telemedicine, like informatics, applies advancements in health technologies to the healthcare setting. Using such innovations and technologies improves clinical quality, particularly in rural areas'.[234]

433. *Telehealth* suggests a broader application that considers the activities of health professionals including nurses, psychologists and others. The use of information technologies is an integral part of the electronic delivery of healthcare.[235]

II. Scope of e-Health

434. Any discussion of e-health as a tool may involve all or some of the following services and systems including the collateral issues that arise.

- *Telemedicine,* that is, medical practice that eliminates patients travelling to access all types of physical and psychological assessments.
- *Consumer Health Informatics* which refers to the methods and systems that provide health information to consumers, for example, how to ensure that information on an Internet site is accurate and complete, how to ensure that the system gives access to a high quality of healthcare and health information.

232. *Ibid.*
233. Health Informatics Society of Australia at http://www.hisa.org.au.
234. Preston, J (1993) The Telemedicine Handbook: Improving Health Care with Interactive Video (1993) quoted in Mitchell, J (1993) *From Telehealth to E-Health. The Unstoppable Rise of E-Health* at p. 8. *See also* Crowe, B (1993) Telemedicine in Australia: a discussion paper, Australian Institute of Health and Welfare, February 1993.
235. Mitchell, J (1998) Fragmentation to Integration: The Telemedicine Industry in Australia, Canberra: AGPS at p. 9.

- *Electronic Health Records Systems* enable communicating patient data between different healthcare professionals including general practitioners (GPs), specialists, pharmacists and healthcare teams.
- *Health Knowledge Management* provides specialist information to practitioners and healthcare workers through medical journals, best practice guidelines and epidemiological tracking services and resources such as Medscape and MD-Linx.[236]
- *Virtual Health Teams* of healthcare professionals to care for a patient who collaborate, cooperate and communicate information on patients using digital equipment.
- *M-Health* which includes the use of digital mobile devices (mobile telemedicine) that collect, aggregate and summarize patient level health data that are conveyed to practitioners, specialists and researchers in real-time.
- *E-Health Grids* that involve the deployment of powerful computing systems and data management capabilities that aggregate and network huge volumes of heterogeneous data. Distributed computing in the guise of 'clouds' and off-site storage capabilities place powerful tools in the hands of healthcare professionals to assist in the care of patients.[237]
- *Health-care Information Systems* include systems based on software that assist in appointment scheduling, patient data management, work schedules and other tasks associated with the care of patients. In addition, such systems may also interact with other private and public healthcare system in terms of billing, benefits and rebates as well as the interchange of patient data and medical diagnosis.[238]
- *Health Robotics* involves the use of robotics in the delivery of healthcare.
- *E-health Intellectual Property and Bio-Ethics Issues* relate to unanswered legal and ethical questions about patent protection given advances in gene technology and nano technology. Nanotechnologies, such as cellular or sub cellular sensors or computers, generate novel methods and tools for collecting, storing, and analysing Internet-accessible health data.[239]
- *E-health Payment Systems* involve the issue of electronic systems of payment for health services.[240]

---

236. Medscape is an online destination used by medical practitioners and other healthcare professionals for timely medical information. *See* https://www.medscape.com/. MD-Link is a web-based program for online medical services at https://themdlink.com/ that allows referring medical doctors access to their patients' treatment results in a timely and secure manner.
237. *See* Fingberg, J *et al.* (2006) *Integrating Data Custodians in eHealth Grids – Security and Privacy Aspects* at https://www.semanticscholar.org/paper/Integrating-Data-Custodians-in-eHealth-Grids-%E2%80%93-and-Fingberg-Hansen/9f4bf16d368f0779ad3700251efa17d7f73f2995.
238. Spil, T & Kijl, B (2009) 'E-health Business Models: From pilot project to successful deployment': IBMA Business Review, Volume 1, (2009) at http://www.ibimapublishing.com/journals/IBIMABR/volume1/v1n5.pdf.
239. *See* generally Australian Office of Nanotechnology (AON) at http://www.innovation.gov.au/.../australianofficeofnanotechnology.aspx; and Office of Gene Technology Regulator (Australia) at http://www.ogtr.gov.au/.
240. *See* for example, Final Report of the Expert Group on e-Invoicing (2009) at http://ec.europa.eu/internal_market/consultations/2009/e-invoicing_en.htm.

- *Globalization /Internationalization of healthcare delivery* involves the challenges posed by national borders and the legal issues created by the increasing delivery of healthcare services across national borders.
- *Dispute Resolution* and the use of technology to provide online resolution of disputes emanating from healthcare delivery.
- *E-health policy issues* among others relate to questions of access for all citizens to the healthcare system, especially those in remote or rural areas.
- *Disaster Recovery/Environmental Law issues* relate to the implications of technology on strategies to prevent and manage pandemics and other disasters.
- *E-health as Export* and the legal and strategic economic issues in the growth and development of e-health as a major export.
- *Risk management/legal liability* issues involving the risks inherent in e-health developments and how best to manage those risks and who should be legally and financially accountable.
- *E-health economics* includes issues of competition and consumer protection law and policy.[241]

§2. National e-Health Strategic Developments

435. E-health can be traced to well before 1996 when the Howard Coalition government came into office as the previous Labor government and the various state and territory governments had already committed funding to a variety of e-health projects. These projects were part of the national health information and technology strategy under the auspices of the Australian Health Ministers' Conference (AHMC). The desire to propel the provision and delivery of the health industry into the information age played a major part in this thinking.[242]

436. In early 2008 Australian Health Ministers, through the Australian Health Ministers' Advisory Council (AHMAC) commissioned Deloitte National E-Health and Information Principal Committee to develop a strategic framework and plan to guide national coordination and collaboration in e-Health.[243] As part of this process, Deloitte conducted a series of national consultations with all stakeholders at every level and in all sectors of the health industry. The national e-Health strategy developed by Deloitte provides an appropriate basis to guide the development of e-Health in Australia.[244]

437. The national e-Health strategy adopts an incremental and staged approach developing e-Health capabilities that leverage currently available capacities, manage underlying variations across the health sector and levels of government; and allow flexibility for change from lessons learnt and technologies developed. The

241. *See* generally United Nations (2010) E-Government Survey 2010 - Leveraging e-government at a time of financial and economic crisis: http://www.epractice.eu/en/library/313483.
242. For instance, Medicare benefits could only be claimed for face-to-face consultations under the *Health Insurance Act* 1973 (Cth).
243. Australian Health Ministers' Conference (AHMAC) (2008) *op cit.*
244. *Ibid.* AHMAC.

strategy reinforces the existing collaboration of Commonwealth, State and Territory governments on the core foundations of the Electronic Health Records (EHR) system and identifies priority areas where these may be extended to support health reform in Australia.

I. e-Health Record Systems in Australia

438. Consideration of EHR systems in Australia begun around the 2000s. An initial system of the kind envisaged was MediConnect, which electronically collected stored information about medicines and exchanged such information among doctors, pharmacists and individuals. In 2004, MediConnect completed its field test in Launceston and Ballarat and ceased as a stand-alone system by December.

439. From experiences gained from the e-health trials HealthConnect was launched as a network of EHR that involved the collection, storage and exchange of individual health information on the network.[245]

440. The HealthConnect programme, began in 2005 and completed in 2009, consisted of a set of different projects undertaken individually by all the states and territories except Queensland. The programme is credited to have provided significant insights to the establishment of e-health infrastructure across Australia.[246]

441. In 2005 the National Electronic Health Transition Authority (NEHTA) was established to coordinate the national EHR project.

II. e-Health Identifiers

442. In 2010, the *Healthcare Identifiers Act* 2010 (Cth) was proclaimed.[247] The Act aimed to ensure that healthcare is matched to health information. A correct match is achieved by assigning an identifier to each healthcare provider or healthcare recipient and where the identifiers are used in the Personally Controlled Electronic Health Record (PCEHR) system.

443. In 2012, the *Personally Controlled Electronic Health Records Act* 2012 (Cth) was enacted to support the effective operation of the PCEHR system. The Act's four main areas are:

245. Medicare, MediConnect (2012) at http://www.medicareaustralia.gov.au/provider/patients/mediconnect.jsp.
246. NEHTA (2011) Concept of Operations: Relating to the introduction of a Personally Controlled Electronic Health Record System (2011) at http://www.yourhealth.gov.au/internet/yourhealth/publishing.nsf/Content/PCEHRS-Introtoc/AUD File/Concept%20of%20Operations%20-%20Final.pdf.
247. *See Healthcare Identifiers Act* 2010 (Cth) text at http://classic.austlii.edu.au/au/legis/cth/consol_act/hia2010199/.

1. the governance of the PCEHR system;
2. registration of individuals, healthcare provider organizations, individual healthcare providers and other actors in the system;
3. collection, use and disclosure of health information included in a registered individual's e-Health record; and,
4. penalties and enforcement. For the first time mandatory privacy breach reporting obligations have appeared in a regulation in Australia.[248]

444. Between 2010 and 2012, the Australian government invested AUD 467 million in the development of a national PCEHR system which was launched on 1 July 2012.[249]

445. Core functionality of the PCEHR was designed to ensure that the interactions between patients and healthcare providers eliminated the inconsistency held in paper-based files and non-shared databases held in different locations. The system aimed to eliminate the lack of standardization in records that previously led to medical errors. The records would also address inadequate information, unplanned hospital admissions, prescribing errors such as undergoing the same tests for different providers.

446. The implementation of the PCEHR gave rise to policy and economic uncertainties. The challenges included the lack of a unified approach within the multi-tiered government system in Australia, the lack of transparency in the operations of NEHTA,[250] the opt-in model for individual registration, privacy concerns and the effectiveness and usability of the system.[251] These issues would eventually spell the demise of the PCEHR to be replaced by My Health Record.

447. In 2014, the federal Health Minister commissioned a review into the PCEHR to identify and mitigate the issues identified above. Recommendations of the review that have been adopted include the renaming the PCEHR as My Health Record; a move to an opt-out system rather than opt-in; the establishment of the Australian Digital Health Agency (ADHA) in July 2016; a focus on clinical content; and a more transparent approach to safety and security.[252]

---

248. Bloom, G (2012) The National Systems of Personally Controlled Electronic Health Records, *HWL Ebsworth* (Oct 17, 2012) at http://www.hwlebsworth.com.au/latest-news-apublications/publications/health/item/756-the-nationalsystem-of-personally-controlled-electronic-healthrecords.html.
249. Xu, J *et al.* (2013) Implementation of e-Health record systems in Australia, *The International Technology Management Review.* V 3 (2013) No 2, 92-104.
250. Dearne, K (2012) Sceptics warn of risks and inadequacies in shared e-health records system, *The Australian* (Jun 30); and Glance, D (2012) Everything you need to know about Australia's e-health record, *The Conversation*, (Mar 1) at http://theconversation.edu.au/everything-youneed-to-know-about-australias-e-health-records-5516.
251. Australian Digital Health Agency (2015) MyEHR to National eHealth Record Transition Impact Evaluation; 11 Aug 2015 and see https://www.digitalhealth.gov.au/initiatives-and-programs/my-health-record.
252. The Hon Peter Dutton MP e-Health Record Review at http://www.health.gov.au/internet/ministers/publishing.nsf/Content/health-mediarel-yr2013-dutton028.htm.

III. National Digital Health Strategy

448. In 2017, the Agency launched the National Digital Health Strategy.[253] The goals of the Strategy include better care coordination; fewer preventable hospitalizations; improved self-care; reduced duplication and operating costs; and improved patient and provider experiences.[254]

449. The ADHA established in 2016 by the federal government to lead the development and implementation of the National Digital Health Strategy and its priority outcomes. Digital health is seen as a key to improving service delivery and positive health outcomes. The catalyst to encourage e-Health is left to healthcare providers, entrepreneurs and others in using tools and new ways to use data.

450. In 2019, the Australian government expanded My Health Record to all Australians unless they have 'opted-out'. Almost five million Australians now have a record (20 per cent of the population) and, with opt-out participation arrangements implemented from 2018, an estimated 98 per cent of the population would have a My Health Record.[255]

451. Over 6 million Australians have been registered in My Health Record with over 23 million records have been populated with the relevant data.[256]

452. Empirical research has also shown a greater uptake of the record system in remote Australia.[257]

453. As part of the National Digital Health Strategy interoperability is seen to be the key to patient safety as well as the coordinated care and efficient delivery of healthcare services and equity within the health system.[258] The Strategic Interoperability Framework provides the scaffold to build on compliance and regulation that accords with government policy.[259]

---

253. Australian Digital Health Agency *Australia's National Digital Health Strategy* at https://www.digitalhealth.gov.au/about-the-agency/publications/australias-national-digital-healthstrategy.
254. *Ibid.*
255. Australian Digital Health Agency (2017) My Health Record Latest Statistics: Commonwealth of Australia; 2017 at https://myhealthrecord.gov.au/internet/mhr/publishing.nsf/Content/news-002.
256. Australian Digital Health Agency (2021) statistics https://www.digitalhealth.gov.au/sites/default/files/documents/myhealthrecord-statistics-june21.pdf (June).
257. NEHTA (2015) MyEHR to National eHealth Record Transition Impact Evaluation. Phase 1 evaluation report (10 July) at http://webarchive.nla.gov.au/gov/20151020064041/http://www.nehta.gov.au/get-started-with-ehealth/ehealth-benefits/case-studies/northern-territory/918-myehr-tonational-ehealth-record-transition-evaluation.
258. Australia's National Digital Health Strategy at https://www.digitalhealth.gov.au/australias-national-digital-health-strategy.
259. Australian Digital Health Agency (2017) Strategic Interoperability Framework November 2017 at https://www.digitalhealth.gov.au/sites/default/files/2020-12/Strategic_Interoperability_Framework_Summary_Report_v3.0_2017.pdf.

454. Australia has attained the top rank in the world for its open data policies that have created an environment for interoperability and the efficacious use of available public sector data as a national resource.[260]

455. Many Australians have been engaged with digital technology in relation to their health. Research has uncovered that most Australians would like their doctor to suggest health information websites (77 per cent) and 73 per cent have already used the Internet to research a health issue. However, only a small proportion of the population (6 per cent) manage to find an online health source that they trust.[261]

456. Of all Australian Google searches, one in twenty are health related.[262]

457. Interestingly, most older Australians (69 per cent of those aged 65 and over) have used the Internet to look up health information.[263]

458. Taken together, this data demonstrates that most Australians are using digital technology as part of their daily life.[264]

§3. Regulatory and Legal Frameworks

459. The evolution of e-health in Australia as elsewhere poses regulatory challenges that will need to be overcome if e-health is to function effectively. While, the general law is applicable in most cases, arguably the greatest challenge to e-health is that the Internet is borderless. Over and above this, a complex network of federal, state and territory legislation govern the management of personal healthcare information and clinical processes such as medicines management, registration and regulation of healthcare professionals and the very business of e-health.

460. The *My Health Records Act* 2012 (Cth) governs the operations of the My Health Record system and the Healthcare Identifiers Service, as well as the oversight and mandate for the digital health agenda under the Australian Digital Health Agency.[265]

260. Global Open Data Index, Tracking the State of Open Government Data: Open Data for Development Network, Open Knowledge International at https://index.okfn.org/.
261. Perillo, A (2019) Connecting consumers to their digital health: Perspectives on consumer's opportunities in the Digital Healthcare revolution: Telstra Health at https://www.health.qld.gov.au/__data/assets/pdf_file/0023/441518/qcs-pp-1608-perillo.pdf.
262. Ramaswami, P (2015) A remedy for your health-related questions: health info in the Knowledge Graph: Google; 2015 at https://googleblog.blogspot.com.au/2015/02/health-info-knowledge-graph.html.
263. Research Australia (2016) Australia Speaks! Research Australia Opinion Polling 2016 Sydney at http://researchaustralia.org/wp-content/uploads/2016/01/Research-Australia_Polling-Report-2016.pdf.
264. Australia's National Digital Health Strategy 2020 at https://www.digitalhealth.gov.au/about-us/national-digital-health-strategy-and-framework-for-action.
265. *See* text of the Act at http://www.austlii.edu.au/au/legis/cth/consol_act/mhra2012180/.

461. A review of the enabling legislation for the My Health Record system and the Healthcare Identifiers Service is to be undertaken every three years.[266]

I. e-Health Legislation

462. There are no specific legislation covering the e-health sector other than the regulation and rules governing competition, consumer law, liability and enforcement. For instance, the framework governing competition and consumer protection is the *Competition and Consumer Act* 2010 (Cth) (CCA) and the embedded Australian Consumer Law (ACL).

463. Other legislation which touches on e-health includes the *Therapeutic Goods Act* 1989 (Cth) (TGA Act) that regulates all therapeutic goods such as medical devices and medicines including regulations governing complementary over-the-counter prescriptions in the *Therapeutic Goods Regulations* 1990 (Cth), and the *Therapeutic Goods (Medical Devices) Regulations* 2002 (Cth).

464. Any e-health technologies that collect personal information need to comply with the *Privacy Act* 1988 (Cth) since health information is considered highly sensitive personal information. Strong protections under the *Privacy Act* 1988 (Cth) centre on its collection and handling of health information by all agencies that provide e-health services. The OAIC is the regulator of the use of health information in an individual's health records such as the My Health Record and healthcare identifiers operated by Medicare.

II. Licensing and Registration

465. In Australia, professional registration is a requirement for many health-related occupations. Thus, to practice as a health professional such as a doctor, nurse, or dentist one needs to be registered with the relevant registration board. Registration is state based in Australia.[267] The provision of telehealth services across state borders raises the issue of whether a health professional is practising outside the jurisdiction in which they are authorized to practice. This may be very relevant in the context of e-health across borders and where jurisdictions may be borderless.

466. To practice outside of the jurisdiction of registration is to contravene the provisions of the relevant registration with no automatic indemnity cover were this to happen.

---

266. In 2021 a review of the *My Health Records Act* 2012 (Cth) was led by Professor John McMillan. A recommendation that ss 44 & 51(3) to the *My Health Records Act* 2012 (Cth) be amended to introduce positive obligations on the ADHA has been made. *See* OAIC Annual Report Digital Health 2020-21 at https://www.oaic.gov.au/__data/assets/pdf_file/0013/10831/digital-health-annual-report-2020-21.pdf.
267. For example, *Medical Practice Act* 1992 (NSW), *Nurses Act* 1991 (NSW), and the *Dentists Act* 1989 (NSW).

467. However, it is to be noted that while mutual recognition schemes have operated since 1993 registration in the relevant state must still occur.[268]

468. All therapeutic goods need to be registered on the Australian Register of Therapeutic Goods (ARTG) before being made available for sale in Australia. This includes computer software that meets the definition of a 'medical device' under the TGA Act. Amendments to the TGA Regulations since 25 February 2021 provide new classification rules to categorize software-based medical devices with preprogrammed or programmable hardware that have the potential to cause harm through the provision of incorrect information be defined as a medical device.[269] This amendment ensures alignment with Australia's trading partners.[270]

III. Enforcement and Regulators

469. The *Australian Competition and Consumer Commission* (ACCC) is empowered by the CCA. The ACCC's Digital Platforms Branch is responsible for the ongoing scrutiny of digital platform markets. In general, while the ACCC's scrutiny of digital platforms are not targeted on e-health, the outcomes of these investigations and inquiries have strong implications for e-health businesses.

470. Similarly the TGA regulates medical devices. Its regulations, include computer software as a medical device because the information about symptoms for diagnosis and mobile apps coupled with devices for calculating medical dosages, are integral in e-health settings.

471. The Privacy Commissioner under the *Privacy Act* 1988 (Cth) is bestowed with a range of privacy regulatory powers as well as investigative and enforcement powers to respond to privacy breaches.

472. The OAIC in undertaking its remit, cooperates with healthcare agencies and providers to ensure best privacy practices.

473. A healthcare company that fails to obtain consent to collect health information from an individual is in breach of Australian Privacy Principles 3 (APP3) regarding the collection of sensitive information.

---

268. *See also Mutual Recognition Act* 1992 (Cth), *Mutual Recognition (NSW) Act* 1992 (NSW), *Mutual Recognition (Australian Capital Territory) Act* 1992 (ACT), *Mutual Recognition (Northern Territory) Act* (NT), *Mutual Recognition (Queensland) Act* 1992 (Qld), *Mutual Recognition (South Australia) Act* 1993 (SA), *Mutual Recognition (Tasmania) Act* 1993 (Tas), *Mutual Recognition (Victoria) Act* 1998 (Vic), *Mutual Recognition (Western Australia) Act* 1995 (WA).
269. *See* TGA (2021) at https://www.tga.gov.au/medical-devices-reforms-medical-device-software-regulation and at *Therapeutic Goods Legislation Amendment (2021 Measures No.2) Act* 2021 (Cth) at http://www5.austlii.edu.au/au/legis/cth/num_reg_es/tgla2021mn1r2021202100450628.html.
270. *See* Australian Regulatory Guidelines for Medical Devices (ARGMD) at https://www.tga.gov.au/publication/australian-regulatory-guidelines-medical-devices-argmd. The new classification rules are similar to the European Union Medical Devices Regulations 2017 at https://eur-lex.europa.eu/legal-content/EN/TXT/?uri=CELEX%3A32017R0745.

474. A breach of an APP is an 'interference with the privacy of an individual' under section 13(1) of the *Privacy Act* 1988 (Cth) and may lead to regulatory action and penalties.

475. Enforcement provisions of the *Privacy Act* 1988 (Cth) are provided under Parts 6 and 7 of the *Regulatory Powers (Standard Provisions) Act* 2014 (Cth) where enforceable undertakings and injunctions may be issued.

476. The OAIC is tasked with reporting digital health compliance and enforcement activity, in accordance with section 106 of the *My Health Records Act* 2012 and section 30 of the *Healthcare Identifiers Act* 2010 (HI Act).[271] Both Acts contain provisions that protect and restrict the collection, use and disclosure of personal information.

477. In 2020-2021, the OAIC received seven privacy complaints relating to the My Health Record system four of which were finalized. In 2019-2020 there was one complaint and two from 2020 to 2019. There was one privacy complaint relating to the HI Service in 2020-2021 which is ongoing and three data breach notifications during the reporting period.

478. The OAIC undertook assessments of mobile health apps 2020-2021. The scope of assessments considered the handling of personal information to the My Health Record system by Chamonix and Telstra Health and their respective mobile applications. In the case of Chamonix's Healthi app only read access is given to a user's My Health Record and the app has no other functionality. Telstra Health's HealthNow app provides a range of e-health services to users including a 'view-only' access to a user's My Health Record. Reasonable steps had been taken to document all processes and practices and to notify all HealthNow users of APP 5 matters relating to the notification of the collection of personal information.[272]

479. Health data collected in addition to personal information will require additional consent under the *Privacy Act* 1988 (Cth). The Act distinguishes between the use and disclosure of personal information for 'primary purposes' versus 'secondary purposes'.

480. The *primary purpose* is the specific purpose for which the health information was collected. The context in which the health information was collected is relevant to this concept. A *secondary purpose* is any use or disclosure for reasons other than the primary purpose. Secondary purposes are prohibited unless the secondary purpose falls within a specific permitted exception.

---

271. OAIC Annual Report Digital Health 2020-21 at https://www.oaic.gov.au/__data/assets/pdf_file/0013/10831/digital-health-annual-report-2020-21.pdf.
272. *Ibid.* OAIC Annual Report Digital Health 2020-21. *See also* OAIC https://www.oaic.gov.au/privacy/australian-privacy-principles-guidelines/chapter-5-app-5-notification-of-the-collection-of-personal-information.

481. APP 11 imposes a general legal obligation on agencies to take reasonable steps to protect personal information it holds from misuse, interference and loss and from unauthorized access, modification or disclosure. As noted, there are no specific obligations on the e-health sector for IT related security standards for the handling of health data.

482. However, there are specific standards such as information security management in health using the international standard ISO/IEC 27002 and the *National eHealth Security and Access Framework* v 4.0. Compliance with these standards is voluntary.

483. The OAIC and the ADHA have published an Information Security Guide for Securing Personal Information for small healthcare businesses.[273] IT service providers who engage with government health agencies will typically be required to meet certain minimum IT security standards.

IV. Liability Regimes: ACL and Tort Law

484. The ACL consumer protection provisions applies to e-health goods and services including:

- a prohibition on misleading or deceptive conduct and false or misleading representations made in the course of advertising goods and services;
- consumer's automatic quality guarantees to goods and services. Suppliers, and in certain cases, manufacturers are required to remedy a failure to comply with the guarantees and to compensate consumers for reasonably foreseeable loss caused by the failure;
- enabling plaintiffs to recover losses from manufacturers who supply products with safety defects;
- setting out an 'unfair contract terms' regime that governs terms contained in standard form consumer or small business contracts. It is unlawful to make unfair contract terms and civil penalties apply.

485. In August 2021 the Australian government concluded consultations to make unfair contract terms unlawful (currently rendered void) and subject to civil penalties. As well consumers may bring class actions for misleading or deceptive conduct, consumer guarantee failures or product safety breaches.[274]

486. Under the TGA Act any consumer or supplier wishing to import and supply a medical device in Australia is required to meet the Essential Principles on

273. *See* OAIC at https://www.oaic.gov.au/privacy/guidance-and-advice/guide-to-securing-personal-information; https://www.oaic.gov.au/engage-with-us/consultations/guide-to-securing-personal-information-update, and https://www.digitalhealth.gov.au/sites/default/files/2020-11/Information_security_guide_for_small_healthcare_businesses.pdf.
274. *See* Australian Treasury at https://treasury.gov.au/consultation/c2021-201582.

safety and performance.[275] Failure to do so may result in civil or criminal penalties under the Act. Essential principles require the minimization of risks associated with the design, long-term safety and use of the device and by implication the minimization of cybersecurity risks.

487. The provision of e-health services and products raise liability issues. While the traditional legal obligations of health professionals, such as the duty to exercise reasonable care, and the duty to maintain the confidentiality of patient information remain, to achieve the standard of care in e-health is particularly challenging such as alleged negligence on the part of a health professional.

488. It is arguable that in e-health more than in face-to-face consultations the duty of care is greater compared with face-to-face patients together with the associated 'material risks' of any proposed treatment from a distance.

489. Other potential liability issues may arise from possible missed diagnoses where advice is provided from a distance because of poor imagery, inadequate equipment, or simply missing serendipity.

490. The relationship between an e-health professional and patient via electronic means such as email communication may open new areas of liability. One such is in the context of sensitive medical information where the need to protect patients privacy is utmost. Unless encryption of communications is used as a standard operating procedure the information might be compromised and privacy jeopardized. Moreover, it is implicit that the advice given in an e-health context may be no different to that in a face-to-face consultation; and analogous to advise given via telephone communication. But uncertainty exists and, in the e-health context caution is required until some of these issues are resolved either by legislation or litigation.

V. Litigation

491. The ACCC recently brought proceedings that focus on misleading and deceptive conduct in the use of consumer data in various sectors. An example in e-health is the proceedings against Health Engine (an online health directory) for misleading consumers in the use of their data and the publication of patient reviews and ratings. On 20 August 2020, by consent of the parties, the Federal Court ordered that Health Engine pay AUD 2.9 million in penalties for engaging in misleading and deceptive conduct.[276]

275. *See* Therapeutic Goods Authority (2021) at https://www.tga.gov.au/form/essential-principles-checklist-medical-devices as at 15 Sept 2021.

276. *See* ACCC at https://www.accc.gov.au/media-release/healthengine-to-pay-29-million-for-misleading-reviews-and-patient-referrals.

VI. Advertising and Marketing

492. The advertising and marketing of all e-health products to ensure that the marketing and advertising of therapeutic goods to consumers is conducted in a manner that promotes the quality use of goods, is socially responsible and does not mislead or deceive consumers. These safeguards are spelt out in the *Therapeutic Goods Act* 1989 (Cth), which regulates all therapeutic goods; the *Therapeutic Goods Regulations* 1990, which include provisions about advertising therapeutic goods and information about both ingredients and patient information; and the Australian Register of Therapeutic Goods and the *Therapeutic Goods Advertising Code (No 2)* 2018 (Cth).

493. The advertising and marketing of e-health services is governed by the *Health Practitioner Regulation National Law Act* 2009 (Cth). The Australian Health Practitioner Regulation Agency (AHPRA) sets out guidelines for advertising regulated health services.[277]

494. The Australian Pharmaceutical Manufacturers Association (APMA) Code of Conduct now superseded by Medicines Australia Code Edition 19 prohibits advertising of prescription medicines directly to consumers.[278]

495. The general rules that apply to registered trademarks under the *Trade Marks Act* 1995 (Cth) in relation to passing off and misleading and deceptive conduct are relevant in marketing and advertising e-health products and services.

VII. e-Commerce

496. There are no specific rules governing e-commerce for e-health services and products. Thus, e-contracts require compliance under general contract law as there are no specific technology rules. Hence, businesses must take all reasonable steps to present contract terms to the customer and to ensure that the customer has indicated consent to those terms.

VIII. Emergency Measures: COVID-19 Pandemic

497. In view of the COVID-19 pandemic and emergency measures the ACCC has granted interim authorization to the Medical Technology Association of Australia (MTAA) to allow its members and others such as suppliers or distributors of medical equipment, to share information between each other, coordinate orders and

277. *See* AHPRA Advertising Guidelines at https://www.ahpra.gov.au/publications/advertising-hub/advertising-guidelines-and-other-guidance/advertising-guidelines.aspx.
278. *See* TGA ss 42C & 42D and Medicines Australia Code Edition 19 at https://www.medicinesaustralia.com.au/code/about-the-code/. *See also* https://www.nps.org.au/australian-prescriber/articles/the-australian-pharmaceutical-manufacturers-association-code-of-conduct-guiding-the-promotion-of-prescription-medicines.

supply requests, prioritize requests and jointly tender to supply COVID-19 medical equipment.[279] Such an interim authorization is aimed at providing statutory protection from court action for conduct that might otherwise raise concerns under the competition provisions of the CCA.

498. Legislation enacted under the *Therapeutic Goods (Medical Devices – Accredited Pathology Laboratories) (COVID-19 Emergency) Exemption* 2020 (Cth) allows for the rapid supply of COVID-19 diagnostic tests to all Australian accredited pathology laboratories. The emergency exemption to TGA assessments permits the importation, manufacture and supply of COVID-19 diagnostic tests to be supplied immediately to accredited pathology laboratories.

IX. Security Obligations: Critical Infrastructure Act

499. The Australian government released the Exposure Draft *Security Legislation Amendment (Critical Infrastructure) Bill* 2020 in November. The draft Bill is an initiative of Australia's Cyber Security Strategy 2020, which aims to protect Australia's critical infrastructure providers from cyber threats by amending the *Security of Critical Infrastructure Act* 2018 (Cth). The amendment will impose security obligations on eleven new sectors, including 'healthcare and medical'. The Bill was passed on 22 November 2021 as the *Security Legislation Amendment* (*Critical Infrastructure*) *Act* 2021 (Cth).

279. *See* MTAA at https://www.mtaa.org.au/mtaa-covid19-update-21.

Chapter 3. Australian Electoral System

§1. Introduction

500. Australia is a representative democracy that is built upon an electoral system that is total, free and fair. As a federation, elections at the federal, state and territory level occurs once every three or four years or earlier if confidence in a government is lost. Every registered citizen over the age of 18 gets to cast a compulsory vote[280] and candidates are selected on a preferential system to elect members in federal elections for the House of Representatives (the lower house) and a form of proportional representation for electing Senators to the Senate (upper house).[281]

501. There are 151 members in the Australian House of Representatives elected from single member electorates that are designed to be approximately equal in population. The Senate consists of seventy-six members consisting of thirteen from each State and two from each Territory.

502. Australia was the first country to introduce the secret ballot (the Australian Ballot) providing privacy to voters at polling places and preventing coercion of voters.[282] Section 233(1)(a) of the *Commonwealth Electoral Act* 1918 (Cth) (CEA) codifies the principle of voter secrecy by requiring voters to 'retire alone to some unoccupied compartment of the booth, and there, in private, mark his or her vote on the ballot-paper'.[283]

503. Section 234 of the *Commonwealth Electoral Act* 1918 (Cth) governs the provision of assistance to certain voters.[284]

504. The Electoral Council of Australia and New Zealand (ECANZ) holds the view that 'a secret ballot is typically argued to provide a necessary, though not always sufficient safeguard against fear and intimidation'.[285]

---

280. Hill, L (2002) On the Reasonableness of Compelling Citizens to 'Vote': The Australian Case. *Political Studies*, 50(1):80-101, March 2002, at http://journals.sagepub.com/doi/abs/10.1111/1467-9248.00360, doi:10.1111/1467-9248.00360.
281. Preferential voting allows a voter to mark candidates in order of preference. In counting, the votes are allocated to first preference candidate and then progressively allocated to following candidates as earlier preferences are taken out from the count. For Senate elections the system is designed to ensure that each party wins seats in proportion to the percentage of voters who supported them. *See* Bennett, B & Lundie, R (2007) Australian Electoral Systems. Technical Report, Parliament of Australia. Department of Parliamentary Services, 2007, at http://www.aph.gov.au/About_Parliament/Parliamentary_Departments/Parliamentary_Library/pubs/rp/RP0708/08rp05.
282. Implemented in Victoria and South Australia in 1856 the 'secret ballot' inaugurated a voting revolution around Australia and the democratic world. *See* Mercurio, B (2003) 'Discrimination in electoral law: Using technology to extend the secret ballot to disabled and illiterate voters' [2003] AltLawJl 85; (2003) 28(6) *Alternative Law Journal* 272; and at http://www.austlii.edu.au/au/journals/AltLawJl/2003/85.html.
283. *See* text of the Act at http://www.austlii.edu.au/au/legis/cth/consol_act/cea1918233/s233.html.
284. *See* text of the Act at http://www.austlii.edu.au/au/legis/cth/consol_act/cea1918233/s234.html.
285. ECANZ (2013) Internet voting in Australian election systems at ttps://www.ecanz.gov.au/sites/g/files/net4931/f/internet-voting-australian-election-systems.pdf.

505. The Australian Electoral Commission (AEC) was established by the *Commonwealth Electoral Act* 1918 delivers the franchise for every Australian citizen's right to vote.[286]

506. The AEC is an independent statutory body that is responsible for conducting federal elections. Similar electoral commissions exist in the states and territories to conduct their respective elections. The AEC maintains an impartial and independent electoral system for eligible voters through active electoral roll management, efficient delivery of polling services and targeted education and public awareness programmes.[287]

507. The AEC's administration of federal referenda is undertaken in accordance with the *Referendum (Machinery Provisions) Act* 1984 (Cth).[288]

508. There are a total of nine electoral systems in Australia, one for each of the Commonwealth, the states and the two self-governing territories.[289]

509. State, territory and local council elections are conducted by other electoral management bodies in accordance with separate legislation.[290]

510. The mandate for the enfranchisement to vote is derived from the Australian Constitution as well as all other supplementary legislation. In addition, the right is derived by reason of Australia's accession to international treaties and agreements adopted under local law.

511. Australia has a written constitution, as do the states, which provides for the conduct of elections and methods of balloting. Sections 8 and 30 of the Australian Constitution expresses the principle that at federal elections in choosing members and senators 'each elector shall vote only once'.[291]

512. The Universal Declaration of Human Rights (UDHR) proclaimed at the UN General Assembly in December 1948 provides entitlement to the rights and freedoms without distinction of any kind as set forth in the declaration (Article 2) and everyone's right to take part in the government of the country either directly or through freely chosen representatives (Article 21).[292]

---

286. *See* s. 6 *Commonwealth Electoral Act* 1918 (Cth) at http://classic.austlii.edu.au/au/legis/cth/consol_act/cea1918233/.
287. *See* Australian Electoral Commission at https://www.aec.gov.au/About_AEC/.
288. *See* text of the Act at https://www.legislation.gov.au/Latest/C2004A02908.
289. Arguably there is a tenth electoral jurisdiction – Norfolk Island, that operated as a self-governing territory between 1979 and 2015. *See* the *Norfolk Island Act* 1979 (Cth) (repealed), and the *Norfolk Island Legislation Amendment Act* 2015 (Cth).
290. *See* the Australian elections portal at https://www.ecanz.gov.au/electoral-systems/australia.
291. *See* APH at https://www.aph.gov.au/constitution.
292. *See* Office of the High Commissioner for Human Rights (OHCHR) at https://www.ohchr.org/en/udhr/documents/udhr_translations/eng.pdf.

513. The International Covenant on Civil and Political Rights (ICCPR) Article 25 provides that every citizen shall have the right and the opportunity without any distinction and without unreasonable restrictions to take part in the conduct of public affairs, directly or through freely chosen representatives and to vote and be elected at genuine periodic elections that are universal and equal suffrage to be exercised by secret ballot.[293]

514. International standards with regards to electoral democracy are also embodied in several other documents, and to which Australia is a signatory. These documents include:

- the Declaration on Criteria for Free and Fair Elections (the IPU Declaration) adopted by the Inter-Parliamentary Council of the Inter-Parliamentary Union (IPU) in March 1994;
- the Convention on the Rights of Persons with Disabilities Article 29 provides that persons with disabilities can effectively fully participate in political and public life on an equal basis with others and the right and opportunity for persons with disabilities to vote and be elected; and,
- the Code of Conduct for Ethical and Professional Administration of Elections published in 1998 by the International Institute for Democracy and Electoral Assistance (International IDEA) highlights the importance of transparency, accuracy and provision of services to voters.

§2. The Electronic Voting Paradox

515. The system of voting for federal, state and territory elections predominantly use paper ballots cast in secret with winner determined by hand-counting, performed in the presence of scrutineers appointed by the candidates. Any design of electronic online voting must achieve these same goals. But, ironically, these ideals present unique security and privacy challenges.[294] The vexed paradox is that Internet voting will both enhance as well as derogate from the secrecy of the ballot – the need to identify a registered voter on the one hand and the need to keep secret the vote cast on the other.[295]

516. While Australia has adopted compulsory voting for all citizens over 18, this very rule provides an under-recognized component of electoral security.[296] The

293. *See* OHCHR at https://www.ohchr.org/documents/professionalinterest/ccpr.pdf.

294. For a study which sets out a wide range of potential technical risks associated with Internet voting, see Jones, DW & Simons, B (2012) *Broken Ballots: Will Your Vote Count?* CSLI Publications, Stanford, California, Ch. 11 cited in Eldridge, M (2018) *supra*.

295. *See* a discussion by Smith, R (2002) Electronic voting: benefits and risks, *Trends & issues in crime and criminal justice* no. 224, Canberra: Australian Institute of Criminology at https://www.aic.gov.au/publications/tandi/tandi224.

296. *See* the *Commonwealth Electoral Act* 1918 (Cth) s. 245(1) which states that: 'It shall be the duty of every elector to vote at each election'.

compulsory voting rule secures against voter suppression tactics that may have been used to undermine elections elsewhere in the world.

517. To date, electronic voting has mostly been used for special categories of voters such as those with disabilities and low vision and for those on special assignments such as Australian Defence Force (ADF) and Australian Federal Police (AFP) personnel in remote locations and scientists in Antarctica and not an option for mass voting.[297]

§3. Modalities of Electronic Voting

I. Electronic Voting

518. Electronic voting is a broad church. The various types and modalities of such voting need identification and clear language of what is intended and meant.

519. An AEC 2001 report observes that 'in any discussion on electronic voting, it is important from the outset to be clear about what type of electronic voting is being discussed … some forms of electronic voting are simply not possible in the context of the Australian election environment'.[298]

520. At its simplest e-voting could simply be 'email voting' undertaken via an electronic mailing system. The use of the World Wide Web (WWW) may be considered 'web-based voting'. Others include 'kiosk' voting, 'mobile Internet' voting and 'remote Internet voting'.

521. E-voting covers the technology used to facilitate the casting of a vote in an election.[299] Various technologies used in e-voting include:

– *electronically assisted voting* that enables visually impaired voters to complete a ballot paper with the help of an operator, through audio prompts on a phone or an electronic voting machine;
– *isolated static electronic voting* where voters cast their votes at polling stations on a stand-alone computer or a local area network without an Internet connection; and,
– *internet voting* through various means including static voting at polling places via dedicated computers or networks, mobile Internet voting using devices provided by polling officials; and remote Internet voting where voters use any device with an Internet connection.

297. *See* Taylor, G (2015) 'Electronic Voting in Australia', in Maurer, A, Barrett, J (eds), *E-Voting Case Law: A Comparative Analysis*, Routledge, London, p. 233.
298. Australian Electoral Commission (2001) "Electoral Voting and Electronic Counting of Votes", Australian Electoral Commission, March 2001, p. 1.
299. Lundie, R (2016) Electronic voting at federal elections at https://www.aph.gov.au/About_Parliament/Parliamentary_Departments/Parliamentary_Library/pubs/BriefingBook45p/ElectronicVoting.

522. Supplementary electronic technologies to support the electoral process include:

- electronic electoral rolls that enable voters to enrol and update their enrolment online;
- electronically certified lists that enable voters to be marked off in real-time at polling stations and that also allow for declaration votes to be dealt with more quickly; and,
- electronic scanning and counting of ballot papers.

523. Mercurio (2003) has used the term ‘computerized voting’ to describe a variety of mechanical voting such as lever-arch or punch card machines, as well as using a computer terminal or similar audio or voice-recognition software which stores votes and may or may not have the functionality to tabulate votes.[300]

II. Mechanisms of Electronic Voting Systems

524. Electronic voting systems can broadly be divided into two categories – *poll-site* electronic voting where voters physically attend a polling place and ballots are cast and counted electronically; and, *remote electronic voting* where votes are cast from a distance using a personal device linked to the Internet as a transfer mechanism.[301] In such a system voters cast a ballot in an uncontrolled location and perhaps also on an insecure device that may be subject to a hacking intrusion.

525. Poll-site electronic voting systems. Poll-site electronic voting systems where government-controlled polling sites involve the use of electronic means for casting ballot, counting votes or both can take on different modes of operation. Such systems may be described as follows:

- Kiosk electronic poll-site voting is best understood as electronically assisted voting. The ‘closed’ system kiosks assist eligible voters (such as the vision-impaired) to cast their vote with the assistance of electronic voting equipment.[302] Such equipment are only available at authorized voting centres.[303]
- Direct Recording Electronic (DRE) systems that involve both electronic ballot casting and electronic vote counting.

---

300. For a more detailed definition and discussion on computerized voting, see Mercurio, B (2003) ‘Beyond the Paper Ballet: Exploring Computerised Voting’ in Orr, G, Mercurio, B & Williams, G (eds), *Realising Democracy: Electoral Law in Australia* (2003) 230-42.
301. Holmes, B (2012) e-Voting: The Promise and the Practice. text, Parliament of Australia. Department of Parliamentary Services, Parliamentary Library, October 2012 at http://www.aph.gov.au/About_Parliament/Parliamentary_Departments/Parliamentary_Library/pubs/BN/2012-2013/EVoting.
302. This is analogous to the US-style voting machines such as punch card and direct record type voting machines.
303. ACE Electoral Knowledge Network, ‘Focus on E-Voting’ at https://www.aec.gov.au/.

- ThreeBallot systems where voters cast three ballots: exactly two in favour of a candidate to support them, and exactly once in favour of a candidate to oppose them. Each ballot is also marked with a unique randomly generated ballot ID number.[304]
- Scantegrity voting system that combines cryptographic principles with paper ballots and optical scan machines.[305]
- STAR-Vote a poll-site electronic voting system designed to provide a DRE-style interface to the voter that is software independent with a voter-verifiable audit trail and full end-to-end verifiability.[306]
- Prêt à Voter, an electronically verifiable voting system which employs a split ballot paper and randomized candidate lists for each ballot.[307]

526. Remote electronic voting systems. Remote electronic voting systems do not require attendance at poll-sites but at locations that are convenient to the voter. Neither the client machines nor the locations are under the control of election officials and voters can cast their votes from practically any place using the Internet as a transfer mechanism. Such systems include the following:

- The ACT's electronic voting and counting system EVACS, the first of its kind to be deployed for parliamentary elections in Australia. Used for the 2001 ACT Legislative Assembly election it has since been utilized at all subsequent elections. The system employs standard personal computers as voting terminals with voters using an e-voting card to authenticate their votes. Secure local area networks are used, and no votes taken or transmitted over a public network like the Internet.[308]
- The iVote NSW system used in the 2015 NSW State Election based on a proprietary Scytl iVote online voting system. The iVote system also incorporated a telephone verification service which allowed voters to confirm that votes cast on the iVote website had been correctly recorded.[309] The WA State Election in 2017 has a similar system called iVoteWA.

---

304. Rivest, RL (2018) The ThreeBallot Voting System. Working Paper, Caltech/MIT Voting Technology Project, October 2006 at http://dspace.mit.edu/handle/1721.1/96593 cited in Eldridge, M (2018) A trustworthy Electronic Voting System for Australian Federal Elections at https://arxiv.org/pdf/1805.02202.pdf.
305. Chaum, D, Essex, A, Carback, R, Clark, J, Popoveniuc, S, Sherman, A & Vora, P (2008) Scantegrity: End-to-End Voter-Verifiable Optical- Scan Voting. IEEE Security Privacy, 6(3):40-46, May 2008, doi:10.1109/MSP.2008.70 cited in Eldridge, M (2018) *supra.*
306. Bell, S *et al.* (2013) STAR-Vote: A secure, transparent, auditable and reliable voting system. USENIX Journal of Election Technology and Systems (JETS), 1(1):8 cited in Eldridge, M (2018) *supra.*
307. A modified version of this system, the vVote, poll-site electronic voting system was used in the 2014 Victorian State election.
308. ACT Government (2020) Electronic voting and counting (EVACS) at https://www.elections.act.gov.au/elections_and_voting/electronic_voting_and_counting.
309. Brightwell, I, Cucurull, J, Galindo, D, & Guasch, S (2015) An overview of the iVote 2015 voting system. Tech. rep. New South Wales Electoral Commission (2015); and Halderman, JA & Teague, T (2015) The New South Wales iVoteSystem: Security Failures and Verification Flaws in a Live

– Telephone voting involves a telephone service to cast a vote.
– The Estonian i-voting system, first used in 2005 elections, is the digital equivalent of the 'two-envelope' method for postal voting.[310]
– The Helios Online Voting System, was the first publicly available implementation of an online open-audit voting system allowing for any observer to cryptographically verify that election results are sound.[311]
– Pretty Good Democracy (PGD) is a remote online voting system based on code voting.[312]

§4. States and Territories Electronic Voting Legislation

I. The Commonwealth

527. The *Commonwealth Electoral Act* 1918 (Cth) provides for electronically assisted voting in Part XVB sections 202AA–202AF. Similar state and territory legislation facilitate electronic voting as discussed below.

528. A report and recommendation of the Federal parliament's Joint Standing Committee on Electoral Matters (JSCEM) marks the advent of electronic voting in Australia.[313] At a federal level were the trials of electronically assisted voting for blind and low vision (BLV) voters and for Australian Defence Force (ADF) and Australian Federal Police (AFP) personnel at the 2007 federal elections.[314]

529. The trial for BLV voters in 2007 was restricted to thirty pre-poll voting sites with the technology based on a desktop computer with a monitor, telephone style keypad and earphones. The facility only provided a 'vote only' function and did not store any vote data on the computer. Barcodes were used to record a printed vote record placed in an envelope and deposited in a pre-poll ballot box. A total of 850

Online Election, in Haenni, R, Koenig, RE & and Wikström, D (eds.) *E-Voting and Identity* in Lecture Notes in Computer Science, no. 9269 pp. 35-53, Springer International Publishing, September 2015 DOI:10.1007/978-3-319-22270-7_3 at http://link.springer.com/chapter/10.1007/978-3-319-22270-7_3 cited in Eldridge, M (2018) *supra.*

310. Vinkel, P (2011) Internet Voting in Estonia in Laud, P (ed.) Information Security Technology for Applications, *Lecture Notes in Computer Science*, pages 4-12. Springer Berlin Heidelberg, October 2011. DOI:10.1007/978-3-642-29615-4_2 at http://link.springer.com/chapter/10.1007/978-3-642-29615-4_2 cited in Eldridge, M (2018) *supra.*

311. Adida, B (2008) Helios: Web-based Open-Audit Voting. In USENIX security symposium, volume 17, pages 335-348, 2008 cited in Eldridge, M (2018) *supra.*

312. Ryan, P & Teague, V (2009) Pretty Good Democracy in Christianson, B *et al.* eds., Security Protocols XVII, number 7028 in *Lecture Notes in Computer Science*, pages 111-130 Springer Berlin Heidelberg, April 2009. DOI: 10.1007/978-3-642-36213-2_15 at http://link.springer.com/chapter/10.1007/978-3-642-36213-2_15 cited in Eldridge, M (2018) *supra.*

313. Joint Standing Committee on Electoral Matters (2005) and *Joint Standing Committee on Electoral Matters Report* on the 2007 federal election electronic voting trials: interim report of the inquiry into the conduct of the 2007 election and matters related thereto. text, March 2009 at http://www.aph.gov.au/Parliamentary_Business/Committees/House_of_Representatives_Committees?url=em/elect07/report.htm.

314. *See* ECANZ (2013) *supra.*

votes were cast over 29 locations during a two-week voting period in the 2007 elections. This demonstration trial showed that secure, secret and independent voting could potentially be adopted at a larger scale.

530. The ADF remote electronic voting trial used the Defence Restricted Network (DRN) not available on the Internet. As a secure environment voting was restricted to ADF personnel located overseas who had access to the DRN. However, the trial excluded Royal Australian Navy ships because of technology constraints. Of the 2012 registered voters of the ADF about 75 per cent used the remote electronic voting system.

531. Electronic voting however had its precedents in territory and state elections. The ACT's Kiosk system has been in place since 2001 and this was followed by Tasmania's kiosk-based system in 2006 and Victoria's kiosk-style voting machines. Later systems featured the Tasmania Express Voting in 2010 and the remote telephone and Internet voting system known as iVote in NSW in 2011.

532. Federal legislation and as well as state and territory electoral laws in Australia make provisions for voters who are unable to cast an independent vote to appoint a person or a polling official to complete their ballot paper according to instructions. Alternative methods include Braille embossed ballot papers that have been facilitated by the respective state Electoral Commissions such as WA which provided magnifiers and CCTV magnifiers in 1996, electronic voting machines in the ACT in 2001 and Braille embossed ballots in Victoria, NSW and Queensland in 2002.

533. The progress towards electronic means of recording votes that are both secure and secret has been slow in development in federal, state and territory elections. The uptake has been variable with no compelling arguments forwarded by either states or territories to encourage the change-over to electronic-based elections. All jurisdictions specify broad categories of who may vote with penalty provisions that apply to those violating electoral rules.

II. New South Wales

534. The Electoral Commission has the power to approve procedures for technology assisted voting subject to several procedural criteria.[315] Penalties apply to provisions relating to secrecy and the protection of hardware and software from interference.[316]

315. Parliamentary Electorates and Elections Act 1912 (NSW) s. 120AC.
316. *Parliamentary Electorates and Elections Act* 1912 (NSW) s. 120AG and s. 120AI respectively.

535. The *Electoral Act* 2017 (NSW) also provides in section 156 for the independent auditing of technology assisted voting; section 157 the independent monitoring of technology assisted voting; and section 159 secrecy relating to technology assisted voting.[317]

536. The *Parliamentary Electorates and Elections Further Amendments Act* 2010 (NSW) was passed Parliament in November 2010 to provide the legislation for iVote.

537. Recent experiences in the latest state elections in 2021 suggests mixed results with the iVote system in NSW. On 17 March 2022, the Supreme Court of NSW delivered judgment in relation to an application brought by the NSW Electoral Commissioner concerning the operation of the iVote system in three local government elections held in December 2021. This application was brought in the public interest, to support the integrity of the election system. The Court decided that the problem that occurred for some Internet voters in these areas was a material irregularity and that the elections in Kempsey, Singleton and Shellharbour Ward A are void. This finding was despite only 148 people had been unable to vote in the three local council regions, the result should be set aside, and new elections called.[318]

538. The NSW Electoral Commissioner has determined not to use iVote at any intervening by-elections between 1 July 2022 and 25 March 2023.[319]

539. However, the NSW Electoral Commissioner has recommended to the NSW government that ordinary telephone voting be made available for BLV electors. This option has been delivered successfully at the recent four State by-elections and at two local government by-elections under COVID-19 special temporary arrangements.

540. The NSW Electoral Commissioner has reported that from the results of recent surveys the Commission undertook that most voters' experiences with iVote at the Local Government elections in December 2021 were positive. Almost triple the number of voters successfully used the system than at any previous election.[320]

---

317. These provisions have since been criticized for lacking rigour and protections to enable the public to have confidence that e-voting in NSW is accurate, accountable and transparent. *See* Teague, V & Keyzer, P (2020) Electronic Australian Elections: Verifiability of Accuracy is a Design Goal, which Must be Mandated by Law and Deliberately Designed into Electronic Electoral Processes, *Law in Context: A Socio-legal Journal*, V.37(1) and at https://journals.latrobe.edu.au/index.php/law-in-context/article/view/119/208.

318. *See NSW Electoral Commissioner v. Kempsey Shire Council (No 2)* [2022] NSWSC 282 at https://www.caselaw.nsw.gov.au/decision/17f913a39e2ade551b821020#.

319. *See* https://www.elections.nsw.gov.au/NSWEC/media/NSWEC/Legislation/Tab-1-Determination-not-to-use-technology-assisted-voting.PDF.

320. *See* https://www.elections.nsw.gov.au/About-us/Media-centre/News-media-releases/Electoral-Commissioner-iVote-determination (16 Mar 2022).

III. Victoria

541. The *Electoral Act* 2002 (Vic) provides for electronic voting at an electronic voting centre for specified electors.[321] The Act also provides for the Victoria Electoral Commission (VEC) to ensure that the systems are secure from interference and that the integrity of voting is maintained.[322] These provisions enabled the VEC to conduct computerized vote counting for Legislative Council elections.[323]

542. Electronic voting was first introduced for the 2006 Victorian state election, following the passage of the *Electoral and Parliamentary Committees Legislation (Amendment) Act* 2006 (Vic). Subsequently the *Electoral Amendment (Electoral Participation) Act* 2010 (Vic) amended the electronic franchise to include electors with a motor skill impairment, electors whose first language is not English and those with low or no English literacy.

IV. Queensland

543. The *Electoral Act* 1992 (Qld) has no specific provisions for electronic balloting in state elections save for an elector requesting a ballot paper from an issuing officer.[324] The Electoral Commission of Queensland may provide electronically assisted telephone voting to electors who cannot vote without assistance.[325]

V. Western Australia

544. The *Electoral Act* 1907 (WA) prescribes specific ballot paper requirements with polling places having separate compartments furnished with a pencil.[326] Amendments to the *Electoral Act* 1907 (WA) in 2016 permitted the implementation of the iVote for a state election.

VI. South Australia

545. The *Electoral Act* 1985 (SA) specifies the marking of a ballot paper by a voter and done so in private.[327] South Australia does not currently provide an electronic voting option for South Australian state elections.

321. *Electoral Act* 2002 (Vic) s. 110D and Part 5 of the Electoral Regulations 2012 (Vic).
322. *Electoral Act* 2002 (Vic) s. 110F.
323. Victorian Electoral Commission, 'VEC's Election Management Systems', Victorian Electoral Commission, Melbourne.
324. *Electoral Act* 1992 (Qld) s. 107(3).
325. *Electoral Act* 1992 (Qld) s. 121.
326. *Electoral Act* 1907 (WA) s. 113 and s. 110 respectively.
327. *Electoral Act* 1985 (SA) ss 76 & 79 respectively.

VII. Tasmania

546. The *Electoral Act* 2004 (Tas) permits the Commission to approve any procedures that are reasonable and appropriate to assist an elector, external to Tasmania, to vote.[328]

VIII. Australian Capital Territory

547. The *Electoral Act* 1992 (ACT) provides that ballot papers may be in electronic form and that Commission may approve a computer program to be used for electronic voting.[329] The devices and programs for electronic voting are to be always kept secure from interference and paper ballots may be available at a polling place.[330]

548. The *COVID-19 Emergency Response Legislation Amendment Act* 2020 (ACT) introduced temporary amendments to the Electoral Act 1992 for the October 2020 election. The amendment included the deployment of an overseas electronic voting solution for eligible ACT electors who were abroad at that time. The amendments expired in April 2021.

IX. Northern Territory

549. The *Electoral Act* 2004 (NT) gives the Electoral Commissioner the power to approve electronic or other automated systems for targeted groups of voters which include disabled voters and for attendance at voting to be undertaken in private.[331] The Northern Territory introduced the ACT's eLAPPS electronic mark-off system for the 2016 NT election.

§5. Proposed Voter Identity Legislation

550. The federal parliament has introduced the *Electoral Legislation Amendment (Voter Integrity) Bill* 2021 a voter identification bill. Initial reading of the Bill suggests that it can potentially be racially discriminatory in effect.[332] This arises because while most Australians have some form of formal identification such as a driver's licence, a minority such as Aboriginal and Torres Strait Islander people do not.

328. *Electoral Act* 2004 (Tas) s. 113(1) and s. 132 respectively.
329. *Electoral Act* 1992 (ACT) ss 114 & 118A.
330. *Electoral Act* 1992 (ACT) ss 118B and 118B respectively.
331. *Electoral Act* 2004 (NT) ss 85A and 53 respectively.
332. *Electoral Legislation Amendment (Voter Integrity) Bill* 2021 at https://www.aph.gov.au/Parliamentary_Business/Bills_Legislation/Bills_Search_Results/Result?bId=r6811.

551. Furthermore, section 73M of the Bill seeks 'regulations [that] must provide for an electronically assisted voting method to be used by Antarctic electors to vote at referenda.'

552. Voter ID is also politically sensitive given how it has demonstrably been 'weaponized' in the recent 2020 US elections.[333]

553. Thus far a long-standing tradition is that in federal elections in Australia at least, it is not necessary to produce an ID to vote.[334]

§6. Future Prospects for Electronic Voting Systems

554. During the 2013 Australian federal election, a loss of almost 1,400 Western Australian Senate ballots resulted in a Special Election being held several months after polling day.[335]

555. In its inquiry into the 2013 federal election, the Joint Standing Committee on Electoral Matters (JSCEM) undertook an assessment of electronic voting options.[336] The report of the JSCEM identified:

- 'significant questions over the capacity of an electronic voting solution to be both cost-effective and protect the security and sanctity of the ballot in the Australian context', and concluded that 'there can be no widespread introduction of electronic voting in the near term without massive costs and unacceptable security risks;' and,
- concern over the potential for electronic voting to 'further disengage the community' from the political process.

556. According to the JSCEM, the outcome of the trial on electronic voting resulted in an average cost per vote cast of AUD 2,597 for electronically assisted voting for blind and low vision electors, and AUD 1,159 for remote online voting for ADF personnel via the DRN. This compared to an average cost per vote of AUD 8.36 for ordinary paper ballots. Based on the outcomes of these trials, the JSCEM recommended that the systems be discontinued at future federal elections.[337].

---

333. Dixon, R (2021) 'Proposed voter ID laws pose a risk to our democracy' at https://www.smh.com.au/politics/federal/proposed-voter-id-laws-pose-a-risk-to-our-democracy-20211031-p594p6.html.

334. Lowrey, T (2021) Voter Id Laws at https://www.abc.net.au/news/2021-10-28/voter-id-laws-to-require-proof-could-disenfranchise-vulnerable/100575812.

335. Joint Standing Committee on Electoral Matters, *second interim report on the inquiry into the conduct of the 2013 federal election: An assessment of electronic voting options*, Canberra, November 2014.

336. *See* http://parlinfo.aph.gov.au/parlInfo/search/display/display.w3p;query=Id%3A%22publications%2Ftabledpapers%2Fb2a871d0-8106-42e3-8481-8749744020e7%22.

337. Holmes, B (2012) e-Voting: The Promise and the Practice. text, Parliament of Australia. Department of Parliamentary Services, Parliamentary Library, October 2012 at http://www.aph.gov.au/About_Parliament/Parliamentary_Departments/Parliamentary_Library/pubs/BN/2012-2013/EVoting.

557. Another view expresses a lack of confidence with the integrity of electronic voting systems. 'With electronic voting, whether online or on stand-alone voting machines, everything happens inside the invisible cave of computer memory. It is impossible to see what is going on at the time the votes are tallied. How can you know that the votes were counted correctly? You just have to trust the system.'[338]

558. The fundamental principles of exercising one's voting rights are that one's vote is secret and that one does not need to prove how one voted. Seemingly electronic voting breaks both these fundamental principles when such systems' integrity can be compromised, and voter identity and vote secrecy no longer guaranteed.[339]

559. When one votes in an election, one should be sure that no one else can vote in one's name and no one else can vote more than once in an election. Using blockchain technology, there is a suggestion that it can help make Australian elections more reliable, fair, safe and secure. Blockchain technology is an emergent distributed ledger technology that may be used wherever a verified and trusted transaction is required.[340] Using the blockchain for voting would allow for a location agnostic, 'tamper proof' system that would provide traceability, prevent manipulation, yet allow anonymity and be resistant to denial of service (DDOS) attacks.[341]

§7. Postscript

560. For there to be a nationwide adoption of electronic voting there might need a generational and a paradigmatic change in perceptions, attitudes and trust in the alternate means of exercising one's democratic franchise. The extant modalities of electronic voting must guarantee both security and secrecy both tenets in choosing a democratic government system. The will of the people is as important as the perceptions of the reality of the system itself. Such perceptions will influence the choice of which systems to adopt. There does not seem to be compelling reasons to adopt a different *modus operandi* as far as electing legislatures is concerned. According to ECANZ the status quo should be maintained because 'broadly speaking, all jurisdictions in those countries have succeeded in delivering the franchise

---

338. Stilgherrian (2019) Flaws found in NSW iVote system yet again at https://www.zdnet.com/article/flaws-found-in-nsw-ivote-system-yet-again/.
339. Peake, R (n.d.) Why can't we vote on the Internet? at https://reporter.anu.edu.au/why-cant-we-vote-internet, *ANU Reporter* Vol 47 no 4.
340. *See* CSIRO at https://data61.csiro.au/~/media/D61/Files/Blockchain-reports/Blockchain-RisksandOpps-HTML.html?hash=B30AF266CCDE4BC81684C676AE70E61E72E9E995&la=en. *See also* Blockchain Voting at https://www.voteaustralia.org.au/blockchain_voting that describes the Australian startup Horizon State that has created a verified, secure voting systems.
341. *See* Duckett, C (2016) Australia Post details plan to use blockchain for voting at https://www.zdnet.com/article/australia-post-details-plan-to-use-blockchain-for-voting/ and Palmer, D (2016) Australia Post plans blockchain-based e-voting system at https://delimiter.com.au/2016/08/23/australia-post-plans-blockchain-based-e-voting-system/.

effectively over a sustained period of time, through credible and transparent elections which have enjoyed high levels of community trust'[342] and equivalent electronic voting systems may be unable to achieve such high standards.

342. *Supra,* ECANZ (2013) Internet voting in Australian election systems.

Chapter 4. Other e-Government Services

561. Other e-government services that should be noted include an Australian national e-conveyancing system and a national e-invoicing system that encompasses all jurisdictions. These developments address the challenges of cyber developments and the government's Digital Vision 2025 Strategy.[343] These e-government and other services are discussed next.

§1. Introduction

I. e-Conveyancing National Law (ECNL)

562. The e-Conveyancing National Law (ECNL) is a significant e-government project from 2011. The project aims to develop a national online conveyancing system to be run by the National E-conveyancing Office (NECO) that was initially funded by the NSW Department of Lands.

563. A National E-conveyancing System (NECS) was created by Australian State and Territory governments in 2005. The NECS aims to deliver a truly national e-conveyancing system with a single point of entry operating in each jurisdiction.[344]

564. As background, in March 2008, the Council of Australian Governments (COAG) committed to the development of NECS and in March 2009 published a National Partnership Agreement (NPA) on twenty-seven areas of regulatory reform, including NECS. As with most intergovernmental agreements (IGA) the broad framework of overarching principles is the model law legislation to be adopted in every Australian jurisdiction. Practical details to make e-conveyancing work is the follow-up in administrative regulations, protocols, standards, procedures and guidelines to be established for those who use the system.

565. The IGA for an Electronic Conveyancing National Law was signed in 2011 and a set of documents were developed to establish the legal framework to implement e-conveyancing. The users included legal practitioners, conveyancers and financial institutions to electronically prepare and lodge land property dealings with title registries; to transmit settlement funds and pay associated duties and tax; and to remove the need to physically attend property settlements.

566. The ECNL was first implemented in NSW as an Appendix to its *Electronic Conveyancing (Adoption of National Law) Act* 2012 (NSW).

---

343. *See* DTA https://www.dta.gov.au/sites/default/files/files/digital-transformation-strategy/digital-transformation-strategy.pdf.

344. For a detailed assessment of e-Conveyancing in Australia see Clark, E (2011) E-Conveyancing in Australia: An Important Step Along the Journey, [2011] *Journal of Law and Information Science* 5; (2011) 21(1) 62.

567. Thereafter, the ECNL was implemented in other States and Territories as either application or corresponding legislation. *Application legislation* is an Act that adopts the Appendix to the NSW legislation. *Corresponding legislation* is an Act that is essentially the same as the Appendix to the NSW legislation.

II. e-Conveyancing State and Territory Legislation

568. The specific e-conveyancing legislation in each State and Territory is as follows:

- *Electronic Conveyancing (Adoption of National Law) Act* 2012 (NSW) [345] (1 January 2013).
- *Electronic Conveyancing (Adoption of National Law) Act* 2013 (Vic) [346] (14 March 2013).
- *Electronic Conveyancing National Law (Queensland) Act* 2013 (Qld) [347] (17 May 2013).
- *Electronic Conveyancing Act* 2014 (WA) [348] (3 June 2014).
- *Electronic Conveyancing National Law (South Australia) Act* 2013 (SA) [349] (21 January 2016).
- *Electronic Conveyancing (Adoption of National Law) Act* 2013 (Tas) [350] (19 November 2013).
- *Electronic Conveyancing National Law (ACT) Act* 2020 (ACT) [351] (13 May 2020).
- *Electronic Conveyancing (National Uniform Legislation) Act* 2013 (NT) [352] (17 July 2013).

III. National e-Conveyancing System (NECS)

569. After the COAG agreement, the NSW, Queensland and Victorian Governments established National e-Conveyancing Development Ltd (NECDL)[353] to accelerate the development of NECS and to allow other jurisdictions to join in the operation of NECS.[354]

---

345. *See* text of the Act at http://www.austlii.edu.au/au/legis/nsw/consol_act/econla2012451/.
346. *See* text of the Act at http://classic.austlii.edu.au/au/legis/vic/consol_act/econla2013451/.
347. *See* text of the Act at http://www.austlii.edu.au/au/legis/qld/consol_act/ecnla2013448/.
348. *See* text of the Act at http://www.austlii.edu.au/au/legis/wa/consol_act/eca2014235/.
349. *See* text of the Act at http://www.austlii.edu.au/au/legis/sa/consol_act/ecnlaa2013517/.
350. *See* text of the Act at http://www.austlii.edu.au/au/legis/tas/consol_act/econla2013451/.
351. *See* text of the Act at https://legislation.act.gov.au/a/2020-15/.
352. *See* text of the Act at http://www.austlii.edu.au/au/legis/nt/num_act/ecula201313o2013560/.
353. *See* National e-Conveyancing Council at https://www.arnecc.gov.au/about_us/.
354. Effective 3 Mar. 2014, NECDL changed its name to Property Exchange Australia Ltd (PEXA) at https://www.pexa.com.au.

570. An Australian Registrars National E-conveyancing Council (ARNECC) was established in 2011 to ensure a consistent national approach in the regulation of NEC.[355] This Council was formed under the IGA in the ECNL for the purposes of coordinating a national approach among the States and Territories in the regulation of an electronic environment for completing conveyancing transactions. ARNECC membership comprises the Land Titles Registrars from each Australian state and territory or nominee.

571. The Strategic Statement issued by ARNECC in May 2014 sets out the purpose, focus and priorities for the benefit of participants in the conveyancing industry throughout Australia. The aim is on developing, implementing and nurturing a safe, reliable, national and sustainable electronic environment for completing conveyancing transactions.

572. The objectives of the NECS activities are to develop a system that enables practitioners electronically to:[356]

- prepare land title deals and related instruments needed to register changes in property ownership and interests;
- settle financial transactions (that is, exchange property settlement monies including payment of duties, taxes and disbursements);
- comply with the tax and duty requirements of the relevant State or Territory revenue office;
- lodge land title instruments for registration with the relevant State or Territory land registry; and,
- receive prompt confirmation of the lodgement and registration of land title instruments.

573. The regulatory framework under the existing ECNL includes Model Operating Requirements (MOR) and Model Participation Rules (MPR) as requirements that subscribers to the Electronic Lodgement Network (ELN) must meet to be able to transact on the ELN.

IV. Review and Performance of the ECNL

574. A 2019 *Review of the Intergovernmental Agreement for an Electronic Conveyancing National Law* has found that the IGA has met its objective of establishing a framework to facilitate the implementation of e-conveyancing and has partially met its objective of ongoing management of the regulatory framework.[357]

355. Information on ARNECC activities and the legal framework to support the NEC is found at http://www.arnecc.gov.au.
356. National Electronic Conveyancing System (2010) *What's in* at http://www.necs.gov.au/What-s-In/default.aspx.
357. Dench McClean Carlson (2019) *Review of the Intergovernmental Agreement for an Electronic Conveyancing National Law* at https://dmcca.com.au/wp-content/uploads/2019/12/ IGA-Review-Final-Report-19-12-18.pdf.

575. However, conveyancing practitioners and financial institutions have requested improvements in several areas. For example, with the advent of two new ELN operators, some matters that were left to the management of the sole operator may need to be coordinated or managed by government.

576. The existing governance and regulatory arrangements for the land titling components of e-conveyancing are fit-for-purpose for the future and provide appropriate accountability to participating governments on those matters, but the regulatory arrangements for financial payment and settlement, for the collection of duties and taxes and for market regulation need to be defined and explicitly stated.

577. More critically, the market regulator ACCC in a report to State and Territory policy agencies on e-conveyancing market reform has posited the view that considering the mandating of e-conveyancing and the emergence of competition in various state jurisdictions, the regulatory framework for e-conveyancing in Australia may no longer be fit-for-purpose.[358]

§2. E-INVOICING IN AUSTRALIA

I. e-Invoicing: Background

578. E-invoicing allows the digital exchange of invoices between a supplier's and a buyer's software or systems using a secure network and a common proven standard.

579. The Australian Treasury, citing Deloitte Access Economics, estimates that every time a paper invoice is replaced by an e-invoice there is a cost savings of AUD 20 to the businesses involved.[359] Given that over 1.2 billion invoices are exchanged in Australia annually and with 89 per cent of small and medium enterprises (SME) still using paper-based invoices, it is self-evident that e-invoices can deliver significant benefits to the economy. With over 1.2 billion invoices exchanged in Australia annually, savings to the economy are estimated to be AUD 28 billion over ten years.[360]

580. In 2019, Australia adopted the Pan-European Public Procurement OnLine (Peppol) framework. Peppol is an internationally recognized framework for

358. *See* ACCC (2019) report on e-conveyancing market reform at https://www.accc.gov.au/about-us/consultations-submissions/accc-submissions and at https://www.accc.gov.au/system/files/Letter%20to%20ARNECC%20Chair%20and%20state%20and%20territory%20policy%20agencies%20-%20December%202019.pdf.

359. The Treasury (2020) Options for mandatory adoption of electronic invoicing by businesses (November) at https://treasury.gov.au/sites/default/files/2020-11/c2020122716.pdf.; and *see also* Deloitte Access Economics 2016 *The Economic Impact of E-invoicing*.

360. *See* Digital business plan to drive Australia's economic recovery at https://www.pm.gov.au/media/digital-business-plan-drive-australias-economic-recovery, Australian Government media release 29 Sep. 2020.

e-Invoicing and e-Procurement, used by over thirty countries in Europe, Asia and North America. While there has been interest in the potential benefits of Peppol e-Invoicing in Australia, voluntary adoption has been modest in both the public and private sectors.

581. As part of Budget 2020-2021, the government announced that it will seek to accelerate the adoption of Peppol e-Invoicing, starting with the public sector. The government will mandate that all Commonwealth government agencies must be able to receive Peppol e-Invoices by 1 July 2022.[361] This will include Business-to-Government (B2G) and vice versa G2B e-commerce.

582. The potential benefits of adopting e-invoicing include efficient processing of invoice processing compared to paper-based time consuming procedures; faster payments to suppliers; more secure and accurate delivery of invoices to correct buyers given the use of Peppol network of in-built database of addresses; compatibility with extant electronic data interchange (EDI) systems; data-driven decision-making in near real-time; the environmentally friendly elimination of paper-based invoices; and the potential to connect once but trading with many.[362]

II. e-Invoicing Legislation

583. The ATO has been provided with legislative powers under section 3G(1) of the *Taxation Administration Act* 1953 (Cth) to develop and administer the framework to implement e-invoicing into the Australian economy. The ATO manages the local invoice specifications (that is, goods and services tax (GST)) and regulates the use of e-invoicing to ensure standards are being met and operates the national e-invoicing system.

584. The ATO is the Australian Peppol Authority. Currently, Australia is the only country that has its tax authority act as the Peppol Authority.

585. Each PEPPOL Authority refers to OpenPEPPOL, the international non-profit organization that has been given responsibility for developing and disseminating the PEPPOL standard.[363]

586. PEPPOL Access Point is a businesses' connection to the PEPPOL network. Typically, it is a service purchased from a service provider. Using this access point businesses may be able to exchange electronic documents with other companies that are also linked to an access point.

361. *Ibid* The Treasury (2020).
362. *See* ATO (2021) at https://www.taxathand.com/article/17442/Australia/2021/Federal-government-consults-on-Introduction-of-electronic-invoicing.
363. *See* PEPPOL at https://peppol.eu/about-openpeppol/what-is-openpeppol/. *See also* Zachariasen, DN (2021) What is Peppol? Six most important things to know at https://peppol.com/blog/what-is-peppol/.

III. e-Invoicing Policy and Other Legislation

A. *Mandate*

587. The debate as to whether e-invoicing may be made mandatory for the country is dependent on Commonwealth powers residing with the government. In Australia, the Constitution limits the Commonwealth's powers in relation to the regulation of businesses. So one means is for such a mandate to be legislated via amendments to existing corporation legislation. Perversely, this may leave unincorporated businesses such as sole traders are not subject to a mandate.

588. Of the fifteen countries currently with Peppol Authorities (twelve European countries, Australia, New Zealand and Singapore), only Italy has mandated e-Invoicing for business transactions (effective from January 2019). Outside of this, countries such as Argentina, Brazil, Chile, Mexico and Peru have all mandated e-Invoicing for business transactions, with the aim of combatting the black economy and tax evasion.

589. A KPMG Report notes that the EU mandated e-invoicing in 2020, with a five-year implementation timeframe of 2025, to give business enough time to be educated and prepare.[364]

B. *Resource Management Guides Policy*

590. Another legislative means of implementing e-invoicing and to capture all types of businesses is the use of Resource Management Guides (RMG) policy issued by the Treasury and Finance Department.

591. One such is the *Supplier Pay On-Time or Pay Interest Policy* (RMG 417).[365] This policy came into effect 1 January 2020, introducing five-day payment terms where PEPPOL-compliant e-Invoicing capability exists. RMG 416 (dated November 2016) – *Facilitating Supplier Payment Through Payment Card* has also been merged into RMG 417, resulting in all supplier payment arrangements now found in the one guide.

592. Under the *Payment Times Reporting Act* 2020 (Cth)[366] the definition of a large or medium taxpayer for the tax agent lodgement programme (AUD 10 million turnover) will capture around 30,000 businesses in Australia and the same threshold of AUD 100 million turnover will capture around 3,400 businesses in Australia.[367]

364. *See* KPMG Report (2021) https://assets.kpmg/content/dam/kpmg/au/pdf/2021/options-for-mandatory-e-invoicing-adoption-kpmg-submission.pdf.
365. *See* Department of Finance at https://www.finance.gov.au/publications/resource-management-guides/supplier-pay-time-or-pay-interest-policy-rmg-417.
366. *See* text of the Act at http://classic.austlii.edu.au/au/legis/cth/num_act/ptra2020282/.
367. *See* Treasury at https://treasury.gov.au/sites/default/files/2020-11/c2020122716.pdf.

C. Business Transactions Through Payment Systems

593. Following the ATO, new legislation requires organizations that process transactions for their business clients through an electronic payment system to report these transactions in a business transaction through payment systems (BTTPS) report.[368] A payment system is defined by the *Payment Systems (Regulation) Act* 1998 (Cth).[369]

594. The information reported will be used to pre-fill income tax returns to make it easier for individuals and businesses to lodge; and ensure businesses comply with their tax obligations, including lodging their tax returns and reporting their income.[370]

D. Interoperability Framework

595. An interoperability framework has been proposed by the Australian Digital Business Council (ADBC) that aims to provide efficacy in e-invoicing. Such a framework will provide certainty on how a prescribed set of established open standards can be used to extend e-Invoicing to all Australian businesses; minimize the cost of implementation for software providers; and enhance business interactions (especially for SME) by making invoicing an automatic digital interaction.[371]

IV. e-Invoicing Trans-Tasman Developments

596. An Australia-New Zealand government electronic invoicing arrangement has been signed in 2018. The objective of this arrangement is to create and maintain a common Australia and New Zealand e-invoicing approach to improve productivity and reduce the costs of doing business for both government and industry through an interoperable single digital economic market.[372]

---

368. ATO (2017) Business transactions through payment systems report at https://softwaredevelopers.ato.gov.au/BTTPS.
369. *See* text of the Act at https://www.legislation.gov.au/Details/C2016C00591.
370. *See* ATO at https://www.ato.gov.au/Business/E-invoicing/E-invoicing-for-businesses/.
371. *See* Australian Digital Business Council (2016) *e-Invoicing Interoperability Framework* (July 2016, Version 1.0) at http://digitalbusinesscouncil.com.au/interoperability-framework/.
372. *See* Treasury at https://treasury.gov.au/trans-tasman-electronic-invoicing-arrangement; and *see also* Treasury (2018) *Discussion Paper Early Thinking: Operational governance for trans-Tasman e-Invoicing*, (October) at https://treasury.gov.au/sites/default/files/2019-03/c2018-t331468-openpeppol-aisbl_3.pdf.

Part III. Online Transactions

Chapter 1. Online Transactions

§1. Introduction

597. Information technology presents many challenges to traditional notions of law that requires a major paradigm shift. These include rights to privacy, protection against defamation by email, computer crime, trust services and electronic data interchange, intellectual property questions, transborder data flow issues, rules of evidence, and use of expert systems. As technology transcends national boundaries and globalization continues, the trend is towards developing uniform international laws. New technology brings with it challenges as well as opportunities. [373]

598. e-Commerce refers to commercial services on the Internet that encompasses business-to-consumer (B2C) services, business to business (B2B) services such as using electronic data interchange (EDI), and e-Markets as deployed in financial markets and airline booking systems.[374] The various permutations of the business-to-government (B2G), consumer-to-government (C2G), and government-to-government (G2G) transactions suggest the complexity of the task.

599. e-Business refers to the commercial operations and procedures when engaging in e-commerce. In recent times mobile e-commerce (m-commerce) conducted on mobile devices has become commonplace. Web 2.0 i-Commerce system refers to the use of the Internet that deploys user-generated content (UGC) and the participatory web.

§2. e-Commerce and the Internet

600. As Australia moves from an industrial to an information society in the Fourth Industrial Revolution, commerce will increasingly take place in an

373. Electronic Commerce Expert Group (ECEG), *Electronic Commerce: Building the Legal Framework* (ECEG Report) (March 1998), www.law.gov.au/aghome/advisory/eceg/single.htm and Australian Taxation Office at (ATO), Electronic Commerce Report, *Tax and the Internet* (August 1997), https://www.ato.gov.au/ecp/ecp/htm.
374. De Zwart, M (2000) Electronic Commerce: Promises, Potential and Proposals, 21(2) *UNSW Law Journal* (May 2000) at http://www.law.unsw.edu.au/unswlj/ecommerce/zwart.html. Abstract.

electronic world as opposed to a physical one.[375] The most obvious development is the growth of business on the Internet.

601. According to modelling by Australia Post online shopping in Australia reached 8 per cent of total traditional retail sales at the end of 2017, a 1 per cent rise on the year before. Australians spent AUD 21.3 billion buying goods online, an increase of 18.7 per cent. The online spending growth outstripped traditional retail by 16.2 per cent.[376]

602. Beyond Australia 99.9 per cent of global online spend sits outside of Australia. Online shopping is growing around the world, with the global e-commerce goods market worth USD 1.57 trillion in 2017. That figure is set to increase by a further 19 per cent in 2018 and reach over USD 2 trillion by 2019. Today, Australia's top five export markets are China, Japan, Republic of Korea, United States and India. Collectively, these countries represent 58.4 per cent of Australia's total export market.[377]

603. As the world of commerce is transformed from a paper-based to a digital one, in Australia, as elsewhere, the law is struggling to keep up. However, the government has moved to establish the legal infrastructure that achieves an appropriate balance between the promotion of e-commerce and regulations to satisfy concerns about consumer protection, privacy and security. As e-commerce activity is not restricted by physical borders, Australia's laws in this area takes note of what is happening globally as it attempts to influence international treaties and agreements consistent with the promotion of world trade.

604. In 1998 the Australian government set up an Electronic Commerce Expert Group (ECEG) to report on the need for legislation to support the regulation of e-commerce transactions.[378]

605. In one sense, e-commerce is a new and largely unregulated frontier where digital marketers are free to ride the electronic range. In another sense, however, e-commerce is heavily regulated. All Australian legislation apply to e-commerce including several emerging laws and codes which are designed specifically to deal with the Internet and other forms of new technology.[379] In addition, as e-commerce

375. Schwab, K (2017) *The Fourth Industrial Revolution,* London: Portfolio Penguin.

376. Australia Post, *e-Commerce: Inside Australian Online Shopping* (2018), at https://auspost.com.au/content/dam/auspost_corp/media/documents/2018-ecommerce-industry-paper-inside-australian-online-shopping.pdf. The data in the report are based on analysis of goods bought online and delivered by Australia Post between January 2016 and December 2017. It also draws on modelled estimates from Australia Post consumer surveys, statistics from the Australian Bureau of Statistics (ABS) and publicly available information.

377. *Ibid.* citing Euromonitor sources.

378. ECEG (1998) *Electronic Commerce: Building the Legal Framework* (April) at https://www.law.gov.au/aghome/eceg/ecegreport.html.

379. National Advisory Council on Consumer Affairs (1998) *Consumer Protection in Electronic Commerce: Principles and Key Issues* (April) at https://www.dist.gov.au/consumer/eleccomm/princip.html.

spreads across national borders, the laws of many other countries may become applicable too. The problem then is that there may be too many laws that claim jurisdiction and the resultant uncertainty about which laws will govern a particular transaction, plus the uncertainty of how paper-based laws will deal with such new realities such as digital signatures and digital contracts.[380]

606. The implication is that there will be a greater reliance on the common law and resort to legislation where private regulation proves unsatisfactory. For legal practitioners this means that there is little available in the form of case law or adapted legislation that regulates this space. Instead, lawyers must become familiar with frequent changes to codes and industry standards.

§3. *The Electronic Transactions Act* 1999 (ETA)

607. The *Electronic Transactions Act* 1999 (Cth) (ETA) is based on the ECEG Report which recommended that Australia enact legislation based on the UNCITRAL Model Law on Electronic Commerce.[381] The ETA received Royal Assent in December 1999 and commenced by Proclamation on 15 March 2000.[382]

608. The ETA prevents the invalidation of transactions merely because they have been conducted electronically.

609. From 1 July 2001, the ETA applies to all Commonwealth legislation (other than those specifically excluded by the regulations).

610. The *Electronic Transactions Regulations* 2000 (Cth) list the provisions of 157 federal Acts and Regulations which continue to be exempted from the operation of the ETA.[383]

611. In general, the ETA allows e-commerce to fit into the same legal framework as traditional paper-based transactions. The goal is to ensure that the technological developments brought about by e-commerce can be dealt with within the existing legal system, while allowing business and consumers to determine the most effective technological choice for their purposes.[384]

---

380. ASIC (2000) Electronic Applications Policy Proposal Paper at https://download.asic.gov.au/media/1342052/ppp-elecapp.pdf.
381. UNCITRAL Model Law on Electronic Commerce with Guide to Enactment 1996, General Assembly Resolution 51/162 at http://www.uncitral.org/uncitral/en/uncitral_texts/electronic_commerce/1996Model.html.
382. *See* text of the Act at https://www.legislation.gov.au/Details/C2011C00445.
383. For a listing of legislation to which the Act does not apply, see text of the Act at https://www.legislation.gov.au/Details/F2011C00367.
384. Giles, D (2000) You've Got Mail … or Have You?, 3 *Internet L. Bull.* 12, 14 (2000).

612. Progressively from 1999 onwards the Commonwealth, States and Territories have all passed legislation mirroring the Commonwealth Act.[385]

613. The key differences between the State and Territory legislations and the ETA are that the State and Territory legislations apply to the interpretation of the common law as well as legislation; does not differentiate between communications with private organizations and communications with government bodies; and does not provide for a staged introduction of the ETA.

614. The ETA is built on three underlying principles of functional equivalence where paper and electronic documents will be on the same legal footing; technology neutrality where there is no discrimination between different forms of technology; and a principled approach to electronic signatures.[386]

615. A graphical summary of the *ETA* is shown in Figure 5.

385. *See Electronic Transactions Act* 2000 (NSW); *Electronic Transactions Act* 2000 (Victoria); *Electronic Transactions Act* 2000 (SA); *Electronic Transactions Act* (Tasmania) 2001; *Electronic Transactions Act* 2001 (Queensland); *Electronic Transactions Act* 2000 (WA); *Electronic Transactions Act* 2000 (Northern Territory); and *Electronic Transactions Act* 2001 (ACT).

386. UNCITRAL Uniform Rules on Electronic Signatures – Australian Issues Paper, http://law.gov.au/publications/ecommerce/welcome.html; Sneddon, M (2000) Legislating to Facilitate Electronic Signatures and Records: Exceptions, Standards and the Impact of the Statute Book, 21(2) *UNSW Law Journal* (May 2000), http://www.law.unsw.edu.au/unswlj/ecommerce/sneddon.html.

Figure 5 A Graphical Summary of the ETA

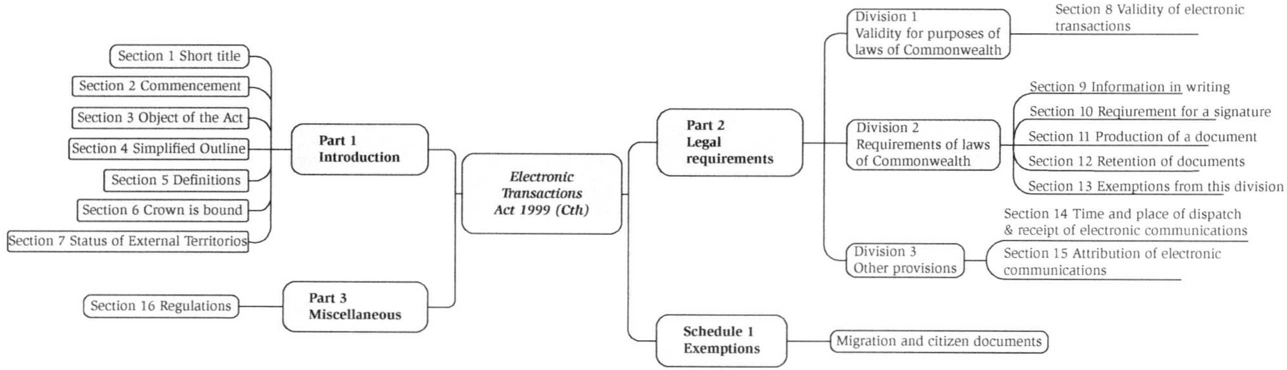

Source: Summarized from details of the ETA legislation at https://www.legislation.gov.au/Details/C2005C0048.

616. A distinction is made between a *digital signature* and a *digitized signature*. A *digital signature* refers to the use of a cryptic mathematical function and private key verification scheme to determine the identity of a person, purported to have made the signature. Many, if not all digital signatures rely on public key cryptography as their identity verification core including proprietary products such as Adobe EchoSign and DocuSign. However, *digitized signatures* refer to the scanned signature superimposed upon a document such as a letter or contract or just text on an email. For purposes of the ETA there is no difference between electronic and digitized signatures.[387]

617. A person must consent to receiving electronic communications from the government. Consent can be inferred from a person's conduct. Express consent is not required. The consent provisions, however, do not extend to Commonwealth entities. Herein lies an inconsistency as it would be impossible to fulfil the government's wish and commitment to delivering all Commonwealth services electronically. Some provisions of the ETA are vague, and it may take a few court challenges to give full meaning to the Act.[388]

618. As the Commonwealth is excluded from the operation of the consent provisions, it must accept all electronic communications. However, the Commonwealth is given certain specific powers. Being able to satisfy a legal requirement electronically is conditional upon a person complying with any IT requirement for communication with a Commonwealth agency, including any electronic signature technology that must be used and any action a person must take to verify receipt of information.

619. The ETA also sets out default rules that apply in the absence of any contrary agreement between the parties, regulating what is deemed to be the time and place of dispatch and receipt of electronic communications and the attribution of electronic communications.

620. The ETA also provides that any other laws that deal specifically with the use of electronic communications to satisfy writing, signature, production, or retention requirements will be preserved.[389] The ETA does not override any existing laws that deal specifically with these matters.

387. *See* Bolam, P & Choi, R (2012) Electronic Signatures: When Are They Effective?, *Internet L. Bull.* 118-120 (October 2012).

388. For example, the ETA leaves to the courts the decision as to whether the postal acceptance rule would apply to a particular contract; if it does, presumably, the time, place of dispatch and receipt of communications provisions found in s. 14 of the ETA would come into play and be applied. *See* Forder, J & Quick, P (2001) *Electronic Commerce and the Law* 67-74 (Milton).

389. The Australian Archives developed three general information papers about how to keep track of incoming and outgoing electronic communications. *See* Australian Archives website at https://www.naa.gov.au.

621. The workability issue stems from the Commonwealth's decision to leave it to the States and Territories to adopt the model legislation. The Commonwealth rejected the option of a comprehensive federal legislation because of concerns that such a scheme would be open to constitutional challenge.

Chapter 2. Electronic Contracts

622. e-Contracts encompass only those types of contracts that one could make with the 'click' of a mouse online in an e-business transaction. The question is whether e-contracts are legally recognized.

623. A UN Working Group on E-commerce examined the feasibility of developing a Convention that dealt with electronic documents of title and electronic contracting. This resulted in the UN Convention on the Use of Electronic Communications in International Contracts (CUECIC) adopted by the General Assembly on 23 November 2005.[390] The CUECIC updates the Model Law on E-commerce 1996. The Convention provides legal certainty where electronic communications are used by private parties in international e-commerce.[391]

624. The Convention addresses issues such as the location of parties, time of contract formation, the distinction between offers and invitations to make offers, time and place of offer and acceptance, automated transactions and the information to be made available to parties. The principles of functional equivalence and technology neutrality are maintained. The 2005 UN CUECIC was signed by Australia and eighteen other countries.

625. To enable Australia to fully accede to the CUECIC in 2010 the Standing Committee of Attorneys-General (SCAG) and Attorneys-General resolved to adopt nationally consistent amendments to their respective e-commerce laws.[392] As a result the *Electronic Transactions Amendment Act* 2011 (Cth) contains provisions addressing the issues raised by the CUECIC including invitations to treat in the electronic context; the rules on electronic signatures; use of automated message systems in e-contracting; determination of the location of parties; default rules for the time and place of dispatch and receipt of electronic communications; and, keystroke errors that have unintended consequences for contract formation.[393]

626. Other issues about acceptance of a contract in online environments include the question of jurisdiction and where the contract is formed and whether the postal rule is applicable in such environments. In the case of a 'clickwrap' contract one may ask whether acceptance of the contract formed in the country where customer clicks the '*I accept*' icon or where the server for the website is located or when the acceptance is communicated to the suppliers in their country of location. Common

390. UNCITRAL UN Doc A/60/515 (23 Nov. 2005) at http://www.uncitral.org/uncitral/en/uncitral_texts/electronic_commerce/2005Convention.html.
391. For details of the draft Convention, see AGD (2008) Australia's accession to the UN Convention on the Use of Electronic Communications in International Contracts 2005: Proposed amendments to Australia's electronic transactions law – Consultation paper (November), at http://www.ag.gov.au/Consultations/Documents/AustralianecommercereviewUNConventiononElectronicCommunications/UN%20Convention%20on%20ecommerce.pdf.
392. *Ibid.* AGD (2008).
393. *See* text of the Act at https://www.legislation.gov.au/Details/C2011A00033.

law principles suggest that a contract will be formed when acceptance is in fact communicated to the offeror – the receipt rule.

§1. Principles of Contract Law

627. Contracts are the most common legal institution in everyday life. Contracts are entered into in various ways, sometimes formally by signing documents and having it witnessed and sealed and sometimes informally without documents but with just the shaking of hands on a 'gentleman's agreement'.

628. The function of a contract is to signify an agreement that becomes operative when two parties intend it to be binding, that is, committed to the agreement after an offer has been accepted and there is a 'meeting of the minds'. The contract also spells out the respective roles of the parties and the terms the parties agree to be bound.[394]

629. As contracts can take different forms, it is very important to understand any terms used in the preceding bargaining meetings. As both sides strive for 'certainty' as well as to cover as many contingencies as possible, and especially in online environments, contracts should be comprehensive and unambiguous to avoid difficulties in interpretation later.

§2. Elements of a Contract

630. A contract is a legally enforceable agreement. Most rules of contract law in Australia derive from the common law, although there are different statutory provisions in each of the States and Territories covering various aspects.

631. In an electronic context, contracts may be formed by an exchange of email, through a page on the website, at an online auction, or through an online portal. As in the common law, a binding contract, and an intention to create legal relations is formed where there is an *offer* which is *accepted*; *valuable consideration* for the promises given; and *consensus* as to the subject and all major aspects of the contract.

I. Offer and Acceptance

632. For a contract to come into being, there must be a firm 'offer' by one party that is 'accepted' in its precise terms by another. There is very little that may be

394. *See* generally Seddon, NC & Ellinghaus, MP (1997) Cheshire and Fifoot's *Law of Contract* (7th Australian ed., Butterworths). *See also* McBurnie, D & Levinson, E (2001) *Contract: Sales of Goods over the Internet. E-Commerce: The Implications for the Law Series* (The Law Book Co.).

required to constitute offer and acceptance.[395] The *Carlill* case also demonstrates how a contract may be concluded at 'arm's length' since there was no face-to-face contact, unlike most bargains made in the marketplace between two traders. This is especially apposite in an online context where the two parties may not have met face-to-face but have negotiated over the Internet.

633. In an online context, the invitation to treat may be either posted electronically on a website, on an electronic mailing list, or sent by email to a specific recipient. But to avoid the possibility that the invitation may constitute a unilateral contract, that is, a contract taken up by a customer without reference to the offeror, websites now customarily include disclaimers indicating that statements made are neither offers nor unilateral contracts but are mere invitations to treat.[396]

A. *Terms and Conditions*

634. On the Internet an offeror may wish to incorporate standard terms and conditions into a contract by including these on the web page. Thus, in order that these standard terms and conditions form part of the contract, the offeror must put these to the offeree so that they have a reasonable opportunity to read them. To minimize legal risks, it is prudent to set out all the terms and conditions in full and up front in such a manner that the offeree cannot avoid seeing them.

635. Potential liabilities may also be minimized by using disclaimers or exclusions. The effectiveness of these disclaimers is underpinned by contract law in the sense that information and services will only be provided if the person reading it agrees to the disclaimer. In general, such disclaimers or exclusions must be brought to the attention of a user and accepted by the user with a positive act (for example, by clicking the*I Agree* icon) for disclaimers and exclusions to be enforceable.

636. Furthermore, terms and conditions of a website may place limits on those users of the website. These depend on several factors including the geographical area, the purpose, or their contribution to the site. However, the terms and conditions of a website may not exclude or restrict all liability arising from the operation or functioning of the website in all circumstances.

637. The design of the website is thus critical. When a purchaser presses the 'place order' button, a page incorporating the terms should appear automatically. The purchaser must then be made to click on a 'submit offer on these terms' button to send the order to the seller. Hence, on the assumption that the display of information on the website is an invitation to treat, the website visitor makes an offer (offeror) in relation to the good or service displayed, and the seller (offeree) communicates acceptance of that offer to the offeror on the website. Contract law will

395. *Carlill v. Carbolic Smoke Ball Co.* [1893] 1 QB 256 illustrates the criteria in contract formation.
396. *See* Chissick, M & Kelman, A (1999) *Electronic* Commerce*: Law and Practice* (Sweet & Maxwell Ltd).

generally regard that a contract has formed. The jurisdiction of the website visitor is the place where the communication of the acceptance was received. It follows that if the offeree uses another method to communicate acceptance, for example, by posting a letter, the place where the letter was received is where the contract is formed.

B. Invitations to Treat

638. The online request for tender (RFT) is a classic example of an invitation to treat. While not a contract, the negotiations and agreements that follow an RFT may result in a contract.

639. Similarly, websites and electronic mailing lists may be interpreted as advertisements and shop fronts that display goods and prices and give customers an opportunity to look at their goods before purchase. Such activities are then simply invitations to treat rather than offers. So is the example of an auctioneer's call for bids on an online auction site. This is a first step toward an offer and eventual purchase.

C. Electronic Agents

640. One issue that is emerging is the question of whether machines can accept offers. In the so-called ticket cases, in *Thornton v. Shoe Lane Parking* [1971] 1 All ER 686, the court held that a car park machine had made an offer which was accepted when the customer put money into the slot in the machine.

641. Where online businesses are bound by contracts 'accepted' by their computers, such businesses are also bound even if, for example, a computer were to misbehave in a peculiar way because of a hardware fault. Computers may be programmed to reject contracts in which the customer may have altered some of its terms. Online business contracts, therefore, are often inflexible, and terms cannot be added or deleted by customers. Any such variations would thus require a face-to-face discussion, negating the very essence of engaging in online business.

642. Sometimes computers may be programmed to carry out transactions automatically. For example, electronic agents might be used to initiate or respond to electronic messages without review by a human; as an online shopping agent programmed to surf the Internet and make purchases; or, as an inventory control system programmed to place orders when stocks reach set levels, for example, in electronic data interchange (EDI) systems.

643. Smart self-executing contracts that are programmed with electronic agents have now evolved and acquired a degree of sophistication that these sorts of contracts are becoming widely used. A later discussion in this chapter on smart contracts is given in §6 on Smart contracts and block chains below.

644. The legal status of electronic agents remains untested. However, if an electronic agent has been programmed to respond to certain criteria and circumstances, then by extension such acts are by, and with a person's authority to implement their intentions and, therefore, can make and accept contractual offers on their behalf. The proviso is that such contracts are unexceptional and without the need to modify terms and conditions.

D. Other Methods of Communication

645. Courts have examined whether the postal rule is applicable to other methods of communication such as telex and facsimile documents.[397] Thus, whether the communication is instantaneous will be a significant factor in determining whether the postal acceptance rule will apply, but this is not decisive because no test case has been mounted with, for example, 'clickwrap' agreements.

646. The practice of the fax-then-mail procedure designed to ensure a paper record of an agreement invites a different legal problem. A party seeking to resile from the agreement communicated by fax could argue that the fax was not the final communication and that the deal was open until the original paper was mailed. In such a case, the parties may need to agree to an operative communication method. Arguably, the postal acceptance rule may apply to an email message and an acceptance effective once the email was sent.

647. The jurisdiction of the contract in that case will be that of the offeree. It has been argued that the rule should not apply to email acceptance because this would place an unfair burden on offerors.[398] Moreover, the sender of an email would know if a message has been received via error messages received or automatic responses to message receipts. At the same time, an email message may become lost or garbled in transmission, and this may again place greater burdens on the offeror than may be warranted if the postal acceptance rule were to be applied to acceptances by electronic means.

648. An Australian Direct Marketing Association (ADMA) Code of Practice 2006 was developed to set standards of conduct for direct marketers, minimize the risk of breaching legislation, promote a culture of best practice, serve as a benchmark in settling disputes and increase business and consumer confidence in doing business with ADMA members who are bound to the provisions of the Code.[399] Where there is any conflict or inconsistency between the Code and any Commonwealth, State or Territory legislation or regulation, that legislation or regulation shall

---

397. *Entores Ltd. v. Miles Far East Co.* [1955] 2 QB 327 suggests that the postal acceptance rule will not apply to methods of communication which are 'virtually instantaneous' – phone, fax and telex, but not by telegram.

398. Downing, S & Harrington, J (2000) The Postal Rule in Electronic Commerce: A Re-Consideration, 5 *Commun. L.* 43, at 44.

399. *See* ADMA Code of Practice 2006 at http://www.adma.com.au/assets/Uploads/Comply-Documents/ADMA-Code-of-Practice3.pdf.

prevail to the extent of the conflict or inconsistency. ADMA members must comply with all Commonwealth, State or Territory legislation relating to business and direct marketing practices.

II. Valuable Consideration

649. Valuable consideration is merely something given in return for a promise, the price for a promise indicating that something more than mere good intentions is involved. In law, valuable consideration may consist either in some right, interest, profit, or benefit accruing to one party, or some forbearance, detriment, loss, or responsibility given, suffered, or undertaken by the other.[400]

650. On the Internet valuable consideration could be the giving of a credit card number even though no funds are transferred. This may occur when credit card numbers are sought as 'security' to further the purposes of the negotiations. A problem that may arise is when erroneous or stolen credit card numbers are used. Here the conventional practice is for the merchant-offeror and credit card provider to assume the burdens of the risks of non-payment for goods and services rendered.

III. Consensus

651. The central question is to what extent has there been agreement or consensus between the parties. Ergo, if there are outstanding issues to which there is no agreement, and which is considered essential, then it will be extremely unlikely that there can be a legally enforceable contract.

652. Arguably in an online contract, silence may amount to acceptance despite the general rule to the contrary. To protect oneself, sellers should generally spell out their terms and conditions clearly on the website, and it is assumed that the seller will accept his or her own terms and conditions and will accept any order placed by customers. Because of such risks, it may be prudent for sellers to specify how they will accept offers made by customers. Equally, mere inaction cannot constitute acceptance. Thus, the statement 'if I do not hear from you, I assume that you agreed to this contract' is ineffectual and unenforceable at law.

§3. Requirements for a Written Document

653. Sometimes agreements cannot be enforced unless in writing. For example, the sale of a house or land must be in writing.

400. *Currie v. Misa* (1875) L.R. 10 Ex. 162 per Lush J.

654. The formal requirement of writing may be satisfied in an electronic environment with the use of digital signatures section 9 of the ETA and corresponding State and Territory legislation. The ETA also provides for recognizing electronic signatures under section 10.

655. Oral contracts may be entered into and are bound by the 'parole' evidence rule. This is a rule of evidence that prohibits any party to a written contract from adducing evidence to contradict, vary, add to, or subtract from its terms. The parole evidence rule is, however, no more than a general rule to which there are numerous exceptions. At present it is evident that this rule is inapplicable in an electronic environment that has yet to develop sophisticated voice-recognition technology to the extent where it may be used as a matter of course in business negotiations and contract formation purposes.

§4. Terms of a Contract

656. The terms of a contract are designed to give efficacy to the intention of the parties. The *terms of any contract* can be viewed as either being express or implied. The former is relatively easier to deal with since they are the ones that the parties have discussed and decided to include in the contract. *Implied terms* may be a bit more intractable as these could be imposed by relevant legislation.

I. Express Terms

657. Under English and Australian laws, where there is a written contract and on what appears whole and complete on its face, a court will presume that the words contain the entire contract and are not to be varied by any oral terms.

658. A trend emerging in the process of contract formation in e-commerce is where the vendor will require its customers to download terms and conditions from a website and then to accept these by signing a hard copy and returning it to the other party by post. This act creates a higher degree of certainty in the transactions, for not only is there notice made of such terms, but also the agreement to specific terms of the contract. Doing so will avoid misinterpreting representations made either in writing or in negotiations and later in the execution of the contract.

659. It is necessary to take note of the difference between a term of a contract and a mere representation. For example, in the purchase of a computer system, a buyer relied on the promises of a salesperson that the system could do certain things. When the system was found to have been unable to perform such things, there may be no requirement in the contract that it did so.[401] To form part of the contract, both parties must have intended that the statements of the salesperson formed part of the contract. Thus, in e-contracts where there are no signed documents between parties,

401. *Christopher Hill Ltd v. Ashington Piggeries Ltd* [1969] AC 441.

the terms and conditions may be incorporated into a contract provided that reasonable notice of the terms is given to each party.

660. Two further issues are of material importance. The first issue is the timing and placement of the statement. Any representation made during early negotiations but not repeated later is unlikely to form part of the contract. Likewise, a representation made after the formation of the contract will unlikely form part of the contract. Thus, customers should be made aware of relevant documents or web pages containing contractual terms and conditions; otherwise, these may not be part of the contract so formed. There is also the question of whether the notice on the web page, for example, would objectively be expected to contain contractual terms. In commercial websites it is expected that a reasonable person would easily discover such terms and conditions.

661. A second issue concerns the skill and expertise of the person making the statement. Where the person making the representation is placed in a position to know the truth of the statement, a court will be more willing to infer an intention that the statement forms part of the contract. This is especially important in the sale of electronic products, where technical specifications can be accurately given rather than simply a general statement as to the reliability of the system.

662. Online the terms to a contract may be particularly difficult to find especially where a website that offers to supply goods and services has its terms located elsewhere on the website or in an obscure hypertext link. There is no certain way to ensure that the customer has accessed these terms, let alone read them. Therefore, the question arises as to whether the offer and terms have been adequately communicated to the offeree. To ensure that customers to websites read such terms and conditions web customers may be forced to scroll through a set of screens and click the '*I Agree*' button before being permitted to proceed to the next step. This 'clickwrap' technique provides an effective way of ensuring that terms and conditions of the proposed contract have been communicated to the customers. Numerous cases have demonstrated the legal validity of clickwrap acceptances.[402]

II. Implied Terms

663. Implied terms are those which are not agreed to by the parties explicitly at the time of agreement, but which the courts and legislators have decided to import on behalf of the parties.

402. *Hotmail Corp. v. van Money Pie Inc.* 1998 WL 388389, 47 USPQ 2d 1020 (BNA) (ND Cal. 16 Apr. 1998) but not *Ticketmaster Corp. v. Tickets.com Inc.* 54 USPQ 2d (BNA) (1344 US D. Cal. 27 Mar. 2000) because the information was placed at the end of the web page.

664. Implied terms may arise in several ways, including industry practice, terms implied by the courts, and implication by statute.[403] Online there are certain accepted practices and usages that are familiar to all in the industry. For example, software development contracts neither assign copyright nor source codes to users. On a literal interpretation of the contract, the user who is paying for a software package has neither copyright nor usage rights to the program. However, there is an implied understanding that the user may have a right to the program along with a duty to keep the source codes confidential. A further implied term may be that the user has no right to sublicense the software to other parties to use the program.

665. Implied terms might become contentious in bespoke software. Bespoke software, by definition, is supplied pursuant to a direct contract between a programmer and a client.[404] The software may not exist at the time of the contract. Property rights might vest in the client in the contract[405] or the agreement could only be in the leasing and use of the software.[406]

III. Shrink-Wrap and Web-Wrap Terms

666. Software licences were used originally as a means of protecting suppliers when copyright laws did not cover computer software. The supplier 'lent' or gave 'on license' or 'bailed' the goods for the use of the licensee in return for a fee. In recent times, software suppliers introduced licences as a means of reminding buyers of the rules governing copyright as customer protection laws. Thus, 'box-top' licences and 'break-seal' licences purport to bind consumers to a contract when the customer opens the software package and hence signifies acceptance of terms and conditions.

667. The enforceability of ordinary principles of contract law with the advent of mass marketing on the Internet has brought in the issue of whether there is appropriate notice of, and assent, to the terms. Especially when inspecting electronic goods, one may need to open the box or break the seal to read the conditions attached to the contract.

668. Shrink-wrap agreements commonly accompany software products in which terms are sealed inside shrink-wrapping and/or appear when software is installed. The terms of these agreements are not accessible until after a product is purchased and opened/installed. The outside of the wrapping may or may not indicate that terms are forthcoming. Where terms are displayed upon installation, the user may also be required to click an '*I Agree*' or similar icon before installation can be completed.

---

403. Knight, P & Fitzsimons, J (1990) *The Legal Environment of Computing* 124-126 (Sydney: Addison-Wesley Pub. Coy.).
404. Smith, G (1996) *Software Contracts, in Computer Law* Ch. 2, 53-80 at 74 (Reed C ed., 3d ed., Blackstone Press Ltd).
405. *Saphena Computing Ltd v. Allied Collection Agencies Ltd* [1995] FSR 616.
406. *John Richardson Computers Ltd v. Flanders* [1993] FSR 497 at 516-19.

669. Clickwrap agreements indicate a party's assent to terms of an agreement offered online by clicking on an '*I Agree*' or similar icon.

670. Browse-wrap agreements are used by many websites and deem that the act of browsing the website constitutes acceptance of their terms. While broadly the law of contract holds that terms cannot be incorporated into a contract after acceptance of an offer, the question of incorporation of terms is particularly relevant to shrink-wrap and browse-wrap agreements, where purported terms are not notified until after a product is purchased or until after access to a website has been granted.

671. As Australian courts have yet to consider whether shrink-wrapped terms can be properly incorporated into a contract, the generally accepted position is that these terms may be enforceable because of the so-called ticket cases. In Australia, the purchaser is generally considered to be the offeror, and the vendor the offeree, for the purposes of retail sales. However, the ticket cases have held that a ticket received after payment of a service may represent an offer containing terms that are accepted when the recipient goes ahead with the contract. A term may be incorporated if reasonable notice of the term is given and there is a reasonable opportunity to reject the term, prior to the assumption of binding contractual obligations. The more unusual and/or harsher a term, the greater the effort that must be made to bring it to the attention of the party to be bound.

672. Such developments have given rise to two concerns about mass-market agreements. The first is that the public cannot or may not ordinarily be able to negotiate their own terms. The second is that the standard terms may override exceptions granted in an Act or to impose other undesirable restrictions.[407]

673. As previously noted, certain jurisdictions have required that all terms and conditions to the contract be placed outside the package to overcome the rule against introducing terms and conditions after a contract has been agreed to. Licence conditions are included to give warranty protection in limiting liability, to control the use of the software, and, under consumer protection laws, the terms under which goods may be returned because of defects. The issue revolves around whether reasonable notice of the terms was provided to the customers prior to, or contemporaneously with, the formation of the contract. The reliance on shrink-wrap contracts suggests that contracts are formed once the customer opens the package and discovers the preprinted terms and conditions.[408]

674. In B2B transactions where each business may use its own forms and standard contracts, there is a danger that there will be potential conflicts in terms of a contract. In such situations, it is essential that the conflicting terms and conditions

407. Founds, G (1999) Shrink-wrap and Click-wrap Agreements: 2B or Not 2B? 52 *Fed. Commun. LJ* 100.

408. *See* US cases that reject the view on additional terms in shrink-wrap contracts: *Step-Saver Data Systems Inc. v. Wyse Technology and Software Link Inc.*, 939 F.2d 91 (3rd Cir. 1991); and *Arizona Retail Systems Inc. v. Software Link Inc.*, 831 F. Supp. 759 (D Ariz 1993).

be avoided through the development and use of standardized forms that both businesses can use. This is to avoid the classic legal dilemma of the 'battle of the forms'.

§5. Collateral Issues

675. Contractual issues discussed previously, however, cannot be taken in isolation. This is because there are interactions between the law of contract and tort, between contract and statutory provisions, and the issue of copyright and ownership after a contract has been fulfilled.

I. Ownership of Property

676. Where copyright has been assigned, the customer should require the delivery of the source code. If no assignment is made, an express licence in comprehensive terms is thought mandatory and desirable with the source code put in escrow generally known as source code escrow.[409] This is a mechanism by which the source code of a computer program and all relevant documents are given to an independent third party for safekeeping in the unlikely event that the supplier goes out of business or is unable to support the software.

677. A further development is 'Internet escrow' especially where auctions and e-commerce are undertaken. The escrow works by placing money in the control of an independent and licensed third party to protect both the buyer and seller in a transaction. When both parties verify that the transaction has been completed according to the terms of their respective agreement, the money is released. If at any point there is a dispute between the parties in the transaction, the process moves into a dispute resolution mode. The outcome of the dispute resolution process will determine what happens to the money in escrow.

II. Minors and Agents

678. In the electronic environment, it would be remiss not to mention capacity and authorization to enter contracts. The common law presumption is that a person who enters a contract has full capacity to do so. However, there are a group of persons who may be barred from entering contracts, such as minors, mentally disabled persons, drunks and bankrupts. Each of these actors gives rise to unique issues in the context of contracts concluded online. As the offeror may have no knowledge of

---

409. 'Escrow' is an old legal term with origins in the law of deeds. A deed is binding upon delivery, so an escrow agent is usually an independent third party who holds a sealed deed and guarantees its delivery to an intended party once certain conditions are met. This is useful in cases where a software developer goes out of business and the customer needs access to the source code to modify and update.

the identity of the customer and the offeror will need to explicitly ask for more information and a confirmation that the person has capacity to enter contracts. The issue of the capacity of minors is therefore of most significance in e-commerce. In addition, the use of debit cards by minors, whether it be their own or those of an adult (but used without permission) may raise further issues.

679. All Australian jurisdictions have statutes that set the age of majority at 18.[410] Transactions are usually binding on a child only if they can be shown to be for the child's benefit. Where no such benefit exists (for example, the purchase of a car for which the child could neither possibly complete nor practically use), then the contract is not binding, and the merchant may have to bear the loss from a failure of the minor to comply with the terms of the contract.

680. In the case of agents, common law suggests that where an agent has actual authority to conclude a contract on behalf of a principal, the latter will be bound by the contract formed. However, it may arise that where an agent does not in fact have authority but concludes a contract, the validity of the contract may hinge on other indicia. The absence of ostensible authority will place the agent personally liable to contracts agreed to.

681. On the Internet, businesses would have to overtly ask for such authority before a contract can be said to have been formed. The presumptions of section 128 of the *Corporations Act* 2001 (Cth) may apply. Persons dealing with a company are entitled to make assumptions that the person is assumed to be an officer or agent of the company they are dealing with. To support this assumption companies and businesses have developed policies and practices in the use of email and the Internet. Agents and employees are provided with online identifiers and overt authority to enter contracts with the world at large.

III. Consumer Protection

682. Consumer protection laws also impinge on e-contract formation. In particular, the *CCA* especially Part V Schedule 2 Pt 2-2 that deals with consumer protection and how corporations may engage in certain conduct in trade and commerce.[411]

683. The Australian government has recently initiated the consultation process to strengthening protections against unfair contract terms for consumers and small

410. *See*, for example, *Age of Majority Act* 1974 (ACT); *Minors (Property and Contracts) Act* 1970 (NSW). Legislation in New South Wales, South Australia and Tasmania provides that a person acting as a guarantor of a minor's contract can be enforced against the guarantor. Minors can also generally be sued on cheques, bills of exchange, or promissory notes. The signature of a minor is valid to draw, issue, or indorse.

411. *See also* Finch, B (1999) Consumer Protection on the Internet, in *Going Digital 2000: Legal Issues for e-Commerce, Software and the Internet* (A. Fitzgerald, A *et al.* eds, Sydney: Prospect Media).

businesses.[412] This exposure draft legislation would amend the Australian Consumer Law and the *Australian Securities and Investments Commission Act* 2001 (Cth) to implement the agreed reforms.

§6. Smart Contracts and Blockchain

684. Recently an emerging technology known as blockchain has the potential to revolutionize e-contracts for financial transactions and services. Such a distributed ledger technology (DLT) may be applied wherever a verified and trusted transaction is required such as smart contracts.

685. Smart contracts are those whose terms are recorded in a computer language that can be automatically executed by a computing system using a suitable distributed ledger system.[413] The term blockchain has been given to such a distributed ledger system.

686. Blockchain is a distributed recordkeeping system where each user can keep a copy of the records, which uses encryption of communications to provide for auditable transactions. The digitally recorded data in packages are called blocks. Each block is 'chained' to the next block using a cryptographic signature. This allows blockchains to be used like a ledger which can be shared and accessed by anyone with the appropriate permissions.

687. Using blockchain, each smart contract is traceable to a user, each set of transactions is verifiable, and the data in the blockchain cannot be edited without a user's knowledge. These blockchain features allow two or more parties without a trusted relationship to engage in reliable transactions without relying on intermediaries or central authority (for example, a bank or government agency). The transactions execute automatically on the occurrence of predefined triggers without third-party intervention. These actions are hard-wired into the code that execute the smart contract. A good example is the electronic transfer of payment by a certain date. Another is that the smart contract could act as an effective escrow agent for conditional payments in the execution of a contract.

688. Smart contracts have been used in security trades, buying and selling real estate and pricing and the purchasing of certain types of advertisements on Google negotiated autonomously between computers without any human intervention.[414]

---

412. *See Treasury Laws Amendment (Measures 3 for a later sitting) Bill* 2021*: Unfair contract terms reforms* at https://treasury.gov.au/sites/default/files/2021-08/c2021-201582_edl.pdf. Consultations closed on 20 Sep. 2021 with the progress of the bill being anticipated.

413. *See* Allens & Linklaters LLP Blockchain Reaction at https://www.allens.com.au/globalassets/pdfs/specials/blockchainreport.pdf.

414. *See* Giancaspro, M (2018) That contract your computer made could get you in a legal bind, *The Conversation* (April 11) at https://theconversation.com/that-contract-your-computer-made-could-get-you-in-a-legal-bind-94583.

689. *Ethereum* is a blockchain-based platform that executes smart contracts and transfers value using digital currency. Written in a computer programming language known as Solidity an agreement can be precisely defined and automatically executed *sans* uncertainty engendered with the use of ambiguous words.[415]

690. In Australia, arguably, the regulatory framework governing the use of smart contracts is the *Electronic Transactions Act* 1999 (Cth) section 15C which provides for contracts that are formed entirely through the interaction of automated message system. Such contracts are '... not invalid, void or unenforceable on the sole ground that no natural person reviewed or intervened in each of the individual actions carried out by the automated message systems or the resulting contract'.

691. The legal risks that may arise from such smart contracts could include among others:

- the validity of an implied agency relationship in certain circumstances such as the implied authority written in the coding of the smart contract provided to a 'computer';[416]
- the intention to create legal relationships in the autonomous execution of the code in the smart contract software;
- the extent to which smart contracts are valid and enforceable under existing contract law; and,
- the liability of a principal where a smart contract produces an outcome which is undesirable or not by the intention of the parties.

I. Australian Guidelines

692. The Australian Treasury and CSIRO's Data61 have undertaken a review to examine distributed ledger technology's general potential usage and its implications for government and industry.[417]

693. The Digital Transformation Authority released a guide – *Blockchain Overview: Australian Government Guide* 2018. The DTA has observed that 'blockchain is good for low trust engagement where you do not know who you are dealing with, you have low trust in that person or business, but you have a series of ledgers that can give you some validation. [However] generally speaking when government is engaging with someone, we want to have a trusted relationship with them'.[418]

---

415. *See* Smart Contracts at https://ethereum.org/en/developers/docs/smart-contracts/anatomy/#top.
416. *See* above in Chapter 2 Electronic Contracts §2. Elements of a Contract I. Offer and Acceptance *supra.* for a discussion of whether machines can enter a contract and the roles of agents.
417. *See* Department of Industry, Innovation & Science (2017) *The Digital Economy: Opening up the conversation,* https://industry.gov.au/innovation/Digital-Economy/Documents/Digital-Economy-Strategy-Consultation-Paper.pdf; and, http://www.data61.csiro.au/en/Our-Work/Safety-and-security/Secure-Systems-and-Platforms/Blockchain.
418. Hamilton, P (2019) Public sector digital transformation: a quick guide, Parliamentary Library's Cyber and Digital Research Group, Politics and Public Administration Section at https://www.aph.gov.au/About_Parliament/Parliamentary_Departments/Parliamentary_Library/ pubs/rp/rp1819/Quick_Guides/PSDigitalTransformation.

694. The Australian National Blockchain Roadmap highlights some of the opportunities blockchain technology can enable across the whole economy and provides the signposts for the future development of this technology.[419]

II. Emergent Issues

695. Some emergent issues with blockchains have been identified including:

- The legal standing of smart contracts and the role of each government agency in the development of smart contracts and associated templates.
- Where a smart contract may not be capable of recognizing when it is an unfair smart contract.
- The challenges of understanding and resolving regulatory problems for a rapidly evolving technology and the need for an innovative regulatory system that focusses on opportunities.
- The identity of participants in blockchain systems and the manner in which to trust the identity of participants. This identity issue also involves the privacy of information on a blockchain. Such privacy concerns include maintaining the balance between transparency in open blockchains, the security of such systems, provenance, integrity and accuracy of data. A further consideration is its use as evidence for regulatory and enforcement purposes..

419. *See* PM&C at https://digitaleconomy.pmc.gov.au/sites/default/files/2021-07/digital-economy-strategy.pdf. *See also* Assir, H, Nanda, P & Mohanty, M (2021) A novel e-Government Framework using Blockchain *Journal of Information Assurance & Cyber Security* Vol. 2021 at https://ibimapublishing.com/articles/JIACS/2021/164568/164568.pdf.

Chapter 3. Digital Signatures

§1. Introduction

696. The *Electronic Transactions Act* 1999 (Cth)[420] section 10 provides the requirements for an e-signature. As enacted in the respective State and Territory *Electronic Transaction Acts,* a stated a requirement under a Commonwealth, State or Territory law for a person's signature to be provided, will be satisfied by an electronic communication that uses a method which identifies the person and indicates their approval of the information communicated.

697. Specific legislative provisions will override the general provisions on signatures under the ETA legislation.

698. However, digital signatures raise other important issues that are unaddressed by the ETA. In implementing public key infrastructure (PKI) and public key authentication framework (PKAF) (discussed in the next chapter), the government has put in place certain principles and standards by which electronic signatures may be used in electronic communications with public agencies. The concern is the extent to which an individual may be able to have more than one digital persona – individually as a person and corporately as a company or business entity. Next, there is the issue of whether the digital signature is to be used for security and authentication or whether there will be privacy concerns.[421]

699. PKI is an integrated system of non-government certification bodies that have developed methods for cross-verification of an authority. This system ensures authenticity by assuming that each authority wishes to protect and enhance its reputation. This assumption is then tested as each authority checks the security of another authority's system. In this way, one authority often carries the seals of others as a testament of its own reliability. In return, that authority will test and seal numerous others.

700. Digital signatures are perceived to be foolproof. However, the very basis of its integrity depends on how secure is the process by which the e-signature was created. While it is true that even with handwritten signatures there may be forgeries similar to the vulnerability of biometric systems, users need to be reassured of the security of e-signatures. Authentication of e-signatures is very different from its security. The use of e-signatures in electronic communications with a public agency suggests a loss of anonymity.

---

420. *See* text of the Act at https://www.legislation.gov.au/Series/C2004A00553.

421. There remain unresolved privacy issues. *See* Australian Privacy Commissioner, *Privacy Issues in the Use of Public Key Infrastructure for Individuals*, 2001 at https://www.privacy.gov.au/publications/dpki.html.

§2. Case Notes

701. An Australian court was prepared to accept the 'typed' name of the sender at the end of an email as the sender's signature in *McGuren v. Simpson* [2004] NSWSC 35 at [22].

702. The issue of whether a resolution of a Board member that had been sent by email was validly received was reviewed in *Legal Services Board v. Forste*r [2010] VSC 102. The judge held that the Board had consented to the Board member providing their signature by email and it was clear from the email message that the Board member had intended the typed name to represent their signature.

703. In *eBay International AG v. Creative Festival Entertainment Pty Ltd* (2006) 170 FCR 450; [2006] FCA 1768 at [48] Rares J held that a contract was formed when the consumer clicked the 'Send this Order' button on the website.

704. In *Getup Ltd v. Electoral Commissioner* (2010) 268 ALR 797; [2010] FCA 869 Perram J ruled in favour of a political activist group Getup by holding that the requirement to sign the electoral enrolment form was satisfied by a member of the group using a digital pen on a laptop computer and transmitted to the Electoral Commission through the Internet.

705. The case of *Leo v. Paulsen* [2010] QCAT involved the making of an offer of settlement to another party sent by email to the applicant. The Tribunal held that the offer was valid for the purposes of the relevant Queensland Act and was signed in accordance with section 14 of the *Electronic Transactions Act* 2001 (Qld). Similarly, it was possible for a party to submit an objection to a development proposal in electronic form via the City Council's online facility in the case of *Harding v. Brisbane City Council* [2008] QPEC 75.

706. There are also some pitfalls when signing contracts and deeds. In *Bendigo & Adelaide Bank v. Rickard* [2019] SASC 123 a court held that a deed was not properly signed as it did not meet the traditional legal requirements of signed, sealed and delivered as the electronic signature on the deed was not executed on a single document.[422]

§3. Model Laws

707. Through the *Corporations Amendment (Meetings and Documents) Act* 2022 (Cth) enacted in February 2022, the *Corporations Act* 2001 (Cth) has been amended to permanently allow companies and their agents to sign documents electronically.[423] The *Corporations Amendment Act* 2022 has introduced amongst others, technology-neutral signing with either signing by hand or using electronic

422. *See* AUSTLII at http://www.austlii.edu.au/cgi-bin/viewdoc/au/cases/sa/SASC/2019/123.html.
423. *See* text of the Act at https://www.legislation.gov.au/Details/C2022A00009.

means, entire contents requirements previously required under the *Treasury Laws Amendment (2021 Measures No. 1) Act* 2021 (Cth) have been removed, split execution is now permissible with two officers signing on behalf of a company using different methods; and electronic signing by an agent is recognized.

708. Remote witnessing is now permanent in NSW with the passage in November 2021 of the *Electronic Transactions Amendment (Remote Witnessing) Act* 2021 (NSW). This amendment permits remote witnessing of certain documents, including deeds and agreements. Similarly in Queensland under the *Justice and Other Legislation Amendment Act* 2021 (Qld) remote witnessing is made permanent.

709. The UNCITRAL Model Law on Electronic Signatures was adopted by the UN General Assembly on 5 July 2001.[424] The principles of functional equivalence and technology neutrality have been retained.[425]

710. The UNCITRAL Model Law on Electronic Signatures was adopted by Australia on 5 July 2001.[426]

424. UNCITRAL (2001) *Model Law on Electronic Signatures* (2001), at http://www.uncitral.org/english/texts/electcom/ml-elecsig-e.pdf.
425. UNCITRAL (2001) *Model Law on Electronic Signatures,* is available at: http://www.uncitral.org/uncitral/en/uncitral_texts/electronic_commerce/2001Model_signatures.html.
426. *Ibid.* UNCITRAL (2001).

Chapter 4. Trust Services: Certification and Security Tools

§1. Introduction

711. E-commerce is dependent on hardware and software tools as well as administrative and legal infrastructure to provide the appropriate mix of rights and responsibilities. Such elements are also necessary to provide both businesses and consumers the appropriate level of trust and certainty of outcome so that businesses and consumers will have confidence in e-commerce transactions. As the transactions are undertaken electronically and hence are 'faceless' interactions, offers and acceptances, payments and other business require some sort of security technology and procedures. Trust services, certification and security tools provide these assurances which are discussed next.

§2. Public Key Infrastructure (PKI)

I. Developments in Australia

712. Public key infrastructure (PKI) is a set of roles, policies, hardware, software and procedures needed to create, manage, distribute, use, store and revoke digital certificates and manage public key encryption.[427]

713. In May 1998, the Office of Government Information Technology (OGIT) released the Gatekeeper Report (1998), which outlined a strategy for the development and use of public key technology (PKT), or a generic PKI, for electronic transactions with, between and within Commonwealth agencies.[428]

714. The Gatekeeper PKI Framework governs the way the Australian government uses digital keys and certificates to assure the identity of subscribers to authentication services.[429] The Project Gatekeeper established an authority to develop an accreditation process for private certification authorities (CAs) to gain accreditation. Policy requirement in the Gatekeeper PKI Framework states that Australian government agencies must only use digital keys and certificates issued by a gatekeeper-accredited organization for PKI authentication. The framework sets out the requirements for organizations to become accredited to issue digital keys and certificates for use in government for PKI-based authentication.

715. PKI subscribers can include individual users, organizations and devices, such as applications and computers.

---

427. *See* PKI at https://www.ssh.com/academy/pki.

428. Gatekeeper Public Key Infrastructure framework at https://www.dta.gov.au/our-projects/digital-identity/join-identity-federation/accreditation-and-onboarding/gatekeeper-public-key-infrastructure-framework.

429. *See* Digital Transformation Agency at https://www.dta.gov.au/sites/default/files/files/digital-identity/Gatekeeper/Gatekeeper-PKI-Framework-v3_1.pdf.

II. Workability of Public Key Infrastructures

716. PKI promises much but problems remain. Identified security and policy issues take time, money and training for the people involved. These problems have led some researchers to be concerned whether PKI as it currently exists will meet the standard required under the ETA that the digital signature be in all circumstances 'as reliable as was appropriate for the purposes for which the information was communicated'.[430] Other problems with PKI include its cost, the fact that businesses with subsidiaries may need multiple certificates, and that public keys are required and must be distributed to all parties.

§3. Digital Certificates, e-Procurement and e-Tendering

717. Digital Certificates (DC) provide a partial solution to identity problems. DC are issued as part of the Goods and Services Tax (GST) registration process. Such a certificate purports to prove the identity of any person when dealings are undertaken over the Internet. The certificate not only enables businesses to identify themselves to government agencies such as the ATO, but also to other business partners. Companies will be able to display their Australian Business Number (ABN) and their DC on their web pages.[431]

718. The DCs are a device to allow all Australian businesses to conduct secure transactions with the government. This is a necessary component of the legal and technical infrastructure required for online procurement.

719. The DC scheme applied initially to Commonwealth agencies only.

720. Electronic procurement (e-procurement) refers to the automation of any part of the procurement to payment process with e-commerce tools. Among an array of such tools include electronic catalogues, electronic purchase orders and automated approvals. As the name implies an e-catalogue provides a list of supplier products that is accessible through the Internet. E-catalogues are best sent to end users for retail goods that are described as 'high volume low value' products. Such e-catalogues may be managed in-house, outsourced to a third party, or hosted and managed by the supplier.[432]

---

430. *See* Smith, (2001) Public Key Infrastructures: Debunking the Myths, 3 *Internet L. Bull.* 122.
431. Davidson, J (1999) Taking Care of Business on the Web, *Australian Financial Review* (23 Jul.).
432. *See* Australian Government, Department of Finance and Administration (2002) *Procurement,* at http://www.finance.gov.au/procurement/; Department of Finance and Administration (DOFA) (2012) *Commonwealth Procurement Guidelines and Best Practice Guidance,* Canberra, Australia; DOFA (2012) Australian Government *Commonwealth Procurement Rules*, at http://www.finance.gov.au/sites/default/files/cpr_commonwealth_procurement_rules_july_2012.pdf; and Vaidya, K, Sajeev, ASM & Callender, G (2006) Critical Factors that Influence E-procurement Implementation Success in the Public Sector, 6 *Journal of Public Procurement* 70-99 (2006).

721. The key element to the Australian government's e-procurement strategy is an *e-tendering* system to procure and purchase goods and services. Mostly regulated by common law principles of contract law and protocols such as the Australian Standard Code of Tendering (AS 4120-1994) and other state specific and industry-specific codes several Australian e-tendering systems are in use. The Commonwealth's AusTender system and the NSW's e-Tendering website are examples.[433]

§4. E-COMMERCE TRUST MECHANISMS AND SECURITY TOOLS

722. Other electronic tools for security and authentication include secure sockets layer (SSL) and secure electronic transaction (SET) protocols for sending sensitive financial data such as credit card information over the Internet.

I. Secure Socket Layers (SSL)

723. SSL protocol is a non-proprietary (open) worldwide standard for authentication, data encryption-decryption and privacy protection over a network such as the Internet.[434]

724. SSL provides a high level of data integrity and security by encrypting the entire data stream and by sending it over a secure channel. SSL has since been superseded by the transport layer security (TLS) protocol.

725. Versions of both SSL and TLS are in widespread use in applications such as web browsing, email, Internet faxing, instant messaging and voice over Internet protocol (VOIP) telephone services. SSL connections are established through the purchasing of SSL certificates from a certificate authority before they are associated with a web server.

II. Secure Electronic Transaction (SET) Protocol

726. SET protocol is a non-proprietary (open) industry standard developed jointly by MasterCard and Visa for secure online e-commerce, credit card transactions over a network such as the Internet.[435]

727. Under SET, a buyer provides credit card numbers to the merchant in encoded form. The merchant cannot decode the numbers but can forward these to the card issuer for verification and approval. SET by itself is not a payment system

433. *See* the Commonwealth's AusTender site at http://www.tenders.gov.au/federal/index.cfm and NSW's e-Tendering system at http://www.tenders.nsw.gov.au.
434. *See* Security Encyclopaedia at https://www.hypr.com/secure-sockets-layer/.
435. *See* Investopedia at https://www.investopedia.com/terms/s/secure-electronic-transaction-set.asp.

but a set of protocols. SET uses DCs and public key cryptography to allow parties to identify themselves to each other and to exchange information securely.

728. Key features of SET include the confidentiality of information, the integrity of the data transmitted, cardholder account authentication and merchant authentication.

III. Virtual Private Networks (VPN)

729. VPN are systems that allow businesses to access their internal networks and computers over the Internet or other public network using encrypted ‘tunnels’ to ensure that data cannot be accessed without authorization. VPN involve the use of advanced encryption and ‘tunnelling’ technologies to use the Internet to create a ‘virtual’ private network that uses the public facility of the Internet.[436]

730. Some government departments in Australia and many businesses with mobile workforces use VPN to create mobile offices where employees can still communicate in a secure environment. Unfortunately, VPN can be expensive to implement and are not suitable for B2C transactions.

IV. Passwords and Passcodes

731. Passwords and passcodes are the most common form of security protection, but also one of the least secure. The advantages of password and passcode protection are that it is easily understood, easy to change and inexpensive. The disadvantages are that it can be compromised by users, does not authenticate the data being transferred, and can often be transmitted insecurely. However, ‘two-factor’ authentication tools permit validation of passwords and passcodes whereby a security code is used to the authenticate identity of the user. The codes are sent to a mobile phone and the code received is then entered on the relevant section of the webpage to the authenticate identity of the user.

§5. Secure E-mail Access

732. A common element of much of e-commerce is the use of email. Email is particularly vulnerable because it is written in Simple Mail Transport Protocol (SMPT), a protocol that enables email to be sent between different servers that is encoded in plain text in the American Standard Code for Information Interchange (ASCII) standard data-transmission code, used by computers to represent both textual data and input which in turn is readable by most computers.[437]

---

436. *See* VPN Tunnelling discussion at http://compnetworking.about.com/od/vpn/a/vpn_tunneling.htm.
437. *See* ASCII at https://www.thefreedictionary.com/SMPT, and https://www.britannica.com/topic/ASCII.

733. Unauthorized access to someone else's email can give rise to a host of legal issues, depending on the context. If the information is confidential, a breach of confidence action could be brought. If the information is protected by contract, then contract remedies would ensue. If one wilfully intercepted the email, then the *Telecommunications (Interception) Act* 1979 (Cth) sanctions may apply.

734. Where conduct involves the unauthorized access to a computer, various criminal laws may apply. In criminal matters the *Crimes Legislation Amendment Act* 1989 (Cth) outlaws wrongful gaining of access to computers,[438] altering data,[439] or impeding access to computers.[440] The *Crimes Act* 1914 (Cth) prohibits the use of communications for improper purposes, the intentional or reckless causing of communications in the course of carriage to be received by a person or service other than to whom it was directed, and the wrongful sending of signals to satellite without lawful authority or excuse.[441]

735. Monitoring the email and Internet use of employees is also arguably a breach of the *Telecommunications (Interception) Act* 1979 (Cth). The Act prohibits the interception of communications passing over a telecommunications service (section 7).

736. The screening of employee emails is an issue relating to employment agreements. Thus far there have been no case in Australia on whether the screening of emails would constitute an infringement of the *Telecommunications (Interception) Act* 1979 (Cth). A key matter is whether employees are advised of the screening. There is arguably no wrong if this is part of the employment contract and has been accepted as a condition of employment.

737. It is unlikely that retaining emails and storing them on a server or other digital storage device would breach the Act. This is because storing messages is unlikely to constitute electromagnetic energy passing over a telecommunications system. Storage is not itself part of the communication. An employer's computer network may be viewed as a 'telecommunications service' – a system for carrying communications by either guided or unguided electromagnetic energy.

438. *Crimes Act* 1914 (Cth) s. 76B and D.
439. *Ibid.*
440. *Ibid.*
441. *Ibid.*

Chapter 5. Online Financial Services

§1. Introduction

738. Financial transactions and payments systems in the electronic environment present many new and interesting challenges, not least of which is how to adapt existing methods to new ways of working electronically. At the same time, these also present many financial and legal risks to businesses as well as to consumers, but which in turn gives rise to many new business opportunities to those who can provide assurances to create trust in the electronic environment.

739. In taking Australia's digital pulse, a Deloitte Access Economics (2021) report highlighted the growth of e-commerce in the light of the COVID-19 lockdowns throughout the nation during 2020 and 2021. The limited access to physical stores has driven the growth in e-commerce throughout 2020. According to a survey of Australian businesses in August 2020, the shift to online activity increased the average online revenue between AUD 105,000 and AUD 708,000 for small businesses.[442] It also projected that the shift to digital purchases would persist with home deliveries expected to remain 25 per cent higher than before March 2020.

740. The Wallis Inquiry (1996) into the financial system in Australia had previously observed that the Internet would transform banking business for financial institutions and customers alike.[443] With the substantial investment in upgrading telecommunication infrastructure to accommodate wireless and broadband technology as well as the uptake of information technology by most Australians, the scope for electronic banking and payments systems has widened considerably. While it can be expected that penetration of the technology will be deep, the Wallis Inquiry report identified security and reliability as the two key issues requiring immediate resolution.

741. The implications for the Australian payment systems are profound with the need for tighter regulations, regulatory control and enforcement and keeping up with trends in e-commerce and technology.

742. This chapter avoids any discussion of the mechanics and processes taking place behind the payment systems such as clearing and settlement and netting arrangements. Clearing is an accounting process and the formal acceptance of the transferred liability. Settlement is the process that resolves mutual liabilities of the parties involved at the end of a clearing cycle. Netting refers to the replacement of obligations between parties with a single obligation calculated by the summing of

---

442. Deloitte Access Economics (2020) Australia's eCommerce revolution: how it saved businesses in COVID-19 and future strategies to thrive (report commissioned by Australia Post, October) at https://auspost.com.au/content/dam/auspost_corp/media/documents/ ecommerce-report-2020.pdf.
443. Treasury (Wallis Inquiry) (1996) Financial System Inquiry Final Report at https://treasury.gov.au/publication/p1996-fsi-fr.

all obligations owed by each of the parties. Whilst vital these processes are opaque to consumers within the payment systems.

743. This chapter also avoids discussing Financial Market Infrastructures (FMI) despite being key components of the financial system and delivering services critical to the smooth functioning of financial markets. Such infrastructures underpin the securities and equity markets but are strictly not consumer retail payment systems *per se.*[444]

§2. Payment Systems

744. According to the Reserve Bank of Australia (RBA) the country's central bank, a 'payments system' refers to how consumers, businesses and financial institutions transfer funds to one another to satisfy their respective obligations.[445]

745. These transfers use payment instruments such as cash, credit and debit cards, cheques and electronic funds transfers. Payment systems ensure the seamless and unseen arrangements movement of funds from one account at one financial institution to another.

746. The RBA's *Consumer Payments Survey* in 2019 has shown that cash as a payment method remains widespread.[446] The survey in 2019 shows a continued substitution away from cash towards electronic methods. Cash payments accounted for 27 per cent of the number and 11 per cent of the value of all consumer payments in 2019. Cash withdrawn through automated teller machines (ATM) is the most common method which accounted for 72 per cent of the total number of cash withdrawals and 62 per cent of the value of the withdrawals in 2019.

747. The trend is for a strong preference to use electronic payment methods rather than cash for day-to-day payments.[447] Many consumers now tap their cards or sometimes mobile phones on payment readers for small purchases. Increasingly consumers are taking advantage of a range of innovative payment services facilitated by mobile technology and other digital payment credentials such as a digital wallet.

---

444. The RBA and ASIC have co-regulatory responsibilities under the *Corporations Act 2001* (Corporations Act) for securities settlement facilities and other activities. *See* https://www.rba.gov.au/payments-and-infrastructure/financial-market-infrastructure/principles/implementation-of-principles.html.

445. *See* Reserve Bank Australia (2021) Payments System at https://www.rba.gov.au/payments-and-infrastructure/payments-system.html.

446. *See* RBA *Consumer Payments Survey* 2019 at https://www.rba.gov.au/payments-and-infrastructure/consumer-payments-survey/.

447. *See* Caddy, J, Delaney, L & Fisher, C (2020) *Consumer Payment Behaviour in Australia: Evidence from the 2019 Consumer Payments Survey*, Research Discussion Paper 2020-06 (September), Payments Policy Department, Reserve Bank of Australia; also at https://www.rba.gov.au/publications/rdp/2020/2020-06.html.

748. Non-cash payments accounted for most of the value of payments in the Australian economy. On average, in 2020 non-cash payments worth about AUD 275 billion were made each business day approximately 14 per cent of annual GDP.[448]

749. It is notable that in 2020 less than two cheques were written per person in Australia, a reduction from close to fifty cheques written in the mid-1990s.

750. In contrast the use of electronic payment instruments at retail level has been growing rapidly. In 2020 both purchases and cash withdrawals using either a credit or debit card averaged about 420 per person, an increase of about 61 per cent from the level five years prior.

§3. Regulatory Frameworks

751. The regulatory framework governing payment systems in Australia is underpinned by the following legislations:

- *Reserve Bank Act* 1959 (Cth);
- *Payment Systems (Regulation) Act* 1998 (Cth) (PSRA);
- *Payment Systems and Netting Act* 1998 (Cth) (PSNA);
- *Corporations Act* 2001 (Cth) Part 7.3;
- *Cheques Act* 1986 (Cth);
- *Anti-Money Laundering and Counter-Terrorism Financing Act* 2006 (the AML/CTF Act);
- *Proceeds of Crime Act* 1987 (Cth);
- *Competition and Consumer Act* 2010 (Cth) (CCA);[449]
- *Payment Systems (Regulation) Act* 1998 (Cth) section 18;
- *Anti-Money Laundering and Counter-Terrorism Financing Act* 2006 (Cth) (AML/CTF Act) amended in 2018 to include regulation of digital currency exchanges (DCE).

I. Reserve Bank of Australia (RBA)

752. In general, the RBA has regulatory responsibilities for the payments systems and plays a key role in the operations of the system. The Payments System Board (PSB) of the RBA oversees the payments system in Australia. It is responsible for promoting the safety and efficiency of the payments systems.[450]

---

448. *Ibid.* Reserve Bank Australia (2021).
449. The *Competition and Consumer Act* 2010 (Cth) replaced the *Trade Practices Act* 1974 (Cth). (TPA).
450. Details on the structure and operations of the Australian payments system can be found in *Payment Systems in Australia* (Bank for International Settlements' website Red Book 2011 at https://bis.org/publ/cpss97_au.pdf) and the activities of the Bank's Payments System Board are reported in its Annual Reports at https//rba.gov.au/publications/annual-reports/psb/.

753. The RBA also has a formal regulatory role to ensure that the infrastructure supporting the clearing and settlement of transactions in financial markets is operated in a way that promotes financial stability.

754. The RBA is also empowered to set Financial Stability Standards for clearing and settlement facilities.

755. The RBA's operational role in the payments system includes owning and operating Australia's real-time gross settlement (RTGS) system and Reserve Bank Information and Transfer System (RITS). These systems provide facilities for the final settlement of payments between financial institutions, serve as banker to the Australian government and manage Australia's foreign exchange reserves.

756. The RTGS system operated by the RBA settles payments arising from a range of sources such as foreign exchange settlements and transactions.

757. The RITS Regulations and Conditions of Operation (RITS Regulations) provide the legal structure for RITS. The RITS Regulations set out the rules for the operation of RITS and the rights and obligations of participants and the RBA. The legal basis of RITS is established by contract, and standard agreements are executed to bind each party to the RITS Regulations. RITS is owned and operated by the RBA.

II. Other Public and Private Sector Regulators

*758. Australian Competition and Consumer Commission (*ACCC). The ACCC is Australia's competition regulator. It is responsible for ensuring that private sector arrangements comply with the competition and access provisions of the *Competition and Consumer Act* 2010 (Cth).

759. In February 2016, the Parliament passed legislation amending the *Competition and Consumer Act* 2010 (Cth), enabling the ACCC to issue infringement notices to entities that it considered were surcharging more than 'permitted surcharge' levels, with the definition of permitted surcharge to be defined in a Reserve Bank standard or in a regulation.

760. Australian Securities and Investments Commission (ASIC). ASIC was established on 1 July 1998. It has responsibility for market integrity and consumer protection across the financial system, including payment transactions.

761. Australian Prudential Regulation Authority (APRA). APRA was established on 1 July 1998. It is the prudential regulator of the Australian financial services industry. APRA operates under the *Australian Prudential Regulation Authority Act* 1998 (Cth) and its powers derive from the *Banking Act* 1959 (Cth), the *Insurance Act* 1973 (Cth), the *Life Insurance Act* 1995 (Cth) and the *Superannuation Industry (Supervision) Act* 1993 (Cth).

762. Australian Transaction Reports and Analysis Centre (AUSTRAC). AUSTRAC is Australia's anti-money laundering and counterterrorism financing (AML/CTF) regulator and specialist financial intelligence unit (FIU).

763. Council of Financial Regulators. The Council of Financial Regulators is a non-statutory body that contributes to efficiency and effectiveness of regulation. However, the Council is not a regulator.

764. Australian Payments Clearing Association (APCA). APCA was established in 1992 to coordinate and manage development of industry policies and rules for several payments clearing arrangements. APCA manages five clearing systems authorized by the ACCC.

765. EFTPOS Payments Australia Limited (EPAL). EPAL was established in April 2009 to manage and promote the EFTPOS (proprietary debit) system.

766. Financial Ombudsman Service (FOS). FOS is a free, independent dispute resolution scheme funded by participating providers of financial services.

767. Financial Sector Advisory Council (FSAC). The Financial Sector Advisory Council provides advice to Australia's Treasurer on financial sector developments and policies.

§4. Regulation of Payment Instruments

768. The strategic objectives for the Australian payment systems include the ability for users to make real-time payments; send more complete remittance information with payments; address payments in a relatively simple way; and make and receive payments outside normal business hours.

769. Under Part 3 of the *Payment Systems (Regulation) Act* 1998 (Cth), the Reserve Bank may designate a payment system if it considers that designating the system is in the public interest. It may then impose an access regime or establish standards to be complied with by participants in the system.[451]

770. The regulation of the relevant payment systems includes payment cards (designation, standards, guidance in the standards, access regimes, undertakings); and ATM System (regulations and exemptions discussed below).

771. A Standard is determined under section 18 of the *Payment Systems (Regulation) Act* 1998 (Cth).

---

451. *See* RBA Payments and Infrastructure (2022) at https://www.rba.gov.au/payments-and-infrastructure/.

772. An Access Regime is imposed under section 12 of the *Payment Systems (Regulation) Act* 1998 (Cth).

773. Undertakings are Statements made to do or refrain from certain actions under the relevant sections of the *Payment Systems (Regulation) Act* 1998 (Cth).[452]

I. Cheques and Paper-based Instruments

774. The *Cheques Act* 1986 (Cth) allows cheques to be drawn on authorized deposit-taking institutions (ADI) (that is, banks, building societies, credit unions and special service providers).

II. Electronic Credit Transfers and Direct Debits

775. Electronic funds transfer means any transfer of funds other than by cheque, draft, or similar paper instrument that is initiated through an electronic terminal, telephone, computer, magnetic tape, or electronic media to order, instruct, or authorize a financial institution to debit or credit an account.

776. Electronic money includes both chip card-based and digital stored value systems that function as a medium of exchange but differs in two very important respects from 'cash' such as notes, and coins issued by a central bank. Electronic money is neither legal tender nor a sovereign currency nor fiat that is accepted for the payment of debts; it is an obligation of a private company rather than of the central bank. In addition, electronic money products are traceable to the payer. In contrast to cash where the payer is anonymous.

777. In Australia, the Reserve Bank issues currency notes, and the Treasury issues coins.

778. Electronic credit transfers and direct debits are means of making payments in Australia. These transactions are made under the framework rules set by the Bulk Electronic Clearing System (BECS) but credit transfers are made through separate bank-owned system such as BPAY.

III. Payment Cards

779. Debit cards, also known as charge cards, allow access to deposit funds in customers' accounts. In Australia, banks, credit unions and building societies are the

452. ACCC (2021) Visa undertakes to address competition concerns over debit card payments, 10 Mar. 2021 at https://www.accc.gov.au/media-release/visa-undertakes-to-address-competition-concerns-over-debit-card-payments.

main issuers of debit cards, which can be used in ATMs, and electronic funds transfers point of sale (EFTPOS) terminals. Debit cards can access proprietary domestic Australian or international EFTPOS systems. Access requires a personal identification number (PIN) to initiate electronic transactions. On the contrary, direct debits such as automatic payment arrangements are another means where bills and other debts are paid through financial institutions by consumers to merchants.

780. Charge and retailer cards allow payment to be deferred from the date of purchase until the account due date; some provide revolving credit.

781. Credit cards are issued mainly by banks. Credit cards provide prearranged revolving credit, up to a specified limit. Payments for goods and services and withdrawals of cash are made against the line of credit. The RBA introduced reforms to the credit card schemes in 2002. These reforms set standards that cap the level of interchange fees, a cap on allowing merchants to surcharge customers using credit cards for payment and liberalize access arrangements for credit card schemes.[453]

782. Prepaid cards take a variety of forms: reloadable or not reloadable; linked to an account in the name of the cardholder or non-specific account; limited to use at a single merchant (or defined group of merchants).

783. Smart cards and stored value cards (SVCs) are electronic cash in which an embedded microprocessor chip is used to pay for goods and services, operating in much the way as telephone cards commonly used worldwide.

784. Smart cards can be used as a credit card, a debit card to execute account transfers, or as something more secure than the magnetic stripe card. Where a smart card functions as a stored value card, it has been called an electronic purse or an e-wallet.[454] The Department of Finance and Deregulation, through the AGIMO has developed a National Smartcard Framework (2008) for smart cards. This framework provides mechanisms that evidence identity and service requirements by specifying minimum requirements for applications and infrastructure interoperability. This framework has been developed in consultation with Australian government agencies, state and territory governments and industry.[455]

785. Contactless card payments and mobile wallets are becoming more popular especially with micropayments for small-value transactions. Contactless transactions are initiated by tapping either a physical card or mobile device and authenticating it with a pin. Consumers are also increasingly storing their card details in mobile wallets on their smart phones and other electronic devices.

---

453. *See* RBA (2002) at https://www.rba.gov.au/payments-and-infrastructure/review-of-card-payments-regulation/banks-card-system.html (August).
454. Newman, S & Sutter, G (2002) *Electronic Payments – The Smart Card: Smart Cards, E-payments & Law – Part I*, 18 *Computer Law & Security Report* 235 (2002); Privacy Committee of New South Wales (1995), *Smart Cards: Big Brother's Little Helpers* (Sydney: NSW Parliament).
455. AGIMO (2008) *Australian Government Smartcard Framework* at http://www.agimo.gov.au/infrastructure/smart_cards.

786. Mobile wallets are applications on a mobile device like a smartphones or other payment-enabled mobile device that stores card details and allows in-person payments to be made by using the near field communication (NFC) functionality of the mobile device by tapping the device on or near a compatible terminal. Mobile wallets can sometimes also be used to make online payments.

IV. Automatic Teller Machines (ATM)

787. Automated teller machines (ATM) introduced since 1981 have been a widespread feature in many shopping centres and other locations. In the beginning financial institutions and independent deployers developed their own ATM networks, groupings of institutions developed, over time to provide mutual access arrangements. ATMs allow cash withdrawals and account balance enquiries; some also provide facilities for deposits, transfers between accounts and ordering of cheque books and statements. The RBA reforms in 2002 include a cap on connection cost that can be charged to new entrants to the system and the prohibition on interchange fees.[456]

V. Third-party Bill Payments

788. The main providers of third-party bill payment services are Australia Post, the national postal service, and BPAY, a bank-owned service company.

789. Australia Post provides bill payment services for over 1,000 billers. Payments can be made by telephone, the Internet or over the counter at Australia Post outlets, although not all billers accept payment using all three of these options.

790. BPAY facilitates bill payments by allowing customers of participating financial institutions to arrange for the transfer of funds from their deposit or credit card account using phone banking or Internet banking services.

VI. Alternative Payment Instruments

791. New Internet payment systems have also begun operations over recent years, including PayPal, which holds member accounts for online transactions, funded by either a direct debit from a deposit account with a financial institution or by a credit or scheme debit card payment. PayPal is an authorized deposit-taking institution in Australia.

---

456. *Supra*, RBA (2002).

792. Cryptocurrencies (such as bitcoin) are designed as an alternative means of payment to sovereign currencies and may also be held for investment or speculative purposes.[457]

793. A notable development in the Australian retail payments system over the past few years has been the emergence of buy-now-pay-later (BNPL) services such as AfterPay and ZipPay.[458] These services enable consumers to obtain goods and services immediately and make subsequent payments in a series of interest-free instalments, typically drawn from a linked debit or credit card. However, such services may avoid the responsible lending requirements of the *National Consumer Credit Protection Act* 2009 (Cth) such as lending money without verifying a person's income or credit history.[459]

794. Prepaid transport cards such as MyWay, Myki and Opal are in use across public transport systems in Australia.[460] More recently some public transport terminals have enabled fares to be paid directly by tapping a debit or credit card on the terminal rather than having to use a specific transport card.

§5. Trends and Developments in Regulatory Enforcement

I. Electronic Funds Transfer Code

795. The *Australian Electronic Funds Transfer Code of Conduct* (EFT Code) (2012) sets out the procedures governing the relationship between users and providers of EFTs.[461] The operation of the code is monitored by the Treasury and the ACCC.

796. The EFT Code provides protection to customers by governing unauthorized EFT transactions, transaction errors, liability for EFT losses and against whom claims may be made.

797. The EFT Code excludes the need for credit card transactions authorized by a manual signature as it is not an 'access method'.

---

457. Dark C, Emery, D, Ma, J & Noone, C (2019), 'Cryptocurrency: Ten Years On', *RBA Bulletin*, June at https://www.rba.gov.au/publications/bulletin/2019/jun/cryptocurrency-ten-years-on.html.
458. *See* Afterpay and Zip respectively at https://afterpay.com.au and https://zip.co.
459. *See* ASIC at https://asic.gov.au/regulatory-resources/credit/credit-general-conduct-obligations/national-credit-code/. *See also* Dutta, S *et al.* (2019) How Zip Pay works and why the extra cost of 'buy now, pay later' is still enticing, *The Conversation* Feb. 14 and at https://theconversation.com/how-zip-pay-works-and-why-the-extra-cost-of-buy-now-pay-later-is-still-enticing-110429/.
460. *See* Transport Canberra at https://www.transport.act.gov.au; Public Transport Victoria at https://www.ptv.vic.gov.au/tickets/myki and Transport NSW at https://transportnsw.info/tickets-opal/opal/top-up-your-opal-card respectively.
461. *See* EFT Code at http://www.asic.gov.au/asic/pdflib.nsf/LookupByFileName/EFT-Code-as-amended-from-1-July-2012.pdf/$file/EFT-Code-as-amended-from-1-July-2012.pdf.

798. The EFT Code currently applies only to transactions initiated by an individual using an electronic terminal, an EFT card and a PIN. While some smart card transactions require a PIN to complete, most will not. Internet banking is outside the scope of the Code, unless it involves the use of a smart card and PIN, and the Code does not apply to digital cash transactions or BPAY transactions.

799. EFT transactions are now regulated by the *e-Payments Code* (2013) a voluntary code of practice which is administered by the ASIC for compliance and review.[462] The Code sets out the obligations of businesses to consumers, consumer rights and responsibilities and what to do in the event of a complaint or dispute, such as unauthorized transactions. The Code covers ATM transactions, EFTPOS purchases, purchasing goods by credit card either online or by phone, mobile phone or Internet banking, telephone banking and transactions using stored value facilities such as debit cards.

800. The e-Payments Code complements other regulatory requirements and obligations under the *Corporations Act* 2001 (Cth) and the *National Consumer Credit Protection Act* 2009 (Cth) (NCCP).

801. ASIC approves codes as set out in Regulations Guide RG 183 in accordance with section 1101A of the *Corporations Act* 2001 (Cth). This is a statutory power to approve voluntary industry codes of conduct. However, ASIC does not have to power to mandate industry codes. Industry must decide in the first instance whether to develop a code, and then whether to have that code approved by ASIC.

802. RG 183 describes key features of an effective code regime that applies to the financial services industry. In certain circumstances a breach of a code is a breach of a contract with a financial institution. This gives the consumer a right to take legal action for breach of contract.

II. National Payments Platform

803. Launched in February 2018, the New Payments Platform (NPP) is open access infrastructure for fast payments in Australia. The NPP was developed with industry collaboration to enable households, businesses and government agencies to make payments, with near real-time funds availability to the recipient, on a 24/7 basis.[463]

462. The e-Payments Code is at https://asic.gov.au/regulatory-resources/financial-services/epayments-code/.
463. *See* RBA at https://www.rba.gov.au/payments-and-infrastructure/new-payments-platform/about-npp.html.

804. Twelve Authorised Deposit-Taking Institutions (ADI) committed to funding to build and operate the NPP in 2014 and became the founding members of NPP Australia Limited.[464]

805. The NPP platform was built using ISO20022 to enable more data to travel with a payment.[465]

806. The NPP provides consumers with the ability to make real-time, data-rich account-to-account bank transfers using PayIDs.

807. A *PayID* – the NPPs addressing service, is a simple unique identifier which links to a customer's transaction account so that fast payments can be made to that account through the NPP. A PayID is often an email address, phone number or ABN.[466] It allows users to link easy-to-remember pieces of information, such as their phone number or email address, to their account. Users can provide their PayID, instead of their Bank State Branch (BSB) number, a six-digit code that represents a bank, state, and branch location, and account number, to people or organizations they wish to receive payments from in real-time.

808. *PayTo* is a new, digital way for merchants and businesses to initiate real-time payments from their customers' bank accounts. It was previously known as the Mandated Payments Service.

809. Businesses have taken advantage of 'overlay services' known as Osko developed by BPay. '*Overlay services*' are the services which businesses can use to deliver a better customer experience. Overlay service providers have control over defining their service levels, commercial terms, branding, governance, processes and rules allowing the experience to be uniform across the industry.[467] Osko Payments permits customers to send and receive money near instantaneously between participating banks and financial institutions on a 24/7 basis.

810. NPP transactions have been growing steadily since its launch in 2018. Over 2 million PayIDs had been created as of end September, and over 35 million payments worth about AUD 30 billion had been sent through the platform. The average value of an NPP payment is nearly AUD 1000.

III. Neo-banks

811. With the decline in the use of cash for transactions, the emergence of distributed ledger technology, blockchain and cryptocurrencies and the broader

464. *See* NPPA at https://nppa.com.au/.
465. *See* NPPA ISO 20022 at https://nppa.com.au/the-platform/iso-20022-message-capabilities/.
466. *See* Rush A and R Louw (2018) 'The New Payments Platform and Fast Settlement Service', *RBA Bulletin* (September) at https://www.rba.gov.au/publications/bulletin/2018/sep/the-new-payments-platform-and-fast-settlement-service.html.
467. *See* OSKO Payments at https://osko.com.au.

digitalization of the economy, there is a growing interest in the possibility of central banks issuing a new digital form of money, known as central bank digital currency (CBDC) somewhat like a digital version of cash. The RBA is exploring the creation of a CBDC for wholesale and retail markets.[468]

812. Neo-banks provide all their services online or through apps. Neo-banks use AI and machine learning such as chatbots and digital agents to provide a sense of personal service, replacing call centres and physical branch locations.

813. Although the neo-bank service model is different to traditional banks, these institutions must go through the same regulatory requirements. They all have an ADI institution licence from the APRA and like other banks must hold AUD 250,000 per person per ADI in case the institution stops operating or becomes insolvent.

IV. Digital Assets

814. While digital assets and crypto assets are generally not prescriptively regulated in Australia certain digital asset businesses must register with AUSTRAC to manage potential security and financial risks.

815. Digital assets that meet the definition of 'financial product' under the *Corporations Act* 2001 (Cth) are subject to regulatory oversight by ASIC and must hold an Australian Financial Services Licence (AFSL).

816. Section 764A of the *Corporations Act* 2001 (Cth) describes a 'digital asset' as a facility specifically taken to be a financial product for the purpose of Chapter 7. The definition here is the same as that in the *Anti-Money Laundering and Counter-Terrorism Financing Act* 2006 (Cth) and the *Australian Securities and Investment Commission Act* 2001 (Cth).

817. Crypto assets are not financial products and crypto asset services are generally not regulated by ASIC.

818. ASIC InfoSheet 225 describes how obligations under the *Corporations Act* 2001 (Cth) and the *Australian Securities and Investment Commission Act* 2001 (Cth) may apply to initial coin offerings (ICO) or other digital asset offering for businesses involved with crypto assets.

819. The Australian Taxation Office (ATO) oversees the collection of tax revenue arising from digital asset businesses and transactions and provides guidance on the circumstances in which tax accrues.

---

468. *See* RBA (2021) at https://www.rba.gov.au/publications/annual-reports/psb/2021/about-the-payments-system-board.html#glance-3-1.

820. Non-fungible tokens (NFTs) are crypto assets which 'may represent the original or licensed literary and artistic works of an author or authors or the unique contractual terms between parties'. The most prominent examples of NFTs are digital artworks.[469]

821. Richardson (2022) has observed that there remain issues around unregulated coin offerings, unregistered securities, de-banking and stories of scams or frauds.[470] The opinion piece cites Axie Infinity, one of the industry's most valuable NFT gaming businesses, reported that it was the victim of around a USD 625 million decentralized finance hack or fraud. The conclusion is that a free market without regulation or legally enforceable contracts is bound to be infested with frauds with no legal recourse or protection.

822. One estimate of the global current aggregate market value of the digital assets is about AUD 2.8 trillion with about 221 million users worldwide having traded a cryptocurrency or used a blockchain-based application in June 2021. This is an increase of 66 million users from the end of May 2020.[471]

V. Cryptocurrency

823. Australian laws neither equate digital currency with 'fiat' or sovereign currency, nor does it treat cryptocurrency as 'money'.[472]

824. Various forms of cryptocurrency exist including digital cash,[473] Digicash,[474] e-cash,[475] netCash[476] and bitcoins.[477]

469. The Senate Select Committee on Australia as a Technology and Financial Centre (2021) at https://parlinfo.aph.gov.au/parlInfo/download/committees/reportsen/024747/toc_pdf/Finalreport.pdf;fileType=application%2Fpdf.
470. Richardson, T (2022) Cash-driven NFTs a vulgar misappropriation of art, *Australian Financial Review* 2-3 April, p 25.
471. Moore, T (2021) 'Digital assets sector 'too big to ignore': Bank of America', *Australian Financial Review* at https://www.afr.com/companies/financial-services/digital-assets-sector-too-big-to-ignore-bank-of-america-20211005-p58x7w (accessed 5 Oct. 2021).
472. *See* Hutcheon, S (2014) Cracking the Cryptic World of Virtual Cash, *Sydney Morning Herald*, 9 (8-9 Feb. 2014).
473. *See* Digital Cash at https://www.cs.bham.ac.uk/~mdr/teaching/modules06/netsec/lectures/DigitalCash.html.
474. *See* Digicash at https://cmcrc.com/better-than-blockchain-digital-financial-instruments/.
475. *See* e-cash at https://www.chaum.com/ecash/.
476. Neuman, BC & Medvinisky, G (1995) NetCheque, NetCash, and the Characteristics of Internet Payment Services, 1(1&2) *J Electronic Publishing*, (January) DOI: http://dx.doi.org/10.3998/3336451.0001.126 and at https://www.semanticscholar.org/paper/NetCheque%2C-NetCash%2C-and-the-Characteristics-of-Neuman-Medvinsky/fd023521e6676d6dcdc4794161b6401f9c2b3697.
477. *See* Simonite, T (2011) *What Bitcoin Is, and Why It Matters. Can a booming 'crypto-currency' really compete with conventional cash?* at https://www.technologyreview.com/s/424091/what-bitcoin-is-and-why-it-matters/.

825. The RBA describes cryptocurrencies as having their own 'currency' unit and are not denominated in the currency of any sovereign issuer. The distinguishing feature of most cryptocurrencies is that they use distributed ledger technology (DLT) also known as blockchain and cryptography to store digital 'coin' ownership records and transactions in a digital ledger that is distributed (and synchronized) across several 'nodes' (or computers) rather than relying on a central party to operate the system. Cryptocurrencies such as bitcoins cannot replace money issued by central banks. A central bank provides a stable unit of account for the economy.

826. The ANZ Bank has created a stablecoin A$DC (pronounced A-dollar-DC) pegged to the Australian dollar hence reducing the risks of buying digital assets.[478]The stablecoin as its name suggests is a type of digital asset designed to maintain a stable value relative to another asset and may be used to access other cryptocurrencies or to earn income in decentralized finance (DeFi) systems. For example, there will be no need to convert AUD to USD before purchasing a USD stablecoin known as the USDCoin (USDC).

827. In creating the stablecoin ANZ engaged blockchain partner Fireblocks and digital asset management firm ZeroCap to create A$DC cryptocurrency. The A$DC is unlike other cryptocurrencies where values fluctuate in line with demand and liquidity, stablecoins are pegged to the value of real-world assets, like hard currency or precious metals. ANZ reported that it has minted AUD 30 million worth of A$DC using a smart contract based on the Ethereum system. Working with its advisers ZeroCap, ANZ has also created a custodial infrastructure for consumer protection and willing to be regulated under the new Australian crypto licensing regime once it is established.

828. Structurally stablecoins can either be asset based such as fiat coins backed by dollar funds, or asset collateralized by reference to a single asset or basket of assets such as commodities or crypto assets, or algorithmic stablecoins whose value is through a predetermined algorithm.[479] Algorithmic stablecoins are neither redeemable to nor backed by one-to-one dollars.[480] Recent events however have demonstrated the volatility of the stablecoin market and 'meltdown' of algorithmic stablecoins.[481] These developments highlight the growing risks and increasing

---

478. *See* ANZ media release at https://media.anz.com/posts/2022/03/anz-completes-landmark-stablecoin-payment. *See also* Eyers, J (2022) ANZ leads way with first Aussie dollar stablecoin, *Australian Financial Review,* 24 Mar 2022, p. 13.
479. *See* G7 Working Group on Stablecoins, *Investigating the impact of global stablecoins* (Report, October 2019) and ASIC, Submission 61, Senate Select Committee on Australia as a Technology and Financial Centre (June 2021).
480. Benjamin S (2020) 'Stability, Elasticity, and Reflexivity: A Deep Dive into Algorithmic Stablecoins' *Mechanism Capital* (21 Dec. 2020) at https://www.mechanism.capital/algorithmic-stablecoins/.
481. Sier, J & Shapiro, J (2022) A week of Terra: Behind the collapse of $26B stablecoin, *Australian Financial Review* 14-15 May 2022.

regulator concerns.[482] Statements from the RBA suggest a greater need for regulation of stablecoins.[483]

829. There are currently no specific regulations dealing with blockchain technology in Australia.[484] The Report by the Senate Select Committee on Australia as a Technology and Financial Centre makes twelve recommendations one of which proposes the legal recognition of digital autonomous organizations (DAO) and digital currency exchanges (DCE).

830. DAO are self-regulating organizations the comprise of members linked on a blockchain through NFTs and smart contracts which serve as a digital constitution. The goal of DAO is to free modern commerce from administrative inefficiencies, centralized control and fraud. The legal issues that DAO pose are legal liability and accountability.

831. Australia as a common law jurisdiction deems DAO to be treated as a form of partnership or unincorporated association. This implies that individual members of a DAO are exposed to unlimited personal liability for the entity's entire operation, regardless of any actual knowledge or control. The proposal is that the DAO be treated as a limited liability company, thus enabling it to hold property and to enter contracts and the benefits such a legal entity entails.[485]

832. DCE are subject to light touch registration with AUSTRAC despite handling billions of dollars' worth of assets. The recommendation of the Senate Select Committee (2021) is for a new market licence regime for DCEs.

833. Various cryptocurrency networks have also implemented 'smart' or self-executing contracts permitted under the *Electronic Transactions Act* 1999 (Cth) (ETA) and the equivalent Australian state and territory legislation.

834. Cryptocurrencies do not fall within the definition of a 'foreign currency' for tax purposes.[486] That view is based on the concept of a 'currency' compared to 'fiat currencies', such as the Australian dollar. The ATO, for income tax purposes, views cryptocurrency as an asset that is held or traded rather than as money or a foreign currency. A profit on sale or disposal is treated as a capital gain and hence considered as a capital gains tax (CGT) asset.

---

482. Denton J (2022) Cryptocurrency's stable coin proves to be anything but *The Australian* 16 May 2022 and at https://www.theaustralian.com.au/business/cryptocurrencys-stablecoin-proves-to-be-anything-but/newsstory/8d29a0653e7f97e5512beab4e3d70cda.
483. Eyers, J (2022) Stablecoins need regulation: RBA *Australian Financial Review* 14-15 May 2022, p. 26.
484. But see ASIC' *(INFO 2019 Evaluating distributed ledger technology* (March 2021) that outlines an approach to regulatory issues.
485. *Supra, The Senate Select Committee (2021).*
486. *See* ATO Submission (2021) at https://www.aph.gov.au/DocumentStore.ashx?id=f634981b-7748-4186-8945-3f7d28dd3568&subId=712323.

835. ATO data analysis shows an increase in trading since 2020. It is estimated that there are over 600,000 taxpayers that have invested in digital assets in recent years.[487]

836. Recent survey data shows that 25 per cent of Australians either currently or have previously held cryptocurrencies, making Australia one of the biggest adopters of cryptocurrencies on a per capita basis.[488]

837. Loan activities in relation to cryptocurrency may fall within the scope of credit and such services may be caught under the *National Consumer Credit Protection Act* 2009 (Cth) (NCCP Act) s. 30. The relevant entities may need to hold an Australian credit licence or be otherwise exempt from the requirement to be licensed.[489]

838. ASIC recently announced that an Australian crypto lender Helio Lending Pty Ltd has been charged with falsely claiming that it had an Australian Credit Licence.[490] Helio Lending offered cryptocurrency-backed loans to consumers, using the digital currency as security over the loan.

839. Cryptocurrencies have been said to be speculative and volatile to work as a means of to exchange wealth. Australian Financial Complaints Authority (AFCA) currently has limited scope to resolve consumer complaints arising from cryptocurrency dealings, because AFCA is only able to consider complaints against financial firms that are members of AFCA.[491]

840. To date, there has been no explicit regulation or case law surrounding the treatment of cryptocurrency in Australian succession law.

841. Foreign companies that are considered as carrying on a business in Australia such as issuing cryptocurrency or operating a platform developed using ICO proceeds, may be required to establish a local presence under ASIC rules.

842. Australia is supportive of the work that is underway at the OECD through Working Party to develop a tax transparency framework for crypto assets and digital money products. The proposed framework seeks to address the risks associated with the lack of transparency in crypto assets and digital money products, by establishing a new reporting regime for these types of financial products.[492]

---

487. *Supra*, ATO Submission 2021 *The Senate Select Committee (2021).*
488. *Supra, The Senate Select Committee (2021).*
489. *See* ASIC National Credit Code at https://asic.gov.au/regulatory-resources/credit/credit-general-conduct-obligations/national-credit-code/.
490. *See* ASIC (2022) at https://asic.gov.au/about-asic/news-centre/find-a-media-release/2022-releases/22-085mr-cryptocurrency-lender-charged-for-false-australian-credit-licence-claims/.
491. *See* AFCA at https://www.afca.org.au/.
492. *See* OECD (2020) *Taxing Virtual Currencies: An Overview of Tax Treatments and Emerging Tax Policy Issues*, October 2020 at https://www.oecd.org/tax/tax-policy/taxing-virtual-currencies-an-overview-of-tax-treatments-and-emerging-tax-policy-issues.htm.

VI. Consumer Protection

843. ASIC has committed to supporting financial innovation. ASIC is part of the Global Financial Innovation Network (GFIN), formally launched in January 2019, by a group of financial regulators across twenty-nine member organizations. The GFIN is dedicated to facilitating regulatory collaboration in a cross-border context and provides more efficient means for innovative businesses to interact with regulators, in robo-advice or digital advice models.

844. The provision of robo-advice involves algorithms and technology to provide automated financial product advice without a human advisor. For investment or fund businesses seeking to operate in Australia in providing digital or hybrid advice (including investing in cryptocurrencies) licensing obligations under the *Corporations Act* 2001 (Cth) will apply.

845. ASIC guidance contained in *Regulatory Guide 255: Providing digital financial product advice to retail clients* details issues that digital advice providers need to consider. This complements ASIC's existing guidance on providing financial product advice together with *Regulatory Guide 36: Licensing: Financial product advice and dealing.*

846. Financial product advisers also need to consider their conduct and disclosure obligations outlined in ASIC's *Regulatory Guide 175: Licensing: Financial product adviser - conduct and disclosure.*

847. It is to be noted that the *Financial Sector Reform Amendments and Transitional Provisions Act* 1998 (Cth) (FSR) deals with financial markets and financial products and proposes to harmonize the regulation of the financial industry through uniform licensing requirements. While aimed primarily at breaking down the regulatory distinctions between securities, futures, derivatives and other financial products, the proposed reforms impact on e-payments. This is due to the proposed broader definition of a 'financial product' and the uniform regulation of 'financial service providers'. Such a definition is wide enough to capture payments systems providers, electronic cash issuers and smart cards. The FSR will also impose stringent point of sale (POS) disclosure requirements that could also have an impact on e-payments schemes.

§6. Afterword

848. The legal implications of new technology like blockchains loom large in this postscript. Apart from data portability where the data are 'locked' within the chain and unable to be used in other systems, additional concerns include those of keeping secure the encryption keys and the locking of resources that inhibit any other transaction with that asset, the potential collusion among groups of users on blockchains to mine blocks by recreating the blockchain, and the level of user savviness and safety of consumers in the widespread use of this technology. As the public and private sector interest in blockchain technology continues apace the legal and economic implications need closer attention.

849. From the consumer point of view it is important to ensure that electronic payment systems are low cost, accessible and safe. As the transactional use of cash declines, it will also be important to consider the needs of those members of society who continue to rely heavily on cash for their day-to-day payments. The instance of de-banking, also known as un-banking, such as the withdrawal of bank branch services, may push consumers to go totally online and to wholly engage with the payment system.

850. The growth of e-cash portends a further shift towards electronic payment methods. The potential of transferring funds instantaneously by any means may make it difficult for governments to monitor or regulate. E-cash raises other regulatory issues and dilemmas. Customers can choose between different currencies. This could result in loss of revenues from tax avoidance and loss of income earned by central banks (*seigniorage*).[493] There are also issues of crime such as money laundering and the privacy of such transactions. If there is going to be a close monitoring of all electronic activity, people may feel that their privacy has been invaded. The advent of digital cash and other forms of electronic money may render government-issued media of exchange obsolete. The overall impact of e-cash, however, will depend on the pace and direction of technological change and response to this by consumers, businesses and governments.

851. Trends in electronic payments systems on the one hand have provided incentives to reform regulations to encourage the use of e-money, while also ensuring that it does not have unintended consequences such as undermining the tax base. On the other hand, poorly designed regulatory responses by governments could unnecessarily impede electronic payment systems that could result in the loss of economic activity in the financial, retailing and other sectors and a loss of tax revenues to countries with better regulatory environments.

493. *Seigniorage* – the profit made by a government by issuing currency such as the difference between the face value of coins and their production costs.

Chapter 6. Law of Evidence in the Digital Environment

§1. Introduction

852. The general rules of evidence state that material presented in courts must be 'facts'. What are deemed as facts will have to be proven as well as to overcome the chief obstacle to admissibility – the hearsay rule. The use of electronic evidence as instruments of persuasion must surmount other obstacles such as whether computer-generated evidence may be treated as substantive or 'real' evidence in court, and whether the evidence are facts or depictions of facts.

853. Evidence is thus the introduction of material offered in court to persuade a trier of fact about the truth or falsity of a disputed fact. The law of evidence is a challenge to the introduction, relevancy and admissibility of evidentiary material in an adversarial court system. These rules apply whether in civil or criminal proceedings.

854. Evidence has relevance if it has probative value. This means that its presentation to the court can go to prove a material fact. Such material facts may be proved either by direct or circumstantial evidence. Hence, the strong distinction between the admissibility of evidence as opposed to the 'weight' of that evidence when presented.

855. The present concern is to consider the kinds of digital evidence that may be admissible and those that may satisfy an exception to the hearsay rule. All Australian states and territories have legislation that admit certain documents as an exception to the hearsay rule. In general, such legislation indicate the requirements for the authentication of paper documents or electronic documents.

856. Authentication is the process by which proof is provided that an electronic document has been produced by standard hardware and software, that the data processing is checked, the data are secure from loss and alteration and that the printouts accurately represent the data stored in a computer's memory system.[494]

857. Hearsay is an out-of-court assertion brought into court to prove the truth of the matter so asserted. However, hearsay is not ordinarily admissible because the person who made the out-of-court assertion cannot be cross-examined before the judge or jury. The hearsay rule thus is a rule against secondhand evidence.

858. Electronic evidence is deemed to be out-of-court statements and when offered in court may be deemed hearsay. To overcome this obstacle there is a reliance on exceptions that may apply such as declarations in public documents,

494. In the landmark English case *Statute of Liberty* [1968] 2 All ER 195 it was held that a record produced by a machine was 'real' evidence. The recordings from a radar reading of ship movements and locations that had been set by a purely mechanical means without human intervention were deemed admissible.

statutory exceptions, computer outputs and business records. The testimony of expert witnesses may also be persuasive as an exception. For these exceptions, reliance must be placed on the relevant legislation and circumstances of the case.

§2. The Law of Evidence

859. The law of evidence in Australia is a mixture of statute and common law together with rules of court. In Australia, if the legal proceeding is in a federal court (that is, the High Court, Federal Court, Family Court or the Federal Magistrates Court) or an ACT court, the Commonwealth *Evidence Act* 1995 (Cth) applies.[495] The New South Wales,[496] Victorian[497] and Tasmanian[498] Evidence Acts generally mirror the Commonwealth Evidence Act and its admissibility requirements as do those of the ACT[499] and Northern Territory.[500] In other jurisdictions, the laws of evidence may vary.

860. The Commonwealth *Evidence Act* 1995 (Cth) provides for documents created and maintained in paper and electronic form to be admitted in evidence before federal courts.

861. The *Evidence Act* 1995 (Cth) section 51 abolishes the original document rule, includes a narrower hearsay rule and wider exceptions and easier proof of, and presumptions about, business and official records, and documents recording an electronic communication.

862. The rules of evidence prescribe the standards to which a fact must be proved, that is, in civil proceedings facts must be proved on the balance of probabilities, and in criminal proceedings, facts must be proved beyond reasonable doubt. Such rules of evidence are concerned about the form of 'evidence' given or presented to a court, and whether that information can be admitted to the proceedings.

863. The term 'document' is defined in the dictionary to the *Evidence Act* 1995 (Cth).[501] A document also includes any part, copy, reproduction or duplicate of a document. Metadata, as information embedded in a document is generally considered part of a 'document'.

---

495. *Evidence Act* 1995 (Cth), which commenced on 18 Apr. 1995.
496. *Evidence Act* 1995 (NSW), which commenced on 1 Sep. 1995.
497. *Evidence Act* 2008 (Vic), which commenced on 1 Jan. 2010.
498. *Evidence Act* 2001 (Tas), which commenced on 17 Dec. 2001.
499. *Evidence Act* 2011 (ACT), which commenced on 1 Mar. 2012.
500. *Evidence (National Uniform Legislation) Act* (2012) (NT), which commenced on 1 Jan. 2013.
501. *Evidence Act* 1995 (Cth) Dictionary definition: *document* means any record of information and includes: (a) anything on which there is writing; or (b) anything on which there are marks, figures, symbols or perforations having a meaning for persons qualified to interpret them; or (c) anything from which sounds, images or writings can be reproduced with or without the aid of anything else; or (d) a map, plan, drawing or photograph.

I. Commonwealth Uniform Evidence Law

864. There were hopes that when the *Evidence Act* 1995 (Cth) was passed that it would lead to uniform legislation throughout Australia. However, this has not yet occurred.[502]

865. Federal courts and courts in the Australian Capital Territory apply the law found in the *Evidence Act* 1995 (Cth) and some provisions have a wider reach. New South Wales, Tasmania and Norfolk Island[503] have passed mirror legislation. These statutes are substantially the same as the Commonwealth legislation but not identical. In New South Wales and Tasmania, state courts exercising federal, or state jurisdiction and some tribunals apply the law found in the mirror legislation.[504]

866. For various reasons, three 'hold out' states of Western Australia, South Australia and Queensland have not indicated a present or future intention of relinquishing control of their respective Evidence Acts.[505]

867. The uniform Evidence Acts in its entirety are not a code of the law of evidence and has not been intended to operate as such. It does not exclude the operation of other laws regarding the admissibility of evidence.[506]

868. The rules of evidence are unaffected by the *Electronic Transactions Act* 1999 (Cth) (ETA). Indeed, the ETA promotes confidence in electronic transactions by confirming that a permission or requirement under a law of the Commonwealth to provide information in writing, a signature, or to retain information can be met by electronic means unless specifically excluded by other Commonwealth legislation, or the *Electronic Transactions Regulations* 2000 (Cth).

869. The ETA does not define an electronic document, *per se*. Electronic documents tendered in court is information stored and transmitted in digital form. These electronically generated documents may be produced in hard copy form.

II. Declarations in Public Documents

870. The law of evidence provides that such declarations or certified copies may be tendered in court to prove the facts stated. This rationale being that the document exists for public use on a public matter, is open to public inspection and is

502. *See* Australian Law Reform Commission (2010) Uniform Evidence Law ALRC Report 102 ch.2 The Uniform Evidence Acts at https://www.alrc.gov.au/publication/uniform-evidence-law-alrc-report-102/2-the-uniform-evidence-acts/the-movement-towards-a-uniform-evidence-law/.
503. *Evidence Act* 2004 (Norfolk Island) which commenced on 28 Sep. 2004.
504. *Supra,* Australian Law Reform Commission (2010).
505. *Evidence Act* 1906 (WA), *Evidence Act* 1929 (SA) and *Evidence Act* 1977 (Qld). *See* discussion in Hemming, A (2017) Adoption of the uniform evidence legislation: so far and no further? in *Critical perspectives on the uniform evidence law*, Federation Press, Sydney, Australia, pp. 34-52.
506. *Supra,* Australian Law Reform Commission (2010).

made by someone who has a duty to satisfy themselves as to the truth and accuracy of the matter contained in the document. Examples could include computational accuracy of calculations of a particular type of microchip and the like.

III. Certain Statutory Exceptions

871. In NSW documentary evidence must relate to a fact in issue where an oral testimony of the fact stated in the document would have been admissible in the proceedings.[507]

872. In Victoria, secondhand and more distant hearsay is admitted where the document forms part of a record relating to or made during business from information supplied by someone with personal knowledge (*Evidence Act* 1958 (Vic) sections 54-55).

873. Queensland legislation replaced the continuous record requirement for the admission of records made with the knowledge of the speaker or during proceedings. Such 'reported hearsay' is admissible so long as it is traceable to a person who spoke with personal knowledge of the matter (*Evidence Act* 1977 (Qld) sections 83-91).

874. In Western Australia there is neither a provision for the authentication of documents nor the need of continuous records before secondhand information is admitted (*Evidence Amendment Act* 1898 (WA) sections 89-96).

875. The ACT legislation permits opinion evidence only where the witness is unavailable (*Evidence Act* 1971 (ACT) sections 21-27). Such statements must be made while memory is fresh and is admitted only at the end of an examination-in-chief.

876. The Tasmanian legislation is like ACT law in that it applies to both criminal and civil matters. Courts have been given wide discretion to exclude evidence under the provisions (*Evidence Act* 1910 (Tas) sections 33-39, 40A).

IV. Computer-Generated Output

877. NSW, Tasmania, the Northern Territory and the Commonwealth (including the ACT) have incorporated computer output in their business records

507. *Evidence Act* 1898 (NSW) ss 14B-14C. Relevant sections of the other state enactments are: *Evidence Act* 1958 (Vic.) ss 3(1), 54, 55; *Evidence Act* 1971 (ACT) ss 6, 28-31; *Evidence Act* 1977 (Qld) ss 92-94; *Evidence Act* 1929 (SA) ss 34c-34d; *Evidence Act* 1906 (WA) and *Evidence Amendment Act* 1987 (WA) ss 79B–79C; *Evidence Act* 1910 (Tas) ss 81A–81D.

legislation.[508] While Western Australia, Queensland and Victoria have defined a document so as to incorporate information stored and generated by computers, in South Australia a document is narrowly defined to apply to documents printed by computers.[509] Except for Western Australia, Queensland and Victoria, all other jurisdictions require that the maker authenticate a document. South Australian legislation is most onerous as three specific requirements must be met.

878. The Queensland *Evidence Act* 1977 section 95 'admissibility of statements produced by computers' may be relied upon for evidentiary purposes.

V. Business Records

879. All Australian jurisdictions admit business records in evidence.[510]

§3. Evidence in an Electronic Environment

880. Electronic data interchange (EDI) is an industry standards-based computer to computer exchange in inter- and intra-organization business documents and information. [511] Automated electronic creation and revision of documents and messages are possible. EDI as a communications tool reduces the likelihood of legal disputes and offer a higher level of technical security than in a paper environment.[512]

881. Smart contracts and blockchains discussed earlier are also examples in which documents that are produced autonomously and in response to the satisfaction of certain algorithmic criteria. However, such documents pose challenges to traditional legal systems.

882. In traditional legal analysis, paper-based documents serve three basic functions. It has an informative function, an evidential function and a symbolic function. These functions may be said to be absent with electronic messages which may

508. The relevant statutory provisions are *Evidence Act* 1989 (NSW) s. 14CN; *Evidence Act* 1929 (SA) Pt. VIA; *Evidence Act* 1958 (Vic.) s. 55B; *Evidence Act* 1971 (ACT) ss 39-45; and *Evidence Act* 1977 (Queensland) s. 95. At common law see: *Mehesz v. Redman (No. 2)* (1980) 26 SASR 244 and *R v. Weatherall* (1981) 27 SASR 238.

509. This is to be distinguished from a computer-assisted work. A *computer-assisted work* is one in which an operator used a computer to produce some final product such as a grid of letters in a crossword puzzle. *See Express Newspapers Plc v. Liverpool Daily Post and Echo Plc* [1985] 1 WLRC 1089.

510. *Evidence Act* 1898 (NSW) ss 14CD–14CH; *Evidence Act* 1929 (SA) ss 45a–45b; *Evidence Amendment Act* 1984 (SA) s. 45C; *Evidence Amendment Act* 1981 (Tas) Div. 2B).

511. EDI is seen as an essential prerequisite in Just-in-Time / Quick Response inventory and production systems where limited stock holdings are dependent on rapid and accurate communication of purchasing needs. *See* Swatman, PMC & Everett, JE (1991) 'Australian involvement in electronic data interchange — 1989' *The Australian Computer Journal*, v. 23 (February), pp. 22-32.

512. Walden, I (1990) 'EDI and the law' in Edwards, C, Savage, N & Walden, I (eds.) *Information Technology and the Law*, (2nd ed.) Basingstoke: Macmillan, pp. 239 – 252 at p. 240-1.

be described as ephemeral and hence difficult to produce an acceptable record to a court's satisfaction. However, such reservations have now been dispelled by the *Electronic Transactions Act* 1999 (Cth) which has put electronic documents on an equal footing as paper-based ones.

I. Electronic Mail

883. The question whether emails are admissible in court as business records has been considered in various court cases. In *Aqua-Marine v. Reef Fisheries (No 4)* [2011] FCA 578 a Federal Court of Australia adopted a broad approach and held that an email was admissible under section 69 of the *Evidence Act* 1995 (Cth).

884. Justice Austin in *ASC v. Rich* [2005] NSWSC 741 held that emails between the Chief Operating Officer of OneTel Europe and a non-executive director of One-Tel Ltd were an exception to the hearsay rule, as they were business records within the definition in section 69 of the *Evidence Act* 1995 (Cth).[513]

885. There is a general rule that secondary documents are inadmissible if a primary document is available. In the case of electronic documents, there may be numerous copies generated, each identical with the other. It is arguable that in the case of emails the 'original' is the initial data message in a sender's computer with the recipient only receiving a copy. Thus, in court whether an electronic document is admitted into evidence will depend upon the foundation that is laid for that document.

886. In *Buterea v. Director of Public Prosecution for the State of Victoria* (1987), 164 C.L.R. 180, the HCA held that the 'best evidence' rule would not apply to exclude an audiotape copy where a foundation had been laid regarding the original tape, the accuracy of the recording process, and of the taped copy.

887. The *Evidence Act* 1995 (Cth) section 51 has since abolished the 'original document rule' (best evidence rule); instead evidence of the contents of a document may be given in several alternate ways including: the tendering of the original physical or digital copy, a transcript of a document recording words or a business record in physical or digital form.

II. Other Media

888. The use of short messaging service (SMS) or instant messaging applications such as WhatsApp, Telegram and others have become commonplace both official as well as unofficial communications. Provided that these types of messages have been ruled admissible they may be tended in court and led in evidence under the relevant Evidence Acts in Australia.

---

513. *See* text of the Act at https://www.legislation.gov.au/Details/C2021C00472.

889. The question whether screenshots from computer monitors or smartphones may be tendered as electronic evidence has been considered. The issue was presented to a Canadian court which held that the threshold of authenticity remains pivotal in its admissibility.[514] Where a presenter is unable to speak of the authenticity of the screenshot, its admissibility could be in doubt.[515]

§4. ELECTRONIC ARCHIVING REGULATORY ENVIRONMENT

890. Information management legislation provides the National Archives of Australia (NAA) the sole responsibility for electronic archiving.[516] The primary legislation for the NAA is the *Archives Act* 1983 (Cth).[517] Section 3 of the Act specifies that a 'Commonwealth record' may be in any form including electronic and as defined in section 2B of the *Acts Interpretation Act* 1901 (Cth).

891. All Commonwealth agencies are required to make and keep records of their business activities irrespective of how these activities are transacted. All Commonwealth agencies are affected by a variety of legislation that may relate specifically to an agency's unique business or may apply to the public sector. The relevant regulations are given below.

892. Archives Act 1983 (Cth).[518] The Act empowers the National Archives to identify the archival resources of the Commonwealth; preserve and make publicly available the archival resources of the Commonwealth; preserve Commonwealth recordkeeping, by determining standards and giving advice to Australian government agencies.[519] The Act also makes government agencies responsible for the destruction, transfer, or alteration of Commonwealth records (section 24), subject to National Archive's authorization; transfer of Commonwealth archives to the National Archives (section 27); and, to satisfy records management requirements.

893. Archives Regulations 2018 (Cth).[520] The Regulations require Australian government agencies to keep, in writing, information relating to the destruction, transfer of custody or ownership and damage to or alteration of a Commonwealth record in an agency's custody.

514. *R v. Martin* 2021 NLCA 1 at https://records.court.nl.ca/public/supremecourt/decisiondownload/?decision-id=7321&mode=stream.
515. *See* Safeer, R (2021) *R v. Martin:* Shedding Light on Screenshots as Electronic Evidence at http://www.thecourt.ca/r-v-martin-shedding-light-on-screenshots-as-electronic-evidence/.
516. *See* National Archives of Australia, Information Management Legislation at https://www.naa.gov.au/information-management/information-management-legislation.
517. *See* text of the Act at https://www.legislation.gov.au/Details/C2021C00366.
518. *See* text of the Act at https://www.legislation.gov.au/Details/C2019C00179.
519. *See* NAA at https://www.naa.gov.au/node/170.
520. *See* text of the regulations at https://www.legislation.gov.au/Details/F2018L00343.

894. Crimes Act 1914 (Cth).[521] The Act protects official information. It sets out penalties for unauthorized disclosure, such as in the instance that a person intentionally destroys or make inaccessible information known to be required as evidence in a federal judicial proceeding (section 39); a Commonwealth officer publishes or communicates information gained by virtue of being a Commonwealth officer, unless authorized to do so (section 70); a person receives or communicates official secrets (section 79).

895. Electronic Transactions Act 1999 (Cth).[522] The Act permits the use of electronic transactions for public sector activities and enables business and community to use electronic communications in their dealings with government. It makes a transaction valid even if it was an electronic communication (section 8(1)). The Act outlines requirements for electronic documents (section 11) including production; integrity; retention; and copyright.

896. Electronic Transactions Regulations 2000 (Cth).[523] The regulations describe how to give or serve documents by electronic means (Part 3). Documents sent to an email address must be in a format that can be saved and printed (section 10(4)).

897. Evidence Act 1995 (Cth).[524] The Act describes how documents, analogue or digital, must be presented as evidence before federal courts, including original documents, as well as copies, extracts from, or summaries of, original documents (section 48); the abolition of the original document rule (section 51); and the use of Commonwealth records (sections 155, 156 and 182).

898. Freedom of Information Act 1982 (Cth).[525] The Act provides a right of access to most government-held documents, other than exempt documents.

899. Privacy Act 1988 (Cth).[526] The Act regulates the handling of personal information about individuals, including collection; use; storage; and disclosure.

900. Privacy Regulation 2013 (Cth).[527] The regulations require Australian government agencies to take reasonable steps to destroy or de-identify personal information that they hold once it is no longer needed, unless exceptions apply including to Australian Privacy Principles (APP).

901. Public Governance, Performance and Accountability Act 2013 (Cth).[528]

---

521. *See* text of the Act at https://www.legislation.gov.au/Series/C1914A00012.
522. *See* text of the Act at https://www.legislation.gov.au/Details/C2011C00445.
523. *See* text of the regulations at https://www.legislation.gov.au/Details/F2019C00345.
524. *See* text of the Act at https://www.legislation.gov.au/Details/C2018C00433.
525. *See* text of the Act at https://www.legislation.gov.au/Details/C2019C00055.
526. *See* text of the Act at https://www.legislation.gov.au/Series/C2004A03712.
527. *See* text of the regulation at https://www.legislation.gov.au/Series/F2013L02126.
528. *See* text of the Act at https://www.legislation.gov.au/Series/C2013A00123.

The Act details how Commonwealth entities should use and manage public resources, including Commonwealth records (Parts 2-4).

902. *Public Service Act* 1999 (Cth).[529] The Act provides guidance on records management in the Australian Public Service (APS). The APS is open and accountable to the Australian community under the law and within the framework of ministerial responsibility (section 10(4)); APS employee compliance with all applicable Australian laws in their APS role (section 13 (4)); and employees must use Commonwealth resources in a proper manner (section 13 (8)).

I. Impact of the Rules

903. An immediate impact of the rules on the NAA is the adoption and use of current international best practice for managing electronic data as records and for all Commonwealth, State and Territory agencies to establish identifiable corporate recordkeeping systems. This includes the custody of and appropriate destruction policies of archival electronic records in relevant circumstances.

904. The *Building Trust in the Public Record: Managing Information and Data for Government and Community* Policy extends the National Archives' previous policies: *Digital Transition* (2011) and *Digital Continuity 2020* (2015). The Building Trust policy supports agencies to effectively manage information assets under their guardianship and provides an overarching framework for good information management practice.[530]

905. The *Digital Continuity 2020* Policy plays a key role in supporting the Australian government's digital transformation initiatives and driving e-Government.[531] The policy enables the integration of information governance principles and practices into the work of agencies and their governance arrangements. The strategic policy statement goals are that Commonwealth government agencies will manage their information assets, transition to entirely digital work processes and have interoperable information, systems and processes that meet agreed standards in the future.

906. The Digital Continuity Policy applies to Australian government digital and non-digital records, information and data which are created, collected, received and kept as part of government business. The policy uses the term 'information asset' to refer to records, information and data collectively and 'information management' to refer to their collective management.

529. *See* text of the Act at https://www.legislation.gov.au/Details/C2019C00057.
530. National Archives of Australia (2021) Building trust in the public record. Managing information and data for government and community at https://www.naa.gov.au/information-management/informationmanagementpolicies/building-trust-public-record-policy/building-trustpublicrecord-managing-information-and-data-government-andcommunity# intro.
531. National Archives of Australia (2015) Digital Continuity 2020 Policy at https://www.naa.gov.au/information-management/information-management-policies/ digital-continuity-2020-policy.

907. The National Archives established the *Information Management Standard for Australian Government* in 2017.[532] This standard is consistent with the international and Australian standard *AS ISO 15489.1 (2017) Information and Documentation - Records Management, Part 1: Concepts and Principles.*

908. The NAA 2017 Standard sets out principles for the management of information to support agencies to meet business, government and community needs and expectations.[533]

909. To achieve their respective strategic goals Commonwealth government agencies are required to create and manage their information as a public resource in accordance with the *Archives Act* 1983 (Cth) and the *Public Governance, Performance and Accountability Act* 2013 (Cth) as well as the Protective Security Policy Framework, Commonwealth Resource Management Framework and internal corporate controls.

532. The authority is found in s. 2A of the *Archives Act* 1983 (Cth) where the NAA is mandated to determine standards and provide advice on managing Australian Government records.

533. Information Management Standard for Australian Government (2021) at https://www.naa.gov.au/information-management/information-management-standards/information-management-standard-australian-government.

Chapter 7. Consumer Protection: Online Sales and Service

§1. INTRODUCTION

910. In Australia there are no specific legislation on consumer protection for online sales and service. However, the consumer protection laws that govern traditional forms of business and commerce apply equally in an online environment.

§2. FRAMEWORK FOR CONSUMER PROTECTION

I. Constitutional Bases

911. In Australia, the States and Territories have a general power to make laws regarding consumer protection matters within the scope of the Territories powers in section 122 of the *Australian Constitution*. The Commonwealth does not have the constitutional power to make consumer protection laws generally but may make laws with respect to the conduct of corporations and with respect to interstate trade under its general powers in section 51. The Commonwealth may also make consumer protection laws in respect of financial products and services, because of the referral of legislative competence from the states under the *Corporations Agreement 2002*.[534]

912. In 2009, the States and Territories also referred their specific powers concerning consumer credit by signing the National Credit Law Agreement 2009. Made in accordance with COAGs' agreement in March and June 2008 regulation for the responsibility of consumer credit was transferred to the Commonwealth. A uniform approach to consumer credit laws with a national licensing scheme – the *National Consumer Credit Protection Act* 2009 (Cth) replaced the Uniform Credit Laws Agreement 1993, which underpinned the State-based Uniform Consumer Credit Code.[535] On 29 June 2017, technical amendments were made to the National Credit Law Agreement 2009 reflecting the establishment of the Legislative and Governance Forum on Corporations by the Corporations Agreement and include reference to the *Competition and Consumer Act* 2010 (Cth).[536]

II. Background to the Australian Consumer Law

913. As background, the ACL was implemented through enactment of the *Trade Practices Amendment (Australian Consumer Law) Act (No. 1)* 2010 (Cth) and the

534. *See Corporations Amendment Regulations 2002 (No.2)* 2002 (Cth) text at https://classic.austlii.edu.au/au/legis/cth/num_reg_es/car200222002n16415.html.
535. *See* text of the Act at http://classic.austlii.edu.au/au/legis/cth/consol_act/nccpa2009377/.
536. *See* National Credit Law Agreement at https://federation.gov.au/sites/default/files/about/agreements/Revised-National-Credit-Law-Agreement.docx.

Trade Practices Amendment (Australian Consumer Law) Act (No 2) 2010 (Cth). Schedule 2 to the *Competition and Consumer Act* 2010 (CCA) sets out the full text of the ACL.[537]

914. The Australian Consumer Law (ACL) commenced on 1 January 2011, creating a national policy framework designed to enhance consumer choice and protection.

915. The ACL is a national *application law* (generic) which applies in the same way to all sectors and in all Australian jurisdictions. This means that all consumers and businesses in Australia enjoy the same rights and have the same obligations, irrespective of which state or territory they engaged in transactions. As an application law the ACL has been drafted to reflect that it is a law of the Commonwealth and of each State and Territory. Consequently, all of the provisions have been drafted to apply to the conduct of 'persons' rather than 'corporations'.[538]

916. The ACL is *atypical* of Australian legislation in that it provides a single legislative framework across all jurisdictions supported by Commonwealth, state and territory regulators.

917. Consumer affairs ministers form the Consumer Affairs Forum (CAF) under a broad COAG framework.[539] CAF is responsible for the administration and development of the ACL and for other specific issues under the Intergovernmental Agreement (IGA) for the Australian Consumer Law and the Trans-Tasman Mutual Recognition Agreement.

918. Under the IGA the objective of CAF 'is to improve consumer well-being through consumer empowerment and protection, to foster effective competition and to enable the confident participation of consumers in markets in which both consumers and suppliers trade fairly'.[540]

919. Consumer Affairs Australia New Zealand (CAANZ) is a forum of consumer affairs agencies in Australia and New Zealand, established to support the formal responsibilities of CAF. CAANZ.

---

537. *See* Schedule 2 CCA at http://classic.austlii.edu.au/au/legis/cth/consol_act/caca2010265/toc-sch2.html.
538. Part XI of the CCA applies the ACL as a law of the Commonwealth and references to 'persons' apply, for the purposes of the ACL, to 'corporations' as a law of the Commonwealth.
539. Legislative and Governance Forum on Consumer Affairs with Consumer Affairs Australia and New Zealand (2018) *Strategic Agenda 2018-2022*, August at https://consumer.gov.au/sites/consumer/files/2018/11/FINAL-Strategic-Agenda-2018-2022.pdf.
540. *See* Inter-Governmental Agreement at https://consumer.gov.au/sites/consumer/files/2015/06/acl_iga.pdf p.3.

§3. Australian Consumer Law (ACL)

920. In broad terms the ACL applies to all Australian businesses that deal with consumers. The ACL regulates: standards of business conduct; unfair contract laws; harmful business practices; specific B2C transactions; basic consumer rights; and consumer product safety.

921. A '*consumer*' under section 4 of the ACL is a person who has acquired goods or services of any kind valued at less than AUD 40,000 or if more than this value is of a kind ordinarily acquired for personal, domestic or household use. This definition was expanded on 1 July 2021 with the monetary threshold increasing to AUD 100,000.

922. Chapter 2 of the ACL establishes the general standards of business conduct. Prohibitions of misleading or deceptive conduct,[541] unconscionable conduct and unfair contract terms. All consumer contracts and small business contracts that are standard form contracts must not contain 'unfair terms'.

923. Part 1 of Chapter 3 of the ACL sets out specific protections against certain defined business practices that are deemed unfair.

924. Under the ACL it is illegal to engage in unconscionable conduct such as taking unfair or unjust advantage which may include exploiting someone who is suffering from a certain disability.

925. Unfair practices include a wide range of prohibitions against or protections relating to bait advertising; wrongly accepting payment; unsolicited supplies; pyramid schemes and referral selling; component or part pricing; door-to-door unsolicited sales; lay-by agreements; and gift cards.

926. Part 2 of Chapter 3 of the ACL provides certain requirements that businesses must comply with when participating in certain transactions, for example the system of statutory consumer guarantees and unsolicited selling law.

927. Online businesses have legal responsibilities including handling online payments, customer privacy and online reviews.

928. The ACL creates 'consumer guarantees' regarding the quality and function of goods and services that automatically apply to every supply to a 'consumer'. These cannot be waived, limited, or excluded, or misrepresented. Sections 54 to 56 of the ACL provide consumer guarantees as to acceptable quality, the fitness of goods for disclosed purposes and the correspondence between goods and their description.

---

541. *See* ACL misleading or deceptive conduct in Sch. 2 Pt 2-2 s. 18.

929. Liability for the consumer guarantees lies with both the supplier of the good or service and/or the manufacturer of the goods.

930. Consumer guarantees do not apply where the goods were bought from a one-off private sale, bought at auction, purchased for the purpose of resupply, goods lost or destroyed, consumer not taking reasonable care of goods, damaged by consumer's abnormal use, consumer examined the goods before purchase and should have seen obvious faults or defect was brought to the consumer's attention prior to purchase.

931. Under the ACL product safety law applies to consumer goods and product-related services supplied in Australia. The ACL also outlines responsibilities of suppliers under the national product safety framework.

932. Chapter 4 of the ACL creates a criminal offence regime for certain provisions rules on defences, prosecution timeframes, compensation and penalties for offences.

933. For civil matters, the usual statute of limitations applies, that is, within six years of the alleged breach of the ACL, while for criminal matters, prosecutions must be brought within three years.

934. Chapter 5 of the ACL includes enforcement powers, penalties and remedies that can apply for breaches or suspected breaches of the ACL.

935. The ACL is administered and enforced jointly by the ACCC and the State and Territory consumer protection agencies, with the involvement of ASIC on financial services matters.

936. National enforcement powers include enforceable undertakings; substantiation notices; and public warning notices.

937. National consumer law remedies include civic pecuniary penalties; disqualification orders; non-punitive orders; adverse publicity orders; declarations; injunctions; damages; compensatory orders, and redress for non-parties.

938. Certain defences are available for breaches of the ACL including specific defences concerning country-of-origin representations.

I. Enforcement of ACL

939. National, state and territory consumer agencies jointly administer and enforce the ACL.

940. The relevant agencies states and territories are:

- Australian Capital Territory. Access Canberra[542] administers the ACT Fair Trading Act 1992.[543]
- New South Wales. NSW Fair Trading[544] administers the NSW Fair Trading Act 1987.[545]
- Northern Territory. Consumer Affairs[546] administers the NT Consumer Affairs and Fair Trading Act 1990.[547]
- Queensland. The Queensland Office of Fair Trading[548] administers the QLD Fair Trading Act 1989.[549]
- South Australia. Consumer and Business Services[550] administers the SA Fair Trading Act 1987.[551]
- Tasmania. The Consumer, Building and Occupational Services[552] administers the Australian Consumer Law (Tasmania) Act 2010.[553]
- Victoria. Consumer Affairs Victoria[554] administers the Australian Consumer Law and Fair Trading Act 2012.[555]
- Western Australia. Department of Mines, Industry Regulation and Safety[556] administers the WA Fair Trading Act 2010.[557]

941. ASIC enforces the consumer protection provisions of the ASIC Act and the *National Consumer Credit Protection Act* 2009 (Cth).

942. Recent litigations have clarified the overseas reach of the ACL. The Full Federal Court has held that the ACL applies to overseas-based online operators that sell product into Australia in *Valve Corporation v. Australian Competition and Consumer Commission* [2017] FCAFC 224. The court clarified the test for determining the place where a representation on the Internet is made and it was held that the online distribution of games involves the supply of a 'good' within the meaning of the ACL.

---

542. *See* text at https://www.accesscanberra.act.gov.au/app/home/fairtrading/.
543. *See* text at http://www.legislation.act.gov.au/a/1992-72/default.asp.
544. *See* text at https://www.fairtrading.nsw.gov.au/.
545. *See* text at https://www.legislation.nsw.gov.au/view/html/inforce/current/act-1987-068.
546. *See* text at https://consumeraffairs.nt.gov.au/.
547. *See* text at https://legislation.nt.gov.au/en/Legislation/consumer-affairs-and-fair-trading-act-1990.
548. *See* text at https://www.qld.gov.au/law/laws-regulated-industries-and-accountability/queensland-laws-and-regulations/fair-trading-services-programs-and-resources.
549. *See* text at https://www.legislation.qld.gov.au/view/html/inforce/current/act-1989-084.
550. *See* text of the Act at https://www.cbs.sa.gov.au/.
551. *See* text of the Act at http://www.legislation.sa.gov.au/LZ/C/A/FAIR%20TRADING%20ACT%201987.aspx.
552. *See* Tasmania CBOS at https://www.cbos.tas.gov.au/home.
553. *See* text of the Act at https://www.legislation.tas.gov.au/view/html/inforce/current/act-2010-040.
554. *See* Consumer Victoria at http://www.consumer.vic.gov.au/.
555. *See* Consumer Victoria at https://www.consumer.vic.gov.au/resources-and-tools/legislation/legislation-we-administer#a##a.
556. *See* WA Consumer Protection at https://www.commerce.wa.gov.au/consumer-protection.
557. *See* text of the Act at http://www8.austlii.edu.au/cgi-bin/viewdb/au/legis/wa/consol_act/fta2010117/.

943. Australian courts appear not to shy away from assuming Australian jurisdiction over Internet-related activities if a relevant party is a resident in Australia.[558]

§4. ONLINE SALES AND SERVICES LITIGATION

944. Some examples of online sales and services litigation that demonstrate the application of the ACL in online environments are given below. The cases underline the agnostic nature of the application of the consumer protection law to both the face-to-face and virtual markets.

945. The *Trade Practices Act* 1974 (Cth) (TPA) was held to apply in *ACCC v. Internic Technology Pty. Ltd.* (1998) FCA 818 where the ACCC sued Internic for operating a website that made false, misleading and deceptive representations as to the nature of its domain name registration services. It was found that the site 'www.internic.com' operated by Internic was misleading because it falsely represented that the site was affiliated with InterNIC, which was the sole body authorized to issue domain names and which had a website, 'www.internic.net'.

946. In *ACCC v. Abel Rentacar Pty. Ltd.* (1999) FCA 314 it was found that advertisements on the website stating without qualification that cars could be hired for AUD 29 per day were misleading, and the Court ordered them removed from the Internet website operated by the respondent.

947. In *Australian Competition & Consumer Commission v. Chen* [2002] FCA 1248 (8 October 2002) the respondent as operator of the websites (and apparently based in the US), had breached sections of the Act in relation to misrepresentation and misleading and deceptive conduct. The websites allegedly fraudulently imitated the Sydney Opera House official site and customers who had ordered tickets from the websites had either been overcharged or had not received their tickets at all. While the websites were hosted and operated from overseas, the court was satisfied that the actual misrepresentation and the basis for the cause of action had taken place in Australia.[559] This was sufficient for the court's jurisdiction under the TPA to apply. Accordingly, the court made orders for the service of proceedings on Mr Chen, as well as interim orders requiring that Mr Chen restrain from publishing or operating the websites and to 'remove' the websites to make them inaccessible to persons or computers within Australia.[560]

---

558. *See Australian Competition and Consumer Commission v. European City Guide SL* [2009] FCA 1206. The respondent was found to have engaged in misleading and deceptive conduct in circumstances where the business was registered, and all relevant business activities conduced in Spain.
559. *See also* Allens Arthur Robinson 'Australian laws can apply to entities outside national borders' at https://data.allens.com.au/pubs/pdf/cmt/foecomnov02.pdf.
560. The ACCC action had the assistance of the International Consumer Protection and Enforcement Network (ICPEN) and the US Federal Trade Commission. *See* Australian Competition and Consumer Commission (2003) *Global Consumer Scams: The ACCC's International Role*, Canberra. *See also* ACCC at https://www.accc.gov.au/media-release/court-declares-imitation-sydney-opera-house-website-illegal.

948. Australia's two biggest competing airlines, Jetstar and Virgin Australia were fined AUD 545,000 and AUD 200,000 respectively for misleading practices described as 'drip pricing'.[561] Drip pricing is where a price advertised online is increased incrementally throughout the purchase process via undisclosed fees or charges. The ACCC had alleged that the airlines engaged in misleading conduct by not disclosing hidden charges on top of advertised prices on their mobile websites. In 2015, the court found that the airlines had engaged in misleading and deceptive (drip) pricing practices.

949. In *ACCC v. Apple Pty Ltd (No 4)* (2018) ATPR ¶42-605, Federal Court of Australia, 18 June 2018 found that the respondent in trade or commerce had engaged in misleading or deceptive conduct, or conduct that was likely to mislead or deceive, in contravention of s 18 of the ACL; and in connection with the supply of iPhone and iPad devices (including all hardware and software), made false or misleading representations concerning the existence, exclusion or effect of the consumer guarantees under Part 3-2 of the ACL, and the rights or remedies available under Part 5-4 of the ACL, in contravention of section 29(1)(m) of the ACL. The court imposed a pecuniary penalty of AUD 9 million in respect of its contraventions of section 29(1)(m) of the ACL.[562]

950. In *ACCC v. Jetstar Airways Pty Ltd* [2019] FCA 797 (30 May 2019), the Federal Court of Australia has ordered Jetstar Airways Pty Ltd to pay AUD 1.95 million in penalties for making false or misleading representations about consumer guarantee rights under the ACL.[563]

951. In *Australian Competition and Consumer Commission v. Sony Interactive Entertainment Network Europe Limited* [2020] FCA 787; 381 ALR 531; 145 ACSR 353 Sony Interactive Entertainment Network Europe Limited was found to have engaged in conduct that was misleading or deceptive, or likely to mislead or deceive, in contravention of section 18 of the ACL; and/or made false or misleading representations regarding the existence, exclusion or effect of any condition, warranty, guarantee, right or remedy in contravention of section 29(1)(m) of the ACL. A pecuniary penalty of AUD 3.5 million was imposed on the respondent.[564]

---

561. *See Australian Competition and Consumer Commission v. Jetstar Airways Pty Limited* [2015] FCA 1263 (17 Nov. 2015); and *Australian Competition and Consumer Commission v. Virgin Australia Airlines Pty Ltd* (No 2) [2017] FCA 204. *See also* Timebase (2015) report 'Australian Airlines fined three quarters of a million dollars for drip pricing' at https://www.timebase.com.au/news/2015/AT452-article.html.
562. *See* CCH at https://pinpoint.cch.com.au/document/legauUio3032610sl989474813/australian-competition-and-consumer-commission-v-apple-pty-ltd-no-4.
563. *See* ACCC at https://www.accc.gov.au/media-release/jetstar-to-pay-195-million-for-false-or-misleading-claims-on-refunds, and Timebase report at https://www.timebase.com.au/news/2018/AT04895-article.html.
564. *See* Federal Court of Australia case note at https://jade.io/j/?a=outline&id=750722.

§5. Trends and Proposals for Reform

952. Recent litigations have pointed to the trend of increasing pecuniary penalties issued by the Courts for consumer law breaches. The ACCC outlined its compliance and enforcement priorities in February 2021.[565] The ACCC will focus particularly on the impact of the COVID-19 pandemic including sales practices of the travel and aviation sectors; pricing and selling practices of essential services such as electricity and telecommunications; competition and consumer issues relating to digital platforms; and the financial services sector.

953. Amendments to clarify what constitutes a 'major failure' to comply with the ACL and inserting additional test into the definition of a major failure with respect to goods and services in the ACL are found in *Treasury Laws Amendment (2020 Measures No. 6) Act* 2020 (Cth).[566]

954. Under the ACL a major failure in a good or product occurs where a reasonable consumer would not have purchased the good or product had they known about the problem. It could also be where the good or product is significantly different from the sample or description at the time of purchase, unfit for normal purpose and unable to be easily fixed, or unsafe.[567]

955. Proposals to strengthen and broaden the existing unfair contract terms regime under the ACL as well as making illegal unfair contract terms have been underway since September 2021.[568]

565. *See* Sims, R (2021) ACCC 2021 Compliance and Enforcement Priorities at https://www.accc.gov.au/speech/accc-2021-compliance-and-enforcement-priorities.
566. *See* text to the Act at https://www.legislation.gov.au/Details/C2020A00141 that amends Schedule 2 s. 260 of the CCA.
567. *See* ACCC Consumer guarantees at https://www.accc.gov.au/consumers/consumer-rights-guarantees/repair-replace-refund.
568. *See* Treasury (2021) strengthening protections against unfair contract terms exposure draft legislation at https://treasury.gov.au/consultation/c2021-201582.

Chapter 8. Online Liability

§1. Introduction

956. The Australian government is responsible for laws and regulations relating to Internet governance and online safety. This responsibility includes online services and infrastructure, Internet governance, cybersecurity, competition and online harms.

957. A central question in liability law is *who* did *what* wrongful conduct. In cyberspace, the way the law defines the role of participants in the online activity and the operation of the online facilities is particularly apposite. Ironically in the cyber environment, the virtually limitless number of end users, their 'anonymity', and the automated nature of the facilities (hardware and software with embedded artificial intelligent algorithms) make it difficult to identify both the 'who' and the 'what' conduct to help resolve the question of online liability.

958. So the pertinent question is: what is meant by 'online' to satisfy both the who and the what conduct to sheet home liability on a party? The generic term used to describe the relevant parties is to refer to these as Internet intermediaries, carriage service providers, Internet service providers, content hosts, search engines, social media platforms and e-commerce and payment providers. All these actors play a role in enabling (and restricting) the information that people can see and post online.

959. Unsurprisingly, there is no one preeminent legal theory that imposes a legal standard of responsibility on online intermediaries. For that it may be necessary to examine each of the theories of law which includes copyright, defamation, consumer protection and statutory liability to discover primary roles and responsibilities.

960. This chapter begins with a discussion of the nomenclature used to describe Internet intermediaries, followed by a section on common law and statutory liability, and a final section on trends in liability law.

§2. Framework for Liability

961. To properly understand liability law, a framework that identifies individual actors and their respective roles and responsibilities may be required. Each of these may assume differing levels of liability with different rules and sanctions. This framework may be constructed by putting together the different terminologies that describe the online activities of intermediaries. The terminology used may assist in a proper definition and identification of the relevant theory of law.

I. Definitions and Terminology

962. The online activity of a digital 'warrior' may be conceived by drawing an interlocking Venn diagram of three irregular circles with each interlocking part in greater or less prominence depending on their respective roles. To this may be added the view that an actor could be in one or more roles at different times and even at the same time.

963. One circle of the Venn diagram describes basic Internet services that include the deployment of application software such as the proprietary Microsoft 365 office suite, and Google Docs suite with its email services such as Outlook and Gmail. An Internet service is a method of communication between two electronic devices over a network.

964. A second circle of the diagram interlock these basic services with digital platforms applications that may include the hardware infrastructure. Such platforms include social networks and publishing services; gateways like search engines; and marketplaces such as Amazon, ebay as well as other functions. These functions could include review websites for online and offline retailers and services, podcast aggregators that pull content and miscellaneous related media content together, for example, Apple Podcast through to Really Simple Syndication (RSS) feeds. In RSS feeds websites share and exchange content with each other using human- and machine-readable Extensible Mark-up Language (XML); as well as short (SMS) and instant messaging services (iMS); for example, on Twitter and Facebook.

965. A third interlocking circle of the diagram consists of forum administrators – an intermediary with soft skills at its core. The online forum model also permits third-party commentary. The online forum could be run by an individual, a company or a community group hosting a Facebook page or conversations with instant messaging threads.

966. Having described such an ecosystem of actors – Internet intermediaries – the potential liability for violating consumer protection laws, deliberate or inadvertent copyright infringements and defamatory comments made by third parties can be quite large. Today, anyone with an Internet connection may publish or make comment on any subject to the world at large. Any actor may be able to either heighten or to minimize the risk of harm in social and economic settings. In the latter, the business model may be designed to profit from network effects of their posts such as in the stock market. Whether these sites could be held responsible for the content posted, created and authored by third parties is thus the pivotal legal issue.

A. Internet Intermediary

967. The Organisation for Economic Cooperation and Development (OECD) has defined Internet intermediaries as entities that bring together or facilitate transactions between third parties on the Internet.[569] This umbrella term may be used to cover the broad range of online services and platforms discussed in this chapter. Such intermediaries exist to provide basic Internet services, host digital platforms and are Internet forum administrators for third parties. The latter create content, products and services.

968. Internet intermediaries are also mere conduits like those performed by telephone lines and postal services. The intermediaries facilitate access to services on the Internet, but neither actively participate nor profit from the generation and dissemination of user-generated content.

969. The *Telecommunications Act* 1997 (Cth) section 7 defines the term 'carriage service intermediary' to refer to a person who is a carriage service provider (as defined in section 87) who supplies or proposes to supply a carriage service to the public using a network unit owned by one or more carriers.

B. Digital Platform

970. A digital platform is provided by an Internet intermediary for user-generated content to be posted and shared with all users. This service will allow third-party comments and reviews as well as aggregating and curating user-generated content from other sources. This can include search engines where search results are curated.

C. Internet Service Provider

971. An ISP connects its subscribers to the Internet by supplying hardware facilities and access equipment, such as modems and subscriber lines.[570] The ISP may host virtual ISPs, provide free Internet services and other services on the Internet.

972. In a codified form, an ISP according to the *Broadcasting Services Act* 1992 (Cth)[571] is a person who supplies, or proposes to supply, an Internet carriage service to the public.

D. Internet Content Host

973. An Internet content host according to the *Broadcasting Services Act* 1992 (Cth) is defined as a person who hosts Internet content in Australia, or who proposes

569. Organisation for Economic Cooperation and Development (OECD) (2010) 'The Economic and Social Role of Internet Intermediaries' at http://www.oecd.org/digital/ieconomy/44949023.pdf.
570. Riordan, J (2016) *Liability of Internet Intermediaries*, Oxford University Press.
571. Clause 8 Schedule 5 Online Services.

to host Internet content in Australia.[572] This has the same meaning as a content service provider defined in section 97 of the *Telecommunications Act* 1997 (Cth).

974. Internet content providers services include web site building, mailboxes, social media, host to Internet content and access to Internet search engines.

975. Given the range of actors, the responsibilities and liability of Internet intermediaries should be related to their different roles and functions. Careful consideration needs to be given to the nature of the different responsibilities of each actor. Thus, with reference to online safety, the range of mischiefs that may be perpetrated by third parties on the Internet could include cyberbullying, abusive commentary or 'trolling', the non-consensual sharing of intimate images, grooming for the purpose of child sexual abuse, cyber-flashing,[573] doxing[574] and cyberstalking'.[575]

976. The general tests for liability are intention, the active or passive role of the actor and the knowledge that each intermediary possesses.

§3. Common law and Statutory Liability

977. Online liability is governed either by common law or statute or a combination of both. This is predicated upon the nature of the mischief and the appropriate application of standards and tests. Given the wide reach of liability issues the following is a highly selective discussion of four different liabilities, namely online liability for copyright infringement, defamation, consumer protection and statutory infringements.

I. Online Liability under Copyright law

978. Online liabilities for copyright infringements by Internet intermediaries may be direct or indirect. Direct liability includes demonstrating ownership of the allegedly infringing material and that the infringer had violated an exclusive right granted to a copyright holder. Indirect liability, is characterized by Internet

572. Clause 5 Schedule 7 Content Services.
573. *Cyber-flashing* is the sending of obscene pictures to others over peer-to-peer Wi-Fi networks, such as the app AirDrop on Apple iPhones.
574. *Doxing* is to search for and publishing of private or identifying information about a particular individual on the Internet, typically with malicious intent.
575. Australian Government Department of Infrastructure, Transport, Regional Development and Communications (2019) *Online Safety Legislation Reform – Discussion Paper* (11 December) at https ://www.communications.gov.au/have-your-say/consultation-new-online-safety-act, p. 14.

intermediaries not themselves directly engaged in the infringing activity but because of their ownership and operation of equipment and services that facilitate copyright infringement.[576]

A. Intermediary Liability

979. Section 13(2) of the Australian *Copyright Act* 1968 (Cth) states that the exclusive right to do acts comprised in the copyright in a work, adaptation or subject matter 'includes the exclusive right to *authorize* a person to do that act' in relation to that work, adaptation or subject matter. A person who authorizes another to do an act without the licence of the copyright owner and without legal justification infringes the copyright in the work or subject matter.[577] An online intermediary will be liable under the Act where a third party is given authorization and the intermediary does not have a licence to do so.

980. The intermediary may also be secondarily liable in authorizing the infringement.[578]

981. Secondary infringement liability. However, if the customers of an ISP infringe copyright and the ISP does not take steps to stop it from occurring, is the ISP liable for copyright infringement? In *Roadshow Films Pty Ltd v. .iiNet Ltd (No 3)* (2010) 263 ALR 215 the Full Federal Court found that iiNet Ltd. (iiNet) was not liable as iiNet had not authorized any copyright infringement by its customers.

982. This decision cited with approval the landmark High Court case of *University of New South Wales v. Moorhouse & Angus & Robertson (Publishers) Pty Ltd* (1975) 133 CLR 1. As well the court relied on mandatory factors in the *Copyright Act* 1968 (Cth) section 101(1A) which included the test of whether a party had the power to prevent the infringing acts; the nature of relationship between a party and its customers; and, whether the party took reasonable steps to prevent infringing acts.[579]

983. While the *iiNet* case dealt with secondary infringement, in *Optus v. NRL* the court was called upon to decide who bore liability for primary infringement of

576. The US *Copyright Act* 1976 17 U.S.C.A.Pub.L. 94–553 s 106 identifies direct liability, vicarious liability and contributory liability. In addition, the *Digital Millennium Copyright Act* 1998 (DMCA) Pub.L.No. 105-304, 112 State 28, 60 (1998) limits ISP liability by allowing them to avoid both copyright liability and liability to subscribers by following the specific guidelines set out in the Act.

577. *Copyright Act* 1968 (Cth) s. 36(1), 101(1).

578. *Australasian Performing Right Assoc. Limited v. Jain* (1990) 26 FCR 53, 57 (Full Fed. Ct.).

579. *Roadshow Films Pty Limited v. iiNet Limited* [2011] FCAFC 23. *See also* discussions in Fairbairn, F & Webb, T (2011) 'When is an ISP liable for its users' copyright infringements?' at https://www.claytonutz.com/knowledge/2011/may/when-is-an-isp-liable-for-its-users-copyright-infringements; and Giblin, RK (2012) Australia's High Court rules on ISP's liability for user infringements. *Journal of Intellectual Property Law & Practice*, 7(8), 559-560.

copyright via the Internet.[580] The preferred view of the Full Court was that Optus and the subscriber acted in concert to produce the copies and were jointly and severally liable for the copyright infringement.

B. Authorization Liability

984. A person secondarily liable for the unlawful actions of another person for authorizing copyright infringements was considered in the Australian High Court case in *Adelaide Corporation v. Australian Performing Rights Association* (1928) 40 CLR 481. The case cited with approval the landmark case on authorization liability in the High Court decision of *University of NSW v. Moorhouse* (1975) 133 CLR 1; (1975) 6 ALR 193.

985. Following *Moorhouse,* a new section 39A was promptly introduced into the *Copyright Act* 1968 (Cth) to protect libraries against authorization liability. A notice is fixed on photocopy machines, for example, could avoid any such liability.

986. The amendment to the Copyright Act follows the Agreed Statement to the 1996 *WIPO Copyright Treaty* (WCT) in which '... the mere provision of physical facilities for enabling or making a communication does not in itself amount to communication within the meaning of this Treaty or the Berne Convention'.[581]

987. Also section 112E of the *Copyright Act* 1968 (Cth), inserted pursuant to the *Copyright Amendment (Digital Agenda) Act* 2000 (Cth), provides that a person 'who provides facilities for making, or facilitating the making of, a communication is not taken to have authorized any infringement of copyright in an audiovisual item merely because another person uses the facilities so provided to do what is provided and included in the copyright'. These are described as 'safe harbour' defences to infringement.[582]

C. Exemptions from Liability

988. Internet intermediaries may also seek exemption from liability for a lack of knowledge in the sense of being unaware of infringing materials passing and stored

580. *Singtel Optus Pry Ltd v. National Rugby League Investments Pty Ltd (No 2)* (2012) 199 FCR 300; 285 ALR 157; [2012] FCA 34; BC201200207" (2012) 24(8) *Intellectual Property Law Bulletin* 202.

581. This agreed statement relates to Article 8 of the WCT. *See also* Lindsay, D (2012) 'ISP liability for end-user copyright infringements: the High Court decision in Roadshow Films v iiNet'. *Telecommunications Journal of Australia* 62 (4): 53.1-53.24 at http://tja.org.au.

582. Four safe harbour defences from s. 112E of the *Copyright Act* 1968 (Cth) include: s. 112AC content service providers (CSP) providing facilities or services and transient storage'; s. 116D CSPs cache copyright material automatic process; s. 116AE CSP hosting services store at direction of a user of copyright material; and s. 116AF CSPs referral services referring to an online location using GPS tools technology.

through their servers. Additionally, they could plead the due diligence exemption by stating that they had taken all precautions to prevent infringement and were not negligent in their actions.

989. In Australia the concept of diffusion rights under copyright law includes the transmission of the work to users and subscribers of copyright materials.

990. In the lead case of *Telstra v. Australasian Performing Rights Association* infringement occurred when Telstra played music of the association-owned copyright to persons 'on hold' on the telephone.[583] The majority of the High Court held Telstra infringed the association's right to cause the works to be transmitted to the subscribers by a diffusion service (when the caller used a conventional phone).[584]

991. The *Copyright Amendment (Digital Agenda) Act* 2000 (Cth) was passed to provide greater certainty about the various obligations ISPs owed to copyright owners. The Act includes exceptions for the temporary reproduction or copies of copyrightable material. The amending act also responds to ISP's concern regarding the uncertainty of liability arising from copyright infringements by customers. The uncertainty has been removed by limiting and clarifying the liability of ISPs in relation to both direct and authorization liability. ISPs are immunized against liability for authorizing copyright infringement in the absence of contributory negligence. ISPs may also escape liability for merely providing the facilities to enable infringements to occur.[585]

II. Online Liability for Defamation

992. Defamation is a common law tort whereby a communication, publication or broadcast of material to two or more people which causes a third party's reputation to be injured. This communication could be expressed verbally, in writing or as pictures. The legal test is whether an ordinary reasonable person would think less of that person because of the defamatory material.

---

583. *Telstra Corporation Limited v. Australasian Performing Right Association Limited* [1997] HCA 41; (1997) 38 IPR 294.
584. The 'diffusion right' in the *Copyright Act* 1968 (Cth) is in s. 31(1)(a)(v). When used a mobile phone, the High Court unanimously held that Telstra had infringed the Association's right to broadcast the works. The 'broadcast right' in the *Copyright Act* 1968 (Cth) is in s. 31(1)(a)(iv). *See* Telstra [1997] HCA 41; 38 IPR 294, 304, 316, 340.
585. *See* ss 39B and 112E of the *Copyright Amendment (Digital Agenda) Act* 2000 (Cth). *See also* Mercurio, B (2002) 'Internet Service Provider Liability for Copyright Infringements of Subscribers: American and Australian Developments' [2002] MurdochUeJlLaw 51; (2002) 9(4) *Murdoch University Electronic Journal of Law*; and Fairbairn, J & Webb, T (2011) When is an ISP liable for its users' copyright infringements? at https://www.claytonutz.com/knowledge/2011/may/when-is-an-isp-liable-for-its-users-copyright-infringements.

A. *The Voller Case*

993. Dylan Voller sued several media outlets over comments about him that were published on Facebook.[586] The High Court by a majority held that the liability of a person as a publisher depends upon whether that person, by facilitating and encouraging the relevant communication, 'participated' in the communication of the defamatory matter to a third person. The majority rejected the appellant's argument that for a person to be a publisher they must know of the relevant defamatory matter and intended to convey it.

994. The *Voller case* confirms that an Internet intermediary, hosting an organization or person to post comments by third parties, may be liable for any defamation in the comments others may make. While larger Internet intermediary organizations may have the resources to keep track of posts, individual persons hosting sites may have difficulty in controlling and mitigating potentially defamatory posts from third parties.

995. The High Court's decision in the *Voller case* held to an orthodox interpretation of 'publication' under defamation laws. In effect the court rejected the argument made by the media company appellants that they should not be liable for defamatory posts on Facebook pages that they controlled, because they did not intend the material to be posted.

996. This decision introduces uncertainty about what is required for the host of an online comment to be considered a participant in the publication process. Entities which provide infrastructure for defamatory comments can be held liable as publishers with or without notice. The defence of innocent dissemination may only be argued after the tort of defamation has been established.[587]

B. *Publication*

997. Publication is a term of art and is an essential element of Australian defamation law. Material must be published before it can be deemed defamatory. The principle laid in *Webb v. Bloch* (1928) 41 CLR 331 confirmed in *Trkulja v. Google LLC* [2018] HCA 25. A person making material available to a third party is a 'publisher' once the matter becomes readable on a media and is comprehensible to the third party.

586. *Fairfax Media Publications Pty Ltd v. Dylan Voller; Nationwide News Pty Limited v. Dylan Voller; Australian News Channel Pty Ltd v. Dylan Voller* [2021] HCA 27.

587. *See* Qui, G (2021) What new defamation ruling means for your social media at https://www.artslaw.com.au/defamation-and-the-voller-case/; and Lynch, K & Nunan, M (2021) The Voller Appeal: High Court confirms liability for third party Facebook comments at https://jws.com.au/en/insights/articles/2021-articles/the-voller-appeal-high-court-confirms-liability.

998. In *Trkulja v. Google LLC [2018] HCA 25* the High Court held that Google Inc could be liable as a publisher prior to notice of the defamatory matter posted on the Google webpage.

999. However, previously in *Google Inc v. Australian Competition and Consumer Commission (ACCC)* (2013) 294 ALR 404; 87 ALJR 235; [20131 HCA; Google was held to be merely a 'means of communication between advertisers and consumers' in their sponsored links service called Google Ads and therefore was relieved of any liability.

1000. It is now generally understood that an ISP that merely provides a service over which others can publish, and access defamatory material is not likely to be liable for 'publishing' that content. A distinction is thus made between active publishing and passive facilitation. The ISP in other words is a conduit and therefore not likely to be liable for the publication of the defamatory material.

1001. In 2015 Google was found liable in the Supreme Court of South Australia for publishing defamatory material when its search engine that provided links which contained an extract of text that carried defamatory imputations.[588] Previously in 2012 liability subsists when an image search results in images from third-party pages in such a way that gave rise to a defamatory imputation.[589]

1002. Defamation is private law. The question of who is and is not a publisher is determined by common law and operates irrespective of whether online or offline publishers make it.

1003. Protections for digital publishers include the innocent dissemination defence, 'safe harbour' provisions, and 'takedown' notices.

1004. Innocent dissemination defence can also be pleaded in tandem with the immunity provided by the *Broadcasting Services Act* 1992 (Cth) Clause 91 Schedule 5.[590]

C. Jurisdictional Issues

1005. One should also be mindful of technological innovations that now include hosts existing on 'clouds' and 'cloud service providers'. The liability of these hosts and providers on the Internet should be like the other Internet intermediaries discussed previously. Cloud services offer remote computational and storage services

588. *Duffy v. Google Inc* [2015] SASC 170; (2015) 125 SASR 437. Upheld on appeal in *Google Inc v. Duffy* (2017) 129 SASR 304.
589. *Trkulja v. Google (No 5)* [2012] VSC 533 (12 Nov. 2012).
590. Clause 91(1) of Schedule 5 to the *Broadcasting Services Act* 1992 (Cth) inserted in 1999, provides immunity to 'Internet service providers' and 'Internet content hosts' in certain circumstances in relation to third-party material.

for on-demand access to the Internet. With respect to the latter, webmail and big data databases are now increasingly being delivered via cloud infrastructure located in remote sites.[591]

1006. A general legal principle governing a tort is that the law of the place where it took place is usually applied. When a website publishes defamatory or misleading information, the court where the victim is located may assert its jurisdiction. However, on the Internet the identification of the location may prove difficult. Several cases have illustrated the difficulties that cross-jurisdictional postings on the Internet pose.

1007. In *Macquarie Bank Ltd. & Anor v. Berg* (1999) NSWSC 526; Simpson J of the NSW Supreme Court refused to grant an injunction against an alleged defamatory Internet website based in an offshore jurisdiction.

1008. The High Court in *Dow Jones and Company Inc. v. Gutnick* (2002) 210 CLR 575 held that the location is where the defamatory material on the Internet was downloaded. The respondent could litigate his claim in Australia since it is where the circle of people in which his reputation was likely to be damaged by the article and where the damage was suffered.

1009. Defamation is a strict liability tort. Arguably, intermediaries may simply remove content to avoid being sued. However, there may be a possible chilling effect on freedom of speech and inventiveness.

III. Consumer Protection Law

1010. Consumers are protected from misleading and deceptive conduct under provisions of the *Australian Consumer Law* (ACL) Schedule 2 to the *Competition and Consumer Act* 2010 (Cth). Such representations may occur online or offline; onshore or offshore.

1011. In *Australian Competition and Consumer Commission (ACCC) v. European City Guide SL* [2009] FCA 1206 a Federal Court granted leave to the ACCC to serve an originating process on a respondent domiciled abroad. The respondent caused to be published in Australia leading and deceptive representations which contained deliberate mistakes intended to prompt businesses to respond.

1012. Network service operators as intermediaries may also be liable for chat rooms and websites that provide financial advice. Pursuant to Chapter 7 of the *Corporations Act* 2001 (Cth), ASIC established a single licensing regime for financial service providers (discussed in this book in Chapter 7 Consumer Protection: Online

591. *See* further commentary on the role of technological innovation in Pappalardo, K and Suzor, N (2018) 'The Liability of Australian Online Intermediaries' *Sydney Law Review* 40 (4) p 472-473.

Sales and Service §2 Framework for Consumer Protection). 'Financial service' is defined broadly and includes the provision of financial product advice.

1013. An ISP that acts as a mere conduit and does not exercise control over those providing the financial advice might be outside the reach of the regime. In Australia, the offer of securities on the Internet and accessible from here means that Australian law will apply.[592]

A. *Fake Reviews*

1014. Online reviews are subject to the ACL. A false review can be potentially misleading and deceptive. The false review is intended to persuade a customer to think and act in a certain way based on false information.

1015. In 2016 Builders Champion Homes commenced court proceedings against forty-five families in New South Wales who were dissatisfied with the construction of their homes and left negative reviews on a website at http://www.productreview.com.au. The customers posted the reviews under headings that recommended consumers avoid the building company. However, the litigation was withdrawn before a final decision.[593]

1016. In *Google v. ACCC* (2013) 249 CLR 435 the High Court held that Google was not liable when it created a system to enable third parties to create advertisements that were reproduced on Google's search results pages. The High Court found that Google did not 'endorse' advertisements submitted by third parties and published on its own web pages on the basis that the content of the material was wholly determined by the advertiser and published automatically by Google. Google 'did not itself engage in misleading or deceptive conduct or *endorse or adopt* the representations which it displayed on behalf of advertisers'.[594]

1017. The decision in *Google v. ACCC* can be contrasted with the earlier Federal Court of Australia decision in *ACCC v. Allergy Pathway (No 2)* [2011] FCA 74; (2011) 192 FCR 34 where the respondents were found to have breached their undertaking not to engage in misleading and deceptive conduct when they failed to remove comments posted by third parties on their Facebook page. Allergy Pathway was liable for contempt of court on the basis that it knew about the comments and failed to remove them.[595]

---

592. Australian Securities and Investments Commission Policy Statement No. 141, issued on 2 Mar. 2000.
593. Williams, S (2016) Building company withdraws legal action over negative online reviews, (June 2) at https://www.domain.com.au/news/legal-action-pulled-after-taking-aim-at-negative-online-reviews-20160602-gpa4hh/.
594. *Google v. ACCC* (2013) 249 CLR 435, 459 (per French CJ, Crennan and Kiefel JJ).
595. *ACCC v. Allergy Pathway (No 2)* [2011] FCA 74; (2011) 192 FCR 34, 37 & 42 (per Finkelstein J). The undertaking was given in the context of litigation brought by the ACCC. The respondents were also found to have breached the undertakings through material that they themselves had posted.

B. Hacking and Spoofing of Email Addresses

1018. Hacking and spoofing of an email is a type of online scam.[596] However, the legal position is uncertain when attempting to establish liability. Arguably the hacked party is considered the one at fault if the email is the cause of malicious damage or loss to another party because of negligence or other reasons. A distinction must be made between the actual hacking of a businesses' server and the spoofing of a businesses' email address.

1019. Hacking involves a hacker gaining access to a businesses' email or IT system and impersonating the email address of the business or a member of staff.

1020. Spoofing is about making it appear that the email is coming from a trusted sender, while the email originates from an external source.

1021. Where the case is simply one of spoofing, there should be no liability or responsibility on part of the supplier whose email address and invoices originating therefrom were spoofed. However, the customer is still liable to pay the outstanding amounts to the supplier. On the contrary, if the case was one of an actual hacking of the businesses' server the degree of liability would depend on the circumstances of the case.

1022. An invoice fraud scheme is one that involves a cybercriminal masquerading as a trusted supplier and sending a fake invoice to that supplier's customer email address.

C. Vicarious Liability for Employee Internet Misuse

1023. Employers have successfully sued under the doctrine of vicarious liability where their employees have harassed other employees in the workplace, for instance. The High Court has held in several cases that an employer may be vicariously liable for intentional, criminal acts on the part of an employee when there is 'a sufficiently "close connection" between the employer's enterprise' and the employee's offending conduct, even if the conduct is not authorized by the employer.[597]

1024. Employers may also be held liable for a wider range of employee misconduct. The potential for abuse of email and Internet facilities provided at the workplace is virtually limitless.[598]

---

596. Carlill, J (2020) Australia: Legal liability when your business email has been hacked (16 November) at https://www.mondaq.com/australia/white-collar-crime-anti-corruption-fraud/1006152/legal-liability-when-your-business-email-has-been-hacked.

597. *New South Wales v. Lepore and Another; Samin v. Queensland and Others; Rich v. Queensland and Others* 195 ALR 412 (2003) 195 ALR 412, at 481 per Kirby J.

598. Stephens Lawyers (2010) 'Legal Traps: The Internet & the Office - Employer Liability for Employee Internet misuse' at https://stephens.com.au/wp-content/uploads/2016/11/May-2010-Legal-Traps.pdf.

1025. In a case before the Queensland Anti-Discrimination Tribunal in 2006, Ms Webb successfully established that whilst employed with Queensland Health, she was sexually harassed by a male co-worker whose unwanted conduct included the sending of pornographic emails. Webb had informed her employer of the harassment but was told no action could be taken until she lodged a formal complaint.[599]

1026. The liability of employers and company directors for workplace bullying and harassment was highlighted in Victoria in 2010 in the wake of the *Panlock* case. Brodie Panlock, a waitress at Café Vamp in Melbourne, committed suicide because of 'relentless bullying' by co-workers on the Internet. Under the *Occupational Health and Safety Act* 2004 (Vic), WorkSafe successfully prosecuted the company as employer, the company director and manager and two employees.[600]

1027. To avoid liability from staff misuse of the Internet and email, the recommendation is to devise and implement a comprehensive policy, providing employee training and guidance. A workplace Internet browsing, and email policy should also be implemented.[601]

IV. Statutory Liability

A. Vilification

1028. Although untested in Australia, social networking Web 2.0 sites such as Facebook (Meta), Twitter, MySpace and YouTube, could raise new discrimination issues in the workplace.

1029. Intermediaries who provide a forum for third-party content can be liable under the *Racial Discrimination Act* 1975 (Cth) when those comments amount to vilification under the act.[602] Section 18C of the Act makes it unlawful to 'do an act'[603] that is reasonably likely to 'offend, insult, humiliate or intimidate' a person or group where that act is motivated by 'race, colour or national or ethnic origin'.

1030. In the two decisions *Silberberg* and *Clarke* the courts considered the provision in the context of an online forum. However, the courts have come to contrasting conclusions as to when a secondary actor will be liable for providing the

---

599. *Webb v. State of Queensland* [2006] QADT 8 (23 Mar. 2006).

600. 16 May 2008 — *Case* No: 3625/06. Record of investigation into death at https://www.coronerscourt.vic.gov.au/sites/default/files/2018-12/panlock.pdf and *see also* Gleeson, S (2010) 'Brodie's Law – Panlock case Bullying / Harassment Psychological factors Workplace Culture' at https://www.rtwmatters.org/article/article.php?id=1648.

601. *Office of the Privacy Commissioner*, 'Guidelines on Workplace Email, Web Browsing and Privacy', available at http://www.privacy.gov.au/materials/types/guidelines/view/6056.

602. *See* text of the Act at http://www.austlii.edu.au/au/legis/cth/consol_act/rda1975202/.

603. The reference to 'an act', in this case, specifically includes an omission: see *Racial Discrimination Act* 1975 (Cth) s. 3(3): 'refusing or failing to do an act shall be deemed to be the doing of an act and a reference to an act includes a reference to such a refusal or failure'. *See* text for s. 18C at http://www.austlii.edu.au/au/legis/cth/consol_act/rda1975202/s18c.html.

facilities for another to make vilifying comments.[604] The contrasting views lie primarily in the intentional element of the provision.

1031. In *Silberberg*, Gyles J found that there was insufficient evidence to draw that conclusion — the first respondent's failure to remove the offensive comments was 'just as easily explained by inattention or lack of diligence'.[605]

1032. In *Clarke* Barker J held that where the respondent 'actively solicits and moderates contributions from readers', the 'offence will be given as much by the respondent in publishing the offensive comment as by the original author in writing it'.[606]

B. Abhorrent Violent Material

1033. The *Criminal Code Amendment (Sharing of Abhorrent Violent Material) Act* 2019 (Cth) requires online intermediaries, including social media services and digital platform providers, to take steps to remove abhorrent violent material that is accessible in Australia.[607]

C. Summary

1034. Intermediary liabilities may lie on intent as well as the third-party action. The design and operational aspects of the system may help explain the facilitation of the defamatory statements as would answers as to whether there were active or passive actors. There would be liability by omission in that there was a failure to act with or without prior or any knowledge.

1035. The *Manila Principles on Intermediary Liability* is a joint civil society statement on best practices, informed particularly by freedom of expression and privacy rights under international law.[608] The Manila Principles set out a guide for intermediary liability law that does not require intermediaries either to proactively monitor content or to substantially evaluate the validity of allegations that third-party content is harmful.

---

604. *Silberberg v. Builders Collective of Australia Inc* [2007] FCA 1512; (2007) 164 FCR 475 ('Silberberg'); *Clarke v. Nationwide News Pty Ltd* [2012] FCA 307; (2012) 201 FCR 389 ('Clarke').
605. *Silberberg* [2007] FCA 1512; (2007) 164 FCR 475, 486 [35].
606. *Clarke* [2012] FCA 307; (2012) 201 FCR 389, 412 [110].
607. Irwin, E & Selvadurai, N (2021) Imposing liability on online intermediaries for violent user-generated content: an Australian perspective at *Richmond Journal of Law and Technology* (2021) v. 28(1), pp. 1-4 and at https://researchers.mq.edu.au/en/publications/imposing-liability-on-online-intermediaries-for-violent-user-gene.
608. *Manila Principles on Intermediary Liability* at https://www.manilaprinciples.org/.

V. Trends in Common Law and Statutory Developments

A. *Common Law*

1036. The common law as developed in Australia however has yet to construct a clear theory that determines when an intermediary who creates a technology or system enabling wrongful behaviour will be liable. One of the basic organizing principles of the common law system is that there is usually no liability without fault. With few exceptions, the common law does not impose obligations on institutions or individuals to protect the rights of another against harm caused by third parties. This notion is most expressed in the rule that there is no general duty to rescue.[609]

B. *Reform of Defamation Law*

1037. A general lesson arising from the *Voller* case discussed above is that the judgment extends well beyond Facebook and the Internet.[610] The judgment will apply to all people and organizations that maintain their own websites and social media pages, including non-media companies, not-for-profit organizations, government bodies and individuals.

1038. In November 2004, the former Standing Committee of Attorneys-General agreed there was a need for uniform state and territory legislation to reform the law of defamation in Australia. The Attorneys-General agreed to support the enactment in their respective jurisdictions of Model Defamation Provisions.

1039. In February 2018 the NSW government completed a statutory review of that state's *Defamation Act* 2005 (NSW). The review identified several areas in the Act which would benefit either from amendment or modernization. Implementation for reform in NSW and most jurisdictions arising from the review is ongoing to date.[611]

C. *Copyright Liability Protections*

1040. On 29 December 2018 the *Copyright Amendment (Service Providers) Act* 2017 (Cth) came into force. The amendments extend safe harbour protections to broader categories of service providers in the disability, education, library, archive

609. The first main exception at common law is where there is a non-delegable special duty and a relationship of control (for example, parents and children, prisoners and their guards); and a second exception that a defendant has had some role in creating the risk from which the plaintiff needs rescuing. *See* Pappalardo, K & Suzor, N (2018) 'The Liability of Australian Online Intermediaries' [2018] SydLawRw 19; (2018) 40(4) Sydney Law Review 469.

610. *Ibid. Voller supra.*

611. NSW (2018) *Attorneys-General Review of Model Defamation Provisions – Stage 2 Discussion paper* at https://www.justice.nsw.gov.au/justicepolicy/Documents/review-model-defamationprovisi ons/ discussion-paper-stage-2.pdf.

and cultural sector. It further limits their liability for copyright infringements that occur while carrying out certain activities within their remit.[612]

1041. On 26 July 2019, the ACCC published its *Digital Platforms Inquiry Final Report* making important findings about the functions of digital platforms and recommendations for reform in the areas of competition law, media regulation and privacy law.[613]

D. *Online Disinformation and Misinformation Code*

1042. On 22 February 2021 the Digital Industry Group Inc. (DIGI) launched a new code of practice to reduce the risk of online misinformation causing harm to Australians. According to DIGI, the Australian Code of Practice on Disinformation and Misinformation has been adopted by Adobe, Apple, Facebook, Google, Microsoft, Redbubble, TikTok and Twitter.[614] In adopting the code all signatories have committed to safeguards to protect Australians against harm from online disinformation and misinformation, and to adopt a range of scalable measures that reduced its spread and visibility.

1043. 'Disinformation' is harmful, false or misleading online content spread among users of digital platforms via spam and other types of deceptive, manipulative or bulk, aggressive behaviours including behaviours intended to artificially influence users' online conversations and/or to encourage users to spread online content.

1044. 'Misinformation' is false or misleading online content that is spread by users of digital platforms, the spreading of which is reasonably likely to cause harm but may not be clearly intended to cause harm. The content may often be legal.[615]

§4. Postscript

1045. Australian courts like those around the world are having difficulties to identify when an online intermediary who is not morally responsible for a wrong

612. IPAustralia Liability of hosting platforms: 'safe harbour' at https://www.ipaustralia.gov.au/ip-for-digital-business/grow/liability-of-hosting-platforms%E2%80%90safe-habour.
613. ACCC (2020) *Digital Platform Services Inquiry. Interim Report* at https://www.accc.gov.au/publications/serial-publications/digital-platform-servicesinquiry-2020-2025/digital-platform-services-inquiry-september-2021-interim-report.
614. *See* DIGI Code at https://digi.org.au/disinformation-code/.
615. *See* ACMA's Disinformation Report at https://www.acma.gov.au/articles/2022-03/release-acmas-disinformation-report, 21 Mar. 2022.

should nevertheless be expected to do something to prevent it.[616] The *Voller* defamation case may be seen as a significant landmark in Internet governance. However, this must be balanced against the need to support legitimate socially beneficial online speech. Complex policy questions such as these need resolution to help make it easy to navigate the law in cyberspace.

616. Pappalardo, K & Suzor, N (2018) 'The Liability of Australian Online Intermediaries' (2018) 40(4) *Sydney Law Review* 469 and at http://classic.austlii.edu.au/au/journals/SydLawRw/2018/19.html.

Part IV. Digital Property Rights

§1. Introduction

1046. Intellectual property (IP) refers to the property of the mind and is any intangible 'thing'. 'Intellect' from the Latin root *intellectus* means the power of knowing. IP can be an invention, original design, or the practical application of an idea. IP law protects the rights in these creative and inventive endeavours and gives certain exclusive economic rights for a limited time to profit from these creative works and inventions.

1047. However, the claim to property rights depends on fact situations – employers have prior claims as do independent contractors. Partners developing an invention may jointly claim ownership of the IP.

1048. Ownership of IP is the legal recognition and reward for creative effort. The law also enables the community-at-large to access and benefit from the products of IP. As the protection is for rights rather than the physical property IP is a form of intangible property.

1049. IP is a generic label that encompasses a bundle of rights that protect innovation and reputation. IP encompasses patents, copyright, trademarks, designs, circuit layouts, plant breeder rights, confidential information (or trade secrets) and a miscellany of other such as moral rights and *sui generis* (one of a kind) rights.[617]

1050. Digital property rights run parallel to traditional IP rights in that such property are in a digital form. These digital products are as valuable as any other property and require protection from exploitation, loss, theft and inadvertent slippage into the public arena.

1051. Digital property rights may be seen as the next generation of IPR placing digital property rights at the same level as patents, copyright and trademarks. So data, circuit layouts for computing and other digital products are part of the digital property rights realm. The data in the form of emails, word processing documents, spreadsheets, photo images, audio files and movies acquire digital property rights, albeit mostly in intangible form.

---

617. IPAustralia (2004) What is Intellectual Property? at http://www.ipaustralia.gov.au/ip and Attorney General's Department (AGD) (2003) A Short Guide to Copyright at http://www.law.gov.au/.

1052. In the digital world IP rights fleet between the public and private domains and the question of ownership can be somewhat 'fuzzy' with such boundaries easily transgressed. In the digital environment information and data sent online with ease also means easy replication and the production of derivative works. The practical difficulty is in tracing the lineage, the author and owners of the work whilst separating the original from the imitation.

1053. Various Australian government publications and reviews return to the theme that IP rights is crucial to the promotion of innovation.[618] Arguably according to the government innovation is integral to the competitiveness of organizations and nations, and innovation drives economic growth. The conferring of enforceable rights on those who produce creative intellectual output incentivizes people to engage in creative endeavours and intellectual property protection offers rewards for the investment of time and effort.

1054. The legal framework facilitating the protection of IP and digital rights in Australia is by common law, equity and statute. At common law the protection of IP rights in goods and services is found in goodwill or commercial reputation attached to a name, mark, or trade dress (get-up). In equity, trade secrets and confidential information is protected by the equitable action of breach of confidence and rights protection through a confidentiality agreement. Other types of protection include moral rights,[619] geographical indications,[620] photographs and fonts.

618. *See* Copyright Convergence Group (1994) Highways to Change, Canberra: AGPS, Department of Industry, Science and Resources 1999, Shaping Australia's Future. Innovation Framework Paper, Canberra: AGPS and at http://industry.gov.au/library/content_library/shaping.pdf and Australia House of Representatives Standing Committee on Legal and Constitutional Affairs (1999), Advisory Report on the Copyright Amendment (Digital Agenda) Bill 1999, Canberra: Australian Parliament House.

619. The *Copyright Amendment (Moral Rights) Act* 2000 (Cth) recognizes the moral rights of creators and authors in their works even if they may have assigned their copyrights to someone else.

620. Geographical indications identify a good as originating from a locale where the quality, reputation or other characteristic of a product is essentially attributable to that geographic region, for example, *Champagne, Bordeaux* and *Cognac* readily identify regions in France that produce these wines and spirits. Some indications refer to the 'process' or a variety of fruit, for example, Dijon mustard, Shiraz wine.

Chapter 1. Patent Protection for Software

§1. Introduction

1055. The *Patents Act* 1990 (Cth) protects rights of inventors in their inventions provided certain threshold requirements have been satisfied such as novelty, inventiveness, utility and non-obviousness. A patent grants monopoly rights to inventors of new inventions.

1056. Depending on the invention, the monopoly is for a limited period of ten to twenty years for the inventor to exploit the invention. Patent registration in Australia is usually filed with the *de jure* patent office IPAustralia.

1057. Software patents, such as a system for placing purchase orders online, is patentable. But artistic creations, mathematical models, plans, schemes, or other purely mental processes are unpatentable.

1058. Digital patents refer to patents covering computer-implemented inventions most typically those methods that are performed using software. It is not the software code that is protected but the design processes that deliver functionality. The software operates in a manner that impacts on the world around it.[621]

1059. In the digital space the question is whether one may obtain a patent for methods or algorithms when they are implemented using a computer. Case law and common law discussed below suggests that the answer lies in whether the 'substance' of the invention is a patentable technical innovation or a non-patentable business innovation.

1060. The '*substance*' of the invention refers to how the invention works. The 'substantive' contribution is in the improvements that the invention makes over what is already known in that field. So, if the invention is one where the computer is used for more than its expected routine functions, the invention will pass the '*manner of manufacture*' test and these non-routine functions, involving a technical innovation, makes it a patentable invention. This test is apart from the threshold novelty and inventive step tests.

1061. Using a computer for its known functions such as data storage, display, data processing is said to be within a method of doing business and thus the invention cannot be patented. This is because the substance of the invention does not involve a new or novel technical innovation. An example is a phone app, and while it performs its functions within a new business model, the substance of many such apps is unpatentable.

---

621. Sparrefors, R, Werner, T & Ehrving, J (2019) Understanding digital patents at https://www.konsert.com/insight/understanding-digital-patents/. Categories of digital patents based on their technological content include technical approach patents, functional operation patents and use case application patents. Digital patents can cover one, two or all three categories.

1062. An ongoing debate in Australia is whether a 'business method' implemented using computer technology is patentable manner of manufacture under section 18(1)(a) of the *Patents Act* 1990 (Cth). Case law suggests that the answer rests on the creation of a 'technical improvement' in computer technology to be patentable.[622] Australian approach to software patents have been evident in the recently litigated cases discussed below.[623]

§2. Case Law and Legal Framework

1063. The patentability of computer-implemented inventions has been the subject of litigated cases. The 'method of manufacture' criterion has been in the forefront of the cases argued in addition to whether the invention is a subject matter for the grant of a patent. As well other criteria of prior art and general knowledge and whether the inventive step is an improvement have been raised. The cases also point to a relaxation by the Australian Patents Office (APO) on the strict view of patenting computer-mediated inventions.

1064. Importantly, the characterization of an invention is a matter of law and not of expert opinion. A two-step test has been used to decide whether an invention was a mere business method which is unpatentable as opposed to the computerization of a method beyond the use of the ordinary functions of a computer which makes the invention patentable.

1065. Finally, the question of whether an AI system is capable of being named as an 'inventor' of patentable subject matter has also been argued in court.

1066. In *Commissioner of Patents v. RPL Central*, the Full Federal Court has rejected a computer-implemented invention for failing to constitute patentable subject matter.[624] The Full Court emphasized that the question of patentable subject matter should be approached as a matter of substance, rather than form, consistent with other recent appellate decisions in *Myriad*[625] and *Research Affiliates.*[626] Essentially, the business method could be implemented using merely standard or generic operation of computers, and so was not patentable. In May 2016 the High Court of

622. Leigh, R (2021) Patentability of computer-implemented 'business methods' in Australia—a closer look at the 'technical improvement' test, *Journal of Intellectual Property Law & Practice*, Vol. 16, Issue 3, March, pp. 271-277 and at https://doi.org/10.1093/jiplp/jpab079.

623. For example in of the decision at first instance of *Encompass Corporation Pty Ltd v. InfoTrack Pty Ltd* [2018] FCA 421 (29 Mar. 2018) at http://www.austlii.edu.au/cgi-bin/viewdoc/au/cases/cth/FCA/2018/421.html?context=1;query=Encompass;mask_path=au/cases/cth/FCA where the claims of two of Encompass' innovation patents were determined to be not directed to a 'manner of manufacture'.

624. *Commissioner of Patents v. RPL Central Pty Ltd* [2015] FCAFC 177 (11 Dec. 2015) at http://www.austlii.edu.au/cgi-bin/sinodisp/au/cases/cth/FCAFC/2015/177.html.

625. *D'Arcy v. Myriad Genetics Inc* [2015] HCA 35 (7 Oct. 2015) at http://www.austlii.edu.au/cgi-bin/sinodisp/au/cases/cth/HCA/2015/35.html.

626. *Research Affiliates LLC v. Commissioner of Patents* [2014] FCAFC 150 (10 Nov. 2014) http://www.austlii.edu.au/cgi-bin/sinodisp/au/cases/cth/FCAFC/2014/150.html.

Australia dismissed an application for special leave to appeal the *RPL Central* decision of the Full Court of the Federal Court of Australia.[627]

1067. The Full Bench of the Federal Court affirmed the existing principles about the patentability of computer-implemented inventions in *Encompass Corporation Pty Ltd v. InfoTrack Pty Ltd* [2019] FCAFC 161; 372 ALR 646. The relevant invention claimed to be a method and apparatus for displaying information. Using generic computer technology for its well-known functions to apply instructions to an abstract idea is not a manner of manufacture which makes the invention unpatentable. The manner of manufacture criteria used by the court is whether the invention is a proper subject matter according to developed principles for grant of a patent as well as the substance of the invention and not its form. In the instance case it seems irrelevant to examine prior art and common general knowledge to consider whether the invention is an improvement. There is also the risk of conflating the issues of novelty or an inventive step with manner of manufacture.

1068. In the case of *Facebook, Inc.* [2020] APO 19 the APO may be signalling a relaxation of its previously strict views on the requirements for patent of a computer-implemented invention.[628] The invention claimed was one which tracked when an ad on a social media platform about a phone app (Advertised App) was clicked on by someone so they could download the app from an app store. The invention overcomes the problem of 'sandboxed' data where one's app data are separate from another app's data and the two apps are unable to communicate with each other or have access to each other's cookies.

1069. The APO Delegate noted the importance of understanding the state of the art in terms of whether an invention is a manner of manufacture; the distinction between the result of the invention and the substance of the invention that advances more than an abstract idea. The APO Delegate found that the invention was a patentable subject matter that was properly defined by the claims.

1070. The Full Court of the Federal Court in *Commissioner of Patents v. Rokt Pte Ltd* [2020] FCAFC 86 unanimously held that Rokt's 'digital advertising system' implemented using a computer's well-known functions was not patentable. This decision reversed the decision of a trial judge which found Rokt's invention was patentable.

1071. The invention claimed was that it was a computer-implemented method for linking a computer user to an advertising message. However, the Commissioner in arguing that the invention was an advertising scheme concluded that the invention used a computer and the Internet to implement an abstract idea. In the Court's view it had to characterize the invention *as a matter of law* and not a question of fact.

---

627. *RPL Central Pty Ltd v. Commissioner of Patents* [2016] HCASL 84 (5 May 2016).
628. *See Facebook* case at http://www.austlii.edu.au/cgi-bin/viewdoc/au/cases/cth/APO/2020/19.html.

1072. The Federal Court in *Aristocrat Technologies Australia Pty Limited v. Commissioner of Patents* [2020] FCA 778 overturned a decision of the APO in relation to a set of innovation patents directed to gaming machines. The approach of his Honour Justice Burley was to respond to two questions. An initial question is to ask whether the claimed invention was for a mere scheme or business method of the type that is not a proper subject matter of a grant of a letters patent. And if the answer was in the affirmative, to then ask whether the computer-implemented method is one where invention lay in the computerization of the method. Justice Burley found that the claims to patent were an eligible subject matter for a patent to be granted. Having answered the initial question in the negative, his Honour found it unnecessary to consider the second question of the two-step test.

1073. In *Thaler v. Commissioner of Patents* [2021] FCA 879 the Federal Court held that an artificial intelligence (AI) system is capable of being named as an 'inventor' of patentable subject matter. This decision suggests that AI systems can be 'inventors' for the purposes of the *Patents Act* 1990 (Cth). But it also means that while AI systems cannot be 'owners' of patents, a patentee can derive certain rights and entitlements to a patent from an AI inventor. The decision is in contrast with legislative requirements for human authors in other areas of intellectual property in Australia such as copyright. The decision may make Australia a more appealing place for new patent filings in the AI space although it may raise collateral issues of AI 'inventors' and capacity as a legal person.

1074. As background, Dr Stephen Thaler is the creator and owner of DABUS, the 'device for the autonomous bootstrapping of unified sentience'. DABUS is an AI system, trained through a combination of supervised and unsupervised learning. Dr Thaler claimed that DABUS 'invented' an improved, interlocking container for food products and named DABUS on the application as the inventor. In February 2021, the Deputy Commissioner of Patents found that to treat an AI system as an 'inventor' would be inconsistent with section 15 *Patents Act* 1990 (Cth).[629] Further, the Deputy Commissioner held that the failure to nominate a valid inventor meant that Dr Thaler's application for a patent had lapsed. Dr Thaler sought judicial review at the Federal Court which set aside the Deputy Commissioner's decision.

1075. On appeal to the Full Court of the Federal Court in *Commissioner of Patents v. Thaler* [2022] FCAFC 62 in April the Court unanimously allowed the Commissioner's appeal and reversed the earlier decision. Central to the Full Court's decision was the observation that the law relating to the entitlement of a person to the grant of a patent is premised upon an invention that arises *from the mind of a natural person or persons.* Also according to the Full Court, the *Patents Act* 1990 (Cth) does not contemplate beings other than human being having the capacity to make representations or indeed misrepresentations that may render a patent liable

629. *Stephen L. Thaler* [2021] APO 5 (9 Feb. 2021).

to be revoked.[630] In the absence of a successful appeal to the High Court of Australia patent applications in Australia must name a human inventor or at risk of lapsing.

1076. International addenda. The UK, EU and US patent offices have all found that AI cannot be a legal inventor for the purposes of a patent registration. Each of those jurisdictions has rejected Dr Thaler's patent applications on the basis that listing an AI system as an inventor does not meet the relevant requirements for patentability.[631]

§3. Postscript

I. Innovation Patents

1077. Australia has a two-tier patent system – the standard and the 'innovation' patent. The innovation patent was introduced with the *Patents Amendment (Innovation Patents) Act* 2000 (Cth). The amendment offers short-term protection for inventions that do not meet the higher thresholds of the standard patent.[632] However, the *Intellectual Property Laws Amendment (Productivity Commission Response Part 2 and Other Measures) Act* 2020 phased out the innovation patent system from 25 August 2021.

II. Patent Box Scheme

1078. 'Patent box' is a generic term for regimes that apply a concessional tax treatment to profits derived from eligible IP. Currently, over twenty jurisdictions, including the UK, Singapore and many European countries have patent boxes or other regimes that offer concessional tax treatments to IP derived profits.

1079. On 11 May 2021, the Australian government announced that it will introduce a patent box scheme for eligible corporate income associated with new patents in the medical and biotechnology sectors.[633] The patent box will apply to companies for income years commencing on or after 1 July 2022.

1080. The patent box scheme legislation is the *Treasury Laws Amendment (Tax Concession for Australian Medical Innovations) Bill* 2022 (Cth). The aim of the

630. *See* full text of the decision at https://www.judgments.fedcourt.gov.au/judgments/Judgments/fca/full/2022/2022fcafc0062.
631. UK Intellectual Property Office, applications GB1816909.4 and GB1818161.0; European Patents Office, applications EP 18 275 163 and EP 18 275 174; United States Patent and Trademark Office, application 16/524, 3250.
632. *Patents Amendment (Innovation Patents) Act* 2000 (Cth) at http://classic.austlii.edu.au/au/legis/cth/num_act/papa2000400/longtitle.html.
633. The consultation document for the patent box scheme is at https://treasury.gov.au/consultation/c2021-177849.

policy is to encourage companies to base their medical and biotechnology research and development (R&D) operations, and commercialize innovation, in Australia and to retain associated patent profits in Australia.[634] The scheme is in place for medical technology companies and to businesses that commercialize patented agricultural and veterinary chemicals and technologies with the potential to lower emissions.[635]

III. Crown Use of Copyright Material

1081. The High Court decision in *Copyright Agency Limited v. New South Wales* [2008] HCA 35 suggests a need for a special defence outside the operation of section 183 of the *Copyright Act* 1988 (Cth) (CA) that permits certain public uses of copyright material deposited or registered in accordance with statutory obligations under State or Commonwealth law. Section 183 states that copyright in a literary work (which ordinarily would include a computer program) is not infringed by the Commonwealth or a State where the copyright is used for the services of the Commonwealth or State without permission from the copyright owner.

1082. The *Intellectual Property Laws Amendment (Productivity Commission Response Part 2 and Other Measures) Act* 2020 amended the Crown use provisions for patents and designs where governments may exploit patented inventions and registered designs without authorization from the rights owner. Crown use can be invoked for the provision of a service primarily provided or funded by any government. Commonwealth, State or Territory governments are now required to seek a negotiated outcome with the rights owner before invoking it.

1083. However, in practice the law is far from certain. In South Australia Working Systems Software, a subsidiary of Global Health, commenced court action against the South Australian government when it continued using the CHIRON patent administration system after its licence agreement ended. Global Health claimed that the SA Government infringed its copyright in the CHIRON system and sought damages and an injunction to prevent continued use of the system.[636] From media reports the SA Government has decided to stop its use of the software and vacated the trial.[637]

634. *See* ATO at https://www.ato.gov.au/General/New-legislation/In-detail/Direct-taxes/Income-tax-for-businesses/Patent-Box---extension-to-the-agricultural-and-low-emissions-technologies-sectors/.
635. *See* media release by the Treasurer Josh Frydenberg 'Patent Box legislation introduced into Parliament to support investment and jobs' at https://ministers.treasury.gov.au/ministers/josh-frydenberg-2018/media-releases/patent-box-legislation-introduced-parliament-support (10 Feb. 2022).
636. *See* Donnellan, A (2016) Software legal battle could put SA patients' safety at risk, Government outlines in court documents (18 Jun) at https://www.abc.net.au/news/2016-06-18/software-legal-battle-could-put-sa-patients-safety/7522934.
637. *See* Cowan, P (2016) SA govt settles unlicensed software lawsuit at https://www.itnews.com.au/news/sa-govt-settles-unlicensed-software-lawsuit-432608.

Chapter 2. Copyright Protection for Software

§1. Copyright and Computer Programs

1084. A computer program is deemed to be a 'literary work' under section 10 CA where the programmer is the owner of copyright in the computer program. Computer software is IP and is also protected by patent law.

1085. Copyright protection is automatic when recorded in tangible form. However, copyright extends only to expressions of an idea but not to the ideas, procedures, methods of operation or mathematical concepts. The *Patents Act* 1990 (Cth) sections 13-17, on the contrary, bestows an exclusive grant to an invention which may be a product or process for a new way of doing things or offers a novel technical solution to a problem.

1086. Copyright is formality free in any state that is a party to the Berne Convention for the Protection of Literary and Artistic Works. Patents are granted after an examination process by a government agency. The law relating to the patentability of software is not harmonized internationally.[638]

1087. The differences between copyright and patent of computer software hinges on answering the question of what is being protected. Copyrights offers protection to creativity and expression whereas patents aim to protect the functionality of a computer program and its products.

1088. Computer code, like other literary works are automatically protected by copyright. Subject to exceptions, only the copyright owner has the exclusive right to reproduce a literary work in which copyright subsists, pursuant to section 31 of the CA. So the reproduction of another programmer's code without consent is an infringement of copyright section 36. In addition, the section provides that the work is reproduced in 'material form' and unnecessary that the work is reproduced in full. Section 10 of the Act defines 'material form' to include a substantial part of the work.

1089. What constitutes substantial part was litigated in the case of *IPC Global Pty Ltd v. Pavetest Pty Ltd (No 3)* [2017] FCA 82. Code from a dynamic-link library and several test modules used in IPC's version of the software was copied by Pavetest. The court found in favour of IPC holding that Pavetest had infringed IPC's copyright by copying a substantial part of their software.

1090. Computer code is protected but not its function. Copyright is not infringed just because two programs or algorithms perform identical functions. The expression of the code is protected and is usually referred to the idea-expression dichotomy in copyright.

638. *See* WIPO at https://www.wipo.int/copyright/en/activities/software.html.

1091. In *TICA Default Tenancy Control Pty Ltd v. Datakatch Pty Ltd* [2016] FCA 815, the defendant company, Datakatch, was incorporated by three ex-employees of TICA Default Tenancy Control Pty Ltd.[639] Datakatch operated business critical software which performed essentially the same function as TICA's software. The Federal Court determined that it was most unlikely the code was copied and there was no breach of copyright based on expert witness testimony. Ironically TICA was successful in prosecuting for a breach of confidence by Datakatch.

1092. The threshold to protect computer software is relatively low. Where technical requirements of the programming code mandate that there is only one way to achieve a certain result as a fact then that software so developed is rendered uncopyrightable.

1093. Copyright protects the whole program so long as it represents creativity.[640] In *Computer Edge v. Apple Computer Inc* (1986) 161 CLR 171, Apple failed to prove to the that EPROMS[641] containing an object code version of Apple's APPLESOFT software, infringed Apple Computer's copyright.[642]

1094. However, in *Autodesk Inc v. Dyason* (1992) 173 CLR 330 the issue was whether an EPROM breached Autodesk's copyright in its AutoCad program.[643] Initially the court found that copyright subsisted in a 127-bit sequence lookup table contained in a source program, and that the EPROM was a reproduction of the lookup table. However, in a reconvened sitting the application was ultimately denied by a majority of the High Court. Their Honours found that the 127 bits was a substantial part of a copyright work.

1095. In computer programming, the author may be one of the following persons: the programmer, the person who conceived the idea, which was implemented by the programmer, the operator of the computer on which the program runs, or the

---

639. *See* case notes at http://www.austlii.edu.au/cgi-bin/viewdoc/au/cases/cth/FCA/2016/815.html.
640. Coding for computer software may be divided into three levels including a user interface, application programming interfaces (APIs), algorithms and data structures. (1) *Level One: User Interface.* This involves how the user interacts with the program. (2) *Level Two: API.* This involves how the software is used by another program. The API may be protected by two areas of law – copyright and trade secrets. (3) *Level Three: Algorithms and Data Structures.* This includes the substantive features of the software. This level may be protected by trade secret law. *See* Bullock, S (2017) *Is There Legal Protection for Software?* (2017), at https://www.legalteamusa.net/is-there-legal-protection-for-software/.
641. *See* Wikipedia at https://en.wikipedia.org/wiki/EPROM. Erasable programmable read-only memory (EPROMS) is a type of programmable read-only memory (PROM) chip that retains its data when its power supply is switched off.
642. *See* case note at https://computerlaw.com.au/doku.php?id=case_links#computer_edge_v_apple_computer_inc.
643. *See* case note at https://computerlaw.com.au/doku.php?id=case_links#autodesk_inc_v_dyason.

person who commissioned the work produced by the computer.[644] In other words, the author is a 'natural' person.[645]

1096. Copyright provides the right holder an exclusive right to copy the work and to make it available to anyone. However, copyright does not extend to the usage of the work, for example, one may read a book without permission. To instal and run a program there is a need to make copies and the permission is granted by way of a licence. The exhaustive rights to copyright extend only to the first sell of a work and reselling a legal copy does not infringe copyright even though reselling software requires new copies.

1097. The Internet provides a rapid and widespread method of disseminating information. Some works disseminated on the Internet have an implied licence in its usage. In *Trumpet Software Pty Ltd v. OzEmail Pty Ltd* & Ors [1996] FCA 560 copyright was found to subsist in software ('Winsock') which was available for distribution freely on the Internet as 'shareware'. The Federal Court found that copyright works distributed in Australia on the Internet retained their copyright and are subject to an implied licence. The court held that the Internet service provider OzEmail had infringed Trumpet Software's copyright in Trumpet Winsock 2.0 by arranging for the program and a set of altered data files to be distributed with other software on diskette as a giveaway inserted in copies of computer magazines.

1098. De-compilation (sometimes referred to as 'reverse engineering') of the computer software is permissible if only to obtain the information necessary to achieve the interoperability of an independently created computer program – section 47D of the CA. However, the caveats are that there is an existing right to use the program, that the information is not readily available elsewhere and that the information may not be used for other purposes.

1099. In *Coogi Australia Pty Ltd v. Hysport International Pty Ltd* (1998) 41 IPR 591 infringement of copyright in a computer program was alleged where the respondent had reverse engineered a fabric produced by a computer-controlled knitting machine. Hysport did not have access to any literary form in which the original Coogi program was expressed but had only the manufactured garment. The Federal Court held that it would not be possible to establish infringement of copyright in software where the alleged infringer had merely reverse engineered the object to discover how it had been constructed and then written a program to facilitate making the object.

---

644. *See* Ricketson, S (1984) *The Law of Intellectual Property* (Law Book Company 1984) at p. 442 and the English position in *Express Newspapers Inc. Plc. V. Liverpool Daily Post and Echo Plc.* (1986) 5 IPR 193 which distinguishes between 'works' generated by a computer and 'works' produced with the aid of a computer.

645. *See* IPAustralia (2017) *Australia and the Future of Intellectual Property* at https://www.ipaustralia.gov.au/sites/default/files/ip_australia_and_the_future_of_intellectual_property.pdf.

§2. Other Protection Measures

I. Trademarks

1100. Trademarks as brands are preferred means for marketing computer programs. Trademark protects brands, like the name of the program, a logo, or a graphic symbol and distinguishes a program from competing programs. However, trademarks neither protect the program itself nor r does it prevent the unauthorized copying of the program code. Especially in mass markets, brands can be very valuable, it is easy and relatively inexpensive to register a trademark. But trademarks need to be defended through a registration process.

II. Embedded Software

1101. Embedded software is normally found in programs that control devices other than the usual computer. These programs have been written for a specific piece of hardware. The embedded software may be copyrightable like any software and as part of hardware may be easier to patent than inventions in stand-alone software.

1102. The Therapeutic Goods Administration (TGA) regulates software-based medical devices; including software that functions as a medical device (SaMD), and software that controls or interacts with a medical device either from within the device or externally. The *Therapeutic Goods (Medical Devices) Regulations* 2002 (Cth) were amended to clarify existing requirements and to introduce new requirements for software-based medical devices commending in February 2021. Among the amendments include clarification of the boundary for regulated software products and new classification rules.

III. Open-Source Software Licences

1103. The legal issues for the use of free and open-source software (OSS) include warranties and indemnities, licensing and software patents.[646] The protection of such software lies apart from copyright laws. Free software is distributed with source code disclosed or open at the point of distribution. Legally binding obligations such as GNU General Public Licence (GPL) is one example where users are free to modify software code but to disclose their modifications.[647]

1104. 'Open-source' software refers to computer programs that allows users to modify, access and shared freely. This accessibility is enabled as the digital material is designed so that the individual components and underlying elements are publicly

646. Fitzgerald, B & Suzor, N (2005) 'Legal Issues for the Use of Free and Open Source Software in Government' [2005] MelbULawRw 13; (2005) 29(2) *Melbourne University Law Review* 412.

647. Free Software Foundation (1991) *The GNU General Public License: Version 2.0* (June 1991) The GNU Project at http://www.gnu.org/licenses/gpl.html.

accessible. OSS has its source code publicly available under the terms of a copyright licence. The OSS will allow general use, inspection, modification and enhancement of the source code by any competent person.

1105. This contrasts with proprietary closed source software which is unavailable to anyone except under limited circumstances such as a licence agreement. Here only permitted uses are governed by the licensing agreement and any unauthorized use is in infringement of the copyright.

1106. A notable obligation imposed by OSS licences is the requirement to include certain copyright notices and in limited cases, to make available certain programming codes. The Apache Licence for example, permits the creation of derivative works and free redistribution of the original material and any derivative works created therefrom with certain provisos. One proviso is that the modified files carry prominent notices stating that the files have been changed in addition to attribution, copyright, patent or trademark notices.[648]

§3. Case Notes

1107. In *Data Access Corporation v. Powerflex Services Pty. Ltd. and Others* (1999) 45 IPR 353 Data Access claimed that Powerflex had infringed its copyright by copying reserved words as well as three macros and the Huffman compression table that it developed. [649]

1108. Data Access were successful at first instance in the Federal Court[650] but that decision was overturned on appeal to the Full Court of the Federal Court[651], except regarding the finding that PFXplus infringed copyright in the Huffman compression table. The High Court[652] upheld the decision of the Full Court of the Federal Court.

1109. The practical effect of the High Court's decision in Powerflex is that while programmers are not permitted to copy source code, they are permitted to adopt the structure, commands and user interface of a competitor's program.

1110. The *Copyright Amendment (Computer Programs) Act* 1999 (Cth) amended the CA by inserting sections 47B–47H to permit the owner or licensee of a computer program, in specified circumstances, to make a copy of the program during the normal use of the program, as a backup copy or to study the program and to make a copy or adaptation of the program to correct an error, for security testing or to make an interoperable program.

---

648. Apache Licence 2.0 at https://www.apache.org/licenses/LICENSE-2.0.
649. *See* Evenden, R (2001) Copyright protection of computer programs *in Australia ANZ Computers & Law Journal* pp. 24-37 at http://kirra.austlii.edu.au/au/journals/ANZCompuLawJl/2001/7.pdf.
650. *Data Access v. Powerflex case* at (1996) 33 IPR 194.
651. *Data Access v. Powerflex case* at (1997) 37 IPR 436.
652. *Data Access v. Powerflex case* at (1999) 45 IPR 353.

1111. It is conjectured that in some rare circumstances, copyright in software may be infringed even without taking a copy of the code itself. For example, if using an original computer program for 'inspiration' the same functionality may be provided by writing a new program having the same or very similar program components even where none of the original code is used.

1112. The ecosystem for smart phone applications (apps) including those of Apple, Google Android, Microsoft Windows have their own rules, guidelines and technical constraints which may limit copyrightability. Industry standards in the mobile telecommunications may also set constraints. This is because certain functionality is required to be implemented in a standard way to make it interoperable with other systems, leaving little room for creativity. Generally, smart phone applications are copyrightable and patentable like any computer program with their own licensing policies

1113. For example, Facebook apps with 'Software-as-a-Service' (SaaS) sitting on top of the Facebook platform suggests limited applicability for IP protection. To comply with the technical environment, the platform necessarily constraints the functionality and implementation of the app. But apps are copyrightable as with any computer program.[653]

1114. In *Leica Geosystems Pty Ltd v. Koudstaal (No. 3)* [2014] FCA 1129, Leica Geosystems the plaintiff company, was a supplier of software and services to the mining industry and the defendant was a software engineer formerly employed by the plaintiff who had commenced employment with a competitor.[654] Leica suspected the defendant had copied large amounts of source code and other files to a personal external hard drive prior to leaving the company. Leica successfully applied to the Federal Court for Anton Piller style orders.[655] The order empowered the legal representatives of Leica to enter the residence of their former employee to search for and seize any source code and any data storage device suspected of containing software material belonging to Leica. The court awarded damages to Leica for the infringement of their copyright by the employee.

1115. A recent New South Wales Supreme Court decision in *EIFY Systems Pty Ltd v. 3D Safety Services Pty Ltd* [2017] NSWSC 1310 reaffirmed the application of Australian copyright law to computer programs.

1116. EIFY Systems Pty Ltd provided an online induction programme (eInduct) which provided qualifications to personnel to work on sites. In 2011 EIFY Systems and 3D Safety Services Pty Ltd entered a joint venture to provide online training and management systems to construction and mining clients. The joint venture was

---

653. *Supra,* Bullock (2017) Legal Protection for Software.
654. *See* case notes summary at https://jade.io/summary/mnc/2014/FCA/1129.
655. Anton Piller order is that it can be obtained without notifying the person against whom it is sought. This can assist in securing evidence that is at risk of being destroyed, for example, source code taken from a company server using an external drive.

unsuccessful and short-lived. By 2012 3D Safety Services had begun developing its own online induction study scheme which resembled EIFY's product in terms of its function, structure and organization. EIFY sued 3D Safety Services and its directors for breach of copyright.

1117. The Court found that EIFY's claim to copyright encompassed the whole of the eInduct system. The result was a claim to protect a combination of know-how (which is not protected) and information that may or may not have been confidential to EIFY. The court found that the Directors of 3D Safety Services had not breached their contractual duty of confidence arising from the terms of use. The Court found EIFY's claim conflated the eInduct system with the code that underpinned the system. Copyright can subsist in the code, but not in the system. The source and object code of a computer program are protected under section 21(5) of the CA.

1118. The Federal Court decision in *Campaigntrack Pty Ltd v. Real Estate Tool Box Pty Ltd* [2021] FCA 809 has important implications for copyright enforcement in software in Australia.[656] The decision confirms that copyright may subsists not only in relation to a software system as a whole but also in subsets of instructions within the overall program in the software. The court in this case confirmed that a subset of instructions or statements may constitute a 'computer program' within the whole system. The court held that the relevant files were computer programs with separate functions 'of sufficient substance for each file to be regarded on its own as an "original work"'.

656. *See* case notes and summary at https://www.jade.io/article/824275.

Chapter 3. Trademarks in a Digital Context

§1. Introduction

1119. The *Trade Marks Act* 1995 (Cth) protects the marks used by traders in relation to their goods and services to indicate the origins and trade connection of those goods and services.[657] A trademark indicates to the public that goods come from a particular source. A trademark or brand name in layperson's language is a visual symbol denoted by a word signature, name, label, numerals, colours, shape, sound, scent or a combination of these used by a person on goods or services or other articles of commerce to distinguish it from other similar goods or services.[658] The trademark symbol ™ is used as the identifier for the source of that product or service. The ® symbol indicates that this word, phrase or logo is a registered trademark for the product or service. The trademark also serves to prevent consumer confusion. A trademark protects a product's identification but does not protect a product.

§2. Legal framework

1120. Trademark law in Australia is governed by the *Trademarks Act* 1995 (Cth) and the *Trademarks Regulations* 1995 (Cth). For the purposes of the legislation goods and services are described using specifications in the WIPO Nice Classification System.[659] The Nice Classification was established by the Nice Agreement (1957) for the international classification of goods and services applied for the registration of marks for thirty-four classes of goods and eleven classes of services.

1121. In Australia, the term of a trademark registration is ten years which may be renewed. There is no mandate to register a trademark but when registered the owner of the trademark assumes a monopoly on its use for the company's goods or services.

1122. Two businesses can use an identical brand name. However, the law in Australia will not allow the use of the same brand name for the same goods or services, and the company that is allowed use of the name is usually determined on a first come first served basis.[660]

1123. In some circumstances two companies can both use a trademark at the same time – the law calls this 'honest concurrent use'. Also, two companies can use

657. *See* text of the Act at http://classic.austlii.edu.au/au/legis/cth/consol_act/tma1995121/.
658. *See Trade Marks Act* 1995 (Cth) ss 6 and 17.
659. Nice Classification see https://www.wipo.int/classifications/nice/en/.
660. *See* discussion Givoni, S (2021) Same Same but Different Different at https://www.sharongivoni.com.au/same-same-but-different-different/.

the same trademark is if they are in a different category of goods or services and if there is no risk of consumer confusion.[661] For example, Dove chocolates and Dove soap.

1124. Trademark registration means there is an exclusive right to its use by the owner. It may be considered an asset that may be bought and sold, and registration protects against infringement in its use. Where a trademark is used dishonestly the registered trademark owner may seek compensation from the infringer. Unregistered trademarks may have to rely on the common law under passing off doctrines or as codified in the *Australian Consumer Law* (ACL) provisions to seek redress.

1125. It has been conjectured that 'use as a trademark' is probably the most difficult concept in trademark law.[662] This is because of the myriad interpretations of the three lettered word made even more difficult in the digital world. 'Use' as in deployment and 'use' as in illustration are challenging of itself let alone whether the term is used figuratively, metaphorically or literally. The litigated cases discussed below amply illustrate the legal difficulties and perverse consequential results.

I. Unregistered Trademark

1126. Unregistered trademarks are protected under the common law and enforced by the tort of passing off and by an action for misleading and deceptive conduct contrary to the ACL.

1127. Similarly, domain name registration to denote a presence on the Internet does not create any proprietary rights but can provide protection where reputation is established in the same way as unregistered trademarks.

1128. The Full Federal Court in *Kraft Foods Group Brands LLC v. Bega Cheese Limited* [2020] FCAFC 65 unanimously upheld the decision of the trial judge in *Kraft Foods Group Brands LLC v. Bega Cheese Limited (No 8)* [2019] FCA 593, dismissing the appeal by Kraft Foods Group Brands LLC (Kraft) and H.J Heinz Company Australia Limited. As a result Bega Cheese Ltd. will retain the right to use the Peanut Butter Trade Dress, which it acquired through purchasing the peanut butter business of Mondelez Australia in 2017. The Full Court also confirmed that an unregistered trademark cannot be assigned without associated business goodwill as part of a sale of the business because business goodwill cannot be attached to individual assets.

1129. As it remains unsettled as to whether brand owners can validly license common law trademarks, the legal advice is that brand owners should register all

661. *See* ss 6, 10, 23 and 120 of the *Trade Marks Act* 1995 (Cth) for statements on the meaning of substantially identical or deceptively similar trademarks.
662. *See* Lisbon, D (2018) The 'use as a trademark' requirement in keyword search advertising at http ://www.austlii.edu.au/au/journals/WAStuLawRw/2018/3.html.

distinctive product packaging and get-up as a trademark in Australia.[663] The decision reinforces the benefits of brand owners registering all distinctive product packaging and get-up as a trademark in Australia rather than relying on unregistered common law rights. The wide reach of the Internet makes registration of marks even more important.

1130. In *Lamont v. Malishus & Ors* (No. 4) [2019] FCCA 3206 in a decision in the trademark dispute over use of the name 'MALISHUS' the Court found infringement of MALISHUS trademark registration. The Court found that use of the malishus.com domain name by the respondents was *use* of MALISHUS as a trademark in relation to clothing in Australia. The Court also found that offers for sale of clothing to Australian consumers, made via the respondents Facebook page, also constituted infringement.

1131. However, the mere registration of a domain name does not amount to infringement, and as there was no 'use' of the malishus.com.au domain name, the registration of that domain name did not infringe Lamont's registrations. The Court found that Lamont was unable to establish a sufficient reputation in MALISHUS in Australia to find a claim for misleading or deceptive conduct under the ACL.

1132. This case confirms that while the mere registration of a domain name does not amount to infringement, its use in relation to the sale of products targeting the Australian online and real-world market may infringe an Australian trademark registration, as may other uses on the website.[664]

§3. Trademark Infringements Online

1133. Trademark infringements online may arise in several other ways. The depiction of a trademark on a toy replica, advertisements placed on results in online searches, the use of metatags in keyword search algorithms, in online retailing promotions and on media mastheads are some examples. In litigated cases the word 'use' is a major consideration as is the subtlety of interpreting the word 'visibility' of such use.

---

663. *See* Anstey, P, Barrett, A & Smith, K (2020) 'Goodwill and trademarks: crunchy not smooth' at https://www.ashurst.com/en/news-and-insights/legal-updates/ip-at-ashurst-update-goodwill-and-trade-marks-are-crunchy-not-smooth; and McGuire, S & Hoad, R (2020) 'Round 2: A fight about much more than peanuts: Kraft beaten by Bega in crunch trademark appeal' at https://www.claytonutz.com/knowledge/2020/april/round-2-a-fight-about-much-more-than-peanuts-kraft-beaten-by-bega-in-crunch-trade-mark-appeal.

664. *See* a discussion in Mytton, K & McManis, S (2019) 'When Does Use On A Website Infringe An Australian Trademark Registration?' at https://ipta.org.au/news/when-does-use-on-a-website-infringe-an-australian-trade-mark-registration/. Compare this with the reported WIPO ruling where the Lord of the Rings creator JRR Tolkien's estate successfully blocked a crypto-currency called JRR Token. *See* BBC News (2021) Tolkien estate blocks JRR Token cryptocurrency https://www.bbc.com/news/technology-59373968.

1134. The digital world has come to disrupt traditional trademark law with the latter's orientation towards the origins of physical goods and services. The conceptual challenge of digitization is that it is not that there are inadequate rules but that digital technology calls into question the tangible and intangible distinction between goods and services.

I. Trademarks and Digital Goods

1135. Digital goods in this context include many media products such as music, software and services in the 'cloud' such as software-as-a-service (SAAS). The digital files, computer data, software and systems that are used to produce these goods and services may be intangible, but their products may be physical. Digitization adds a further layer to the traditional distinction between goods and services.

1136. As technology enables the separation of the design of goods on the one hand from their production on the other, trademarks may increasingly be unnecessary to identify the origins and producers of those goods.

1137. An example from the US illustrates the dilemma for trademarks and trade dress. In 2016 BMW sued an online virtual modelling company TurboSquid for selling digital model replicas of BMW vehicles.[665] According to BMW, TurboSquid's 'marketing of 3D virtual models' of BMW vehicles for use in video games infringed BMW's trademarks and trade dress and its design patents. The 3D virtual models were in the form of digital files that could be used in 3D printers to produce either the physical model or a virtual depiction on the Internet and in games modules.

1138. The case was dismissed, presumably after the parties had reached a settlement pretrial.[666] However, the implication here is that there is a weakening of trademark law's core principle of the 'origin' of the goods. It is settled law that use 'as a trademark' is use of the mark as a 'source of origin' in the sense that it indicates a connection in the course of trade between goods or services and the person who applies the mark to goods or services. Users and buyers of the digital files may now simultaneously be 'producers' – producers and users of these goods facilitated by the 3D printing of digital files.[667] The 'origin' of the goods and services seem now to have been blurred.

II. Online Triggered Ads

1139. Online marketing strategies have become a crucial channel for many businesses in advertising their products and services. Some of these include purchasing

665. *BMW of North America LLC v. TurboSquid, Inc., No.* 2:16-CV-02500 (D.N.J. May 3, 2016).
666. *See* discussion in McKenna, MP & Osborn LS (2017)' Trademarks and digital goods', 92 *Notre Dame L. Rev* 1425 (2017) and at https://scholarship.law.nd.edu/ndlr/vol92/iss4/2.
667. *Ibid.* McKenna & Osborn.

strategic domain names, using search engine optimization services (SEO), and using paid search engine advertising (PSEA).

1140. SEOs improve a website's online visibility through the strategic use of metatags and other website information to improve 'organic' search results. Metatags are snippets of text that describe and index a webpage's content and form a part of the Hypertext Markup Language (HTML) code. Metatags are not visible on the webpage *per se;* however, they can be found in the page's source code.

1141. PSEAs on the contrary involve businesses nominating search terms they wish link to ads for their products or services. These are usually marked as 'Ad' or 'Sponsored' in the search result displays to indicate that they are paid ads. When users enter the search terms an automated auction process occurs to determine whether the business' ad is displayed.

1142. Metatags can be highly effective in manipulating search traffic either onto a website or perversely to divert search engines away from a website.[668]

1143. One common example is a search engine with Google AdWords where certain terms (including trademarks) appear in Google searches. Such processes have given rise to trademark disputes in Australia[669] and elsewhere.[670]

1144. Google AdWords is an Internet search engine that uses an auction-based system whereby a company will bid for search terms that it wishes to link to its advertisements. The Google search engine displays two types of search results: organic results and sponsored links. Organic results are those links that have been found by a search engine. Sponsored links are advertisements which Goggle AdWords programs allows advertisers to create, change and monitor. These are triggered by keywords supplied by the advertiser to Google. When a search is undertaken using those purchased words, the company's advertisement appears on the search results page. The mere use of the purchased words triggers a particular outcome when the word is typed into the search engine. This process is described as search engine marketing.

---

668. *See* Llewelyn, D & Reddy, P (2020) 'Metatags Using Third Party Trademarks on the Internet' in Alpin, T (Ed.) (2020) *Research Handbook on Intellectual Property and Digital Technologies* (Edward Elgar Publishing), Chapter 20. Available at SSRN: https://ssrn.com/abstract=3683824.

669. Kallenbach, P (2005) 'Will triggered ads trigger trademark litigation in Australia?' MinterEllison 28 Jun. 2005. *See also* DLA Piper (2019) 'Online marketing and trade marks: To infringe, or not to infringe?' at https://blogs.dlapiper.com/legal-advertising-and-marketing/2019/03/online-marketing-and-trade-marks-to-infringe-or-not-to-infringe/.

670. In the UK for example see Iserles, I (2013) 'M&S's use of Google AdWords infringes Interflora's trademark' at https://www.ashurst.com/en/news-and-insights/legal-updates/m-and-s-use-of-google-adwords-infringes-interflora-s-trade-mark/ which discusses the infringement where 'reasonably well-informed and observant Internet users' to believe, erroneously that the advertiser is connected to the trademark owner. In Spain see Ceniceros IT (2018) 'Spain: Sometimes, Google AdWords Cause Trademark Infringement: Decisions of The Provincial Court of Madrid on June 8, 2018' at https://www.mondaq.com/trademark/763518/sometimes-google-adwords-cause-trademark-infringement-decisions-of-the-provincial-court-of-madrid-on-june-8-2018.

1145. The issue arising from the above discussion is the dichotomy between 'use' and 'descriptive use' in deploying these keywords in Google AdWords searches.

1146. In *Lift Shop Pty Ltd v. Easy Living Home Elevators Pty Ltd* [2014] FCAFC 75 the Full Court determined that the only functional significance of the words 'Lift Shop', as they were used by Easy Living, was to describe the character of its business. There was found to be no trademark infringement if the alleged infringer is simply using the words in a descriptive sense.[671] Moreover, the received view is that there can be no monopoly over descriptive words that form part of a trademark.

1147. There are, however, some circumstances where particular words used are other than in a descriptive way. For example, Google AdWords does not restrict the use of trademark terms in keywords. This does not mean that it is lawful to 'use' a competitor's trademark.

1148. Australian courts have been divided about whether metatags constitute trademark 'use'. Australian courts have held that using another party's registered trademark as a Google Adword is not a trademark infringement but putting the keyword in a website source code can be.[672]

1149. The practice of putting a competitor's registered trademarks in website source code is to improve the searchability of their websites. Such use of metatags has resulted in a few trademark infringement cases involving competitors using competing brand names within their own metatags to obtain top ranking search results. Top ranks matter as the advertised product appears first in the search results displayed. The issue here is whether the use of a competing brand name in a metatag by a business who is not the owner of that registered trademark constitutes an infringement.

1150. In *Complete Technology Integrations Pty Ltd v. Green Energy Management Solutions Pty Ltd*, [2011] FCA 1319; (2011) AIPC ¶92–431 the Federal Court of Australia categorically stated that trademarks as metatags do not constitute use of a trademark as understood under trademark law because the use is 'invisible'.

1151. In *Veda Advantage Ltd v. Malouf Group Enterprises Pty Ltd* [2016] FCA 255 the Federal Court held that the mere purchase and use of a registered trademark

---

671. *See* Webb, T & Landerer, N (2014) 'Don't expect exclusive use online if your trademark contains descriptive words' at https://www.claytonutz.com/knowledge/2014/september/don-t-expect-exclusive-use-online-if-your-trade-mark-contains-descriptive-words.

672. Neil, J & Moore, B (2017) 'Fair shake of the source bottle - Full Federal Court confirms trademark use in source code can be trademark infringement' at https://www.claytonutz.com/knowledge/2017/july/fair-shake-of-the-source-bottle-full-federal-court-confirms-trade-mark-use-in-source-code-can-be-trade-mark-infringement.

as a Google AdWord was not 'use' of a trademark a requirement necessary to establish trademark infringement under the Trademarks Act. The Google AdWords were considered 'invisible to consumers'.[673]

1152. The lessons from this case provide a useful framework for businesses using Google AdWords as a marketing tool. Where one use's other businesses' trademarks, it may be prudent to ensure either that the keyword selected is hidden from public view or is descriptive in nature.[674]

1153. However, a Full Federal Court has recently confirmed that the use of another's registered trademark in the source code of a website can amount to trademark infringement.[675]

1154. In *Accor Australia & New Zealand Hospitality Pty Ltd v. Liv Pty Ltd* [2017] FCAFC 56 a website operator was sued for infringing a registered trademark by including the source code in one of the operators' website. The Full Federal Court affirmed that including trademarks in a website's source code could be considered 'use' of a trademark, in the infringing sense required by the Trade Marks Act, because the source code 'was visible to those who know what to look for … and influenced search results'; and, trademark in the website source code infringed Accor's registration because the website was promoting services for which the trademark was registered, and the particular metatag was not using the trademark in a descriptive sense.

1155. 'Visibility', where absent cannot function as a 'badge of origin' to establish trademark infringement. A trademark may be used in a descriptive sense and demonstrably shown that it has not used the trademark 'as a trademark'.

1156. A competitor may purchase and use another party's registered trademark as a Google AdWord, no matter how distinctive it is, and may avoid any liability for trademark infringement unless accompanied by other conduct.

1157. The cases discussed also suggest that it is technically possible to infringe trademarks by implementing the Google AdWords program. The use of such source code may also constitute a breach of section 18 of the *Australian Consumer Law*

673. *See* Burrows, M (2017) 'Is the use of a trademark in AdWords an infringement?' at https://www.dundaslawyers.com.au/is-the-use-of-a-trade-marks-in-adwords-and-infringement/. *See also* Smith, D (2019) 'Can I Use a Competitor's Trademark as a Keyword on Google AdWords?' at https://legalvision.com.au/can-i-use-a-competitors-trade-mark-on-google-adwords/.
674. *See* VonMuenster (2021) 'Can I use competitor trademarks in my SEO and Adwords?' at https://www.vonmuensterlegal.com/using-competitor-trade-marks-seo/.
675. *Supra*, Neil, J & Moore, B (2017). *See also* Burrows, M (2020) 'Can meta tags constitute trademark infringement?' at https://www.dundaslawyers.com.au/can-meta-tags-constitute-trade-mark-infringement/.

2010 (Cth) (ACL)[676], as it in fact did in the *Veda Advantage* case. The breach of the ACL arose because the display of the keywords wrongfully implied a commercial relationship between the two entities.[677]

1158. In Australian *Competition & Consumer Commission v. Employsure Pty Ltd* (NSD20/2022) ACCC commended civil proceedings against Employsure alleging that it engaged in misleading conduct in breach of the ACL through its use of Google Ads campaigns in 2016-2018.[678] The Google Ads advertisements featured headlines such as ‘Fair Work Ombudsman Help – Free 24/7 Employer Advice’ among other search terms. At first instance the Federal Court dismissed the ACCC’s case and found that Employsure’s Google Ads advertisements did not misrepresent to small businesses that Employsure was, or was affiliated with, a government agency. The decision was overturned by the Full Federal Court in August 2021. The court imposed a penalty of AUD 1 million on Employsure for breaching sections 18 and 29 of the ACL. ACCC has appealed the penalty on the basis that it is ‘manifestly inadequate’ having regard to the nature of the conduct and the size and financial position of Employsure. This action is also in pursuit of ACCC’s priorities for 2022-2023 which is to monitor ‘consumer and fair-trading issues relating to manipulative or deceptive advertising and marketing practices in the digital economy’.[679]

1159. Section 120(1) of the *Trademarks Act* 1995 (Cth) provides that a person infringes a registered trademark if the person uses as a trademark as a sign that is substantially identical with, or deceptively similar to, the trademark, in relation to goods or services in respect of which the trademark is registered.

III. Online Retailing

1160. In *Pinnacle Runway Pty Ltd v. Triangl Limited* [2019] FCA 1662 (10 October) the Federal Court considered whether Pinnacle’s trademark DELPHINE, which was registered in class 25 for clothing, headwear and swimwear, was infringed by use of the word DELPHINE as a style of one of Triangl’s bikinis. Triangl sold a range of approximately thirty-five styles of bikini over the Internet.[680]

1161. The Court held that there was no trademark infringement of Pinnacle’s mark because Triangl had not used DELPHINE as a trademark. The Court found that the overall ‘context or setting in which Triangl used the name DELPHINE on its website is of critical importance’.

676. *See* text of the *ACL* at http://www.austlii.edu.au/au/legis/cth/consol_act/caca2010265/sch2.html.
677. One view is that as trademark law is not an all-embracing law against competition, it would be preferable to do so under general advertising law. *See* Llewelyn, D & Reddy P (2020) *supra.*
678. *See* details at https://www.comcourts.gov.au/file/Federal/P/NSD20/2022/actions.
679. *See* ACCC Priorities at https://www.accc.gov.au/media-release/compliance-and-enforcement-priorities-for-2022-23.
680. *See* case notes at http://www.austlii.edu.au/cgi-bin/sinodisp/au/cases/cth/FCA/2019/1662.html?query=.

1162. Consumer purchases in e-commerce are increasingly made online in response to direct marketing emails, Instagram posts and personal choices in shopping online. The Court recognized such retail practices and that a product listing on an online store is much more than just an ad. It '... sets out the essential terms of the proposed transaction, which will be completed if the consumer clicks on another button on the website and provides his or her credit card details'. In relation to the use of DELPHINE on direct email marketing material, the fact it was sent only to subscribers to Triangl's email list was considered by the judge to 'increase the improbability that they [consumers] would perceive that DELPHINE was being used as a trademark or as indicating the trade source of the swimwear'.[681]

1163. This case provides an important precedent for brands and online retailing and highlights the importance of 'context' in particular cases. To e-commerce businesses and consumers, the subtlety of how consumers interact with and interpret the content of online retail platforms is significant for trademark law. As well the case points towards future directions in similar trademark infringement litigation.

IV. Online Branding

1164. Registering a brand or trademark is not compulsory. Trademark registration only protect trademarks in respect of the goods and/or services claimed in the relevant registration.[682] A trademark bestows IPR in the item or aspect that has been registered. Such registrations permit owners to enforce their rights from the date on which the application was filed (the priority date). As noted previously common law unregistered trademark rights can sue for passing off and misleading and deceptive conduct under the ACL.[683] This latter route to enforce rights often involves higher costs as it is usually necessary to prove evidence of business reputation in the relevant brand.[684]

1165. As outlined in section 6 of *Trademarks Act* 1995 (Cth) different aspects of branding may be trademarked, including any letter, word, name, logo, signature, numeral, device, brand, heading, label, ticket, aspect of packaging, shape, colour, slogan, sound or scent – or any combination of these.

1166. Another means of proactively protecting online branding is to strategically purchase domain names. While Part 17 section 185 of the *Trade Marks Act*

681. *See* Ryan, M (2020) 'The Curious Case of Pinnacle and the Bikinis' at https://ipta.org.au/news/the-curious-case-of-pinnacle-and-the-bikinis/ and Gilbert & Tobin (2020) 'Catching trademark law up with the reality of online retail: Pinnacle Runway Pty Ltd v Triangl Limited' at https://www.gtlaw.com.au/insights/catching-trade-mark-law-reality-online-retail-pinnacle-runway-pty-ltd-v-triangl-limited.

682. *See* s. 68 of the *Trade Marks Act* 1995 (Cth).

683. *See* ACL at https://consumerlaw.gov.au/.

684. *See* Neil, J & Martine, S (2020) 'Don't put a mask on your trade marks: how to protect your brand during the COVID-19 pandemic' at https://www.claytonutz.com/knowledge/2020/may/don-t-put-a-mask-on-your-trade-marks-how-to-protect-your-brand-during-the-covid-19-pandemic.

1995 (Cth) provides for defensive trademarks, there may be some who purchase domain names with strategic and ulterior motives. For example, cybersquatters could seize domain names with the sole intention of selling them for profit.[685]

1167. Domain names usually reflect a chosen business name or brand. In such instances there is arguably an obvious connection with a product or service offering. One view is that this link has led to Australian court rulings that the way a domain name directs users to such a business offering would be sufficient for it to be considered a 'use as a trademark' and thereby could be found to amount to a trademark infringement.[686]

1168. Business name registration with the Australian Securities and Investments Commission (ASIC) is necessary as it provides recognition as a legal entity such as a company, partnership or sole proprietorship. As well the registration is part of the Australian Taxation Office's (ATO) remit on company and other tax. Within limits, registration of a business name does not provide exclusive ownership of a name or the right to stop others from registering a similar name.

1169. For those in media services the name, logo, masthead, slogans, design elements of a website may help subscribers and advertising customers recognize and identify a brand. Such clients associate these as part of the brand's reputation that has been built up over time.[687]

1170. According to the Australian Retail Association (ARA) Retail Institute a key component online reputation management is to ensure that the result listings of search engines reflect the benefits that a company provides. Any malicious attempts to discredit or lower consumer confidence should be vigorously challenged with appropriate countermeasures. The online brand management campaign should be to keep reputation untarnished and enhance consumer confidence.[688]

V. Groundless Trademark Infringement

1171. Under Australia's *Trademarks Act* 1995 (Cth) Part 12, section 120 infringement is found if a mark, which is substantially identical or deceptively like the complainant's registered trademark, is being used as a trademark in relation to

685. *See* Neil, J & Lobb, R (2018) 'Evicting cybersquatters: what to do when someone registers your brand as a domain name' at https://www.claytonutz.com/knowledge/2018/september/evicting-cybersquatters-what-to-do-when-someone-registers-your-brand-as-a-domain-name.
686. *See* DLA Piper (2019) 'Online marketing and trade marks: To infringe, or not to infringe?' at https://blogs.dlapiper.com/legal-advertising-and-marketing/2019/03/online-marketing-and-trade-marks-to-infringe-or-not-to-infringe/.
687. Clark, L (2020) 'Do you need to trademark your media title or masthead?' at https://www.targetedmediaservices.com.au/do-you-need-to-trade-mark-your-media-title-or-masthead/.
688. *See* ARA Retail Institute Legalities of Online Brand Protection at https://blog.retail.org.au/newsandinsights/legalities-of-online-brand-protection.

the specific goods or services for which the trademark is registered. The mark in this instance is used as an indication of origin.

1172. Section 129(5) of the *Trademarks Act* 1995 (Cth) empowers a person threatened with an action for trademark infringement to seek a declaration from the Court that the threats are 'groundless' and consequently be restrained from making them.[689]

1173. In *Stone & Wood Group Pty Ltd v. Intellectual Property Development Corporation Pty Ltd* [2016] FCA 820 the Federal Court neither found that any trademark infringements nor was the threatened action made out.[690]

VI. Trademark Dilution

1174. Trademark dilution involves an unauthorized use of another's trademark on products that do not compete with, and have little connection with, those of the trademark owner.[691] For example, a famous trademark used by one company to refer to hair care products might be diluted if another company began using a similar mark to refer to breakfast cereals or spark plugs. Hence, dilution comprises of two principal harms, namely, blurring and tarnishing.[692]

1175. In Australia while the issue of the dilution or misappropriation of the value of a famous trademark is provided under section 120(3) *Trademarks Act* 1955 (Cth)[693] The High Court decision in *Campomar Sociedad Limitada v. Nike International Ltd* [2000] HCA 12; (2000) 202 CLR 45 suggests that section 120(3) is an anti-dilution provision.[694]

689. *See* Burrows, M (2016) 'Groundless threats of trademark infringement' at https://www.dundaslawyers.com.au/groundless-threats-of-trade-mark-infringement/.
690. *See* case notes at http://www.austlii.edu.au/cgi-bin/sinodisp/au/cases/cth/FCA/2016/820.html?stem=0&synonyms=0&query=stone%20and%20wood. *Advanced Data Integration Pty Ltd v. ADI Ltd* [2004] FCA 731 at http://www.austlii.edu.au/au/cases/cth/FCA/2004/731.html was cited as authority that the s. 129(5) defence, the "due diligence" aspect applied in this instance.
691. Bajpai, A *et al.* (2019) 'Keywords and Infringement of Trademark in Cyberspace', *National Journal of Cyber Security Law* Vol.2(1) and at http://lawjournals.celnet.in/index.php/njcsl/issue/view/34.
692. Legal Information Institute at https://www.law.cornell.edu/wex/dilution_(trademark).
693. *See* Fitzgerald, B & Sheehan, E (1999) Trademark dilution and the commodification of information: Understanding the 'cultural command', *Macarthur Law Review* Vol.3, pp. 61-68.
694. *See* case notes at http://www.austlii.edu.au/au/cases/cth/FCA/2000/1099.html and a critique by Handler, M (2008) 'Trademark Dilution in Australia?' [2008] UNSWLRS 48 at http://classic.austlii.edu.au/au/journals/UNSWLRS/2008; and Gonsalves, M & Flynn, P (2006) 'Dilution Down Under: The Protection of Well-Known Trademarks in Australia' [2006] *European Intellectual Property Review* 174 at http://classic.austlii.edu.au/cgi-bin/LawCite?cit=%5b2006%5d%20European%20Intellectual%20Property%20Review%20174.

1176. Dilution differs from normal trademark infringement in that there is no need to prove a likelihood of confusion to protect a mark. Instead, all that is required is that use of a 'famous' mark by a third party causes the dilution of the 'distinctive quality' of the mark.[695]

1177. In *Halal Certification Authority v. Flujo Sanguineo Holdings* [2021] FCA 1399, the Federal Court dismissed Halal Certification Authority Pty Ltd's claims of trademark infringement, misleading or deceptive conduct and passing off against the Flujo Group of companies relating to the use of a halal-related trademark and ordered that its registration for that mark be cancelled.[696] To be liable for trademark infringement, the alleged infringer must use a trademark 'as a trademark'. In this case, the requirement that the trademark be 'used as a trademark' was not met, with the court citing the 'small size and relatively obscure placement' of the trademark on the product packaging, contrasted with the 'large and dominant size' of the product's core branding.

§4. Australian Trends

1178. The current Australian Trade Mark Online Search System (ATMOSS) in Australia will cease operation, and from 11 February 2017 trademark searching may be made through the new 'Australian Trademark Search'.

1179. IP Australia ran a pilot for a Smart Trade Marks project in 2018 designed to allow consumers and importers to instantly check if a product has a registered Australian trademark.[697] The system will also enable brand owners to protect themselves against misuse and counterfeit as well as to connect digitally to the government register to prove that they are the authentic owner of a brand.[698] As trials are underway a report and results from the pilot and efficacy of this project is anticipated in the near future.

1180. A proposal has been made that distributed ledger technologies (DLT) may be deployed to automate the management of trademark licences and rights.[699] Blockchains as used in self-executing smart contracts could both monitor and collect micropayments automatically instead of a fixed-licence fee subscription business model. Similarly, blockchains could be used to collect royalties of digital

---

695. In the US fair use is not actionable as dilution. This includes advertising or promotions that permit consumers to compare goods or services; identifying and parodying, criticizing or commenting on the owner of the mark or the goods and services connected with the mark. News commenting or news reporting and non-commercial use of mark are also non-actionable under dilution laws. *See* Rosznyai, LF (2005) *Trademarkdilution.com: Nissan Motor Co. v. Nissan Computer Corp., and the Evolving Law of Trademark Dilution on the Internet*, 2 Shidler J. L. Com. & Tech. 2 (2005) at: https://digitalcommons.law.uw.edu/wjlta/vol2/iss1/2.

696. *See* Case Notes at http://www.austlii.edu.au/au/cases/cth/FCA/2021/1399.html.

697. *See* IPAustralia at https://www.ipaustralia.gov.au/beta/smart-trade-mark.

698. *See* IPAustralia at https://smarttrademark.search.ipaustralia.gov.au/.

699. *See* Bacina, M (2019) Trademarks and Blockchain: Technology Update at https://piperalderman.com.au/insight/trade-marks-and-blockchain-technology-update/.

media such as songs, videoclips and others in an automated processing of small payments. Even as indicators of authenticity and origin such as logos, QR codes and near field communication (NFC) chips are used in trademark identifiers, on the Internet counterfeiters may circumvent the territoriality of trademark registration systems.

1181. Many everyday products have become the victims of trademark genericization. This is because the trademark has morphed from a single product identified under a name to an entire product category, for example, Kleenex as a trademark name and a general reference to tissues in everyday speech. This transformation is described as 'genericide'.

1182. The non-official advocacy group Bitcoin Foundation[700] has opposed the idea of registering 'Bitcoin' as a trademark, arguing that '[Bitcoin] is a generic term like the terms used for other currencies such as "dollar", "euro," "yen," etc.' and that the term 'Bitcoin' should be preserved for public use.[701] Whether it is successful will depend in large measure on the use of the term to generally describe it as a medium of value exchange. If this is the case, then the argument is that it should not be registrable unless it can be shown that it has acquired a secondary meaning. On the contrary, even if terms like 'bitcoin' and 'blockchain' were not descriptive, it may be submitted that they have become generic terms used to describe the technology itself and hence should not be registered to one trader.[702]

§5. Global Impacts

1183. Competition law, as applied by several competition authorities in the EU, might place obstacles on trademark owners trying to implement a distribution policy that they believe best to protect them from trade in counterfeit goods on online selling platforms.

1184. To prevent unfair competition the need for an intelligent trademark legal precedent recommendation system has been proposed. Using information technology and AI a continuously updated trademark case data system has been devised. Such a system will assist trademark owners rapidly identify similar cases in support of their trademark infringement allegations.[703]

700. *See* Bitcoin Foundation generally at https://bitcoinfoundation.org/.
701. *See* Bitcoin Foundation on trademarking bitcoins at https://bitcoinfoundation.org/the-bitcoin-foundations-view-and-policy-on-trademarking-bitcoin/.
702. *See* Stern, J (1983) 'Genericide: Cancellation of a Registered Trademark', 51 *Fordham L. Rev.* 666 (1983). Available at: https://ir.lawnet.fordham.edu/flr/vol51/iss4/4.
703. *See* Trappey, CV, Chang, A-C, & Trappey, AJC (2021) 'Building an Internet-based Knowledge Ontology for Trademark Protection', *Journal of Global Information Management*, v.29(1) Jan-Feb 2021 and at https://www.igi-global.com/gateway/article/full-text-pdf/268709&riu=true.

1185. In the US the *Anticybersquatting Consumer Protection Act* 1999 authorizes the development of the digital trademark right.[704] Under this new right, a trademark owner can petition a domestic court to transfer a foreign registrant's domain name to the trademark owner. The property transfer order has a global effect, enjoining the foreign registrant from further use of its property in its home country. This is a curious development in trademark law in that legal protection for trademarks is territorial and that trademark rights exist in each country solely according to that country's law. The new digital trademark right may represent a unilateral imposition of domestic US law on foreign nationals has been critiqued in academic circles.[705]

1186. Monitoring of global digital content published on websites are difficult to trace and to identify the identities and country of origin of the IP infringers even more so. The protection of well-known marks may have to rely on global treaties and agreements. The TRIPS Agreement is an influential international treaty on IPR.[706] Art 16 stipulates that a registered trademark owner shall have an exclusive right to prevent others from obtaining consent to use their exclusively owned IP protecting their brand or trademark.[707] The work of TRIPS in this area of digital trademark protection will be influential in the future.

704. *Anticybersquatting Consumer Protection Act*, Pub. L. No. 106-113, Title III, 113 Stat. 1501A-545 (1999) (codified at 15 U.S.C. § 1125(d) (2000)).

705. *See* Nguyen, X-TN (2003) *The Digital Trademark Right: A Troubling New Extraterritorial Reach of United States Law*, 81 NCL Rev. 483 (2003). At: http://scholarship.law.unc.edu/nclr/vol81/iss2/3.

706. World Intellectual Property Organization (WIPO) (1996) *Implications of the TRIPS Agreement on Treaties Administered by WIPO. See* https://www.wipo.int/edocs/pubdocs/en/intproperty/464/wipo_pub_ 464.pdf (July 20, 2019). *See also* WIPO Standing Committee on the Law of Trademarks, Industrial Designs and Geographical Indications, *Draft Provisions on the Protection of Well-Known Marks*, WIPO Document SCT/2/8, Geneva, 7-12 Jun. 1999, p. 18, at https://www.wipo.int/edocs/mdocs/sct/en/sct_2_1/sct_2_3-main1.doc.

707. World Trade Organization (WTO) (1994) *Agreement on trade-related aspects of intellectual property rights* (TRIPS Agreement) at https://www.wipo.int/wipolex/en/other_treaties/text.jsp?file_id=305736, 20 Jul. 2019.

Chapter 4. Digital Design Protection

§1. Introduction

1187. The *Designs Act* 2003 (Cth) protects rights in relation to the appearance of an article so long as its features are novel or original. This Act places a higher threshold of distinctiveness for registration. To be registered, designs must be *new* – not known or previously used, and *original* – a design not previously applied to the product. Registration of a design may subsist for up to sixteen years. Some designs may also qualify for protection under copyright law. Registered designs make up the fourth of the main pillars of Australia's statutory intellectual property system.

1188. Australia grants statutory protection for the overall product's visual appearance. Such an appearance includes one or more of its visual features including its shape, configuration, pattern, or ornamentation.

1189. In this scheme, designs sit astride the gap between copyright on the one hand and patents on the other. Copyright protects artistic creations of a work which have not been industrially applied, patents protect the workings and function of an invention. Trademarks protect a brand; the design domain is in protecting the visual appearance of a product and in its manufacture and industrial applications. This protection of designs is to ensure the laws are 'sufficiently strong to prevent excessive copying' on the one hand and not 'so restrictive that they act as a barrier to further innovation' on the other.[708]

1190. In 2020 IPAustralia received a total of 7,165 applications for design rights, a 4 per cent decrease from 2019. In Australia 6,332 designs were registered in 2020 representing an 11 per cent annual decline.[709]

1191. Australian residents were named as applicants on 2,581 design right applications in 2020 representing a decline of 3 per cent from the previous year. Ninety-five per cent of resident applications listed only one Australian applicant, with a small number of multiparty applications – 113 from Australian co-applicants and 10 from Australians with international co-applicants.

1192. Non-residents accounted for 4,560 applications in 2020, a decline of 5 per cent from the level in 2019. Most design right applications in Australia come from single non-resident applicants (4,488 of all filings), with a smaller number (72) from non-resident co-applicants without involvement of Australian residents. The non-resident share of total applications has steadily increased over the past decade, from 60 per cent in 2011 to 64 per cent in 2020.

---

708. ACIP *Review of the Designs System: Issues Paper* September 2014 available at https://www.ipaustralia.gov.au/sites/default/files/options-paper-for-the-review-of-the-designs-system.pdf.

709. *See* IPAustralia *Australian Intellectual Property Report 2021* at https://www.ipaustralia.gov.au/ip-report-2021/chapter-4-designs.

§2. DESIGNS LAW

1193. Designs law in Australia has had a history of sporadic legislative changes.[710] The *Designs Act* 2003 (Cth) was introduced to replace the *Designs Act* 1906 (Cth). In 2021 after many years of investigation, consultation and review of Australia's registered designs laws, the *Designs Amendment (Advisory Council on Intellectual Property Response) Act* 2021 (Cth) came into force.

1194. Australia belongs to the International Convention for the Protection of Industrial Property (the Paris Convention). Over 170 countries are party to the 1883 Paris Convention.[711]

1195. Australia is not a contracting party to the Hague System and cannot accept applications under it. The Hague System for the International Registration of Industrial Designs (the Hague System) allows anyone to register up to 100 designs in many countries or regions. This may be done through a single application.[712]

I. *Designs Act* 2003

1196. The *Designs* Act 2003 (Cth) repeals the *Designs Act* 1906 (Cth) and consists of twelve chapters. Since 2012 the Advisory Council on Intellectual Property (ACIP) undertook a review and broad consultation on the Australian Designs System to assess its effectiveness in stimulating innovation and encouraging economic growth and reported in May 2015.[713] Among some of the major recommendations included the proposal for an unregistered design right, bridging the gap between copyright and design protection, the consideration of the treatment of virtual or non-physical designs and clarification of existing legislation.

II. *Designs Amendment (ACIP Response) Act* 2021

1197. The *Designs Amendment (Advisory Council for Intellectual Property Response) Act* 2021 (Designs Amendment Act) (Cth) is the culmination of public consultations and responses to submissions received.[714] The Act received royal assent in September 2021 and puts in place several recommendations by the ACIP accepted by the government.[715]

---

710. Caine, E & Christie, A (2005) 'A quantitative analysis of Australian intellectual property law and policy-making since federation' (2005) 16 *Australian Intellectual Property Journal* 185, 193-4.
711. *See* WIPO Paris Convention at https://www.wipo.int/treaties/en/ip/paris/.
712. *See* WIPO The Hague System at https://www.wipo.int/hague/en/.
713. *See* ACIP, Review of the Designs System (5 May 2015) at http://www.acip.gov.au/reviews/all-reviews/review-designs-system/.
714. *See* IPAustralia at https://www.ipaustralia.gov.au/about-us/public-consultations/implementing-accepted-recommendations-acips-review-designs-system and submissions collected at a Consultation Hub at https://consultation.ipaustralia.gov.au/policy/design-reforms-implement-acip-recs/.
715. *See* IPAustralia at https://www.ipaustralia.gov.au/sites/default/files/government_response_-_acip_designs_review_-_final_pdf.pdf.

1198. The amendments allow registered designs system to better support designers and encourage innovation in Australia. In addition to the introduction of a grace period for applying to register a design, thus providing an important safety net for designers, additional changes streamline the design application process and clarify gaps in existing law.

1199. Grace period. The Designs Amendment Act now permits a grace period of twelve months prior to filing to protect its newness.[716] The grace period will not apply to official publications of a design by the Designs Office in Australia or any similar office in a foreign jurisdiction to avoid extending the six-month period. The Paris Convention provides six months – the foreign filing exception – within which they can file in other Convention countries using the earlier 'Convention priority date'.[717]

1200. This grace period may also be interpreted as a new safety net either for accidentally failing to register a design in time or for innocent infringements. This grace period in allowing designers to delay filing an application for a registered design may potentially create difficulties for third parties who may independently come up with a design during this period.

1201. The grace period introduces a defence to infringement if a person starts using a design before it is published on the Register – that is, during the grace period. The defence continues to apply after the design has been filed, so that the third party can continue use of the design after it is registered without infringing it.[718]

1202. Design infringements. Exclusive licensees may now sue third parties for registered design infringements. This brings design law in line with other IPR such as patent, trademark and plant breeder's rights where licensees have been able to do so.

1203. Informed user. The *Designs Amendment Act* 2021 clarifies that the notion of a 'familiar person' with a notional standard of the 'informed user'. This amendment enshrines the approach taken by the Federal Court in *Multisteps Pty Ltd v. Source & Sell Pty Ltd* [2013] FCA 743. IPAustralia and the courts will now have more certainty and clarity about the views they can consider when assessing the substantial similarity in overall impression of designs, encompassing a broader range of consumers, experts and skilled persons

716. *See* commentary by Stewart, D & English, B (2021) 'Finally! A grace period. The proposed amendments to Australia's Designs Act 2003' at https://bennettandco.com.au/areas/intellectual/finally-a-grace-period-the-proposed-amendments-toaustralias-designs-act-2003/.
717. Paris Convention for the Protection of Industrial Property 1883 at https://www.wipo.int/treaties/en/ip/paris/.
718. *See* Wrigley, J & Sgourakis, C (2021) 'Australian designs law undergoes a welcome update', at https://www.corrs.com.au/insights/australian-designs-law-undergoes-a-welcome-update.

1204. Publishing a design. The current provision that a person for a fee may 'publish' rather than 'register' a design was intended to establish a design into the prior art base. As this has been rarely accessed, this mechanism has since been removed from the legislation.[719]

1205. Inadvertent disclosures. Where a design has been disclosed inadvertently such as at a trade show or in pre-launch publicity, it is still possible to seek design registration. Likewise, it will be possible to test proof of concepts to assess commercial potential and marketability of the product before registration of the design at various fora.

1206. Court revocation of registration. A court may revoke a design registration on the ground that 'the certificate of examination was obtained by fraud, false suggestion or misrepresentation' under the *Designs Amendment Act* 2021.

§3. Digital Design Assets and Online Services

I. 3D Printing

1207. Three-dimensional (3D) printing is described as a disruptive technology, which promises to transform art and design, science and manufacturing, and the digital economy.[720] *The Economist* previously declared that 3D printing would prompt the 'third industrial revolution'.[721]

1208. There is hope expressed that non-commercial 3D printing of designs would not infringe design rights so long as it was for purely personal use.[722] While it may appear that 3D printing seemingly would facilitate copyright infringement[723] another commentator suggests that it intersects with trademark law which would together shape the next battleground for IP law overreach.[724]

1209. Using computer-aided design (CAD) software and 3D object scanners, 3D objects may be created through the printing a series of layers. 3D printing involves layering of materials such as plastics, composites or biomaterials to create objects of any shape, size, rigidity and colour, subject to dimensional constraints of the

719. A search of the online system shows that only 25 designs are currently listed as published in Australia. *See* https://www.ipaustralia.gov.au/tools-resources/forms/request-publication-design.
720. Rimmer, M (2017) 'The maker movement: Copyright law, remix culture and 3D printing' *The University of Western Australia Law Review*, v.41(2) pp. 51- 84 and at http://www8.austlii.edu.au/cgi-bin/viewdoc/au/journals/UWALawRw/2017/5.html.
721. The Economist (2012) *The Third Industrial Revolution* (21 April).
722. Bradshaw, S, Bowyer, A & Haufe, P (2010) 'The Intellectual Property Implications of Low-Cost 3D Printing' (2010) 7(1) SCRIPTed at http://www.law.ed.ac.uk/ahrc/script-ed/vol7-1/bradshaw.asp.
723. *Supra*, Rimmer (2017).
724. Scardamaglia, A (2015) 'Flashpoints in 3D Printing and Trade Mark Law', (2015) 23(2) *Journal of Law, Information and Science* 30.

printer. 3D printing is described as an 'additive manufacturing' process as it successively adds materials to create an object. This contrasts with 'subtractive manufacturing' in traditional processes which remove materials through milling, machining, carving, shaping or other means.[725]

1210. With 3D printing three business models for digital designs have been identified namely: the user model, the distribution model and the print services model. Each of these are either a product or a service but raise similar legal issues. Users may reproduce unauthorized versions of an object that embodies a registered design in digital and physical form. The legality of such reproduction depends on whether these are either for personal use only or for commercial purposes as in the distribution model. 3D print services have been able to flourish on the Internet given the numerous online filesharing platforms supplying 3D object templates.

1211. The *Designs Act* 2003 (Cth) provides a system of registered designs and protection for those designs registered on the Design Register.[726] A 'product' means something that is manufactured or handmade. Visual features are defined to include 'shape, configuration, pattern or ornamentation of the product'. Such features can encompass the 3D and 2D aspects of a design which may or may not serve a functional purpose.[727]

1212. It is interesting to note that the protection of 2D designs is extended to reproductions in 3D form under the CA but is silent in the *Designs Act* 2003 (Cth).[728] So in the 3D printing context the original 3D digital design embedded in the CAD file can be protected under copyright and the product as a registered design. However, current Australian legislation denies protection of artistic works commercially exploited as 3D designs.[729]

A. *Infringements*

1213. Adams (2015) published a comprehensive review of 3D printing technology and Australian designs law.[730] Adams suggests that the 3D printing of a registered design would constitute an infringement under section 71 of the *Designs Act* 2003 (Cth). Under this section users commissioning a 3D print may infringe the design and the implied primary and vicarious liability contained therein. Secondary infringement is incurred for the importation for commercial purposes and there is

725. Lipson, H (2013) Fabricated: The New World of 3D Printing (John Wiley).
726. *Designs Act 2003* (Cth) ss 39-56. Design owners may choose instead to publish their design to prevent others from registering similar designs: *Designs Act 2003* (Cth) ss 57-59.
727. *Designs Act 2003* (Cth) s. 6(1), s. 7 and s. 7(2) respectively.
728. *Copyright Act* 1968 (Cth) s. 21(3).
729. *See Gold Peg International Pty Ltd v Kovan Engineering (Aust) Pty Ltd and Others* (2005) 225 ALR 57, 108 (per Crennan J).
730. Adams, M (2015) 'The 'Third Industrial Revolution': 3D Printing Technology and Australian Designs Law', *Journal of Law and Information Science* 2015 v.24(1) pp. 56-82 and at http://www8.austlii.edu.au/cgi-bin/viewdoc/au/journals/JlLawInfoSci/2015/11.html.

an implied territorial limit in that printing takes place within Australia – section 71(b)–(e). A defence may be open to users creating a digital copy of a design as is the printing of spare parts whilst exercising a right to repair section 72 generally and the so-called after-market defence provided under section 72(1)(a).

B. Defences

1214. Adams (2015) further notes that it is important to differentiate individuals as private users as against service providers for identification of infringements. However, territorial limits suggest that the 3D printing should occur within Australia for there to be an infringement.[731] Online file sharing services hosting design files will incur no infringement if the printing is incidental to the acts specified under section 71 of the Act. This is characterized as intermediary liability in the absence of authorization provided for under section 10(1)(a)–(e). However, service providers, such as those who host 3D template files online, would not be considered in common law as joint tortfeasors if there is no common design in their endeavours. A differentiation is made between procuring and mere facilitation infringement.

C. Identified Gaps

1215. Gaps in legal protection of designs have been identified in the *Designs Act* 2003 (Cth) where it has been unable to deal with the nascent 3D printing technology.[732] The Act is currently ill-equipped to respond to products in a physical and a digital form. Designs law is the only IP regime that has not addressed the evolution into the digital age.

II. Graphical User Interfaces (GUI)

1216. Virtual designs or non-physical designs affect the appearance of digital assets implemented via software on digital screens, such as those relating to monitor displays, GUI and screen icons.

1217. A GUI is the visual display through which a user interacts with software. The user interface (UI) refers to the underlying *non-graphic* code of a software program. The GUI refers to the visual elements, that is, the 'look' of the program. UIs remain virtually unprotected under current Australian IP laws even though it is apparent that it may be protected under various overlapping legal regimes such as copyright, trade dress and design patents.[733]

---

731. *See Led Technologies Pty Ltd v. Elecspess Pty Ltd.* (2008) 80 IPR 85.
732. *Supra*, Adams, M (2015).
733. In the US, Stigler has described how copyright protection for GUIs is thin. The more utilitarian or useful a work is, the narrower (or thinner) its scope of protection. Only an exact copy will be found

1218. User interface design is the process designers use to build interfaces in software of computerized devices and which focus on look or style.[734] The aim of designers is to create interfaces which provide easy and pleasurable access to the devices. The term 'user experience (UX) design' covers the entire spectrum of the user experience.[735]

1219. One form of GUI designs is where users interact with visual representations on digital control panels such as a computer's desktop on a monitor screen. Another is with voice-controlled interface (VUI) where a voice is used to control functions and applications. Examples include Siri on the iPhone and Alexa on Amazon device. A final form is gesture-based interfaces through bodily motions that allow users to engage with 3D design spaces. Examples include virtual reality (VR) and augmented reality (AR) games and functions.

1220. In Australia, the *Designs Amendment Act* 2021 GUI is excluded. GUIs may be registered with only the need to pass a limited formalities check. However, passing examination-certification to enforce the design may be slightly more difficult. While there are many registered designs that relate to GUIs and other non-physical designs, only a very few of these are certified. As a result, the status of protection of non-physical or virtual designs in Australia is uncertain.

1221. Some GUIs have been certified, for example, Apple Inc's Garage Band display screen[736] and Shenzhen Royole Technologies Co. Ltd's wearable display screens with GUl.[737]

1222. It appears that IPAustralia has potentially shifted its views considering the decision in *Apple Inc* [2017] ADO 6 in which Apple failed to have an adverse examination decision for its 'display screen' overturned.

1223. The ACIP recommendations contained in the *Review of the Designs System* suggested the reconsideration of the treatment of virtual or non-physical designs.[738] In particular, the recommendation was for the consideration of such designs in an active state not just resting state, when evaluating the validity and

---

not infringe. *See* Stigler, R (2014) Ooey GUI: The Messy Protection of Graphical User Interfaces, 12 *Northwestern Journal of Technology and Intellectual Property,* 215 (2014) at https://scholarlycommons.law.northwestern.edu/njtip/vol12/iss3/3.

734. *See* User Interface (UI) Design at https://www.interaction-design.org/literature/topics/ui-design.

735. The analogy used is to think of UX design as a car with UI design as the driving console and ancillary equipment.

736. *See* IPAustralia at https://search.ipaustralia.gov.au/designs/search/details/201214383?s=baf7c5c4-e1e4-4c32-9b30-17385d8fcdd1&page=1&sort=PRIORITY&fs=CERTIFIED.

737. *See* IPAustralia at https://search.ipaustralia.gov.au/designs/search/result?s=7ca27d2b-a73d-4ca8-8ec8-050d9aa55797&fs=CERTIFIED.

738. Advisory Council on Intellectual Property (2014) *Review of the Designs System: Options Paper* (December) at https://www.ipaustralia.gov.au/sites/g/files/net856/f/options-paper-for-thereview-of-the-designs-system.pdf.

potential granting an enforceable right.[739] In 2015, the ACIP recommended GUIs be examined in their 'active state', citing widespread support for such change. However, the government has left this recommendation out in the *Design Amendments Act* 2021 (Cth) a topic discussed further under trends in designs legislation below.

III. Typefaces and Fonts

1224. The design of typefaces and fonts used in media production needs closer examination and consideration because the protection of the design aspects from the point of view of 'creativity' have mostly been undertaken under copyright law.

1225. A *typeface* is technically 'a set of letters, numbers, or other symbolic characters, whose forms are related by repeating design elements consistently applied in a notational system and are intended to be embodied in articles whose intrinsic utilitarian function is for use in composing text or other cognizable combinations of characters'.[740]

1226. A *font*, on the contrary, is 'an article in which a typeface resides as the implement of printing technology, regardless of the medium or form'. A font (the product of a foundry) refers to the complete character set in one specific point size and style of type within a type family, for example, *Helvetica*. While a typeface is the artistic creation of a typeface designer, most likely produced in digital format, a font is the result of an industrial process to enable the reproduction of typefaces in the printing process.[741]

1227. In Australia, a newspaper masthead comprising Chinese calligraphic characters is an 'artistic work' capable of copyright protection as well as being a trademark capable of protection under the *Trade Marks Act* 1995 (Cth). In *Australian Chinese Newspapers Pty. Ltd. v. Melbourne Chinese Press* (2003) 58 IPR 1 the court was satisfied that the requisite level of thinking had gone into the creation of the work and masthead and therefore an original artwork capable of copyright protection. The art and the creation of the characters were sufficiently expressive, and the artist had exhibited a sufficient degree of thinking in producing the work.[742]

1228. In *Lott v. JBW & Friends Pty. Ltd* (2003) 58 IPR 1 a copyright claim in computer-aided typography fonts in a brochure was argued. At first instance the decision in the Magistrates Court a copyright was found to subsist and had been infringed. On appeal to the Supreme Court, the respondents had stated that they

739. *See* IPAustralia at https://www.ipaustralia.gov.au/policy-register/reconsider-treatment-virtual-or-non-physical-designs-eg-allow-consideration-such.

740. Cabarga, L (2004) *Logo, Font and Lettering Bible,* Writer's Digest Books, at 12.

741. *See* a discussion of the terminological distinction between fonts and typefaces in Carroll, TJ (1994) Protection for Typeface Designs: A Copyright Proposal, 10 *Santa Clara Computer & High Tech Law Journal* 139, 169-70 (1994).

742. Pappas, C (2004) 'Can copyright subsist in Chinese characters?' *Intellectual Property Law Bulletin*, vol. 16(9) February/March, pp. 150.

were commissioned to produce a brochure *Opera in the Outback*. There was a dispute over unpaid fees as well the respondents had sought damages for twenty occasions of infringement of copyright. The respondents claimed that they designed and crafted the graphic bar using words supplied by choosing typefaces and font used as well as all the graphic design in the letters, the angle of curves above and below the words and setting the words in colour using different hues. It was claimed that the graphic bar was only licensed for use on the brochure.

1229. The Supreme Court found that the respondents had designed the graphic bar; that they owned the copyright in it; that the Director of the Company that had commissioned the design and authorized the publication of the graphic bar in advertisements was personally liable for the breach of copyright. The Court found that the agreement was clear, and the licence was limited to the use of the graphic bar on the brochure.

A. *Denial of Design Law Protection*

1230. There may be three reasons in denying design law protection to typefaces and fonts. First, to acquire design registration and certification the artistic elements of the digital typeface must be new and innovative as well as physically separate. In the digital age, physical separation occurs in the software code that generates the digital typefaces. The software code is generally copyrightable.

1231. In Australia copyright protection is denied for typefaces based on functionality grounds.[743] A typeface's artistic elements are usually not *physically* separable from the functional elements in the sense generally contemplated by copyright law. The individual fonts need to be recognizable as letters in the absence of which it would not be able to perform its function.

1232. It may be postulated that copyrighting typeface software code may potentially allow typeface designers to use as a backdoor to protect their otherwise uncopyrightable designs.

1233. Another line of argument for rejecting protection for designs under copyright law is that the typeface code may lack sufficient creativity. Moreover, industry practice among typeface designers is that they do not actually create and write the necessary code but instead use off-the-shelf proprietary programs such as FontLab Studio or TypeTool to create typefaces.

1234. Furthermore, even where the code is under copyright protection, the copyright does not necessarily extend to the design of the resulting typeface *per se*. Copyrighting the code and copyrighting the products are two different things.

743. In the US typefaces do not qualify for copyright protection. *See* Lipton, JD (2009) To © or Not to ©? Copyright and Innovation in the Digital Typeface Industry, 43 *U.C. Davis Law Review* 143 (2009) at https://scholarship.law.pitt.edu/fac_articles/184.

Through reverse engineering, or even independent coding, it may be possible for font designers to generate a very similar looking typeface using a different code.

1235. Second, technological protection measures (TPM) when implemented on the typeface code, are technically complex and difficult to operationalize. Apart from its cumbersome implementation and complexity, the technical difficulty is that typefaces are system-level resources, unlike music, videos or e-books which are applications that are deployable instantly.

1236. Third, design law also raises questions as to whether typefaces meet the statutory newness and distinctive criteria. As digital objects in computer memory and in code form, there is no physical article of manufacture that embodies the typeface. It is thus unclear whether design law can meaningfully apply.

1237. From a patent law point of view much of typeface software may be insufficiently novel or may be too obvious to attract registration as a patent. In online typeface and font marketplaces, such as fontspace.com and myfonts.com, most digital font developers rely on copyrights, contractual licenses and to some extent trademarks, to protect their fonts, rather than use a design patent.

1238. Software code for typefaces is a patentable subject matter if it otherwise meets the novelty and non-obviousness requirements of the patent law.

1239. Industry norms suggest that while font designers are concerned about unauthorized copying, they expect and understand that some degree of copying is necessary and accept this as a normative matter.[744]

1240. Design registration has proven to be an effective tool for enforcing IP rights against online sales of counterfeit goods.[745] Compared to patent registration obtaining a design certification is relatively quick. Online marketplaces typically have fora to assist with takedown listings proven to be infringing on a design registration. eBay has established their Verified Rights Owner Program (VeRO), Amazon employs an Amazon Brand Registry and AliExpress (along with all other Alibaba platforms) provides an Alibaba Group IP Protection Platform. Takedown of registered design articles of a proven infringing listing is usually much less contentious and involved compared to a patent-related request.

1241. Lipton (2009) has conjectured that the uncertainties surrounding the legal protection of digital typefaces may be resolved through a form of international *sui generis* IP protection.[746] Internationally, the Vienna Agreement for the Protection of

744. *I.* Lipton 2009.
745. *See* Shaw, E (2020) 'How can design registration help stop online sales of counterfeit products?' at https://www.spruson.com/designs/how-can-design-registration-help-stop-online-sales-of-counter feit-products/.
746. *Supra*, Lipton 2009.

Type Faces and Their International Deposit of 1973 could be a consideration.[747] Previously, the US Congress has provided *sui generis* protection for digital databases to overcome concerns that many of these databases fail to meet the originality requirements of copyright law.[748] It is arguable that such a suggestion is viable for the protection of fonts.

§4. Trends in Design Regulation

I. Unregistered Designs Right (UDR)

1242. The idea of an unregistered design right (UDR) was contemplated in the ACIP Review but was excluded from the *Designs Amendment Act* 2021.[749] A UDR would provide automatic protection when a design comes into existence. The introduction of this right would prevent 'freeriding' from third parties and relieve designers having to undergo the rigours of the registration and certification process. Designers may balk at this having to register as costs might usually outweigh benefits. Additionally, in the fashion industry, designs have a very short-lived shelf life and may form part of a larger range. Together with automatic rights under copyright law it is argued that its introduction could promote further innovation and investment in the Australian design industry.[750]

1243. However, the introduction of any version of a UDR is unlikely in Australia as the ACIP's final report into the Australian designs system recommended that Australia should not introduce UDRs.[751] The government subsequently agreed with ACIP and indicated that the introduction of a UDR will not be supported.[752]

II. Design-Copyright Law Overlap

1244. It is believed that sole traders and businesses have not sought design registration for their products because of the expense or neglecting to get legal advice prior to selling their designs.[753] This exposes them to their designs being obviously

747. *See* the Vienna Agreement for the Protection of Type Faces and Their International Deposit of 1973 at http://www.austlii.edu.au/au/other/dfat/seldoc/1973/2203.html.
748. Cross, JT (1994) Protecting Computer Databases under the United States Copyright Laws: Implications of the Feist Decision, in *Computers and Law* 113-127 (Carr, I & Williams, K (eds), London: Intellect Books 1994).
749. ACIP (2014) Review of the Designs System: Issues Paper (September) at https://www.ipaustralia.gov.au/sites/default/files/options-paper-for-the-review-of-the-designs-system.pdf.
750. Bell, V (2014) 'Opening "Pandora's box": ACIP's review of the Australian designs system', (2014) 27(7) *Australian Intellectual Property Law Bulletin*.
751. Advisory Council on Intellectual Property at https://www.ipaustralia.gov.au/sites/g/files/net856/f/acip_designs_final_report.pdf.
752. Australian Government (2016) Government response – ACIP Review of the Designs System (2016) 8-9.
753. *See* Givoni, S (n.d.) Avoiding the Gaps in the Copyright/Design Overlap at https://www.sharongivoni.com.au/avoiding-the-gaps-in-the-copyrightdesign-overlap/.

copied. To ensure protection under copyright law, their products must fall under one of the exceptions to the copyright design overlap.

1245. Sections 74-77 of the CA govern the copyright designs overlap. Where a design has already been registered or applied industrially,[754] under these provisions, it is not an infringement of the underlying copyright to reproduce the work by embodying the corresponding design in a product.[755] These provisions remove copyright protection for industrially applied designs.[756]

1246. The rationale behind copyright-designs overlap is to prevent a design that *could* be registered and commercialized under the *Designs Act* 2003 (Cth) for a period of ten years protection from enjoying the lengthy protection afforded by the CA – life of the author plus seventy years.

1247. However, the most contentious exception is whether a design can be considered as work of artistic craftmanship. This question 'turns on assessing the extent to which the particular work's artistic expression, in its form, is unconstrained by functional considerations'.[757] In *Burge v. Swarbrick* [2007] HCA 17 the High Court concluded that the design was substantially dictated by functional considerations and the aesthetic appeal of the look was a secondary concern. The design was held neither to constitute a work of artistic craftmanship for the purposes of attracting copyright protection nor designs protection due to the failure to register the design.

III. Design Law Reform

1248. IPAustralia Designs Reform Project initiative is founded on a holistic review of the design ecosystem and its potential impact on the Australian economy, the drivers of design innovation and the role of design rights.[758] On the horizon is a discussion of virtual and non-physical designs and the protection of designs in iteration. There is also the prospect of using blockchain technology to protect designs.

754. 'Industrially applied' means to apply the design to more than fifty articles: *Copyright Regulations* 1969 (Cth) reg 17. The policy intention is to deny cumulative protection of artistic works commercially exploited as 3D designs. *See Gold Peg International Pty Ltd v. Kovan Engineering (Aust) Pty Ltd and Others* (2005) 225 ALR 57, 108 (per Crennan J).
755. 'Corresponding design' is defined as the visual features of shape or configuration, which, when embodied in a product, result in a reproduction of the work: *Copyright Act 1968* (Cth) s. 74(1).
756. And copies have not been sold or exposed for sale (s. 77) or is a 2D design that has been applied to the surface of an article (s. 74).
757. *See Burge v. Swarbrick* [2007] HCA 17, 83-84.
758. *See* IPAustralia Design Reform Project at https://www.ipaustralia.gov.au/designs/design-initiatives.

A. Virtual and Non-physical Designs

1249. IPAustralia's Policy Register,[759] has listed a reconsideration of its treatment of virtual or non-physical designs such as GUIs and to allow such designs to be considered in an active state not just resting state, when assessing its validity and the granting of an enforceable right. The potential for policy and legislative reform in this space is apparent given the increasingly important and essential feature of such applications in design registrations and certification especially for virtual and digital designs.

1250. The current policy guidance is that for design registration the product should be specified as an electronic device including a GUI or display screen or similar and avoid identifying it as a GUI alone and avoiding an examiner querying the GUI product names.[760] To be successful in the registration of a design there should be an overt statement of newness and distinctiveness as a feature of the GUI.

B. Protection of Designs in Iteration

1251. IPAustralia is currently undertaking a review of issues surrounding the protection of designs in iteration. Under the *Designs Act* 2003 (Cth) protection is for the overall visual appearance of a product. The implied requirement is that designers must have an effectively completed design before they can access the design rights system. IPAustralia has found that an emergent theme in its various reviews of the design system has been that for many designers the linear design registration system is incompatible with the iterative nature of the design process involving research and development, testing and refining their design before market exposure.[761] This incompatibility creates difficulties for businesses seeking to develop a protection strategy, particularly in the timing of when to apply for design protection. Applying for protection early risks in going to market with a design that is either not optimized and/or has iterated and is out of step with what's protected, whereas waiting to apply for protection risks disclosure and compromising any future protection at all.

1252. The cost of protection itself a barrier for some designers, especially when what they are seeking to protect may not be the final product. A measure of cost-effectiveness protection during the iteration process might be desirable and permit designers to spend more time innovating, leading to better design in the marketplace.

---

759. *See* IPAustralia Policy Register at https://www.ipaustralia.gov.au/policy-register/reconsider-treatment-virtual-or-non-physical-designs-eg-allow-consideration-such.

760. *See* IPAustralia Examiner's Manual at http://manuals.ipaustralia.gov.au/design/chapter-7.-product-name.

761. *See* IPAustralia Protection of Designs in Iteration at https://www.ipaustralia.gov.au/policy-register/protection-designs-iteration.

C. Designs and NFT Fashion Tokens

1253. Non-fungible tokens (NFT) have entered the design vocabulary even when fashion design houses have registered their designs using blockchain technology.[762]

1254. Non-fungible tokens refer to cryptographic assets on a blockchain with unique identification codes.[763] Unlike fungible cryptocurrencies where one may have smaller denominations of a cryptocurrency, NFTs cannot be traded or exchanged at equivalency because there is only one of a kind. Examples of NFTs include a unique digital artwork, a unique sneaker in a limited-run fashion line, a domain name or a ticket that gives access to an event.

1255. Using blockchain technology (literally a chain of blocks) it is possible to track a particular product after it leaves the manufacturer, including checking which store sold the goods and who the purchaser was. Similarly, it is possible to verify whether an article is authentic. Such security measures are a means of protection and a method to combat counterfeiting. An entire production process may easily and quickly be checked for authenticity as well as passing on IPR related to the design or trademark to consumers.

1256. The French luxury goods company LVMH (Moët Hennessy Louis Vuitton) uses a platform called *Aura Blockchain* to track its products and to verify their authenticity.[764] The corporation's premise is to extend the blockchain network to monitor its brands and designs within its group. Blockchain functionality is also extended to include IP protection and prevent fraudulent advertising.

1257. Aura Blockchain matches a product ID to a client ID through a chain of secure, non-reproducible, digital blocks. This platform will enable consumers to access the history of a product and proof of its authenticity at every step of the value chain, from raw materials to point of sale. Consumers can thus follow the entire life-cycle of a product with trusted data throughout, and with no need for third-party verification.

D. Australian Determinations on Blockchains

1258. In Australia a recent determination of a delegate to the Commissioner of Patents held that certain blockchain inventions constituted patentable subject matter even if they only use generic computer implementation.

---

762. *See* Villa, A (2021) Gucci Sells NFT Inspired by Latest Collection at Christie's, *Art News*, (June 2, 2021) at https://www.artnews.com/art-news/market/gucci-nft-auction-christies-1234594632/. An auction bid for USD20,000 has been made and proceeds from the sale will be donated to UNICEF USA to support the non-profit's COVAX initiative, which supports global access to COVID-19 vaccines.

763. *See* Investopedia at https://www.investopedia.com/non-fungible-tokens-nft-5115211.

764. *See* LVMH at https://www.lvmh.com/news-documents/news/lvmh-partners-with-other-major-luxury-companies-on-aura-the-first-global-luxury-blockchain/.

1259. Two recent cases are apposite here. First in *Advanced New Technologies* Co. *Ltd.* [2021] APO 29 The patent application purported to minimize the risk of security breaches with respect to private and confidential information in the blockchain. The invention claimed was the avoidance of recording and dissemination of raw data across the entire network by converting it into non-recognizable form and then using it to confirm consensus between nodes.

1260. In the second case *Commonwealth Scientific and Industrial Research Organisation* [2021] APO 43 the patent application purported to improve the ability of an entity to monitor the compliance of other entities that were a party to a process in a way that would mask the confidential information. The claimed invention used blockchain technologies to compare the actions of the monitored entity against a machine-readable version of the desired process.

1261. In separate decisions, the delegate considered that blockchain inventions are computer-implemented technologies that are not inherently unpatentable. Despite the claimed inventions' use of generic computer processes and were not necessarily directed to solving a technical problem, the delegate considered that the claimed inventions constituted patentable subject matter as they each provided a technical solution to a problem.

1262. However, it is noted that later decisions are at variance with the two cases discussed above. The Full Federal Court of Australia delivered their judgment in *Commissioner of Patents v. Aristocrat Technologies Australia Pty Ltd* [2021] FCAFC 202 and *Repipe Pty Ltd v. Commissioner of Patents* [2021] FCAFC 223 shortly after the delegate's decision. These latter decisions emphasize that computer-implemented inventions must represent an *advance in computer technology.* Merely providing a technical solution to a problem which does not lie in the field of computer technology may be insufficient cause for the award of a patent.

1263. The High Court has granted special leave to appeal the decision in *Commissioner of Patents v. Aristocrat Technologies Australia Pty Ltd* [2021] FCAFC 202. Successful special leave applications are relatively rare, as the High Court must be satisfied the appeal involves a question of general principle of law sufficient to warrant the grant of special leave or be in the public interest.[765] *Repipe Pty Ltd v. Commissioner of Patents* [2021] FCAFC 223 also filed a special leave application to the High Court on 6 January 2022, but an outcome is still pending to date.

1264. In summary, while a delegate's decisions indicate that blockchain inventions are not inherent unpatentable, section 18(1) of the *Patent Act* 1990 (Cth) might require more than the mere provision of a technical solution. This is particularly so if the problem which the invention solves does not lie in the field of computer technology.

765. High Court of Australia Application granted [2022] HCA Trans 025 (10 Mar. 2022).

§5. CONCLUSION

1265. The impact of digitization on creative industries such as design has yet to be comprehensively assessed. Whether such technologies provide incentives for innovation and creativity or have a chilling effect is yet to become apparent. Equally scant are case law and litigation that address such questions. The Australian government has acknowledged that it will continue to monitor technological developments and their implications for the designs system.[766]

1266. Adams (2015) is of the view that designs law is currently ill-equipped to respond to the situation where products can enjoy a life in physical and digital forms. It is more likely that online services will assist registered design owners by implementing self-regulation and innovative solutions that protect the digital equivalents of registered design owners and deter the manufacture of copied designs.[767] It is moot whether digital designs residing on the Internet will properly be protected and defended from infringements.

766. *See* Productivity Commission (2016) *Intellectual Property Arrangements: Draft Report* (2016) at http://www.pc.gov.au/inquiries/completed/intellectual-property/draft.
767. *Supra*, Adams, M (2015).

Chapter 5. Copyright Protection for Digital Assets

§1. Introduction

1267. Administratively the Department of Infrastructure, Transport, Regional Development and Communications is responsible for managing the CA for policy and other matters. A recent study by PriceWaterhouseCoopers for the period 2006-2018 has found that Australian copyright industries relying on copyright protection in 2018 contributed AUD 24 billion to the Australian economy, equivalent to 6.8 per cent of Australia's GDP, employed about 1.034 million people and AUD 4.8 billion in exports.[768]

1268. During the period of the COVID-19 pandemic the copyright industries have been affected in several ways. With more time at home and dependent on online content, the changes to online activity and habits have been modified. Of significance is the increased screen content consumption of online subscription services (29 per cent increase), free video streaming services (23 per cent increase) and other websites and apps (16 per cent increase).[769]

1269. In 2020, the proportion of respondents to the Online Copyright Infringement Survey who reported consuming music and movies from an unlawful source was broadly consistent compared to 2019.[770] The pattern of visits to piracy sites in 2020 are similar across industries and overall visits to piracy sites have decreased since 2017. Further the data also show that 34 per cent of users who downloaded or accessed content online between March-June 2020 had consumed some content that was likely to be unlawful. Of these 13 per cent were more concerned about lawfulness of their consumption during the pandemic and 3 per cent less concerned.

I. Background to Copyright Legislation

1270. The *Copyright Act* 1968 (Cth) (CA) protects the rights of authors and creators in their 'works' of original creative effort. Such rights include the right to reproduce the work and to make copies and the right to present it to the public. Copyright subsists in the physical and online world. Copyright does not exist apart from the Act and vests in the creator as soon as the work is created even though it

768. *See* PriceWaterhouseCoopers 2020 The economic contribution of Australia's copyright industries 2006-2018 at https://www.copyright.org.au/static/ACC_pdf/The_economic_contribution_of_Australia%E2%80%99s_copyright.pdf.
769. Department of Infrastructure, Transport (2020) Regional Development and Communications, *Media Content Consumption Survey 2020*, p. 26.
770. Department of Infrastructure, Transport, Regional Development and Communications, *Copyright Infringement Survey 2020*, pp. 5-9 based on an internal analysis of data from MUSO Piracy by Industry. *See* MUSO at https://www.muso.com/.

may be unpublished. There is no registration requirement in Australia. This exclusive property right is also an economic right as a royalty is the monetary consideration received by the owner of a copyright in a work from a person with a licence to take copies of that work.

1271. Copyright is primarily concerned with the prevention of unauthorized copying. It is a right that prevents the unauthorized reproduction by a third party of the form in which a person has chosen to express ideas.[771] The right is conferred automatically with no formalities other than affixing the copyright notice and symbol – the letter c enclosed in a circle thus © and the name of the creator and date.

1272. Since 1968 there have been over sixty major or minor amendments to the CA. Some of the copyright amendments are noted below.

1273. *Copyright Amendment (Moral Rights) Act* 2000 (Cth) ensures that Australia complies with its obligations under article 6 bis.122 of the 1928 Berne Convention for the Protection of Literary and Artistic Works.[772]

1274. *Copyright Amendment (Digital Agenda) Act* 2000 (Cth) proposes simplified regimes and technology-neutral right of communication to the public.

1275. *Copyright Amendment Act* 2006 (Cth) to comply with the *Australia-United States Free Trade Agreement* 2004 and the introduction of technological protection measures and address issues of copyright exceptions.

1276. *Resale Royalty Right for Visual Artists Act* 2009 (Cth) in relation to the right of resale (*droit de suite*).

1277. *Copyright Amendment (Online Infringement) Act* 2018 (Cth) (CAOIA) to provide tools that rights holders use to respond to commercial-scale widespread copyright infringement on websites operated outside Australia.

1278. *Copyright (Disabilities and Other Measures) Act* 2017 (Cth) simplification of statutory licences, libraries to make preservation copies, and fixed term of protection of unpublished works and making accessible format versions for people with disabilities.

1279. *Copyright Amendment (Service Providers) Act* 2018 (Cth) expands the safe harbour system to include cultural, education and disability institutions as a 'first step' in modernizing Australia's safe harbour scheme.

1280. The CAOIA expands the remit in relation to online infringements.

771. Ricketson, S (1989) The use of copyright works in electronic databases, Law Inst. J. 480-482.
772. For text of the Copyright Amendment Act see http://www.austlii.edu.au/au/legis/cth/num_act/cara 2000342/ and Bern Convention text at https://wipolex.wipo.int/en/text/283698.

II. Overview: *Copyright Act* 1968 (CA)

1281. The CA copyright protects Part III 'works' grouped by category such as: literary, dramatic, musical, artistic, and Part IV 'subject matter other than works', such as film, sound recording, television and sound broadcasts and published editions.

1282. Each category attracts certain exclusive rights to the copyright owner (section 32) provided the author is a 'qualified person', the work is 'original' and the work is in 'material form'. The copyright lasts the life of an author plus seventy years after death of the author (section 33). Rights may be sold or transferred and the assignment of copyright in IT must be in writing section 196(3).

1283. A 'fair dealing' clause permits users to copy limited amounts of a work for personal research or study purposes (sections 40-43). Technically copyright is infringed when reverse engineering (or de-compilation) someone else's computer program.

1284. Section 10(1) defines 'literary work' to include a table or compilation, whether in a visible form or otherwise and includes a computer program or compilation of computer programs.

III. Online Information Technology Data

1285. In general, most materials published on the Internet is protected by copyright. The concept of fair dealing simply says that if someone obtains a copyrighted product legally then that person may legitimately use such copies for personal purposes. However, when that person redistributes the material, then copyright is infringed. This is despite the information being value-added to and augmented, or even given away free by the latter user.

1286. While it is nearly impossible to prevent illegal copying using technology, there have been attempts to ensure the origins of material are maintained. On maps and images, one could use watermarks (sometimes called 'fingerprinting') inserted unobtrusively and invisible to the naked eye, to discourage counterfeiting. Alternatively, one could introduce 'copyright traps' in the form of including false but insignificant features such as misspelling names, inserting (or omitting) cul-de-sacs in streets, encoding messages or random colours into the bits that constitute a raster image which will be preserved even if the image is altered in anyway. Adding redundant code in software that are hidden in the computer program may arguably be used to prove provenance and ownership.

1287. If data were distributed for viewing only then the data could be degraded sufficiently to make it useful for viewing only but not much else. Alternatively, a geographic information system (GIS) raster map in GIF or JPEG format[773] may look nice but would be of little use without the extensive metadata on the projection used to generate the pixel coordinates. Vector maps may be drawn with false coordinates using map centimetres instead of real-world meters which would look acceptable on a computer screen but will not be positionally correct on a mapping system. All these technological features are meant to provide an audit trail of evidentiary material if litigation were to take place and proof of ownership were to be required by the courts.

1288. The term digital rights management (DRM) describes a technology for identifying, trading, protecting, monitoring and tracking all forms of rights usages over both tangible and intangible information assets including management of right holder's relationships. Geospatial DRM manages all rights, not only the rights applicable to permissions over digital geographic data. Technological protection methods (TPM) describe the technology to embed artefacts to prevent as well as detect copyright infringements.

1289. Article 11 of the WIPO *Copyright Treaty* 1996 (WCT) encouraged member states to pass laws that would prohibit circumvention of TPMs used to protect copyright information, such as passwords and copy controls – also known as anti-circumvention laws. The *Copyright Amendment (Digital Agenda Act)* 2000 (Cth) section 116A of the CA introduced the anti-circumvention notion enshrined in art. 11 WCT into Australian law.

1290. An early case involving circumvention devices under Australian copyright law was *Kabushiki Kaisha Sony Computer Entertainment v. Stevens* [2002] FCA 906. A mod-chip permitted the extension of functionality of the PlayStation allowing games from other regions as well as unauthorized copies to be played on the PlayStation. The regional access code was held not to be a TPM as it was not designed to prevent access to the copyright content or to act as a copy control mechanism of the copyright content.

1291. In recent times, online geo-blocking is used to control access to digital content on the Internet from music to computer games and software. Geo-blocking is the restriction of access based on the physical address of a user. One geo-blocking mechanisms is to use the Internet protocol address filter on a user and the other is credit card discrimination. In address filtering, a user's location based on

773. Graphics interchange format (GIF) a common raster graphics data format to display images. Raster data in this format is compressed for simple graphics with up to 256 colours. Joint Photographic Experts Group (JPEG) is an industry committee that develops standards for digital photographs. This acronym is commonly used for raster data formats and the data files are compressed to optimize the true-colour images of photographs and remote sensing images. However, this format is 'lossy' in that a small amount of data is lost in the compressing process giving a lower quality image than the original.

the Internet protocol address of the device used to access the service may be blocked. Credit card discrimination uses the billing address of a user's credit card to restrict access.[774]

1292. While access control mechanisms are a means to protect copyright information to assist monitoring licensing and distribution of digital assets it is also a business tool. Control mechanisms may be used to facilitate price discrimination between geographic regions to maximize profits and as a means of controlling the staggered release dates of digital material coordinated on a global basis.

§2. Evolution of Safe Harbour Principles

I. History of Safe Harbours in Australia

1293. The concept of a copyright safe harbour scheme was first introduced by the US as part of its *Digital Millennium Copyright Act 1998* (DMCA) to 'facilitate the robust development and worldwide expansion of electronic commerce, communications, research, development, and education in the digital age'.[775]

1294. Safe harbour laws were introduced in Australia as part of amendments to implement the *Australia-United States Free Trade Agreement* (AUSFTA) in 2005.[776] Under the Agreement Australia was required to introduce a safe harbour scheme based substantially on the US system, and with the same goals and basic operation. In 2018, the government expanded the safe harbour system to include cultural, education and disability institutions as a 'first step' in modernizing Australia's safe harbour scheme.[777]

II. Case law

1295. Litigation on safe harbour principles and the liability of Internet intermediaries discussed below relate to the of authorization of copyright infringement and the liability of service providers for content uploaded by users.[778]

---

774. *See* discussion in Burke, T (2017) Jumping the wall: Geoblocking, circumvention and the law in *University of Western Australia Law Review* v.42(2) pp. 56 – 68 and at: http://classic.austlii.edu.au/cgi-bin/sinodisp/au/journals/UWALawRw/2017/24.html.

775. *See* US S. Rep. No. 105-190, at 1 (1998).

776. *US Free Trade Agreement Implementation Act 2004*, Part 11.

777. *See* the *Copyright Amendment (Service Providers) Act* 2018 (Cth) at https://www.legislation.gov.au/Details/C2018A00071. In implementing the AUSFTA, Australia inadvertently limited the coverage of scheme to the narrower term 'carriage service providers' which is defined by the *Telecommunications Act* 1997 (Cth) as including only commercial ISPs and not to all online service providers. The Productivity Commission has recommended that all service providers be included was accepted by the government. *See Productivity Commission Inquiry Report no.78, Intellectual Property Arrangements* (23 Sep. 2016) Recommendation 19.1 available at http://www.pc.gov.au/inquiries/completed/intellectual-property/report/intellectual-property.pdf.

778. *See* Weatherall, K (2018) *Internet Intermediaries and Copyright – A 2018 Update*, (February 2018) at http://digital.org.au/sites/digital.org.au/files/documents/Weatherall%20on%20Internet%20Intermediaries%20and%20Copyright%20-%20Update%20Final.pdf.

1296. In *Roadshow Films Pty Ltd & others v. iiNet Ltd* [2012] HCA 16, (2012) 248 CLR 42, an alliance of thirty-four company members of the Australian Federation Against Copyright Theft (AFACT) and other movie and television studios unsuccessfully claimed that iiNet authorized primary copyright infringement. The claim was that iiNet failed to take reasonable steps to prevent its customers from downloading and sharing infringing copies of films and television programmes using BitTorrent a peer-to-peer file (P2P) sharing communication platform.

1297. In *Pokèmon Company International, Inc. v. Redbubble Ltd* [2017] FCA 1541, the issue was whether platforms were liable for content uploaded by their users.[779] Redbubble was found to have authorized the infringing content uploaded by its users and were found to be directly liable for the infringements despite its best practice takedown procedures.

III. Legislative Responses

1298. The copyright safe harbour scheme is set out in sections 116AA–116AJ of the CA. It is intended to encourage rights holders and online service providers to work together when dealing with copyright infringement.

1299. The safe harbour scheme grants online service providers protection when their facilities are used to infringe copyright. Service providers are protected from financial liability for user infringements if certain steps have been taken to limit the impact on copyright owners. The important part of the scheme is the notice and takedown system as prescribed by Part 6 of the *Copyright Regulations* 2017 (Cth).

1300. The Australian safe harbour scheme previously applied only to commercial carriage service providers as defined by the *Telecommunications Act* 1997 (Cth). However, the *Copyright Amendment (Service Providers) Act* 2018 (Cth) extended the safe harbour to all carriage service providers including cultural, educational and disability groups where they provide online services to the public.

1301. The services to which the safe harbour apply include providing facilities to access the Internet (section 116AC); automatic caching (section 116AD); storing or hosting materials for clients section 116(AE); and linking to third-party materials (section 116AF).

§3. Code and Other Protection Measures

1302. Electronic documents may be secured by adding some specific features that allow simple copyright protection, authentication, document tracking or

779. The Redbubble's takedown process is described in *Pokèmon Company International, Inc. v. Redbubble Ltd* [2017] FCA 1541 at http://www.judgments.fedcourt.gov.au/judgments/Judgments/fca/single/2017/2017fca1541.

investigation of counterfeiting and forgeries. While TPMs have been used to protect copyright infringements, new developments in information science have extended such protections.

1303. The Digital Object Identifier (DOI) is an emerging international standard for identification of published material online. It forms the foundation layer technology that may incentivize publishers on the Internet to protect copyright, compensate content creators for their work and benefit consumers with a system that is sophisticated, seamless and easy to use.[780]

1304. At the systems level Khadim *et al.* (2015)[781] present a novel method for information hiding in text to provide copyright protection to preserve the integrity of information. The proposed scheme uses special objects like text watermarking to hide information, but which preserves information. The research has been shown to be robust and the method masks 'imperceptibility' to users but ensures the integrity of the document.

1305. Analysis by Ahvanooey *et al.* (2018)[782] reviewed information hiding techniques for copyright protection of text documents. The study argues that protection of texts to provide proof of ownership and provenance may be enhanced by digital watermarking and steganography techniques.

1306. Digital text watermarking is a data hiding technique which conceals a code or copyright information. Steganography hides secret messages in text media to transmit the secret information. Both techniques can be applied to sensitive documents as the inherent imperceptibility and robustness of the code can be ideal for detecting copyright infringement in text documents. Stojanov *et al.* (2014) have proposed a new property coding in text steganography of Microsoft Word documents. The encoding adds specific features that allow efficient copyright protection, authentication, document tracking and the investigation of counterfeiting and forgeries.[783]

780. *See* http://www.doi.org. *See* a discussion by Rosenblatt, W (1997) The Digital Object Identifier: Solving the Dilemma of Copyright Protection Online, *Journal of Electronic Publishing*, v.3(2) December and at https://quod.lib.umich.edu/cgi/t/text/idx/j/jep/3336451.0003.204?rgn=main;view=fulltext#top.

781. Khadim, U *et al.* (2015) Information hiding in text to improve performance for word document, International Journal of Technology and Research pp. 50 – 55 at https://www.researchgate.net/publication/281740572_Information_Hiding_in_Text_to_Improve_Performance_for_Word_Document.

782. Ahvanooey, MT *et al.* (2018) A comparative analysis of information hiding techniques for copyright protection of text documents, Security and Communication Networks, Wiley-Hindawi at https://www.hindawi.com/journals/scn/2018/5325040/.

783. *See* Stojanov, I *et al.* (2014) A new property coding in text steganography of Microsoft Word documents, in SECUREWARE 2014 The Eighth International Conference on Emerging Security Information, Systems and Technologies, and https://www.researchgate.net/publication/268515701_A_New_Property_Coding_in_Text_Steganography_of_Microsoft_Word_Documents.

§4. *Copyright Amendment Online Infringement Act* 2018

1307. The *Copyright Amendment (Online Infringement) Act* 2018 (Cth) (CAOIA) brings a wider range of online products, technologies and services under the umbrella of Australia's anti-piracy regime and copyright infringement. The amendment makes it harder for Australians to engage in digital piracy by downloading music, films and other digital content for free. The amendments will capture online locations that have the 'primary' effect of infringing or facilitating infringement of copyright; render online search engine providers susceptible to blocking injunctions; and provide adaptive blocking orders that can block new mirror or proxy websites.

I. Existing Blocking Regime

1308. In its current form the CA section 115A allows copyright owners to apply to the Federal Court of Australia for an injunction requiring that a carriage service provider to take reasonable steps to block access to an online location located outside Australia. The grant of an injunction must show that the online location has infringed or facilitates an infringement of copyright and have the primary purpose of infringing or facilitating the infringement of copyright whether located in Australia or elsewhere.

1309. The first injunction was ordered in December 2016 by Nicholas J in *Roadshow Films Pty Ltd v. Telstra Corporation Ltd* [2016] FCA 1503. Order 13 provided a mechanism for the copyright holder to approach the Court to have the terms of the existing injunction apply to a domain name, URL or Internet protocol address for the new location/s of the online location the subject of the injunction.

1310. Since then injunctions to block access have been granted with reference to a range of online locations where infringing content is made available including 'Solar Movie', 'The PirateBay', 'Torrentz', 'TorrentHound' and 'IsoHunt'.[784]

1311. In addition to targeting unlawful streaming and torrent indexers, applications have also been deployed to disable a broader range of technologies. For example, the Federal Court judgment in *Roadshow Films Pty Ltd v. Telstra Corporation Ltd* [2018] FCA 582 has the effect of disabling the HDSubs+ App which targets ancillary services that allow an 'app' or device to function.

II. Changes to Blocking Regime

1312. The CAOIA extends the scope of the current website blocking regime by broadening the threshold test of 'primary purpose of infringing copyright'; extending the potential application of injunctions to 'online search engine providers'; and

784. *Ibid. Roadshow Films* (2016).

providing an adaptive style of injunction where ISPs and online search engine providers can continue to block domain names, URLs and Internet protocol addresses without the need for a Court order.

1313. The COIA authorizes the blocking of access to websites that infringe copyright in situations where the party responsible for infringement is presumed to be located outside Australia. Rights holders will no longer need to put on evidence to prove this fact of the website location situated outside the jurisdiction. Whether the intended effect of this aim is practical remains to be seen as infringers can work from unknown locations, hide behind anonymous accounts or use VPNs.

1314. The making of blocking orders under section 115A(5) is discretionary under a statutory test where a Court may take into account proportionality; the public interest; and, the 'flagrancy' of the infringement when determining whether to grant the injunction.

1315. The CAOIA will enable applicants to seek injunctions against 'online search engine providers' and carriage service providers and not just ISPs requiring them to take steps to block search results that refer users to the relevant online location or infringing website.

1316. However, to mitigate the effects on small search engine providers who might be caught by the expanded regime, section 115A(8B) provides that the minister may specifically exclude online search engine providers or a class of online search engine providers from the application of the blocking injunction.

1317. The provision of adaptive injunctions will dispense the need for parties to return to the Court to vary existing orders where the copyright owner and ISP (or search engine provider) agree that a new domain name, URL or Internet protocol address has started to provide access to an online location specified in an earlier order.

1318. The categories of copyright which can be used as the basis for the site blocking orders and deindexing orders are not closed. The cases that have been brought before the courts so far have been literary works and cinematographic films.

§5. Afterword

1319. The blocking provisions of the CAOIA on CSPs seemingly has a broad reach. However, whether such injunctions can require CSPs to take down online locations that carry products that infringe trademark owners' rights will be closely watched by providers of services and users of such services.

1320. The question has been asked as to whether the legislation that blocks so-called piracy sites are a solution to the problems associated with online piracy.

As evidenced by subscription-based business model solutions such as those provided by Freemantle Media and Netflix demonstrate, Australians appear to be satisfied with the processes and access to the content they want to watch.[785]

1321. A Senate Environment and Communications Committee report of 26 November 2018 recommended that the amendments to the CAOIA be reviewed two years after their enactment.[786]

1322. There has been strong criticism and opposition to the CAOIA within Australia.[787] Following the stand taken in the *Equustek* litigation in Canada by Google, it can be expected that a vigorous defence may be forthcoming from Google and other service providers in Australia.[788] The Canadian case provides evidence of the extraterritorial application of an injunction against a non-party to litigation when the order is fair and equitable. It further demonstrates that 'the Internet has no borders – its natural habitat is global'.[789]

1323. The tension between human authorship requirement in copyright laws has been further tightened with the increasingly prevalent computer-generated elements and the use of AI in the production of digital assets and services.

1324. A looming challenge to copyright is that posed by non-fungible token (NFT) transactions. Unlike fungible tokens such as cryptocurrencies like Bitcoin, non-fungible tokens represent one of a kind, unique individualized units. These digital assets are built and reside on blockchain networks. The 'token' portion of the digital asset tracks its identity and attributes ownership to the current owner recorded as chains in a block in an encrypted digital public ledger of recorded transactions.

1325. NFTs give rise to novel IP rights issues. Unlike cryptocurrencies NFTs do not represent a store of value in and of themselves. Their value derives from the rights attaching to the underlying assets. 'NFTs have opened up a Pandora's box with respect to the enforcement of IP rights, where the value ascribed to an NFT as a whole is greater than the sum of its parts'.[790] NFTs have become a way for creators to monetize their art, photos, videos, audio and other digital files by selling NFTs as proxy certificates of authenticity. However, as NFTs are licences to use the

---

785. *See* Scott, MC (2015) There are better ways to combat piracy than blocking, *The Conversation* 23 Jun. 2015 at https://theconversation.com/there-are-better-ways-to-combat-piracy-than-blocking-websites-43701.
786. *See* Senate Environment and Communications Committee on 26 Nov. 2018 at https://www.aph.gov.au/Parliamentary_Business/Committees/Senate/Environment_and_Communications/OnlineInfringementBill/Report.
787. *See* Rimmer, M (2019) Australia's Stop Online Piracy Act: Copyright Law, Site-blocking, and Search Filters in an Age of Internet Censorship, *Canberra Law Review* (2019) (16(1) pp. 10-64, and at http://classic.austlii.edu.au/cgi-bin/sinodisp/au/journals/CanLawRw/2019/4.html.
788. *See Google Inc. v. Equustek Solutions Inc.* [2017] 1 SCR 824 at https://scc-csc.lexum.com/scc-csc/scc-csc/en/item/16701/index.do.
789. Supreme Court of Canada in *Google Inc.* v. *Equustek Solutions Inc.*, 2017 SCC 34.
790. Tan, P (2021) 'NFTs and the IP conundrum' at https://law.asia/nfts-ip-conundrum/.

underlying digital asset, it does not confer the copyright in that production to the buyer. Some NFTs only confer licences to use for personal, non-commercial purposes of the digital asset. Hence, novel legal questions for this new technology have arisen, such as whether copyright subsists in the NFT, enforcement of rights, whether copyright can *prima facie* be infringed and what, if any, defences apply.[791]

1326. As the minting and sale of NFTs is unregulated but also highly accessible to an international audience it has indeed a Pandora's box. NFTs will emerge to test the applicability of existing general law and copyright laws.

791. *See* Taylor, M (2021) Digital assets: surging popularity of NFTs raises important legal questions at https://www.ibanet.org/surging-popularity-of-NFTs-raises-important-legal-questions; and Chindlund, GJ & Gordon, KS (2021) What are the copyright implications of NFTs? at https://www.reuters.com/legal/transactional/what-are-copyright-implications-nfts-2021-10-29/.

Chapter 6. Protection for Electronic Databases

§1. Introduction

1327. The European Union *Database Directive* refers to a *database* as 'a collection of independent works, data or other materials arranged in a systematic or methodical way and individually accessible by electronic or other means'.[792] Databases may either be autonomously generated by machines and by machine intelligence; compiled systematically rather than 'creatively' or involve a process of selection only after the compilation has been created. The content of the data may be 'personal' relating to the subject themselves or 'non-personal' data relating to business or other kinds of scientific data.

1328. In terms of property rights electronic databases may be no different from non-electronic databases (for example, printed paper copies of data) and probably raise no novel copyright issues. Some databases do not qualify for copyright protection because there may be no originality in the selection and arrangement of the information.[793] In a work that records facts whether it be an encyclopaedia, a map, a directory, a catalogue, a database or some other factual compilation, there is neither copyright in the facts nor in each individual fact so presented. The author or creator however may have copyright in the form in which the facts are presented where there has been an intellectual effort in the selection or arrangement of the facts.

1329. Copyright protection of compilations is said to be 'thin'. It means that even a slight variation from the original will likely be permissible as careful imitators may escape infringing property rights by producing immaterial variations.

1330. Originally, the term *thin copyright* was coined to describe protection for map products.[794] Thin copyright provides protection against the 'grosser forms' of copying and encourages the adding of value either through verification or revision or through improvements in presentation.[795] In other words, a veneer of copyright protection is afforded to, say an electronic database for geographical data which is

---

792. *Directive of the European Parliament and of the Council on the Legal Protection of Databases,* 96/9/EC (11 Mar. 1996) Art. 1(2).

793. Lindsay, P (1993) Copyright Protection of Electronic Databases, 4(1) *Journal of Law and Information Science* 287-292 (1993). This contrasts with the EU *sui generis* database right that protects the 'sweat of the brow' of a database producer who has made a substantial investment in either obtaining, verifying or presenting the contents of a database. *See* Art 7 s. 1 of the European Union Council *Directive 1991 Legal Protection of Computer Programs* 91/250/EEC OJ L 122/42 of 17 May 1991.

794. *See* Karjala, DS (1994) 'Copyright in electronic maps', *Proceedings of the Conference on Law and Information Policy for Spatial Databases,* Tempe AZ, October, NCGIA & Center for the Study of Law, Science and Technology, Arizona State University College of Law (1994), at http://www.spatial.maine.edu.tempe/karjala.html. And in 35 *Jurimetrics J.* 395-415 (1995).

795. Gorman, RA (1992) The Feist Case: Reflections on a Path-Breaking Copyright Decision, 18 *Rutgers Computer & Tech LJ* 731 (1992).

made up of various elements including compilations that are 'normally' not copyrightable and those 'creative' elements which are copyrightable. When assembled the new work may attract thin copyright as it is ostensibly a newly created original work. Thus, while there may appear to be infringements of copyright works, the new work has added new value to the original by way of revision, updating and improvements in content and presentation.

§2. Legal Framework for Electronic Databases

1331. A legal framework for the protection of electronic databases is necessary because of the nature of the design, deployment and usage. The data stored in electronic databases may be structured, semi-structured and unstructured. Structured data are highly organized in predefined fields that assist in search and analysis. Unstructured data are neither organized nor formatted in any predefined manner and thus harder to interrogate and use. Database know-how ably assist the capacity to index and query unstructured data and thus handle large files such as visual media and photogrammetric images of the earth.

1332. The *Copyright Amendment (Digital Agenda) Act* 2000 (Cth) is designed to fulfil obligations under the Internet Treaties (for example WIPO and TRIPS) for the protection of databases and computer programs.

§3. Copyright in Electronic Databases

1333. In general, under the CA a database will be protected if the data compilations fall within the 'literary works' category (section 10(1); is expressed in material form includes any form of storage entered into a computer or stored in some machine-readable form; meets the originality test; and, has a relevant connection with Australia such as being published in Australia or produced by an Australian resident.

1334. Under Australian copyright law, facts and data in themselves are not protected by copyright. However, a collection of data, a dataset, or a database may be protected by copyright if it is sufficiently original. The issue of originality is dependent on whether it has been produced with independent intellectual effort. Originality is not defined in the Act and has been the subject of much debate and litigation.

1335. The selection of facts, its inclusion or exclusion and its arrangement and presentation may be crucial in deciding whether copyright protection is available. However, with electronic data there is doubt whether computer-produced data can claim copyright protection, whether such data are original and if so, the identity of the author. Also collated information in the form of an electronic database has become subject to interpretation. Subject to these provisos, an electronic database may be entitled to the same amount of protection under the CA as a printed database.

1336. The operation of Australian copyright law regarding databases is consistent with the *TRIPS Agreement* (Articles 9.2 and 10.2) and the *WIPO Copyright Treaty* (Articles 2 and 5), which require that copyright protection is extended to 'compilations of data or other material ... which by reason of the selection or arrangement of their contents, constitute intellectual creations'.[796]

I. Sufficiently Original Electronic Databases

1337. Databases generated from remote sensing satellite data raise doubts as to whether the data in its raw form is a 'work' and merits copyright protection. The decision whether raw data and databases qualify for copyright protection will depend on the degree of originality, the arrangement of the data and the skill in constructing the database. Uncertainty also arises as to who the 'author' of the resulting work might be, if indeed there is a human 'author' at all. In *Telstra Corporation Ltd v. Phone Directories Company Pty Ltd* (2010) FCAFC 149 the directories produced by defendants' original works and the human authors could not be identified.

1338. Electronic databases are subject to constant revisions and updates. One view is that each revised and updated version should be entitled to a separate copyright claim. The issue arises when someone other than the owner makes minor changes to an existing database. The implication here is that the person making the changes may not claim copyright in the amended version. Indeed, that person may have infringed copyright in the absence of permission to use and to amend the data.

1339. The question of the 'authorship' of a compilation is further clouded with the rapid evolution of technology. For example, intelligent computer software could be programmed to automatically add further information to a database to the extent that the compilation is virtually being assembled by a 'robot' computer (bot). This introduces doubt as to whether the original compiler of the database still retains a claim to copyright and whether the original compiler may claim copyright to the whole work including the data added by either a bot or another user.[797]

1340. At the other end of the spectrum, examples of factual compilations considered by courts to be original literary works include:

- a lookup table in a computer program in *Autodesk Inc v. Dyason* [1992] HCA 2;
- a pseudo-random data table used by a computer program to compress data in *Data Access Corporation v. Powerflex Services Pty Ltd* [1999] HCA 49;

796. *See* World Trade Organization (1994) *Agreement on Trade-Related Aspects of Intellectual Property Rights,* http://www.wto.orglenglish/tratop-e/trips-e/t-agm0_-e.htm (Apr. 15, 1994) and see World Intellectual Property Organization, *WIPO Copyright Treaty* http://www.wipo.int/treaties/en/ip/wct/trtdocswo033.html#P83_10885 (Dec. 20, 1996).

797. Cross, JT (1994) Protecting Computer Databases under the United States Copyright Laws: Implications of the Feist Decision, in *Computers and Law* 113-127 at 115 (Carr, I & Williams, K eds, London: Intellect Books 1994).

- poker machine prize scales in *Milwell Pty Ltd v. Olympic Amusements Pty Ltd* [1999] FCA 63;
- data compiled from survey forms about usage of copyright materials for educational purposes in *Copyright Agency Ltd v. Queensland Department of Education* [2007] FCAFC 80; and,
- a customer database list in *Vivid Entertainment LLC & Ors v. Digital Sinema Australia Pty Ltd & Ors (No.3)* [2007] FMCA 748.

II. Case Notes

1341. The following case notes sketch the evolving nature of the copyrightability of electronic databases no doubt reflecting the dynamic nature of the technology but also changing attitudes and contextual economic circumstances.

1342. In *Telstra Corporation Ltd v. Desktop Marketing Systems Pty Ltd* (2001) 181 ALR 134 and the follow-up appeal in *Desktop Marketing Systems Pty Ltd v. Telstra Corporation Ltd* (2002) 119 FCR 491, the issue was whether Telstra's White Pages and Yellow Pages, which arranged names, addresses and telephone numbers of individuals alphabetically, and the headings book, were original literary works. The Federal Court and the Full Federal Court on appeal unanimously held that Telstra's White Pages, Yellow Pages and headings book were original literary works. It was held that factual compilations could qualify as original literary works based on the skill, judgment and knowledge exercised in selecting or arranging the facts or on the ground that substantial labour and expense were incurred in collecting the information as opposed to the so-called industrious collection or sweat of the brow efforts.

1343. In *IceTV Pty Ltd v. Nine Network Australia Pty Ltd* (2009) 239 CLR 458 the High Court considered the meaning of the term 'originality' under copyright law. Originality requires that the literary work is traceable to an identifiable author and is the result of some 'independent intellectual effort' or 'sufficient effort of a literary nature' and that it was not merely copied from another work. The authors of a compilation would be those who gathered or organized the collection of material and selected, ordered, or arranged its presentation in material form. This decision sets a higher threshold for originality.

1344. In *Telstra Corporation Ltd v. Phone Directories Company Pty Ltd* (2010) 264 ALR 617 Telstra claimed copyright in the content, form and arrangement of the individual listings and enhancements in the White Pages and the Yellow Pages; the overall arrangement; and the headings, arrangement of listings under headings and cross-referencing. Both the Federal Court at first instance and the Full Federal Court on appeal found that the directories produced by Phone Directories Company were not original works. The human authors could not be identified and even if identifiable the human authors did not exercise 'independent intellectual effort' or 'sufficient effort of a literary work' in creating or presenting the works.

1345. In *Acohs Pty Ltd v. Ucorp Pty Ltd* [2010] FCA 577 and *Acohs Pty Ltd v. Ucorp Pty Ltd* [2012] FCAFC 16, Acohs claimed copyright in the Material Safety Data Sheets (MSDS) it prepared for companies and their obligations when supplying hazardous substances. The Federal Court and the Full Federal Court held that MSDS written by Acohs' employees constituted original literary works as the author was required to select materials. However, MSDS that were merely transcribed from existing MSDS were not original because the transcribers did not make any original contribution as the system dictated the layout, presentation and appearance of the MSDS. The computer programmers who wrote the underlying code could be considered authors of the MSDS.

1346. In *Dynamic Supplies Pty Ltd v. Tonnex International Pty Ltd* [2011] FCA 362, copyright was claimed in a compatibility chart for Dynamic's printer and computer consumables. The Federal Court held that this compilation was an original literary work as it comprised a unique layout presenting nine columns of interconnected, cross-referenced information. The court confirmed that simplicity does not deprive a work of originality unless the simplicity is a demonstration of the absence of skill or effort.

1347. In *Sanofi-Aventis Australia Pty Ltd and Others v. Apotex Pty Ltd (no 3)* [2011] FCA 846 the Federal Court held that the product information document for a medicine was an original literary work due to its overall form, arrangement, content and presentation. Specialized knowledge, creative skills and judgment were required to select information from the available information, and interpret, analyse and arrange this information into the form of the product information document.

A. Human Author

1348. For copyright purposes the case notes suggest that it may not be necessary to name each author of the database but that it need only be demonstrated that an author exists and exercised intellectual effort in the databases' compilation. Originality may be demonstrated by establishing a framework for the contents of a database, the selection of data, the assembly of content and in deciding on how fields and indexes are used in the schema of the database. In the *Telstra v. Phone Directories 2010 case* the full Federal Court had noted that it is uncertain that at what point human input will be too remote from computer-driven processes of creating the database.[798] With advances in AI technologies incorporating machine learning models and the like, it would be conceivable that technology will approach the notion of a 'singularity' so that human input into a work would seem so remote that human authorship will disappear and be lost.

---

798. *See Telstra Corporation Ltd v. Phone Directories Company Pty Ltd* (2010) 264 ALR 617 *and Telstra Corporation Ltd v. Phone Directories Company Pty Ltd* (2010) FCAFC 149.

1349. As discussed previously under patents in *Thaler v. Commissioner of Patents* [2021] FCA 879 the Federal Court held that an artificial intelligence (AI) system is capable of being named as an 'inventor' of patentable subject matter. On appeal the Full Court of the Federal Court has reversed this decision. For the purposes of the *Patents Act* 1990 (Cth) the inventor and of the patent must be a human inventor.[799]

1350. In the UK, the *Copyright, Designs and Patents Act* 1988 (UK) c. 48 provides for the notion of 'computer-generated' works, which have no human author (section 178). For literary, dramatic, musical or artistic works that are computer-generated, the author, for copyright purposes, is taken to be 'the person by whom the arrangements necessary for the creation of the work are undertaken' section 9(3). India, New Zealand and Hong Kong have similar provisions regarding human authors.[800]

§4. Other Legal Protections for Electronic Databases

I. Patent

1351. It may be possible to seek protection of aspects of electronic databases in the form of patents where criteria are met under the *Patents Act* 1990 (Cth) and the *Patents Amendment (Innovation Patents) Act* 2020 (Cth).

1352. Whether the software is bespoke or commercial-off-the-shelf (COTS) programmes are used to design, develop and disseminate the electronic database, such inventions are capable of software patent protection. The patent protection available includes protection of the schema, the structure of the database tables and the functional relationships between the tables. But such patents might be limited to the software used for the database management system, for example, the limited protection of the database as a collection of data or to its structures. The underlying data, datasets and the associated data structures that comprise the database may not be protected by patent law. The use of open-source software tools to design the electronic databases may lack 'novelty' and may be unable to attract patent registration.

II. Contract

1353. Adequate protection of databases may be proffered by the common law of contract between the owners and presumptive users of the database but not third-party infringement because of the absence of a privity to the contract. While standard form contracts tend to favour owners of databases it is difficult to monitor its

799. *See Commissioner of Patents v. Thaler [2022] FCAFC 62* at https://www.judgments.fedcourt.gov.au/judgments/Judgments/fca/full/2022/2022fcafc0062.

800. *Copyright Act* 1957 (No 14 of 1957 India) s. 2(d)(vi); *Copyright Act* 1994 (1994 No 143;(NZ) s. 5(2); and *Copyright Ordinance* (Cap 528; HK) s. 11(3).

use and enforce contractual provisions. This is predicated on the existence of IPR in the database. An in-depth discussion of contracts for electronic assets is in Part III Chapter 2 Electronic Contracts *supra.* of this volume.

III. Confidential Information

1354. The consumer data rights framework is identified as a possible regulatory tool to address data portability of the database that encompasses personal data. The next chapter discusses this right Chapter 7 Electronic Data Rights §2 II. Consumer Data Right Legislation *infra.*

1355. But just as important is the potential that the databases might enable producers of new services to have access to the data to assist in driving external benefits from increased data use, higher productivity and cognate innovation.

1356. The law of confidential information preserves the trade secrets or business in confidence information in economic and similar kinds of databases. Such protections could include client databases, marketing strategies and financial data as well as business processes.[801]

IV. Passing-Off, Misleading and Deceptive Conduct

1357. Almost all other offences contained in Australian IP legislation relate either to misrepresentations as to whether a patent, trademark, design is registered, or dishonesty dealing with the registration process.

1358. The Australian consumer law ACL generally applies to statutory guarantees and warranties, unfair contracts regime, misleading or deceptive conduct and the making of false or misleading representations about goods or services.[802] These provisions also offer protection of databases.

1359. Passing off, misleading and deceptive conduct may also be found in online interactions such as the use of hyperlinks. Online deep hyperlinking is the use of a hyperlink that points to a specific location containing some web content on a website rather accessing the contents through the website's home page. The deep linked URL contains all the information needed to point to a particular item inside a website. When used in conjunction with website 'frames', hyperlinks make the contents of another website viewable from its own site. Hence the legal issue of deep linking

801. In *Coco v. AN Clark (Engineers) Ltd* [1969] RPC 41, Megarry J found that three elements necessary to establish a breach of confidence are that the information (1) must be of a confidential nature; (2) must have been communicated in circumstances importing an obligation of confidence; and (3) must have been an unauthorized use to the detriment of the party communicating it.

802. Misleading or deceptive conduct (s. 18 of the ACL, formerly s. 52 of the *Trade Practices Act* 1974 (Cth); unfair practices (including unconscionable conduct, misleading or deceptive conduct and unfair contracts) under Chapter 2 and Part 3-1 of the ACL.

and framing is the deception and infringement of copyright and trademark laws arguably because the website alters the appearance of the framed website.[803]

1360. Another potential source of infringement is the use of 'electronic agents' where computer algorithms deploying web spiders and web robots to automatically browse, retrieve and store web content. The implication being these some of these activities might infringe the property rights of a database owner.[804]

V. Cybercrime Provisions

1361. Cybercrime laws in Australia provide an additional layer of database protection. Section 477.1 of the *Criminal Code Act* 1995 (Cth) prohibits 'unauthorized access, modification or impairment with intent to commit a serious offence' on computer systems. Section 477.3 of the Act relating to unauthorized impairment of electronic communication together with other offences under the *Cybercrime Legislation Amendment Act* 2012 (Cth) (CLAA) that target hacking and other computer misconduct has potentially wide reach and carries heavy penalties.

VI. Property Interests and Unfair Competition

1362. A database owner may hold 'quasi-property' interests in information against a competitor where that information contains an economic value. Applied *ex-post* for the protection of databases, the focus of interest comes into being after the database has been compiled, structured and developed. The business model of many businesses online is one where consumers themselves are the subject matter of the data collected and developed so that seemingly bespoke 'personalized' ads and services may be directed towards the consumer. Intelligent agents or bots are deployed in such data aggregation processes. The economic value of such data is dependent on the nature of the data, the purpose of the appropriation and what data are appropriated.

VII. Technological Protection Measures

1363. A variety of non-legal defences against unlawful access to, and appropriation of, electronic compilations have been developed by the database industry. These technological 'self-help' measures considerably aid in bridging the gaps left by other forms of database protection.

---

803. *See* deep linking and framing at https://en.wikipedia.org/wiki/Copyright_aspects_of_hyperlinking_and_framing.
804. *See* Grosse-Ruse, (2001) 'Electronic Agents and the Legal Protection of Non-creative Databases' (2001) 9(3) *International Journal of Law and Information Technology* 295.

1364. A popular mechanism used by many database owners to limit access to their online and compact disk read-only-memory (CD-ROM) products is the use of passwords. Databases and compilations ranging from the *Australian Prescription Products Guide* to the *Attorney-General's Information Service* require users to enter their login name and password to gain authorized access to the contents of the product. Password protection is almost always used in conjunction with other means of database protection.

1365. Search-only or read-only databases are common practices used by major media and financial platforms. Examples of such practices used by online newspaper publishers such as the *Sydney Morning Herald* for its database of archived articles;[805] Bloomberg and Reuters[806] are subscription-only services for databases behind a 'pay-wall'. Often the term 'freemium' is used to describe a business model where a basic product or service is provided free-of-charge, but a premium is charged for additional features, services and online access to the database.

1366. Encrypted databases are commonly used to protect data from compromise or abuse. Through encryption data is controlled by ensuring that only authorized users who have been granted the relevant 'key' can view the data in human readable 'clear text'.[807]

1367. Other technological protection devices that will enable tracing the source of illegal copies include 'digital watermarks' to mark the provenance of the database, 'copyright traps' where spurious or redundant data are added to catch unsuspecting abusers and tracing offenders.

VIII. Market-Based Approaches

1368. Business practices and market-based approaches to safeguard investments in databases have been implemented through the production of customized versions of databases. Bespoke versions of compilations for different market segments enlarges market share as well as making it difficult for data pirates to compete whilst at the same time protecting the database producer.

§5. Postscript for Electronic Databases

1369. Databases represent great investment of time, skill and capital to put together. The issue of copyright protection in databases thus distils to questions of access and monopoly rights, economics and policy. The ascendancy of one over the

805. *See* Sydney Morning Herald report at https://www.smh.com.au/business/markets.
806. *See* Bloomberg at https://www.bloomberg.com/subscriptions; Reuters at https://www.reuters.com/markets/commodities/.
807. *See* National Research Council (1999) *A Question of Balance – Private Rights and the Public Interest in Scientific and Technical Databases* at http://www.nap.edu/html/question_balance/ch3.html.

other may delineate the boundaries of protection for creators of electronic databases. Little or no protection will give insufficient incentives to develop and maintain databases. Too much protection may stifle research, development and learning and at the same time encourage the negative aspects of monopoly power and civil disobedience.

Chapter 7. Electronic Data Rights

§1. Introduction

1370. The terms 'data privacy' (personal data) and 'data protection' are often used interchangeably, but important differences exist. Data privacy defines who has access to data, while data protection provides tools and policies that restrict access to the data. Data privacy is about what people who have collected consumer data lawfully can and should do with it and what control consumers have over that retention and use of data. Data protection ensures that consumer data is safeguarded from unlawful access by unauthorized parties. While data privacy is more about policy and regulation, that is, legal matters; data protection are the tools and procedures to enforce the policy and regulation including prevention of unauthorized access or misuse of the data.

1371. Users control the privacy part of the data while agencies and companies ensure protection of the data. Questions of data security and confidentiality, usage of the data as intended, and dissemination, retention and extinction are issues in relation to data subject rights.

1372. In sum, the issues distil as to how consumer data on the one hand are created and collected, its control of how the data are used and the retention of sovereignty over the data. On the other hand, in the exercise of rights in a situation where an imbalance of bargaining power exists. The data right applies both to individuals and businesses.

§2. Consumer Data Right Legislation

1373. As part of ongoing Australian government policy on the digital economy and consumer protection, the Consumer Data Right (CDR) was introduced to provide consumers greater control over their consumer data. Such a right enables a consumer to direct a data holder to provide their CDR data to an approved data recipient in a CDR compliant manner.[808] This is an opt-in scheme and consumers may choose to withdraw their data at any time, what it may be used for and to who it is disclosed to including its deletion once the need for the data has been exhausted.

1374. The *Treasury Laws Amendment (Consumer Data Right) Act* 2019 (Cth), was inserted in a new Part IVD of the *Competition and Consumer Act* 2010 (Cth).[809]

808. The legislation and explanation of the consumer data right are found at the OAIC's site at https://www.oaic.gov.au/consumer-data-right/cdr-legislation and at https://www.oaic.gov.au/consumer-data-right/what-is-the-consumer-data-right respectively.
809. *See* text of the Act at https://www.legislation.gov.au/Details/C2021C00151.

1375. The *Competition and Consumer (Consumer Data Right) Rules* 2020 (the CDR Rules) supplies the framework for the operation of the CDR.[810] These rules define the elements for consent, the accreditation framework and the privacy aspects of the scheme.[811]

1376. Included in the rules are 'data standards' established by the Data Standards Body, that include standards on the format and the process for transferring data.[812]

1377. Thus, far the minister has designated two sectors to be part of the CDR system. For the banking sector the *Consumer Data Right (Authorised Deposit-Taking Institutions) Designation* 2019 (Cth) prescribes among other things 'open banking';[813] while for the energy sector the instrument is the *Consumer Data Right (Energy Sector) Designation* 2020 (Cth).[814] These instruments set out the classes of information that are subject to the CDR as well as the custodian of the relevant information that may be required to be transferred at the consumer's request.

1378. The lead government agencies responsible for the governance and monitoring of the CDR are the Office of the Australian Information Commissioner (OAIC), the Australian Competition and Consumer Commission (ACCC) and the Federal Treasury.[815]

1379. The thirteen legally binding CDR privacy safeguards in the *Competition and Consumer Act* 2010 (Cth) set out privacy rights and the strict obligations on businesses collecting and handling consumer data.[816] The agency that deals with strictly privacy issues of consumers is the OAIC.

---

810. *See* text of Part IVD of the Act at https://www.legislation.gov.au/Details/F2021C00076.
811. The *Competition and Consumer (Consumer Data Right) Amendment Rules (No. 3)* 2020 (Cth) introduced new functionality in relation to consents and the sharing of CDR data by non-individuals and business partnerships.
812. The data standards are available on the Consumer Data Standards website at https://consumerdatastandards.gov.au/.
813. *See* text of the Act at https://www.legislation.gov.au/Details/F2019L01153.
814. *See* text of the Act at https://www.legislation.gov.au/Details/F2020L00833.
815. As noted previously, a discussion of the privacy aspects of the CDR is avoided here as the topic is dealt with in Kluwer's *International Encyclopaedia of Privacy and Technology Law – Privacy and Data Protection*.
816. Part IV D s. 56 EQ(1)(a) of the *Competition and Consumer Act* 2010 (Cth) provides guidelines for privacy safeguards. For details see OAIC at https://www.oaic.gov.au/consumer-data-right/cdr-privacy-safeguard-guidelines.

Chapter 8. Legal Protection of Circuit Layouts

§1. Introduction

1380. The passage of the Australian *Circuit Layouts Act* 1989 (Cth) (CLA) arose from three congruent imperatives.[817] First, the protection accorded to computer chip designs by copyright, trade secret and patent law was deemed inadequate albeit the right is a derivative of copyright law principles. The second is the Treaty on Intellectual Property in Respect of Integrated Circuits (IPIC Treaty).[818] Australia participated in the negotiation of this treaty under the auspices of the WIPO in 1989. The treaty committed signatories to passing legislation to protect semiconductor chip designs. Third, negotiation over IPR protection, as part of the Uruguay Round of the General Agreement on Tariffs and Trade (GATT) negotiations, resulted in the TRIPS Agreement.[819]

1381. Australia and 120 other member nations adopted the TRIPS Agreement. Under TRIPS the minimum standards signatories must meet are mandated in the agreement. Within TRIPS there is a provision dealing specifically with semiconductor chip design layout protection.

1382. A semiconductor chip is a tiny electronic integrated circuit (IC). So-called because a semiconductor is neither fully conducting nor fully non-conducting; rather, it can be fabricated to partially conduct electricity in ways selected by its designers. It is called an IC because the electrical circuit is integrated with the semiconductor material, usually silicon. Engineers design the circuit layout (topography) of the chip's electric circuits. The layouts are roughly analogous to an architect's plans for a house.[820]

1383. The Australian CLA draws heavily on earlier legislation in the US *Semiconductor Chip Protection Act* 1984 (SCPA).[821] But there are significant differences in the definition, the creativity requirement, registration and the requirement that innocent infringers pay a reasonable royalty.

1384. The CLA definition of an 'integrated circuit' section 5 protects ICs formed on any material while the US section 901(a)(1) refers to a narrower 'semiconductor chip product'. Section 11 of the CLA requires some form of 'creativity' to attract any protection absent in the SCPA. There are no registration requirements under the CLA such as section 908 of the SCPA. The CLA section 20 contains a broad defence

817. *See* text of the Act at http://classic.austlii.edu.au/au/legis/cth/consol_act/cla1989203/s5.html.
818. *See* WIPO at https://www.wipo.int/edocs/pubdocs/en/wipo_pub_202.pdf.
819. *See* WIPO TRIPS at https://www.wto.org/english/docs_e/legal_e/27-trips_03_e.htm.
820. *See* Wikipedia Integrated Circuit at https://en.wikipedia.org/wiki/Integrated_circuit and Investopedia on semiconductors at https://www.investopedia.com/terms/s/semiconductor.asp.
821. US 17 USC. ss 901-914.

for innocent infringement while the SCPA requires innocent infringers to pay a reasonable royalty section 907(a)(2).

1385. The US SCPA introduces a new form of IP protection not for the semiconductor chips themselves, but for their most easily copied part, the circuit layout designs or 'mask works'.[822]

1386. Relevant legislation protecting circuit layouts in the UK,[823] Europe[824] and Japan.[825] predate those of Australia.

§2. *Circuit Layouts Act* 1989 (CLA)

1387. The CLA provides a *sui generis* form of intellectual property protection for circuit layouts commencing on 1 October 1990. Under the CLA there are no registration requirements. As with similar principles that underlie copyright law, circuit layout rights automatically protect original layout designs for IC and computer chips.

1388. The owner of an original circuit layout has exclusive rights to copy the layout in a material form; make IC from the layout; and exploit it commercially in Australia.[826]

1389. Commercial exploitation must occur within ten years of creation of the layout. Exclusive rights continue for a period of ten years, so that the maximum possible protection period is twenty years from the year of making a circuit layout.

1390. A graphical summary of the main divisions of the CLA is shown in Figure 6.

822. US 17 USC. ss 901-914.
823. UK Semiconductor Products (Protection of Topography) Regulations 1987 (SI 1987 No. 1497), later replaced by Design Right (Semiconductor Topographies) Regulations 1989 (SI 1989 No. 1497).
824. *See* EU Council Directive at 87/54/EED, OJ No. L 24, 27 Jan. 1987, p. 3.
825. *See* Japan Act Concerning the Circuit Layout of a Semiconductor Integrated Circuit law effective 1 Jan. 1986.
826. *See* IPAustralia on circuit layout rights at http://www.ipaustralia.gov.au/get-the-right-ip/other-types-of-IP/circuit-layout-rights/.

Figure 6 A Graphical Summary of the CLA

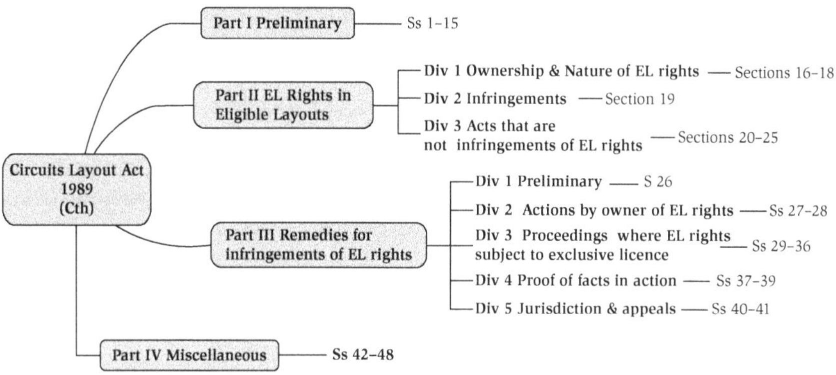

§3. Relationship with Other Areas of IPR

1391. It may cost tens of millions of dollars and take several years to research and develop a new generation semiconductor chip, yet that same chip can be disassembled, its essential design or layout photographed, and a perfect copy fabricated for a tiny fraction of that cost and in just a few months. Today, however, many believe that changes in technology and fabrication techniques have made circuit layout design piracy much less feasible than it once was, rendering *sui generis* legal protection less necessary than had originally been thought.

1392. This alleged ease of 'reverse engineering' neutralizes the protection chip designs might otherwise be provided by trade secret law. Patent law does not provide satisfactory protection because chip designs are developed more by 'sweat of the brow' effort than by the inventiveness that is the *sine qua non* of patent protection. Copyright law provides inadequate protection for computer chips because of the fundamental rule that copyright law does not protect useful or utilitarian articles standing alone.

1393. Traditional forms of intellectual property protection are inadequate to protect designers of semiconductor chips. Although the CLA draws heavily from copyright law concepts and somewhat less from patent law principles the CLA provides a unique form of intellectual property protection.

1394. The interrelationship with other areas of intellectual property has meant that enactment of the CLA has required consequential amendments to the CA section 10(1); and the *Designs Act* 2003 (Cth) sections 4(1) and 6.

1395. Australian copyright legislation explicitly precludes the possibility that certain aspects of IC may also be protected under copyright or patent law. The definition of 'artistic work' under the CA section 10(1), expressly excludes 'circuit layout'. Thus, the design drawing of a circuit layout, the photolithographic mask and a photograph of a layer could not be considered as forms of 'artistic work' under Copyright legislation. However, the layout data (for example, a written logic statement as opposed to the physical form of the logic device itself) incorporated in an IC may be a 'literary work' as it is 'written' and in 'material form' and given that the definition of 'material form' under the CA includes any form of notation or code irrespective of whether the recording is visible. As a literary work, the IC would arguably be protected should it be infringed if copied by a design drawing, photolithographic mask or layout data or an IC in the same form.

1396. Object code, which may be stored electro-physically as a pattern of electronic circuitry, is protected with amendments to the CA section 10(1) definition of a computer program. As the logic instructions inherent in an IC constitute a computer program and protection is available under copyright law.[827]

§4. Protection under the CLA

1397. The five criteria for protection of circuit layouts to confer monopoly rights include originality section 11, eligible persons section 5, eligible foreign country section 14, commercial exploitation section 8 and eligible layout (EL) section 5.

1398. An EL defined in section 5 of the CLA is an original circuit layout; the maker of which was, at the time the layout was made, an eligible person; or, that it was first commercially exploited in Australia or in an eligible foreign country.

1399. The Act presumes that the maker of an EL is the first owner of the layout's EL rights holds those EL rights exclusively under the CLA section 16(1). Section 17 provides that person or country has exclusive rights to copy the layout, directly or indirectly, in material form, section 17(a); to make an IC in accordance with the layout or a copy of it, section 17(b); and, to commercially exploit the layout in Australia, section 17(c).

1400. The eligible person or foreign country is afforded these exclusive rights for the duration of the protection period, which is generally ten calendar years after the eligible layout was first commercially exploited (section 5).

827. *See Autodesk v. Dyason* (1992) 173 CLR 330. *See also* Christie A (1995) *Integrated Circuits and Their Contents: International Protection* Ch. 13 (Law Book Company 1995).

§5. COMMERCIAL DEALINGS

1401. EL rights are personal property and as such may be assigned or licensed under the CLA section 45(1).

1402. The Act makes various provisions for prospective ownership of future EL rights. This means that if a person who would be the owner of prospective EL rights upon their coming into existence assigns those rights in whole or part via a signed writing to an 'assignee', then when the rights come into existence those rights vest in the assignee or his or her successor in title, section 44(1).

1403. EL rights are entitled to protection even with no label or mark attached. Specifically, the Act provides that if at the time an EL was first imported or distributed by way of trade, the layout bore a prescribed label or mark, such label or mark constitutes *prima facie* evidence that any person dealing at or after that time with the layout has been notified of the subsistence of EL rights in the layout, section 44(2).

1404. The protection provided to the owner of EL rights is not to disrupt normal commerce by impeding the proper availability of IC used in machinery and consumer appliances, section 24.

1405. Although the owner of the EL rights can still prevent the copying of the circuit layouts, it cannot control the importation or distribution of the legitimately acquired chips. Thus, section 24(1) has the effect of ensuring that there is no prohibition on parallel importing of IC, also known as grey or direct importing, made in accordance with an EL.

1406. The CLA rules deal with the importation of IC chips embedded with copyrighted software, section 24. This provision involves the interplay of the CLA with the CA and addresses the situation where an IC contains a copy or an adaptation of a copyrighted computer program.

1407. Section 37 of the CA provides that it is an infringement of copyright to import a protected article into Australia if the importer knows or should have known that the making of the article would, if it were made in Australia by the importer, constitute an infringement. Section 38 provides that a copyright is infringed by the selling, leasing, or exhibiting of an item in Australia if the importer knew or should have known that the article, if it had been made in Australia by the importer, would have constituted a copyright infringement.[828]

828. Although these restrictions on parallel importation have been heavily criticized, as in the 1992 Report of the Price Surveillance Authority on its Inquiry into Prices of Computer Software finding that retail computer software prices in Australia are on average 49 per cent higher than in the US, the April 1995 report of the Copyright Law Review Committee recommended their retention.

1408. Parallel importing of computer programs is permitted by the CLA if those programs are stored in IC, whether those circuits are contained in kitchen appliances or computer game circuit boards, creating a limited exception to CA provisions. This exception is required to accomplish the CLA's purposes, which has not included the prohibition on the importation of legitimately manufactured circuits.[829]

1409. Relevantly, the Australian government sought to clarify matters through introduction of the *Copyright Amendment (Parallel Importation) Act* 2003 (Cth) which made provisions for parallel importing affecting the 'grey market'.[830]

§6. Acts of Infringement

1410. An EL right is infringed by a person who during the protection period and not having a licence from the owner copies or authorizes the copying of the layout in a material form;[831] makes or authorizes the making of an IC in accordance with the layout; or commercially exploits, or authorizes the commercial exploitation of the layout in Australia 'if the person knows or ought reasonably to know, that he or she is not licensed by the owner of that right to do so' CLA section 19. The first two types are described as 'primary' or 'direct' infringement; the next refers to 'secondary' or 'indirect' infringement.[832] Thus, infringement can occur without copying or making or commercially exploiting the entire EL. Pursuant to section 13 of the CLA, if an infringing act as described above applies in respect of only part of an eligible layout, the EL rights will have been partially infringed.

1411. Section 23 of the CLA contains exceptions to the infringement provision. Copying an eligible layout for the purposes of evaluation and analysis leading to the development of a new hybrid original circuit layout based on such analysis is not an infringement of EL rights.

§7. Remedies for Infringements

1412. The CLA limits the rights to bring an action to the owner of EL rights and the exclusive licensee of the owner, Part III sections 27-30. A non-exclusive licensee may not sue for an infringement.

---

829. Under current law parallel importation of IC is treated differently from the parallel importation of computer programs. This creates a difference in treatment of parallel importation of computer programs depending on whether they are stored in an IC or not.
830. *See* a discussion Jones, R (2000) Parallel imports & intellectual property restraints. *The Australian Competition & Consumer Commission's Perspective*, 14 April IM Regional Seminar on Competition Law and Policy for Asia-Pacific at https://www.accc.gov.au/speech/parallel-imports-intellectual-property-restraints.
831. 'Material form' is defined in s. 5 as 'any form of storage (whether visible or not) from which the layout, or a substantial part of it, can be reproduced'.
832. *Nintendo Co. Ltd. v. Centronics Systems Pty* [1994] 121 ALR 577.

1413. The CLA specifies various remedies for infringements of EL rights. The court may 'grant an injunction of either damages or an account of profits', section 27(2). In assessing damages, the court considers the flagrancy of the infringement; any benefit accruing to the defendant because of the infringement and all other relevant matters, section 27(3). Having considered all these factors, the court may award 'such additional damages as it considers appropriate in the circumstances', section 27(4). In an action in which the owner and exclusive licensee's interests are involved, the court in assessing damages must consider 'any pecuniary remedy already awarded to the other party', section 33.

1414. In cases of innocent infringement, the plaintiff is not entitled to damages, 'but is entitled to an account of profits in respect of the infringement, whether any other relief is granted or not', section 35.

1415. Under the CLA where a person, including the owner of EL rights, uses 'circulars, advertisements or otherwise, threatens a person with an action or proceeding in respect of an infringement of EL rights, the person threatened may bring an action for a declaration to the effect that the threat is unjustifiable, an injunction to stop the threat, and may recover any damages sustained, against the person making the threats unless that person can show that there was an infringement of the EL rights of the person making the threat', section 28.

§8. Defences

1416. General defences are provided under Part II Div 2 section 19 of the CLA which identifies activities that are 'not infringements of EL rights'.

1417. In *Centronics Systems Pty Ltd; Tiberio Salice and Fabrizio Latin v. Nintendo Company Ltd* [1992] FCA 584; (1992) 111 ALR 13 (1992); 24 IPR 418 (1992); and 39 FCR 147 in the Federal Court raised important questions relating to the construction and application of sections 19 and 20 of the CLA that exempts activities from infringement. The Federal Court allowed the appeal on the interpretation of EL rights that applied to both the circuit layout and to an IC made in accordance with the circuit layout.

1418. In *Lumen Australia Pty Ltd v. Frontline Australasia Pty Ltd* [2018] FCA 1807 the Federal Court found that the Lumen Australia designed and manufactured an engine control units constituted an original circuit and EL layout first commercially exploited in Australia in 2011 with protection ending in 2021.[833] The Court found that the defendants Frontline Australasia Pty Ltd and Love Strategic Investments Pty Ltd competitors of Lumen, had copied and subsequently commercially exploited the Lumen layout, or a substantial part of the Lumen layout, in a material form and made an IC in accordance with the Lumen layout, without licence or authority from Lumen.

833. *See* case note at http://www.austlii.edu.au/cgi-bin/viewdoc/au/cases/cth/FCA/2018/1807.html.

1419. Statutory defences are available under innocent commercial exploitation of the technology. While knowledge of the existence of another's EL rights is not required for infringement of the CLA, section 21(1) the CLA provides a defence for innocent commercial exploitation in sections 20-25. These include copying for private use, copying for teaching or research purposes, evaluation, or analysis, permitted use under licence, for purposes of defence or security.

1420. The CLA is silent on the issue of which party bears the burden of proof in relation to a reverse engineering defence. However, Australian courts have ruled that the burden of proof lies on the party asserting such a defence.[834]

1421. Originality is defined in section 5 of the Act, under 'eligible layout'. For example, in *Nintendo Co. Ltd. v. Centronics Systems Pty* [1994] 121 ALR 577 a defendant produced a scaled-down version of the plaintiff's layout. The court held that this layout involved no evaluation or analysis, no intellectual or unique design work, and was therefore not 'original'. It was therefore not exempted from infringement of the EL right protection.

1422. Common law defence for circuit layouts may be available where it is argued that the idea/expression in underlying copyright defence is ineligible for protection.[835] The form of the layout is protected under the CLA. Applying the idea-expression principle in this way, it may be a defence that the alleged layout in question copies only the function, but not the form of the protected layout and does not constitute an infringement under the CLA.[836]

§9. Procedural Matters

1423. The CLA specifies that an action must be brought within six years from the date when the infringement took place, Part III, Division 2, section 28.

1424. The CLA creates some evidentiary presumptions. 'EL rights will be presumed to subsist in the circuit layout to which the action relates if the defendant does not put in issue the question of whether those rights subsist in the layout'. Where EL rights subsist in the layout, the plaintiff claiming to be owner will be presumed to be the owner if the defendant does not put in issue the question of ownership, Pt III Div 4 section 37.

1425. The CLA confers jurisdiction on the Federal Court of Australia with respect to actions in relation to infringements of EL rights under section 47. The

834. This was applied by the court at first instance in *Nintendo v. Centronics Systems* (1991) 23 IPR 119, at 132.

835. *See* Christie, A (1995) *Integrated Circuits and Their Components: International Protection* pp. 131-135 (North Ryde, NSW: The Law Book Company Limited).

836. As the 'literary' distinctiveness inherent in a circuit layout is low, practitioners searching for copyright parallels in this area should compare alleged infringements with such items as compilations and directories.

CLA further provides that jurisdiction, when exercised by the Supreme Court of a State or Territory, is to be exercised by a single judge of the Court. An appeal in relation to a matter under the CLA and from a decision of a court of a State or Territory lies either to the Federal Court of Australia, or by special leave of the High Court (section 41).

Chapter 9. Internet Domain Names

§1. INTRODUCTION

1426. Domain Name System (DNS) is a naming system for accessing resources on the Internet. The system coordinates Internet addresses and domain names the two kinds of unique identifiers that make Internet connection via the World Wide Web possible for personal computers and other devices. The Australian '.au' domain name system is administered by.au Domain Administration (auDA). auDA has a range of policies in relation to the registration and use of '.au' domain names.

1427. Amendments to the *Telecommunications Act* 1997 (Cth) and the *Australian Communications Authority Act* 1997 (Cth) clarified that any Australian domain authority was subject to *Telecommunications Act.* The statutory scheme permitted intervention by either the national communications regulator or the national competition regulator to preserve the public interest such as market competition.

1428. Domain names are integral to the smooth operation of portals that exist on the Internet. For users, domain names are important for 'landing' at the relevant website and web page. In Internet searchers owners of websites and web pages would welcome unambiguous addresses to attract as many 'landings' as possible. Unfortunately, there are those who welcome landings when use is made of ambiguously misspelt domain names to trap the unwary as well as the inattentive users and in some cases the abusive users of the Internet.

1429. Domain names may contradict traditional trademark legislation. The latter may confer 'rights' in IPR whereas no such right exists in the former. The ideal would be one where both the domain name and trademark are one and the same and points equivocally to a business enterprise or an entity. The common misconception is that a trademark is the same as a business name, company name or domain name. Having a trademark registration does not automatically entitle one to a domain name licence.

1430. To establish an online presence it would be prudent to register one's domain name. But it would be useful to discover if the domain name is available and not already registered by someone else. This is like using some else's trademark as one's brand hence opening oneself to legal action from the trademark owner. This can occur for names which are the same as or like their trademark.

§2. THE DOMAIN NAMES SYSTEM

1431. Every computer connected to the Internet and every web page is allocated a number under the Internet protocol system and Internet protocol address.[837] This

837. Technically TCP/IP refers to the transmission control protocol Internet protocol – a standardized set of rules that allows computers to communicate over long distances. *See* TCP/IP at https://www.britannica.com/technology/TCP-IP.

number or address enables computers connected to the Internet to locate each other. Each address consists of twelve digits separated by full stops (.) into four groups of three numerals, for example, 123.456.789.876.

1432. A domain name is also termed a uniform resource locator (URL). As numbers are difficult to remember, a system of names was developed to represent the numbers. People can more easily remember Amazon.com than the URL number behind it.

1433. URLs are structured into four or more segments. First, the transfer protocol is stated (hypertext transfer protocol (http) or file transfer protocol (ftp)). Second, a network sector is given (for example, www for the World Wide Web). Third a domain name is used. This domain name is divided into a unique segment (for example, the trade name of a business) and a generic portion (the Top-Level Domain (TLD) which indicates the type of entry owning the domain name (for example, government body, commercial entity, educational institution). Fourth, the domain name category or typology. Finally, the country code, for example, '.au' for Australia. All segments can be seen in the example of a domain name of the University of Canberra: http://www.canberra.edu.au.

1434. Domain names under generic Top-Level Domain Names (gTLDs) may be registered with one of more than 2,000 Internet Corporation for Assigned Names and Numbers (ICANN) accredited registrars, or their resellers.

1435. ICANN was established in 1998 as a private non-profit corporation that runs the domain system via a memorandum of understanding with the US Department of Commerce and renewed in September 2002.[838] The ICANN website links to the various registrars' registration website.[839]

1436. The registrars remain responsible and accountable for all domain names sold by their resellers. ICANN maintains a list of current ICANN-accredited registrars on its website.[840] Domain name registrations under country code Top-Level Domain Names (ccTLDs) is made through the ccTLD operators.[841]

1437. The original generic TLDs described the type of organization involved. These included: '.com' for commercial corporations; '.org' for various organizations that do not fit other categories; '.net' for organizations involved in Internet operations; '.edu' for educational institutions; '.gov' for government departments and other entities; '.mil' for military and defence entities; and '.int' for international organizations.

---

838. *See* http://www.icann.org/registrars/accredited-list.htm. This page links to the various registrars' registration website. For information on the various geographic domains, *See* http://www.iana.org/cctld.html. The ICANN website is at http://www.icann.org/registrars/accredited-list.htm.
839. For information on the various geographic domains see IANA at http://www.iana.org/cctld.html.
840. *See* ICANN at https://www.icann.org/registrar-reports/accredited-list.html.
841. *See* ICANN at https://www.icann.org/resources/pages/register-domain-name-2017-06-20-en.

1438. In addition to the above the ICANN added seven more gTLDs: '.biz' for businesses; '.info' for unrestricted general use; '.pro' for professional firms like doctors and lawyers; '.name' for individuals; '.museum' for museums; '.coop' for cooperatives; and '.aero' for air transport industries.[842]

1439. There is also the ccTLD which adds a country designation following the categories of domains listed previously. In the case of Australia, the ccTLD is '.au'.

1440. Since 2005, ICANN's Generic Names Supporting Organization (GNSO), the main policymaking body for gTLD, initiated a policy development process to consider the introduction of new gTLDs. Significant expansion of gTLD offerings are in the process of being implemented in 2021.[843]

1441. It is possible for the same domain name to exist on another domain at a different level, for example www.domainname.com (global) and www.domainname.com.au (Australian). The same domain name may also exist at the same level but on a different domain (that is, www.domainname.com.au and www.domainname.net.au). There may also be similar sounding or similar looking domain names on the same domain, some may be deliberately misspelt or transposed letters in the name.

I. Domain Names Administration in Australia

1442. Domain name registration in Australia began with the Internet Assigned Numbers Authority (IANA), the predecessor to ICANN. IANA granted responsibility for the 'au' ccTLD to Mr Elz in 1986 when the domain name system was first introduced into Australia. In 1996, Mr Elz signed a five-year licence with the University of Melbourne's commercial unit, Melbourne IT, to register second level '.com.au' domains. Since that time eleven second level domains have been established under the '.au' ccTLD. These include: asn.au, com.au, conf.au, csiro.au, edu.au, gov.au, id.au, info.au, net.au, org.au and oz.au.

1443. In 1999 the Australian non-profit company, auDomain Administration Limited (auDA), was established and endorsed by the Australian government as the body to manage the 'au' ccTLD. Mr Elz sub-delegated to auDA his management authority over the second level 'com.au' which comprises about 85 per cent of all domain names. In July 2000, auDA entered into a controversial agreement with Melbourne IT not to register '.com.au' domains until after Melbourne IT's rights to register domain names through Mr Elz's authority expired in October 2001.

---

842. The US has been lobbying for a specialized 'Kids domain that would provide an online safe-haven for children'. *See* http://www.newsbytes.com/news/01/167478.html.

843. *See* GNSO Final Report. Introduction of New Generic Top-Level Domains, 8 Aug. 2007 at https://gnso.icann.org/en/issues/new-gtlds/pdp-dec05-fr-parta-08aug07.htm; and also at https://gnso.icann.org/sites/default/files/policy/2021/presentation/draft-2councilrecommendationsnew-gtld-subsequent-procedures-pdf-24mar21-en.pdf.

1444. In May 2001, auDA approached ICANN, seeking the management of the entire 'au' ccTLD domains to be formally re-delegated to auDA. An agreement to this effect was signed in October 2001. In November 2001, auDA assumed technical and administrative control over the entire.au domain space. This marked a major step to the introduction of a new system of 'au' ccTLD management that would permit competition in domain name services. Under the new system, AusRegistry Pty Ltd was awarded the tender to provide registry services for the 'com.au', 'net.au', 'asn.au', 'id.au', and 'org.au' domains.

1445. auDA has also developed a policy based on the Uniform Domain Name Dispute Resolution Policy (UDRP)[844] in relation to the 'au' ccTLD. It also developed a Code of Practice governing Domain Name Suppliers.[845] Finally, auDA also undertook a consumer protection role by providing consumer briefings and other domain name issues.[846]

1446. auDA operates under *Telecommunications Act* 1997 (Cth) that reflects the federal government's powers under the Australian Constitution. auDA has progressively developed new policies and introduced competition for the delivery of domain-related services. auDA is neither a government-owned corporation nor established by specific Commonwealth legislation. However, its powers and responsibilities are delineated by federal law such as by the *Telecommunications Legislation Amendment Act* 2000 (Cth) and the *Australian Communications Authority Act* 1997 (Cth) with reference to electronic addressing responsibilities of the ACA (now ACMA) and Australian Competition and Consumer Commission (ACCC).

§3. Licensing and Registration of Domain Names in Australia

1447. Licensing of domain names is carried out by registrar companies on behalf of auDA on a first in, first served basis.[847]

1448. Upon the issue of a domain name, it no longer becomes assignable to anyone else. The registrant has exclusive right to use the domain name for a limited period from one to five years which can be renewed under the terms of the licence. The licence agreement used in Australia provides that the licence neither confers any property or legal rights to that domain name nor does it provide any immunity regarding an objection from another party about either the registration or the use of the domain name. The licence is revocable either upon the decision of a domain name dispute resolution panel or a court order.[848]

844. *See* UDRP at https://www.icann.org/resources/pages/help/dndr/udrp-en.
845. *See* Code of Practice for Domain Name Suppliers at http://www.auda.org.au/.
846. For a list of auDA policies see http://www.auda.org.au/policy/.
847. A list of accredited registrars may be found at https://www.auda.org.au/registrars/accreditted-registrars/.
848. *See* AUDA at https://www.auda.org.au/docs/auda-registrar-agreement.pdf.

1449. Cybersquatting is the registration and use of domain names that are either identical or like trademarks, service marks, company names or personal names. These registrants have the intention to profit from the goodwill of the actual trademark owner. 'Cybersquatters' seek to gain financially from their domain registration. One means of doing this is by posting paid links or advertising related to the trademark to attract users seeking information related to that trademark. In some instances, the 'cybersquatter' domain name owner will offer to sell it to the 'aggrieved' trademark owner for an inflated price.

1450. Cybersquatting is illegal and is being addressed by the federal government and ICANN. The illegality stems from the alleged breach of the ACL under misleading and deceptive conduct section 18, as well as allegations of trademark infringement or allegation of the tort of passing off. A deeper discussion of the misuse of the domain name system is found in Part VI Cybercrime, Chapter 4 §1 Criminal Misuse of the Domain Name System *infra*.

1451. One emerging issue in Australia, as elsewhere in the world, is the registration of domain names that are not in the English language. While 75 per cent of domain names are registered in English, yet only 17 per cent of the world speaks English.[849]

1452. Most domain name registrations are in the English language, and many businesses are looking towards registration in other languages. The US company Verisign's subsidiary, Network Solutions and others have started registration services for language domains in sixty different languages.[850]

1453. Until recently, the only languages available were English, Chinese, Korean and Japanese. The Chinese Internet Network Information Centre (CNNIC), an administrative agency responsible for domain name registrations under the Cyberspace Administration of China, has vigorously opposed the monopoly by US companies and sought to take control of Chinese registries. The Singapore-based I-DNS is another player in the Asian domain name market.[851]

1454. In mid-2014, auDA announced a review of its Policy Rules and Guidelines for Community Geographic Domain Names (CGDN). auDA adopted a policy on the issuing of domain names in the open Second Level Domain Names (2LD) category, with a set of general policies underscored by specific criteria regarding eligibility.[852]

---

849. *See* Babbel at https://www.babbel.com/en/magazine/how-many-people-speak-english-and-where-is-it-spoken.

850. *See* the US domain name registrar NSI at http://www.nsi.com.

851. *See* CNNIC at https://www.cnnic.com.cn/ and the Singapore-based I-dns at http://www.i-dns.com.

852. *See* auDA at https://www.auda.org.au/policy/policy-rules-and-guidelines-community-geographic-domain-names-cgdns-2008-04.

§4. DOMAIN NAMES DISPUTE RESOLUTION PROCEDURES

1455. Under ICANN rules, all domain name registrars must follow the UDRP. Under the policy, most types of trademark-based domain name disputes must be resolved either by agreement, court action, or arbitration before a registrar will either cancel, suspend, or transfer a domain name. Disputes alleged to arise from abusive registrations of domain names such as cybersquatting, may be addressed by administrative proceedings which the holder of trademark rights initiates by filing a complaint with an approved dispute resolution service provider.

1456. To invoke the policy, a trademark owner should either file a complaint in a court of proper jurisdiction against the domain name holder (or where appropriate an *in rem* action concerning the domain name), or in cases of abusive registration, submit a complaint to an approved dispute resolution service provider.

1457. Disputes over the Australian level domain.au are heard by the auDA's Australian Domain Name Administrator, while disputes over top-level domains such as.com and .net are heard by either the World Intellectual Property Organisation – WIPO Arbitration and Mediation Center[853] or the Forum (formerly the National Arbitration Forum).[854] As administrative dispute resolution procedures the decisions may be overturned by a competent court decision.

1458. In 2010 the auDA published 2010-05 au Dispute Resolution Policy (auDRP) setting out the list of approved auDA providers as an alternative to litigation for the resolution of domain name disputes between the registrant of an.au domain name and the party with competing rights in the domain name.[855]

I. Australian Dispute Resolution Procedures

1459. Many ccTLDs, including Australia, have chosen to use the UDRP as a starting point and then modify it to suit the local context. Many countries have adopted a mediation procedure as the first step before escalation to formal arbitration.[856] However, given there are almost 200 different countries involved in Domain Name registration, it would appear desirable that all domain name disputes adopted the same UDRP procedure.[857]

853. *See* WIPO Arbitration and Mediation Center at http://www.wipo.int/amc/en/domains/ and National Arbitration Forum at http://domains.adrforum.com/.

854. *See* The Forum at https://www.adrforum.com. The Forum, formerly known as the National Arbitration Forum is an American organization founded in 1986 provides arbitration and mediation services to businesses, based in Minneapolis headquarters and offices in New Jersey.

855. *See* AUDA at https://www.auda.org.au/index.php/policies/index-of-published-policies/2010/2010-05/.

856. *See* Nominet Registry at https://www.nominet.uk/domain-solutions/.

857. *See* UDRP Policy at https://www.icann.org/resources/pages/help/dndr/udrp-en.

1460. At a global scale all disputes are submitted to the WIPO subject to the UDRP at first instance. Other accredited dispute resolution providers include the Forum and the Asian Domain Name Dispute Resolution Centre (a joint initiative of the China International Economic and Trade Arbitration Commission and the Hong Kong International Arbitration Centre).

1461. There are subtle yet very important differences between the auDRP and the UDRP. The decisions of panellists deciding cases under the auDRP can turn on these differences. Decisions under the auDRP are unique and need to be considered separately from decisions under the UDRP even though both processes are similar. The most obvious difference is filing a complaint in relation to eligibility grounds in the '.com.au' versus '.com' space where a direct link to Australia is essential in the former. The auDA uses the term 'name' instead of 'service mark' which is wider in definition to include a person, company, business or other legal or trading name. Thus, the net is cast wider to capture registrants who have done so in bad faith.

II. Domain Name Versus Trademark

1462. The fact that either a company or a business has incorporated under a name does not automatically give it rights to obtain a domain name registered under that name. Someone else may have already registered that name as a domain name or may be using that name as a trademark, either of which may preclude anyone else from registration of that domain name.

1463. In contrast a trademark has recognized IPR and the trademark will normally prevail over a domain name. Companies will pragmatically seek to register domain names that incorporate their key trademarks. However, if two companies have virtually identical trademarks, but relating to different classes of goods or services, the domain name rights will normally go to the first entity to register.

1464. The Australian experience of cybersquatting is nowhere near that in the US.[858] This is because the registration process in Australia (1) requires that the putative domain name holder to have a legitimate business interest in Australia in acquiring that name; and (2) the registration process itself checks the registration application against the trademark database to look for prior registrations of the name.

1465. In *Ariix LLC v. Mahilall (No 2)* [2014] FCA 494 a Federal Court restrained the respondent from using as part of a domain name 'Ariix' name or any other name, word, or mark substantially identical with or misleadingly, deceptively,

858. *See* WIPO's Anti-Cybersquatting Service Surpasses 50,000 Cases amid COVID-19 Surge, Geneva, November 30, 2020 at https://www.wipo.int/pressroom/en/articles/2020/article_0026.html.

or confusingly similar. In addition, the court ordered the transfer of domain ownership from the respondent to the applicant. This case involved a concerted attempt by a cybersquatter through 'injurious falsehood and intimidation' to 'pass off' a site as representative of another.

1466. In *Tyre Depot Holdings Pty Ltd v. Tyre Kingdom Pty Ltd*, WIPO Case No. DAU2014-0016 (2014) the complainant brought an action against the respondent over the domain 'tyredepot.com.au' which the respondent held. The auDRP found the domain to be identical or confusingly similar and determined that due to the 'significant reputation' enjoyed by the complainant in the name Tyre Depot and that the website was essentially a 'shell' with no substance to it and hence the respondent could claim no rights or legitimate interests in respect of the domain name. The domain name had been registered by the respondent in bad faith with reference to the offer to transfer the domain name in exchange for payment and the domain name from 'preventing the complainant from reflecting its Tyre Depot mark'. The decision mandated the transfer of the registration of the domain name to the complainant.

III. Critique of the UDRP Processes

1467. Domain name dispute resolution procedures have the advantage of speed and low cost but there are also attendant disadvantages. Under the UDRP and procedures modelled upon it, there is no opportunity for discovery as that which is available in normal commercial arbitration processes. In contrast to the full range of awards available through litigation and even arbitration, UDRP awards are limited to either cancellation or de-registration of the offending domain name; or transfer of the domain name to the legally entitled owner.

1468. Furthermore, the URDP procedure does not permit the resolution of other issues and is not appropriate for the resolution of complex legal issues. There can be no award of damages or other relief.

1469. Finally, parties may appeal an UDRP decision in the courts, but this is rare. This is because decisions are not binding, plaintiffs may in fact pursue litigation in a court of law and the URDP avenues of redress contemporaneously.[859]

§5. Reform

I. Australian Reforms

1470. The 2015 auDA Review Panel Interim Report recommended several reforms to be adopted and implemented:[860] No restriction is to be placed on the

859. UDRP decisions are listed on the ICANN website at http://www.icann.org/udrp.

860. *See* https://www.auda.org.au/assets/Policies/auDA-Policy-Review-Panel-Interim-Report-15-May-2015.pdf.

number of domain names a single entity may hold; .au domain names continue to be licensed only to Australian entities; applicants must declare a *bona fide* intention to use the domain name; there has to be a direct connection between the domain name licence holder and the domain name, though this need not be the company name or trading name; the existing prohibition on registering generic and geographic domain names should continue; a limited number of second level domain names should be introduced as new gTLDs; and, a new dispute resolution policy be developed wholly adopting ICANN UDRP but adjusted for Australian conditions.

1471. The new '.au' registry has ushered in a lighter touch regulatory regime. Companies can now have more than one Australian 'com.au' name and can register names according to trademarks.[861] According to auDA's rules, domain names ending in.au must have an Australian link or presence, such as an Australian Business Number (ABN) registration or trademark.[862] New rules came into effect from 12 April 2021.[863]

1472. The new rules are stricter, and it will no longer be possible to rely on vague and misused 'close and substantial connection' rule. There must now be an identical match between the domain name and the trademark registration.

1473. The auDA announced plans in 2021 to make available a shortened Australian country domain by releasing a brand new second level domain (2LD) for eligible Australian businesses such as the highly anticipated <.au> namespace.[864]

II. ICANN Reforms

1474. For several years the role and future of ICANN has been the subject of much debate.[865] Among the suggested reforms include greater accountability by ICANN and to give other governments greater say through ICANN's Government Advisory Committee (GAC).

1475. An important issue is that ICANN defines and enforces intellectual property rules regarding entitlements in domain names. The implication is that the rules will inevitably have a significant impact on the ability of Internet users to access information and therefore, the meaningful exercise of the right to freedom of expression.

---

861. Lindsay, N (2002) Looser Domain Name System Takes Over, *Australian Financial Review* 45 (1 Jul. 2002).
862. *See* AUDA at https://www.auda.org.au/policy/2012-04-domain-name-eligibility-and-allocation-policy-rules-open-2lds.
863. *See* the new auDA rules at https://www.auda.org.au/au-domain-names/new-au-licensing-rules.
864. For a complete overview of eligibility criteria for different 3LD domain variations of the auDA Licensing Rules see http://www.auda.org.au/policies/index-of-published-policies/2019/auda-licensing-rules/.
865. *See* White Paper by the US National Telecommunications and Information Agency of the Department of Commerce at http://www.ntia.doc.gov.

1476. Several other concerns have also been raised about ICANN's legitimacy in taking policy decisions in certain areas due to its corporate governance arrangements.[866] These concern the lack of independence from the US government as regards the IANA function; the lack of representation of developing countries within ICANN; the disproportionate influence of the GAC; the lack of accountability of the Board; and the non-universality of the support for ICANN and its role.[867]

1477. Another issue with the new domain names rules is that they are open to two types of abusers such as cybersquatters, who have no legitimate interests; and those who have limited rights in one area and want generic positioning unavailable under trademark law.

1478. The Australian government has requested that WIPO undertake a Second Domain Name Process given the ongoing disputes about geographic indications and terms, International Non-proprietary Names (INN), names of international intergovernmental organizations (IGO), personal names and trade names.[868] As part of this process, WIPO considered protection of geopolitical terms (for example, .eu for Europe) and geo-ethnic terms (for example, Indigenous Aboriginal names).

1479. In 2006 ICANN informed the Secretariat that while it had not been possible to achieve consensus among ICANN's constituencies concerning the recommendations of the Second WIPO Internet Domain Name Process, that progress might be possible with the protection of names and acronyms of IGO.

1480. Subsequently, ICANN in 2007 recommended that new gTLD agreements may provide protection for the names and acronyms of IGOs at the second level through a Dispute Resolution Procedure (separate from the UDRP) incorporated in new gTLD contracts. To date such policy remains under consideration for implementation.[869]

1481. Another suggested reform is the extension of the UDRP to handle generic drug and government names. No doubt the popular domain name dispute resolution service offered by WIPO will gradually be extended to cover new domain areas such as government organizations, generic names for pharmaceutical substances and international organizations.[870]

866. *See* ICANN at http://www.article19.org/resources.php/resource/37494/en/icann-reform:-recommendations#sthash.MQQMsJrt.dpuf.

867. A group calling itself the 'People for Internet Responsibility' issued an open letter in March 2012, 'Overcoming ICANN: forging Better Paths for the Internet' describing ICANN a 'failed experiment' and recommending the immediate transfer of Internet-related function performed by ICANN to another non-profit organization. *See* http://www.pfir.org/statements/icann.

868. *See* Hon Richard Alston, Minister for Communications, Information Technology and the Arts letter to WIPO Director-General Dr Kamil Idris at https://www.wipo.int/amc/en/processes/process2/rfc/letter2.html.

869. *See* WIPO at http://www.wipo.int/amc/en/processes/process2/; and *ibid.* GNSO Final Report. Introduction of New Generic Top-Level Domains.

870. *See* WIPO at The Recognition of Rights and the Use of Names in the Internet Domain Name System: Report of the Second WIPO Internet Domain Name Process, a t http://wipo2.wipo.int.

Part V. Cybersecurity Legal Issues

Chapter 1. Cybersecurity

1482. In the third decade of the twenty-first century citizens are becoming even more embedded in digital society and life. Everyday as one wakes one is immediately linked to something digital. From the digital alarm clock to the smart watch that one straps onto one's wrist to the musical tones of the radio or phone gently waking us up to the kettle and toaster ready to begin its programmed tasks. These digital assets are the modern day 'work-horses' that assist in daily living. Unseen and working in the background are other assets that monitor the household including the baby cam hung over the crib, the talking doll, the smart fridge that are all linked to the digital world of the so-called Internet of Things (IOT) and to other smart devices. Even the 'air gap' between the computer and the wall and cables linking the computer to the Internet is susceptible to monitoring and feeding data in unseen ways to automated data capturing devices located somewhere else.[871] All these functionalities of digital assets seemingly also march to the tune of policies and governance rules devised by governments and private agencies.

1483. Welcome to the cyber world to what innocuously appears to be a secure and safe one. The above is but a brief introduction to the many facets and paradigms that cybersecurity deals with.

1484. There is no general and single definition of cybersecurity and cyberspace. The 'cyber' is derivative of, and appropriated from, Norbert Wiener whose book *Cybernetics* published in 1948. According to Weiner cybernetics is the 'science of control and communications in the animal and machine'.[872]

1485. For the purposes of this discussion cybersecurity is the security of a nation in cyberspace. The entire digital infrastructure and all those services that are a part of the cyberspace that exist to deliver an experience to the human user. These infrastructures must be kept secure from threat actors that directly target elements of cyberspace. Such elements include the networks, the data, the services as well as

871. Greenberg, A (2018) Mind the Gap: This Researcher Steals Data With Noise, Light, and Magnets, Feb. 7 at https://www.wired.com/story/air-gap-researcher-mordechai-guri/ and Mordechai G, Bykhovsky D, & Elovici Y (2018) aIR-Jumper: Covert Air-Gap Exfiltration/Infiltration via Security Cameras & Infrared (IR) (September) at https://arxiv.org/abs/1709.05742.

872. *Cybernetics* comes from the Greek word *kybernetikos* – good at steering. *See* https://www.britannica.com/science/cybernetics.

other human users. Malfeasant actors, some of whom might be 'state-actors' (acting on behalf of nation-states) may also use these digital tools to launch attacks on industry and governments through cyberspace. To respond to such attack vectors, governments and institutions through policy and legislation, set up systems that supply information and system security, mandate device security, provide governance mechanisms and collaborate globally to ensure international interoperability and defences.

1486. This chapter focusses on the legal issues related to protecting critical digital assets and infrastructure and the liability and loss that may result from any lack of security. It is also about the legal issues related to the protection of federated computer systems and networks either locally or globally as well as the threats to data and information security. Invariably such measures will lead to security legislation designed to deter threat actors and prevent cybercrime that cause loss and damage assets.

§1. Introduction

1487. Cybersecurity is understood to be the practice of defending networks and digital assets from malicious attacks. Such practices involve the commitment and action across all regulators and users with proper governance and policies, user capacity building and local and international cooperation.

1488. In 2017 the International Telecommunications Union (ITU) placed Australia in the top ten for preparedness of the 162 countries surveyed. Australia was placed just below the leaders Singapore and the US but ahead of Canada and France.[873]

1489. Cybersecurity remains a top business priority as the number of undetected security breaches grows. The *Telstra Security Report 2019* is a major study that benchmarked performances among major economies globally.[874]

1490. Data from the report makes sobering reading.[875] The report found that:

- 89 per cent of Australian businesses estimate that breaches went undetected an increase of 12 per cent since 2018;
- 65 per cent of Australian businesses were interrupted by a breach, an increase of 5 per cent since 2018;

873. International Telecommunications Union (ITU) (2017) *Global Cybersecurity Index 2017,* ITU Geneva, p 17 at https://www.itu.int/dms_pub/itu-d/opb/str/d-str-gci.01-2017-pdf-e.pdf.
874. The *Telstra Security Report 2019* is a report of the research conducted by analyst firm GlobalData. The research involved interviews with 1,298 security professionals across 13 countries in November and December 2018. Sixty-one per cent of the surveys were conducted in Asia-Pacific (APAC) and 39 per cent in Europe.
875. *See Telstra Security Report 2019* at https://www.telstra.com.au/content/dam/shared-component-assets/tecom/campaigns/security-report/Telstra%20Security%20Report%202019%20(1).pdf.

- 55 per cent of Australian businesses reported that they received fines for being in breach of legislation enacted in the past two years; and,
- 48 per cent of Australian businesses experienced a security attack in the past twelve months.

1491. Australian businesses are better prepared for cyberattacks with incidence response plans in place for over 77 per cent of local businesses. The introduction of new regulations such as the forced public disclosure of security breaches, companies have become more conscious of the threat to reputational damage, erosion of customer trust and negative performances in the company's bottom line.

1492. Selected information from the report have pointed to human error as a major risk factor. This has been caused by inadequate business processes and inadequate employee education in security policies. Targeted attacks on employees were cited as the highest risk to security by 36 per cent of respondents.

1493. About 19 per cent of Australian respondents surveyed estimated that over half of data breaches affecting their company went undetected in the past year. This is even though 74 per cent of Australian businesses reporting that they have strong systems to verify a critical incident had taken place.

1494. For cyber criminals, ransomware is still the most profitable attack weapon of choice. Among Australian respondents 32 per cent showed that weekly or monthly interruptions were due to ransomware attacks. Unfortunately paying the ransom does not guarantee a retrieval of data. Over half of Australian businesses that experienced ransomware in the past year reported paying the ransom compared to 47 per cent in the previous year. Of those who paid 77 per cent were able to retrieve the data compared with 86 per cent the year before.

1495. Lessons garnered from the research include general best practices that businesses should consider as part of their security strategy. These may comprise of multilayered defences; undertaking continual systems and infrastructure reviews; training employees to improve security and resilience; and responding to and managing business risks of cybersecurity attacks. Whether these are adequate responses are addressed in the next chapter.

Chapter 2. National Security Framework

1496. A security framework is a set of documented processes that defines policies or procedures around how security controls can be implemented and managed on an ongoing basis.[876] Considered below different sections outline and discuss the cybersecurity threat environment and trends during the 2020-2021 financial year; the challenges, issues, and impacts; and the cybersecurity strategies proposed and adopted.

§1. Introduction

1497. The cybersecurity threat environment in Australia is managed by several government agencies, chief among these are entities under the Department of Home Affairs and the Australian Signals Directorate (ASD).

1498. The Australian Cyber and Infrastructure Security Centre (CISC) is a portfolio of the Department of Home Affairs that undertakes cybersecurity policy functions.[877] The CISC regulatory functions are governed by the *Security of Critical Infrastructure Act* 2018,[878] the *Telecommunications Act* 1997,[879] the *Aviation Transport Security Act* 2004,[880] the *Maritime Transport and Offshore Facilities Security Act* 2003[881] and the *AusCheck Act* 2007.[882]

1499. The CISC collaborates with industry and provides best practice advice; identification and mitigation of all hazard risks; critical infrastructure modelling; setting standards, accreditation and regulatory reform policy; compliance and regulatory functions that prioritize education and partnerships; and provides a background checking service in aviation and maritime sections.

1500. CISC has a role in enhancing the security and resilience of critical infrastructure assets. In continuing the work of the former Critical Infrastructure Centre, the work is guided by the Australian *Critical Infrastructure Resilience Strategy* 2015, collaboration across industry and all levels of government, keeping existing regulations up to date and managing national security risks to Australia's critical infrastructure.[883]

---

876. *Ibid.* Telstra Security Report 2019, p. 31.
877. *See* CISC at https://www.cisc.gov.au/what-is-the-cyber-and-infrastructure-security-centre.
878. *Security of Critical Infrastructure Act* 2018 (Cth) at https://www.legislation.gov.au/Details/C2018A00029.
879. *Telecommunications Act* 1997 (Cth) at https://www.legislation.gov.au/Details/C2017C00179.
880. *Aviation Transport Security Act* 2004 (Cth) at https://www.legislation.gov.au/Details/C2004A01242.
881. *Maritime Transport and Offshore Facilities Security Act* 2003 at https://www.legislation.gov.au/Details/C2017C00120.
882. *AusCheck Act* 2007 (Cth) at https://www.legislation.gov.au/Details/C2007A00053.
883. *See Critical Infrastructure Resilience Strategy* 2015 at https://www.cisc.gov.au/what-is-the-cyber-and-infrastructure-security-centre/critical-infrastructure-resilience-strategy.

1501. The Australian Cybersecurity Centre (ACSC) as part of the ASD is tasked with the protection of Australian national cybersecurity.[884] In bringing together cybersecurity capabilities from across the Australian government, ACSC provides advice and information on cybersecurity protection, alerts, technical advice, monitoring of cyber threats and supporting business, government, law enforcement and academic partners.

1502. The ACSC *Annual Cyber Threat Report 2020-21* includes contributions from the Defence Intelligence Organisation (DIO), the Australian Criminal Intelligence Commission (ACIC), Australian Federal Police (AFP), Australian Security Intelligence Organisation (ASIO), the Department of Home Affairs and industry partners.[885] The report for the financial year 1 July 2020 to 20 June 2021 includes unclassified cyber information since ASD became a statutory agency in July 2018. The following statistics are from the ACSC Report.

1503. During the financial year 2000-2020 the ACSC received over 67,500 cybercrime reports, an increase of nearly 13 per cent from the previous financial year. A higher proportion of cybersecurity threats was categorized as 'substantial' (categories1-3) in impact with some cases of data and/or services made offline. The less severe impacts (categories 4-6) related to low-level malicious activity such as targeted reconnaissance, phishing, or non-sensitive data loss. The increased frequency of cybercrime was accompanied by an increased complexity and sophistication of cybercriminal operations. part of this was due to the access to cybercrime services such as ransomware-as-a-service (RaaS) helped via the dark web supplying a market to a growing number of malicious actors.

1504. No sector of the Australian economy was immune from cybercrime and malicious cyber activity.

§2. Key Cybersecurity Trends 2020-2021

1505. The ACSC Report identified key cybersecurity threats and trends in the 2020-2021 financial year summarized as follows:

- *Exploitation of the pandemic environment.* The targeting of the healthcare sector with spear phishing emails related to COVID-related topics was most evident. State and criminal actor criminal activity focused on IP and sensitive information about Australia's response to COVID-19 as well as attempting to leverage critical services to increase motivation of victims to pay ransoms.

884. *See* ACSC at https://www.cyber.gov.au.
885. *See* ACSC Cyber Threat Report at https://www.cyber.gov.au/sites/default/files/2021-09/ACSC%20 Annual%20Cyber%20Threat%20Report%20-% 202020-2021.pdf.

- *Disruption of essential services and critical infrastructure.* About a quarter of cyber incidents during the 2020-2021 financial year were associated with critical infrastructure or essential services especially the health, food distribution and energy sectors.
- *Ransomware.* The ACSC received nearly 500 ransomware cybercrime reports showing a 15 per cent increase compared with the previous financial year in ransomware cybercrime extortions from vulnerable and critical members of society. Ransomware incidents disrupted a range of sectors including professional, scientific and technical organizations.[886] Phishing campaigns, targeted spear phishing, remote access through vulnerable machines and the use of publicly available exploits were the most common vectors for deploying ransomware.
- *Rapid exploitation of security vulnerabilities.* Cyber criminals are reported to be exploiting security vulnerabilities of digital assets 'at source' – at the point of development and deployment. Including pursuing publicly disclosed vulnerabilities, these state and non-state actors exploit public disclosures in software patch releases and technical write-ups especially when proof-of-concept codes routinely identify the vulnerabilities in systems when released.
- *Supply chains in software and services.* The threat of supply chain compromises remains high as vendors and customers struggle to protect their networks against highly resourced actors with capabilities to infect widely used software products.
- *Business email compromise.* With many Australians working remotely from home during the pandemic business email compromises made up nearly 7 per cent of cybercrime reports received. The estimated average loss per successful event in compromised emails increased to more than AUD 51,000 – approximately one-and-a-half times higher than the previous financial year.

1506. Such threats and trends in cybersecurity attacks point to common issues and challenges with accompanying impacts on society and the economy. These issues need addressing at a policy and legislative level.

I. Cybersecurity Issues

1507. A summary of the ACSC Report will identify four issues that are critical to cybersecurity:[887]

1. Information and system security include the trustworthiness, confidentiality, integrity and availability of information. Trusted sources of information underpin system security.
2. The governance of IT systems by government entities and by manufacturer standards and best practice. These affect users, network access and service providers. Through common law contracts, treaties and agreements there is

886. Haskell-Dowland, P (2021) Holding the news to ransom? What we know so far about the Channel 9 cyber attack *The Conversation,* Mar 30 at https://theconversation.com/holding-the-news-to-ransom-what-we-know-so-far-about-the-channel-9-cyber-attack-158069.
887. *Supra*, ACSC *Cyber Threat Report 2021.*

to be found a complex layer of responsibility and accountability in cyberspace that is often not policed and watched.

3. Device securities include applications, servers, routers, appliances and the devices themselves. The global nature of the supply chain for device and software manufactures show that devices built or assembled in one country is fabricated to standards of another country where it is sold. Such devices might be connected to the Internet and infected with malware from a third country and used against users in a fourth country often with little or no user action or awareness. Such is the nature of the IOT and the international character of cybersecurity.
4. Policy considerations are critical in providing oversight, developing cybersafe strategies, incentivizing behaviours and regulating industry. Anticipating developments and innovating strategies and legislating to counter threats to cybersecurity are part of such policies.

II. Cybersecurity Challenges

1508. From the summary, the challenges to Australian cybersecurity are both the identification of the actors and the recognition of technical and 'soft' vulnerabilities.

1. *Threat actors.* Five such actors may be identified and self-described by their nomenclature including: criminals, spies, non-state adversaries, hacktivists and terrorists. The *Australian Cybersecurity Strategy 2020* described these threat actors as nation-states and state-sponsored actors, financially motivated criminals, issue-motivated groups and individuals and terrorist groups and extremists with different intentions and sophistication of their tradecraft.[888]
2. *Vulnerabilities.* Both threat attackers and threat defenders are in a race to counter one another. Attackers probe weaknesses in the systems while defenders try to address known vulnerabilities. Such vulnerabilities include 'insiders' (that include poorly skilled personnel and weak cybersecurity policies) and supply chains that are open to attack and intrusion. 'Trojan-like' insertion of malware or hardware during development or acquisition, and proof-of-concept codes may lead to zero-day vulnerabilities with no established fixes.[889]

888. *See Australian Cyber Security Strategy 2020* at Australia's Cyber Security Strategy 2020 at https://www.homeaffairs.gov.au/cyber-securitysubsite/files/cyber-security-strategy-2020.pdf, p. 12-13.

889. Zero-day vulnerability is a vulnerability in a system or device that has been disclosed but is not yet patched, sometimes even the vendor is unaware of. An exploit that attacks a zero-day vulnerability is called a zero-day exploit with zero-days to fix it. *See* https://www.kaspersky.com.au/resource-center/definitions/zero-day-exploit.

III. Cybersecurity Effects

1509. The threat environment within which cybersecurity attacks and exploits take place have identified negative consequences. Cyber theft and cyber espionage result in financial, proprietary and personal data loss. While these losses benefit the attacker it perversely takes place without the knowledge of the victim. Distributed denial of service (DDOS) attacks slows a computer system down.[890] Botnet malware make IT and operational technology (OT) systems and devices behave erratically and go out of control. Attacks on industrial control systems especially critical infrastructure leading to the destruction of equipment and perturbing supervisory control and data acquisition (SCADA) systems. Such attacks on components of critical infrastructure may have collateral effects on national security, the economy, livelihoods and safety of individual citizens. Finally, identification of these issues, challenges and impacts suggest a central role for governments in making new laws and regulations to manage and monitor cybersecurity and installing intrusion protection systems. Legislative actions to address these are described in the following section.

§3. Australian Cybersecurity Strategy

1510. Australia's current cybersecurity strategy is set out in the *Cybersecurity Strategy 2020 Report* released on 6 August 2020.[891] This strategy is based on several recommendations made by the Cybersecurity Strategy Industry Advisory Panel report 2020[892] and builds upon its earlier *Cybersecurity Strategy* 2016.[893]

I. Cybersecurity Strategy 2016

1511. The key achievements of the 2016 *Strategy* include the opening the Australian Cybersecurity Centre (ACSC); the establishment of Joint Cybersecurity Centres (JCSC) to engage state and territory governments and industry; increasing cyber skills and education investments; establishing the 24/7 Global Watch; appointing the Ambassador for Cyber Affairs; and, establishing AustCyber, the Australian Cybersecurity Growth Network and the Cybersecurity Cooperative Research Centre.

890. Holmes, D (2016) Making Sense of the Last Month of DDoS Attacks (Oct 27) at https://f5.com/Portals/1/Cache/Pdfs/5041/making-sense-of-the-last-month-of-ddos-attacks.pdf.
891. *See Australia's Cyber Security Strategy* 2020 at https://www.homeaffairs.gov.au/cyber-securitysub site/files/cyber-security-strategy-2020.pdf.
892. *See Cybersecurity Strategy Industry Advisory Panel (CSIAP) Report* 2020 at https://www.homeaf fairs.gov.au/cyber-security-subsite/files/2020-cyber-security-strategy-iap-report.pdf.
893. Australia's Cyber Security Strategy 2016 at https://www.homeaffairs.gov.au/cyber-security-subsit e/files/PMC-Cyber-Strategy.pdf.

II. Cybersecurity Strategy Industry Advisory Panel Report 2020

1512. The Cybersecurity Strategy Industry Advisory Panel (CSIAP) formed in November 2019 was briefed to provide advice from an industry perspective on best practices in cybersecurity and related fields; emerging cybersecurity trends and threats; key strategic priorities for the Cybersecurity Strategy 2020; significant obstacles and barriers for the delivery of the Cybersecurity Strategy 2020; and the effect of proposed initiatives on different elements of the economy, both domestic and international

1513. After broad consultation and careful deliberation, the Cybersecurity Strategy Industry Advisory Panel developed a series of recommendations. The panel's recommendations are structured around five key pillars:[894]

1. *Deterrence*: deterring malicious actors from targeting Australia.
2. *Prevention*: preventing people and sectors in Australia from being compromised online.
3. *Detection*: identifying and responding quickly to cybersecurity threats.
4. *Resilience*: minimizing the impact of cybersecurity incidents.
5. *Investment*: investing in essential cybersecurity enablers.

1514. In structuring the framework the panel developed a vision where 'strong cybersecurity that enables Australians to prosper' guided its deliberations.[895] In its recommendations the panel attempted to strike a balance between realizing the opportunities that a cyber safe and secure economy presents Australia, and countering threats to the economy, safety, sovereignty and national security.

III. Cybersecurity Strategy 2020

1515. The Cybersecurity Strategy 2020 was launched as a countermeasure to address the threat environment affecting both public and private sectors in Australia. Cyberattacks from state-sponsored and cyber criminals are demonstrative of the need for greater global cooperation and collaboration to fight the current scourge and the need for more financial resources to do so.

1516. In the 2020 Strategy the government committed AUD 1.67 billion over ten years (compared to the AUD 230 million in the 2016 Strategy) to improve Australia's cybersecurity.[896] The measures to do so include proposed legislative changes to expand current critical infrastructure legislation, potential new directors' duties, the introduction of voluntary codes and the establishment of a standing 'Industry Advisory Committee'.

---

894. *Ibid.* CSIAP Report 2020 p. 5.
895. *Ibid.* CSIAP Report 2020 p. 19.
896. *Ibid. Cybersecurity Strategy 2020* p. 6.

1517. The Australian government's vision is to create a more secure online world for businesses and the essential services upon which all Australians depend on.[897] The Australian government will strengthen the protection of Australians, businesses and critical infrastructure from the most sophisticated threats. State and territory and local governments have a corresponding role in protecting their systems from cyberattacks. Businesses will take responsibility for securing their products and services and protecting their customers from known cyber vulnerabilities. The community will take responsibility for practising secure online behaviours and making informed purchasing decisions.

A. *Features of an Enhanced Framework for Cybersecurity*

1518. The government's proposed enhanced cybersecurity framework comprises of three key elements:[898]

1. positive security obligations include a set of enforceable baseline protections against all hazards for critical infrastructure and systems that are implemented through sector-specific standards proportionate to risk;
2. enhanced cybersecurity obligations that establish the ability for government to request information to contribute to a near real-time national threat picture; owner and operator participation in preparatory activities with government;[899] and, the co-development of a scenario based 'playbook' that sets out response arrangements; and,
3. government assistance for entities that are the target or victim of a cyberattack on Australian systems through the establishment of a government capability and authorities to disrupt and respond to threats that have significant impacts on Australia's economy, security, or sovereignty in an emergency.

1519. To achieve the vision and strategies of the *Cybersecurity Strategy 2020* a total of AUD 1,670 million funding commitments over the next ten years has been made under four heads of expenditures:[900]

1. Cyber enhanced situational awareness and response AUD 1,350 million.
2. Strengthening Australia's counter cybercrime capacity AUD 164.9 million.
3. Grow Australia's skills AUD 90.2 million.
4. Support to small and medium enterprises (SME) and vulnerable Australians AUD 63.4 million.

---

897. *Ibid. Cybersecurity Strategy 2020* p. 9.
898. *See* Department of Home Affairs Protecting Critical Infrastructure and Systems of National Significance Consultation Paper August 2020 at https://www.homeaffairs.gov.au/reports-and-pubs/files/protecting-critical-infrastructure-systems-consultation-paper.pdf p. 10.
899. Such activities include situational awareness and participation in preparatory activities in cybersecurity activities and playbook in response to range of scenarios. *ibid.* Department of Home Affairs Protecting Critical Infrastructure 2020 document.
900. *Ibid. Cyber Security Strategy 2020* Appendix A Funding Commitments p. 47.

§4. AUSTRALIAN ELECTRONIC SURVEILLANCE POLICY

1520. The Department of Home Affairs released a discussion paper outlining proposals for regulatory changes that has potential significant impacts on the telecommunications industry.[901] The proposal to move to 'technology-neutral' definitions of key concepts and extending the reach of the regime to industry sectors and operators of online platforms. The proposals signal a recognition that Australia's legal and regulatory framework relating to government electronic surveillance powers needs reform and rationalization. Legislation has lagged the rapid evolution of communications technologies with legal frameworks reflecting assumptions and definitions dating back to the 1960s. The proposals also pick up on many themes arising from the Richardson Review,[902] as well as recent reforms in the industry assistance regime under Part 15 Industry Assistance of the *Telecommunications Act* 1997 (Cth); the metadata retention regime; the mandatory privacy breach scheme; and cybersecurity incident notification and government assistance requirements under the *Security of Critical Infrastructure Act* 2018 (Cth).

1521. A key driver of the reforms is the government's anxiety of 'going dark' where law enforcement and national security agencies are unable to access encrypted communications or conducted in a form not dealt with adequately in existing legislation. The reform is designed to include providers of a range of digital and 'over the top' messaging services as part of their products and services. Included are a number of 'guiding principles' to include surveillance legislation that will be technology neutral and the definition of what constitutes a 'communication' and to distinguish between content and non-content information. The expansion is aimed at capturing the range of information and data transmitted electronically.

1522. Recommendation 75 from the Richardson Review is the development of a new single national surveillance act that better protects individuals' information and data; ensures law enforcement and security agencies have the necessary powers they need to respond to security threats; is clear, transparent and usable for operational agencies; is modernized, streamlined and as technology-neutral as possible; and contains appropriate thresholds in the use of these intrusive powers.

---

901. Department of Home Affairs (2021) Reform of Australia's electronic surveillance framework. Discussion Paper at https://www.homeaffairs.gov.au/reports-and-publications/submissions-and-discussion-papers/reform-ofaustraliaselectronic-surveillance-framework-discussion-paper.

902. Dennis Richardson AC (2020) *Comprehensive Review of the Legal Framework of the National Intelligence Community* at https://www.ag.gov.au/national-security/publications/report-comprehensive-review-legal-framework-national-intelligence-community.

Chapter 3. Regulation and Sector-Specific Obligations

§1. Introduction

1523. The regulatory framework for cybersecurity includes those laws that relate to critical infrastructure, privacy, consumer and data protection law and corporations law. Other regulatory measures include voluntary and quasi-legal obligations for company directors, and private sector codes of practice for smart devices and business policies for supply chains.

1524. The *Security of Critical Infrastructure Act* 2020 (Cth) (SOCI Act) is one of the most relevant Australian laws for cybersecurity. Other legislation that applies broadly across the economy are the *Privacy Act* 1988 (Cth), *Australian Consumer Law* (ACL)[903] and *Corporations Act* 2001 (Cth).

1525. Critical infrastructure operators and businesses in safety-critical industries have additional cybersecurity obligations, for example directors' duties. In addition, policies directed towards safer and stronger cybersecurity include industry codes of practices for smart devices and opportunities to create a more robust digital economy through clear, consistent and enforceable cybersecurity practices in supply chain management.

§2. Security of Critical Infrastructure Legislation

1526. The Australian Government's Critical Infrastructure Resilience Strategy currently defines critical infrastructure as:

> those physical facilities, supply chains, information technologies and communication networks, which if destroyed, degraded or rendered unavailable for an extended period, would significantly impact on the social or economic well-being of the nation, or affect Australia's ability to conduct national defence and ensure national security.[904]

1527. The SOCI Act was introduced to Parliament on 10 December 2020.[905] The SOCI Act seeks to manage national security risks of sabotage, espionage and coercion posed by foreign involvement in Australia's critical infrastructure.

1528. The SOCI Act was amended on 2 December 2021 by the *Security Legislation Amendment (Critical Infrastructure) Act* 2021 (Cth).

903. Australian Consumer Law (ACL) is set out in Schedule 2 of the *Competition and Consumer Act* 2010 (Cth) (previously known as the *Trade Practices Act* 1974 (TPA)) at https://www.legislation.gov.au/Latest/C2018C00437.
904. *See* Australian Government *Critical Infrastructure Resilience Strategy Plan (2015). See also*, https://www.nationalsecurity.gov.au/Media-and-publications/Publications/Documents/national-guidelines-protectioncritical-infrastructure-from-terrorism.pdf.
905. *See* SOCI Act at https://www.legislation.gov.au/Details/C2018A00029.

1529. The SOCI Act currently covers specific entities in the electricity, gas, water and ports sectors. The list of entities has since be enlarged and the SOCI Act as amended in 2021 now applies to twenty-two asset classes across eleven sectors including: communications, data storage or processing, financial services and markets, water and sewerage, energy, healthcare and medical, higher education and research, food and grocery, transport, space technology and defence industry (SOCI Act section 8D).

1530. A *critical infrastructure sector asset* is one if it is an asset that relates to a critical infrastructure sector (SOCI Act section 8E).

1531. Key elements of the SOCI Act are:

- Div 2 sections 19-22 a Register of Critical Infrastructure Assets is required to be kept by its owners. The register provides details of critical infrastructure ownership and control in high-risk sectors;
- Div 3 sections 23-25 provides for the mandatory cyber incident reporting of critical and other cybersecurity incidents to the ACSC online cyber incident reporting portal;[906]
- government assistance is to be provided as a last resort as a way of responding to serious cyber incidents that affect Australia's critical infrastructure;
- the Secretary of the Department of Home Affairs is empowered to obtain more information from owners and operators of assets to support the work of the ACSC (sections 23-25); and,
- Part 3 Directions by the Minister section 31-15 provides for the Minister for Home Affairs to be given directional powers to direct an owner or operator of critical infrastructure to do, or not do, a specified thing to mitigate against a national security risk where all other mechanisms to mitigate the risk have been exhausted.
- Entities that are subject to positive security obligations (PSO) are required to identify material risks to the critical infrastructure that they operate and to take steps to mitigate the risks to prevent incidents and strategies to minimize the impact of realized incidents.

§3. Privacy, Data Protection and Consumer Law

1532. Businesses not covered under sector-specific legislation, estimated around two-thirds of the Australian Securities Exchange (ASX) ASX200 companies, will be covered broadly across the economy by relevant laws such as the *Privacy Act* 1988 (Cth), the ACL. Regulations applicable to cybersecurity include the following:

906. *See* ACSC cyber incident portal at http://cyber.gov.au.

I. *Privacy Act* 1988

1533. A direct right of action for privacy breaches is currently being explored as part of the Review of the *Privacy Act* 1988 (Cth).[907] This implies that in certain circumstances victims of cybersecurity incidents involving personal information could take businesses, who have not taken reasonable steps to protect this personal information, to court and seek damages.

1534. In February 2018, the *Privacy Amendment (Notifiable Data Breaches) Act* 2017 (Cth) amended the *Privacy Act* 1988 (Cth) to require entities to, as soon as practicable, provide notice to the OAIC and affected individuals of an 'eligible data breach', where there are reasonable grounds to believe than an 'eligible data breach' has occurred. This process is called the Notifiable Data Breaches Scheme (NDB Scheme).

1535. OAIC suggests in its submission that under the auspices of Australian Privacy Principles (APP) APP11, an accreditation or certification scheme may assist entities meet Privacy Act obligations and provide consumers evidence-based information about the cyber credentials of entities with which they may engage.[908] APP11 requires 'reasonable steps' be taken to protect personal information from misuse, interference and loss from unauthorized access, modification or disclosure.

II. *Australian Consumer Law* (ACL)

1536. Existing laws, such as the ACL and the tort of negligence have played a prominent role in legal action for physical goods. However, these laws do not appear to have been used to compensate consumers for cybersecurity incidents.

1537. The ACL is designed to regulate the conduct of businesses and to protect the rights of consumers in Australia. Under the ACL misleading or deceptive conduct or making false representations about goods and services may include false representation of security standards or security measure.

1538. ACL consumer guarantees help ensure that goods (including digital goods) are of acceptable quality and fit-for-purpose, and that services (including digital services) are provided with due care and skill. For ACL to apply directly to cyber incidents there will be a need to characterize transactions for a 'good' and 'service.[909]

---

907. *See* Attorney General's Department Consultation on the Review of the *Privacy Act* 1988 at https ://www.ag.gov.au/integrity/consultations/review-privacy-act-1988.

908. *See* OAIC Submission at https://www.homeaffairs.gov.au/reports-and-pubs/files/cyber-strategy-20 20/submission-197.pdf.

909. *See* discussion in Department of Home Affairs, *Strengthening Australia's cyber security regulations and incentives: An initiative of Australia's Cyber Security Strategy 2020* at https://www.ho meaffairs.gov.au/reports-and-publications/submissions-and-discussionpapers/cyber-security-regula tions-incentives, pp. 52 – 55.

§4. Directors' Duties

1539. The *Corporations Act* 2001 (Cth) provides that company directors and officers have a duty to act in good faith in the best interests of the company and for proper purpose. Such personnel are required to act with due care and diligence as director or officer in all circumstances.[910]

1540. The Australian Securities and Investments Commission (ASIC) provides guidance for Australia's integrated corporate markets, financial services and consumer regulator and organizations through its 'cyber resilience good practices'.[911] The good practices recommend, among others, periodic review of cyber strategy by a board of directors, using cyber resilience as a management tool. For corporate governance, good practices are reflected in responsive actions such as keeping cybersecurity policies and procedures up to date; collaborating and information sharing; managing third-party risks and implementing continuous monitoring systems for cybersecurity purposes.

1541. Specific duties for company directors relating to cybersecurity is outlined in the Australian Prudential Regulatory Authority (APRA) Prudential Standard 234 on Information Security.[912] The standard provides that a board of APRA-regulated entity is ultimately responsible for the information security of the entity; and, the board must ensure that the entity maintains information security in a manner commensurate with the size and extent of threats to its information assets, and which enables the continued sound operation of the entity.

§5. Smart Devices and Internet of Things Code of Practice

1542. The Australian government released the voluntary *Code of Practice: Securing the Internet of Things for Consumers* (IOT Code of Practice) on 3 September 2020.[913] The IOT Code of Practice thirteen principles signal government expectations to manufacturers about the security of smart products.

1543. These principles align with international approaches, such as the UK's Code of Practice[914] and the European Telecommunication Standards Institute (ETSI) baseline standard on smart devices.[915]

---

910. *See Corporations Act* 2001 (Cth) at https://www.legislation.gov.au/Details/C2019C00216 Chapter 2D Officers and Employees, Part 2D.1 Duties and powers ss 180-190C.

911. *See* ASIC Cyber resilience good practices at https://asic.gov.au/regulatory-resources/digital-transformation/cyber-resilience/cyber-resilience-good-practices/.

912. *See* APRA Prudential Standard 234 at https://www.apra.gov.au/sites/default/files/cps_234_july_2019_for_public_release.pdf.

913. Australian Government (2020) *Code of Practice: Securing the Internet of Things for Consumers* at https://www.homeaffairs.gov.au/reports-and-pubs/files/code-of-practice.pdf.

914. UK Department of Digital, Culture, Media and Sport (2018) *Code of Practice for Consumer IoT Security*, at https://assets.publishing.service.gov.uk/government/uploads/system/uploads/attachment_data/file/773867/Code_of_Practice_for_Consumer_IoT_Security_October_2018.pdf.

915. European Telecommunication Standards Institute (ETSI) (2020) *Cyber Security for Consumer Internet of Things: Baseline Requirements*, standard ESTI EN 303 645 at https://www.etsi.org/deliver/etsi_en/303600_303699/303645/02.01.00_30/en_303645v020100v.pdf.

1544. Many smart devices have been identified to have poor cybersecurity.[916] A study by Data61 found that nearly 50 per cent of consumers incorrectly believe that cybersecurity is built-in to all smart devices sold in Australia.[917]

1545. The proposal to have labelling schemes for IOT smart devices may be a pathway to changing consumer behaviour. These suggestions emulate other widely used labelling and safety accreditation in Australia for nutritional information and energy, water and fuel efficiency, and star rating systems for road vehicles.[918]

1546. The Internet of Things Alliance Australia (IoTAA) has developed a Security Trust Mark primarily for commercial and industrial applications.[919] The issue is whether such trust marks are either adopted voluntarily or made mandatory.

1547. In considering such issues it is necessary also to have a better understanding of smart devices and their features. Smart devices can simultaneously be a 'good' as in a product as well as a 'service' and may need closer definition under ACL, for example.

1548. The three important features of smart devices are:

1. the physical device itself, an object with a sensor or multiple sensors that are bundled together;
2. the operating system, which is the software that runs the basic functions of the device; and,
3. the user interface, which allows the user to interact with the device.[920]

1549. The smart device has some connectivity, which allows the device to connect to other systems and networks. Through this connectivity, smart devices can collect and store device data through cloud-based data processing and connect to smart home ecosystems such as Google Home and Alexa.

§6. SUPPLY CHAIN

1550. The *Cybersecurity Strategy 2020* has underscored the importance of supply chains in an economy-wide approach to raise business' cybersecurity

916. *Ibid.* see discussion in Department of Home Affairs *Strengthening* document, Chapter 6 ff.
917. Data61 (2020) *Results of the IoT Consumer Focused Survey*, unpublished report produced for the Cyber Security Cooperative Research Centre cited in *ibid.* Department of Home Affairs *Strengthening* document.
918. *Ibid.* see discussion in Department of Home Affairs *Strengthening* document.
919. *See* Internet of Things Alliance Australia's submission to the Cyber Security Strategy at https://www.homeaffairs.gov.au/reports-and-publications/submissions-and-discussion-papers/cyber-security-strategy-2020.
920. *Ibid.* Department of Home Affairs *Strengthening* document, Annex A Understanding the cyber security of smart devices in Australia, pp. 61-64.

capabilities.[921] Global interconnectedness, whether in terms of communications or in trade, has demonstrated the need for internationally aligned standards for interoperability, trade and interpersonal relationships. All parts of the supply chain for smart devices and delivery of services have their respective roles to play. A breakdown in the supply chain would have repercussions further along the distribution channels. Government and business support may be a catalyst for innovation and development of technologies. Above all else, trust drives investment in cybersecurity.

1551. The *Cybersecurity Strategy 2020* has proposed the:[922]

– adoption of a *security-by-design* approach with decision makers and suppliers (similar to the steps taken in the United Kingdom);
– monitoring and building on existing government initiatives that promote innovation in sovereign cybersecurity research and development; and,
– establishing a 'Cybersecurity Best Practice Regulation Task Force' to work with businesses and international partners to ensure cybersecurity is built into digital products, services and supply chains.

1552. With the *Strategy*, the Australian government will co-design supply chain principles for decision makers and suppliers, to encourage security-by-design; transparency; and autonomy and integrity in investment, procurement and security.

921. *Ibid. Cybersecurity Strategy 2020,* Actions by businesses pp. 28-34.
922. *Ibid. Cybersecurity Strategy 2020,* Security by design p. 32.

Chapter 4. Public and Private Sector Responsibilities

1553. Apart from the 'hard' legislative requirements and obligations described above, the public and private sectors have responsibilities and obligations to their respective regulators that are either mandatory or voluntary. Each sector has its own regulator, standards and code of practice. A selection of the obligations for the financial, health, communication, infrastructure (including electricity, gas, water and sewage) and other sectors are given below.

§1. Financial Sector

1554. The Department of Home Affairs estimates that about one-third of ASX 200 companies are covered by the SOCI Act.[923] In the finance sector entities regulated by the APRA and the Reserve Bank of Australia (RBA) are subject to standards that deal specifically with operational risks including cybersecurity. Indirectly other regulators such as the ASIC and Foreign Investments Review Board (FIRB) monitor licensee and foreign ownership obligations of critical infrastructure industries.

1555. APRA's *Prudential Standard CPS 234 Information Security* effective since July 2019 requires a regulated entity to take precautions to manage information security risk. All APRA-regulated entities are required to develop and maintain information security protection that are appropriate given the importance of the data they hold and the seriousness of the threats that they face.

1556. Prudential Standard CPS 234 applies to all 'APRA-regulated entities', which includes authorized deposit-taking institutions (that is, banks and other financial institutions), general insurers, life insurance companies, private health insurers and registrable superannuation entity licensees, as well as any third parties that manage these entities' information assets.

1557. Prudential Standard CPS 231 Outsourcing requires that all APRA-regulated entities must ensure that APRA is given certain audit rights in connection with a material outsourcing arrangement.[924] The application of this standard to cybersecurity relates to the realities of outsourcing IT and OT functionalities when using cloud services.

1558. ASIC regulates other financial services and credit providers which includes general licensee obligations under the *Corporations Act* 2001 (Cth) section 912A to manage cyber risk.[925] ASIC has also released new guidance for social

923. *Supra*, Department of Home Affairs *Strengthening paper*.
924. *See* APRA Prudential Standard CPS 231 at https://www.apra.gov.au/sites/default/files/Prudential-Standard-CPS-231-Outsourcing-%28July-2017%29.pdf.
925. *See Corporations Act* 2001 at https://www.legislation.gov.au/Details/C2019C00216.

media finance influencers or *finfluencers* warning against producing content that may be misleading or cross over from information to financial advice.[926]

1559. The significant expansion of the definition of 'critical infrastructure asset' under the SOCI Act is expected to result in many more transactions being subject to FIRB approval requirements. This is because the proposed changes include a new requirement to obtain FIRB approval when an entity acquires a 10 per cent or more interest in any 'national security business', which includes 'responsible entities' and 'direct interest holders' of critical infrastructure assets within the meaning of the *Security of Critical Infrastructure Act* 2018 (Cth).[927]

§2. Health Sector

1560. The Australian Cybersecurity Centre (ACSC) reported that the health sector is most often targeted by ransomware attacks, accounting for 20 per cent of all such attacks in Australia.[928] The SOCI Act as amended now includes the health and medical sector within the ambit of critical infrastructure sectors. Sector entities now must register those assets and comply with certain security obligations. They will also be able to access government assistance in an incident which would have a serious impact on national security or the country's social or economic stability.

1561. In addition, software classified as a medical device (SaMD) is included within the SOCI Act regime. The SaMD will continue to be regulated by the Therapeutic Goods Authority (TGA).[929] Software (including mobile apps) is deemed to be a medical device if it fits within the definition under section 41BD of the *Therapeutic Goods Act* 1989 (Cth). Many mobile apps are simply sources of information, or tools to manage a healthy lifestyle. The TGA does not regulate health and lifestyle apps or other software that do not meet the definition of a medical device.

§3. Communications Sector

1562. The *Telecommunication and Other Legislation Act* 2017 (Cth), known as the Telecommunication Sector Security Reforms (TSSR),[930] amended the

926. *See* ASIC at https://asic.gov.au/about-asic/news-centre/find-a-media-release/2022-releases/22-054mr-asic-issues-information-for-social-media-influencers-and-licensees/. Perversely influencers peddling buy now, pay later (BNPL) or cryptocurrency products, both of which are not deemed financial or credit products under Australian law and are therefore out of bounds of the financial advice regulations.

927. *See* s. 8A for meaning of 'influence and control' and generally in Part 7 Div 2 Treatment of certain entities and s. 56 treatment of unincorporated foreign companies under the SOCI Act.

928. Australian Cyber Security Centre, Ransomware in Australia (Website, October 2020) at https://www.cyber.gov.au/sites/default/files/2020-10/Ransomware%20in%20Australia%20%28October%202020%29.pdf.

929. *See* TGA Software as a medical device at https://www.tga.gov.au/regulation-software-based-medical-devices.

930. TSSR https://www.homeaffairs.gov.au/nat-security/Pages/telecommunications-sector-security-reforms.aspx.

Telecommunications Act 1997 (Cth) to establish a regulatory framework to better manage the national security risks of espionage, sabotage and foreign interference to Australia's telecommunications networks and facilities.[931] The TSSR strengthens Australia's protection against threats to designated telecommunications sector and certain electricity, water, gas and port assets. Hence, all these designated critical infrastructure entities and assets identified under the SOCI Act have enhanced cybersecurity obligations.[932]

1563. TSSR commenced on 18 September 2018 with the following key elements:

– *Security obligation*: all carriers, carriage service providers and carriage service intermediaries will be required to do their best to protect networks and facilities from unauthorized access and interference – including a requirement to maintain 'competent supervision' and 'effective control' over telecommunications networks and facilities owned or operated by them.
– *Notification obligation*: carriers and nominated carriage service providers will be required to notify the government of planned changes to their systems and services that could compromise their capacity to comply with the security obligation.
– *Information gathering power*: the Secretary of the Department of Home Affairs has the power to obtain information and documents from carriers, carriage service providers and carriage service intermediaries, to monitor and investigate their compliance with the security obligation.
– Directions power: the Home Affairs Minister has a new directions power, to direct a carrier, carriage service provider or carriage service intermediary to do, or not do, a specified thing that is reasonably necessary to protect networks and facilities from national security risks.[933]

1564. The *Telecommunications and Other Legislation Amendment (Assistance and Access) Act* 2018 (Cth) (Assistance and Access Act) Schedule 1 Part 1 Main amendments to the *Telecommunications Act* 1997 (Cth) section 5 requires all carriers, carriage service providers and carriage service intermediaries to protect their telecommunications networks and facilities from unauthorized interference or access to confidential communications. A further requirement of the Act is competent supervision and effective control over the networks and facilities owned or operated by them.[934]

1565. The reforms place obligations on providers in the telecommunications sector to ensure the security of their networks and to notify the government of changes with potential security impacts. The reforms also enable government to

931. *Telecommunications Act* 1997 (Cth) Part 14 Div 2 Obligations.
932. *Ibid. Cyber Security Strategy 2020* p. 29.
933. *Ibid.* TSSR https://www.homeaffairs.gov.au/nat-security/Pages/telecommunications-sector-security-reforms.aspx.
934. *See* TOLA 2017 legislation at https://www.legislation.gov.au/Details/C2017A00111.

obtain information to monitor compliance and to direct providers to do 'a specified thing that is reasonably necessary to protect networks and facilities from national security risks'.[935]

1566. In the telecommunications sector, the cyber threat environment includes crime, espionage and theft that happens at a scale and unprecedented speed. Many technical solutions have been put in place to thwart these challenges. However, as noted previously, personnel, staff and user communities have been identified as the 'soft' (weakest) link in cybersecurity as it relates to human beings. To reframe this challenge, a proactive stance is proposed by Telstra that involves senior executives whereby senior management engages in and contributes to the minimization of cybersecurity risk.

1567. In May 2020, Telstra announced its Cleaner Pipes initiative, which is an upgrade to Telstra's Domain Name System (DNS) filtering processes.[936] Such a process automatically blocks millions of malware communications as they try to cross Telstra 's infrastructure every week.[937]

1568. Another contribution that Telstra has made is to promote its Five Knows of Cybersecurity mantra.[938] This refers to the five things businesses should know to effectively manage risk. It includes *knowing*:

1. the value of their data;
2. who has access to their data;
3. where their data is;
4. who is protecting their data; and,
5. how well their data is protected.

§4. ELECTRICITY, GAS, WATER & SEWAGE SECTOR

1569. More than perhaps any other industry, the infrastructure industry relies on operational technology (OT) to monitor and control physical processes or devices. OT is widely deployed within critical infrastructure industry as exemplified by SCADA.

1570. OT monitors and controls devices and processes of physical operational systems such as assembly lines, utility distribution networks, production facilities,

935. *See* Schedule 1 of the *Telecommunications and Other Legislation Amendment Act* 2017 (Cth) at http://classic.austlii.edu.au/au/legis/cth/num_act/taolaa2017483/sch1.html.
936. *Ibid. Cyber Security Strategy 2021* p. 31.
937. *See* Telstra Cleaner Pipe initiative at https://exchange.telstra.com.au/safer-online-and-the-new-normal/.
938. *See* Telstra' Five Knows at https://www.telstra.com.au/content/dam/shared-component-assets/tecom/campaigns/security-report/Telstra%20Security%25; and Telstra Five Knows of Cyber Security at https://www.telstra.com.au/content/dam/tcom/business-enterprise/security-services/pdf/5-knows-of-cyber-security.pdf.

roadway systems and others.[939] OT has traditionally operated in isolation from enterprise or broader networks. Increasingly, however, OT is converging with IOT enabled devices.[940] For example, in the mining industry, in response to the COVID-19 pandemic, IOT devices have been integrated with machinery to deliver real-time information to maintenance technicians who cannot attend on-site. This protects the health and well-being of all staff whilst facilitating the real-time monitoring of mission-critical mining systems.[941]

1571. However, this convergence of IT with OT significantly increases the risk of a cyberattacks or other cyber incidents. Such incidents risk the operations and physical facilities of electricity, gas, water, telecommunications or other critical infrastructure being disrupted and damaged.

1572. Cyberattacks against OT systems can be financially motivated (for example, the theft of confidential or sensitive data or the deployment of ransomware against critical systems). They can also be undertaken for political or other reasons with potentially dire consequences on the health of all staff in the industry.[942]

1573. As outlined in the *Cybersecurity Strategy 2020* the Department of Home Affairs has strong ongoing engagement with critical infrastructure entities. Use of fora such as the Trusted Information Sharing Network for Critical Infrastructure Resilience (TISN) provide cross-sector dialogue, facilitate ongoing feedback on the security environment for all entities.[943] TISN is an agency made up of industry and government representatives that meet to share information on issues relevant to the resilience of Australian critical infrastructure.

§5. Other Sectors: Higher Education

1574. An ASIO Director General Review has found that there have been unprecedented incursions of foreign interests in the higher education sector during 2017-2018.[944]

939. *See* Gartner definition of OT at https://www.gartner.com/en/information-technology/glossary/operational-technology-ot.
940. *See* Deloitte (2020) Managing the successful convergence of IT and OT at https://www2.deloitte.com/content/dam/Deloitte/global/Documents/Risk/gx-deloitte-managing-the-successful-convergence-of-it-andot.pdf.
941. *See* Australian Strategic Policy Institute (2019) *Protecting national critical infrastructure in an era of IT and OT convergence* at https://www.aspi.org.au/report/protecting-critical-national-infrastructure-era-it-and-ot-convergence.
942. *Ibid.* Deloitte 2020.
943. *See* TISN at https://www.directory.gov.au/portfolios/home-affairs/trusted-information-sharing-network-critical-infrastructure-resilience.
944. Australian Security Intelligence Organisation, Annual Report 2017-18 (Annual Report, 25 Sep. 2018) at https://www.asio.gov.au/sites/default/files/ASIO%20Annual%20Report%20to%20Parliament%202017-18.pdf.

1575. Foreign interference is distinguishable from foreign influence. *Foreign influence* is conducted openly and transparently and is a normal aspect of international relations and diplomacy. *Foreign interference* occurs where activities are carried out by, or on behalf of, foreign actors. They are coercive, deceptive or corrupting and contrary to Australia's sovereignty, values and national interests. Such interference and influence can take place covertly and at times in the normal course of business.[945]

1576. A University Foreign Interference Taskforce (UFIT) was established by the Department of Education, Skills & Employment (DESE) to provide better protection for universities from August 2019.

1577. UFIT developed the *Guidelines to Counter Foreign Interference in the Australian University Sector* released on 13 November 2019.[946]

1578. The Guidelines to counter foreign interference in the Australian university sector were developed collaboratively between the Australian government and the university sector to build awareness and resilience to foreign interference within a university. The objectives of the Guidelines are to support universities to develop new, or examine existing tools, frameworks and resources to assess and mitigate risks from foreign interference. The Guidelines promote greater consistency across the sector and used by each university proportionate to their organizational risk.

1579. Cybersecurity for the university sector is discussed separately in the Guidelines and in summary requires public universities to:[947]

- understand and proportionately mitigate cyber business risks, using techniques like threat models where possible, to inform their cybersecurity strategy;
- implement a cybersecurity strategy that treats cybersecurity as a whole-of-organization human issue and incorporates an appropriate controls framework; and,
- participate in communities of best practice, which share cyber intelligence and lessons across the sector and government.

1580. A regulation affecting universities is the *Foreign Relations (State and Territory Arrangements) Act* 2020 (Cth), commencing on 10 December 2020 established the Foreign Arrangements Scheme (FA Scheme). The FA Scheme requires public universities to notify, through an online public register, new, prospective and existing arrangements with foreign governments and foreign universities 'without institutional autonomy'.[948]

---

945. DESE Guidelines Foreign Interference at https://www.dese.gov.au/guidelines-counter-foreign-interference-australian-university-sector/resources/guidelines-counter-foreign-interference-australian-university-sector, p. 5.
946. *See Guidelines* at https://www.dese.gov.au/guidelines-counter-foreign-interference-australian-university-sector.
947. *Ibid. Guidelines* on Cyber security at pp. 20-21.
948. Department of Foreign Affairs and Trade, Foreign Arrangements Scheme, 'What does the scheme do?' https://www.foreignarrangements.gov.au/about-the-scheme/what-does-the-scheme-do.

1581. The scheme creates an approval process for 'core' foreign arrangements and a notification process for 'non-core' foreign arrangements. A core foreign arrangement is an arrangement between a core State/Territory entity and a core foreign entity.

1582. A non-core foreign arrangement is an arrangement between:

– a core State/Territory entity and a non-core foreign entity;
– a non-core State/Territory entity and a core foreign entity; or
– a non-core State/Territory entity and a non-core foreign entity.

Chapter 5. Cybersecurity Strategy Reform 2021

1583. In its development and evolution, Australia's privacy, consumer and corporations laws were intended for sector-specific application but were silent on cybersecurity issues. To address limitations in addressing cybersecurity threats, the current cybersecurity framework is continually being reviewed.

1584. In 2021 the Australian government began fresh consultations on proposed regulatory changes targeted at improving the country's cybersecurity infrastructure and readiness.[949] The government sought feedback on potential new policies in three key areas of action:

1. minimum expectations on businesses to manage cyber risk that includes governance standards for large businesses; minimum standards for personal information; and standards for smart devices;
2. transparency and disclosure for consumers and businesses about the risks associated with certain technologies such as labelling for smart devices; responsible disclosure policies; health checks for small businesses; and,
3. protection of consumer rights by establishing clear legal remedies for consumers should a cybersecurity incident occur.

§1. Governance Standards

1585. The reform proposes additional cybersecurity governance standards should apply to a wider range of businesses. The current critical infrastructure owners are obligated under the SOCI Act and financial institutions by APRA's prudential standard CPS 234 with cybersecurity obligations.

§2. Minimum Standards for Personal Information

1586. The consideration here is whether a technical standard or 'code' under the *Privacy Act* 1988 (Cth) could encourage the adoption of improved cybersecurity practices. Compliance could be mandatory or tied to regulatory incentives. Such a code could be targeted at specific technologies or data, high-low impact cybersecurity controls and minimum requirements like the Australian Taxation Office's (ATO) Digital Service Provider Operational Framework.[950] The *Privacy Act* 1988 (Cth) presently is limited in its application to 'personal information' and applies to entities whose annual turnover of more than AUD 3 million.

---

949. *Ibid.* Department of Home Affairs 2021 Discussion Paper *Strengthening*.
950. *See* ATO DSP Framework at https://softwaredevelopers.ato.gov.au/RequirementsforDSPs.

§3. Standards for Smart Devices

1587. Smart or IOT devices that connect to the Internet are vulnerable to cybercriminal exploitation resulting in the loss of private and valuable information either stored online or when the device is in use. The issue for consultation is whether a mandatory product standard for smart devices requiring baseline cybersecurity requirements, such as those specified in the EU standard for IOT baseline requirements ERSI EN 303 645, should be implemented.[951]

1588. On 3 September 2020, the Australian government released the voluntary *Code of Practice: Securing the Internet of Things for Consumers.*[952]

1589. Additional feedback is sought on the adoption of a cybersecurity labelling scheme for smart devices and adoption of a 'star' rating proposal and use-by-date labels for cybersecurity devices.

§4. Responsible Disclosure Policies

1590. The consultation sought views on voluntary and regulatory proposals for responsible disclosures that allow software developers make patch systems before a vulnerability is discovered and exploited in a cyberattack. Such disclosures are already in place and encouraged with the ACSC taking a lead role.[953]

§5. Small Business 'Health Checks'

1591. Feedback is also sought on voluntary cybersecurity checking system run by the government at low or no cost. Small businesses and SMEs are much less likely to have supply chain risk management strategies. Where a disruption occurs to other organizations, it may affect directly, or indirectly other entities connected to the Internet. Small businesses and SMEs may not have processes or dedicated cybersecurity teams to respond to cyberattacks.

§6. Legal Remedies for Consumers

1592. The reforms proposed addresses how regulation can be strengthened to better protect consumers from cybersecurity threats. At present consumers have

951. *See* ETSI Cyber: Cyber Security for Consumer Internet of Things: Baseline Requirements at https://www.etsi.org/deliver/etsi_en/303600_303699/303645/02.01.01_60/en_303645v020101p.pdf.
952. Australian Government 2020, *Code of Practice: Securing the Internet of Things for Consumers*, available at https://www.homeaffairs.gov.au/reports-and-pubs/files/code-of-practice.pdf.
953. *Ibid.* Department of Home Affairs 2021 Discussion Paper *Strengthening*.

limited legal options to seek remedies or compensation for cybersecurity incidents. Proposals for amendments to the Australian Consumer Law and the *Privacy Act* 1988 (Cth) are aimed at redressing and to protecting consumers generally.

Chapter 6. International and Global Citizenship

1593. The obligations in the SOCI Act will apply to all owners of critical infrastructure facilities and entities regardless of nationality. The government is mindful of its free trade agreement obligations and will obtain legal advice before using the ministerial directions power to ensure that any use of the power is consistent with such obligations.[954]

1594. The Australian government launched the *2021 Cyber and Critical Technology International Engagement Strategy* on 21 April 2021. This strategy builds on the *2017 International Cyber Engagement Strategy,*[955] The *2021 Strategy* provides a framework to guide Australia's international engagement and to ensure cyberspace and critical technologies support the goal of a safe, secure and prosperous Australia, Indo-Pacific and world.[956]

1595. Key to the *2021 Strategy* is a package that will support cyber and critical technology resilience including:

- co-sponsorship of a proposal to establish a new United Nations Program of Action for Responsible State Behaviour in Cyberspace;
- launching of the flagship Cyber and Critical Tech Cooperation Program with funding of AUD 20.5 million to strengthen cyber and critical technology resilience in Southeast Asia; and,
- contributing AUD 17 million to support neighbouring countries in the Pacific to strengthen their cyber capabilities and resilience to fight cybercrime, improve online safety and counter disinformation and misinformation.

1596. Australia has reaffirmed its commitment to act in accordance with the United Nations Framework for responsible state behaviour in Cyberspace (2018).[957] The four pillars of the Framework include: international law, norms, confidence building measures and capacity building. In 2019 the Department of Foreign Affairs and Trade (DFAT) began consultations and invited submissions on how Australia observes and implements the four pillars of the Framework.[958]

---

954. *See* Department of Home Affairs (2018) *Security of Critical Infrastructure Act* 2018 (Cth) Free trade obligations at https://www.homeaffairs.gov.au/about-us/our-portfolios/national-security/security-coordination/security-of-critical-infrastructure-act-2018; and also the discussion on access to global markets and a more certain regulatory environment in DFAT International Cyber Engagement Strategy (2017) at https://www.internationalcybertech.gov.au/about/2017-International-Cyber-Engagement-Strategy, p. 14ff.
955. *Ibid.* DFAT *International Cyber Engagement Strategy 2017.*
956. *See* DFAT *Cyber and Critical Technology Engagement Strategy 2021* at https://www.internationalcybertech.gov.au/.
957. *Supra,* DFAT *Cyber and Critical Technology Engagement Strategy 2021* p. 37. *See also* https://www.internationalcybertech.gov.au/public-consultation-responsible-state-behaviour-in-cyberspace.
958. *Ibid.* DFAT responsible state behaviour.

1597. All members of the UN have agreed to abide by the Charter of the UN in its entirety. The Charter is applicable in cyberspace and essential to maintaining peace and stability and promoting an open, secure, stable, accessible and peaceful ICT environment.[959]

1598. The Australian Strategic Policy Institute (ASPI), in collaboration with the United Kingdom Foreign, Commonwealth and Development Office (FCDO) and DFAT produced a collection of downloadable UN cyber norms resources for general use.[960]

1599. Australia continues to engage with regional partners to help mature cybersecurity and incident response capabilities and posture in the Indo-Pacific.[961] This aligns with the *Boe Declaration on Regional Security* (agreed by Pacific Leaders in 2018), which confirmed cybersecurity as a key emerging security challenge for the region, and builds on the *ASEAN Leaders' Statement on Cybersecurity Cooperation* (agreed by ASEAN Leaders in 2018), and bilateral agreements with Singapore, Indonesia and Thailand. The ACSC leads operational and technical cybersecurity engagement, including with regional partners through the Pacific Cybersecurity Operational Network (PaCSON) and the Asia Pacific Computer Emergency Response Team (APCERT).

§1. Paris Call for Trust and Security in Cyberspace

1600. An international agreement on cybersecurity principles was launched by the French President Emmanuel Macron in November 2018 as part of the Internet Governance Forum held at UNESCO and the Paris Peace Forum.[962] Nine common principles to secure cyberspace from threats that endanger citizens and infrastructure have been adopted. The signatories included more than 81 nations, 36 public authorities and local governments, 390 organizations and members of civil society and 706 companies and private sector entities, 90 charitable groups and universities, but not the Russia or China. The US signed the Internet Governance Forum agreement in 2021.[963]

1601. While the agreement does not command any specific legislation, the principles include agreements to promote human rights on the Internet, thwart election hacking, cease the theft of intellectual property via hacking and to stop malicious cyber activities especially the ones threatening or resulting in significant, indiscriminate or systemic harm to individuals.

959. *See* UN GA resolutions A/RES/68/243; A/RES/70/237 at https://undocs.org/A/RES/70/237.
960. *See* ASPI at https://www.aspi.org.au/cybernorms.
961. *Supra,* DFAT *Cyber and Critical Technology Engagement Strategy 2021* p. 49.
962. *See* Paris Peace Forum at https://pariscall.international/en/.
963. Falconer, R (2021) U.S. joins global cybersecurity partnership ignored by Trump at https://www.axios.com/us-joins-global-cybersecurity-partnership-ignored-by-trump-1c7cd0a1-17fa-4ab8-ba1f-001639a04bf7.html.

1602. It is notable that the signatories include the Microsoft-led Cybersecurity Tech Accord[964] and the Siemens-led Charter of Trust.[965]

964. *See* Cybertech Accord at https://cybertechaccord.org/.
965. *See* Charter of Trust at https://new.siemens.com/global/en/company/stories/research-technologies/cybersecurity/cybersecurity-charter-of-trust.html.

Part VI. Cybercrime

Chapter 1. Introduction

§1. Crime Versus Cybercrime

1603. Crime is an intentional act that is deemed socially harmful or dangerous, prohibited and punishable under criminal law.[966] The main sources of criminal law in Australia are the *Crimes Act* 1914 (Cth) and the *Criminal Code Act* 1995 (Cth) and parallel laws in the States[967] and Territories[968] and the decisions of the courts. The regime is 'interlocking' where there is an intersection of federal with state and territory laws, that is, where for example, Commonwealth law is at its constitutional limits and where assistance of state or territory law is required. Any interpretation of criminal law is based on principles such as the *mens rea* (guilty mind), *actus reus* (act or omission constituting the action charged) and the mental state of the accused person at the time of the alleged crime. To determine whether conduct is deemed a crime may require reference to the relevant provisions of the criminal code or statutory law. The general principles in criminal law being the rule against retroactivity, intention and criminal responsibility.

1604. Cybercrime. There is no universally accepted definition of 'cybercrime'. In Australia, the term 'cybercrime' is used to describe both crimes directed at computers or other digital assets (such as hacking and denial of service attacks); and crimes where computers or digital assets are an integral part of an offence (such as online fraud which also includes advanced fee scams, online auction frauds, fraudulent lottery schemes, identity theft, modem and webpage hijacking and the distribution of child exploitation material).[969]

966. *See* Crime at https://www.britannica.com/topic/crime-law.
967. *See Crimes Act* 1900 (NSW) as amended; *Criminal Code Act* 1899 (Qld); *Crimes Act* 1958 (Vic); *Criminal Law Consolidation Act* 1933 (SA); The Criminal Code; and *Criminal Code Act* 1913 (WA).
968. The Australian Capital Territory (ACT) replicates the *Crimes Act* 1900 (NSW) as amended.
969. *See* Australia Analysis and Policy Observatory (2013) *National Plan to Combat Cybercrime* at http://apo.org.au/node/35312. *See also* Cross C, Smith R & Richards K (2014) Challenges of responding to online fraud victimization in Australia, *Trends & Issues in Crime and Criminal Justice* no. 474, Canberra: Australian Institute of Criminology at https://www.aic.gov.au/publications/tandi/tandi474.

1605. Often the discussion is on 'traditional' crimes such as theft and 'new' crimes where computers are involved such as phishing. Cybercrime is a crime committed using technology mediated on the Internet. While cybercrime is spoken about separately to traditional crime there are no differences as it is carried out by the same type of criminals for the same type of reasons. These criminals include professional thieves, criminal gangs, disgruntled employees, activists, disillusioned youth and state adversaries. The motivations remain the same from boredom and vandalism to ideological or political support, malice, revenge, financial gains, terrorism, notoriety and sensationalism. Probably the differences may lie in the scale of the attack, the reach and the speed of cybercrime attacks.

§2. Classification of Cybercrime

1606. Whereas computer crime has traditionally involved the illegal entry into and manipulation of computer systems, cybercrime increasingly involves activity on the Internet that cross multiple national and international borders and jurisdictions. The latter issue of jurisdiction brings greater levels of complexity to detection and enforcement.

1607. The Internet has brought about the need to regulate its use and to legislate against a variety of new abuses and frauds online.

1608. A variety of cybercrimes committed by individuals, organized groups, 'state' actors as well as other modes of criminal activity has been variously classified.

1609. Teunissen *et al.* (2021) has distinguished between cyber-dependent crimes and cyber-enabled crimes.[970] Cyber-dependent crimes are those that can only be committed using information communication technologies (ICT). These include activities such as hacking, spreading of viruses and other malware so-called pure cybercrimes as they are directed *against* machines and networks.

1610. By contrast, cyber-enabled or technology-enabled crimes are traditional crimes that could be committed without using digital equipment and other technology, but which use these tools to increase the scale or reach of their crimes.[971] Criminal offences *using* the machine include identity theft, fraud, stalking and harassment. In committing such conventional crimes there is a perceived lower risk of detection.

970. Teunissen C, Voce I & Smith R (2021) *Estimating the cost of pure cybercrime to Australian individuals*, Statistical Bulletin no. 34. Canberra: Australian Institute of Criminology. https://doi.org/10.52922/ sb78269.

971. *See* Choo, RK-K, Smith RG & McCusker, R (2007) *Future Directions in Technology-enabled Crime: 2007-09,* AIC Research & Public Policy Series No. 78 at https://www.aic.gov.au/publications/rpp/rpp78.

1611. Teunissen *et al.* (2021) further refine pure cybercrime into three broad types: computer access crimes (CAC); computer disruption crimes (CDC); and, computer malfunction crimes.[972]

1612. In all cybercrimes, criminal intent is an important element for successful prosecutions. Unauthorized access to another's computer system, especially where there is no deletion or alteration of data, is generally actionable under common law provisions dealing with fraud, forgery, theft, damage to property and similar doctrines such as trespass. All Australian jurisdictions have reformed and standardized its criminal laws to accommodate designated harms caused by computer crime.

1613. A classification of cybercrime could begin under different 'heads' from two viewpoints. First, conceptually cybercrime is one where the target is the computer (or IT system) itself. This framework will possibly capture all such crimes that target the computer. The key element is the manipulation of machines using malware.

1614. The second is to characterize cybercrime where the computer is used as a tool – a computer-mediated crime. Within this class, particular crimes might be described as those that are 'financial' in nature, crimes against businesses, persons and personnel and against governments and nation-states. An important element here is the manipulation of people ('warmware') sometimes described as social engineering.[973]

1615. In their examination of the misuse of the domain name system (DNS) Krone & Smith (2020) used a three-fold typology: where it is used as a target, as a vector to launch cyberattacks and as a platform for misuse. In software engineering terms the DNS as a *target* of misuse includes attacks on the network architecture; alternative root systems; root zone attack; routing via the border gateway protocol (BGP);[974] DNS hijacking; and cache poisoning or spoofing. Where the DNS is used as a *vector* the misuse can include cross-site scripting; hacking; botnets; denial of service attacks; and spam. In social engineering terms the DNS may be used as a

---

972. *Supra,* Teunissen 2021.

973. Cited in Krone, T & Smith RG (2020) *Criminal misuse of the Domain Name System,* AIC Research Report 03 at https://www.aic.gov.au/sites/default/files/2020-05/research_report_03.pdf. Wall (2007) describes the computer as a target offence as *computer integrity crimes* and computer as a tool offence as *computer-assisted crime. See* Wall DS (2007) *Cybercrime: The Transformation of Crime in the Information Age,* Cambridge: Polity Press. Gordon & Ford (2006:1-2) argue that cybercrime indicates a distinct sphere of criminal behaviour and crimeware that includes trojans, viruses, bots, spyware and worms that are instrumental in facilitating certain cybercrimes. *Type I* offences consist of discrete crimeware victimizations, often based on exploitation of software vulnerabilities. *Type II* offences are based on interaction with a victim and characterized using software other than crimeware usually involving repeated contact. *See* Gordon S & Ford R (2006) On the definition and classification of cybercrime in the *Journal in Computer Virology* 2: 13-20.

974. One example of BGP misuse is a bitcoin-stealing offence committed using the compromised administrator account of an ISP. *See* Litke P & Stewart J (2014) BGP hijacking for cryptocurrency profit at https://www.secureworks.com/research/bgp-hijacking-for-cryptocurrency-profit.

platform for phishing; technical support scams; geo-blocking and circumvention of identification; fraud detection; and marketing and price differentials.

1616. However, it is noted that the categories cannot be put neatly into either software or social engineering types. Some forms of cybercrime combine both types.[975] The categories of cybercrimes in Figure 7 are non-exclusive as a particular type might appear in one or more classes. The intention is to better depict the various types of cybercrimes in a non-exhaustive listing and as a framework to describe variations of cybercrimes.

1617. Figure 7 serves as a conceptual framework for presenting information in Chapters 4 and 5 here in Part VI where the computer is a target and the computer is a tool or attack vector. Items in bold lettering denote a more detailed treatment while contextual material is given within the text.

975. *See* Choo & McCusker (2007) *supra* at p. xvi and p. 8.

Figure 7 A Conceptual Framework for Classifying Cybercrimes

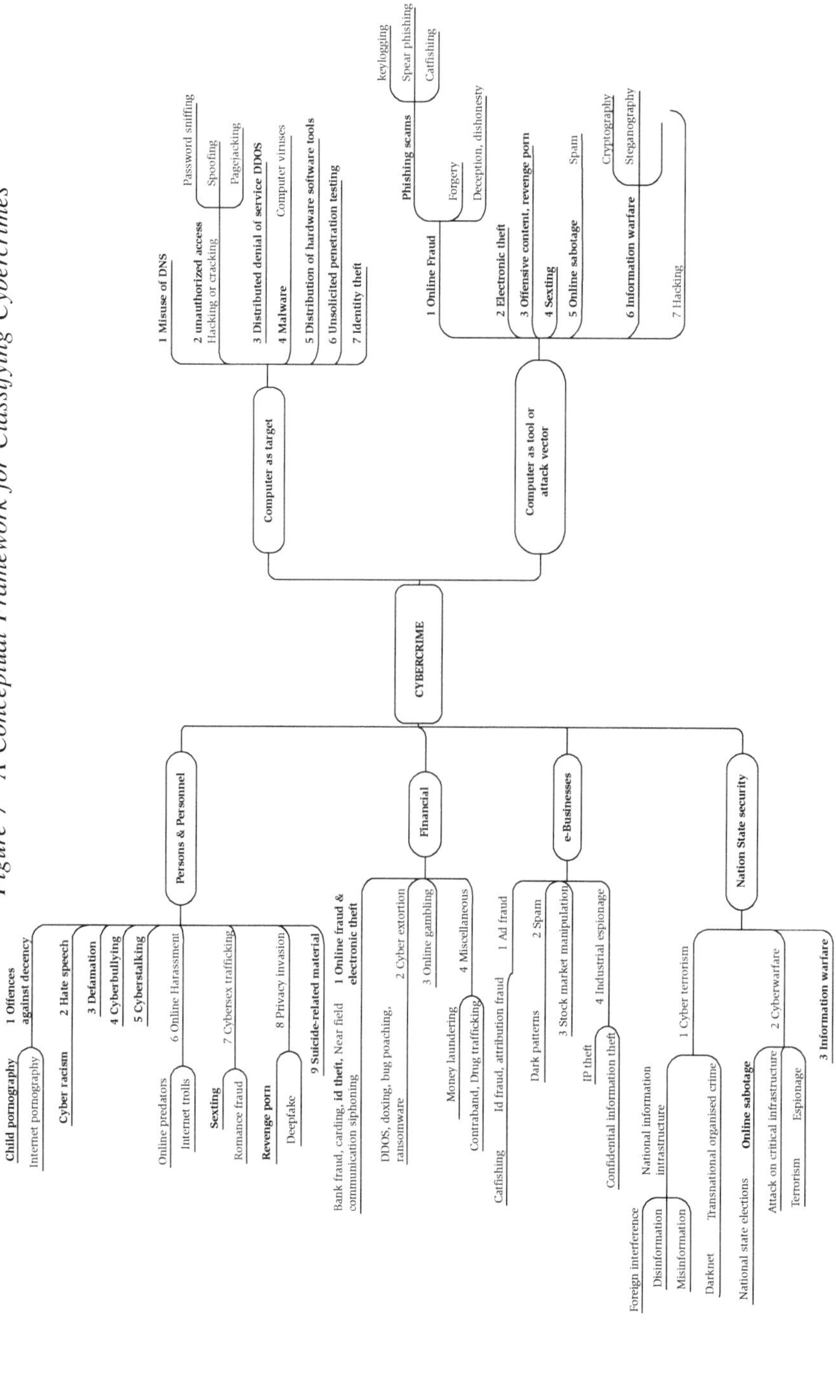

§3. NATURE AND EXTENT OF CYBERCRIME

1618. Reliable statistics regarding the extent of cybercrime taking place within Australia are difficult to obtain. However, given the high levels of connectivity and computer and mobile phone use in Australia, it may be surmised that the level of cybercrime is both significant and increasing. This may be inferred from various government reports and studies undertaken in Australia in the past decade.

1619. A report by the Australian Business Assessment of Computer User Security (ABACUS) based on a nationwide survey in 2009 undertaken by the Australian Institute of Criminology (AIC) demonstrated the prevalence and nature of computer security incidents experienced by Australian businesses. The survey highlighted that:

- given that the average Australian household owns a personal computer or laptop or both (1.61 computers per household in 2009) the incidence for cybercrime occurring at home is considerable.[976]
- fourteen per cent of Australian businesses experienced one or more incidents of cybercrime in the period 2006-2007.[977]

1620. The Computer Emergency Response Team (CERT) Australia Cybercrime Security Survey 2012 found that:

- over 20 per cent of organizations were aware of or experienced a cyber incident in the previous twelve months, with 20 per cent of these organizations experiencing more than ten incidents. Of the organizations which are aware that they experienced cyber incidents, 17 per cent suffered from loss of confidential or proprietary information, 16 per cent encountered a distributed denial of service (DDOS) attack and 10 per cent financial fraud;
- over 44 per cent reported the incident to a law enforcement agency, whereas only 13 per cent sought civil remedies through litigation;
- over 20 per cent chose not to report the matter to a law enforcement agency because of the fear of negative publicity;
- the most common responses as to why incidents were successful, were that they used powerful automated attack tools, or exploited unpatched or unprotected software vulnerabilities, or because of misconfigured operating systems, applications or network devices; and
- over half of all organizations increased their expenditure on IT security in the previous twelve months.[978]

---

976. Skelton, P. (2009) *The 2009 Digital Atlas of Australia* at https://connectedmag.com.au/2009-digital-atlas-australia/ (6 May 2009).
977. Richards, K. (2009) *Australian Business Assessment of Computer User Safety Survey* at https://aic.gov.au/publications/rpp/rpp102 and at http://www.aic.gov.au/crime_types/in_focus/cybercrime.html.
978. Australian Government, *Cybercrime & Security Survey Report 2012*, University of Canberra at http://www.canberra.edu.au/cis/storage/Cyber%20Crime%20and%20Security%20Survey%20Report%202012.pdf.

1621. According to Australia's *National Plan to Combat Cybercrime* (2013) discernible trends include:[979]

- the growth in the number, sophistication and impact of cybercrimes that poses a serious and evolving threat to Australian individuals, businesses and governments;
- while is difficult to quantify, the total costs evident from operational agencies, suggests that economic costs of cybercrime in Australia are substantial. Many instances of cybercrime go unreported but non-government estimates put the cost of cybercrime in Australia as high as AUD 2 billion annually; and
- online criminals committing crimes across multiple borders and targeting large numbers of victims simultaneously. Tools that have many legitimate uses, like high-speed Internet, peer-to-peer file sharing and sophisticated encryption methods, are being used to help criminals carry out and conceal their activities.[980]

1622. In Australia one industry estimate put the cost of cybercrime to be at least AUD 1 billion over the previous twelve months in 2013.[981]

1623. In 2018, AUD 490 million in financial losses were reported to Scamwatch, the Australian Cybercrime Online Reporting Network (ACORN) and other state and territory government agencies. These losses represented an increase of 44 per cent over the AUD 340 million reported in 2017, demonstrating the significant impact of scams on the Australian public.[982] The Australian Competition and Consumer Commission (ACCC) believes that many scams are not reported and that the true cost of scams is likely much higher than the reported figure.[983]

1624. In the same year, 22 per cent of total reported scams were reported to the ACCC's Scamwatch (representing AUD 107 million in financial losses). Of the scams reported to the ACCC, 4 per cent of scams and 15 per cent of total financial losses occurred on social media or online forums and 6 per cent of such scams and 16 per cent of total losses were reported as originating on the Internet.

1625. Consumers reported losses of AUD 15.7 million from scams occurred on online platforms and AUD 16.5 million from scams occurring on the Internet in 2018.[984] Victims of social media based dating and romance scams reported losses of AUD 9.3 million and victims of social media based investment scams reported losses of AUD 3.3 million in 2018.

---

979. *See* Department of Home Affairs (2013) *National Plan to Combat Cybercrime* at https://www.homeaffairs.gov.au/criminal-justice/files/national-plan-combat-cybercrime.pdf.
980. *Ibid.*
981. *See* Symantec (2013) *Norton Report: Total Cost of Cybercrime in Australia amounts to A$1.06 billion* media release 13 October www.symantec.com/about/news/resources/press_kits/detail.jsp?pkid=norton-report-2013.
982. ACCC (2019) Targeting scams: report of the ACCC on scams activity 2018, (May 2019) p. iii.
983. *Supra*, ACCC (2019) Targeting scams.
984. *Supra*, ACCC (2019) Targeting scams, p. 13.

1626. In a report estimating the cost of pure cybercrime to individuals in Australia in 2019, Teunissen *et al.* (2021) have observed that the total economic impact was approximately AUD 3.5 billion.[985] This estimate is made up of AUD 1.9 billion in money directly lost by victims, AUD 597 million spent in dealing with the consequences of the loss, and AUD 1.4 billion spent on preventative measures. The victims recovered AUD 389 million.

1627. This may be contrasted to the global cybercrime survey data from over 10,000 adults in ten countries.[986] The data there showed that over a third of respondents experienced a cybercrime of some kind between 2018 and 2019. In Australia, 57 per cent of respondents indicated that they have been a cybercrime victim with 33 per cent indicating that they had been victimized in the past twelve months.[987]

1628. For various reasons computer crime often goes unreported. Business victims fear the loss of control over the cost and direction of their case. Many victims fear reputational damage by letting others, especially customers or clients, know that their system had been breached. There is also the fear of potential legal liability for loss of customer data and the possible reduction in shareholder value resulting from the breach of security.

985. *Supra,* Teunissen *et al.* (2021).
986. *Supra,* Teunissen *et al.* (2021) citing NortonLifeLock 2020 *2019 Cyber Safety Insights Report.* https://au.norton.com/nortonlifelock-cyber-safety-report.
987. *Supra,* Teunissen *et al.* (2021).

Chapter 2. Commonwealth Cybercrime Legislation

1629. Commonwealth, State and Territory laws dealing with computer crime have been characterized as diverse in policy and piecemeal in application.[988] The implementation of the Commonwealth Criminal code provisions under the *Cybercrime Act* 2001 (Cth) has achieved some uniformity in NSW, Victoria, SA and the ACT, with NT law based loosely on the model provisions.

1630. Responsibility for combating the different forms of cybercrime in Australia is shared between Australian government law enforcement agencies state and territory agencies. All jurisdictions have criminal laws directed at the various forms of cybercrime. In addition to formal legislation and case law, there are also 'soft law' mechanisms such as mandatory industry codes, voluntary codes of best practice and best practice guidelines which also seek to mitigate, prevent, aid the fight against cybercrime.

1631. At the Commonwealth level, offences under the *Crimes Act* 1914 (Cth), *Criminal Code Act* 1995 (Cth) (Criminal Code), the *Cybercrime Act* 2001 (Cth) and the *Telecommunications (Interception and Access) Act* 1979 (Cth) cover most crimes directed at computers and Internet systems, such as unauthorized access and distributed denial of service (DDoS) attacks as well as the use of digital devices as a platform and vector for criminal activities. Powers to prosecute offences for the misuse of telecommunications services for criminal purposes, such as the online distribution of child exploitation material are available under specific legislation. Other legislation relating to sharing of violent material online, sex offences against children and minors, money laundering and counter terrorism, suicide related material offences, online safety and anti-discrimination laws are specific aspects of criminal activity. These provisions are supported by a range of powers which can be exercised by law enforcement and national security agencies in the detection, disruption and investigation of those offences.

1632. Each State and Territory has primary responsibility for laws dealing with online versions of personal and property crimes, such as stalking, theft and fraud. Legal frameworks for State and Territory agencies to detect, disrupt and investigate offences also exist.[989]

1633. The Standing Committee of Attorneys-General presented a National Model Criminal Code[990] (Model Code) in 2009 which adopted terminology consistent with the Council of Europe's *Convention on Cybercrime.* The Model Code is

---

988. *See* Model Criminal Code Officers Committee (MCCOC) (2001) Damage and computer offences, MCCOC Report, Canberra: AGD.
989. *See* Lim, YF (2002) *Cyberspace Law: Commentaries and Materials*, Ch. 7 (Oxford University Press).
990. *See* Model Criminal Code (2009) at https://www.ag.gov.au/crime/publications/model-criminal-law-officers-committee-reports, (May).

the foundational basis for criminal laws in NSW, Victoria, SA, the ACT, the Northern Territory and Commonwealth legislation. However, Queensland, WA and Tasmania have yet to adopt the Model Code.

1634. The *Cybercrime Act* 2001 (Cth) passed on 27 September 2001 amended the *Criminal Code Act* 1995 (Cth) through the addition of new updated computer offences based upon the December 1992 Model Criminal Code Damage and Computer Offences Report developed through Commonwealth, State, and Territory cooperation.[991] The Act also repealed existing offences in Part VIA of the *Crimes Act* 1914 (Cth), enacted in 1989 that predate existing technologies. The *Cybercrime Act* 2001 (Cth) inserted Part 10.6 dealing with offences prohibiting misuse of telecommunication networks for a range of illicit purposes and Part 10.7 dealing with computer offences in the *Criminal Code Act* 1995 (Cth).

1635. This chapter focusses on describing some of the principal provisions of criminal and cybercrime Commonwealth laws. The relevant Commonwealth cybercrime legislations to be discussed include:

- *Crimes Act* 1914
- *Criminal Code Act* 1995 (Criminal Code)
- *Cybercrime Act* 2001
- *Cybercrime Legislation Amendment Act* 2012 (CLAA)
- *Telecommunications (Interception and Access) Act* 1979 (TIAA)
- *Broadcasting Services (Online Services) Act* 1992
- *Crimes Legislative Amendment (Telecommunications Offences and Other Measures) Act* 2004
- *Enhancing Online Safety Act* 2015
- *Crimes Legislative Amendment (Sex Offences Against Children) Act* 2010 (SOAC)
- *Criminal Code Amendment (Protection of Minors Online) Act* 2017
- *Enhancing Online Safety (Non-consensual Sharing of Intimate Images) Act* 2018
- *Criminal Code Amendment (Sharing of Abhorrent Violent Material) Act* 2019 (SAVM)
- *Criminal Code Amendment (Suicide Related Material Offences) Act* 2005
- *Anti-Money Laundering and Counter Terrorism Financing Act* 2006 (AML/CTF Act)
- *Racial Discrimination Act* 1975.

991. *See* Model Criminal Code Damage and Computer Offences Report 1992 archived at https://web.archive.org.au/awa/20100518121436mp_/http://www.scag.gov.au/lawlink/SCAG/ll_scag.nsf/vwFiles/crime-(composite-2007)-website.pdf/$file/crime-(composite-2007)-website.pdf, and at https://www.ag.gov.au/crime/publications/model-criminal-law-officers-committee-reports.

§1. *CRIMES ACT* 1914 AND *CRIMINAL CODE ACT* 1995

1636. The *Crimes Act* 1914 (Cth) sets out Commonwealth powers, authorities and obligations for dealing with Commonwealth criminal offences and related matters.[992]

1637. The *Criminal Code Act* 1995 (Cth) codifies the general principles of criminal responsibility under laws of the Commonwealth.[993]

1638. Offences relating to the telecommunications services in the *Criminal Code Act* 1995 (Cth) are outlined in Part 10. More specifically Part 10.6 makes it an offence to do any of the following using a carriage service:

- section 474.15 and section 474.16: make an unlawful or hoax threat respectively;
- section 474.17: menace, harass or cause offence;
- section 474.19, section 474.20: access, transmit, publish, possess, control, produce, supply or obtain child pornography respectively;
- section 474.22, section 474.22A, section 474.23: access, transmit, publish, possess, control, produce, supply or obtain child abusive material respectively; or,
- section 474.26, section 474.27: procure, encourage, entice, recruit, groom or induce a person under 16 years of age to engage in sexual activity respectively.

1639. Part 10.6, section 474.25 places obligations on Internet service providers and Internet content hosts like those found in the *Broadcasting Services (Online Services) Act 1992* (Cth). The section requires an Internet service provider or content host to refer details of child abuse material to the Australian Federal Police (AFP) where it becomes aware that the service can be used to access that material.

1640. Parts 10.7 and 10.8 spell out particular cybercrime offences which include: computer intrusions; unauthorized modification of data including destruction of data; unauthorized impairment of electronic communications, including denial of service attacks; the creation and distribution of malicious software; and dishonestly obtaining or dealing in personal financial information.

1641. An extended geographical jurisdiction applies to offences under Part 10.7 of the *Code* in particular Divisions 477 and 478.

1642. A distinction is made between serious computer offences on the one hand and other computer offences. A *serious offence* means an offence that is punishable by imprisonment for life or a period of five or more years (section 477.1).

1643. Part 10.8 refers to financial information offences. The specific sections are:

---

992. *See Crimes Act* 1914 (Cth) at http://www.austlii.edu.au/au/legis/cth/consol_act/ca191482/.
993. *See Criminal Code Act* 1995 (Cth) at https://www.legislation.gov.au/Series/C2004A04868.

- section 480.4: dishonestly obtaining or dealing in personal financial information.
- section 480.5: possession or control of thing with intent to dishonestly obtain or deal in personal financial information.

§2. *Cybercrime Act* 2001

1644. The *Cybercrime Act* 2001 (Cth) enables enhanced investigative powers relating to the search and seizure of electronically stored data.[994] Schedule 1 includes amendments to or repeals applicable items in the *Australian Security Intelligence Organisation Act* 1979 (Cth); *Crimes Act* 1914 (Cth); *Criminal Code Act* 1995 (Cth); *Education Services for Overseas Students Act* 2000 (Cth); and *Telecommunications (Interception) Act* 1997 (Cth).

1645. Under the *Cybercrime Act* 2001 (Cth) Schedule 1 Part 10.7 computer offences include:

- section 476.2 unauthorized access, modification, or impairment.
- section 477.1 unauthorized access, modification, or impairment with intent to commit a serious offence.
- section 477.2 unauthorized modification of data to cause impairment. This is designed to incriminate a person who is reckless as to whether their actions will impair data, for example, circulation of a virus.
- section 477.3 unauthorized impairment of electronic communication, for example, denial of service attack.
- section 478.1 unauthorized access to, or modification of, restricted data, for example, giving password to someone.
- section 478.2 unauthorized impairment of data on a Commonwealth computer disk or a credit card.
- section 478.3 possession or control of data with intent to commit a computer offence.
- section 478.4 producing, supplying, or obtaining data with intent to commit a computer offence. This is targeted at a situation where preparatory action is taken but the intended offence is not completed.

1646. The *Cybercrime Act* 2001 (Cth) includes the following offences: hacking, distribution of viruses, denial of service attacks, unauthorized access with intent to commit a serious offence, misuse of a limited authority, for example, an employee using limited access rights to enter the system and fraudulently transfer funds; and development, supply, or possession of viruses or hacking programs.[995]

1647. The jurisdiction of the *Cybercrime Act* 2001 (Cth) is very wide. The legislation covers offences where the conduct constituting an offence occurs partly in

994. *See Cybercrime Act* 2001 (Cth) at http://classic.austlii.edu.au/au/legis/cth/num_act/ca2001112/.
995. *See* Choo (2007) 'Zombies and botnets', *Trends & Issues in Crime and Criminal Justice* AIC No. 333 at https://www.aic.gov.au/sites/default/files/2020-05/tandi333.pdf.

Australia, where conduct occurs on board an Australian ship or aircraft, and where the person committing the offence is an Australian citizen or an Australian company. In recent years, this has been extended to cover acts committed outside of Australia, but which have consequences within Australia.[996]

1648. The *Cybercrime Act* 2001 (Cth) has been criticized by some as being too vague and over-reaching. However, the limited number of prosecutions to date suggests that the government may have been restrained and conservative in its enforcement.

1649. One example is that the cybercrime policies in Australia do not acknowledge 'computer fraud' as a criminal offence. 'Given the borderless nature of cybercrime, it is an oversight to not have a national approach to computer-related fraud' (Weber 2014: 68).[997] Although as Broadhurst (2017) suggests, the amendments to the *Cybercrime Act* 2001 (Cth) in expanding the definition of cyber offences, possibilities of online crimes have broadened.[998]

1650. Another of the most controversial aspects of the Act is its expanded powers of investigation. These include allowing a magistrate to make an assistance order that requires a specified person (including the owner of a computer system) to provide such information and assistance as is necessary and reasonably practicable to enable access to make a copy or print the data. Computer equipment and storage devices can be examined off-site where it is more efficient and effective. Officers can copy all data on a computer if some of the data contains evidential material or if there are reasonable grounds to suspect it contains such material. Search warrants can be used to access data accessible from the search premises (including data not physically stored at the search premises).[999]

§3. *Cybercrime Legislation Amendment Act* 2012 (CLAA)

1651. The *Cybercrime Legislation Amendment Act* 2012 (Cth) (CLAA) enables Australia to accede to the Cybercrime Convention as well as amending relevant sections in the following four legislations:

---

996. *See Cybercrime Act* 2001 (Cth) s. 15.1.
997. Weber, D (2014) The Cybernetic Sea: Australia's Approach to the Wave of Cybercrime, *QUT Law Review,* 14(2), 52-73.
998. Broadhurst, R (2017) *Cybercrime in Australia,* The Palgrave Handbook of Australian and New Zealand Criminology, Crime and Justice, Cham: Springer International Publishing, pp. 221-235, doi:10.1007/978-3-319-55747-2_15.
999. *See also* Joint Committee on National Crime Authority, investigation on law enforcement implications of new technology, www.aph.gov.au/senate/committee/nca.ctte/; and the Electronic Frontiers Australia's comment on the Cybercrimes legislation at http:// www.efa.org.au/Analysis/cybe rcrime/bill.htm.

1. *Mutual Assistance in Criminal Matters Act* 1987 (Cth) (MACM Act) relating to the cooperation powers of Australian law enforcement agencies with their foreign counterparts;
2. *Criminal Code Act* 1995 (Cth*)* relating to the unauthorized access, modification, or impairment of data and restricted data;
3. *Telecommunications (Interception and Access) Act* 1979 (Cth) relating to the scope of telecommunication interception powers; and,
4. *Telecommunications Act* 1997 (Cth)[1000] relating to the obligation of carriers to preserve stored data and metadata.

I. Mutual Assistance

1652. The CLAA extends the geographic reach of its provisions to conduct which occurs wholly or partly in Australia, on board an Australian aircraft or ship, and to the conduct of Australian nationals abroad in certain circumstances. This is demonstrably a response to the borderless nature of cybercrime.

1653. The Convention on Cybercrime and the CLAA framework facilitate international cooperation between State parties to the Convention through the cross-border preservation and sharing of communication records.

1654. The treaty also requires signatory states to regularize criminal law so that it would prohibit unauthorized access of computer systems, unauthorized interception of computer transmissions, hacking computer systems or data, making devices facilitating such activity and forging computer data. It also criminalizes distribution of material based on their content particularly child pornography.

1655. A vast majority of cybercrime targeting Australian companies originate offshore and from well-organized and resourced entities.[1001] These criminal organizations are either based in or use ICT facilities located in states with poor legislative or enforcement frameworks. The Convention fosters international cooperation and mutual assistance to other member states to find, apprehend and gather evidence of such crime by those responsible.

1656. The CLAA empowers Australia's law enforcement and intelligence agencies to compel carriers to preserve the communication records of persons suspected of cyber-based crimes and to request other parties to the Convention to do the same.

1657. The MACM Act is aimed at regulating the provision of international assistance by Australia in criminal matters when a foreign country makes a request, as well as facilitating the obtaining of international assistance by Australia in criminal

1000. Select Legislative Instrument 2013 No. 4; Explanatory Statement, at http://www.comlaw.gov.au/Details/F2013L00205/Explanatory%20Statement/Text.
1001. *See* King & Wood Mallesons (2014) Australia's cybercrime legislation at https://www.lexology.com/library/detail.aspx?g=4ab62fdd-f177-47eb-b02d-e327cf9833a9.

matters. Several provisions in the MACM Act deal with the recovery of property through the registration and enforcement of foreign orders in Australia. These also include enforcement of foreign forfeiture orders, pecuniary penalty orders, restraining orders, production orders, monitoring orders and search warrants relating to foreign serious offences.

II. Unauthorized Access

1658. The CLAA also expands Commonwealth cybercrime offences by including Commonwealth offences under the *Criminal Code Act* 1995 (Cth). The broadened offences relate to the unauthorized access, modification, or impairment of data and restricted data found in sections 477.2, 477.3 and 478.2 of the Criminal Code.

1659. The CLAA section 477.2 removes limitations that require the relevant data to be owned by the Commonwealth, held by, or on behalf of, the Commonwealth and that the access, modification or impairment was caused via a carriage service. The effect of the amendment is that any unauthorized access, modification, or impairment of any data is now an offence. The amendment captures situations where employees who modify data on-site without authorization or use local networks to conduct such acts are in breach of the legislation.

1660. This section establishes the basis of the exercise of Commonwealth jurisdiction either from the telecommunications powers in the Constitution or in the Commonwealth ownership of the computer or data. The criminal elements include that the person knows that the modification is unauthorized and is reckless as to the impairment, access to, or the reliability, security or operation of such data.

1661. Under section 477.3 of the Criminal Code it is an offence to cause unauthorized impairment of an electronic communication to or from a computer using a carriage service or a Commonwealth-owned computer. The CLAA amendments are based on the Commonwealth's constitutional external affairs powers that include implementation of an international treaty, now means that any unauthorized impairment is an offence. Any conduct that diverts or redirects communications with a computer, such as a distributed denial of service attack is an offence under the Act.

1662. Under the Criminal Code it was an offence to cause unauthorized impairment of the reliability, security or operation of data on a computer disk, credit card, or other storage device, if the Commonwealth owned that device. Section 478.2 of the CLAA has removed that restriction so that it is now an offence to conduct such acts to any such device.

§4. Telecommunication Offences

1663. The Commonwealth has full constitutional powers to make laws in relation to electronic telecommunications, including the Internet. Under section 51(5) of the Constitution it has power to legislate with respect to 'postal, telegraphic, telephonic and *other like services*' [emphasis added]. While the Constitution was drafted when radio and television were not contemplated at the time, both mediums have been held by the High Court to be 'other like services' within the scope of section 51(5). In 1935 the High Court stated that the common characteristic of postal, telegraphic and telephonic services was that '[t]hey are communication services. If a new form of communication should be discovered, it too might be made the subject of legislation as a "like service"'.[1002] The court also rejected the notion that section 51(5) was restricted to services for communication between individuals.[1003] It appears that in creating offences relating to use of telephones, the Internet and other 'carriage services' is clearly within Commonwealth power.

1664. The treatment of Commonwealth legislation under this subheading of telecommunication offences is a means of separating specific elements of electronic communication such as the Internet from telecommunications generally and to appreciate how technological developments telecommunications are being addressed. The relevant legislations are:

- *Telecommunications (Interception and Access) Act* 1979 (Cth) (TIAA Act)
- *Telecommunication Act* 1979 (Cth)
- *Telecommunications Act* 1997 (Cth) INTERPOL and section 313
- *Broadcasting Services (Online Services) Act* 1992 (Cth)
- *Crimes Legislative Amendments (Telecommunication Offences and Other Measures) Act* 2004 (Cth)
- *Crimes Act* 1914 (Cth)
- *Criminal Code Act* 1995 (Cth)

I. *Telecommunication (Interception and Access) Act* 1979 (TIAA)

1665. The TIAA prohibits the *interception* of, and other *access* to, telecommunications except where authorized in special circumstances or for the purpose of tracing.[1004]

1666. The TIAA makes it an offence for a person to intercept or access private telecommunications without the knowledge of those involved in that communication. The TIAA permits access to communications content for law enforcement and national security purposes.

1667. The TIAA protects the privacy of Australians by prohibiting interception of communications and access to stored communications. The privacy of Australians is also protected by Part 13 of the *Telecommunications Act* 1997 (Cth)

1002. *See R v. Brislan; Ex parte Williams* (1935) 54 CLR 262 (radio); and *Jones v. Commonwealth (1965) 112* CLR 206 (television).
1003. *Ibid. R v. Brislan* at 282-3.
1004. *See* text of the Act at https://www.legislation.gov.au/Details/C2021C00341.

that prohibits telecommunications service providers from disclosing information about their customers' use of telecommunications services.[1005]

1668. The Office of Communications Access and Cybercrime (OCAC) is the central liaison point between the telecommunications industry and law enforcement and security agencies regarding the obligations in the TIAA including data retention (discussed in detail in Chapter 7 Cybercrime Law Enforcement and Criminal Procedures, §1. Criminal Procedures I. Data Retention below).[1006]

II. *Telecommunications Act* 1997 Section 313

1669. The Australian Federal Police (AFP) has responsibility for website blocking requests under section 313 of the *Telecommunications Act* 1997 (Cth).[1007] In general section 313 enables Australian government agencies, including state government agencies, to obtain assistance from the telecommunications industry when upholding Australian laws.

1670. More specifically section 313(1) imposes obligations on Internet service providers to do their best to prevent telecommunications networks from being used to commit Commonwealth offences.

1671. Further section 313(3) obliges Internet service providers to give relevant authorities of the Commonwealth, States and Territories any such help as is reasonably necessary for:

- enforcing the criminal law and laws imposing pecuniary penalties;
- the enforcing criminal laws in force in a foreign country;
- protecting the public revenue; or,
- safeguarding national security.

1672. The AFP may use section 313(3) requests to disrupt illegal online activity where other mechanisms have been or are likely to be unsuccessful.

1673. The AFP through the Access Limitation Scheme may deploy section 313(3) requests to block access to INTERPOL's 'Worst of List' of child exploitation websites. When an Australian user attempts to access a website named on the Worst of List, they are redirected to an INTERPOL 'stop page' blocking access to information containing child abuse material. This list is provided to Australian Internet service providers and relies on them to block the identified websites in Australia.

1005. The *Privacy Act* 1988 (Cth) defines 'personal information' in s. 6(1) as any 'information or an opinion about an identified individual, or an individual who is reasonably identifiable. *See* text of the Act at https://www.legislation.gov.au/Series/C2004A03712.

1006. *See* Department of Home Affairs at https://www.homeaffairs.gov.au/about-us/our-portfolios/national-security/lawful-access-telecommunications/data-retention.

1007. *Telecommunications Act 1997* (Cth) s. 313 at https://www.comlaw.gov.au/Details/C2012C00584.

1674. The blocking of known criminal content on the Internet is a proactive, disruptive strategy to help protect children from sexual exploitation and abuse. The websites included on the INTERPOL 'Worst of List' depict some of the most severe child sexual exploitation material.

III. *Broadcasting Services Act* 1992

1675. The *Broadcasting Services Act* 1992 (Cth) broadly covers issues relating to content regulation and media ownership in Australia.[1008] The law stipulates what is regarded as political advertising and the specific conditions which must be met before they are authorized for publication.

1676. To reform and create a platform and technology-neutral legislation the *Enhancing Online Safety Act* 2015 (Cth) incorporated elements of Schedules 5 and 7 of the *Broadcasting Services Act* 1992 (Cth).

1677. The *Criminal Code Amendment (Sharing of Abhorrent Violent Material) Act* 2019 (Cth) (SAVM Act) complements the existing takedown and referral procedures for online services and content under Schedules 5 and 7 of the *Broadcasting Services Act* 1992 (Cth).

1678. Schedule 5 relates to online services and its providers, complaints, industry codes and industry standards, online provider rules, offences and protection from civil and criminal proceedings.

1679. Schedule 7 relates to content services in terms of the classification of content, complaints, industry codes and standards, designated content-hosting service provider determinations, enforcement and protection from civil and criminal proceedings.

IV. *Crimes Legislation Amendment* 2004

1680. The *Crimes Legislation Amendment (Telecommunications Offences and Other Measures) Act (No. 2)* 2004 (Cth) introduced measures dealing with such issues as child pornography, child abuse material, sexual predation and dishonesty in relation to dealing in personal financial information and obtaining financial advantage.[1009]

1008. *See* text of the Act at https://www.legislation.gov.au/Details/C2017C00201.
1009. *See* text of the Act at http://classic.austlii.edu.au/au/legis/cth/num_act/claoaoma22004729/.

V. *Crimes Act* 1914 and *Criminal Code Act* 1995

1681. The *Crimes Act* 1914 (Cth) section 474 makes it an offence to do anything with the intention of dishonestly obtaining a gain or causing a loss to a carriage service provider (CSP) in connection with the supply of a carriage service. It is also an offence to knowingly risk such a loss.[1010] An offence of general dishonesty in relation to a CSP is also available.

1682. Under the *Crimes Act* 1914 (Cth) section 474.17 it is a crime to use the Internet or phone in a *menacing, harassing or offensive* way. It is also an offence to use the Internet or phone to threaten to kill or cause serious harm to another person.

1683. The *Criminal Code Act* 1995 (Cth), more specifically Part 10.6, makes it a criminal offence to interfere with telecommunications, including computer services, the Internet and computer systems. The provisions makes it an offence to interfere with email, tamper with data messages, or cause a telecommunications message to be sent to an unauthorized person.[1011] It is also an offence to use a carriage service to menace or harass another person or use a carrier in a way that would be regarded as offensive to a reasonable person.[1012] It is also an offence to tamper with or interfere in any way with a facility operated by a carrier.[1013]

§5. Protection of Minors Online

1684. The protection of minors online is discussed here to highlight the growing awareness of the menace of crimes perpetrated on a vulnerable section of society as well as the proliferation of harms caused by online predators. The different pieces of legislation demonstrate how sexual offences against children, measures for online safety and the scourge of sharing intimate images on social media such as revenge porn is managed. The specific legislation includes:

- *Crimes Legislative Amendments (Sexual Offences Against Children) Act* 2010 (Cth) (SOAC Act)
- *Enhancing Online Safety Act* 2015 (Cth)
- *Criminal Code Amendment (Protection of Minors Online) Act* 2017 (Cth) ('Carly's Law')
- *Enhancing Online Safety (Non-consensual Sharing of Intimate Images) Act* 2018 (Cth) ('Revenge porn law')

1010. *Ibid.* at s. 474.
1011. *Criminal Code Act* 1995 (Cth), s. 85ZD.
1012. *Ibid.* at s. 85ZE.
1013. *Ibid.* at s. 85ZJ.

I. *Crimes Legislation Amendment* 2010

1685. The *Crimes Legislative Amendments (Sexual Offences Against Children) Act* 2010 (Cth) (SOAC) amends the *Crimes Act* (Cth) 1914 and *Criminal Code Act* (Cth) 1995 and consequential amendments to four acts in relation to: child sex tourism offences; and overseas child pornography and child abuse material offences. The amendments to the *Crimes Act* (Cth) 1914 provides for a scheme for the forfeiture of child pornography and child abuse material and items containing such material. The *Criminal Code Act* (Cth) 1995 is amended in relation to child sex offences involving using postal or similar services, or carriage services.[1014]

1686. Section 272.8 of the SOAC is one of Australia's most cited criminal offences with international reach and regulates conduct which occurs beyond Australia's territorial borders. The section criminalizes sexual intercourse with a child under the age of 16 outside of Australia.

II. *Enhancing Online Safety Act* 2015

1687. The *Enhancing Online Safety for Children Act* 2015 (Cth) was introduced to help protect Australian children from cyber abuse and cyberbullying harm. The Office of the Children's eSafety Commissioner was established to take a national leadership role in online safety for children with an eSafety Commissioner to enforce provisions of the Act.

1688. E-safety is understood to be the safe and responsible use of technology. This includes the use of the Internet and other means of electronic communication like social media. In practice, e-safety is as much about behaviour as it is electronic security.

III. *Criminal Code Amendment* 2017 ('Carly's Law')

1689. The *Criminal Code Amendment (Protecting Minors Online) Act* 2017 ('Carly's Law') amends the *Criminal Code Act* 1995 (Cth) to introduce an offence criminalizing acts done using a carriage service to prepare or plan to cause harm to, procure, or engage in sexual activity with, a person under the age of 16. Consequential amendments are also made to the *Crimes Act* 1914 (Cth) and *Telecommunications (Interception and Access) Act* 1979 (Cth).[1015]

1014. *See* Australian Parliament House (APH) https://www.aph.gov.au/Parliamentary_Business/Bills_Legislation/Bills_Search_Results/Result?bId=r4275 and for the text of the legislation at http://classic.austlii.edu.au/au/legis/cth/num_act/claoaca2010544/.

1015. *See* Australian Parliament House (2017) at https://www.aph.gov.au/Parliamentary_Business/Bills_Legislation/Bills_Search_Results/Result?bId=r5857 (22 Jun) and for a text of the Act at http://classic.austlii.edu.au/au/legis/cth/num_act/ccamoa2017457/sch1.html. *See also* Sutton, M &

1690. The Act enables authorities to prosecute those lying about their age to minors online and intervene before a predator can act. Popularized as 'Carly's Law', the legislation targets online predators preparing or planning to cause harm to, procure, or engage in sexual activity with a child and those who misrepresent their age, with offenders facing ten years' imprisonment. The legislation follows a decade-long campaign by Sonya Ryan, whose fifteen-year-old daughter, Carly, was murdered in 2007 by a man posing as a teenager online.[1016]

1691. The Act amended the *Criminal Code Act* 1995 (Cth) inserts a new offence at section 474.25C 'using a carriage service to prepare or plan to cause harm to, engage in sexual activity with, or procure for sexual activity, persons under 16'. The new offence carries a penalty of imprisonment for up to ten years.

1692. The existing section 474.25 of the *Criminal Code Act* 1995 (Cth) requires an Internet service provider or content host to refer details of child abuse material to the Australian Federal Police, where it becomes aware that the service can be used to access that material.

§6. *Enhancing Online Safety Act* 2018 ('Revenge porn law')

1693. This Act amends the *Enhancing Online Safety Act (Non-consensual Sharing of Intimate Images) Act* 2015 (Cth) ('Revenge porn law') prohibits the posting of, or threatening to post, an intimate image without consent on a social media service, relevant electronic service or a designated Internet service.[1017] The Act also establishes a complaints and objections system to be administered by the eSafety Commissioner and provides the Commissioner with powers to issue removal notices or remedial directions. A civil penalty regime is established and administered by the Commissioner. This will enable the Commissioner to seek a civil penalty order from a relevant court, issue an infringement notice, obtain an injunction or enforce an undertaking, or issue a formal warning for contraventions of the civil penalty provisions. Consequential amendments are also made to the relevant sections of the *Broadcasting Services Act* 1992 (Cth).

1694. The new law labelled locally as 'revenge porn' legislation Sched. 1 section 3 puts in place a complaints and objections system for non-consensual sharing

---

Winter, C (2017) Carly's Law introduced to Federal Parliament to protect minors from online predators at https://www.abc.net.au/news/2017-03-30/carlys-law-introduced-to-protect-minors-from-predators/8400780.

1016. *See* ABC News (2017) 'Carly's Law report: Adelaide man facing child exploitation charges' at https://www.abc.net.au/news/2017-08-09/carlys-law-adelaide-man-charged-with-child-exploitation/8788524. *See* an early case report by Miletic, D (2006) 'Groomer' guilty of procuring girl, 14, for sex at https://www.theage.com.au/national/groomer-guilty-of-procuring-girl-14-for-sex-20060526-ge2e52.html.

1017. *See* Australian Parliament House (2018) at https://www.aph.gov.au/Parliamentary_Business/Bills_Legislation/Bills_Search_Results/Result?bId=s1113 (31 Aug) and text of the Act at http://classic.austlii.edu.au/au/legis/cth/num_act/eossoiia2018592/.

of intimate images and the service of a notice to service providers, end users and host servers to remove an intimate image from a website. Non-compliance with the removal notice will incur a civil penalty of 500 penalty units (AUD 105,000) (Sched. 1 Div. 2 section 44B).

1695. The amendments to the *Criminal Code Act* 1995 (Cth) introduces a definition of 'private sexual material' (section 473.1) and create two new aggravated offences (section 474.17A):

1. a standard aggravated offence for or the use of a carriage service to menace, harass or cause offence via transmission, making available, publication, distribution, advertisement or promotion of private sexual material; and,
2. a special aggravated offence if the above offence is committed and three or more civil penalty orders have already been made against the person.

1696. Consent must be considered when determining offensiveness. These new Criminal Code offences will not apply to a carrier, carriage service provider, Internet service provider or Internet content host. However, those entities will be required to comply with removal notices and take all reasonable steps to ensure the removal of the intimate image within forty-eight hours or face a civil fine of AUD 80,595 and potentially receive a formal warning from the eSafety Commissioner (Sched. 1 Div. 2 section 44C).

1697. Service providers are required to respond promptly to any removal notices they receive in relation to intimate images, and closely monitor their websites for potentially criminal or prohibited activity.

§7. *Criminal Code Amendment Act* 2019 (SAVM Act)

1698. The *Criminal Code Amendment (Sharing of Abhorrent Violent Material) Act* 2019 (Cth) (SAVM Act) amends the *Criminal Code Act* 1995 to introduce new offences that will apply to providers of Internet, hosting or content services.[1018] Such providers must refer details of abhorrent violent material that records or streams conduct that has occurred, or is occurring, in Australia to the AFP.[1019] This referral must be done within a reasonable time after becoming aware of the existence of such material. They are required to remove from, or cease hosting, on their services abhorrent violent material that is capable of being accessed within Australia. The referrals to the AFP will enable the eSafety Commissioner to issue a written notice to a provider of a hosting or content service notifying them that abhorrent violent material can be accessed by, or is hosted on, their service.

1018. Inserted at the end of Division 474 of the *Criminal Code Act* 1995 Subdivision H—Offences relating to use of carriage service for sharing of abhorrent violent material has been added. *See* the text of the Act at https://www.legislation.gov.au/Details/C2019A00038.

1019. *Criminal Code* s. 474.25.

1699. The Act also provides the eSafety Commissioner the power to notify service providers that abhorrent violent material is available on their services. These notices create a presumption that the provider is aware of the material and puts providers on notice that such material should be removed (section 474.35, and section 474.36 respectively).

1700. The new offences apply to any content reasonably capable of being accessed within Australia regardless of where the platform or website operator is located.

1701. The maximum penalties for failing to remove abhorrent violent material include fines of up to 10 per cent of annual group turnover for corporations and imprisonment for up to three years for individual employees that fail to remove or refer content.

1702. This Act was introduced in the wake of the March 2019 Christchurch terrorist attack to create new offences under the *Criminal Code Act* 1995 (Cth) that would require social media platforms and other websites and providers to expeditiously remove abhorrent violent material and refer such material to the Australian Federal Police (AFP).

1703. The Act complements the existing takedown and referral procedures for online content under Schedules 5 and 7 of the *Broadcasting Services Act* 1992 (Cth).

§8. *Criminal Code Amendment* Act 2005

1704. The *Criminal Code Amendment (Suicide Related Material Offences) Act* 2005 (Cth) makes it illegal to use a carriage service to access, transmit or otherwise make available suicide related material, and possession, production, supplying or obtaining suicide related material for use through a carriage service.[1020]

1705. The Act introduces new offences of using a 'carriage service' that includes the Internet, emails, mobile and fixed telephones, faxes, radio and TV; for the purposes of counselling or inciting suicide or promoting or providing instruction on a particular method of suicide. Possession or supply of material that is intended to be used for such offences is also itself an offence.

1706. The Act amends the *Criminal Code Act* 1995 (Cth) by adding Schedule 1 – Suicide related material offences and two sections to the Criminal Code, namely: section 474.29A using a carriage service for suicide related material; and section 474.29B possessing, controlling, producing, supplying or obtaining suicide related material for use through a carriage service.[1021]

1020. *See* text of the *Criminal Code Amendment (Suicide Related Material Offences) Act* 2005 (Cth) at http://www.comlaw.gov.au/Details/C2005A00092.

1021. *See* text of the Act at https://www.legislation.gov.au/Details/C2005A00092.

§9. *Anti-Money Laundering and Counter-Terrorism Financing Act* 2006

1707. The *Anti-Money Laundering and Counter-Terrorism Financing Act* 2006 (Cth) (AML/CTF Act), and the Anti-Money Laundering and Counter-Terrorism Financing Rules (AML/CTF Rules)[1022] aim to prevent money laundering and the financing of terrorism by imposing a number of obligations on the financial sector, gambling sector, remittance (money transfer) services, bullion dealers and other professionals or businesses (known as 'reporting entities') that provide particular services (known as 'designated services'). These obligations include collecting and verifying certain 'know your customer' (KYC) information about a customer's identity when providing those services.[1023]

1708. Division 5A of Part 2 of the AML/CTF Act authorizes the use and disclosure of certain personal information held by a credit reporting body (CRB) to a reporting entity for the purpose of verifying the individual's identity under the AML/CTF Act.

1709. Under the AML/CTF under the relevant sections that characterize offences are:

- section 137 to provide false or misleading documents; punishable by a maximum of ten years imprisonment or 10,000 penalty units, or both.
- section 138(1) for a person to make a false document with the intention that the person or another will produce the false document during an applicable customer identification procedure and the applicable customer identification procedure is under this Act; punishable by a maximum of ten years imprisonment or 10,000 penalty units, or both.
- section 138(3) for a person to knowingly possess a false document with the intention that the person or another will produce it during an applicable customer identification procedure; and the applicable customer identification procedure is under this Act; punishable by a maximum of ten years imprisonment or 10,000 penalty units, or both.
- section 138(5) for a person to possess equipment for making a false document knowing that a device, material or other thing is designed or adapted for the making of a false document (whether or not the device, material or thing is designed or adapted for another purpose); and has the device, material or thing in his or her possession with the intention that the person or another person will use it to commit an offence against section 138(1); punishable by a maximum of ten years imprisonment or 10,000 penalty units, or both.
- section 138(6) for a person to make or adapt a device, material or other thing; and knows that the device, material or other thing is designed or adapted for the

1022. *See* text of the Act at https://www.legislation.gov.au/Details/C2021C00243 and Rules at https://www.legislation.gov.au/Series/F2007L01000.

1023. In 2020, the Federal Court imposed a AUD 1.3 billion penalty on Westpac for 23 million alleged contraventions of AML/CTF programme compliance and transaction reporting obligations under the AML/CTF Act. *See* https://www.austrac.gov.au/news-and-media/our-recent-work/westpac-penalty-ordered.

making of a false document (whether or not the device, material or thing is designed or adapted for another purpose); and makes or adapts the device, material or thing with the intention that the person or another person will use it to commit an offence against section 138(1); punishable by a maximum of ten years imprisonment or 10,000 penalty units, or both.

1710. The AML/CTF Act works alongside the asset recovery provisions contained in the *Proceeds of Crime Act* 2002 (Cth) (POC Act) that enables law enforcement agencies to pursue the recovery of assets linked to offences after a conviction. Similar legislation is found in Australian state and territory for funds generated by criminal offences in the respective jurisdictions.[1024]

1711. The *Financial Transaction Reports Act* 1988 (Cth) (FTR Act) operates alongside the AML/CTF Act. The FTR Act imposes obligations on cash dealers and solicitors to report significant cash transactions of more than AUD 10,000 to the Australian Transaction Reports and Analysis Centre (AUSTRAC).

§10. Anti-Discrimination Laws

1712. Issues relating to online content can be the basis for complaints to the Australian Human Rights Commission under federal anti-discrimination law.[1025] For example, online content that is alleged to constitute sexual harassment or racial vilification or ageism are proscribed behaviour in the following Commonwealth and parallel State and Territory legislations:

- *Racial Discrimination Act* 1975 (Cth)
- *Sex Discrimination Act* 1984 (Cth)
- *Age Discrimination Act* 2004 (Cth)

1024. For example, NSW *Confiscation of Proceeds of Crime Act* 1989 No 90 (NSW) at https://legislation.nsw.gov.au/view/html/inforce/current/act-1989-090; Queensland's *Criminal Proceeds Confiscation Act* 2002 (Qld) (CPCA) at https://www.legislation.qld.gov.au/view/html/inforce/current/act-2002-068; and, Western Australia *Criminal Property Confiscation Act* 2000 (WA)at https://www.legislation.wa.gov.au/legislation/prod/filestore.nsf/FileURL/mrdoc_25306.pdf/$FILE/Criminal%20Property%20Confiscation%20Act%202000%20-%20%5B03-d0-03%5D.pdf?OpenElement.

1025. *See* the text of the respective Acts at the following: *Racial Discrimination Act* 1975 (Cth) at https://www.comlaw.gov.au/Details/C2014C00014, *Sex Discrimination Act* 1984 (Cth) at https://www.comlaw.gov.au/Details/C2014C00002; and *Age Discrimination Act* 2004 (Cth) at https://www.comlaw.gov.au/Details/C2014C00435.

Chapter 3. State and Territory Cybercrime Laws

1713. The discussion here is highly selective if only because national a model cyber law has been proclaimed and applicable for all States and Territories. This discussion highlights those state laws that may be different and unique from the national model law. Like the Commonwealth, most of the Australian States and Territories have specific computer crime legislation.[1026]

§1. NSW Model Criminal Code 2001

1714. NSW has legislation based on the Model Criminal Code Project with the *Crimes Amendment (Computer Offences) Act* 2001 (NSW). The Act seeks to address three categories of activity:

1. intentional and unauthorized access or modification of computer data, or impairment of electronic communication to or from a computer, irrespective of whether there is any intention to commit a serious indictable offence;
2. processing, producing, supplying, or obtaining data with intent to commit computer offences; and,
3. intentional and unauthorized access or modification of restricted computer data, impairment of data held in computer disk, credit card or other data storage devices.[1027]

§2. Queensland Criminal Code 2007

1715. Queensland has adopted a broad definition of cybercrime in the *Criminal Code and Civil Liability Amendment Act* 2007 (Qld). This broad wording arguably includes all crimes under Commonwealth legislation and is designed so that it is technologically neutral; and, less likely to require regular updating given the rapid changes in technology.

1716. Section 408E of the Queensland Act defines *computer hacking and misuse* as the act of a person who uses a restricted computer without the consent of the computer's controller to commit an offence. The maximum penalty is two years imprisonment. The element of the offence includes:

- if the person causes or intends to cause detriment or damage, or gains or intends to gain a benefit, the person commits a crime and is liable to imprisonment for five years;

1026. *See Crimes Act* 1958 (Vic), s. 197; *Crimes Act* 1990 (NSW), ss 194, 201; *Criminal Code* 1913 (WA) ss 441-443, 455; *Criminal Code* (Tas), ss 267-269.

1027. The New South Wales Act has similarities with the UK's *Computer Misuse Act* 1990 at https://www.legislation.gov.uk/id/ukpga/1990/18.

- if the person causes a detriment or damage or obtains a benefit for any person to the value of more than AUD 5,000, or intends to commit an indictable offence, the person commits a crime and is liable to imprisonment for ten years; and,
- a defence to a charge under this section to prove that the use of the restricted computer was authorized, justified, or excused by law.

1717. The Queensland legislation was also amended (section 408D) to make it easier to deal with identity theft. Section 408D of the *Criminal Code Act* 1899 (Qld) makes it an offence to obtain or deal with another entity's identification information for the purpose of committing, or facilitating the commission of, an indictable offence; punishable by a maximum of three years imprisonment.

§3. South Australia *Criminal Law Consolidation Act* 1935

1718. The *Criminal Law Consolidation Act* 1935 (SA)[1028] was amended and consolidated with reference to cybercrime offences namely Part 3, Part 4A and Part 5A. A summary of these is given in the list below:

1719. Part 3 Offences against the person etc.:

- Division 11 A Child exploitation material and related offences.

1720. Part 4A Computer offences:

- section 86C meaning of unauthorized access to or modification of computer data;
- section 86D meaning of unauthorized impairment of electronic communication;
- section 86E use of computer with intention to commit, or facilitate the commission of, an offence;
- section 86F use of computer to commit, or facilitate the commission of, an offence outside the State;
- section 86G unauthorized modification of computer data;
- section 86H unauthorized impairment of electronic communication; and,
- section 86I possession of computer viruses, etc. with intent to commit serious computer offence.

1721. Part 5A Identity theft

- section 144A interpretation;
- section 144B false identity etc.;
- section 144C misuse of personal identification information;
- section 144D prohibited material; and,
- section 144E attempt offence excluded.

1028. *See* text of the Act at https://www.legislation.sa.gov.au/LZ/C/A/CRIMINAL%20LAW%20CONSOLIDATION%20ACT%201935/CURRENT/1935.2252.AUTH.PDF.

§4. Tasmania *Criminal Code Act* 1924

1722. The *Criminal Code Act* 1924 (Tas) has a whole chapter on crimes relating to computer – Chapter XXVIIIA. The following sections refer to:

- section 257B computer-related fraud;
- section 257C damaging computer data;
- section 257D unauthorized access to a computer;
- section 257E insertion of false information as data; and
- section 257F extraterritorial application of this Chapter.

§5. Deception of Person or Machine

1723. In general most Australian jurisdictions have criminal provisions governing fraud that covers both deception in relation to a person and deception of a computer or machine leading to falsification of computer-stored data, credit cards and ATM cards.[1029] Similarly, the provisions dealing with falsification of documents, which previously applied only to written documents, now cover electronic documents such as data stored on a computer or ATM card.[1030] The criminal laws in most jurisdictions have also been amended to include unlawful access to a computer and hacking. In addition, traditional criminal laws dealing with theft, forgery, trespass and burglary may also be applied to cybercrime contexts.[1031]

1029. *See Crimes Act* 1958 (Vic), s. 81(4); *Criminal Code Act* 1924 (Tas), s. 257B.
1030. *See Crimes Act* 1914 (Cth); *Crimes Act* 1958 (Vic), s. 83A; *Criminal Code* 1913 (WA), s. 443.
1031. *See Criminal Code* 1913 (WA), s. 473, in which 'forgery' is defined in such a way that it would cover alteration of computer records.

Chapter 4. Computer and Systems as a Target

1724. Reference is made here to the diagram on cybercrime presented earlier. The focus is directed to the right-hand side of the diagram where two main pillars or parts are labelled 'computer as target' (in this Chapter 4) and 'computer as tool or attack vector' (in the next Chapter 5). From these two pillars are numbered stems to refer to specific items of the cybercrime under discussion. Letters in bold denote detailed content discussion whereas labels in regular print denote a short discussion in passing.

§1. Criminal Misuse of the Domain Names System

1725. Krone & Smith (2020) have reported on an analysis of the criminal misuse of the domain name system (DNS).[1032] The DNS' primary purpose is to permit machines to use the Internet addressing system to make connections between resources. The misuse of the DNS was examined first where the DNS itself is the target of misuse through software engineering: as a mechanism to do harm; a vector to transmit harm; or a platform from which to commit harm. Second, the study analyses human users where the misuse is directed at the manipulation of people through social engineering methods.

1726. The malicious or criminal exploitation of the DNS ranges from the stealing a domain name to registering domain names for phishing attacks. Such attacks may also include gaining access of compromised computers and using botnets to launch other attacks, impersonation of legitimate domain names and using domain names to hide illegal behaviour or evade jurisdiction.[1033]

1727. Prosecuting criminal misuse of the DNS poses several problems including obtaining material evidence, issues of jurisdiction stemming from the borderless Internet, identification of suspects and the process of litigation procedures.

§2. Unauthorized Access: Hacking and Cracking

1728. In general, the terms hacking, and cracking have been used to as alternates to 'unauthorized access' to computer systems. Either term can be used to describe an activity that involves attempts to gain access to computer systems to steal, modify or damage the data in the systems. However, a more accurate description is that cracking techniques are used with malicious intent either to breach

1032. Krone, T & Smith RG (2020) *Criminal misuse of the Domain Name System,* AIC Research Report 03 at https://www.aic.gov.au/sites/default/files/2020-05/research_report_03.pdf.
1033. *Ibid.* Krone & Smith (2020).

computer software or an entire computer security system. Though functionally the same as hacking, cracking strictly has criminal connotations.[1034]

1729. Sometimes hacking is used to test the security of a computer software or system. Such exploits test whether layers of electronic and sometimes physical security layers may be circumvented to gain access to the computer systems. Also known as 'white-hat hackers' or 'ethical hackers' these computer security experts have been employed to undertake the testing. The lessons derived from these tests are then used to 'patch' systems so that criminal intruders may be thwarted because the system builders are already aware of these vulnerabilities and have put in place preventative measures.

1730. Hacking can be typified as 'juvenile delinquency' where underaged children misuse their talents to get unauthorized access to websites. Apparently, these 'show-off' hacks are for no other reason than to demonstrate the vulnerabilities of websites and not committed for financial or other benefit.[1035]

1731. Whether a hack is authorized or not may be determinative of whether the act is a criminal in nature. Such a determination requires information of whether a computer owner has any data access policy; whether and how that policy is communicated to others; how accessible a computer is; and, how accessible the files, directories and other information on that computer are.

1732. Further layers to these complexities are the questions of contractual or moral rights, of implied consent, or the limits of a consent once given.

1733. Australian anti-computer hacking laws are concerned with computer security *per se,* that is, authorized access to the computer, rather than other issues such as privacy and the confidentiality of information.

1734. Unauthorized access to computer and the systems it is connected to give rise to different types of criminal liability. These types are dependent on an accused's intention or how access to the data has been secured.

1735. The four levels of such unauthorized access are:

1. accessing data or impairing an electronic communication with the intention to commit a serious offence;
2. impairing or modifying data or impairing electronic communications if done with the intent to cause or with recklessness to harm or inconvenience;

1034. Alleyne, B (2018) Computer hacking as a social problem, *Cambridge Encyclopedia of Social Problems* at https://research.gold.ac.uk/22394/1/Alleyne%20Hacking_Cambridge%20Encycl%20% 20ACCEPTED.pdf.
1035. *Supra,* Krone & Smith (2020) p. 52.

3. possession, control, production, or supply of data with the intent to commit any of the above offences; recklessness is insufficient; and,
4. accessing data that is subject to an access control restriction.

1736. The *Cybercrime Act* 2001 (Cth) Schedule 1 Part 10.7 criminalizes unauthorized access to data where there is an intent to commit a crime which also includes the modification or impairment of data if accompanied by an intention to cause harm or inconvenience. Other offences under the Commonwealth model are based on breach of access restrictions in relation to data.

1737. Australian anti-hacking laws require an intent to commit a serious offence, or cause harm or inconvenience. Such requirements raise a high barrier for the successful prosecution to evidence that a specific hacking incident is a criminal act such as recklessness as to harm or inconvenience caused by hacking. This criterion necessarily requires the standard of reasonably foreseeable consequences.[1036]

1738. As a general observation all states and territories have laws against simple unauthorized access to or modifying data,[1037] only the Northern Territory, Queensland, Tasmania and Western Australia specifically mention access or modification to gain a pecuniary benefit.[1038] Tasmanian law may be described as a truly cybercrime law specifically targeting computer-related fraud.[1039]

1739. In NSW it is a crime under section 308H of the *Crimes Act* 1900 (NSW) to access or modify restricted data held in a computer with knowledge that such access or modification is unauthorized. An example is logging into another person's online accounts without their permission. The offence attracts a maximum penalty of two years imprisonment.

1740. Western Australia, Queensland and Tasmania, however, have quite different characterizations to regulate unauthorized access offences described below.

I. Western Australia *Criminal Code* 1913

1741. In Western Australia, section 440A of the *Criminal Code* 1913 (WA) was amended in 1990 under the section on 'unlawful operation of a computer

---

1036. *See* Krone, T (2005) Hacking offences, High tech crime brief No. 5 Canberra: Australian Institute of Criminology at https://aic.gov.au/publications/htcb/htcb005; and Krone T (2005) Hacking motives High tech crime brief No. 6 Canberra: Australian Institute of Criminology at https://aic.gov.au/publications/htcb/htcb006.Krone (2005).

1037. *Criminal Code* 2002 (ACT) Pt 4.2; *Crimes Act* 1900 (NSW) Pt 6; *Criminal Code Act* 2009 (NT) Sch 1 Pt VII Div 10; *Criminal Code Act 1899* (Qld) Sch 1 s. 408E; *Criminal Law Consolidation Act* 1935 (SA) Pt 4A; *Criminal Code Act* 1924 (Tas) Sch 1 Ch XXVIIIA; *Crimes Act* 1958 (Vic) Pt 1 Div 3(6); *Criminal Code Act* 1913 (WA) s. 440A.

1038. *Criminal Code Act* 2009 (NT) Sch 1 s. 276B; *Criminal Code Act* 1899 (Qld) Sch 1 s. 408E; *Criminal Code Act* 1924 (Tas) Sch 1 s. 257B; and, *Criminal Code Act* 1913 (WA) Sch s. 440A(3).

1039. *Criminal Code Act* 1924 (Tas) Sch. 1 s.2 57B computer-related fraud.

system'.[1040] The section refers to a person who 'without authorization' accesses 'information stored in a restricted access system' or who 'operates' such a system 'in some other way'. A restricted access system is defined as a computer system or a part or application of a computer system that is accessible only by using a code that is held by the person in control of the computer system or made available on a restricted basis. This provision is particularly applicable where someone hacks a computer from outside the system. However, it introduces considerable difficulties in determining when initially authorized access becomes unauthorized either by exceeding initial permissions or by the subsequent use of data or information accessed.

II. Queensland *Criminal Code* 1997

1742. The Queensland *Criminal Code* 1899 (Qld) amended in 1997 defines 'computer hacking and misuse' as the use of a restricted computer without the consent of the computer's controller.[1041] A restricted computer is defined as one that requires a 'device, code, or sequence of electronic impulses' to gain access. There is a penalty scale of two to ten years maximum term of imprisonment depending on whether: an offender simply uses a computer; causes detriment or damage, or gains or intends to gain a benefit; or the detriment, damage or gain is valued at more than AUD 5,000.

III. Tasmania *Criminal Code Act* 1924

1743. Section 257C of the *Criminal Code Act* 1924 (Tas) requires intention and a lack of 'lawful excuse', in relation to damaging (or destroying, erasing, or altering) computer data or simply accessing a computer or system of computers without authority. However, 'lawful excuse' is undefined.[1042] Unauthorized access is proscribed under section 257D of the *Criminal Code Act* 1924 (Tas).

§3. Distributed Denial of Service (DDOS) attack

1744. The *Criminal Code Act* 1995 (Cth) section 474.14 creates an offence of using a telecommunications network (such as the Internet) with intention to commit a serious offence.

1040. *See* WA *Criminal Code* 1913 (WA) at https://www.legislation.wa.gov.au/legislation/statutes.nsf/main_mrtitle_218_homepage.html.
1041. Queensland *Criminal Code* 1899 (Qld) s. 408E. Computer hacking and misuse at http://www5.austlii.edu.au/au/legis/qld/consol_act/cc189994/s408e.html.
1042. *Criminal Code Act* 1924 (Tas) at https://www.legislation.tas.gov.au/view/html/inforce/current/act-1924-069.

1745. Section 477.3 of the Act criminalizes DDOS typified for the offence of 'unauthorized impairment of electronic communication'. The maximum penalty for contravention of the *Code* is ten years imprisonment.

§4. Infecting IT Systems with malware

1746. Malware infections include ransomware, spyware, worms, botnets and viruses. The act of inserting infections is criminalized under section 478.2 of the *Criminal Code Act* 1995 (Cth) for the offence of 'unauthorized impairment of data held on a computer'. The maximum penalty is two years imprisonment. A state-based offence of this nature is within the 'modification or impairment' aspects of the *Crimes Act* 1900 (NSW) section 308H.

1747. The use of botnets to disseminate spyware may be breach of the relevant sections in the *Privacy Act* 1988 (Cth),[1043] Part 13 of the *Telecommunications Act* 1997 (Cth), and the *Surveillance Devices Act* 2004 (Cth).[1044] Such malware may aim primarily to harvest personal financial information and is collected without the victims' consent.

1748. The *Surveillance Devices Act* 2004 (Cth) is a legislative regime that consists of a combination of state and Commonwealth legislation and common law principles relating to the use of surveillance devices. The Act is broadly based on model surveillance device laws developed in 2003 by the Standing Committee of Attorneys-General and Australasian Police Ministers Council Joint Working Group on National Investigation Powers. The Working Group proposed the adoption of model laws both at the state and federal levels to regulate the use of surveillance devices by law enforcement agencies.

§5. Hardware or Software Tools to Commit Cybercrime

1749. Possession or use of hardware, software or other tools used to commit cybercrime is criminalized by section 478.3 of the *Criminal Code Act* 1995 (Cth), which provides for the offence of possession or control of data with intent to commit a computer offence.

1750. The *Criminal Code Act* 1995 (Cth) section 478.4 prohibits the producing, supplying or obtaining data with intent to commit a computer offence. The offence comprises two elements where a person produces, supplies or obtains data; and the person does so with the intention that the data be used, by the person or another person, in committing an offence against Division 477 Serious computer offences of

---

1043. *See Privacy Act* 1988 (Cth) Part IIIA Credit Reporting Division 6 Unauthorized obtaining of credit reporting information.

1044. *See* text of the Act at https://www.legislation.gov.au/Series/C2004A01387.

Criminal Code Act 1995 (Cth) or facilitating the commission of such an offence. The maximum penalty for a contravention of section 478.4 of *Criminal Code Act* 1995 (Cth) is three years' imprisonment.

1751. An example of a state equivalent can be found in the *Crimes Act* 1900 (NSW) sections 308F and 308G.

§6. Unsolicited Penetration Testing

1752. Penetrating an IT system without the permission of its owner to determine its vulnerabilities and weak points is an offence under the section 478.1 of the *Criminal Code Act* 1995 (Cth). The offence is one of 'unauthorized access to, or modification of restricted data'.

1753. There are presently no laws in Australia which prohibit the use of a 'beacon' or near field communication (NFC) technology, honeypots or sinkholes.

1754. Beacons are remotely hosted graphics inserted into content that trigger a contact with a remote server to reveal the IP address of a computer that is viewing such content.

1755. Honeypots are digital traps designed to trick cyber threat actors into acting against a synthetic network, thereby allowing an organization to detect and counteract attempts to attack its network without causing any damage to the organization's real network or data.

1756. Sinkholes can be measures to redirect malicious traffic away from an organization's own IP addresses and servers, commonly used to prevent DDoS attacks. Sinkhole methods to steer legitimate traffic away from its intended recipient may, however, constitute an offence under section 477.3 of the *Criminal Code Act* 1995 (Cth). It appears that sinkholes can be lawfully used as a defensive practice for research and in reaction to cyberattacks.

§7. Identity Theft or Identity Fraud

1757. Identity fraud offences are criminalized by Division 372 Identity fraud offences of the *Criminal Code Act* 1995 (Cth). The crimes include dealing with identity information, using a carriage service to commit identity information theft, possession of identity information and equipment to steal identity information. An example is the so-called catfishing – pretending one is someone else online to develop a virtual relationship with an unsuspecting stranger and doing so with malicious intent.

1758. Section 372.1A of the *Criminal Code Act* 1995 (Cth) refers to dealing in identification information that involves use of a carriage service. The maximum penalty is five years imprisonment.

Chapter 5. Computer and Systems as a Tool and Attack Vector

1759. The six sections of this chapter discuss the use of the computer and systems as a tool and attack vector as illustrated in Figure 7. Topics shown in bold lettering on the figure denote a detailed discussion of the topic whereas those in normal type means that the topic is discussed cursorily.

§1. Online Fraud: Phishing

1760. Phishing is a form of online fraud proscribed under Commonwealth or State and Territory legislations. The relevant sections under the *Criminal Code Act* 1995 (Cth) are:

- section 134.2(1) – obtaining a financial advantage by deception;
- section 135.1(1) – general dishonesty and obtaining a gain;
- section 135.1(3) – general dishonesty by causing a loss; and,
- section 135.1(5) – general dishonesty by causing a loss to another.

1761. The prosecution must establish that the accused obtains or causes a financial advantage, gain or loss by way of deception or dishonesty. The maximum penalty for each offence is ten years imprisonment.

1762. Charges of online fraud may also be brought under parallel state or territory legislation. In NSW Div 2E Fraud and related offences section 192E of the *Crimes Act* 1900 (NSW) provides for the general offence of fraud.

1763. Online fraud generally covers forgeries, deception and dishonesty. Phishing scams include keylogging where criminals monitor through software the keystrokes on compromised computer keyboards to record sensitive financial information being typed. Spear phishing involves targeting specific individuals in an organization with an email and attachment. The aim is to socially engineer a target's activities to disclose confidential company information. In a phishing scam the attack is directed at everyone on an address list.

§2. Electronic Theft

1764. Electronic theft of data, information and documents may be characterized as a breach of confidence by a current or former employee or as criminal intellectual property infringement proscribed by section 478.1 of the *Criminal Code Act* 1995 (Cth). Under this section an offence is committed if a person modifies restricted data. Modification is defined as the alteration or removal of the data held in a computer, or the unauthorized copying of data from a computer.

§3. Offensive Content and Revenge Porn

1765. Victims of image-based abuse, more commonly named as 'revenge porn', is based on the notion that the perpetrators are people who have been jilted by their partners share graphic images of their 'exes' as a form of retaliation. Such sharing of images is without the knowledge and consent of the victim.

1766. Enhancing Online Safety (Non-consensual Sharing of Intimate Images) Act 2018 (Cth) criminalizes revenge porn.[1045] This Act amends the *Enhancing Online Safety Act* 2015 (Cth). The Act prohibits the posting of, or threatening to post, an intimate image without consent on a social media service, relevant electronic service or a designated Internet service. The Act also establishes a complaints and objections system to be administered by the eSafety Commissioner and provides the Commissioner with powers to issue removal notices or remedial directions. Civil penalties are administered by the Commissioner and enables the Commissioner to seek civil penalty orders from a relevant court. Relevant sections of the *Enhancing Online Safety Act* 2018 (Cth) include:

- section 9B Intimate image;
- section 9E Consent;
- section 19A Complaints;
- section 19B Objection notice;
- section 44B Posting an intimate image;
- section 44D and 44E Removal notice given to the provider of a social media service, relevant electronic service or designated Internet service or to an end user;
- section 44 F Notice to take reasonable steps to cease the hosting of the image; and,
- section 44G Compliance with removal notice.

§4. Sexting

1767. According to Svantesson (2010) sexting is the electronic communication of non-professional images or videos portraying one or more persons in a state of nudity or otherwise in a sexual manner.[1046] Where the content portrays a person who is underaged, the sender, receiver and any intermediary involved in the communication may be charged with child pornography offences under Australian criminal law. Using a carriage service, such as an Internet chat room or using a mobile phone text message, to transmit communications to an underaged person with the intention of procuring that person to engage in sexual activity, is contrary to section 474.26(1) of the *Criminal Code Act* 1995 (Cth).

1045. *See* text of the Act at http://classic.austlii.edu.au/au/legis/cth/num_act/eossoiia2018592/.
1046. Svantesson, D (2010) "Sexting' and The Law - How Australia Regulates Electronic Communication of Non-Professional Sexual Content," *Bond Law Review*: Vol. 22: Iss. 2, Article 3 at http://epublications.bond.edu.au/blr/vol22/iss2/3.

1768. In criminal law that affects sexting, child pornography has by far captured the most attention in prosecutions, in academic debate and media attention. Svantesson (2010) cites examples of criminal law legislation that could arguably be applied to successful sexting criminal prosecution:

- section 474.27A *Crimes Legislation Amendment (Sexual Offences Against Children Act* 2010 (Cth) relating to using a carriage service to transmit indecent communication to person under 16 years of age;
- section 91H(2) *Crimes Act* 1900 (NSW) relating to the production, dissemination or possession of child abuse material; and,
- section 210 *Criminal Code* 1899 (Qld) relating to the indecent treatment of children under the age of 16.

1769. Online sexual predators have been known to make use of chat rooms to prey on unwary children.[1047]

1770. Other actions to prosecute sexting under civil law include defamation, privacy law, surveillance law, nuisance and confidentiality. The regulations are a complex matrix of overlapping state, federal, civil and criminal lawmaking '… the regulation of sexting … haphazard, and in large parts coincidental'.[1048]

1771. Perversely, in a recent study it was found that a preponderance of cases the sexting among teenagers were consensual and with minimal criminality involved.[1049]

§5. Online Sabotage

1772. Online sabotage may happen advertently or otherwise. A form of 'censorship' may be taking place when an agency is able to block certain websites because the content or media on it may be offensive. The agency could use a border gateway protocol (BGP) injection by changing the Internet routing information for that website so that requests would go to the agency's servers.[1050] The changed information will also be sent to the agency's own Internet provider which would then

1047. *See R v. Kennings* [2004] QCA 162 where an offender in a chat room sent emails to an underaged girl for sexual activity. *See also* Miletic, D (2006) 'Groomer' guilty of procuring girl, 14, for sex at https://www.theage.com.au/national/groomer-guilty-of-procuring-girl-14-for-sex-20060526-ge2e52.html and ABC News (2006) Man jailed for pursuing girl online, (21 July) at http://www.abc.net.au/news/2006-07-21/man-jailed-for-pursuing-girl-online/1807308.

1048. *Supra,* Svantesson 2010 p. 57.

1049. Lee M *et al.* (2015) Sexting among young people: Perceptions and practices, *Trends & Issues in Crime and Criminal Justice* no. 508, Canberra: Australian Institute of Criminology, at https://www.aic.gov.au/publications/tandi/tandi508.

1050. Border Gateway Protocol (BGP) is the protocol underlying the global routing system of the Internet. It manages how packets get routed from network to network through the exchange of routing and reachability information among edge routers. *See* a definition at https://www.techtarget.com/searchnetworking/definition/BGP-Border-Gateway-Protocol.

pass it along to the rest of the world. In an instance the website has been sabotaged online and would have disappeared for nearly everyone.

1773. Some BGP injections take place by accident either because spammers have hijacked the domain name address or have set up a fake domain name address. It could also be the work of *agents provocateurs* who inhabit the Internet to spread disharmony among online activists of all persuasions. Such attacks may also be described either as cyberwarfare or cyberwar.[1051]

1774. The security layered onto the Internet by large network providers runs on pure trust. When a provider sends out routing information to others, it is presumed to be correct and accurate. Because of this trust mechanism, some domain names may be hijacked, accidentally or intentionally, at almost any time.

1775. The consequences of these activities are that customer proprietary information may be sent to the hijackers; supply chains may be disrupted; and software-as-a-service applications may go awry.

1776. Online sabotage may arguably be pursued for criminality under the relevant legislations and model provisions in all jurisdictions in Australia. Offences under the *Criminal Code Act* 1995 (Cth) and the *Telecommunications (Interception and Access) Act* 1979 (Cth) cover crimes directed at computers and ICTs, such as sending out spam, unauthorized access to computers and distributed denial of service attacks. The *Spam Act* 2003 (Cth) regulates commercial email.[1052] The Act restricts email spam and some types of phone spam, as well as email address harvesting.[1053]

§6. Information Warfare

1777. Information warfare in a military context is described by Australia's Department of Defence as: '[t]he contest for the provision and assurance of information to support friendly decision-making, whilst denying and degrading that of adversaries'.[1054]

1051. *See* Broadhurst R & Trivedi H (2020) Malware in spam email: Risks and trends in the Australian Spam Intelligence Database, *Trends & Issues in Crime and Criminal Justice* no. 603, Canberra: Australian Institute of Criminology at https://doi.org/10.52922/ti04657; and Alazab M & Broadhurst R (2016) Spam and criminal activity, *Trends & Issues in Crime and Criminal Justice* no. 526, Canberra: Australian Institute of Criminology at https://www.aic.gov.au/publications/tandi/tandi526.

1052. *See* text of the Act at http://classic.austlii.edu.au/au/legis/cth/consol_act/sa200366/.

1053. *See* ACMA (2022) media release dated 8 February, *Unlawful spam costs Sportsbet $3.7 million in penalties and refunds* at https://www.acma.gov.au/articles/2022-02/unlawful-spam-costs-sportsbet-37-million-penalties-and-refunds.

1054. Department of Defence (2020) Information Warfare at https://www.dst.defence.gov.au/sites/default/files/basic_pages/documents/Factsheet%20-%20Information%20Warfare.pdf.

1778. Australia's *International Cyber and Critical Tech Engagement Strategy 2021* in examining Internet shutdowns have identified some of its causes.[1055] The most prominent being political motivations that in many instances amount to the unlawful limitation of human rights such as freedom of expression and of assembly.

1779. According to civil society group Access Now, 1,706 days of Internet access were disrupted by 213 Internet shutdowns across 33 countries in 2019. In 2020 at least 155 Internet shutdown incidents were documented in 29 countries.[1056] They found that Internet shutdowns were increasing in number, lasting longer, affecting more people and targeting vulnerable groups. While seemingly innocuous, such disruptions to the course of business and other activity that are dependent on the Internet, may be interpreted as criminal activities that may be successfully prosecuted under relevant legislation.

1055. *Australia's International Cyber and Critical Tech Engagement Strategy 2021* at https://www.internationalcybertech.gov.au/sites/default/files/2021-05/21066%20DFAT%20Cyber%20Affairs%20Strategy%202021%20update%20Internals%201%20Acc.pdf.

1056. Access Now (2021) Internet shutdowns report: Shattered dreams and lost opportunities — a year in the fight to #KeepItOn (3 March) at https://www.accessnow.org/keepiton-report-a-year-in-the-fight/.

Chapter 6. Traditional Crimes in a Digital Context

1780. Reference is made here to the cybercrime diagram presented earlier (Figure 7). The discussion in this chapter now turns its attention to the left-hand side of the diagram that consists of four main pillars or items – persons and personnel, financial, e-business and nation-state security. From each of these are branch stems relating to specific cybercrimes that refer to an item in question. Letters in bold denote detailed discussion and those in normal print references are made in passing.

§1. Persons and Personnel

I. Offences Against Decency

1781. Section 5 of the *Broadcasting Services Act* 1992 confers on the Australian Communication and Media Authority (ACMA) a broad range of functions and powers to be used in a manner that will produce regulatory arrangements that are stable and predictable; and deal effectively with breaches of the rules established by the Act

1782. ACMA is the authority that monitors the National Classification Scheme Guidelines for television and radio broadcasts.[1057] The Guidelines are based on the principles of classifiable elements, context and impact.[1058] Classification provisions apply to television codes only for all commercial free-to-air and subscription broadcasters, the national broadcasters and community television.[1059] 'Decency' provisions appear only in the commercial radio code.[1060]

1783. A key purpose of the decency provisions is to guide broadcasters in their respective decisions about what content to broadcast. A secondary purpose is to help broadcasters decide if content that some individuals may find inappropriate is nonetheless appropriate in a specific context (having regard to the 'demographic characteristics of the audience of the relevant programme').

1784. In the context of 'decency' offences, reference to the *Crimes Act* 1900 (Cth) section 393 is required, where a person who offends against decency by the exposure of his or her person in a public place, or in any place within the view of a person who is in a public place, commits an offence. Maximum penalty: twenty penalty units, imprisonment for one year or both.[1061]

1057. *See Guidelines for the Classification of Films* under the *Classification (Publications, Films and Computer Games) Act* 1995 (Cth) (revised 2015 (Cth)).
1058. *See* ACMA (2018) Investigation concepts: Decency, classification, and harm and offence at https://www.acma.gov.au/sites/default/files/2020-12/Investigation%20concepts%20Decency%20classification%20and%20harm%20and%20offence.pdf.
1059. ABC *Code of Practice* (2011) (revised in 2016).
1060. SBS *Code of Practice* (2014).
1061. *Crimes Act* 1900 (Cth) at http://www5.austlii.edu.au/au/legis/act/consol_act/ca190082/s393.html.

1785. Online the principal issue is whether the common law offence of outraging public decency can be committed by say, posting a message on an Internet discussion forum or posting 'upskirting' images online. The Internet message or images displayed publicly that would satisfy elements of the offence, but the question remains as to whether the physical or public space may be extended to cyberspace?

1786. Here there are two elements of the offence, first, the nature of the act undertaken; and, second the public element of the offence. Where these have been satisfied under the 'decency' standards prescribed, then *prima facie* an offence has been committed. However, what is a public place or space is problematic.

1787. In legal discourse it is a fiction to describe the Internet as a 'place' in any physical or actual sense. A person can only see a message posted to an Internet forum when the relevant URL address of the website is accessed or downloaded in comprehensible form by someone using a computer or mobile Internet device. It is at the 'places' where they are when they access or download the offending material that their sense of decency may be outraged, not some virtual place. In short, it may be interpreted that for the purposes of the offence, the Internet is the medium, not the place.

1788. The offence of outraging public decency has been used to prosecute upskirting. In Australia, various pieces of state legislation make it an offence to film a person's private parts without consent.[1062]

II. Hate Speech

1789. As a form of cyberbullying, hate speech, publications and demonstrations based on race is unlawful under the *Racial Discrimination Act* 1975 (Cth) section 18c. This section makes it unlawful to do something in public based on the race, colour, national or ethnic origin of a person or group of people which is likely to offend, insult, humiliate or intimidate. In an online digital context it can include racially offensive content that is posted on websites, social media sites and other Internet forums.

III. Defamation

1790. In Australia, defamation laws are a matter for state and territory courts. In November 2004, the Attorneys-General of the States and Territories agreed to

1062. *Crimes Act* 1900 (NSW) s. 91L(1); *Summary Offences Act* 1966 (Vic.) s. 41B; *Criminal Code Act 1899* (Qld.) s. 227A(2); *Summary Offences Act* 1953 (SA) s. 26D; *Police Offences Act* 1935 (Tas.) s. 13A; *Crimes Act* 1900 (ACT) s. 61B(5). *See also* Sarre, R What is 'upskirting' and what are your right to privacy under the law? *The Conversation*, 29 Mar 2021 at https://theconversation.com/what-is-upskirting-and-what-are-your-rights-to-privacy-under-the-law-158060.

support enactment of uniform model provisions *Model Defamation Provisions* (MDP) within their jurisdictions. Since 2005 Australia's states and territories have substantially the same defamation laws.

1791. In 2018 the Council of Attorneys-General reviewed and then amended the MDP and supported the enactment of the *Model Defamation Amendment Provisions 2020* (MDAP) by each State and Territory.[1063] Except for WA and the NT in all other jurisdictions defamation legislations have commenced.[1064] Notably, several amendments have been modelled on the UK *Defamation Act* 2013.

1792. Before the enactment of the MDP, at general law a plaintiff had to prove material loss (or *special damage*) if the publication of defamatory matter was slanderous, but not if it was libellous.

1793. Section 7 of the MDP provides that there is to be no distinction between slander and libel. As a result, all publications of defamatory matter are actionable without proof of special damage.

1794. Generally libel is the publication of defamatory matter in a written or other permanent form while slander is the publication of defamatory matter in a form that is temporary and merely audible. For example, a newspaper article, a Google review or a Facebook post might be libellous. Also, spoken words become libel (not slander) when the words are recorded. For example, it would be libel if someone defamed a personality on the radio, on TV or in a YouTube video.

1795. A person experiencing humiliation, ridicule or contempt because of comments, photos or defamatory material published about them on social media platforms may sue the perpetrator(s) for defamation in a civil suit. It is a criminal offence to publish false information about a person knowing that the information is false and with the intention of causing that person serious harm.[1065] Section 529 of the *Crimes Act* 1900 (NSW) provides for a maximum penalty of three years imprisonment. Similar provisions appear in other state and territory jurisdictions.

1063. Model Defamation Provisions 2020 at https://pcc.gov.au/uniform/2020/Model_Defamation_Amendment_Provisions_2020.pdf. Since 2021 the Council of Attorneys-General has been renamed Meeting of Attorneys-General (MAG).

1064. *See* NSW Review of model defamation provisions at https://www.justice.nsw.gov.au/justicepolicy/Pages/lpclrd/lpclrd_consultation/review-model-defamation-provisions.aspx.

1065. *See* Mitchell, C (2021) Netflix hit by stream of libel lawsuits, *The Australian* 10 November at https://www.theaustralian.com.au/world/the-times/netflix-hit-by-stream-of-libel-lawsuits/news-story/dd4d16817525fd42a5d4a66294252c2d. The US Supreme Court in 1964 set the 'actual malice' standard which makes defamation suits brought by public figures dependent on knowledge of falsity or reckless disregard for the truth. In the US Netflix as a distributor of movies created by someone else has claimed that s. 230 of the US *Communications Decency Act* 1996 provides immunity for Internet platforms with respect to third-party content. *See* https://www.justice.gov/archives/ag/department-justice-s-review-section-230-communications-decency-act-1996.

1796. Significant amendments in 2020 with the MDAP include:

- *Serious harm threshold* section 10A. The new test reframes tort of defamation to make it an element of the cause of action that the publication has caused or likely to cause serious harm to the reputation of the person. The publication of defamatory matter about a person must have or be likely to cause serious harm to the reputation of the person. This is a new element of the cause of action.
- *Single publication rule* Sch 4 cl 1A. Introduction of a single publication rule with a limitation period of one year from date material is first made publicly available or uploaded onto the Internet. This amends existing legislation in the case of online publications where the limitation period restarts whenever a person downloads and comprehends the material from the Internet giving a potentially endless limitation period for such publications. A limitation period for electronic publications is introduced. The new drafting clarifies the date of publication for the purposes of assessing the limitation period. In relation to publication of matter in electronic form; it means the day on which the matter was first uploaded for access or sent electronically to a recipient.
- *Public interest defence* section 29A. The new defence to publication of a defamatory matter is where the matter concerns an issue of public interest; and the defendant reasonably believed that publication was in the public interest. These amend the statutory qualified privilege defence (section 30).
- *Other significant amendments* are defence of contextual truth (section 26); concerns notices (section 12A) and offers to make amends (section 12B); damages cap where appropriate for non-economic loss no longer applies; leave required for multiple proceedings (section 23); honest opinion defences become available (section 31(4)); scientific or academic peer review defence is allowed (section 30A); and capacity to sue clarified (and a new rule on costs (section 10(2)).

1797. However, the amendments have overlooked several issues including the uncertainties on how defamation law should apply to digital platforms. A second stage of reform is under consideration but with no timeline indicated on the Meeting of Attorneys-General website.[1066] Part A of the Stage 2 Review refers to the question of Internet intermediary liability in defamation for the publication of third-party content. It appears that this review is aimed at matters raised in the recent High Court decision in *Fairfax Media Publications Pty Ltd & Ors v. Voller* [2021] HCA 27 where an appeal confirmed the liability of third-party comments and statements on the internet.

1798. Illustrations of the concerns discussed above are to be had from recent significant litigation in the courts one including the mounting of a 'truth defence' in a defamation case. In *Nationwide News Pty Limited v. Rush* [2020] FCAFC 115 Nationwide News appealed after the Oscar winner Rush was awarded almost $2.9 million in damages over defamatory articles published by The Daily Telegraph in

1066. Meeting of Attorneys-General (2021) at https://www.ag.gov.au/about-us/who-we-are/committees-and-councils/meeting-attorneys-general and at https://www.ag.gov.au/about-us/publications/meeting-attorneys-general-mag-communique-november-2021.

2017. The articles alleged that Rush behaved inappropriately towards Eryn Jean Norvill, his co-star in the Sydney Theatre Company production of King Lear. Rush denied the claims. It was argued on appeal that the various imputations carried in the published articles were substantially true, but the argument was not upheld. The Federal Court dismissed all grounds of the appeal.[1067]

1799. In a different case the Court of Appeal set aside an award for economic loss in *Bauer Media Pty Ltd v. Wilson [No.2]* [2018] VSCA 154.[1068] The respondent was forced to pay back AUD 4.1 million of the damages that was awarded. The respondent failed in an appeal to the High Court.

1800. The Federal Court's judgment in *Colagrande v. Kim* [2022] FCA 409 reflects an increasing trend of anonymous online trolls being uncovered and ordered to pay substantial damages. In 2017 Dr Colagrande a cosmetic surgeon was convicted of assaulting a patient. The conviction was overturned on appeal in 2018. Dr Colagrande was dismayed on reading an anonymous online review on a specialist medical review website, RateMDs. When the website refused to retract the review, the doctor was able to find and track down the author of the post and commenced proceedings and successfully sued another rival surgeon Dr Kim for defamation. Dr Colagrande was awarded AUD 430,500 for aggravated damages.

1801. The facts and the award of damages of the case closely mirrors that of *Nettle v. Cruse* [2021] FCA 935. A well-regarded Sydney-based plastic surgeon refused to operate on a patient. The aggrieved patient posted highly defamatory comments on several websites. The surgeon commenced proceedings seeking damages for non-economic loss and a permanent injunction preventing further publication. The complication here was that the defendant had disappeared in the meantime. Nevertheless, the court awarded the surgeon AUD 450,000 in damages.

1802. The lesson from these cases is that an anonymous online review does not necessarily mean that one may remain anonymous. With some determination and detective work those who are defamed can expose desktop trolls to the risk of very substantial damage awards.

1803. The cases signify the consistent approach being taken by the Federal Court in situations where there is malicious reputational damage to a professional practising in a competitive, image-driven industry.

1804. The litigated cases demonstrate the increasingly pervasive influence of the digital age and the 'grapevine effect' of defamatory material when communications move rapidly across the world via the Internet and reach potentially unforeseen

1067. Appeal from *Rush v. Nationwide News Pty Limited (No 7)* [2019] FCA 496. *See* commentary at https://www.abc.net.au/news/2020-07-02/daily-telegraph-loses-defamation-appeal-in-geoffrey-rush-case/12414536.

1068. *See* judgment at https://www.supremecourt.vic.gov.au/court-decisions/judgments-and-sentences/judgment-summaries/bauer-media-pty-ltd-v-wilson-no2-2018-1. *See* commentary at https://www.abc.net.au/news/2018-11-16/rebel-wilson-loses-high-court-bid/10503644.

audiences. Furthermore, finer distinctions could be made in such litigation as to whether it is 'in the public interest' or 'of public interest' generally.[1069]

IV. Cyberbullying

1805. Cyberbullying whilst not constituting a distinct offence under Australian law, the use of mobile phones, email or social networking sites to harass or abuse a person or groups of people are arguably criminal offences.

1806. The use of phones, text messages, emails or online posts to intentionally threaten to kill someone is deemed a criminal offence under section 474.15 of the *Criminal Code Act* 1995 (Cth) with a maximum penalty of ten years imprisonment. It is also a criminal offence under this section to use phones, text messages, emails or online posts to intentionally threaten to cause someone serious harm. Such an offence is punishable by a maximum penalty of seven years imprisonment.

1807. Section 474.47 of the *Criminal Code Act* 1995 (Cth) makes it an offence to use a phone or the Internet to threaten, harass or seriously offend someone. The threatening or harassing message is considered offensive where it would likely cause serious anger, outrage, humiliation or disgust. The maximum penalty for the offence is an imprisonment of three years.

1808. Cyberbullying in the form of online sexual harassment is unlawful under the *Sex Discrimination Act* 1984 (Cth) section 3(c) where the harassment is anticipated to offend, humiliate or intimidate the person to whom the harassment is directed.[1070] The harassment and conduct could include making unwelcome sexual advance or request for sexual favours or other unwelcome conduct of a sexual nature. Such conduct can take the form of sexual text messages or emails, inappropriate suggestions on social media and accessing sexually explicit websites.

1809. A victim of cyberbullying may lodge a complaint of discrimination to any state- or territory-based Anti-Discrimination Board or the Commonwealth Australian Human Rights Commission (HRC).

1810. The safety of children from cyberbullying online is protected in various ways. The Office of the Children's eSafety Commissioner (eSafety Commissioner) was established in July 2015 under the *Enhancing Online Safety Act* 2015 (Cth) to take a national leadership role in online safety for children.[1071]

1069. *See* Douglas, M (2020) Australia's 'outdated' defamation laws are changing but there's no 'revolution' yet, *The Conversation* (28 July) at https://theconversation.com/australias-outdated-defamation-laws-are-changing-but-theres-no-revolution-yet-143532.
1070. *See* text of the Act at https://www.legislation.gov.au/Details/C2014C00002.
1071. *See Enhancing Online Safety for Children Act* 2015 (Cth) at https://www.legislation.gov.au/Details/C2017C00187.

1811. Section 15 of the *Enhancing Online Safety Act* 2015 (Cth) specifies the broad functions of the eSafety Commissioner. The Commissioner administers complaints and takedown services applied to digital platforms, social media services and content hosts including a complaints scheme for cyberbullying of children; removal of cyberbullying material; and removal of image-based abusive materials. The cyberbullying complaints scheme is designed to quickly remove cyberbullying material that is harmful to a child from large social media sites.

1812. The eSafety Commissioner also has carriage of the administration of the Online Content Scheme provided in Schedules 5 & 7 of *Broadcasting Services Act* 1992 for prohibited online material. The regulation of prohibited and potentially prohibited online content is based on the National Classification Scheme. The scheme is complaints-based and applies to content accessed through the Internet and digital devices.

1813. The powers of the eSafety Commissioner in dealing with a cyberbullying complaint also includes issuing of notices to large social media services to remove cyberbullying material targeted at an Australian child from the service; and, giving notice to a person who posts cyberbullying material targeted at an Australian child on either a social media service or a 'relevant electronic service' (for example, email, text message).

1814. The authority to remove material and the issuing of notices are legally binding on all sites and services hosted in Australia but not those hosted overseas.

V. Cyberstalking

1815. Cyberstalking refers to the use of the Internet and other technologies to harass or stalk another person online and is potentially a crime in all jurisdictions in Australia. The cyberstalking can include wilful, malicious and repeated, unwanted phone calls, texts, messages and sending material that may or may not be threatening. Creating fake profiles to continue contacting a person after they have been blocked on their personal account will also count as stalking.

1816. Stalking is a common law offence and is governed by relevant sections in criminal legislation in the states and territories. Elements of the crime include unwanted telephone contact, keeping a person under surveillance by sending electronic messages, and sending offensive materials. The Victorian and Tasmanian legislations explicitly include the sending of electronic messages and the Internet as part of the crime of stalking.[1072]

1072. *See Crimes Act* 1958 (Vic) s. 21A; *Criminal Code Act* 1924 (Tas) s. 192; *Crimes Act* 1900 (NSW) s. 562AB; *Crimes Act* 1900 (ACT) s. 34A; *Criminal Code Act* 1977 (NT) s. 189; *Criminal Code Act* 1899 (Qld) s. 359A; *Criminal Law Consolidation Act* (SA) 1935 s. 19AA; and, *Criminal Code Act Compilation Act* 1913 (WA) s. 338E(2).

1817. Section 60E of the *Crimes Act* 1900 (NSW) criminalizes assaulting, stalking, harassing or intimidating any school student or member of staff of a school while they attend that school. Such an offence carries a maximum penalty of five years imprisonment.

1818. Further, section 13 of the *Crimes (Domestic and Personal Violence) Act* 2007 (NSW) prohibits stalking or intimidation of a person with the intention of causing them to fear physical or mental harm. The prohibited conduct for this offence includes the use of phones, text messaging, email or social media, to stalk or intimidate someone. This offence carries a maximum penalty of five years imprisonment. Similar provisions appear in other states.

1819. In Victoria stalking involves a pattern of behaviour intended to cause harm or arouse fear. Section 13 of the *Crimes (Personal and Domestic Violence) Act* (Vic) 2007 makes clear that the prosecution needs to prove that the accused had an intention to cause the other person to fear physical or mental harm.[1073]

1820. The Victorian case of *Director of Public Prosecutions v. Sutcliffe* [2001] VSC 43 involved the issue of jurisdiction in a stalking case under section 21A of the *Crimes Act* 1958 (Vic). A respondent had committed the offence in Victoria, but the victim of the stalking was in Canada. The judge in that case considered that the relevant section was considered to have implicit extraterritorial operation and to avoid defeating the purpose of the legislation.

1821. Criminal activities that impact on people and personnel include online harassment in the form of online predators and Internet trolls for which specific legislation have been enacted. The extant legislation is evidence that cybersex trafficking on the Internet is being monitored for its impact on online safety for the public generally and minors. The issue of sexting as a form of social media activity may morph into criminality where there is predation of minors and the lack of consent and permission. Anecdotally romance fraud is becoming prominent because of financial losses and where fraud is involved.

1822. Issues of the invasion of privacy online are a topic discussed at length in a different publication of the Kluwer *International Encyclopedia of Privacy and Technology Law – Privacy and Data Protection* imprint. However, from a cybercrime perspective, the topic of privacy is not too distant from revenge porn – where offensive content and images are sent to social media and Internet channels. Included under privacy are 'deepfakes' – the term to refer to a video that has been edited using an algorithm to replace the person in the original video with someone

1073. For a more detailed discussion see Ogilvie E (2000) Stalking: policing and prosecuting practices in three Australian jurisdictions, *Trends & Issues in Crime and Criminal Justice* no. 176, Canberra: Australian Institute of Criminology at https://www.aic.gov.au/publications/tandi/tandi176; and Ogilvie E (2000) *Stalking: Legislative, Policing and Prosecution Patterns in Australia* at Research and public policy series no. 34. Canberra: Australian Institute of Criminology at https://www.aic.gov.au/publications/rpp/rpp34.

else in a way that makes the video look authentic.[1074] It appears that there are few legal options for victims of non-consensual deep fake porn, similar to revenge porn, unless malice, injury, loss or other hurt may be demonstrated and evidenced in a court of law. A law banning such porn may provide a solution to problems caused by such cyber mischiefs.

§2. Financial

1823. The outline stem for financial cybercrime on the diagram includes online fraud and online theft, cyber extortion, online gambling and miscellaneous others including money laundering, contraband and drug trafficking. These financial crimes may take the form of Internet frauds, phone scams and the theft of identities.

1824. Online frauds are those described as bank frauds, carding, id theft and near field communication (NFC) siphoning. Bank frauds include phishing, credit card skimming and loan scams.[1075] Banking fraud is where someone attempts to take funds or other assets from a financial institution or from customers of that institution by posing as a bank official.[1076] A credit card dump is a type of crime in which the criminal makes an unauthorized digital copy of a credit card.

1825. Carding (also known as credit card stuffing and card verification) is the illegal use of a credit or debit card by a thief to pay for products. Carding is performed by bots programmed to software to perform automated operations over the Internet.[1077]

1826. NFC siphoning is undertaken by an application capable of 'sucking' credit card data from contactless credit cards. An app called paycardreader will skim card numbers and expiry dates, along with transactions and merchant IDs. To prevent such skimming some people have used electronic protective shields to house their credit cards.[1078]

1827. Doxing (sometimes written as doxxing) is the act of revealing identifying information about someone online, such as their real name, home address, workplace, phone, financial and other personal information. That information is then circulated to the public, without the victim's permission. Such activity is undertaken typically with malicious intent to harm the victim and to secure agency over that person.[1079]

1074. *See* Merriam-Webster dictionary words at play at https://www.merriam-webster.com/words-at-play/deepfake-slang-definition-examples.
1075. *See* the Australian government's MoneySmart site at https://moneysmart.gov.au/banking/banking-and-credit-scams.
1076. *See* Investopedia at https://www.investopedia.com/banking-fraud-4689709.
1077. *See* Investopedia at https://www.investopedia.com/terms/c/carding.asp.
1078. *See* report at https://www.itnews.com.au/news/android-app-steals-contactless-credit-card-data-305881.
1079. *See* Kaspersky at https://www.kaspersky.com/resource-center/definitions/what-is-doxing.

1828. Bug poaching is a cyberextortion tactic targeting enterprises where a hacker breaks into a corporate network and records a network's private system information and vulnerabilities. The hacker will then contact the corporation with evidence of the breach and demands a ransom.[1080] Such an intrusion is sometimes labelled a 'fake white hat' because the hacker exploits the target enterprises' website to gain access and steal sensitive data displaying fake altruism, by claiming that the hacker is performing a security and vulnerability check of the system.[1081]

§3. E-BUSINESS

1829. Advertising (ad) fraud is a general description of types of crime carried out on online. In one variant ad fraud is carried out by a competitor or fraudulent publishers who deploy software bots to repeatedly click on ads. A variant of this fraudulent technique is to use click farms who pay people to repeatedly click on ads. These clicks purportedly earn micropayments. These micropayments are paid by the advertiser to the publisher and advertising platform for every click on the ad, with the potential to defraud a business of large sums of money.

1830. Other forms of ad fraud may be carried out in combination with identity fraud, where one person uses another person's personal information without permission to commit a crime. Attribution fraud happens when a scammer sends fake Internet traffic through bots using fake web accounts and false cookies. In this type of fraud the bots will click on ads available on a scam page that is faking a famous brand.[1082]

1831. The criminalization of spam has been discussed in Chapter 5 §5 above. However, an extension to spam as a vector is the emergence of the so-called dark pattern. The term was introduced by Harry Brignull, a London-based user experience designer who noticed manipulative and deceptive tricks in software that gets a user to complete an action that they would not otherwise have done.[1083] Some common examples of dark pattern include: bait and switch, disguised ads, forced continuity of subscriptions, hidden costs of products sold online, friend spam, fake price comparison sites and misdirection to fraudulent websites.[1084] These add to the plethora of criminal activity online.

1080. *See* Security Intelligence at https://securityintelligence.com/bug-poaching-a-new-extortion-tactic-targeting-enterprises/.
1081. *See* Security Intelligence at https://securityintelligence.com/posts/ransomware-2020-attack-trends-new-techniques-affecting-organizations-worldwide/.
1082. *See* Forbes at https://www.forbes.com/sites/zengernews/2021/04/23/how-companies-can-deal-with-rampant-digital-ad-fraud/?sh=2879c65e4bf7.
1083. *See* Brignull, H at https://harrybr.medium.com/bringing-dark-patterns-to-light-d86f24224ebf.
1084. *See* discussion by McNealy, J at https://theconversation.com/what-are-dark-patterns-an-online-media-expert-explains-165362.

1832. Industrial espionage is hardly a recent phenomenon. However, the scale and extent afforded by digital media has exposed vulnerabilities for e-commerce and e-business generally.

§4. Nation-State security

1833. In previous chapters cyberterrorism, cyberwarfare and information warfare have been described. An emergent trend is that of the use of the darknet or dark web, a 'parallel' Internet that is used by criminals with something and some activity to hide. The term 'dark web' refers to encrypted online content that is not indexed by conventional search engines. Access to the dark web is only through using specific browsers, such as TOR Browser.[1085] The dark web provides privacy and anonymity compared to traditional websites.[1086]

1834. Darknet markets offer illicit goods for sale, often using cryptocurrencies as a method of payment. Although some products for sale are legal, illicit goods such as drugs, stolen information and weapons are common items in these markets.[1087]

1085. The Onion Router (TOR) Browser is a web browser that anonymizes web traffic using the TOR network to protect a user's identity online. *See* description by *The Guardian* at https://www.theguardian.com/technology/2013/nov/05/tor-beginners-guide-nsa-browser.

1086. *See* Investopedia at https://www.investopedia.com/terms/d/dark-web.asp.

1087. *See* Investopedia at https://www.investopedia.com/terms/d/darknet-market-cryptomarket.asp. *See also* report by *The Guardian* at https://www.theguardian.com/technology/darknet; and the ABC at https://www.abc.net.au/news/2021-01-16/life-on-dark-web-plenty-of-criminals-places-to-hide/13057560.

Chapter 7. Cybercrime Law Enforcement and Criminal Procedures

§1. Criminal Procedures

1835. In general terms, Australian law enforcement efforts in relation to cybercrime involve four major strategies. The first is putting into place regulations and legislation that enable the law enforcement agencies to tackle the major problem areas.

1836. A second strategy is the formation of strategic partnerships in the fight against crime. These partnerships include the law enforcement agencies to work with industry, federal government to work with their state and territory counterparts and national governments to work with each other internationally.

1837. A third major strategy is education, both regarding knowledge to prevent the crime occurring in the first place as well as assistance in helping to solve cybercrime.

1838. Finally, governments at all levels to provide more resources to increase the capacity to combat cybercrime. For example, the Commonwealth government the establishment of 'Crimtrac', which maintains databases such as the National Automated Finger Print Identification System and the National Investigation DNA database. In addition, the AFP and the police forces of the various states and territories have established Cybercrime Units.

1839. Another important development is the establishment of the Australian Hi-Tech Crime Centre (AHTCC).[1088] The centre launched in 2003 is hosted by the AFP and co-located with its Transnational Crime Coordination Centre (TCCC). The focus of such a centre is on serious, organized, and multijurisdictional crime with a focus on cybercrime.

I. Data Retention

1840. The Parliamentary Joint Committee on Intelligence and Security's (PJCIS) review of the mandatory data retention regime describes the framework that governs access to and the retention of telecommunications data.[1089]

1841. Chapter 4 of the *Telecommunications (Interception and Access) Act* 1979 (Cth) (TIAA) provides a framework that authorizes the Australian Security

1088. *See* The Australian Federal Police (n.d.) *High Tech Crime: AFP casts a wide Net* at https://www.afp.gov.au/sites/default/files/PDF/high-tech-crime-afp-casts-a-wide-net.pdf.

1089. *See* The Parliamentary Joint Committee on Intelligence and Security (2020) Review of the Mandatory Data Retention Regime at https://www.aph.gov.au/DocumentStore.ashx?id=284e0a69-91bc-4db1-bfa8-387d9ec36ce7&subId=668160, (16 Apr).

Intelligence Organisation (ASIO) or an enforcement agency to lawfully access, disclose and use telecommunications data without breaching the *Telecommunications Act* 1997 (Cth).

1842. Amendments to the TIAA were made by the *Telecommunications (Interception) Amendment Act* 2006 (Cth) that implement certain recommendations of the *Report of the Review of the Regulation of Access to Communications* prepared by Anthony Blunn AO (the Blunn Report).[1090]

1843. The *Telecommunications (Interception and Access) Amendment (Data Retention) Act* 2015 (Cth) (Data Retention Act) introduced a framework at Part 5-1A in the TIA Act to govern the retention of a prescribed set of telecommunications data for two years by communications service providers of relevant services.

1844. Under the Data Retention Act the relevant sections for data retention obligations are:

- section 187A and section 187C: subject to certain exceptions, carriers, carriage service providers and Internet service providers must retain specified telecommunications data for two years;[1091]
- section 187AA: telecommunications data to be retained is split between six specified categories;
- section 187BA: requires service providers to ensure the confidentiality of retained telecommunications data by encrypting the information and protecting it from unauthorized interference or access; and,
- section 187LA: provides that the *Privacy Act* 1988 (Cth) applies to service providers to the extent their activities relate to retained telecommunication data which for the purposes of the Act is taken to be personal information.

1845. The *Telecommunications Act* 1997 (Cth) protects the privacy of Australians by, among other things, prohibiting service providers from using and disclosing information about customer's use of telecommunication services (sections 276-278). Unauthorized disclosure of telecommunication data carries an imprisonment term of up to two years on conviction.

1846. In the context of the data retention obligations, data is information about a communication – the metadata – rather than the content or substance of a communication.[1092] For telephone calls, data includes the telephone numbers of the people talking to each other and how long they talked for – not what they said. For

1090. Blunn, A (2005) *Report of the Review of the Regulation of Access to Communications,* Canberra: Australian Government Attorney-General's Department. *See* text of the Act at http://classic.austlii.edu.au/au/legis/cth/num_act/taa2006430/.

1091. This obligation overcomes the previous approach labelled a 'quick freeze' system where data are retained only when there is a need to investigate.

1092. Metadata is data about data.

emails, data is information such as the relevant email addresses and when it was sent – not the subject line of the email or its content.[1093]

1847. In a case study, in 2005 a combined ASIO and law enforcement operation prevented a mass casualty terrorist attack in Australia. This resulted in the arrest and conviction of thirteen men on terrorism charges with sentences of up to twenty-eight years in jail. Data was critical to the successful outcome of the investigation and subsequent trial even though covert phone networks were used.[1094]

II. Interception of Electronic Communications

1848. The *Surveillance Legislation Amendment (Identify and Disrupt) Act* 2021 (Cth) authorized three new powers for the AFP and the Australian Criminal Intelligence Commission (ACIC) to identify and disrupt serious online criminal activity.[1095]

1849. Online cyber-enabled criminals use the dark web to buy and sell stolen identities; trade illicit commodities; deal in child abuse material; and, organize and engage in other criminal activities. Such activities use encryption and anonymizing technologies to hide their identities and activities from law enforcement agencies.

1850. To avoid an overreach of agency power, several safeguards have been built into the legislation. The *Telecommunications Act* 1997 (Cth) Part 15 Division 7 and the schedules to the *Telecommunications and Other Legislation Amendment (Assistance and Access) Act* 2018 (the Assistance and Access Act) prohibits building or implementing systematic weaknesses or vulnerabilities in the systems being investigated (section 317ZG); administrative procedures such as the use of a Technical Assistance Request (TAR), Technical Assistance Notice (TAN), or a Technical Capability Notice (TCN) where a warrant or authorization may be required (section 317ZH); and, where the new capabilities must not require the construction of interception capabilities or data retention capabilities (section 317ZGA).[1096]

1093. *See* Department of Home Affairs (2021) at https://www.homeaffairs.gov.au/about-us/our-portfolios/national-security/lawful-access-telecommunications/data-retention-obligations.

1094. *See* Department of Home Affairs (2021) at https://www.homeaffairs.gov.au/about-us/our-portfolios/national-security/lawful-access-telecommunications/data-retention-case-studies.

1095. *See* Department of Home Affairs (2021) at https://www.homeaffairs.gov.au/about-us/our-portfolios/national-security/lawful-access-telecommunications/surveillance-legislation-amendment-identify-and-disrupt-act-2021.

1096. *See* Department of Home Affairs (2021) at https://www.homeaffairs.gov.au/about-us/our-portfolios/national-security/lawful-access-telecommunications/assistance-and-access-limitations-safeguards.

III. Network Searches

1851. The Assistance and Access Act authorizes lawful access to law enforcement agencies whilst at the same time avoiding barriers to e-commerce.[1097] Whilst the Australian government supports cybersecurity tools, like encryption to create a safe online environment for Australians, it has no interest in undermining these critical technologies, such as requiring industry to break encryption.

1852. Unfortunately, the same technologies are being employed by terrorists, paedophiles, drug smugglers and human traffickers to conceal illicit activities and facilitate crime. Criminals have become increasingly sophisticated users of the Internet and rapid technological change has caused valuable sources of evidence and intelligence to diminish. Studies demonstrate that over 95 per cent of the ASIO's most dangerous counterterrorism targets use encrypted communications; encryption impacts intelligence coverage in nine out of ASIO's ten priority cases; and it is estimated that by 2020 all electronic communications of investigative value will be encrypted.[1098]

1853. The Assistance and Access Act equips agencies with the tools they need to effectively operate in the digital era and keep the Australian community safe. The operation of the Assistance and Access Act is subject to ongoing review by the PJCIS and by the INSLM.[1099]

IV. Seizure of Data

1854. The Assistance and Access Act has also provided frameworks, access warrants and penalty clauses that assist law enforcement and intelligence agencies undertake their roles and tasks.[1100] These authorizations are spelt out under five Schedules of the Assistance and Access Act.

- Schedule 1 Industry Assistance of the Act establishes a framework for government and the communications industry to work together on law enforcement and national security investigations.

1097. *See* Department of Home Affairs (2021) at https://www.homeaffairs.gov.au/about-us/our-portfolios/national-security/lawful-access-telecommunications/data-encryption.

1098. *See* Australian Security Intelligence Organisation (2019) Submission No 21 to Independent National Security Legislation Monitor, Review of the *Telecommunications and Other Legislation (Assistance and Access) Act* 2018 (Assistance and Access Act), 23 Sep. 2019.

1099. *See* INSLM (2018) Report at https://www.inslm.gov.au/reviews-reports/telecommunications-and-other-legislation-amendment-act-2018-related-matters.

1100. *See* Department of Home Affairs (2020) at https://www.homeaffairs.gov.au/about-us/our-portfolios/national-security/lawful-access-telecommunications/assistance-and-access-overview (17 March).

- Schedule 2 Computer Access Warrants of the Act creates computer access warrants. Such warrants allow law enforcement to covertly access devices to investigate serious crimes; to search devices such as laptops, mobile phones and USBs, collect information; and, to conceal the fact that a device has been accessed.
- Schedules 3 and 4 of the Act strengthen search and seize powers and extend the maximum penalties associated with the power of a magistrate to require an individual unlock a device where they know the password. Schedule 3 also allows police to access account-based data (that is, social media accounts) via a search warrant.
- Schedule 5 Voluntary assistance for ASIO of the Act provides civil immunity to persons who voluntarily assist ASIO; allows ASIO to apply to the Attorney-General to require a person to unlock a device where they know the authentication protocol; and creates a penalty for non-compliance of a maximum five-year imprisonment.

V. Duties of Intermediaries

1855. The Assistance and Access Act establishes a 'list of acts or things' in section 317E that articulates what assistance can be provided to Australia's law enforcement and intelligence agencies.[1101] The listed acts or things are relevant to each provider in respect of its eligible activities, that is, the services and products that a provider offers or operates in the Australian market. A provider is not required to give help that is unrelated to their relevant eligible activities.

1856. The carriers or carriage service providers are subject to the existing regulatory regime under the Assistance and Access Act. A pecuniary penalty of up to AUD 10 million is imposed each case of non-compliance. An individual may be fined up to approximately AUD 50,000 for each case of non-compliance.

1857. A person may be imprisoned for up to five years for an unauthorized disclosure of information, as detailed in section 317ZF of the Assistance and Access Act.

1858. This legislation does not authorize the government to implement or build so-called backdoors to undermine these systems. Section 317ZG of the Assistance and Access Act includes an express prohibition against building a systemic weakness or vulnerability into a form of electronic protection and ensures that providers cannot be prevented from rectifying a systemic weakness or vulnerability.

1859. The legislation defines systemic weakness as a weakness that affects a whole class of technology but does not include a weakness that is selectively introduced to one or more target technologies that relate to a particular person.

1101. *See* Department of Home Affairs (2020) at https://www.homeaffairs.gov.au/about-us/our-portfolios/national-security/lawful-access-telecommunications/assistance-and-access-industry-assistance-framework (27 August).

1860. The Act ensures that agencies need a warrant or an authorization to access personal information. Section 317ZH Assistance and Access Act prohibits new notices replacing a warrant or authorization if the issuing agency would have otherwise required one for the activity.

1861. For example, law enforcement access to the content of a communication still requires a warrant issued by a judge or Administrative Appeals Tribunal member. Similarly, to require the disclosure of metadata, an authorization under the *Telecommunications (Interception and Access) Act* 1979 (Cth) is still needed.

1862. Under C628:2019 Telecommunications Consumer Protections Code (TCP Code), CSPs must ensure that any information provided or made available to consumers, including the standard form service agreement (SFA), is clear, accurate, free of material omissions, relevant, current, readily available, and, in cases where information is provided, timely.[1102]

§2. Jurisdiction and Court Procedures

1863. In Australia, courts have jurisdiction where a person facing legal proceedings is physically present in a location or territory in which the court operates so that there is a 'territorial nexus'. However, with online activity the situation can be very complicated. There may be multiple jurisdictions to contend with in which the cybercrime is committed in one jurisdiction, the victims located in another and the losses consequently spread over several other territories. There may be different laws in play with various kinds of penalties that may apply.

1864. These sorts of challenges will be familiar to litigators especially the laws of evidence. The requirements of the law such as the presentation of complex and technical evidence; the admissibility of evidence; juror understanding of offence elements; reliance on expert opinion in technology cases and the skill base of lawyers, judges, juries and court officials dealing with high tech forensic issues present unique challenges. On successful prosecution, other challenges will include the reparation for loss, extradition of persons and extraterritorial compliance with court orders.

1865. Reform of the relevant cyber legislation would need to consider new modes of punishment other than forfeiture of equipment and restriction of use orders. Given the nature of some cybercrime offenders' computer skills, such skills could be put to constructive purposes such as supervised community service orders that includes the offender sharing knowledge and providing tutoring in computer skills to communities.

1102. *See* TCP Code at https://www.commsalliance.com.au/Documents/all/codes/c628.

§3. Defences and Mitigating Factors

1866. The *Crimes Act* 1914 (Cth) prescribes the sentences applicable to breaches of Federal legislation. For example, relevant matters for consideration on sentences in NSW are set out as a non-exhaustive list of factors under section 16A of the *Crimes Act* 1900 (NSW). Matters that generally will mitigate a penalty include the timing of any guilty plea, the offender's character, the offender's prior record, assistance provided by the offender to the authorities and the offender's prospect of rehabilitation and likelihood of reoffending. The absence of intent to cause damage or make a financial gain could be considered by a sentencing court as a factor of mitigation. Some of the offences particularized above cannot be 'attempted'; they must be committed. For example, a person cannot attempt to commit the offence of 'unauthorized access, modification or impairment with intent to commit a serious offence'.

1867. Mitigation of penalties and exceptions to offences discussed previously may include those involving altruistic 'ethical hacking' and 'juvenile delinquents' show-off hacking activities where there is no intention to cause damage or to make a financial gain but only to demonstrate the vulnerabilities of computer systems.

1868. Novel defence arguments could include role playing; engaging in sexual fantasies; entrapment; therapeutic behaviours; undertaking research; and forms of Internet addiction disorders.

Chapter 8. National Cybercrime Strategy

1869. The *National Plan to Combat Cybercrime* (2013) provides a consistent strategic direction for agencies involved in combatting cybercrime.[1103] This national commitment is to ensure a safe and more secure digital environment for all Australians based on key principles that underpin the approach. An initiative under the Plan is the ReportCyber which replaced the Australian *Cybercrime* Online *Reporting* Network (ACORN) to enable the public to report cybercrime, obtain information to protect themselves and to ensure agencies can respond more quickly.[1104] Appendix B the National Plan to Combat Cybercrime summarizes these initiatives.

§1. Cyber-safety Legislation

1870. The concept of cyber-safety includes the initiatives to help citizens manage their online behaviour and protect them from harm. Such harm from cyber harassment, cyberstalking and cyberbullying has criminal penalties

1871. In December 2018, the Government announced an AUD 17 million online safety package, to include new resources for parents and carers, an online safety research programme and the development of an Online Safety Charter for digital platforms.[1105]

1872. In the 2018 discussion paper on the *Review of the Enhancing Online Safety Act* 2015 *and the Online Content Scheme*,[1106] the government identified a need for review of the Online Content Scheme.[1107] In particular, the government indicated that 'developments in anonymous and encrypted networking and new hosting arrangements are increasing opportunities for prohibited conduct to be distributed, making it more difficult to determine where it is hosted'. The existing scheme, contained in Schedules 5 and 7 of the *Broadcasting Services Act* 1992 (Cth), is outdated and the eSafety Commissioner has highlighted[1108] that it is 'misaligned with current technologies, usage patterns, community concerns and enforcement mechanisms'.[1109]

1103. *See* Department of Home Affairs National Plan (2013) at https://www.homeaffairs.gov.au/criminal-justice/files/national-plan-combat-cybercrime.pdf.
1104. *See* ACSC Online scams or fraud at https://www.cyber.gov.au/acsc/report.
1105. *See* Prime Minister (2018) at https://www.pm.gov.au/media/keeping-children-safe-online, (18 Dec).
1106. *See* Australian Parliament House (2018) Reviews of the Enhancing Online Safety Act 2015 and the Online Content Scheme: discussion paper at https://parlinfo.aph.gov.au/parlInfo/search/display/display.w3p;query=Id%3A%22library%2Fjrnart%2F6705716%22.
1107. *See* Department of Infrastructure (2015) at https://www.infrastructure.gov.au/have-your-say/reviews-enhancing-online-safety-act-2015-and-online-content-scheme.
1108. *See* eSafety Commissioner (2018) statements at https://parlinfo.aph.gov.au/parlInfo/search/display/display.w3p;query=Id%3A%22library%2Fjrnart%2F6705716%22 (1 June).
1109. *See* Biddington, M (2018) Regulation of Australian online content: cybersafety and harm at https://www.aph.gov.au/About_Parliament/Parliamentary_Departments/Parliamentary_Library/pubs/BriefingBook46p/Cybersafety.

1873. The government tabled the Briggs Review on the *Enhancing Online Safety Act* 2015 (Cth) and the Online Content Scheme in February 2019.[1110] The key recommendation of the review is that 'existing out-of-date and inconsistent legislation should be replaced by a new Online Safety Act and a new single code of industry practice'.

1874. Following a consultation period in early 2019, the government outlined its expectations for industry in relation to protecting children online.[1111] A Draft Online Safety Charter is underpinned by two fundamental principles in which the standards of behaviour online should reflect the standards that apply offline, and, content that is harmful to users, particularly children, should be appropriately restricted.[1112]

1875. The *Online Safety Act* 2021 (Cth) was passed on 23 June 2021 and came into effect on 23 January 2022.[1113] The Act creates the world's first cyber abuse takedown scheme for adults in addition to other online safety protections. The Act implements five 'schemes' to deal with the removal of harmful online material relating to:

1. children (cyberbullying scheme);
2. adults (adult cyber-abuse scheme);
3. the sharing of intimate images without consent (image-based scheme);
4. abhorrent violent material (abhorrent violent material blocking scheme); and,
5. harmful online content (online content scheme).

1876. The Act affects OSPs with Australian end users including electronic services (such as email, instant messaging or chat services); social media services; Internet service providers; app distributor services (such as Apple's App Store or Google's Play Store); and search engines.

1877. Overseas-based OSPs will need to comply with the Act which has extra-territorial application.

1110. *See* Briggs Review (2015) at https://www.infrastructure.gov.au/sites/default/files/briggs-report-stat-review-enhancing-online-safety-act2015.pdf.

1111. *See* Australian Parliament House (2019) at https://parlinfo.aph.gov.au/parlInfo/search/display/display.w3p;query=Id%3A%22library%2Flcatalog%2F01244374%22 (1 Jan). *See also* Australian Parliament House (2018) at https://parlinfo.aph.gov.au/parlInfo/search/display/display.w3p;query=Id%3A%22media%2Fpressrel%2F6396243%22 (12 Dec).

1112. Department of Communications and the Arts (2018) *Reviews of the Enhancing Online Safety Act 2015 and the Online Content Scheme*, Discussion Paper (June), Canberra.

1113. *See* text of the Act at https://www.legislation.gov.au/Details/C2021A00076.

1878. The Act establishes a 'Basic Online Safety Expectations' framework that obliges OSP to take reasonable steps to ensure the safety of users and minimize the extent harmful material is provided on their service.[1114]

1879. The online content scheme regulates offensive content through a complaints-based mechanism and requires OSP to develop mandatory industry codes and standards. It will be mandatory for OSP to implement a restricted access scheme that requires users to declare that they are 18 years or older to access R 18+ or Category 1 content.

1880. The eSafety Commissioner is empowered to issue 'removal notices' to OSP. A removal notice may be issued to an online service provider anywhere in the world so long as the alleged victim is an Australian resident.

1881. Other specific powers of the eSafety Commissioner include compelling online service providers to provide information about the identity of 'trolls' or persons who use fake accounts or anonymity to abuse others; block websites in response to online crises; and, compel search engines and app stores to remove access to websites or app stores that have failed to comply with previous removal orders.

1882. In June 2021 the federal parliament introduced the *Ransomware Payments Bill 2021 (No.2).*[1115] The proposed law would require public and private entities (other than small business) to report any ransomware payments to the Australian Cyber Security Centre (ACSC). Such information may be disclosed to any person for the purpose of informing the recipients about the current cyber threat environment and to law enforcement agencies. Protection from criminal and civil proceedings is proposed because of the notice and disclosure required by the law. The Bill was introduced into the Senate as there was no debate in the lower house.[1116]

1883. The *Crimes Legislation Amendment (Ransomware Action Plan) Bill* 2022 (Cth) was introduced into the House of Representatives on 17 February 2022.[1117] This Bill gives effect to the government's Ransomware Action Plan and creates specific offences for ransomware attacks and related financial crimes. The Bill seeks to deter and safeguard Australians against cyber theft, encryption, extortion and other cyberattack tactics by creating specific ransomware offences by amending relevant sections under the *Criminal Code Act* 1995 (Cth), *Proceeds of Crime Act* 2002 (Cth) and *Crimes Act* 1914 (Cth).

1114. *See* Basic Online Safety Expectations text at https://www.legislation.gov.au/Details/F2022L00062/b98a4f01-6589-4c2e-b7d3-4a1427813a45.
1115. *See* text of the Bill at http://classic.austlii.edu.au/au/legis/cth/bill/rpb20212280/.
1116. *See* Kristina Keneally (2021) media release 12 August at https://www.kristinakeneally.com.au/news/media-releases/labor-introduces-ransomware-bill-in-senate/.
1117. *See* text of the Bill at http://www5.austlii.edu.au/au/legis/cth/bill//////claapb2022496/.

1884. While it is generally not illegal for any organization to pay a ransom, careful decision-making is required in the light of specific offences under the *Commonwealth Criminal Code* and the *AML/CTF Act* 2006 (Cth). It is an offence for payments to be made either for money laundering purposes or to a 'terrorist organisation' of any organization proscribed by UN sanctions or Australia's autonomous sanctions.

1885. On 13 October 2021, the Minister for Home Affairs unveiled a 'new and comprehensive' Ransomware Action Plan.[1118] The plan outlines Australian capabilities and powers to combat ransomware. The plan signposts legislative reforms to introduce mandatory reporting of cyber extortion and criminal offences to deter malicious actors highlighting the importance of information sharing in the fight against cyber criminals. The plan is a part of the government's Cyber Strategy and is the latest in a series of actions taken by the government to combat the escalating threat of ransomware and cyber extortion attacks.

1886. In October 2021 a private member's bill was introduced in federal parliament as the *Social Media (Basic Expectations and Defamation) Bill 2021* to ensure social media users are safe online. The prime minister supported the bill.[1119] The eponymous bill's basic expectations of a social media service is to be mandated and social media companies may be required to show how such expectations have been met. The proposed law would also enable users of social media to make complaints to the eSafety Commissioner about defamatory material on social media platforms.

1887. In November 2021 a follow-up *Social Media (Anti-Trolling) Bill 2022* was announced but yet to be introduced.[1120] Under this law social media companies would be required to obtain each user's name, email address and phone number to limit the creation of anonymous accounts to launch troll attacks. The law will also empower victims of defamation to unmask anonymous user accounts through a complaints mechanism and an 'end user information disclosure order' from a court.

1118. *See* Department of Home Affairs (2021) at https://www.homeaffairs.gov.au/about-us/our-portfolios/cyber-security/strategy/australias-ransomware-action-plan (13 Oct).

1119. *See* text of the Bill at http://www5.austlii.edu.au/au/legis/cth/bill_em/smeadb2021373/index.html; and the prime minister's media release at https://www.pm.gov.au/media/combatting-online-trolls-and-strengthening-defamation-laws.

1120. *See* Attorney General (2021) statement at https://www.ag.gov.au/legal-system/social-media-anti-trolling-bill; and exposure draft of the bill at https://www.ag.gov.au/legal-system/publications/exposure-draft-social-media-anti-trolling-bill-2021.

Chapter 9. International and Regional Agreements

§1. Cybercrime Convention 2001

1888. The Council of Europe approved the *Convention on Cyber-Crime* (Cybercrime Convention also known as the Budapest Convention) on 19 September 2001. The treaty was approved by the forty-three Member States and ratified by Australia in 2010. The treaty creates processes for law enforcement agencies to pursue cybercrime across national borders.[1121] As of November 2013, 41 states ratified the Convention, while a further eleven states have signed the Convention but not ratified the treaty.[1122] Apart from requiring member states to provide mutual assistance to other member states, the Convention aims to facilitate the sharing of intelligence, and to make it easier for member states to collect evidence from foreign jurisdictions.

1889. The Budapest Convention has its roots in early efforts where parliamentarians from the forty-three nations of the Council of Europe proposed transatlantic cooperation to block racist websites and the banning of hate speech. A report found that there were 4,000 race-hate sites in 2001, including 2,500 in the US, compared to only 160 in 1995.[1123] The Council of Europe approved text of a cybercrime protocol outlawing racist speech on the Internet.

1890. In August 2012, the Australian government passed the *Cybercrime Legislation Amendment Act* 2012 (Cth) (CLAA). One of the purposes of the CLAA is to enable Australia to accede to the Council of Europe Convention on Cybercrime (Cybercrime Convention), the only international treaty on cybercrime.

§2. Law Enforcement

1891. Australia's *International Cyber and Critical Tech Engagement Strategy 2020* describes the Australian Federal Police's (AFP) partnership with Interpol's Cyber Fusion Centre in Singapore and Europol's European Cyber Crime Centre to support the identification of new, imminent and evolving cybercrime threats.[1124]

1121. *See* Cybercrime Convention at http://conventions.coe.nt/Treaty/EN/rojets/FinalCybercrime.htm. Background Information and full text of the Convention can be found at the Council of Europe's website, at http://www.coe.int/T/E/Communication_and_Research/Press/Themes_Files/Cybercrime.

1122. Council of Europe list of signatories and ratification of the treaty at https://www.coe.int/en/web/conventions/full-list?module=signatures-by-treaty&treatynum=185.

1123. Tallo's Report Doc. 9263, Racism and Xenophobia in Cyberspace at the Council of Europe website at https://pace.coe.int/en/files/16960 and at https://assembly.coe.int/nw/xml/XRef/X2H-Xref-ViewHTML.asp?FileID=9540&lang=EN.

1124. *See* Department of Foreign Affairs & Trade (2021) at https://www.internationalcybertech.gov.au/sites/default/files/2021-05/21066%20DFAT%20Cyber%20Affairs%20Strategy%202021%20update%20Internals%201%20Acc.pdf, p. 52.

1892. This international initiative accords with the principles outlined in Australia's *National Strategy to Fight Transnational, Serious and Organised Crime.*[1125] The Council of Australian Governments (COAG) agreed to the National Strategy to Fight Transnational, Serious and Organised Crime on 12 December 2018. The strategy outlines the framework in which governments, the private sector, civil society, academia and the community will work together to achieve our vision of an Australia that is secure and cohesive.

§3. COOPERATIVE AGREEMENTS

1893. An aspiration that cybercrime protection will be realized internationally is when developing countries receive help in terms of law their enforcement capabilities. In 2001 thirteen countries, including Australia and the US, signed a memorandum of understanding to help stop the threat of cross-border Internet fraud.[1126] The Internet-based project gathers and share cross-border e-commerce complaints. The objective is that such a move will improve international law enforcement agencies' ability to address cross-border Internet fraud and deception.

1894. Since 2014, the Australian Attorney General's Department (AGD) has partnered with Pacific Island states made up of Tonga, Fiji, Samoa, Vanuatu, Solomon Islands, Niue and Tuvalu to advance cybercrime law reform.[1127] AGD support ranges from assistance in analysing compliance of existing laws with the Cybercrime Convention to assistance with drafting instructions for legislative reforms and the drafting of domestic laws.

I. Christchurch Call

1895. On 15 March 2019, a Facebook live video was broadcast from Christchurch, New Zealand, documenting a terror attack which resulted in the death of 51 people. This attack highlighted weaknesses in social media posts and the lack of protections and gaps in legislation globally.

1896. As a response to the terror attack, the Australian *Criminal Code Amendment (Sharing of Abhorrent Violent Material) Act* 2019 (Cth) (SAVM Act) was swiftly passed making Internet service and social media providers accountable for

1125. *See* Department of Home Affairs (2018) *National Strategy to Fight Transnational Serious Organised Crime* at https://www.homeaffairs.gov.au/nat-security/files/strategy-transnational-serious-organised-crime.pdf, p. 14.
1126. The memorandum of understanding at the US Federal Trade Commission at https://www.ftc.gov/news-events/press-releases/2001/04/united-states-and-twelve-countries-unveil-e-consumergov.
1127. *See* Australia's *International Cyber and Critical Tech Engagement Strategy 2020* p. 55 at https://www.internationalcybertech.gov.au/.

the removal of abhorrent and violent content. The legislation alarmed the international community because of its immediate adoption, perceived unrealistic obligations and harsh penalties, as well as its broad extraterritorial reach.[1128]

1897. The SAVM Act amended the *Criminal Code Act* 1995 (Cth) introduces new offences that apply to providers of Internet, hosting or content services. Such providers must refer details of abhorrent violent material that records, or streams conduct that has occurred, or is occurring, in Australia to the AFP. These reports must be made within a reasonable time after becoming aware of the existence of such material. The providers must remove from, or cease hosting, on their services abhorrent violent material that is capable of being accessed within Australia.

1898. The reports by the AFP will enable the eSafety Commissioner to issue a written notice to a provider of a hosting or content service notifying them that abhorrent violent material can be accessed by, or is hosted, on their service.

II. Australia-US Cloud Act Agreement 2021

1899. Australia signed an agreement with the US government entitled *Agreement between the Government of Australia and the Government of the United States of America on Access to Electronic Data for the Purpose of Countering Serious Crime* (commonly referred to as the Australia-US CLOUD Act Agreement) on 15 December 2021.[1129]

1900. In March 2018, the US Congress passed the Clarifying Lawful Overseas Use of Data Act and the backronym – CLOUD Act – to improve procedures for both foreign and US investigators to obtain access to vital electronic information held by service providers. The CLOUD Act permits the US to enter into agreements with foreign partners that allow their authorities to obtain critical electronic data from communications providers in the other country.[1130]

1901. The Australia-US CLOUD Act Agreement is the first agreement that will be designated under the International Production Order (IPO) framework. The plan is to review the framework by the Australian Parliament and the US Congress before it enters into force, anticipated at the end of 2022. The Australian -US Cloud Act Agreement represents a major step forward for international cooperation in investigating crimes – from cyber and financial crimes, through to terrorism, drug trafficking and human trafficking/exploitation.

1128. *See* Valcic, J (2021) The Sharing of Abhorrent Violent Material Act: The Realities and Implications of Australia's New Laws Regulating Social Media Companies, *Bond Law Review* Vol.33(1).
1129. *See* Department of Home Affairs (2022) at https://www.homeaffairs.gov.au/about-us/our-portfolios/national-security/lawful-access-telecommunications/australia-united-states-cloud-act-agreement, (25 Jan).
1130. *See* US Congress White Paper (2022) at http://www.justice.gov/CLOUDAct, (26 January).

III. *International Production Orders Act* 2021 (IPO)

1902. In keeping with its international commitments the Australian government has ensured that law enforcement and national security agencies have appropriate tools to keep pace with evolving modern technology. As part of this commitment, the *Telecommunications Legislation Amendment (International Production Orders) Act* 2021 (IPO Act) was passed by Parliament on 24 June 2021.

1903. The IPO Act establishes a new international production orders (IPO) framework of reciprocal international agreements under the TIA Act. The IPO enable Commonwealth, state and territory agencies to seek data, via the Australian Designated Authority, from prescribed communications service providers stored in foreign countries with which Australia has a designated agreement.

1904. The IPO Act 2021 will allow relevant law enforcement and surveillance authorities to access data from communications service providers overseas. Likewise Australian-based prescribed communications providers would be subject to similar requirement with incoming IPOs issued by international authorities that have an agreement with Australia.

1905. The IPO Act and the Australia-US CLOUD Act Agreement will enable Australian law enforcement and national security agencies to send IPO directly to communications service providers in the US seeking the disclosure of electronic data, without those orders needing to be separately authorized by US government agencies and courts. This will enhance the effectiveness of Australian investigations and prosecutions of serious crimes.

IV. Australia-UK Cyber and Critical Technology Partnership

1906. On 20 January 2022 Australia agreed a Cyber and Critical Technology Partnership with the UK that will help shape a positive technology environment and maintain an Internet that is open, free and secure.[1131] This partnership aims to foster closer cooperation in tackling malign actors; promote values and a positive vision for technology; strengthen global technology supply chains; and harness technology to solve global challenges.

1131. *See* Minister for Foreign Affairs Statement on the UK-Australia Cyber and Critical Technology Partnership, Media release 20 Jan. 2022 at https://www.foreignminister.gov.au/minister/marise-payne/media-release/statement-uk-australia-cyber-and-critical-technology-partnership, and at https://www.gov.uk/government/news/foreign-secretary-statement-cyber-and-critical-technology-partnership-with-australia.

Summary and Conclusion

1907. Summary and Conclusions reflects on information technology law in Australia and is a postscript to this volume. The themes running through this book are summarized and prospective legislation and policy developments on the horizon are outlined. As the Web 3.0, metaverse and 5G technology would probably dominate the Internet, these megatrends are discussed together with the legal infrastructure that may be necessary to guide, limit, regulate and encourage the development of technology for the benefit of netizens, the nation-state and the world.

§1. Reflections and Postscript

1908. Part I. A key issue emanating from Part I on telecommunication, media and technology regulation is the recognition of the importance that jurisdiction plays not only in terms of its extraterritorial effects but also its role in a borderless cyberspace. The extraterritorial effects of statutory regimes for online securities, financial institutions, advertisements and e-business generally lead to uncertainties as such activities may have to abide to the regulatory dictates of several jurisdictions at once.

1909. It has been suggested that a technological solution may provide a solution to the impasse. New developing technology may permit a business to select their customers and jurisdictional reach of their website through geo-blocking. Software may be written that allows consumers to designate the countries, laws, or protections desired, and an expert system will match those preferences with websites and platforms that meet the specified criteria.

1910. This begs the question as to whether the Internet may spawn a new legal frontier. It is arguable that the Internet may indeed be a new and separate legal frontier. A proposal for reform is to assign Internet law disputes to their own territory, that is, to cyberspace with forms of self-regulation with cyber courts and other mechanisms to resolve disputes. However, it will be difficult to imagine courts giving up such jurisdictional powers especially where consumer protection, enforcement and ethical oversight cannot be assured.

1911. Part II. An unfinished aspect of the discussion online public services in Part II is the voter identification bill introduced in 2021. Initial reactions to the Bill suggest that it could potentially be racially discriminatory in effect given that not every Australian has some form of formal identification. The unintended consequence is that of disenfranchisement. As noted elsewhere voter identification may be weaponized and lead to electoral fraud. The Australian long-standing tradition is that in federal, state and territory elections it is not necessary to produce an ID to vote.

1912. Part III Online Transactions raised a myriad of enigmas as information technology challenges traditional notions of law forcing paradigm shifts. Self -executing smart contracts raise the interesting question of who the principal might be when liability questions arise. There is currently no preeminent legal theory that imposes a legal standard of responsibility for online intermediaries. To discover the primary roles and responsibilities it may be necessary to examine each of the theories of law which includes copyright, defamation, consumer protection and statutory liability.

1913. Cryptocurrencies do not easily sit within the definition of a 'foreign currency' for tax purposes and there are no explicit regulations or case law in Australia concerning the treatment of cryptocurrency in succession law.

1914. While the use of cash continues to decline nation-wide, consumers will need assurances that electronic payment systems are robust and trustworthy given the trends by major financial institutions to de-bank or un-bank by the withdrawal of bank branch services forcing clients to go online.

1915. The growth of e-cash portends a wholesale shift towards electronic transactions. However, this also implies greater difficulties in monitoring and regulating its uses together with issues such as the loss of revenue from tax avoidance, loss of income earned by central banks, crime and money laundering and the loss of privacy. The greater impact of electronic transactions would be the unintended consequences such as the loss of economic activity in the financial, retailing and corporate sectors in addition to the loss of tax revenues to countries with lax regulatory environments – the so-called phenomena of forum shopping or regulatory arbitrage.[1132] Regulatory arbitrage is a practice where firms capitalize on shortcomings in regulatory systems to circumvent unfavourable regulations for tax and other advantages. The need to do so may also signal the need for regulatory clarity.

1916. Part IV Digital Property Rights, apart from canvassing traditional IPR, presents a conundrum in whether an artificial intelligence system that creates 'property' in goods and services is capable of being named an 'inventor' and hence author and owner of a patentable subject matter. The Designs Reform Project initiative for design innovation and design rights is currently examining virtual and non-physical designs and the protection of designs in iteration with the prospect of using blockchain technology as a protection mechanism. How these may evolve is a topic requiring monitoring.

1132. *See* Hayes, A (2021) Regulatory Arbitrage at https://www.investopedia.com/terms/r/regulatory-arbitrage.asp.

1917. It was also suggested that domain names system may contradict traditional trademark legislation. The latter may confer 'rights' in IP whereas no such exclusive digital right exists in the former. The ideal would be one where both the domain name and trademark are one and the same and points equivocally to a business enterprise or an entity. Having a trademark registration does not automatically entitle one to a domain name licence.

1918. Part V. A major conclusion from Part V Cybersecurity Legal Issues is the Richardson Review recommendation to develop a new single national surveillance law that better protects individuals' information and data; ensures law enforcement and provide security agencies the necessary powers they may require to enforce security laws.

1919. Part VI Under the topic of cybercrime the treatment of Commonwealth legislation in the subheading of telecommunication offences is the separation of specific elements of electronic communication such as the Internet from telecommunications generally and technological developments particularly. One of the issues overlooked is the uncertainty on how defamation law should apply on digital platforms. Case law suggests the increasingly pervasive influence of the digital age and the 'grapevine effect' of defamatory material when communications move rapidly across the world via the Internet and reach potentially unforeseen audiences. Finer distinctions would need to be made in such litigation to underscore distinctions with differences as to whether these are 'in the public interest' or 'of public interest' generally.

§2. Prospective Policy and Legal Developments

1920. Information technology presents many challenges to traditional notions of law that requires a major paradigm shift. New technology brings with it opportunities as well. These include rights to privacy, protection against defamation by email, computer crime, trust services and electronic data interchange, intellectual property questions, transborder data flow issues, rules of evidence and use of expert systems. As technology transcends national boundaries and globalization continues, the trend may be towards developing uniform international laws.

1921. The legal implications of new technology like blockchains loom large in this postscript. Apart from data portability where the data are 'locked' within the chain and unable to be used in other systems, additional concerns include those of keeping secure the encryption keys and the locking of resources to inhibit any other transaction with that asset, the potential collusion among groups of users on blockchains to mine blocks by recreating the blockchain and the level of user savviness and safety of consumers in the widespread use of this technology. As the public and private sector interest in blockchain technology continues apace the legal and economic implications will need greater attention. Blockchain technology also comes at an environmental cost due to its high energy demand and carbon footprint for its proof-of-work system.[1133]

1922. Australian courts, like those around the world, are having difficulties to identify the online intermediary who is not morally responsible for a tort but should nevertheless be expected to do something to prevent it. While the *Voller* defamation case may be seen as a significant landmark in internet governance, the result must be balanced against the need to support legitimate socially beneficial online speech. Complex policy questions such as these need resolution to help make it easy to navigate the law in cyberspace.

1923. In June 2021 the federal parliament introduced the *Ransomware Payments Bill 2021 (No.2)*. The proposed law would require public and private entities (other than small business) to report any ransomware payments to the Australian Cyber Security Centre.

1924. In October 2021 a private member's bill was introduced in federal parliament as the *Social Media (Basic Expectations and Defamation) Bill 2021* to ensure social media users are safe online.

1925. In November 2021 a follow-up *Social Media (Anti-Trolling) Bill 2022* was announced but yet to be passed.[1134]

1926. Section 51(5) of the Constitution empowers the Commonwealth government with power to legislate with respect to 'postal, telegraphic, telephonic and *other like services*' [emphasis added]. While the Constitution was drafted when radio and television were not contemplated at the time, both media have been held by the High Court to be within the scope of 'other like services'. The time may well be opportune to overtly consider Internet services as a matter of course to be within the rubric of other like services.

1927. In March 2022 the Department of Prime Minister and Cabinet invited responses to an issues paper on automated decision-making and AI regulation as part of *Positioning Australia as a Leader in Digital Economy Regulation.*[1135] The government is exploring safe and responsible development and deployment of new

1133. Proof of work is a form of adding new blocks of transactions to a cryptocurrency's blockchain. Proof of work is a decentralized consensus mechanism that requires members of a network to expend effort solving an arbitrary mathematical puzzle to prevent anybody from gaming the system. It is widely used in cryptocurrency mining, for validating transactions and mining new tokens. *See* Investopedia at https://www.investopedia.com/terms/p/proof-work.asp.

1134. *See* Attorney General (2021) statement at https://www.ag.gov.au/legal-system/social-media-anti-trolling-bill; and exposure draft of the bill at https://www.ag.gov.au/legal-system/publications/exposure-draft-social-media-anti-trolling-bill-2021.

1135. *See* Prime Minister & Cabinet (2022) at https://www.pmc.gov.au/sites/default/files/automated-decision-making-ai-regulation-issues-paper.pdf.

and emerging technologies such as automated decision-making and AI by modernizing relevant legal frameworks and to increase uptake, investment and consumer confidence. The corpus of work informing this inquiry include the Australian government's AI Ethics Framework (2019), the Commonwealth Ombudsman's Automated Decision Making Better Practice Guide (2019), Human Rights and Technology Final Report (2021), AI Action Plan (2021), Blueprint for Critical Technologies (2021), Regulator Performance Guide (2021) and the Critical Technology Supply Chain Principles (2021).[1136]

1928. The Treasury issued a consultation paper on *Crypto Asset Secondary Service Providers: Licensing and Custody Requirements* in March 2022 with a view to license digital currency exchanges and custody requirements for crypto assets.[1137] The government's proposed approach is to license crypto asset secondary service providers (CASSPrs) and crypto custodians. Such an initiative would satisfy the need for regulatory certainty to encourage innovation and competition and to give consumers greater confidence in dealing with CASSPrs. The outcomes of this consultation are awaited with much anticipation.

1929. A further proposal by Senator Andrew Bragg in April 2022 in relation to crypto reforms is a comprehensive legislative package including a 'Digital Services Act'.[1138] As the main regulatory framework could fall outside the existing Australian Financial Services licensing regime the proposed Act will focus on the ecosystem of those who offer custody, storage, brokering, exchange and dealing services or operate a market in crypto assets for retail clients. No Bill to support this proposal has been put to the parliament.

§3. Disruptive Technologies and Megatrends

1930. At the start of the second decade of the new century the global population is assailed by disruptive technologies and megatrends that have pushed people, governments and corporations to uncertain futures and greater anxiety. The following reflection contemplates scenarios where disruptive technologies together with mega-trends provide grist to cybersecurity legislation and the prevention of cybercrime.

1136. *See* the corpus of work referenced respectively at https://www.ombudsman.gov.au/publications/better-practice-guides/automated-decision-guide; https://humanrights.gov.au/our-work/rights-and-freedoms/projects/human-rights-and-technology; https://www.industry.gov.au/sites/default/files/June%202021/document/australias-ai-action-plan.pdf; https://www.pmc.gov.au/sites/default/files/publications/ctpco-blueprint-critical-technology.pdf; and at https://digitaleconomy.pmc.gov.au/strategy/foreword.
1137. *See* The Treasury at https://treasury.gov.au/consultation/c2022-259046.
1138. Senator Andrew Bragg is the Chair of the Senate Select Committee on Financial Technology and Regulatory Technology. *See* media release at the https://www.andrewbragg.com/post/address-at-blockchain-week-2022.

1931. Disruptive technologies include Web 3.0, 5G computer networks, the IOT, AI and the scalability of computing power. Each of these either separately or in concert have engineered trends where blockchains are becoming mainstream, where NFTs permeate all spheres of industrial and artistic endeavour and cryptocurrencies have promoted decentralized agendas. The anxiety and insecurities that these new ventures produce is exacerbated by those with criminal intent who prey on the unwary and keen on turning a quick profit. The Hollywood wild west or the Ned Kelly world of the bush ranger where there are no laws may seem to be an apt metaphor. But decentralization does not mean unregulated and deregulated. Cyber law is assisted by the convergence of business services from legal services to operational technologies and the IOT where various electronic devices speak to other devices with a common language. Technology offers services in new ways to create new services and whole new industries in support of the Fourth Industrial Revolution.

1932. Web 3.0 is an integral key to the third iteration of the Internet emerging from Web 2.0 centralized platforms. Web 3.0's decentralized, democratic internet may be attractive to some supporters, but implementation would require overcoming hurdles in terms of user interfaces, experiences and content. Web 3.0 is virtualized and is one where websites and apps process information in a smart, human-like way through technologies like data analytics, machine learning, big data and blockchain technology. Web 3.0 will enable a form of peer-to-peer Internet that bypass intermediaries thereby avoiding the exposure of data or target advertising. Trust is provided by blockchain technology making data and information more secure and transparent to all because of the distributed ledger technology. The currency of the Web 3.0 infrastructure will be crypto of various kinds. Unfortunately, cryptocurrencies will also become the new 'frontline' in cybercriminal scams.

1933. 5G technology opens possibilities that are industry-specific from greenhouse automation in agriculture, remote monitoring of stock levels in manufacturing to data analytics for patient outcomes in healthcare and traffic monitoring for smart cities. A recent report by Deloitte Access Economics (2020) has warned that Australia risks losing its world-leading position on 5G and missing out on extra AUD 27 billion of economic growth available this decade unless businesses actively pursue the new technology and governments reset outdated policy.[1139] Among the report's other recommendations include government support for 5G education and skills development campaigns for businesses, tax incentives for 5G investment and be an early 5G adopter itself.

1934. IOTs scale and reach could be much larger than imagined. Faster wireless Internet through 5G network will enable more data to be transmitted between devices. According to Ericsson about 28 billion smart devices will be connected

1139. *See* Deloitte Access Economics (2020) *Mobile Nation 2019. The 5G Future* at https://www2.deloitte.com/au/en/pages/economics/articles/mobile-nation.html.

across the world by 2021.[1140] Furthermore, machine-to-machine communication will be employed in more than 15 billion devices. It is envisaged that around six to seven devices will be carried per person by 2020.[1141] IOT will capture and monitor health data, physical performance in industry, agriculture, transportation and will be wholly cross-sectoral. The potential for increased productivity will become enormous.

1935. AI enabled by 5G will mean greater connectivity between devices with machine learning becoming more effective.[1142] Connected devices with AI will be able to capture data, analyse the data and make decisions and then communicate with other devices. As more data are captured and analysed the insights become more powerful and useful. Most of the computing and machine learning would take place in centralized data centres or in a distributed cloud that runs across multiple locations. The demand for cloud computing would be higher to service the processing power required by AI. Concurrently there will also be the development of custom-made semiconductors and IC chips to accommodate the speed and application-specific requirements and capabilities of AI.

1936. NFTs are unique and one-of-a-kind tokens with data stored on a digital ledger using blockchain technology to authenticate products. Artists can use NFTs to sell their art while high-end haute couture designer houses can guarantee their one-off designs. NFT technology can be used to establish fair payments for the artist who would potentially benefit every time the artwork is sold at higher and higher prices.

1937. But NFTs give rise to novel IP rights issues. Cyber law must recognize the intangibility of digital property rights. A challenging issue that must be addressed is what NFTs represent and what is being bought and sold. As a token it may be subject to different regulatory regimes as a 'currency', for its utility and security. These tokens all carry different rights and are sued for different purposes.

1938. Unlike cryptocurrencies, NFTs do not represent a store of value in and of themselves. Their value derives from the rights attaching to the underlying assets. 'NFTs have opened up a Pandora's box with respect to the enforcement of IP rights, where the value ascribed to an NFT as a whole is greater than the sum of its parts'.[1143] As the minting and sale of NFTs is unregulated but also highly accessible to an international audience it is indeed a Pandora's box. NFTs will emerge to test the applicability of existing general law and copyright laws.

1140. *See* Ericsson (2016) Cellular Networks for Massive IoT: Enabling Low Power Wide Area Applications, Stockholm, Sweden, Jan., pp. 1-13 and at https://www.ericsson.com/en/reports-and-papers/white-papers/cellular-networks-for-massive-iot--enabling-low-power-wide-area-applications.
1141. *See* Ejaz, W, Anpalagan, A, Imran, MA, Jo, M, Naeem, M, & Qaisar, SB (2016) 'Internet of Things (IoT) (2016) 5G wireless communications', *IEEE Access*, vol. 4, pp. 10310-10314.
1142. *See* Department of Industry, Science & Technology (2021) *Australia's AI Action Plan* (June) at https://www.industry.gov.au/sites/default/files/June%202021/document/australias-ai-action-plan.pdf.
1143. Tan, P (2021) 'NFTs and the IP conundrum' at https://law.asia/nfts-ip-conundrum/.

1939. New legal frontiers. Previously it was conjectured that arguably the Internet could represent a new legal frontier that governs cyberspace. This debate is probably for in-depth academic jurisprudence at another forum, but for the moment the indicia of such a legal frontier is presented for further scrutiny. Such indicators include the metaverse, parallel internets and dark webs and decentralized regulatory challenges within the geographically borderless cyberworld.

1940. Cyberlaw is central if e-business is to be mainstreamed and a challenge to bricks-and-mortar enterprises. In a highly disrupted world, e-business is not optional and any business not taking it seriously may not be in business in the long term.

1941. Globally, there have been increasing efforts by private organizations and governments to cooperate on sharing information and tackling cybersecurity issues. Global solutions might be required even for local issues, but this brings to fore geopolitics, world trade, multipartite agreements, treaties and conventions. Simultaneously there is a need to balance national security anxieties with economic concerns and that of sovereignty and independence from interference.

1942. Cyber law regulation and compliance in a digital world can be complex and confusing. In a global economy, human activity – goods and services – move across national borders. In this environment, legal compliance has grown in volume and complexity with the regulatory context constantly changing and with liability even more likely to be personal rather than corporate. Aggressive regulatory agencies and new procedures such as class actions and expanded discovery may make the cost of non-compliance more prohibitive.

1943. Just as cyber law must depend upon traditional metaphors and analogies to extend the Internet, so too, appropriate legal metaphors must emerge which will allow parliaments, courts and regulators to design the appropriate legal infrastructure that will provide the necessary guidance for this new industry to evolve. The difficulty here is that the norms that exist in the real-world do not necessarily transfer easily to the digital realm. Thus, any discussion of the regulation of the Internet may be considered incomplete if the trends arising from regulation is not recognized. There remain pockets of uncertainty and ephemerality in legal constructs and rules in the face of developments in the cyber world. New imaginations might be needed. Whether a light touch regulatory approach suits the cyberworld begs the question.

1944. One illustration is the curious question as to whether cyber law extends beyond the grave. A young Canadian died of septic shock and a perforated intestine and complications related to Crohn's disease recently.[1144] He was the gatekeeper of USD 265 million fortune in cryptocurrency. However, no one has access to the funds because the funds remain sealed in an online black hole with the company

1144. Tomlinson, H (2019) 'Investors shut out of crypto fortune', *The Australian*, 11 Feb. 2019, p. 10. *See* Wired 'Crypto exchange CEO dies holding only key to $137 million' at https://www.wired.com/story/crypto-exchange-ceo-dies-holding-only-key/.

Quadriga, Canada's largest cryptocurrency exchange, claiming that access to the encrypted money died with him.[1145] The same may be said of funds left in dormant accounts and the owner may have deceased leaving behind 'old' digital coins protected by a password. But several legal conundrums remain. What is the legal position of the crypto funds and what laws governing the recovery of the money that the investors have outlaid? Contract law suggests the link between the investors and the currency exchange; succession law suggests examination of a will; encryption may prevent the surrender of passwords; and banking laws may revert such funds, if these could be retrieved, to the Crown.

1945. *The Metaverse.* A report from Citibank defines the metaverse as possibly 'the next generation of the Internet – combining the physical and digital world in a persistent and immersive manner'.[1146] In such a world the authors suggest that the metaverse would be device-agnostic and accessed via PCs, game consoles and smart phones that enhances the way all current activities in commerce, media, education and training, manufacturing and more are undertaken by society. The report estimates that the total addressable market for the metaverse could be between AUD 8 trillion to AUD 13 trillion by 2030 and the total *metaversians* numbering around 5 billion.

1946. Metaverse has nothing to do with Facebook's rebranding as Meta. The metaverse requires one to have an avatar to navigate it together with conceptual understanding, tech savviness and an appreciation of the nuances of the language, words and lexicons used. A popular means of experiencing the metaverse is via a video game using a virtual reality headset. But to really understand the online world of the metaverse one needs to be familiar with the conceptual and the linguistic such as NFTs, blockchains, crypto ecosystems of currencies, central bank digital currencies (CBDC), stablecoins, crypto assets, digital property rights and decentralized finance (DeFi). But this new iteration of the Internet will attract scrutiny and management by regulators, policymakers and governments worldwide. Cybercrime and cybersecurity will require rules against anti-money laundering, financial rules for digital wallets, crypto assets and establishing digital property rights.

1947. It is expected that consumer hardware manufacturers will be portals to the metaverse and potential gatekeepers. The blueprint is already there with the

---

1145. *See* Affidavit filed in the Supreme Court of Nova Scotia by Jennifer Robertson the wife of the CEO to Quadriga Coin Exchange on 31 Jan 2019. *See* https://www.scribd.com/document/398721572/Jennifer-Robertson-Affidavit?irclickid=RfS1eRQk9xyITJW0fEwxs2ifUkGXch1yD1Of2A0&irpid=10078&utm_source=impact&utm_medium=cpc&utm_campaign=affiliate_pdm_acquisition_Skimbit%20Ltd.&sharedid=wired.com&irgwc=1#from_embed?campaign=SkimbitLtd&ad_group=100652X1574425X398bb17cf0b2d0309c0373b5179b5c7f&keyword=660149026&source=hp_affiliate&medium=affiliate.

1146. CITI (2022) Metaverse and Money. Decrypting the Future at https://www.citivelocity.com/citigps/metaverse-and-money/?linkId=159079389&utm_source=sendgrid.com&utm_medium=email&utm_campaign=website (March).

US-International, China firewall-based and emergent Russian Internet metaverse. There is also the likely spectrum-based technology and business model with a centralized versus decentralized metaverse.

1948. A parallel Internet is also contemplated, for example, Russia's sovereign Internet law that promotes Internet independence to the rest of the world orchestrated by the telecommunication agency Rozkomnadzor.[1147] The Great China Firewall-based Internet is one of censorship given that there is just a single gateway into China forcing many to use virtual private networks (VPN) to evade and bypass content restrictions.[1148] Out of these government interventions has arisen the use of the Interplanetary File System (IPFS). The IPFS is a protocol and peer-to-peer network for storing and sharing data in a distributed file system – a decentralized alternative to the World Wide Web.[1149] In Spain the Catalan independence referendum in September-October 2017 was deemed illegal by the Constitutional Court of Spain and many websites were blocked. The Catalan Pirate Party mirrored the website on IPFS to bypass the High Court order of blocking.[1150]

1949. The dark web is a kind of an Internet that operates in the depths of mainstream Internet.[1151] The dark web appearing in the 2000s, also called the darknet, is a secret network that exists underground, websites hidden from general view and conventional search engines. This is because the online content is encrypted and inaccessible unless one uses a specific browser such as the TOR browser and may have content that are password protected. The Onion Router (TOR) was a US Naval Research Laboratory funded project to offer intelligence sources a safe and secure way to communicate from hostile environments. The dark web offers anonymity and privacy providing a social outlet for people who might otherwise be persecuted for their political beliefs and being tracked online and from cyberattacks.

1950. The dark web is the concealed portion of the deep web visible only with the right software and browser. This invisible or hidden web is further hidden by various network security measures like firewalls and encryption. The reputation that it has been linked to criminal intent or illegal content is difficult to refute, but it is not illegal to access the dark web. It is possible to use TOR to browse both the public Internet and the deeper parts of the web in private. However, many TOR-based sited have been hijacked by law enforcement agencies to monitor illegal activities

---

1147. *See* Roskomnadzor – Federal Service for Supervision of Communications, Information Technology and Mass Media at http://government.ru/en/department/58/.
1148. *See* Australia Institute of International Affairs (2019) The Great China Firewall at https://www.internationalaffairs.org.au/news-item/the-great-china-firewall/ (1 June).
1149. *See* IPFS Powers to the Distributed Web at https://ipfs,io; and *see also* Wikipedia InerPlanetary File System https://en.wikipedia.org/wiki/InterPlanetary_File_System.
1150. Balcell, MP (2017) 'Inside Catalonia's cypherpunk referendum', *Eureka Street*. Vol. 27, no. 20. (5 October).
1151. *See* Kaspersky (2022) What is the Deep and Dark Web? https://www.kaspersky.com/resource-center/threats/deep-web; and Bloomenthal, A & Cheng, M What is the dark web? *Investopedia* at https://www.investopedia.com/terms/d/dark-web.asp (22 Feb. 2022).

and drug marketplaces such as the Silk Road. The Silk Road is reputed to be a digital black market platform hosting money laundering activities and illegal drug transactions using cryptocurrencies. Users be aware of their exposure to some types of malwares like keyloggers, botnet malware, ransomware, phishing malware when accessing such sites.

1951. Geographical borders meaningless. On the Internet geographical borders are meaningless. Cyber laws and regulations may need to be transnational and cross-jurisdictional if these are to be effective tools for guidance and deterrence of malicious intentions. In April 2018, the US, UK and Australia issued a coordinated announcement that accused the Russia of a 'malicious Internet offensive' in 2017 that targeted 'government institutions, private sector organizations and infrastructure'.[1152] Australia, Britain, Canada, New Zealand and the US, forming the Five Eyes (FVEY) alliance, are increasing cooperation on the issue of 'foreign interference'. Discussions to date have focused primarily on interference by China and Russia.[1153]

1952. Cryptocurrencies have extended digital frontiers in areas unimagined previously whilst also posing regulatory challenges. Decentralized finance (DeFi) and DAOs pose existential challenges to finance and banking systems. Already the issue of a 'responsible person' in the case of a DAO collapse has exercised the minds of regulators. Such a 'responsible person' is created to provide courts or regulators with some way of attaching liability to a person for DAO failures.[1154] Administration of collapsed cryptocurrency firm Blockchain Global have found potential breaches of director's duties and insolvent trading – and have no definitive answers about who controlled the money put in by traders.[1155]

1953. Laws need to keep pace and up to date. Sophisticated and wholesale investor requirements rules under the *Corporations Act* 2001 (Cth) means one can only invest in early-stage unlisted companies including those serving the cryptocurrency market if one has a certificate from a qualified accountant certifying a prescribed net asset or gross income level. This rule has become inappropriate. Retail investors can freely purchase units in cryptocurrency tokens via an unregulated exchange. All regulated managed funds invested in crypto assets in Australia are 'wholesale' at this stage. The rule is thus ill-suited to a nascent cryptocurrency market. There may be a growing number of well-informed young people who have the

---

1152. MacAskill, E (2018) US and UK blame Russia for 'malicious; cyber-offensive, *The Guardian* (17 Apr.); and Davies, A (2018) Australia joins US and UK in blaming Russian-backed hackers for cyberattacks, *The Guardian* (17 Apr.).
1153. The Five Eyes (FVEY) is an intelligence alliance comprising Australia, Canada, New Zealand, the United Kingdom, and the United States. These countries are parties to the multilateral UKUSA Agreement, a treaty for joint cooperation in signals intelligence. Barkin, N (2018) Exclusive: Five Eyes intelligence alliance builds coalition to counter China, Thomson Reuters (12 Oct. 2018), at https://www.reuters.com/article/us-china-fiveeyes/exclusive-five-eyes-intelligence-alliance-builds-coalition-to-counter-china-idUSKCN1MM0GH.
1154. *See* Eyers, J (2022) Crypto corporate model 'threat to the tax base', *Australian Financial Review* 25 March, p. 20.
1155. *See* Lam, J (2022) Crypto collapse raises issues of ownership, *The Weekend Australian,* 12-13 Mar. 2022, p. 26.

technical knowledge and investment in tricky and complex early-stage crypto ventures. Grandfathers may be sophisticated investors having ticked all the boxes, but they might have an aversion to be involved in the crypto asset market as they may not have the nous as younger Millennials and Gen-Z's.[1156]

1954. Cryptocurrencies are digital but not financial assets and hence unregulated by the financial regulator. Any profits from dealing with cryptocurrencies may be deemed as capital gains by the ATO.

1955. *Singing from same song sheet.* Consumer protection has been the underlying theme in most regulatory activity given the primacy of consumers in any economy. However, such protection should be proportionate to enable innovation. Consumers are in an asymmetrical power relation with suppliers of goods and services implying that such regulations are a necessity but not a sufficient condition.

1956. As depicted in the popular TV Netflix series *Squid Games,* there is an asymmetry in the relationships between the gamers and the controllers in both information provision and in rules of the game. Being poor and seeking a means to escape poverty the players are in an asymmetric relationship with the controllers. The controllers on the contrary seemingly feed on the greed and vulnerabilities of the players and control all the information and rules.

1957. Likewise in the e-commerce world, there is asymmetry in information flows and relationships. Such circumstances give rise to dark patterns and unfair practices in the quest for profits and the ethics of critical technology are called into question. Dark patterns are embedded software that subtly trick users into doing things they did not mean to do. The design elements of a website deliberately obscure, mislead, coerce and/or deceive visitors into making unintended and possibly harmful choices.

1958. *Digital platforms.* Furthering this theme of consumer protection is the streamlining of the government's approach to the regulation of digital platforms in Australia. The harms from a lack of competition to consumers, and business users in a range of areas dominated by large digital platforms require a coordinated approach.

1959. Collaboration among agencies who have a role in regulating digital platforms is vital especially when considering whether to develop regulatory reforms to support competition and protect Australian consumers online. Coordination of the regulation of digital platforms and sharing of information about their approach to issues that cut across the jurisdictional divide is also necessary. In March 2022 the ACCC, ACMA, OAIC and Office of the eSafety Commissioner have together

1156. *See* criteria for sophisticated and wholesale investors at https://asic.gov.au/regulatory-resources/financial-services/financial-product-disclosure/certificates-issued-by-a-qualified-accountant/, for wholesale and retail options at https://treasury.gov.au/sites/default/files/2020-01/wholesale_and_retail_options_paper.rtf.

formed the Digital Platform Regulators Forum (DP-REG).[1157] The forum is designed to effectively access cross-sectoral regulations in relation to competition, consumer impacts, communication and media services, protecting privacy and promoting e-safety online.

1960. However, some solutions to the problems may more likely be technical and social than legal. A good example is the problem of security of signatures, something that is more likely to be resolved by developments in encryption technology than by legal reforms. Indeed, the importance of light touch soft law may emerge in the form of codes, guides, ethical standards, industry standards and the many other rules that regulate human behaviour rather than through the coercive power of the state. The distributed model of Internet governance, belonging to no single country and involving stakeholders from all sectors of society, is an example of new modes of regulation that hold valuable lessons for this new global information society.

1961. Transnational laws. Effective national cyber law and transnational laws and regulations are also needed. Effective laws and strong enforcement are critical if poor consumer experiences result in a loss of faith in e-commerce that is part of the market economy. To restore consumer trust in markets that operate fairly, effectively and to consumer benefit there must be a prevailing culture that encourages such trustworthiness.

1962. In December 2017 Australia together with sixty-seven other nations in Buenos Aires agreed to embark on a formal round of the WTO negotiations to craft a new set of enforceable global rules to govern digital trade.[1158] The aim is to strengthen the trust among digital transaction partners, banning tariffs on low-value goods traded through e-commerce platforms, trade facilitation such as the recognition of digital contracts and signatures, removing barriers on cross-border data flows and forcing foreign firms to open access to their source code as a condition for trade or investment among others.

1963. At the 2021 World Economic Forum Annual Meeting in Davos, Switzerland, Australia and seventy-five other members of the WTO, representing over 90 per cent of global trade, confirmed their intention to commence WTO negotiations on trade-related aspects of e-commerce and on the development of new international rules in digital trade.[1159] With such rules in place cyber law may develop with much vigour to ensure that cybersecurity and for use to pursue cybercriminals in the e-commerce world.

1157. *See* DP-REG at https://www.accc.gov.au/media-release/agencies-form-digital-platform-regulators-forum (11 Mar).

1158. *See* Steve Ciobo (2017) Australia led an initiative at the 11th World Trade Organization (WTO) Ministerial Conference (MC11) on e-commerce, at https://trademinister.gov.au/releases/Pages/2017/sc_mr_171214.aspx.

1159. *See* Simon Birmingham (2021) at https://www.senatorbirmingham.com.au/australia-leads-the-move-to-negotiations-on-digital-trade-rules/ (261 Jan).

Selected Bibliography

AlphaBeta Advisors (2018) *Digital Innovation: Australia's $315b Opportunity*, Report to the CSIRO (Commonwealth Scientific and Industrial Research Organisation) Data 61, AlphaBeta.

Assir, H, Nanda, P & Mohanty, M (2021) A novel e-Government Framework using Blockchain *Journal of Information Assurance & Cyber Security* vol. 2021 at https://ibimapublishing.com/articles/JIACS/2021/164568/164568.pdf.

Australian Bureau of Statistics (2018) *Summary of IT Use and Innovation in Australian Business, 2016-2017,* Catalogue 8166.0.

Australian Bureau of Statistics (2018), *Selected Characteristics of Australian Business,* Catalogue 8167.0.

Australian Bureau of Statistics (2012) *Year Book Australia 2012.* Catalogue 1301.0.

Australian Bureau of Statistics (2010) *Household Use of Information Technology*, Catalogue 8146.0.

Australian Competition & Consumer Commission 2019 *Digital Platforms Inquiry: Final Report*, June 2019 (Canberra: ACCC.)

Australian Computer Society (ACS) (2021) *Australia's Digital Pulse Future directions for Australia's Technology workforce 2021* at https://www2.deloitte.com/au/en/pages/economics/articles/australias-digital-pulse.html.

Australian Government Department of Industry, Innovation and Science (2017) *The Digital Economy: Opening Up the Conversation* at https://www.industry.gov.au/innovation/Digital-Economy/Documents/Digital-Economy-Strategy-Consultation-Paper.pdf.

Australian Institute of Health and Welfare (2019) *Australia's Welfare in brief',* Cat. No. AUS227 (Canberra: AIHW.)

Australian Parliament House, Parliamentary Library 2011, *Parliamentary Handbook of the Commonwealth of Australia* (32nd ed., Canberra: APH).

Banathy, B (1996) *Designing Social Systems in a Changing World* (New York: Plenum Press).

Bhatnagar, SC (2002) *E-government: From Vision to Implementation: A Practical Guide with Case Studies* (Thousand Oaks, CA: Sage Publications).

Broadhurst, R (2017), *Cybercrime in Australia,* The Palgrave Handbook of Australian and New Zealand Criminology, Crime and Justice (Cham: Springer International Publishing), doi:10.1007/978-3-319-55747-2_15.

Business Council of Australia (2013) *Action Plan for Enduring Prosperity* at https://www.bca.com.au/action-plan-for-enduring-prosperity-full-report.

Choo, RK-K, Smith RG & McCusker, R (2009) *Future Directions in Technology-enabled Crime: 2007-09, AIC Research & Public Policy Series No. 78* at https://www.aic.gov.au/publications/rpp/rpp78.

Christie, A (1995) *Integrated Circuits and Their Components: International Protection,* pp. 131-135 (North Ryde, NSW: The Law Book Company Limited.)

Cross C, Smith R & Richards K (2014) Challenges of responding to online fraud victimisation in Australia, *Trends & Issues in Crime and Criminal Justice* no. 474, Canberra: Australian Institute of Criminology, at https://www.aic.gov.au/publications/tandi/tandi474.

Deloitte Access Economics (2020) *Mobile Nation 2019. The 5G Future* at https://www2.deloitte.com/au/en/pages/economics/articles/mobile-nation.html.

Deloitte Access Economics, (2020) *Australia's eCommerce Revolution: How it Saved Businesses in COVID-19 and Future Strategies to Thrive* (Report commissioned by Australia Post, October 2020) <https://auspost.com.au/content/dam/auspost_corp/media/documents/ ecommerce-report-2020.pdf>.

Department of Industry (2018) *Australia's Tech Future* at https://www.industry.gov.au/sites/default/files/2018-12/australias-tech-future.pdf.

Department of Industry, Innovation & Science (2017) *The Digital Economy: Opening up the Conversation* at https://industry.gov.au/innovation/Digital-Economy/Documents/Digital-Economy-Strategy-Consultation-Paper.pdf.

Dutta, S & Lanvin, B (eds.) (2020) *The Network Readiness Index 2020. Accelerating Digital Transformation in a post-COVID Global Economy,* Portulans Institute available at: https://networkreadinessindex.org/wp-content/uploads/2020/11/NRI-2020-V828-11-2020.pdf.

Edwards, C, Savage, N & Walden, I (eds.) (1990) *Information Technology and the Law*, (2nd ed.) (Basingstoke: Macmillan).

Ejaz, W, Anpalagan, A, Imran, MA, Jo, M, Naeem, M, & Qaisar, SB (2016) Internet of Things (IoT) (2016) 5G wireless communications, *IEEE Access*, vol. 4, pp. 10310-10314.

Ericsson (2016) Cellular Networks for Massive IoT: Enabling Low Power Wide Area Applications, Stockholm, Sweden, Jan., pp. 1-13 and at https://www.ericsson.com/en/reports-and-papers/white-papers/cellular-networks-for-massive-iot--enabling-low-power-wide-area-applications.

Finch, B (1999) Consumer Protection on the Internet, in Fitzgerald, A *et al.* eds *Going Digital 2000: Legal Issues for E-Commerce, Software and the Internet* (Sydney: Prospect Media).

Fisher, C, Park, S, Lee, JY, Fuller, G & Sang, Y (2019) *Digital News Report: Australia 2019*, News and Media Research Centre, University of Canberra (June).

Fitzgerald, B & Sheehan, E (1999) Trademark dilution and the commodification of information: Understanding the 'cultural command', *Macarthur Law Review* vol. 3, pp. 61-68.

Gonsalves, M & Flynn, P (2006) 'Dilution Down Under: The Protection of Well-Known Trademarks in Australia' [2006] *European Intellectual Property Review* 174 at http://classic.austlii.edu.au/cgi-bin/LawCite?cit=%5b2006%5d%20European%20Intellectual%20Property%20Review%20174.

Gordon S & Ford R (2006) On the definition and classification of cybercrime in the *Journal in Computer Virology* 2: 13-20.

Hajkowicz SA, Karimi S, Wark T, Chen C, Evans M, Rens N, Dawson D, Charlton A, Brennan T, Moffatt C, Srikumar S and Tong K J (2019) *Artificial Intelligence: Solving Problems, Growing the Economy and Improving Our Quality of Life*, CSIRO Data61 and the Department of Industry, Innovation and Science, Australian Government.

Handler, M (2008) 'Trademark Dilution in Australia?' [2008] UNSWLRS 48 at http://classic.austlii.edu.au/au/journals/UNSWLRS/2008.

Hill, L (2002) On the Reasonableness of Compelling Citizens to 'Vote': The Australian Case. *Political Studies*, 50(1):80-101, March 2002, at http://journals.sagepub.com/doi/abs/10.1111/1467-9248.00360, doi:10.1111/1467-9248.00360.

International Telecommunications Union (ITU) (2017) *Global Cybersecurity Index 2017,* ITU Geneva at https://www.itu.int/dms_pub/itu-d/opb/str/d-str-gci.01-2017-pdf-e.pdf.

Irwin, E & Selvadurai, N (2021) Imposing liability on online intermediaries for violent user-generated content: an Australian perspective, *Richmond Journal of Law and Technology* (2021) v. 28(1), pp. 1-4.

Knight, P & Fitzsimons, J (1990) *The Legal Environment of Computing* 124-126 (Sydney: Addison-Wesley Pub. Coy.)

Krone, T & Smith RG (2020) *Criminal Misuse of the Domain Name System,* AIC Research Report 03 at https://www.aic.gov.au/sites/default/files/2020-05/research_report_03.pdf.

Krone, T (2005) Hacking offences, High tech crime brief No. 5 Canberra: Australian Institute of Criminology at https://aic.gov.au/publications/htcb/htcb005.

Krone T (2005) Hacking motives High tech crime brief No. 6 Canberra: Australian Institute of Criminology at https://aic.gov.au/publications/htcb/htcb006.

Leigh, R (2021) Patentability of computer-implemented 'business methods' in Australia—a closer look at the 'technical improvement' test, *Journal of Intellectual Property Law & Practice*, vol. 16(3) (March), pp. 271-277 and at https://doi.org/10.1093/jiplp/jpab079.

Lim, YF (2002) *Cyberspace Law: Commentaries and Materials* (Sydney: Oxford University Press.)

Linklaters, J (2013) *Generation Next: 5 Pathways to TMT Growth in Emerging Markets* at http://www.tmtgenerationnext.com.

Lipson, H & Kurman, M (2013) *Fabricated: The New World of 3D Printing* (New York: John Wiley).

Llewelyn, D & Reddy, P (2020) 'Metatags Using Third Party Trademarks on the Internet' in Alpin, T (ed.) (2020) *Research Handbook on Intellectual Property and Digital Technologies* (Cheltenham, UK: Edward Elgar Publishing), Chapter 20 and at https://ssrn.com/abstract=3683824.

Mercurio, B (2003) 'Beyond the Paper Ballet: Exploring Computerised Voting' in Orr, G, Mercurio, B & Williams, G (eds), *Realising Democracy: Electoral Law in Australia* (Sydney: Federation Press) pp. 230-42.

Mitchell, J (1998) Fragmentation to Integration: The Telemedicine Industry in Australia (Canberra: AGPS).

National Commission of Audit (2014) Towards Responsible Government Report of the National Commission of Audit. Phase One, February at https://australianpolitics.com/downloads/budgets/2014/14-05-01_commission-of-auditreport1_phase1.pdf.

National Research Council (1999) *A Question of Balance – Private Rights and the Public Interest in Scientific and Technical Databases* (Washington: NAP) at http://www.nap.edu/html/question_balance/ch3.html.

OECD (2020) *Taxing Virtual Currencies: An Overview of Tax Treatments and Emerging Tax Policy Issues*, October 2020 at https://www.oecd.org/tax/tax-policy/taxing-virtual-currencies-an-overview-of-tax-treatments-and-emerging-tax-policy-issues.htm.

Oh, H, Rizo, C, Enkin, M & Jadad, A (2005) 'What is eHealth (3): a systematic review of published definitions', *Journal of Medical Internet Research*, vol. 7(1) at http://www.jmir.org/2005/1/e1/.

Pappalardo, K and Suzor, N (2018) 'The Liability of Australian Online Intermediaries' *Sydney Law Review* 40(4) pp. 472-473.

Ramsfield, J (2000) *The Law as Architecture (American Casebook Series* 1st *ed.)* (New York: West-Thomson).

Riordan, J (2016) *Liability of Internet Intermediaries* (Oxford: Oxford University Press.)

Smith, G (1996) *Software C*^{on}*tracts,* in Reed C (ed., 3rd ed.) *Computer Law* Ch. 2, 53-80 at 74 (London: Blackstone Press Ltd).

Smith, R (2002) Electronic voting: benefits and risks, *Trends & Issues in Crime and Criminal Justice* no. 224, Canberra: Australian Institute of Criminology at https://www.aic.gov.au/publications/tandi/tandi224.

Spil, T & Kijl, B (2009) 'E-health Business Models: From pilot project to successful deployment': IBMA Business Review, vol. 1, (2009) at http://www.ibimapublishing.com/journals/IBIMABR/volume1/v1n5.pdf.

Steward, A (2016) *AGIMO: The Australian Government releases the National Digital Economy Strategy* (2011) at https://www.finance.gov.au/blog/2011/05/31/australian-government-releases-national-digital-economy-strategy/ (last updated 01 Aug. 2016).

Svantesson, D (2010) 'Sexting and The Law - How Australia Regulates Electronic Communication of Non-Professional Sexual Content,' *Bond Law Review* vol. 22(2), Article 3 at http://epublications.bond.edu.au/blr/vol22/iss2/3.

Tan, P (2021) 'NFTs and the IP conundrum' at https://law.asia/nfts-ip-conundrum/.

Taylor, G (2015) 'Electronic Voting in Australia', in Maurer, A, Barrett, J (eds), *E-Voting Case law: A Comparative Analysis* (Farnham, UK: Ashgate).

Telecommunications Industry Ombudsman (2021) *Annual Report 2020-21* at https://www.tio.com.au/sites/default/files/2021-09/TIO_AR_Accessible_LR.pdf.

Teunissen C, Voce I & Smith R (2021) *Estimating the Cost of Pure Cybercrime to Australian Individuals*, Statistical Bulletin no. 34. Canberra: Australian Institute of Criminology. https://doi.org/10.52922/ sb78269.

The Economist (2012) *The Third Industrial Revolution* (21 April) at https://www.economist.com/leaders/2012/04/21/the-third-industrial-revolution.

United Nations (2004) Global E-government Readiness Report: Towards Access for Opportunity, Geneva: Department of Economic and Social Affairs & Division for Public Administration and Development Management (New York: UN Publication).

Valcic, J (2021) The Sharing of Abhorrent Violent Material Act: The Realities and Implications of Australia's New Laws Regulating Social Media Companies, *Bond Law Review* vol. 33(1).

Wall DS 2007 *Cybercrime: The Transformation of Crime in the Information Age* (Cambridge: Polity Press).

WIPO (n.d.) *The Recognition of Rights and the Use of Names in the Internet Domain Name System: Report of the Second WIPO Internet Domain Name Process*, at http://wipo2.wipo.int.

Wiseman, JR (1988) Global Nation: Australia? Australia and the Politics of Globalization (Melbourne: Cambridge University Press).

World Health Organisation (WHO) (2005) *e Health Resolution 2005* at http://www.who.int/healthacademy/news/en/.

Zahir, I & Lov, P (2013) *Evaluating Information Systems* (London: Routledge).

Selected Bibliography

Index

Note: **Bold** letters denote major sections in the text. Underlined text refers to chapters within the sections. Numbers here refer to paragraph numbers.

Index

Index

Index

www.ingramcontent.com/pod-product-compliance
Ingram Content Group UK Ltd.
Pitfield, Milton Keynes, MK11 3LW, UK
UKHW020130290926
15471UKWH00003B/399

9 789403 522968